June 21–25, 2014
Uppsala, Sweden

**Association for
Computing Machinery**

Advancing Computing as a Science & Profession

UPPSALA UNIVERSITET

ITICSE'14
Proceedings of the 2014
Innovation & Technology in Computer
Science Education Conference

Sponsored by:
ACM SIGCSE

Supported by:
Uppsala Universitet, Springer, GitHub

Association for Computing Machinery

Advancing Computing as a Science & Profession

The Association for Computing Machinery
2 Penn Plaza, Suite 701
New York, New York 10121-0701

Notice to Past Authors of ACM-Published Articles

ISBN: 978-1-4503-2833-3 (Digital)

ISBN: 978-1-4503-3110-4 (Print)

Additional copies may be ordered prepaid from:

ACM Order Department
PO Box 30777
New York, NY 10087-0777, USA

Phone: 1-800-342-6626 (USA and Canada)
+1-212-626-0500 (Global)
Fax: +1-212-944-1318
E-mail: acmhelp@acm.org
Hours of Operation: 8:30 am – 4:30 pm ET

Printed in the USA

Foreword

Welcome to ITiCSE 2014 in Uppsala.

The second ITiCSE was in Uppsala 1997 and a delegate inquired late one night; "Mats, could you turn off the sun please". That was in early June and this year the conference will be at a time with fewer hours of darkness as it is close to the Midsummer celebration in Sweden. There are similarities and differences between the two instances of the conference. We will run the conference dinner at the same "nation" as last time and will again have a reception in the main university building, reflecting that traditions are important at our University that was founded in 1477. The conference organizers are researchers from the University's newest research groups, Uppsala Computing Education Research Group (UpCERG), and an even newer center for subject didactic research (MINT). Respecting tradition, but striving for change, the steam train excursion has been updated to a boat trip on the Fyris river out to Skokloster castle (perhaps the most beautiful castle in Sweden). The conference, while being held in the same campus area, will be located at Ångström laboratories (a building that is quite large and in some sense not at all a reflection of its name :-p).

The conference continues to be a truly international conference with 164 submissions from 36 countries on six continents (Africa - 3, Asia - 19, Europe - 38, North America - 51, Oceania - 17, and South America - 7); and that is only considering the first author. These submissions consisted of 150 papers, 4 panels, and 10 working group proposals. Additionally, there were 48 posters and the tips & techniques submissions spanning 19 countries.

All research papers were double blind reviewed by at least three reviewers, though most papers received between four and six reviews. Following the peer review, a meta review was conducted by the members of the programme committee to ensure the reliability of the reviews and to make recommendations to the chairs regarding the acceptance and rejection of each submission. A final selection phase was conducted by the programme chairs who reviewed all reviews and meta-review recommendations before making a final decision on the submission. After this process, 53 research papers with universally high quality (35%) were ultimately selected for presentation and inclusion in the proceedings. The first authors of the 53 papers are distributed over 16 different countries on five continents.

All posters and tips & techniques submissions were double blind reviewed by two members of the programme committee and the chairs for the submission categories before being selected by the programme chairs for final inclusion in the conference. Thirty-six were accepted, representing first authors from 15 countries.

The theme of the conference is "Learning for life" and this will be addressed by our two keynote speakers. Yvonne Rogers from University College London, under the title "New technology, new learning?" will present a perspective on the impact design has on the value of technology for learning, focusing on aspects such as collaboration, mindful engagement, conversational skills and the art of reflection. Jan Gulliksen, of the Royal Institute of Technology in Stockholm, will talk about how to meet educational challenges in the "digital" era with a holistic perspective including the whole population.

There are five accepted working groups dealing with a broad spectrum of topics. They include the role of methodology in education, influences of new technology on education, and pre-university computing education to more specific areas such as peer reviewing and gaming as educational methods, and understanding programming exam questions. Participating in a working group is probably one of the most efficient ways to become part of the ITiCSE community. It provides participants a unique opportunity to work with people from different countries who are interested and knowledgeable in the area of the working group.

Again, we welcome you to Uppsala, to enjoy ITiCSE and Midsummer in Sweden.

Åsa Cajander
Mats Daniels
ITiCSE 2014 Conference Chairs

Tony Clear
Arnold Pears
ITiCSE 2014 Programme Chairs

Table of Contents

Keynote Addresses

Session: New Technology & Learning

Session: Visualisation

Session: Programming

Session: K12 – High School CS

Session: Algorithms

Session: Security & Integrity

Session: Gender & Diversity

Session: Software Engineering

Session: Mobile Development

Session: K12 – High School CS

Session: Software Testing

Session: Collaboration

Session: Digital Fluency

Session: Gamification

Session: Curriculum Concepts

Session: Peer Instruction

Session: CS Ed Research

Session: Motivating Learning

Session: Robotics

Session: Panel

Session: Invited Panel

Session: Tips,Techniques and Courseware

Posters Session I

Posters Session II

Author Index

ITiCSE 2014 Conference Organization

Conference Chair: Åsa Cajander *(Uppsala University, Sweden)*
Mats Daniels *(Uppsala University, Sweden)*

Program Co-Chairs: Tony Clear *(Auckland University of Technology, NZ)*
Arnold Pears *(Uppsala University, Sweden)*

Treasurer & Registration Chair: Cary Laxer *(Rose-Hulman Institute of Technology, USA)*

Working Groups: Alison Clear *(Christchurch Polytechnic Institute of Technology, NZ)*
Raymond Lister *(University of Technology, Sydney, Australia)*

Panels: Viggo Kann *(Royal Institute of Technology, Sweden)*
Roger McDermott *(Robert Gordon University, Scotland)*

Tips, Techniques & Courseware: Lars-Åke Nordén *(Uppsala University, Sweden)*
Jacqui Whalley *(Auckland University of Technology, NZ)*

Proceedings: Michael Goldweber *(Xavier University, USA)*

Posters: Päivi Kinnunen *(Aalto University, Finland)*
Aletta Nylén *(Uppsala University, Sweden)*

Database Coordinators: John Dooley *(Knox College, USA)*
Henry Walker *(Grinnell College, USA)*

Evaluations: Valentina Dagiene *(Vilnius University, Lithuania)*
Isto Huvila *(Uppsala University, Sweden)*

Student Volunteers: Nanna Kjellin Lagerqvist *(Uppsala University, Sweden)*
Thomas Lind *(Uppsala University, Sweden)*
Anne Peters *(Uppsala University, Sweden)*

Website: Björn Victor *(Uppsala University, Sweden)*

Local Committee: Anders Berglund *(Uppsala University, Sweden)*
Anna Eckerdal *(Uppsala University, Sweden)*
Henrik Hedlund *(Uppsala University, Sweden)*

ITiCSE 2014 Working Groups

Working Group 1: Sustainable Gamification Strategy for Education
Co-Leaders: Torsten Reiners (*Curtin University, Australia*)
Lincoln C. Wood (*Auckland University of Technology, New Zealand*)
Hanna Teräs (*Curtin University, Australia*)

Participants: Alexandra Coman (*Ohio Northern University, USA*)
Vladimiras Dolgopolovas (*Vilnius University, Lithuania*)

Working Group 2: Strengthening Methodology Education in Computing
Co-Leaders: Matti Tedre (*Stockholm University, Sweden*)
Justus Randolph (*Mercer University, USA*)
Johannes C. Cronje (*Cape Peninsula University of Technology, South Africa*)

Participants: Ilona Heldal (*University of Skovde, Sweden*)
Rick Detlef (*Hamburg University of Technology, Germany*)
Ville Isomottonen (*University of Jyvaskyla, Finland*)
Jacqueline Whalley (*Auckland University of Technology, New Zealand*)
Anne-Kathrin Peters (*Uppsala University, Sweden*)
Urmas Heinaste (*University of Tartu, Estonia*)
Christina Dörge (*Bremen University of Applied Sciences, Germany*)
Roger McDermott (*The Robert Gordon University, UK*)
Simon (*University of Newcastle, Australia*)
Aljona Sitnik (*Stockholm University, Sweden*)

Working Group 3: Computational Thinking in K-9 Education
Co-Leaders: Linda Mannila (*Åbo Akademi University, Finland*)
Valentina Dagiene (*Vilnius University, Lithuania*)

Participants: Barbara Demo (*University of Turin, Italy*)
Claudio Mirolo (*University of Udine, Italy*)
Amber Settle (*DePaul University, USA*)
Lennart Rolandsson (*Royal Institute of Technology, Sweden*)
Natasa Grgurina (*University of Groningen, Netherlands*)

Working Group 4: Methodology and Technology for In-Flow Peer Review
Co-Leaders: Joe Gibbs Politz (*Brown University, USA*)
Kathi Fisler (*Worcester Polytechnic Institute, USA*)
Shriram Krishnamurthi (*Brown University, USA*)

Participants: Tony Clear (*AUT University, New Zealand*)
Dave Clarke (*Uppsala University, Sweden*)
Matthias Hauswirth (*Lugano, Switzerland*)
Ville Tirronen (*Jyväskylä University, Finland*)
Tobias Wrigstad (*Uppsala University, Sweden*)

Working Group 5: Increasing Accessibility and Adoption of Smart Technologies for Computer Science Education

Co-Leaders: Peter Brusilovsky (*University of Pittsburgh, USA*)
Stephen H. Edwards (*Virginia Tech, USA*)
Amruth Kumar (*Ramapo College of New Jersey, USA*)
Lauri Malmi (*Aalto University, Finland*)

Participants: Luciana Benotti (*National University of Cordoba, Argentina*)
Duane Buck (*Otterbein University, USA*)
Petri Ihantola (*Aalto University, Finland*)
Teemu Sirkiä (*Aalto University, Finland*)
Rikki Prince ECS (*University of Southampton, UK*)
Sergey Sosnovsky (*German Center for Artificial Intelligence, Germany*)
Jaime Urquiza Fuentes (*Universidad Rey, Juan Carlos Spain*)
Arto Vihavainen (*University of Helsinki, Finland*)
Michael Wollowski (*Rose-Hulman Institute of Technology, USA*)

ITiCSE 2014 Reviewers

Raman Adaikkalavan *(Indiana University South Bend)*

Rajeev Agrawal *(North Carolina A & T State University)*

Hend Al-Khalifa *(King Saud University)*

Barbara Anthony *(Southwestern University)*

Michal Armoni *(Weizmann Institute of Science)*

John Aycock *(University of Calgary)*

Doug Baldwin *(SUNY Geneseo)*

David Barnes *(University of Kent)*

Lewis Barnett *(University of Richmond)*

Valerie Barr *(Union College)*

Tim Bell *(University of Canterbury)*

Mordechai Ben-Ari *(Weizmann Institute of Science)*

Marie Bienkowski *(SRI International)*

David Bunde *(Knox College)*

Barry Burd *(Drew University)*

Andre Paul Calitz *(Nelson Mandela Metropolitan University)*

Daniel Canas *(Wake Forest University)*

Steven Case *(University of West Florida)*

Michael E. Caspersen *(Aarhus University)*

Maiga Chang *(Athabasca University)*

Wei Kian Chen *(Champlain Cpllege)*

Li-hsiang Cheo *(William Paterson University of New Jersey)*

Jayan Kurian Chirayath *(Royal Melbourne Institute of Technology)*

David Chiu *(Washington State University, Vancouver)*

John Cigas *(Park University)*

Dawn Cizmar *(St. Edward's University)*

Peter Clarke *(Florida International University)*

Joe Clifton *(University of Wisconsin, Platteville)*

Tim Comber *(Southern Cross University)*

Randy Connolly *(Mount Royal University)*

Stephen Cooper *(Stanford University)*

Michelle Craig *(University of Toronto)*

Joyce Blair Crowell *(Belmont University)*

Jose Cunha *(New University of Lisbon)*

Lawrence D'Antonio *(Ramapo College of New Jersey)*

Douglas Dankel *(University of Florida)*

Renzo Davoli *(University of Bologna)*

Adrienne Decker *(Rochester Institute of Technology)*

Hannah Mary Dee *(Aberystwyth University)*

Katherine Deibel *(University of Washington-Seattle)*

Barbara Demo *(University Torino)*

Zachary Dodds *(Harvey Mudd College)*

Peter Drexel *(Plymouth State University)*

J. Philip East *(University of Northern Iowa)*

Stephanie Elzer *(Millersville University)*

Henry Etlinger *(Rochester Institute of Technology)*

Alan Fekete *(University of Sydney)*

Georgios Fesakis *(University of the Aegean)*

Samantha Foley *(University of Wisconsin-La Crosse)*

Alessio Gaspar *(University of South Florida Polytechnic)*

Rick Gee *(Okanagan College)*

Paul Gestwicki *(Ball State University)*

Michail Giannakos *(Norwegian University of Science and Technology)*

Don Goelman *(Villanova University)*

Michael Goldwasser *(Saint Louis University)*

Jean Goulet *(Universite de Sherbrooke)*

Mary Granger *(George Washington University)*

Simon Gray *(College of Wooster)*

John Hamer *(University of Glasgow)*

Brian Hanks *(BFH Educational Consulting)*

Stuart Hansen *(University of Wisconsin - Parkside)*

Orit Hazzan *(Technion – Israel Institute of Technology)*

Sarah Heckman *(North Carolina State University)*

Michael Helmick *(University of Cincinnati)*

David Hemmendinger *(Union College)*

Tyson Henry *(California State University, Chico)*

Curtis Hill *(Valley City State University)*

Joe Hollingsworth *(Indiana University)*

William Hooper *(Belmont University)*

Hoda Hosny *(The American University in Cairo)*

David Hovemeyer *(York College of Pennsylvania)*

Brian Howard *(DePauw University)*

Janet Hughes *(University of Dundee)*

Steven Huss-Lederman *(Beloit College)*

Jorge Eduardo Ibarra-Esquer *(Universidad Autonoma de Baja California)*

Petri Ihantola *(Aalto University)*

Sridhar Iyer *(Indian Institute of Technology, Bombay)*

Mike Jipping *(Hope College)*

David John *(Wake Forest University)*

Colin Johnson *(University of Kent at Canterbury)*

Anthony Joseph *(Pace University)*

Mike Joy *(University of Warwick)*

Daniel Joyce *(Villanova University)*

David Kauchak *(Middlebury College)*

David G. Kay *(University of California, Irvine)*

Jennifer Kay *(Rowan University)*

Petros Kefalas *(The University of Sheffield International Faculty)*

Mark Kerstetter *(Western Michigan University)*

Nancy Kinnersley *(University of Kansas)*

Paivi Kinnunen *(Aalto University)*

Carsten Kleiner *(University of Applied Sciences & Arts Hannover)*

Michael Kolling *(University of Kent)*

Janet Kourik *(Webster University)*

Joan Krone *(Denison University)*

Jan Kruger *(Unisa School for Business Leadership)*

Benjamin Kuperman *(Oberlin College)*

Stan Kurkovsky *(Central Connecticut State University)*

Zachary Kurmas *(Grand Valley State University)*

Clif Kussmaul *(Muhlenberg College)*

Joan Langdon *(Bowie State University)*

David Largent *(Ball State University)*

Eric Larson *(Seattle University)*

Mary Last

Robert Law *(Glasgow Caledonian University)*

Alina Lazar *(Youngstown State University)*

Arthur Lee *(Claremont McKenna College)*

Byong Lee *(Bennett College)*

Gilliean Lee *(Lander University)*

Chi Un Lei *(University of Hong Kong)*

Charles Leska *(Randolph-Macon College)*

Sergio F. Lopes *(University of Minho)*

Andrew Luxton-Reilly *(The University of Auckland)*

Bonnie MacKellar *(St John's University)*

Dave Mason *(Ryerson University)*

Lester McCann *(The University of Arizona)*

O. William McClung *(Nebraska Wesleyan University)*

Jeffrey McConnell *(Canisius College)*

Sean McCulloch *(Ohio Wesleyan University)*

Hugh McGuire *(Grand Valley State University)*

António Mendes *(Universidade de Coimbra)*

Susan Mengel *(Texas Tech University)*

Jose Carlos Metrolho *(Polytechnic Institute of Castelo Branco)*

Joe Miro *(Universitat de les Illes Balears)*

Roland Mittermeir *(Universität Klagenfurt)*

Patricia Morreale *(Kean University)*

Briana Morrison *(Southern Polytechnic State University)*

Srikanth Mudigonda *(Saint Louis University)*

Michael Murphy *(Concordia University Texas)*

Robert Noonan *(College of William and Mary)*

Lars-Åke Nordén *(Uppsala University)*

Keith O'Hara *(Bard College)*

Rainer Oechsle *(Trier University of Applied Sciences)*

Amos Olagunju *(St. Cloud State University)*

Lawrence Osborne *(Lamar University)*

Iraklis Paraskakis *(University of Sheffield)*

David Parker *(Salisbury University)*

James Paterson *(Glasgow Caledonian University)*

Eileen Peluso *(Lycoming College)*

Teresa Peterman *(Grand Valley State University)*

Andrew Petersen *(University of Toronto Mississauga)*

Chrisila C. Pettey *(Middle Tennessee State University)*

Vreda Pieterse *(University of Pretoria)*

Nelishia Pillay *(University of KwaZulu-Natal)*

Sarah Monisha Pulimood *(The College of New Jersey)*

Muthu Ramachandran *(Leeds Metropolitan University)*

Samuel Rebelsky *(Grinnell College)*

Michael Redmond *(La Salle University)*

Guido Rößling *(TU Darmstadt)*

Suzanne Rivoire *(Sonoma State University)*

Christian Roberson *(Plymouth State University)*

Susan H. Rodger *(Duke University)*

Krishnendu Roy *(Valdosta State University)*

Martin Ruckert *(Munich University of Applied Sciences)*

Roberta Evans Sabin *(Loyola College)*

Mehran Sahami *(Stanford University)*

Ian Sanders *(University of South Africa)*

André Santos *(ISCTE-IUL)*

Otto Seppälä *(Aalto University)*

Amber Settle *(DePaul University)*

Cliff Shaffer *(Virginia Tech)*

Judy Sheard *(Monash University)*

Ching-Kuang Shene *(Michigan Technological University)*

Mark Sherriff *(University of Virginia)*

Yasuto Shirai *(Shizuoka University)*

Peter Smith *(California State University - Channel Islands)*

Jaime Spacco *(Knox College)*

Ben Stephenson *(University of Calgary)*

Fred Strickland *(South University)*

Kazunari Sugiyama *(National University of Singapore)*

Weiqing Sun *(University of Toledo)*

William Thacker *(Winthrop University)*

Megan Thomas *(California State University Stanislaus)*

Rebecca Thomas *(Bard College)*

Neena Thota *(University of Saint Joseph)*

William Turner *(Wabash College)*

Hakan Tuzun *(Hacettepe University)*

Ian Utting *(University of Kent at Canterbury)*

Jan Vahrenhold *(Westfälische Wilhelms-Universität Münster)*

Tammy VanDeGrift *(University of Portland)*

Brad Vander Zanden *(University of Tennessee)*

Yaakov Varol *(University of Nevada Reno)*

Jorge Vasconcelos *(Johns Hopkins University)*

Troy Vasiga *(University of Waterloo)*

Kam Vat *(University of Macau)*

Steven Vegdahl *(University of Portland)*

Gabriela Vilanova *(National Patagonia Austral University)*

Tamar Vilner *(The Open University of Israel)*

David Voorhees *(Le Moyne College)*

Sally Wahba *(Clemson University)*

Jacqueline Whalley *(Auckland University of Technology)*

Elizabeth White *(George Mason University)*

Howard Whitston *(University of South Alabama)*

Linda Wilkens *(Providence College)*

Michael Wirth *(University of Guelph)*

Steven Wolfman *(University of British Columbia)*

Arthur Yanushka *(Christian Brothers University)*

Duane Yoder *(University of West Georgia)*

Daniel Zingaro *(University of Toronto)*

Fani Zlatarova *(Elizabethtown College)*

ITiCSE 2014 Sponsor & Supporters

Sponsor:

Supporters:

UPPSALA
UNIVERSITET

GitHub

New Technology, New Learning?

Yvonne Rogers
University College London
London, UK
y.rogers at ucl.ac.uk

Abstract

There has been a lot of excitement recently about how new technologies can transform learning. MOOCs, the internet of education and flipped classrooms are the latest hotly debated ways of changing how students learn in the modern world. At the same time, a diversity of innovative learning apps has been developed for tabletops, tablets and phones, supporting new forms of learning – mobile, collaborative and situated. New electronic toolkits and programming environments are also emerging intended to introduce new generations to coding and computation in creative and engaging ways – that go way beyond Logo. Never before has there been so much opportunity and buzz to make learning accessible, immersive, interactive, exciting, provocative and enjoyable. To realize the true potential of these latest technological developments, however, requires designing interfaces and apps to not only match learner's needs but also to encourage collaboration, mindful engagement, conversational skills and the art of reflection.

Categories and Subject Descriptors: K.3.2 [**Computers and Education**]: Commputer and Information Science Education – *Computer science education*

Keywords

Human-computer interaction; Technologies to facilitate learning

Short Bio

Yvonne Rogers is a Professor of Interaction Design, the director of UCLIC and a deputy head of the Computer Science department at UCL. Her research interests are in the areas of ubiquitous computing, interaction design and human-computer interaction. A central theme is how to design interactive technologies that enhance life by augmenting and extending everyday learning and work activities.

Yvonne is the PI at UCL for the Intel Collaborative Research Institute on Sustainable Connected Cities which was launched in October 2012 as a joint collaboration with Imperial College. She was awarded a prestigious EPSRC dream fellowship rethinking the relationship between aging, computing and creativity.

From 2006-2011, Yvonne was professor of HCI in the Computing Department at the OU, where she set up the Pervasive Interaction Lab. From 2003-2006, she was a professor in Informatics at Indiana University. Prior to this, she spent 11 years at the former School of Cognitive and Computing Sciences at Sussex University.

Yvonne was one of the principal investigators on the UK Equator Project (2000-2007) where she pioneered ubiquitous learning. She has published widely, beginning with her PhD work on graphical interfaces to her recent work on public visualisations and behavioural change. She is one of the authors of the definitive textbook on Interaction Design and HCI now in its 3rd edition. She is a Fellow of the British Computer Society and the ACM's CHI Academy, and has spent sabbaticals at Stanford, Apple, Queensland University, University of Cape Town, University of Melbourne, QUT and UC San Diego.

ITICSE'14, June 21–25, 2014, Uppsala, Sweden.
ACM 978-1-4503-2833-3/14/06.
http://dx.doi.org/10.1145/2591708.2602688

Meeting the Future Challenges of Education and Digitization

Jan Gulliksen
Royal Institute of Technology
Stockholm, Sweden
gulliksen@kth.se

Abstract

Schools and education are of immense political importance, particularly for the upcoming election, both in the European union and for Sweden. The Pisa surveys show disappointing results for Sweden, and the Swedish Committee for Digitisation has analyzed IT education in the school sector and developed concrete proposals to provide the Swedish government with a basis for future educational policy making. This development also has a great impact on how higher education will need to evolve. Technology, in many ways, changes the playing field for education and life-long learning, and thus the pedagogy and leadership upon which our education is based also needs to change. This talk discusses the current view of education and life-long learning and brings provocative ideas to the table concerning the future of ICT in Education.

Categories and Subject Descriptors: K.3.2 [**Computers and Education**]: Commputer and Information Science Education – *Computer science education*

Keywords
Future of ICT in education

Short Bio

Jan Gulliksen, often referred to by his nickname "Gulan", is a professor in Human Computer Interaction at KTH Royal Institute of Technology. He also holds the position as Dean of the School of Computer Science and Communication at KTH. In 2012, Jan was selected "Sweden's Digital Champion" by the Swedish Government, and he is also Chairman of the Government's Digital Commission.

Before being appointed professor at KTH in 2009, Jan worked as a researcher at Uppsala University. Professor Gulliksen, who has written two books and numerous scientific articles, has focused his research on how the work environment is affected by digitization and how it can be improved by adding more focus on design and usability.

ITICSE'14, June 21–25, 2014, Uppsala, Sweden.
ACM 978-1-4503-2833-3/14/06.
http://dx.doi.org/10.1145/2591708.2602689

SPOC-supported Introduction to Programming

Marco Piccioni
ETH Zurich
marco.piccioni@inf.ethz.ch

Christian Estler
ETH Zurich
christian.estler@inf.ethz.ch

Bertrand Meyer
ETH Zurich
bertrand.meyer@inf.ethz.ch

ABSTRACT

MOOCs (Massive Open Online Courses), which have taken higher education by storm, are an opportunity to elevate the quality of existing residential courses. We report about an experimental attempt during the Autumn 2013 semester at ETH Zurich, involving our "Introduction to Programming" course. We designed and implemented a MOOC infrastructure and used it as a SPOC (Small Private Online Course) to support and complement the existing course. The results reported in this article are encouraging for two reasons: first, the participation level was good, in spite of the fact that the online course was an optional addition to the residential course; second, students really liked the assessments (quizzes and programming exercises), in spite of the fact that assessments did not count towards the course final grade. The data we collected suggest that this may, at least in part, be due to a gamification aspect we introduced in the course: awarding virtual badges for obtaining full points in the quizzes.

Categories and Subject Descriptors

K.3.2 [**Computers and Education**]: Computer and Information Science Education—*Computer science education*

General Terms

Design, Human Factors

Keywords

CS1, MOOC, Pedagogy, SPOC

1. INTRODUCTION

The paper describes our experience with the Autumn 2013 edition of the "Introduction to Programming" course involving 286 freshmen at ETH Zurich. This year we decided to complement the traditional residential course (taught in German, with exercise sessions both in German and in English) with an online counterpart, taught in English and organized like a SPOC. The acronym SPOC was used the first time by Fox [5], who advocates the use of the MOOC "idea" to supplement classroom teaching as opposed to replacing it. In addition to the traditional frontal (live) lectures, exercise sessions, and home assignments, the SPOC provided an online, streamlined version of the above: lectures divided in relatively short lecture segments (17 minutes on average), quizzes both inside and outside the lecture segments, and programming exercises providing automatic feedback. We also introduced badges (awarded for submitting 100% correct answers in quizzes) to increase students' motivation. We summarize the results as follows:

- Students liked the course and responded with enthusiasm to the SPOC;

- Attendance to the live lectures remained stable with respect to the previous year;

- Attendance to each online lecture segment involved 71% of the total number of students on average;

- The average number of attempts to solve the online quizzes was almost five times bigger than the average number of views per online lecture;

- For any given quiz, an average of 48% of the first semester students enrolled in the online course scored 100%, and got the corresponding badge;

- On average, students worked on half of the given programming exercises, and 22% of them worked on 75% to 100% of all the exercises.

- In most cases, students completed programming exercises in a single session lasting an average of 20 minutes, and in 80% of the sessions students' solutions passed all tests.

The above findings suggest that the ideas of awarding a completion badge in quizzes and providing immediate and detailed feedback in programming exercises is effective in motivating the students.

The paper is organized as follows: Section 2 provides some background on our residential "Introduction to Programming" course and its structure; Section 3 describes the software platform we used and the personalizations and additions we provided ad hoc; Section 4 summarizes the data we collected, and our related comments; Section 5 contains our final comments and lessons learned from the experience.

Table 1: Students' initial computing experience

Computer experience	Number of Students	%
Less than 2 years	0	0
2-4 years	4	2
5-7 years	22	8
7-9 years	69	25
More than 10 years	178	65
Total	273	100

Table 2: Students' initial programming experience

Programming Experience	%
Never programmed	16
No O-O experience	25
Less than 100 classes	53
More than 100 classes	6
Total	100

Table 3: Previous knowledge of programming languages

Programming language	%
Java	23
C#	13
PHP	12
JavaScript	10
C++	8
Eiffel	7
Python	7
Others	20
Total	100

Table 4: Students' initial self-assessment

Desired level experience	Number of Students	%
Beginner	99	36
Intermediate	126	46
Advanced	48	18
Total	273	100

2. OUR "INTRODUCTION TO PROGRAMMING" COURSE: STRUCTURE AND STUDENT POPULATION

The residential course is 14 weeks long, excluding exams, which happen approximately 8 months after the course ends. The course includes four hours of live lectures per week over two days, and two hours of exercise sessions per week. The live lectures are of two kinds: traditional, frontal lectures and more interactive, hands-on exercise sessions. There are 10 home assignments and 2 mock exams to simulate a realistic exam setting. The exercise groups typically include 20 students each and are differentiated by skill level and language (English or German). Differentiating the exercise groups according to students' self-assessed skill levels (beginners, intermediate, and advanced) has proven to be quite effective in the last five years, because it enforced more homogeneous groups, which in turn helped to keep students with different backgrounds interested and motivated. Without this differentiation, advanced students tended to loose interest when teaching assistants were slowing down to explain basic concepts to beginners, while beginners tended to become frustrated when teaching assistants were speeding up to keep advanced students interested. The preliminary self-assessment questionnaire was useful to know also about the students' backgrounds.

We now summarize the results of this year's questionnaire. Table 1 clearly indicates that all the students have been significantly exposed to computers (mainly for Internet browsing, social networking, and games) for an average of 8 years (we also know that all of them have either a computer at home or a laptop). Though hardly surprising, it is worth mentioning that we have been having similar results since 2004, so these numbers appear to be rather stable.

To tailor the course to the student population, it is important to know about previous programming experience. The data we gathered on students' such experience is in line with what we observed in previous years. Table 2 shows that more than half of the students attending the residential course come with some object-oriented programming experience, while only 16% have never programmed before. In addition, 18% of the students have a part-time job that re-

quires some programming.

Table 3 shows the aggregated data about relevant programming language knowledge (we only considered answers claiming a "good" and "very good" knowledge) regardless of the knowledge distribution among students. To put the information in the right context, 41% of the total number of students enrolled in the course declared such a (good or very good) knowledge, and among them, the average student declared to know 2.5 programming languages. From the data it is clear that we have to deal with a wide selection of programming languages. This reinforces our choice to focus on the Eiffel programming language [4, 12] that, although not the most adopted for "Introduction to Programming" courses, makes it easier to express and teach the object-oriented concepts and methodology, and allows a gentle introduction to program verification through the Design by Contract technique [10].

Finally, in Table 4 we see students' self-assessed skill level that we used to assign them to a corresponding exercise group in order to avoid the issues of too heterogeneous exercise groups explained earlier.

Our approach to teaching "Introduction to Programming" is an extension of the "Inverted Curriculum" approach [11, 16]. In fact, we integrate the exercises based on the main GUI application (present in the residential course's home assignments) with smaller, self-contained examples and case studies. These allow students to focus on the main concepts in isolation, without the noise that a bigger application inevitably brings. The main application remains useful because it mimics the complexity of software they can find in real world applications, and lets the students cope with the software development activity that has been known for a long time to be the most relevant cost-wise: software maintenance [8].

3. OUR CUSTOMIZED ONLINE LEARNING PLATFORM

The platform we used was made of two distinct parts: a Moodle [2] installation, enhanced with a plugin we programmed to provide quizzes integrated in the online lectures, and a service infrastructure for developing and executing Eiffel programs in the browser, both running on our servers.

3.1 Virtual Learning Environment

For implementing the SPOC we used the Moodle platform, because it is free, open source, widely used, extensible, actively maintained, and with a large user community.

The online course sequence is linear and consists of 14 lectures. Every online lecture is divided into one or more segments (of variable duration), one or more quizzes, and zero or more programming exercises. Topics' durations vary between 5 and 40 minutes, with an average of 17 minutes. To tackle the well known issues deriving from reduced attention span (see for example [13] for an old but still valid reference), we embedded quizzes in the longer online lecture segments. The quizzes provide immediate feedback, can be attempted an unlimited number of times and are not graded. Their purpose is twofold: to allow attention span recovery by breaking the online lecture flow, and to test short-term topic comprehension.

The quizzes for the online lectures appear in a dedicated area next to the (paused) video presentation, allowing for a side-by-side visualization of the quiz and the relevant lecture material. The quizzes are standard multiple choice quizzes, consisting on average of 5 questions with each question offering 7 possible answers.

In general, we designed quizzes and exercises to be useful both in the short term (after taking an online lecture) and in the long term (for reviewing material for the exam, that in our case happens 8 months after the course end).

It is noteworthy to compare the differences between our approach and the "closed laboratory" as advocated by the ACM/IEEE Joint Curriculum Task Force [3, 19]. A closed laboratory model is defined as a:

> "scheduled, structured, and supervised assignment that involves the use of computing hardware, software or instrumentation for its completion. Students attend a closed lab by attending a scheduled session, usually 2-3 hours long, at a specific facility. Supervision is provided by the instructor. [...] Closed laboratories are particularly important in situations where the assignment relies on instructor-student interaction or a team effort among students to complete the work."

In our case the online exercises were intended as mostly optional self-study, they certainly did not rely particularly on instructor-student interaction (though some interactions actually took place, mostly by email) and they typically did not require a team effort among students.

3.2 In-browser programming exercises

We used programming exercises as another form of student feedback for some of the more advanced online lectures. The exercises were designed to train the specific topics, e.g. recursion, by providing an incomplete program that needed to be completed by the students. The correctness of students' solutions was evaluated automatically by running a test-suite on their submitted programs. The number of passing and failing test cases, together with the individual test inputs and outputs, were reported back to the students and they could resubmit new solutions, as many times as they liked. We persisted each student's best solution to allow them to review their submission at a later time. Finally, the programming exercises provided references to the relevant documentation of library classes and APIs for each programming exercise.

The infrastructure used for the programming exercises is a self-contained web service that we developed for this SPOC. The service, publicly available [1], provides basic functionalities for writing and running programs in the browser, thus allowing students to learn and train programming skills without the need to install any software.

For each programming exercise, a lecturer uploads a template program code together with a test suite. Each exercise is then accessible on a separate web page that features a syntax-highlighted code editor, options for compiling and running the program, as well as an output window for displaying the results of running the test suite. And example of such a page is shown in Figure 1. Finally, the exercise pages are integrated into the main SPOC pages, similar to the YouTube lecture videos, through HTML frame tags.

3.3 Assessment of student perception of the SPOC

Overall, students liked the course. With respect to the SPOC section, from Table 5 we see that for most of the students who answered the five questionnaires (in total we collected 318 answers for the various online lectures, quizzes, and programming exercises), the online lectures and quizzes were substantially just at the right difficulty level. The programming exercises were assessed as "too hard" by 23% of the respondents. This is consistent with our experience from previous years.

3.4 Participation

Our SPOC was de-facto open for enrollment to everybody. However, we did not advertise it, because we wanted to focus on our students during the first attempt of running this online course. A the end of the online course we had 327 enrollments, of which 286 were first semester students (determined through analysis of ETH Zurich email domains). Thus, apart from a few early testers and some outsiders constituting 12% of the enrolled participants, the majority of participants of the online course were ETH students.

Table 6 reports the hits per online lecture segment. Assuming that each student accessed each segment once or not at all, these data suggests that each segment was, on average, accessed by 71% of the students. Considering that "Introduction to Programming" students at our university take the exam approximately eight months after having attended the residential course, some may not have done all the exercises or attended all the online lectures during the course period, which is the period we used to collected the data presented here. This implies that our numbers are likely to be conservative estimates.

Table 6: Hits for online lectures, quizzes, and badges awarded. Column "Hits" reports how often a unit was viewed; column "No. segments" reports how many segments were part of a unit; "Quiz hits" reports how quizzes were viewed; "No. quizzes" reports how many quizzes were part of each unit; "No. badges awarded" reports how many badges were awarded in each unit. The second part of the table shows average values for *hits per unit** , *hits per segment*** , *hits per quiz*[†], and *badges per quiz*[‡].

Unit	Hits	No. segments	Quiz hits	No. quizzes	No. badges awarded
Unit 2	968	1	1597	1	254
Unit 3	588	1	2374	1	191
Unit 4	866	2	1790	1	156
Unit 5	915	3	1406	1	169
Unit 6	859	3	1337	1	139
Unit 7	585	3	703	3	488
Unit 8	1191	5	1255	2	314
Unit 9	654	3	935	1	142
Unit 10	870	5	1114	5	601
Unit 11	213	1	803	1	123
Unit 12	228	2	550	1	77
Unit 13	187	1	661	1	131
Unit 14	636	3	847	1	116
Unit 15	434	5	548	1	67
Unit 16	542	4	733	1	65
Total	9736	42	23583	22	3033
Average	649*	232**	—	1072[†]	138[‡]

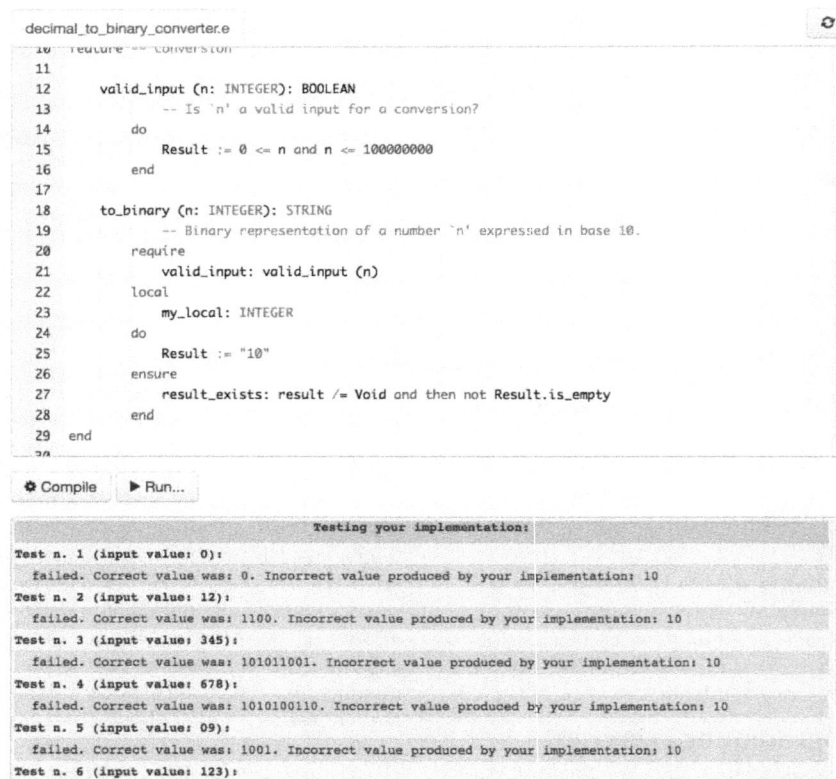

```
10   feature -- Conversion
11
12       valid_input (n: INTEGER): BOOLEAN
13            -- Is 'n' a valid input for a conversion?
14       do
15            Result := 0 <= n and n <= 100000000
16       end
17
18       to_binary (n: INTEGER): STRING
19            -- Binary representation of a number 'n' expressed in base 10.
20       require
21            valid_input: valid_input (n)
22       local
23            my_local: INTEGER
24       do
25            Result := "10"
26       ensure
27            result_exists: result /= Void and then not Result.is_empty
28       end
29   end
```

decimal_to_binary_converter.e

⚙ Compile   ▶ Run...

Testing your implementation:

Test n. 1 (input value: 0):
  failed. Correct value was: 0. Incorrect value produced by your implementation: 10
Test n. 2 (input value: 12):
  failed. Correct value was: 1100. Incorrect value produced by your implementation: 10
Test n. 3 (input value: 345):
  failed. Correct value was: 101011001. Incorrect value produced by your implementation: 10
Test n. 4 (input value: 678):
  failed. Correct value was: 1010100110. Incorrect value produced by your implementation: 10
Test n. 5 (input value: 09):
  failed. Correct value was: 1001. Incorrect value produced by your implementation: 10
Test n. 6 (input value: 123):

Figure 1: Screenshot of an in-browser programming exercise, showing the code editor and the output window which displays the passing and failing test cases.

Table 5: Student evaluation for SPOC online lectures, quizzes, and programming exercises (%)

Assessment	Lectures	Quizzes	Progr. exercises
Too easy	11	11	9
Just right	84	84	69
Too hard	5	5	23

4. COLLECTED DATA AND RESULTS

4.1 Assessment of quizzes

While we allowed just one submission for the standard homework assignments that were independent of the SPOC, we allowed unlimited attempts for the online quizzes, to focus students on the formative aspect of the assessment [15, 17]. With the same objective in mind, we provided detailed feedback in most of the quiz answers [6]. Interestingly enough, we received feedback from the students who asked for even more feedback to foster their learning. Every quiz was made of several questions, and for each quiz attempt the questions were presented in different order and the corresponding answers randomly shuffled. Each quiz attempt was independent from the previous attempts, so students had to provide previously given correct answers again. We intended the quizzes to be not too time consuming (5 to 15 minutes each) and intended to help consolidate the corresponding online lecture topics. We also added to the quizzes a gamification aspect [7]: to motivate students to solve each quiz 100% correctly—a goal we decided to be reasonable given the quiz complexity—we designed and awarded an electronic badge for each entirely correctly solved quiz. There were no penalties for multiple quiz attempts, to encourage motivated students to get the associated badge if they really wanted to.

Indeed the quiz data in Table 6 show that students on average attempted quizzes almost five times more than they viewed online lectures. This is a surprising result, suggesting that the choice of awarding such badges for correct completion may have worked out well. Another interpretation could be that students might have clicked randomly on the quiz answers until they got the completion badge, without actually learning anything. Though this is in principle possible, we believe it is very unlikely: the probability for such students of achieving a 100% score on our quizzes (a quiz has, on average, 5 questions with 7 randomly shuffled answer options per question) is only 0.006%. Thus, it is clear that it would take many more than five attempts to achieve a perfect score in the quiz.

An interesting aspect emerging from our data is that students of our online course took many of the quizzes despite of the fact that quizzes did not influence the final grade. This suggest that the students were not only trying to optimize their learning efforts towards achieving good grades [14, 18] but were also motivated to prove to themselves that they can solve the various quizzes and receive all the badges.

Table 6 shows that for each quiz, an average of 138 students scored 100% and got the corresponding badge. These 138 students constitute 48% of the total number of first semester students enrolled in the online course. An interesting result, considering that only 20 students (6%) participated in all the online course activities.

While the quizzes fall under the category of multiple choice, they vary considerably in structure. For example, to test understanding of source code, we have one type of quiz in which students have to fill in the blanks in an existing incomplete program by choosing among options in several drop-down menus (one option each menu). The catch is that given a set of drop-down menu options, many of them can be correct if considered in isolation. However, only one of them is correct when considered in combination with the options in the other menus.

4.2 Assessment of programming exercises

We also collected basic usage statistics for the programming exercises. For the analysis shown in this section, we focus on the main SPOC target group, consisting of the 286 first semester students. Out of those 286 students, a total of 105 (37%) worked on at least one of the four programming exercises we provided.

For all numbers reported in this section, we removed programming sessions that lasted less than two minutes as they are likely to represent students "having a quick look" but not actually working on the exercise.

We found that, on average, students worked on 1.7 out of the 4 programming exercises. About 22% completed three or four of the exercises.

The work on the exercises spreads over 190 distinct sessions, implying that, on average, a student worked in 1.8 distinct sessions (where a session is recorded as a browser session). This number indicates that, in most cases, students complete an exercise within a single session and do not return at a later time to try the programming exercise again. The average length of a student session, starting from the first compilation until the last compilation/execution, was about 20 minutes with at least 50% of all sessions lasting longer then 15 minutes.

Looking at the number of compilations (2004) and executions (826) of programs that were written by students, we observe, on average, 2.5 times more compilations than executions. We interpret this as an indicator that it takes students 2-3 attempts before they write syntactically correct code that can then be executed. This is in line with the amount of effort we expected from the average student to solve these kinds of programming exercises.

We believe that the feedback about passing and failing test cases motivates students in similar way the badges motivate them to complete the quizzes. We found that in almost 80% of all cases, students continued to work on their exercise solution until it passed all test cases.

While not all students worked on the programming exercises, individual feedback was mostly positive. For example, a student reported that

> "The cool thing about MOOC is you don't need [an IDE] or even a Computer but ...you can't debug it unless you copy it into [the IDE]."

This quote is in line with our impression that the convenience of in-browser programming exercises is appreciated but more advanced features should be added to improve the student's experience.

5. CONCLUSIONS

Research shows that even though MOOCs offer autonomy and connectedness, the lack of support and guidance can be an issue [9]. With our Autumn 2013 "Introduction to Programming" course, we tried to take the best of residential courses and MOOCs by integrating a SPOC into our standard residential course. The results have been encouraging: students' response was positive, and so were the participation and completion rates, given that the material was not mandatory. In addition, we are left with the impression that gamification seems to motivate students to learn.

Individual students' comments included:

> "The MOOC was helpful to understand the theory. "

> "The MOOC is an awesome thing. However, some things could still be improved. Shorter videos and more precise titles are desirable. This way, it could be used as a better learning aid, i.e. looking up a specific topics, watching the same section multiple times."

> "The MOOC is a very good idea to repeat/test what you have learned."

> "The MOOC, which was introduced as a secondary learning instance, complements the lecture perfectly and should absolutely be continued and advanced in the next year. "

As future research, we will analyze the final exam results (once the students have taken the exam) to measure the effect of the SPOC on the students' performance. We are also planning to advertise the online course as a MOOC to the outside world, so others can attend it or use it for teaching. Finally, we will use the insights and findings from this paper to improve our online course for its next iterations in the future.

6. ACKNOWLEDGMENTS

The Authors would like to thank Andre Macejko for his work on the implementation of the Moodle plugin for quizzes in online lectures, Carlo A. Furia for his comments on the paper draft, and the anonymous referees for their useful remarks.

7. REFERENCES

[1] Eiffel 4 mooc. http://se.inf.ethz.ch/data/spoc/. Accessed April 14, 2014.

[2] Moodle virtual learning environment. https://moodle.org. Accessed April 14, 2014.

[3] C. Chang. Computing curricula 2001 computer science: The joint task force on computing curricula. http://www.acm.org/sigcse/cc2001/cc2001.pdf. Accessed April 14, 2014.

[4] E. Committee. *ECMA International Standard 367: Eiffel Analysis, Design and Programming Language*. ECMA International, 2006.

[5] A. Fox. From MOOCs to SPOCs. *Communications of the ACM*, 56(12):38–40, Dec. 2013.

[6] G. Gibbs and C. Simpson. Conditions under which assessment supports students' learning. In *Learning and Teaching in Higher Education*, 2005.

[7] J. J. Lee and J. Hammer. Gamification in education: What, how, why bother? *Academic Exchange Quarterly*, 15(2), 2011.

[8] B. P. Lientz and E. B. Swanson. *Software Maintenance Management*. Addison Wesley, Reading, MA, 1980.

[9] J. Mackness, S. F. J. Mak, and R. Williams. The ideals and reality of participating in a mooc. In *7th International Conference on Networked Learning*, pages 266–274, 2010.

[10] B. Meyer. Applying design by contract. *Computer*, 25(10):40–51, 1992.

[11] B. Meyer. Towards an object-oriented curriculum. In *TOOLS (11)*, pages 585–594, 1993.

[12] B. Meyer. *Object-Oriented Software Construction, 2nd edition*. Prentice Hall, 1997.

[13] J. Middendorf and A. Kalish. The "change-up" in lectures. *The National Teaching & Learning Forum*, 5(2), 1996.

[14] C. Miller and M. Parlett. Up to the mark: a study of the examination game. *Guildford: Society for Research into Higher Education*, 1974.

[15] P. F. Mitros, K. K. Affidi, G. J. Sussman, C. J. Terman, J. K. White, L. Fischer, and A. Agarwal. Teaching electronic circuits online: Lessons from MITx's 6.002x on edX. In *ISCAS*, pages 2763–2766, 2013.

[16] M. Pedroni and B. Meyer. The inverted curriculum in practice. *SIGCSE Bull.*, 38(1):481–485, Mar. 2006.

[17] V. J. Shute. Focus on formative feedback. *Review of Educational Research*, pages 153–189, Mar. 2008.

[18] B. Snyder. The hidden curriculum. In *Learning and Teaching in Higher Education*, 2005.

[19] A. B. Tucker. *Computing Curricula 1991: Report on the ACM/IEEE-CS Joint Curriculum Task Force*. ACM Press, 1991.

Teaching and Learning with MOOCs: Computing Academics' Perspectives and Engagement

Anna Eckerdal
Dept. of Information Technology
Uppsala University
Uppsala, Sweden
+46 18 471 7893
anna.eckerdal@it.uu.se

Päivi Kinnunen
Dept. of Computer Science and
Engineering
Aalto University, Finland
+358 50 436 4699
paivi.kinnunen@aalto.fi

Neena Thota
Faculty of Creative Industries
University of Saint Joseph
Macau, S.A.R.
+853 8796 4400
neenathota@usj.edu.mo

Aletta Nylén
Dept. of Information Technology
Uppsala University
Uppsala, Sweden
+46 18 471 7122
aletta.nylen@gmail.com

Judy Sheard
Faculty of Information Technology
Monash University
Caulfield East, VIC, Australia
+61 3 9903 2701
judy.sheard@monash.edu

Lauri Malmi
Dept. of Computer Science and
Engineering
Aalto University, Finland
+358 50 577 2176
Lauri.Malmi@aalto.fi

ABSTRACT

During the past two years, Massive Open Online Courses (MOOCs) have created wide interest in the academic world raising both enthusiasm for new opportunities for universities and many concerns for the future of university education. The discussion has mainly appeared in non-scientific forums, such as magazine articles, columns and blogs, making it difficult to judge wider opinions within academia. To collect more rigorous data we surveyed teachers, researchers, and academic managers on their opinions and experiences of MOOCs. In this paper, we present our analysis of responses from the computer science academic community (n=137). Their feelings about MOOCs are highly mixed. Content analysis of open-ended questions revealed that the most often mentioned positive aspects included affordances of MOOCs, freedom of time and location for studying, and the possibility to experience teaching from top-level international teachers/experts. The most common negative aspects included concerns about pedagogical designs of MOOCs, assessment practices, and lack of interaction with the teacher. About half the respondents claimed they had not changed their teaching as a result of MOOCs, a small number used MOOCs as learning resources and very few were engaging with MOOCs in any significant way.

Categories and Subject Descriptors

K.3.1: Computer Uses in Education – *computer-managed instruction, distance learning*

K.3.2 [**Computers and Education**]: Computer and Information Science Education – *computer science education*

General Terms

Human factors

Keywords

MOOCs Massive Open Online Courses; e-learning; distance learning; open learning; computing academics; pedagogy

1. INTRODUCTION

The term Massive Open Online Course (MOOC) was coined in 2008 to describe an open online course offered by the University of Manitoba. In 2011, this phenomenon exploded into wider awareness among academics, when top US universities started to give MOOCs and new educational providers joined the field. Since then, discussions on MOOCs have proliferated in blogs, newspaper columns, and magazines [1, 5, 7, 14]. Most discussions are centered on instructional methods, the quality of instruction, and the potential disruption to traditional university education.

Academic research relating to MOOCs has only recently started to appear in journals and conference proceedings. However, most research has focused on the learner perspective and institutional threats and opportunities, leading to a lack of published research on academics' experiences and practices [8]. Teachers are the central stakeholders in this issue. We therefore carried out a survey to learn about academics' awareness, attitudes, and perceptions of MOOCs, as well as their concrete initiatives in relation to MOOCs. Our research focuses on *What are academics' perspectives on current trends relating to MOOCs?* We collected data using a web questionnaire distributed internationally to the computer science/IT education and broader academic community. In this paper, we especially investigate *the computer science/IT academic community views of the pros and cons of MOOCs from the aspect of teaching and learning (RQ1)*. We also investigate *how teachers incorporate MOOCs into their own teaching and their own development of MOOCs (RQ2)*.

In the next section we discuss related research. In Sections 3 and 4 we present our research design and findings, and we discuss and conclude the findings in Sections 5 and 6.

2. RELATED RESEARCH

MOOCs are online courses which are offered free of charge, require no entry requirements, and give no formal accreditation [10]. They typically integrate social networking and are characterized by the provision of online resources. MOOCs are often facilitated by an acknowledged expert in the field. A number of elite universities have led the development of MOOCs: edX, a non-profit organization from Harvard and MIT delivers MOOCs in humanities, computer science, health research, and chemistry; Coursera, an education company that partners with universities, provides some of their existing courses in sciences, humanities, business, and math; and Udacity, a private educational organization focuses on computer science. More recently other universities worldwide have developed MOOCs and number of other platforms now support MOOCs: Futurelearn (UK), OpenHPI (Germany), OpenupEd (pan-European), and Open2Study (Australia).

A recent worldwide survey of educators [15] shows that in 2013 only 13% of higher education institutions offered a MOOC; but 43% plan to offer MOOCs by 2016. The survey found that 84% of the educators surveyed believe that MOOCs complement the education offered by higher education institutions and are most appropriate for continuing education courses. The survey also found that 41% of the educators view the lack of a consistent review and grading system as the biggest drawback of MOOCs.

A number of MOOCs are offered in computer science subjects. Ben Ari [2] proposes that MOOCs offer new opportunities for both students and instructors, and are likely to have an impact on university level computer science courses because of their convenience, potential to lower the costs of running a course, and accessibility to large cohorts of students. Teachers are able to supplement on-campus courses with recorded lectures from MOOCS, facilitating implementation of the "flipped classroom" model where class time is used for discussion of problems with students [9] and to focus more on software development and less on learning syntax [13]. MOOCs also provide the facility to present information to students using different approaches such as instructor-directed, collaborative, or blended learning [3].

For an individual teacher running a MOOC, there are many challenges. The course material may need to be constantly updated and this entails considerable time and effort [17]. Johnson [6], reporting on an experience running a MOOC, claimed that preparing video lectures and composing problems for homework took significant time.

In 2013, a survey [4] of 112,000 undergraduate students about their technology experiences and expectations revealed that students prefer blended learning environments while beginning to experiment with MOOCs. The need to support and challenge students and give them the benefits of interaction with peers remains an unresolved issue [6]. Vardi [16] argues that MOOCS suffer from a lack of clear pedagogical foundations and an inability to cater to the needs of individual students.

Assessments in MOOCs are problematic, as automatic assessment has limited scope, and peer assessment can be too superficial to be truly effective [2, 3]. Another area of concern is the detection of plagiarism and the validation/certification for original work [3]. However, the biggest challenge for MOOC organizers appears to be low completion rates as students drop out in large numbers. A recent study [12] of a million users through 16 Coursera courses shows that course completion rates average only 4% across all courses, with higher completion rates for courses designed with less homework assignments and workload for students.

3. RESEARCH DESIGN

To learn about computing academics' awareness, attitudes and perceptions concerning MOOCs we constructed an online questionnaire, which consisted of both closed, mostly multiple choice or Likert-style questions, as well as several open-ended questions. We constructed the questionnaire[1] as a joint effort of our research team, adopting ideas for questions from the literature and ongoing discussions on several forums. The questionnaire consisted of two parts. The first part (9 questions) was aimed at all academics regardless of prior knowledge or firsthand experience of MOOCs. The second part (11 questions) was aimed at those respondents who had more experiences with and knowledge of MOOCs.

The questionnaire was piloted with a group of 20 academics from different engineering education fields and minor modifications were made based on feedback. Invitations to complete the final questionnaire were posted to several mailing lists (e.g. SIGCSE, PPIG, CSEd) as well as our own personal contact lists in May – June 2013. We also asked our respondents to forward the invitation to their colleagues.

We acknowledge that our data represents only a small number of all computing academics' perceptions at a certain point of time. However, since we were able to receive responses from five continents, 19 countries, and more than 90 universities, we are fairly confident that the results highlight many of the MOOC related topics that are discussed by the international community of computing academics. The questionnaire provided us with rich data. Many respondents had taken the time and effort to elaborate on pros and cons of MOOCs and to provide arguments in open-ended questions. Many of the responses to the open-ended questions were several sentences (or even several paragraphs) long. To enhance the credibility and trustworthiness of the data analysis we provide a description of the analysis procedure in the following paragraphs and in reporting the findings we provide some example quotes from the data to explain and support our conclusions.

3.1 Data analysis

To answer our research questions we analyzed responses from three open-ended questions: "What positive aspects do you see in MOOCs?", "What negative aspects do you see in MOOCs?", and "If you have changed your teaching, please elaborate here on what you have done and your reasons for any changes". In addition, we analyzed responses to a couple of closed questions concerning academics' background, attitudes towards MOOCs, and what effect MOOCs have had on respondents' campus-based courses. The remaining survey questions are not relevant to our current research questions. They will be reported elsewhere.

As there was a scarcity of previous research on academics' perspectives on MOOCs and no relevant frameworks or models were found, we decided to conduct an inductive content analysis [11] to analyze the open-ended responses relating to pros and cons of MOOCs. We proceeded stepwise in our analysis. Four members of our research team individually read the answers to the open-ended questions and made notes on what kind of themes might emerge from the data. They then compared notes and agreed on preliminary categories. To verify that they had a common understanding of the categories two researchers together analyzed about 20% (n=30) of the responses to the question about the positive aspects of MOOCs (positive quotes) and the other two researchers analyzed 20% of the responses to the question about the negative aspects of MOOCs (negative quotes). After that they interchanged the quotes (but not the categorizations) and analyzed them again. They then compared the results, discussed possible

---

[1] http://users.cse.aalto.fi/pakinnun/MOOC/Eckerdal-14_MOOC_questionnaire.pdf

disagreements and made small adjustments to their categories and categorization rules. This process was continued until harmonization was achieved between the coders. After this initial phase of analysis, two members of the team analyzed the rest of the positive quotes and the other two the negative quotes.

The responses to the question concerning the effect of MOOCs on respondents' campus-based courses were analyzed by two researchers. At first one researcher categorized the themes found in the responses and then the other researcher reviewed the results to verify the analysis.

4. FINDINGS

The total number of responses to the survey was 236 of which 137 were teachers from the computing or IT disciplines. Our study focuses on this group.

The gender profile of the computing and IT academics was 71% male and 27% female, with 2% not responding to this question. Most respondents were from North America (43%) or Europe (33%) with the remainder from Australasia (11%), Asia (2%), Middle East (1%) or Africa (1%) and 9% not responding to this question. Overall, 89% of respondents were working as teachers, with the remainder having roles as researchers, educational developers, or postgraduate students. However, all respondents had some teaching experience, with 84% indicating more than 5 years and 74% more than 10 years.

4.1 Attitudes towards MOOCs

This section reports findings related to our first research question (RQ1). The survey participants were asked to identify any attitudes towards MOOCs that they had perceived from discussions amongst their teaching colleagues. The results are shown in Figure 1. The most common attitude amongst teachers was one of concern (55%) or positive (36%). Few were uninterested (14%). Note that multiple responses were allowed for this question.

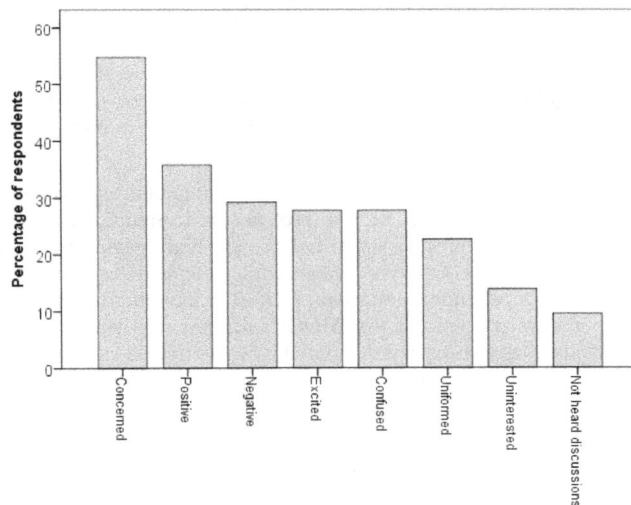

Figure 1: Attitudes of academics towards MOOCs (note that multiple responses were allowed).

We asked the respondents to elaborate on positive and negative aspects of MOOCs in two open-ended questions. A total of 106 (77% of 137 respondents) responded to the open-ended question regarding negative aspects of MOOCs and 107 (78%) answered the question regarding positive aspects. The analysis revealed seven topics that respondents related to being positive and/or negative: *teaching and learning*, *power issues*, *resources*, *educational outcomes*, *cultural issues*, *recruitment*, and *general experience*. Guided by the research questions in this paper we concentrate only on teaching and learning topics raised by our respondents. A more detailed analysis of the teaching and learning topic indicated that it could be divided into five subcategories (*pedagogy and learning environment, affordances of MOOCs, interaction and collaboration, assessment and certification, accessibility*), which we discuss in more detail below. An individual response often included several topics and we therefore included such responses in multiple categories. The most often mentioned positive and negative aspects were related to pedagogy and learning environment and affordance of MOOCs, whereas access to top teachers evoked no negative comments.

4.1.1 Pedagogy and learning environment

Aspects relating to how MOOCs have been designed, the kind of pedagogy that is used, and the quality of courses was one of the most discussed topics in the open-ended questions. Well over half of the responses included this topic. The topic was the one that raised the most negative comments and only about a quarter of the comments on the topic were positive.

The most common focus of the positive comments was the potential for pedagogical improvement. The respondents saw the challenges of MOOCs, i.e., using new technology, dealing with massive numbers of students, and having teaching openly exposed, as factors that may encourage pedagogical development.

> The hype around MOOCs will cause educational institutions to more carefully evaluate their educational outcomes. Moreover, large lecture classrooms supporting a transmissionist view of education will be strongly encouraged to adopt evidence based pedagogical practices which better engage the students.

Other positive aspects mentioned were that online delivery of content caters to different learning styles more than traditional lectures and that presenting course material online can help "*freeing resources for interactive learning/teaching (tutoring)*".

> For many subjects, being able to see concepts illustrated in video is far superior to reading about it in a book or listening to a passive lecture.

Many of the negative comments, however, pointed out that many MOOCs today are based on a transmissive pedagogy rather than on a pedagogy which encourages students to actively interact with peers and experts, despite the research which shows this to be more effective for their learning. One respondent describes the current situation as "*a regression to an educational "stone age"*".

> I worry about the push of poor pedagogy in MOOCs - ignorance of what are appropriate or beneficial learning structures for online learning, and the use of very one-way based communications to drive learning.

Respondents also expressed concerns relating to lack of personal connection and ignoring the interactive nature of the teaching-learning process.

> Education is not a one-way thing; it involves conversation back and forth between the students and the teacher. Taking the people out of it makes education dry and boring.

4.1.2 Affordances of MOOCs

The affordances of MOOCs were mostly discussed in positive terms. The most common argument is summarized in "*Possibility to study subjects which are not taught at home university*". A common suggestion was that MOOCs could provide deeper and broader competences that would prepare students for professional life, offer trendy topics, and supplement existing courses. One respondent reports *"we consider making some MOOC's classes part of the Curriculum"*.

In contrast to this, other respondents predicted that *"to obtain economy of scale, they can only target topics with broad appeal"*. Another limitation pointed to is that *"not all disciplines are suitable to online study"*.

A perspective voiced by a few respondents was the use of MOOCs as a resource for campus courses:

> If well produced, the videos and other materials can be great resources, particularly for other instructors ... could allow faculty (at face-to-face institutions) to focus on facilitating in-class interaction over presenting background material.

Other respondents raised a warning to teachers considering using MOOCs as an addition to their own courses:

> From the teacher's point of view, it is quite possible that many MOOCs will be closed "take it all as is or leave it" packages, with little opportunity for outside teachers to, e.g., compose their own courses from parts of several MOOCs and some study material of their own.

One respondent argued that MOOCs can help students find a future career: *"They offer a way to see if one is interested in a subject without a large up-front investment (tuition, fees)"*.

In contrast, respondents argued that MOOCs do not scaffold students' professional identity development:

> I believe that MOOCs don't support students in their identity development, as university education and education in the physical world can. I think it addresses foremost the students that are already motivated to learn a subject and somehow have a relation to the subject (an identity related to that). Other students might take the course out of curiosity and they might also learn from it, but not grow as a person engaging in a subject, which could be seen as one major goal of education

Furthermore, some respondents commented that MOOCs are not useful in helping students develop critical thinking, teamwork and collaboration, skills that are most important for a new graduate. On the other hand, respondents suggested that MOOCs can help professionals to refresh knowledge and skills *"especially in fields like computer science, where new technologies are frequently changing."*

4.1.3 Interaction and collaboration

Only few respondents mentioned positive aspects relating to interaction and collaboration. These comments highlighted mostly the social networking or interaction between students: *"The peer chats encourage students to lean on and learn from each other, instead of reliance on the professor"*.

Negative comments concerning interaction related to limited interaction between students and teachers in MOOC courses - or lack of interaction altogether. In fact, this was the second most often mentioned negative aspect of MOOCs. Over one third of the respondents commented, for instance, on the quality of the feedback mechanisms or the type of interaction that is possible between students and teachers. Many respondents were concerned about the lack of individual feedback, or any other kind of interaction between students and teachers, due to the massive scale of MOOCs.

> Students have very limited opportunities to receive individual feedback, have questions answered, have misconceptions corrected, etc.

On the other hand, respondents were also worried about how the lack of immediate feedback from students, that one receives when teaching face-to-face, might affect the instructional process.

> Limited direct assistance. Limited feedback from students to instructor, i.e., the questions that come up during or right after a lecture that allow me to adjust immediately to student confusion.

4.1.4 Assessment and certificates

Very few positive comments were made about assessment related topics. In contrast, many negative aspects were identified in the responses. Assessment and recognition of course completion were viewed as being problematic by about one third of the respondents.

The responses conveyed concerns relating to what can be assessed and how assessment can be done in massive courses. For example, multiple choice questions and peer assessment were highlighted as having limitations. Another aspect of assessment mentioned by a number of respondents was related to plagiarism and acknowledgment of who has done the work.

Respondents also raised the issue of the types of certificates awarded to students and how the certificates would be recognized in relation to traditional degree programs and by employers. Several respondents remarked that existing degree programs and employers do not necessarily acknowledge certificates received from MOOC courses.

> I have been told by some employers that they will not accept a PhD from internet based universities. I feel that many of the students that take MOOCs may not investigate this issue prior to taking online courses and will end up with credits that do not apply to any degree or are not accepted by employers.

4.1.5 Accessibility

Nearly one third of the respondents mentioned the possibility to take a MOOC *"anytime, anywhere, at one's own pace"* as positive. However, one respondent pointed out that time and place independence may also have negative consequences. Since students attending a MOOC may be spread around the world it can be difficult, if not impossible, to find a local group of students that can provide the social encouragement needed to endure long enough to pass the course.

Almost a quarter of the respondents also pointed out that MOOCs can reach students that do not have access to traditional higher education. Examples of such students are high school students, *"people who live far from Universities, people without income, people with peculiar work hours, [...]"*. On the other hand, many respondents pointed out that MOOCs are not well suited for all students. Many suspected that only highly motivated students who already have good study skills benefit from MOOCs. Students with weaker academic background will struggle or drop out, if they even enroll.

Furthermore, a quarter of the respondents mentioned *"access to world class teachers"* or *"opportunity to learn from experts in a field"* as being positive. There were no negative comments specifically targeting access to expert teachers, but as we have already reported, many respondents were concerned about the pedagogy used in MOOCs.

4.2 Academics' engagement with MOOCs

This section reports findings related to our second research question (RQ2). When asked about the effect of MOOCs on their campus-based courses 49% of the participants claimed there had been no effect. Some (15%) claimed that MOOCs had inspired changes in their teaching approach or they were incorporating a MOOC into their course. Only one respondent, an experienced teacher, indicated that the course was a MOOC (see Figure 2).

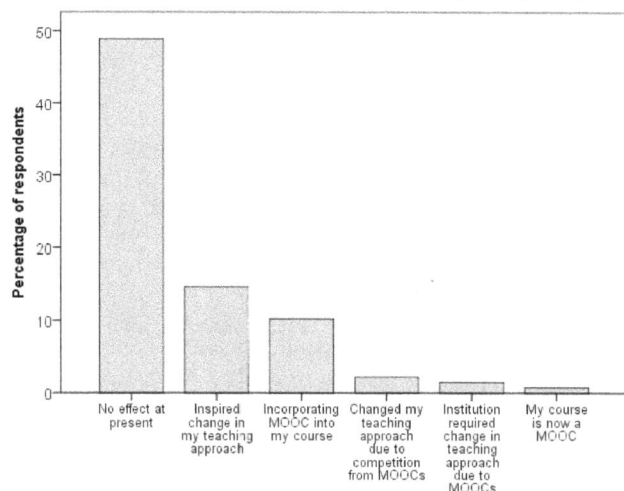

Figure 2: Effect of MOOCs on respondents' campus-based courses (note that multiple responses were allowed).

A question about participants' experience with MOOCs showed that a small number had developed a MOOC (6%) or intended to develop a MOOC (1%). However, a further 12% indicated interest in developing a MOOC. The participants were asked in an open-ended question to elaborate on what they had done to change their teaching practice in response to the MOOCs phenomena. Forty two (31%) responded and provided some explanation.

A number of respondents stated that they had made no changes to their teaching practice. A few mentioned that their teaching practices had or were changing to include elements that were similar to those used in MOOCS, but the introduction of these had not been influenced by the advent of MOOCs.

> I am in the process of adding online materials and automated assessment to courses. This has nothing to do with the MOOC phenomenon. However, what I am doing could transition into something that could drive a successful MOOC.

A small number of respondents stated that they had made no change to their teaching, arguing that their current practices were superior to MOOCs-style education. As one respondent remarked:

> I fail to see how MOOC can be realised without replacing much of the highly valuable personal interaction with domain experts with automated assessment and tutoring systems that mechanise education.

A couple of respondents expressed difficulties with introducing new practices into their local context.

> In the context of MOOCs I have not altered my practise, however I am intrigued by some of the pedagogical changes which this kind of teaching evokes, particularly the social networking aspects.

A number of respondents reported different ways how their teaching practices had changed due to the MOOC phenomena. Some had incorporated elements of MOOCs into their course. Most common were resources such as online quizzes or short videos. One respondent mentioned a change to assessment practice:

> The biggest thing I changed was the nature of student assignments. I have devised ways to force students to produce individualized coursework that cannot easily be plagiarized and that provides good evidence of whether they have actually learned. But such student assignments are more difficult to grade.

The most profound change to teaching practice was the introduction of the "*flipped (inverted) classroom*". About a third of the respondents reported that they were using this teaching model:

> Evaluating the strengths and weaknesses of MOOCs has made me realize the value of the classroom context in traditional teaching, and hence how to make better use of it. I've incorporated more inverted classroom concepts, and more hands-on and team activities into the classroom setting.

Only a small number of participants reported that they were using a MOOC. A few were incorporating MOOCs into their own courses, either using resources from an existing MOOC to supplement their own course: "*I am planning to use videos of lectures from a top-tier university to supplement my own lectures this fall*". Or, in one case requiring students to complete an entire MOOC:

> I am running a course in the fall where each student will sign up for a MOOC of their choice and we will compare/contrast. I want to come up with a proposal for the University's use of such courses.

5. DISCUSSION

The new phenomenon of MOOCs in higher education is clearly in an emergent phase. There is no clear vision of their role in the future. This is demonstrated by the highly mixed opinions in our questionnaire data - the most common attitudes were "*concerned*" and "*positive*". When looking more closely at the arguments behind this split of results, we found slightly more positive aspects than negative aspects mentioned in our open-ended questions. The most commonly mentioned positive aspects were related to increased accessibility to new content (such that is not available locally) and expert international teachers, as well as the typical advantages of on-line courses: freedom of time and place for studying. Many respondents also pointed out that MOOCs can provide free education to non-traditional student groups. Some of these aspects have been mentioned previously in [2, 9, 13, 15].

The negative aspects in respondents' comments focused on the poor pedagogical models applied in MOOCs, e.g., returning to transmissive pedagogies instead of constructivist pedagogies. Other clearly negative aspects were lack of interaction between students and teachers, and the quality of assessment practices. Many comments also presented worries about plagiarism and difficulties to authenticating who was actually doing the work presented by the students. The value and role of MOOC certification thus remains an issue. Our respondents' concerns reflect similar issues being discussed by academics in other forums (see [2, 3, 15, 16]).

When looking at the data from another perspective, we can observe that the positive aspects were discussed in terms of the *potential* of MOOCs for access to content and teachers, and freedom of time and place. These are mainly curriculum and organizational issues. The negative aspects, on the other hand, focus on *current challenges* to the teaching and learning process: pedagogies, interaction, and assessment. Interestingly, accessibility to top level teachers is considered a positive aspect, while the pedagogies that are applied (which the teachers implement) are sources of concern. Many respondents who reported the positive aspect seemed to consider the role of teachers mainly as content experts, not as pedagogical experts. This supports a conclusion that current MOOCs are emphasizing the old-fashioned lecturer-focused transmissive pedagogy.

The academics' descriptions of how the MOOC phenomenon had influenced their teaching further revealed a range of ways that teaching practice has been changed by MOOCs. A few seemed determined not to react to the hype, claiming they were offering students more valuable learning experiences with their current teaching. A number felt their pedagogies were somewhat aligned or aligning with MOOCs for example through providing students with short video 'bites' of lecture material and implementing the flipped classroom model. Others were seeking ways to use MOOCs in some way either as supplementary resources for their teaching, or to replace current course delivery. Very few academics had any deeper involvement with MOOCs.

6. CONCLUSIONS AND FUTURE WORK

MOOCs are a rapidly developing area. Thus, our results present a snapshot of computer science/IT academic community's perceptions and engagement with MOOCs in 2013. The big picture is clearly mixed with positive expectations as well as fears and concerns. Most people in the field are aware of MOOCs but only a small minority report actual changes in their teaching that are related to MOOCs.

The survey clearly identified aspects of MOOCs that need to be addressed by the global community. Firstly, MOOCs should be designed and used with pedagogical models that engage students in active learning. Otherwise there is a risk that their wider adoption forms a step back towards old-fashioned lecture-focused education with transmissive pedagogical thinking. Secondly, serious consideration should be given to the development and use of assessment practices that enable broader evaluation of students' knowledge and skills. It is inevitable that this calls for new research in automatic assessment and feedback methods. Thirdly, with the problems with authenticating student work in MOOCs it is imperative that universities seriously consider their policies in regard to accepting MOOC certificates as part of regular curricula. Overall, many comments in our data suggest that the emergence of MOOCs forces universities to rethink their on-site curricula with new perspectives - what could be the role of MOOCs and what parts of education are best taught in other ways?

We acknowledge that in this kind of research setting we cannot show that our target group forms a representative sample of the CS/IT teaching community. However, the large number of responses we received gives strong support to our belief that our findings reflect the attitudes widely. We intend to repeat the survey next year to find out how this phenomenon is evolving. Our survey has focused on CS/IT academics' perceptions of MOOCs. An equally interesting line of research would be investigating students' experiences of MOOCs. Some scattered research on individual MOOCs exist, but a bigger picture cannot yet be identified. The very recent large survey by Educause [4] found that only a small percent of undergraduate students have taken a MOOC and almost 3 out of 4 students did not even know what MOOCs are.

In the present paper we have focused on teaching and learning related issues in our data set. Our analysis also revealed several other aspects, such as economic issues and use of resources, power issues, and recruitment and dropout rates in MOOCs. We will deal with them in future papers.

7. REFERENCES

[1] Bates, T. *What's right and what's wrong about Coursera-style MOOCs?* [Web log message]. 2012, August 5. http://www.tonybates.ca/2012/08/05/whats-right-andwhats-wrong-about-coursera-style-moocs/

[2] Ben-Ari, M. 2013. *MOOCs on introductory programming: a travelogue.* ACM Inroads, 4, 2 (June, 2013), 58-61.

[3] Cooper, S. and Sahami, M. 2013. Reflections on Stanford's MOOCs. *Commun. ACM*, 56, 2 (February, 2013), 28-30. DOI=10.1145/2408776.2408787

[4] Dahlstrom, E., Walker, J. and Dziuban, C. *ECAR Study of Undergraduate Students and Information Technology.* EDUCAUSE Center for Analysis and Research, Louisville, CO, 2013.

[5] Guzdial, M. *MOOCs today are about less data for the teacher.* [Web log message]. 2013, June 11. http://computinged.wordpress.com/2013/06/11/moocs-today-are-about-less-data-for-the-teacher/

[6] Johnson, D. H. 2013. Teaching a "MOOC:" Experiences from the front line. In *Proceedings of the Digital Signal Processing and Signal Processing Education Meeting (DSP/SPE)* (August 11-14, 2013).

[7] Kolowich, S. *The professors who make the MOOCs.* 2013. http://chronicle.com/article/The-Professors-Behind-the-MOOC/137905/#id=overview

[8] Liyanagunawardena, T. R., Adams, A. A. and Williams, S. A. 2013. MOOCs: A systematic study of the published literature 2008-2012. *The International Review of Research in Open and Distance Learning*, 14, 3 (June, 2013), 202-227.

[9] Martin, F. G. 2012. Will massive open online courses change how we teach? *Commun. ACM*, 55, 8 (August, 2012), 26-28. DOI=10.1145/2240236.2240246

[10] McAuley, A., Stewart, B., Siemens, G. and Cormier, D. *The MOOC model for digital practice.* University of Prince Edward Island, 2010.

[11] Patton, M. Q. 2002. *Qualitative evaluation and research methods.* Sage, Thousands Oaks: CA.

[12] Perna, L., Ruby, A., Boruch, R., Wang, N., Scull, J., Evans, C. and Ahmad, S. The Life Cycle of a Million MOOC Users. In *Proceedings of the MOOC Research Initiative Conference* (Arlington, Texas, USA, December 5-6, 2013).

[13] Severance, C. 2013. MOOCs: An Insider's View. *Computer*, 46, 10 (October, 2013), 93-96.

[14] Touve, D. *MOOC's Contradictions.* 2012, September 11. http://www.insidehighered.com/views/2012/09/11/essay-contradiction-facing-moocs-and-their-university-sponsors

[15] Vala, A. *Adoption of Massive Open Online Courses [Worldwide Survey].* 2013. http://www.huffingtonpost.com/vala-afshar/infographic-adoption-of-m_b_3303789.html

[16] Vardi, M. Y. 2012. Will MOOCs destroy academia? *Commun. ACM*, 55, 11 (November, 2012), 5-5.

[17] Vihavainen, A., Luukkainen, M. and Kurhila, J. 2012. Multi-faceted support for MOOC in programming. In *Proceedings of the 13th Annual Conference on Information Technology Education (SIGITE'12)* (Calgary, Alberta, Canada, 2012). ACM, NY, New York, USA.

Augmenting PBL with Large Public Presentations: A Case Study in Interactive Graphics Pedagogy

Mario Romero[1], Björn Thuresson[1], Christopher Peters[1], Filip Kis[1], Joe Coppard[2], Jonas Andrée[1], Natalia Landázuri[3]

[1]KTH Royal Institute of Technology
Lindstedtsvägen 3, 114 28 Stockholm
{marior, thure, chpeters, fkis, jonandre}@kth.se

[2]Berghs School of Communication AB
Sveavägen 34, 111 93 Stockholm
joe@protothon.com

[3]Karolinska Institutet
CMM L08:03, 171 76 Stockholm
natalia.landazuri@ki.se

ABSTRACT

We present a case study analyzing and discussing the effects of introducing the requirement of public outreach of original student work into the project-based learning of Advanced Graphics and Interaction (AGI) at KTH Royal Institute of Technology. We propose Expo-Based Learning as Project-Based Learning augmented with the constructively aligned goal of achieving public outreach beyond the course. We promote this outreach through three challenges: 1) large public presentations; 2) multidisciplinary collaboration; and 3) professional portfolio building. We demonstrate that the introduction of these challenges, especially the public presentations, had lasting positive impact in the intended technical learning outcomes of AGI with the added benefit of learning team work, presentation skills, timeliness, accountability, self-motivation, technical expertise, and professionalism.

Categories and Subject Descriptors

K.3.2 [**Computers and Education**]: Computer and Information Science Education - *computer science education.*

General Terms

Experimentation, Human Factors.

Keywords

Active Learning, CS Education Research, Graphics/Visualization, Human-Computer Interaction, Outreach, Project-Based Learning, Expo-Based Learning, Large Public Presentations, Public Impact.

1. INTRODUCTION

Consumer electronics are thriving like never before. The January 7, 2014 Las Vegas International Consumer Electronics Show, for example, brought together over 152,000 attendees and produced headline news across the globe for one week. In Computer Science education in general, and in Computer Graphics and Interaction in particular, educators have an unprecedented opportunity to expose students to play a central role in that exhilaratingly large public atmosphere. What will happen to computer science students if they stand center-stage at a public consumer show presenting their original course projects to thousands of people? This is the core question of this paper.

Formally, our research question is:

In the course Advanced Graphics and Interaction (AGI), what are the pedagogical effects of introducing the constructively-aligned requirement of achieving large public impact beyond the course period and participants, students and teachers, through the creation of original interactive graphics systems using project-based learning?

We propose *Expo-Based Learning* (EBL) as Project-Based Learning (PBL) augmented with the constructively-aligned goal of achieving large public impact beyond the course period and participants, students and teachers. We promote this impact through three challenges: 1) large public presentations; 2) multidisciplinary collaboration with communication students from another school; and 3) professional portfolio building. The public presentations challenge the AGI students to meet immutable deadlines, create robust interactive graphics systems, and place them in the hands of a wide audience ranging from toddlers to professors. We grade students based on the impact their project presentations generate at three events: 1) Researcher's Night (ForskarFredag locally in Stockholm); 2) GAMEX; and 3) Open House. Researcher's Night is a yearly exhibition of Europe's leading universities to an audience mostly composed of high school students. GAMEX is a yearly gaming conference gathering over 28,000 attendees across four days. The Open House is a public demonstration to an audience mostly composed of university professors and students. To promote social and cultural relevance, we collaborated with a group of students in a course on Interactive Collaboration (IC) from the Berghs School of Communication. Their role was to co-ideate the development process by challenging what is technically possible and focusing on what is culturally relevant. They were also in charge of producing marketing campaigns for the projects. Finally, to foster lasting impact and motivate the students, we required individual professional portfolios containing a description of their projects, an account of the public impact, and running documented code.

The contribution of this paper is the analysis of the effects of Expo-Based Learning through a case study and a synthesis of actionable insights to reproduce positive results. Succinctly, the public presentations were the greatest motivator for excellence, timeliness, robustness, expertise, and communicativeness. The portfolio served as a strong secondary motivator for the excellence of the work. Finally, when it worked, the collaboration with the communication teams produced some of the most socially outreaching projects in the course. To work, the collaboration required *extraordinary* commitment to communicate and appreciate the different sets of expertise and perspectives.

The following sections present: 2) related work; 3) structure and demographics of AGI and IC; 4) project descriptions; 5) study methodology; 6) results; 7) discussion on implications for course design and implementation; and 8) conclusions and future work.

2. RELATED WORK

The philosophical framework of our version of Advanced Graphics and Interaction (AGI) is constructivist learning, where students gain deep procedural knowledge by building, not memorizing [2, 8, 9]. A core aim is to produce graduates for research and industry who have well-developed practical competencies in addition to strong theoretical foundations [9]. The methodological approach is that of project-based learning [7], with elements of studio-based learning [5]. We judiciously employ Constructive Alignment in every element of AGI. Constructive Alignment maximizes the students' time-on-task by clearly defining the intended learning outcomes (ILOs) of the course and assigning a carefully weighted grading criteria to the learning activities that achieve the ILOs [3]. In particular, we created a detailed breakdown of the public impact elements that students needed to demonstrate for the large public events. We synthesize these grading criteria in the discussion.

While many computer science education researchers have explored the impact of PBL with public presentations on the intended learning outcomes in interactive computer graphics curricula [1, 4], to the best of our knowledge, no one has explored the constructive alignment of evidence-based large public impact through the presentation of course projects at large expos.

3. COURSE STRUCTURE

Advanced Graphics and Interaction (AGI) is the third and last course at KTH's interactive graphics sequence. The sequence starts with Introduction to Visualization and Computer Graphics, which has the pre-requisites of basic programming and mathematics and introduces concepts like geometric transformations, illumination models, rendering, and the principles of interaction programming. The second course, Computer Graphics and Interaction, increases the breadth and depth of the programming and theoretical computer science prerequisites. Ideally, the students who enroll in AGI have followed this sequence. In practice, most of the students in the AGI had followed equivalent sequences. All but one student were capable programmers at the beginning of the course and many had experimented with advanced computer graphics before.

The AGI *Intended Learning Outcomes* (ILOs) are that the students will be able to: 1) Collaborate to build original and stable projects that combine methods in advanced computer graphics and advanced human-computer interaction; 2) Communicate the theory and practice of these methods at a technical and a practical level; 3) Provide informed constructive criticism to the development of the projects from other teams; 4) Demonstrate the projects at large public venues to open audiences; and 5) Collaborate with communication students on the theme and focus of an effective communication strategy for the technical projects.

The course asked for two back-to-back group projects. Figure 1 presents a timeline of the course's milestones: group formation and ideation, project proposal, in-class demonstration, and public presentations. Each project consisted of: 1) a proposal and weekly updates with agile programming methods of developing quickly and discussing collectively what worked, what didn't work, and will work in the coming week [10]; 2) a technical presentation with a demo; 3) large public presentations and hands-on demonstrations of the project results with audience interaction; and 4) a portfolio consisting of a website with a description of the project goals and methods, photographs and videos from the public presentations, documented source code, and stable executable binaries with instructions. The final grade (A, B, C, D,

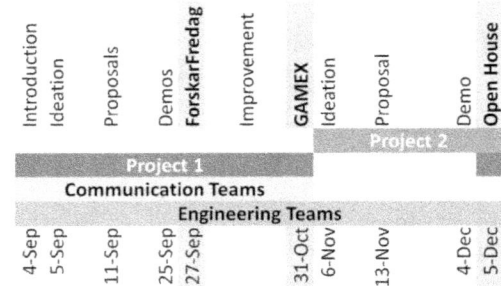

Figure 1. AGI schedule of project milestones.

E) split into Project 1 (50%), Project 2 (40%), and Weekly Assignments (10%). Project 1's grade split into Proposal (10%), Demo (10%), public presentation 1 (10%), public presentation 2 (10%), and public presentation 3 (10%). Project 2's grade split into Proposal (10%), Demo (10%), and public presentation 3 (20%). The grade for the public presentations broke down further into technical and communicative components.

As an integral part of the course, we set up collaboration with the course Interactive Communication (IC) at the renowned Berghs School of Communication in Stockholm, near KTH. The goal of IC was to develop innovative technical concepts with cultural relevance and produce marketing strategies for these concepts. There were 28 master students in AGI (2 women) and 24 first-year students (11 women) in IC who grouped into six projects. We randomly assigned students to different groups balancing their skills across groups. The two schools collaborated only for the first projects, as the IC course ended then. Each group consisted of four or five members from AGI and four from IC. The students met on the first lecture and on the second lecture they were tasked with collectively brainstorming for project ideas. The AGI groups were tasked with proposing technologies for the creation of novel media objects that would not be feasible without the proposed technology. Their instruction was: "focus on the technologies you want to explore." The IC students were tasked with expanding what is technically feasible focusing on what is socially, culturally, and artistically relevant. Their instruction was: "focus on a culturally relevant idea." As a single unit, their task was:

> "Combine at least one advanced computer graphics technique with at least one advanced interaction method and produce a culturally relevant project that will be presented in two large public expos."

AGI consisted of 15 two-hour meetings from September 4 to December 4, 2013, delivered in a state-of-the-art graphics and interaction Visualization Studio (VIC). The goal of studio-based learning was to motivate the students to produce technology that would be integrated to VIC's operations and to facilitate the use of current technology under the expert support of its personnel.

The course included an introduction, two overview lectures of advanced computer graphics and human-computer interaction techniques, and twelve meetings with presentations and discussions focused on the advancement of the projects' milestones described below. Four of these meetings co-occurred with the IC students: 1) Introduction; 2) Ideation; 3) Proposal; and 4) Demo (see Figure 1).

In the introduction, the teacher described the course structure to the students, including the intended learning outcomes and the grading criteria for constructive alignment. During an introductory one-on-one interview, the teacher encouraged the students to use the class as a launching platform to produce a portfolio of their skills through their choice of projects. The argument was to build tangible evidence that future employers will search for and to target the type of job the students would like to pursue.

The students had one week to produce the proposal. Their tasks were to perform a literature review of the area of their choice, determine the boundary of the state-of-the-art, and identify original research that would push this boundary. The teacher guided the work at every step with individual group meetings outside of lecture time. For their proposals, each group presented a project goal, a literature review, a work schedule, and a detailed description of the techniques aimed for the project. The IC groups presented the communication goals and marketing strategy. Other students provided critical feedback, focusing on the feasibility, novelty, and value of the proposal. The teacher moderated the discussions and provided concluding remarks urging the groups to focus on one main goal per project.

After the proposal, the students had two weeks to complete demonstrable prototypes of the projects. The students presented short weekly updates to other members of the class. The teacher and other students provided pointers to potential solutions to challenges. The project in-class presentations included a hands-on demonstration, an oral presentation of the material learned to the rest of the class, and a critical discussion questioning and defending design choices.

The course provided project accountability by replacing individual, written, and private examinations with collective, verbal, and public presentations where students demonstrated their expertise through knowledgeable explanations and justifications of project design choices. The grading was individual. The students publicly presented their first projects in three venues and their second projects in one. The first venue was a yearly European-level education convention, Researcher's Night (ForskarFredag – locally in Stockholm), where all major universities present their research to over 5,000 high school students and teachers during a day-long event at a large public exhibition venue, Medborgarhuset (civic hall). The goal of the convention was to disseminate state-of-the art research and match the interest of the high school students with the educational focus of potentially recruiting universities. Our projects generated one of the highest throughputs in the event, with hands-on interactions and discussions with hundreds of attendees. The teacher instructed the students on informal observation and interview techniques to collect constructive feedback from audience members. The students treated the audience as formative user study participants.

The second presentation venue was a major international gaming fair, GAMEX, held at Stockholm's convention center, Kistamässan, between October 31 and November 3, 2013. The event drew a crowd of over 28,000 attendees. The students took turns to present for four ten-hour days. They presented not only their projects, but everyone's projects. They had to teach each other how to start, troubleshoot, and present all the projects. They were responsible for collecting the evidence of their success in creating impact. They developed pair-wise strategies for taking photographs, observing, and recording video of each other while presenting. The students interacted with thousands of attendees ranging from three-year-old children to 30-year veterans of the gaming industry, from lightning-thumbed teenagers to adults with severe mobility and dexterity limitations.

The third and final presentation venue was a course and studio Open House where the students presented their first and second projects to university professors, researchers, other students, and general guests. We analyze the results and discuss them below.

4. PROJECT DESCRIPTIONS
Table 1 (next page) summarizes the projects. Seven projects belong to the first half of the course. We started with six projects with AGI and IC paired teams. On the first week, SolarSense decided to work separately. Three weeks later, one member of ComposIt decided to work independently and successfully produced WingMan. Two other groups broke up at one and two thirds of the way to GAMEX: InnerVis and Parasomnia, respectively. We analyze this later.

Of the three projects that completed the collaboration, two have continued beyond the course, DangeRoads and FaceUp. SolarSense has also continued beyond the course. Of all the projects, DangeRoads has received the most public attention, with an appearance in the November 27 edition of Stockholm's Metro.

5. STUDY METHODOLOGY
5.1 EBL Evaluation Instruments
We deployed nine formal evaluation instruments on AGI students before, during, and after the course. Unfortunately, we did not have the resources to deploy the instruments on IC students.

1. **Introductory survey**: 12-question online survey querying AGI students' background, skills, interests and expectations from the course; deployed one week before the start of the course.
2. **Introductory individual interview**: 15-minute, one-on-one first-week semi-structured interview deepening the introductory survey and defining the personal intended learning outcomes from the course and introducing the personal portfolio concept as a goal for the course; performed by the instructor.
3. **Review previous course analysis**: Students read and gave constructive critical feedback to the published course analysis from the previous year's AGI [8]. Students received a grade for this report on the first week of class.
4. **Mid-term Evaluation**: 3-question online voluntary survey asking students what is working, what is not working, and what needs to change in the second half of the course.
5. **Self-evidence of participation at GAMEX**: 300-word document, including 5 photographs and a 30-second video, where each student collected evidence of their individual ability to have impact on audience members at GAMEX through the presentation of their projects and the other groups' projects as well. The graded report was due two days after GAMEX.
6. **Focus group reflection**: 1-hour round table transcribed discussion with all class participants on the lessons learned at GAMEX during the class period immediately after it; moderated by the instructor.
7. **Exit survey**: 16-question survey delivered after the final grade for the course with 13 Likert-scale questions with space for open-ended discussion and 3 open-ended questions.
8. **Exit interview**: 30-minute, one-on-one, semi-structured interview inviting the students to reflect on their overall learning experience, what worked, what didn't work, suggestions for improvement, their perceived achievement of personal intended learning outcomes, their perceived value of their individual portfolios, and their perceived value of the three public course presentations; performed by the instructor.
9. **Follow-up online poll**: a one-question follow-up online poll asking students to name the three greatest motivators to work on the course with the ability to add more options or vote on existing responses; deployed five weeks after the course ended.

Photo	Title / Venue	Description	Technologies	std.	Collab.	Prj.
	DangeRoads FF, GX, OH	Texting and driving game humorously exposing the dangers of doing so in real life. http://www.csc.kth.se/utbildning/kth/kurser/DH2413/agi13/dangeroads/	Game Engine Phone steering & text input	5	100% +	1 2
	FaceUp FF, GX, OH	When most are looking down at their phones, FaceUp invites to playfully explore the ceilings of public spaces. http://www.csc.kth.se/utbildning/kth/kurser/DH2413/agi13/faceup/	Water simulation Kinect	5	100% +	1
	ComposIt FF, GX, OH	Create a painting and hear what it sounds like in this continuous sequencer. http://www.csc.kth.se/utbildning/kth/kurser/DH2413/agi13/composit/	Particle systems Visual effects Wacom tablet	4	100%	1
	Parasomnia FF, GX, OH	A game of complementary collaboration where two players must work together to defend their territory from falling meteorites. http://www.csc.kth.se/utbildning/kth/kurser/DH2413/agi13/parasomnia/	Particle systems Special Effects Wii mote	4	60%	1
	InnerVis FF, GX, OH	A training simulator for virtual endoscopic exploration using Nintendo Wii mote control. http://www.csc.kth.se/utbildning/kth/kurser/DH2413/agi13/innervis/	Simulation lighting Wii mote	4	30%	1
	SolarSense FF, GX, OH	Navigate a stereoscopic 3D model of the solar system with your bare hands. http://www.csc.kth.se/utbildning/kth/kurser/DH2413/agi13/solarsense/	Atmospheric scattering Primesense	5	0% +	1 2
	WingMan FF, GX, OH	Wear virtual wings and admire how they look on you from every angle. http://www.csc.kth.se/utbildning/kth/kurser/DH2413/agi13/wingman/	Procedural textures Primesense	1	0%	1
	Dispersion OH	Become the master of light reflecting and dispersing it to avoid obstacles and reach your targets. http://www.csc.kth.se/utbildning/kth/kurser/DH2413/agi13/dispersion/	Optics modeling Phycons Pixelsense	3	NA	2
	Droid 'Ahoy OH	Control the waters of the oceans by tilting your phone. http://www.csc.kth.se/utbildning/kth/kurser/DH2413/agi13/droidahoy/	Fluid simulation Phone gyroscope accel.	5	NA	2
	2.5 D OH	Deep stereoscopic navigation of a 2.5D maze by tilting your head and without 3D glasses. http://www.csc.kth.se/utbildning/kth/kurser/DH2413/agi13/twofiveD/	Shaders blurring Primesense	3	NA	2
	Block Programming Language / OH	Create graphic simulations in just a few lines of code that visualizes the graphics being created. http://www.csc.kth.se/utbildning/kth/kurser/DH2413/agi13/bpl/	Graphical language parser	4	NA	2
	Mysterious Room OH	Visualize the cost-benefit of texture, bump, and parallax bump mapping, versus tessellation. http://www.csc.kth.se/utbildning/kth/kurser/DH2413/agi13/myteryroom/	Parallax bump mapping tessellation	1	NA	2
	Deferred Rendering OH	Hundreds of refracting, reflecting, and diffusing light sources interacting in real-time. http://www.csc.kth.se/utbildning/kth/kurser/DH2413/agi13/defrend/	Deferred Rendering	1	NA	2

Table 1. Advanced Graphics and Interaction 2013 (AGI13) Project Descriptions: column 1 shows sample photographs of students presenting their projects at large public venues to wide audiences, from small children (WingMan) to veterans of the gaming industry (ComposIt) to adults with physical disabilities (SolarSense). Column 2 names the projects and the public venues where they were presented: ForskarFredag (FF), GAMEX (GX), and KTH Open House (OH). Column 3 briefly describes the projects. Column 4 names the computer graphics and interaction technologies adopted for the project. Column 5 (std.) shows the number of AGI students in each project. Column 6 (Collab.) shows the length of the AGI-IC collaboration. The + sign indicates that the project continues after the end of the course. The last column (Prj.) shows whether the project ran over period 1, 2, or both.

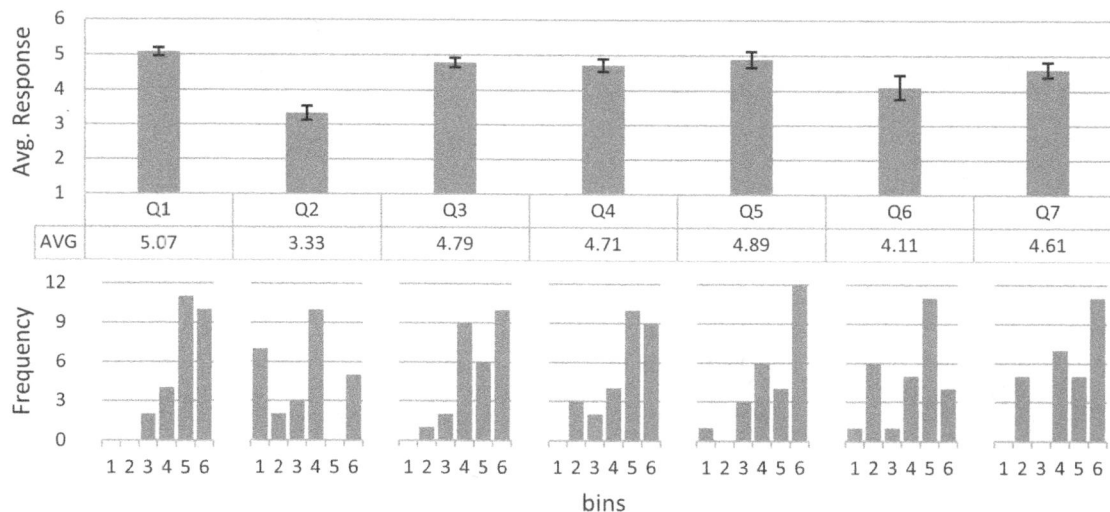

Figure 2. Statistical analysis of response to Likert-scale exit survey questions. Top – averages. Bottom – histogram.

5.2 Analysis Methodology

We gathered the data from the nine instruments above and grouped it into a number of categories using *focused coding* [6]. Focused coding is hypothesis driven. It concentrates on predefined concepts relevant to a study's central research questions, in our case, the pedagogical value of seeking public impact through expos, multidisciplinary collaboration, and portfolios. For inter-coder reliability, we performed two independent analyses of the exit interviews and surveys from two co-authors who were not involved with the course. We ground the results on the categorical structure emerging from focused coding.

6. ANALYSIS OF RESULTS

Figure 2 summarizes the quantitative results of the exit survey. The top row visualizes the average and standard error of the student's answers to each Likert-scale question. The bottom row shows the histogram of the answers. These are the seven questions from the survey that are relevant to this paper. The scale ranges from 1, "I don't agree at all", to 6, "I agree completely". The questions also have an open-ended field which some of the students filled in. We analyze those statements further below. The questions most relevant for this paper are:

Q1. The course contents will be useful for my future career.

Q2. The collaboration with the Berghs School of Communication has positively impacted my learning experience.

Q3. Project 1 contributed to my AGI learning.

Q4. The public presentations of project 1 (ForskarFredag, GAMEX, and Open House) contributed to my AGI learning.

Q5. Project 2 contributed to my AGI learning.

Q6. The Open House presentations of project 2 contributed to my AGI learning.

Q7. In-class discussions contributed to my AGI learning.

Q8. (Open-ended) The three best things with AGI are:

Q9. (Open-ended) These are my ideas for improving AGI:

6.1 Large Public Presentation Impact

The students recognized the challenge of presenting their projects at large venues as a major driving force to: 1) stimulate self-teaching and learning; 2) work hard; 3) effectively balance the group work load; and 4) strategically focus on necessary tasks for completing stable systems given strict time constraints. Most of the students acknowledged that the public presentations contributed to their AGI learning (Q4, Q6). All the students considered the public presentations a positive aspect of the course, and 16 out of 28 students ranked the presentations as one of the top three aspects of the course (Q8). Interestingly, while both projects developed during the course contributed equally to the learning experience (Q3, Q5, p=0.89), the public presentations of the first project at ForskaFredag, GAMEX, and Open House, were, as a whole, ranked statistically higher as a learning tool that the presentation of the second project at Open House (Q4, Q6, p=0.01). Given that the Open House involved a rather small and familiar audience, i.e. peers and professors, while the other two events were much larger and include users of different ages and backgrounds, our observations raise the possibility that the students can greatly benefit from interactions unconventional within purely academic settings. In fact, the learning experience not only occurred during the preparation of the ready-to-display product, but also during the public presentations. The students became aware of the type of interaction a final user would have with their project and witnessed a wide spectrum of the human experience. During the GAMEX focus group, the students expressed their amazement by the candid, fearless, explorative and inquisitive response they observed in children, a large audience for computer interaction, yet an audience rarely encountered by university students. They also realized the importance of being able to explain their work to a non-academic audience, received feedback from the general public, reflected on the pros and cons of their design, and faced the challenge of fixing unexpected problems with their projects on the spot. Of note, due to the logistics of the presentations and the distribution of time slots, all the students were responsible for presenting and fixing all the projects on display. Thus, all the students augmented their learning experience by becoming familiar with concepts, strategies, and systems developed by their peers.

Overall, the students felt extremely rewarded by observing real-world users explore their projects, and having the opportunity to take their results beyond the classroom and into the real world. The student quote below summarizes the overall experience:

"You have to be confident to explain to people this is what I have done, this is how it works, be able to answer questions and be in a public environment. At KTH all the lab assignments are in front of the computers which you know that things will work on. The code will run smoothly. And the person you are presenting to is always someone you have presented to before and knows what you are doing. What we do in this course is present to people who don't have the same understanding of what you are doing. So you have to explain to people in a different way. Also, it is much more likely to break if you are presenting for a long time to a lot of people. You have to be sure that your code doesn't break and know what to do when your code breaks. I think that part is very good. It is most definitely worth the extra effort."

6.2 Portfolio Impact

Students felt that the contents of the class will be useful in their future careers (Q1 AVG: 5.07). In the interviews we asked students if they feel that they have built a portfolio for their future job hunting and the majority response (23 of 28) was "yes", "absolutely". Three students mentioned that their future careers will be in different areas of computation and felt this would not be a proper portfolio. Two students felt their contribution to the projects was not advanced enough to use the projects as a portfolio to showcase their skills. Three groups have continued to develop the projects after the end of the course. FaceUp continues to search for opportunities to commercialize their system to playfully display advertisement on the ceilings of metro stations. DangeRoads is working on a wide beta release of their game. SolarSense is exploring a free release of their software for classroom learning at elementary and high school levels. Students from both AGI and IC have included these and other projects into their public online portfolios. Three AGI students have found internships demoing their specific project contributions.

6.3 Multidisciplinary Collaboration

The collaboration between the engineering and the communication teams evidenced the importance to develop and coach the inter-cultural dialogue between members with very different academic backgrounds. On one side, challenges in this dialogue did not positively impact the learning experience of many of the engineering students (the bimodal distribution of Q2). On the other side, when successful, the collaboration led to the development of some of the projects with farthest social outreach. Among them, DangeRoads, a game on texting and driving, was featured by Stockholm's Metro on November 27, 2013.

Three groups broke apart at different stages of collaboration: SolarSense (0%), InnerVis(30%), and Parasomnia (60%). The main reasons stated were "lack of communication", "lack of compromise", "lack of understanding", and "lack of common goals and working structure."

In this analysis, we focus on the aspects that supported the collaboration, as we expect to develop them in the future. All the students of the three groups that succeeded stated going through a sequence of necessary stages to maintain collaboration: 1) patience; 2) acceptance; 3) appreciation; and 4) admiration. At first, everyone stressed the need to be patient and to listen while they brainstormed project ideas without reaching agreement. In the second stage, they accepted a compromise through listening to each other and being willing to combine their ideas. The concept for the project was mutually decided and, because of that, everyone was engaged. In the third stage, they appreciated the collaboration and trusted each other. Lastly, the admired the value of mutual skills and wouldn't consider working any other way:

"Once we got the project to work, we realized it was looking horrible. At that point we just decided that the communication team should design what it should look like and just tell us what to do".

In summary, the three groups of students realized that listening to each other, trusting each other, and working together was more difficult than they expected, but took them further than they would have gotten on their own.

7. DISCUSSION

The three events utilized in the course (ForskarFredag, GAMEX, and the Open House) are not readily available for all, but although we haven't made any comparative studies, we would argue that they are easily replaced by other expos with equal positive learning outcomes. The common denominator between them is that they demand a thorough preparation of the material to be presented as well as the communicative strategy of the presentation itself. The core event feature for producing learning outcomes for AGI is the *variety of the audience*. Students had to constantly adapt the narrative to get the message across.

The core pedagogical principle for success is the detailed constructive alignment of partitioned goals of the presentations and placing the responsibility to collect the evidence of achieving these goals on the students themselves. At GAMEX, for example, we graded system robustness, student professionalism, ability to present their own project, ability to present all the other projects, and the ability to elicit a constructive response from the audience.

8. CONCLUSION AND FUTURE WORK

We have proposed a new pedagogical framework, Expo-Based Learning (EBL), as Project-Based Learning augmented with the constructively-aligned goal of achieving large public impact beyond the course period and participants. We have demonstrated the lasting positive impact of EBL through a case study in Advanced Graphics and Interaction. Finally, we discussed proposed methods for reproducing the positive results in the case study. As a framework, EBL remains a proposition. Future work must systematically explore multiple contexts with different course content, instructors, cultures, resources, and students.

9. REFERENCES

[1] Anderson, E.F., Peters, C.E., Halloran, J., Every, P., Shuttleworth, J., Liarokapis, F., Lane, R., and Richards, M. 2012. In at the Deep End: An Activity-Led Introduction to First Year Creative Computing. *Computer Graphics Forum: the international journal of the Eurographics Association*, 31 (6), 1852-1866.

[2] Ben-Ari, M. 2001. Constructivism in Computer Science Education, *Journal of Computers in Mathematics and Science Teaching* 20, 1, 45–73.

[3] Biggs, J. & Tang, C. 2011, *Teaching for Quality Learning at University*.

[4] French. J.H. 2012. Evaluating a communication-intensive core course in the CS curriculum. *Journal of Computing Sciences in Colleges*, 28, 2, 197-209.

[5] Hundhausen, C. D., Narayanan, N. H., & Crosby, M. E. 2008. Exploring studio-based instructional models for computing education. *In SIGCSE* (Vol. 8, pp. 392-396).

[6] Lofland, J. and Lofland, L. 1995. *Analyzing Social Settings: A Guide to Qualitative Observation and Analysis,* Wadsworth Publishing Company.

[7] Martí, E., Gil, D., Julia, C. 2006. A PBL experience in the teaching of computer graphics, *Computer Graphics Forum*.

[8] Romero, M. 2013. Project-Based Learning of Advanced Computer Graphics and Interaction, in *EUROGRAPHICS 2013*. Girona, Spain: May 6-10.

[9] Taxén, G. 2003. Teaching Computer Graphics Constructively, *Proceedings SIGGRAPH '03 ACM SIGGRAPH 2003 Educators Program*, 1-4.

[10] Thomas, D. (2005). Agile programming: design to accommodate change. *Software, IEEE*, 22(3), 14-16.

The State Of Play: A Notional Machine for Learning Programming*

Michael Berry
School of Computing
University of Kent
Canterbury, Kent, UK
mjrb5@kent.ac.uk

Michael Kölling
School of Computing
University of Kent
Canterbury, Kent, UK
mik@kent.ac.uk

ABSTRACT

Comprehension of programming and programs is known to be a difficult task for many beginning students, with many computing courses showing significant drop out and failure rates. In this paper, we present a new notional machine design and implementation to help with understanding of programming and its dynamics for beginning learners. The notional machine offers an abstraction of the physical machine designed for comprehension and learning purposes. We introduce the notional machine and a graphical notation for its representation. We also present *Novis*, an implementation of a dynamic real-time visualiser of this notional machine, integrated into BlueJ.

Categories and Subject Descriptors

H.3.2 [**Computers and Education**]: Computer and Information Science Education; H.5.1 [**Information Interfaces and Presentation**]: Multimedia Information Systems—*Animations*; I.6.8 [**Simulation and Modelling**]: Types of Simulation—*Animation, Visual*

General Terms

Human Factors

Keywords

Program visualization, novice programming, Novis

1. INTRODUCTION

It is well understood that programming is a fundamental activity in computer science; it is the process by which conceptual ideas are mapped to instructions that can be understood and interpreted by a machine. The teaching of introductory programming within computer science is essential, and mastery of this skill necessary for students to

---

*This paper expands on a previous short paper, presented at WiPSCE 2013, Aarhus, Denmark.

progress. To be successful in programming, students have to be able to form a valid and consistent mental model of the machine executing their instructions. Forming such a model is not easy, and the computing education community has no agreed, shared abstract model in widespread use. Often, ad-hoc models are formed by instructors or students, but these are not guaranteed to be consistent or correct. A shared, accepted and valid mental model – a notional machine – would benefit both instructors and students in their attempts to teach and learn programming.

1.1 Notional Machines

The difficulties of learning to program are well known; Kim & Lerch, for example, provide a summary[7]. Many students fail or drop out of introductory courses, with a failure rate of 33% reported by Bennedsen and Caspersen not out of line with many courses around the world[2]. A popular hypothesis presented by Boulay[3] states that students find the concepts of programming too hard to grasp, do not understand the key properties of their program, and do not know how to control them by writing code. Boulay took this as a starting point and motivation to formalise the concept of a *notional machine*. A notional machine is an abstraction designed to provide a model to aid in understanding of a particular language construct or program execution. The notional machine does not need to accurately reflect the exact properties of the real machine; it presents a higher conceptual level by providing a metaphorical layer above the real machine (or indeed several such layers) that are hoped to be easier to comprehend than the real machine.

Some teachers, when presented with the idea of a notional machine, are initially skeptical, holding the view that students need to understand what "really happens" to become expert programmers. It should be noted that all models held by almost all programmers are notional, in that they represent simplifications of the real machine. Even discussions about assembly language or machine code are almost necessarily abstractions, since hardware optimisations of modern processors are so complex that they cannot fully be taken into account when reasoning about program execution (other than by a small group of highly trained specialists working on processor design). In addition, details of processor designs are often trade secrets of the manufacturer – we cannot actually know what "really happens".

A meaningful discussion about notional machines therefore does not centre around the question whether or not to use one, but around the most useful level of abstraction to aim for. Whatever the preferred abstraction level, it is important that the notional machine is complete and consistent: it must be able to explain all observable behaviour of the real machine, and reasoning about the notional machine must allow accurate predictions to be made about behaviour of the real machine[4].

The design of the notional machine will typically be heavily influenced by the programming paradigm of the language used for implementation. In this paper, we discuss a notional machine for programs written in Java, therefore representing an object-oriented model.

A notional machine's metaphorical layer can be presented in many forms. Visual metaphors are most commonly used to present state and events that unfold in the actual machine. Visual representations can be replaced or augmented by other media, such as sound.

1.2 The status quo

At present, one of the most common techniques for teachers to explain dynamic elements of object orientation, and the execution of object-oriented programs, is through the drawing of diagrams of objects and classes, often by hand on a whiteboard. No consistent, complete and widely accepted shared notation exists across classrooms, and it is left to the student to form a mental model based on often ad-hoc diagrams the teacher may use. UML provides a variety of standardised notations, but its dynamic diagrams are often perceived as too complex and therefore are not widely used in introductory teaching. Students are often confronted with differing notations to describe the state of a program when switching between teachers, textbooks or tutorials.

One contribution of this work is to provide a shared model and notation that can be used by teachers and lecturers, in textbooks and in discussions. It provides learners with a consistent, correct and useful representation to support the formation of a mental model that transfers to a number of contexts and environments.

The second contribution is *Novis*, an implementation of this notional machine in a software system. Novis is integrated as a new main interface in an experimental version of the BlueJ environment[8], where it replaces the traditional object bench. It uses the notional machine notation to visualise the execution of a Java program in real time. It can show the state of a program at selected points in time of the execution, or it can animate the execution over a period of time.

2. RELATED WORK

Several educational software systems are in use in classrooms that offer presentations and animations of notional machines. UUhistle[12] is a software tool that provides animated, live visualisations of the execution of Python programs. The model employed operates at a fairly low level, animating single statements to illustrate the functionality of single constructs, such as assignment or parameter passing. A related tool, Jeliot[10], operates at a similar conceptual level to UUhistle using the Java language. Both of these tools lose their usefulness once the functionality of the basic programming language constructs is understood by the learner. The level of abstraction is too low to usefully visualise larger examples or more complex data structures, and therefore these tools are often employed for only a few weeks at the beginning of a learning experience. In contrast, a goal for our notional machine design is to be able to visualise somewhat larger examples and to be useful to illustrate or investigate program behaviour even after basic constructs have been mastered.

Also of interest is JGrasp[5]; an integrated environment providing several separate visualisations of parts of the system. Its visualisations operate at a higher level than UUhistle and Jeliot, with a data structure viewer being of specific interest. This viewer shows objects and their relations in a layout and representation purpose-built for several known data structures.

The use and effectiveness of these systems for learning is still under debate. Although literature regarding algorithm visualisation effectiveness is readily available, literature on program visualisation is more scarce. For algorithm visualisations, one meta-study[6] found a high correlation of effectiveness in those studies that actively involved the students. Similar results have not yet been shown for program visualisations. Where literature does exist, it is far from conclusive, with different studies even on the same tool claiming different results. In one study evaluating Jeliot's effectiveness, Moreno and Joy found that on average, the transfer of knowledge from the tool to the student was not successful[9]. However, a different study (also using Jeliot) claims "a significant percentage of students had achieved better results when they were using a software visualisation tool"[11].

For our own work this means that demonstrating the effectiveness of the tool has yet to be demonstrated in future work. No convincing prior work exists that allows reliable conclusions to be drawn about the efficacy of such systems.

3. RESEARCH QUESTIONS

This work supports two distinct and separate use cases: the *comprehension of programming* and the *comprehension of programs*. The first is most relevant for beginning programmers: the goal here is to understand how a computing system executes program code, the mechanics and details of a programming language and the concepts of the underlying paradigm. Typical questions that the system helps to answer in this case are *What does an assignment statement do?* or *How does a method call work?* For experts who have mastered the language this aspect is no longer relevant.

The second use case is to understand and investigate a given program. The goal is to become familiar with a given software system, or to debug a program. Typical questions in this case are *Why does my program behave like this?* or *How many objects are being created when I invoke this method?* This part of the functionality remains relevant even for seasoned programmers.

These use cases lead us to the main aims of the model:

Aim 1 : To provide a shared notation for representing the execution of an object-oriented program within the proposed model.

Aim 2 : To provide a valid mental model for learning and reasoning about object-oriented programming.

Aim 3 : To provide a basis for an implementation in software that can be used to provide a visualisation of the model alongside a running object-oriented program.

These aims further lead us to the two principle research questions:

Research question 1 : What should the notation for a high level, consistent model of a notional machine, developed to aid novices in learning to program look like?

Research question 2 : Can a software tool be created that dynamically visualises the execution of typical beginners' programs using this notional machine notation in a way that is manageable and useful?

For the purpose of RQ1, we define *consistent* to mean that valid reasoning within that model must correctly predict the behaviour of the underlying system. Our targeted problem space covers Java programs of a complexity up to first year university programming problems. Thus, we can explicitly exclude some constructs from our model, if we postulate that they are outside our targeted problem space. This is discussed in more detail below (section 4).

This paper presents the design of the notional machine and does not include an evaluation of its effectiveness for learning or teaching. This will be presented separately in a later paper.

4. PROBLEM SPACE

Our notional machine is aimed at first year programming students and therefore focuses on material typically covered within that year. While the model and software system may well remain useful for tasks in later years, where a conflict between scope and simplicity emerges, simplicity will take precedence for constructs not typically discussed in introductory programming courses.

For a more systematic definition of the problem space, we look at programming examples and projects covered in some popular introductory textbooks. A small number of the most popular introductory Java textbooks (including *Objects First With Java*[1], a book frequently used when teaching with BlueJ) are used to set the scope against which completeness is defined. The notional machine should be able to model and visualise all examples from these books.

4.1 Abstractions

Tying the scope of the notional machine to first year programming examples places implicit bounds on the abstractions that should be shown in the notional machine. Many advanced concepts, such as explicit concurrency and synchronisation, packages, class loading and annotation processing can be excluded from the scope – these are rarely covered in first year programming courses. In addition, we do not aim to illustrate abstractions at the very low level. Simple statements, such as assignments or if-statements, are not represented in the model – the most atomic "step" in the model is defined as a single method execution, and the model focusses on object interaction and method calls. Students typically do not have long term trouble in understanding basic syntax and the behaviour of these simple statements, therefore a visualisation of these would not remain helpful in the longer term.

The abstractions used for presentation of the notional machine centre around objects and classes, and their interactions. Objects and classes are shown with their current state. The state visualised includes both the state of objects and classes at a given point in time, including primitive fields and object references, and the state of any execution currently in progress, visualising the current locus of execu-

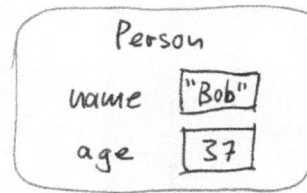

Figure 1: Representation of an object with two fields.

tion as well as the path of invocation (traditionally shown as a stack trace).

5. NOTIONAL MACHINE NOTATION

The notation for the notional machine is designed to be usable in various different media and formats, including line drawings (possibly produced using drawing software), hand drawings on paper (see Figure 1) or a whiteboard, or generated automatically with a software tool (discussed in more detail below).

Some elements of the notation, such as fill colour, are defined but optional and mostly relevant to automatically generated versions of the notional machine diagrams. Hand drawn versions of the diagram are still be readable without the optional elements.

5.1 Notation details

5.1.1 Objects

Objects are represented by rectangles with rounded corners. The object is labelled with its type. The type displayed is the dynamic type, not the type of any declared variable. If fill colours are used, objects are red (Figure 2). Objects do not have unique identifiers, as in some other object visualisation systems. Assigning unique identifiers may sometimes help to talk about the objects, but leads to misconceptions that should be avoided.

A field of an object is presented as a box with a label to its left. The box is white (if colours are used), and it contains the field's value. An object representation contains a list of all its fields. If the value of the field is a primitive or a string, it is displayed in its textual form within the representation of the field. Only instance fields are shown on the object; static fields are displayed on the class instead (see section 5.1.4).

5.1.2 References

If the value of a field is a reference to another object then it is displayed as an arrow originating from the field and pointing to the object that it references (Figure 2).

Strings are treated as a special case. While strings are objects in Java, they are displayed using a literal representation (the characters of the string in double quotes, written directly into the field). The immutability of string objects ensures that this representation does not lead to inconsistent or invalid conclusions, and this representation significantly simplifies many examples. This exception only applies to

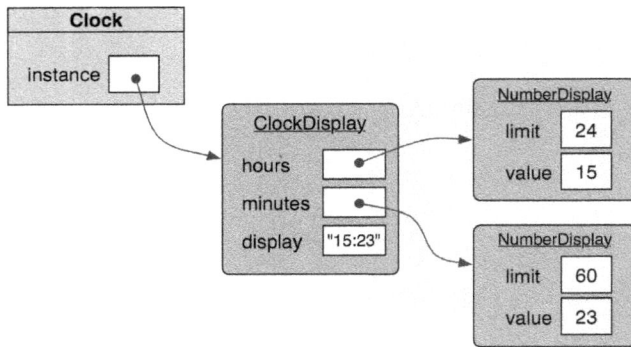

Figure 2: Representation of object references.

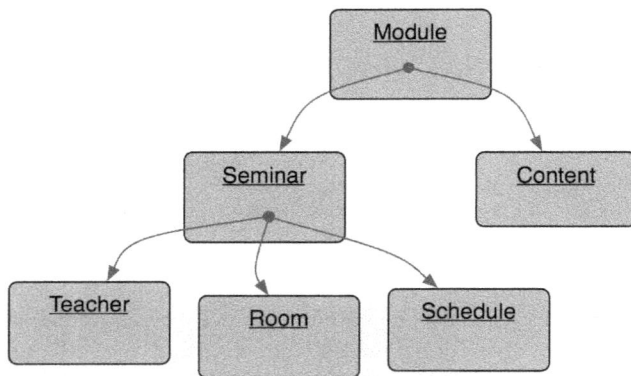

Figure 3: This shows the simplified view – where fields are not of direct interest, they can be omitted as in this example.

strings; all other objects must be represented in their full form via an arrow.

5.1.3 Simplified view

Often the relationships between objects, the object graph, is the sole point of interest. For this case a simplified notation of an object may be used. In this notation fields are omitted and references are drawn originating from the centre of the referring object (Figure 3). Primitive field values are not shown in the simplified view.

5.1.4 Classes

Classes are represented as rectangles with square (not rounded) corners (Figure 2). The class is labelled with its name and static members are displayed in the class icon. If colours are used classes have a light brown sand colour.

The display of static fields in the class is similar to that of instance fields in objects – primitives and strings are displayed inline, object references are displayed with arrows.

5.1.5 Method calls

In addition to the state of objects and classes the notional machine diagram can also show the state of a currently active execution. While the notation described so far represents a classic heap diagram, the execution state at any given point in time is most often depicted as a separate diagram,

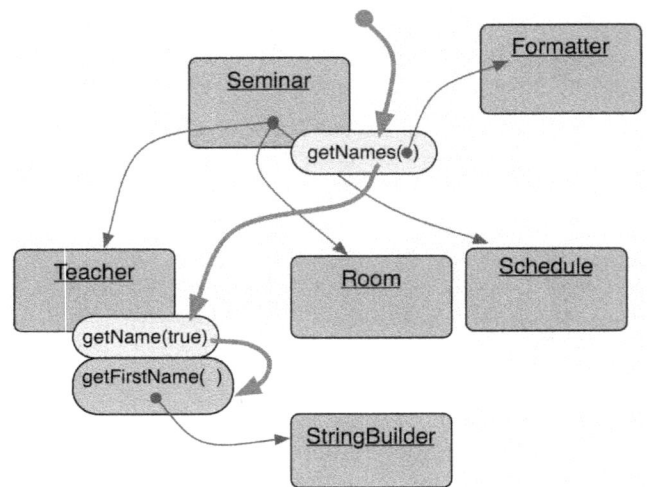

Figure 4: An active method call chain with object parameters.

showing a call stack. In our notation, the execution state is overlayed over the same diagram.

An active method call is represented as an orange (if coloured), oval-shaped label attached to the bottom right of the object that it is called on (Figure 4). The label remains visible as long as the method is active. If this method calls further methods, those are displayed as well, linked by a call chain arrow. In colour representations, the call chain arrow is green. Further method labels may appear attached to the same object or other objects, depending on the receiver of the method call.

The call chain arrow (or, in talking about a notional machine diagram, usually just "call chain") depicts the complete current sequence of open method calls, their dependencies and order. When using this notation on a whiteboard, the call chain is often extended to show nested method calls, and wiped out again to illustrate the completion of a method invocation.

Method labels include the list of actual parameters. For primitives and strings, the parameter value is shown as a literal; for object parameters, a reference to the object is shown originating from the parameter list (see *getNames* method, Figure 4). References from local variables may be shown originating from the method label, below the method name (see *getFirstName* method, Figure 4).

6. SOFTWARE VISUALISATION

Novis, a visualisation creating automatic and animated versions of notional machine diagrams as described here, has been created and integrated into BlueJ's main interface. This implementation can present static notional machine diagrams at selected stages of program execution, or animate ongoing execution in real time.

6.1 Static display

Novis depicts the static view of classes and their references between them as described in section 5.1 (Figure 5). Objects in the diagram are placed automatically when they are created but can be moved by the user; clicking on the

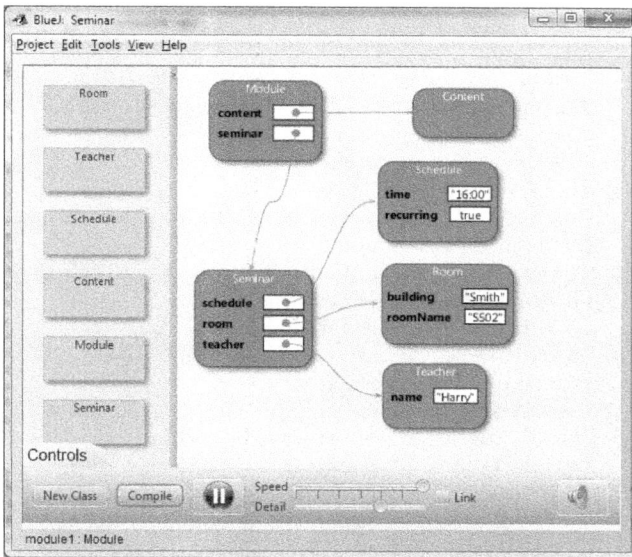

Figure 5: The Novis notional machine visualiser with a simple example.

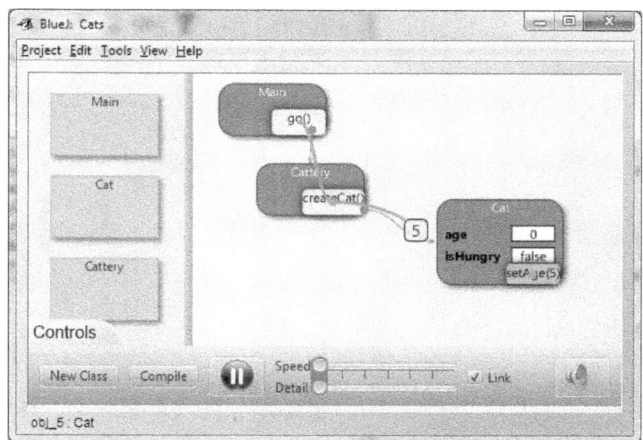

Figure 6: Novis displaying a method call chain.

object toggles between its simplified and detailed state. The reference arrows are placed and updated automatically by the software.

6.2 Object creation and destruction

When an object is created the software searches for an appropriate space in the diagram and "pops" the object into that space (with a short animation) before executing its constructor. The object is initially grey in colour to indicate that it has not been fully instantiated, and then switches to its default red colour on the constructor's completion. User generated objects (created interactively from the class, as was always possible in BlueJ) are removed manually by the user; objects created in code are removed from the diagram whenever they become eligible for garbage collection (not when they are actually collected). In both cases, the objects disappear with a brief "puff of smoke" animation.

6.3 Execution

Methods can be interactively invoked on any object in the traditional BlueJ-style, by right clicking the object and selecting the method from the resulting context menu. A following chain of method calls is then depicted as described in section 5.1.5. As methods are called, the method call labels appear in the animation, drawing the attention of the viewer. The call chain arrow is animated – it extends from its origin to its destination. Parameter values are depicted in a moving animation, following the call chain arrow from the caller to the invoked method (Figure 6).

6.4 Speed and stepping granularity

The notional machine viewer includes a slider to control the speed of the animation. At its maximum setting, no delay is added and the program executes at the maximum speed possible with the current choice of animation detail (see section 6.5, below). At the slowest, a two-second pause is added between each step of the program. The interim

levels have pauses that scale linearly between these two values. A "step" of the program in our context is a method call or a method return – single statement executions are not visualised.

6.5 Level of detail

A second slider in the interface controls the level of detail displayed in the diagram. With full detail visible, the animation performs as described above: objects are shown in detailed view with their fields visible, object creation and destruction are animated, and method calls are dynamically visualised with call chain arrows slowly extending, parameter values passed visually from one method to another, and return values moving the other way at the end of a method execution as the call chain arrow retracts.

This level of detail is useful in early stages of learning, when the focus of the learner is on understanding basics of object interaction and method calls, when examples are small and execution chains short. In later examples, this level of detail becomes a hindrance, illustrating concepts that have already been understood and obscuring information about the program under investigation.

At that stage, the level of detail displayed can be reduced. The visualisation offers seven levels of detail display, gradually reducing or omitting various animations and display elements as the setting is decreased. The lower-detail settings show objects in their simplified view by default, resulting at the extreme end in a "heatmap" view that focuses on object creation, desctruction and activity levels (see section 6.6).

The two sliders – speed and detail – can be linked in the user interface to allow both to be adjusted in a single interface gesture. When linked, they are inversely related: the higher the speed, the less detail is displayed. The linked states represent commonly useful settings when viewing typical examples.

User control over speed and animation detail ensures that our notional machine visualisation addresses a broad range of use cases and remains relevant after the first few weeks of programming instruction. While some settings support the understanding of basic constructs (such as object references and method calls), others allow the investigation of specific

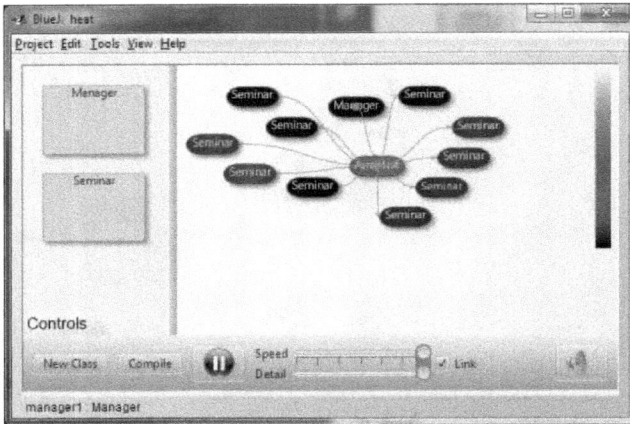

Figure 7: Heatmap view illustrating program activity.

data structures and their associated algorithms, the study of specific programs, or specialised debugging tasks.

6.6 Heatmap

At the lowest level of detail Novis's display turns into a heatmap (Figure 7). Objects are shown in a compact notation using just enough space to display their type, and colour is used to indicate activity. Method calls are not textually displayed; instead, objects "warm up" as methods are invoked, first turning a lighter purple, then red, then yellow with increased activity. All objects cool down gradually when not being active, so that the most recent active objects are easily recognisable. This notation – depicting object creation and destruction, as well as hotspots of activity – provides a quick high level overview of programs with ongoing activity.

7. STATUS AND FUTURE WORK

A prototype implementation of BlueJ with Novis integrated to replace the object bench has been completed, and is currently available for testing and evaluation purposes. The system has been tested with a small number of users with promising results, but no formal user studies have yet been completed.

Work in the near future will concentrate on further testing of usability and effeciveness with first year students, including studies to evaluate effects on program comprehension. The results from these studies will then be used to refine the interface and functionality of the model and corresponding implementation.

8. ACKNOWLEDGEMENTS

We wish to thank Michael Caspersen for many discussions about notional machines and their potential uses in programming education. His ideas were instrumental in starting and shaping this project.

9. REFERENCES

[1] David J Barnes and Michael Kölling. *Objects first with Java: a practical introduction using BlueJ*. Pearson, Boston, 2012.

[2] Jens Bennedsen and Michael E. Caspersen. Failure rates in introductory programming. *SIGCSE Bull.*, 39(2):32–36, June 2007.

[3] Du Boulay. Some difficulties of learning to program. *Journal of Educational Computing Research*, 2:57–73, 1986.

[4] Michael Edelgaard Caspersen. *Educating Novices in The Skills of Programming*. DAIMI PhD Dissertation. Department of Computer Science, 2007.

[5] T. Dean Hendrix and James H. Cross II. jGRASP: an integrated development environment with visualizations for teaching java in CS1, CS2, and beyond. *J. Comput. Sci. Coll.*, 23(2):170–172, December 2007.

[6] Christopher Hundhausen, Sarah A. Douglas, and John T Stasko. A meta-study of algorithm visualization effectiveness. *Journal of Visual Languages & Computing*, 13(3):259–290, June 2002.

[7] Jinwoo Kim and F. Javier Lerch. Why is programming (sometimes) so difficult? programming as scientific discovery in multiple problem spaces. *Information Systems Research*, 8(1):25 –50, March 1997.

[8] Michael Kölling, Bruce Quig, Andrew Patterson, and John Rosenberg. The BlueJ system and its pedagogy. *Computer Science Education*, 13:249–268, December 2003.

[9] Andrés Moreno and Mike S. Joy. Jeliot 3 in a demanding educational setting. *Electronic Notes in Theoretical Computer Science*, 178(0):51–59, July 2007.

[10] Andrés Moreno, Niko Myller, Erkki Sutinen, and Mordechai Ben-Ari. Visualizing programs with Jeliot 3. page 373. ACM Press, 2004.

[11] Sanja Maravic Cisar, Dragica Radosav, Robert Pinter, and Petar Cisar. Effectiveness of Program Visualization in Learning Java: a Case Study with Jeliot 3. *International Journal of Computers Communications & Control*, 6, 2011.

[12] Juha Sorva and Teemu Sirkiä. UUhistle. pages 49–54. ACM Press, 2010.

System for Automatic Generation of Algorithm Visualizations based on Pseudocode Interpretation

Jure Mornar
Siemens Convergence Creators d.o.o.
Put brodarice 6
21 000, Split, Croatia
+385 91 239 08 02
jure.mornar@siemens.com

Andrina Granić
Department of Computer Science
Faculty of Science
University of Split Nikole Tesle 12
21 000, Split, Croatia
+385 91 723 60 36
andrina.granic@pmfst.hr

Saša Mladenović
Department of Computer Science
Faculty of Science
University of Split Nikole Tesle 12
21 000, Split, Croatia
+385 99 342 50 80
sasa.pmfst@gmail.com

ABSTRACT

Algorithm visualization systems have not been as widely adopted by computer science educators as it might be expected from the firm belief that they can enhance computer science education. Two key impediments for widely adopting AV technology in mainstream computer science are: effectiveness and enhancements of learning with visualization and effort needed to create algorithm visualizations. In this paper, we present the interpretation based system capable of automatic creation of algorithm visualizations by interpreting unmodified algorithms written in pseudocode. Although system is interpreting unmodified source code (code without any annotations for triggering appropriate visualization routines), due to the ability to automatically detect interesting events system is able to create visualizations at a sufficiently high level of abstraction so that the emphasis is on algorithmic conceptually relevant principles. Providing users with full control over input data set and by accompanying animation with explanatory messages, highlighting currently executing pseudocode line and providing possibility to inspect variable values at any step visualizations created by our system that can enhance learning and help students mastering algorithms basic concepts.

Categories and Subject Descriptors

H.5.1. [**Information interfaces and presentation**]: Multimedia Information Systems – *Animations*

General Terms

Algorithms, Measurement, Documentation, Design, Languages

Keywords

Algorithm visualization; code interpretation; pseudocode; automatic animation generation; automatic interesting event detection

1. INTRODUCTION AND MOTIVATION

Understanding of computer algorithms is itself a very difficult task which becomes even more difficult when it comes to real programming language implementation when student's attention from algorithmic conceptually relevant principles gets distracted by syntax and semantic details specific to programming language. One of the reasons for this may be that an algorithm describes a process that is both abstract and dynamic, while the methods typically used to teach algorithms are not. Algorithm visualizations (hereafter referred to as "algorithm visualizations" or "AVs") are used in computer science education since the early eighties. By graphically representing computer algorithms, their various states and animating the transitions between them, algorithm visualization technology aims to help computer science students understand how algorithms work. They illustrate data structures in natural, abstract and more conceptual ways instead of focusing solely on variable values, function calls etc. There are various surveys on using visualization as an aid for computer science education.

Although AV's are naturally attractive to educators, who nearly universally view them positively, consistently "liked" by students and despite its intuitive appeal as a pedagogical aid, AV technology has failed to catch on in mainstream computer science education. Two key impediments for widely adopting AV technology in mainstream computer science are: effectiveness and enhancements of learning with visualization and effort needed to create algorithm visualizations. Even though there is a firm belief that graphical representations of algorithms are learning aids, some initial studies designed to substantiate the educational effectiveness of AV's have shown that using visualization is not advantage at all or an advantage that can be only partially attributed to AV technology. However, later studies (e.g., [6]) have shown that AV technology could enhance and improve learning if visualization is interactive enough. In order to be educationally effective system must support student interaction and active learning (support for changing input data sets, making predictions regarding future visualization states, programming the target algorithm, supplement the visualization with appropriate text such as synchronized pseudocode and other descriptions of the algorithm). Besides effectiveness and enhancements of learning with visualization the wide adoption of the visualization system depends on one more important factor – effort needed to create algorithm visualization [13]. Price et al. [16] define four different roles in algorithm animation: user, visualizer, software visualization software developer (or simply developer) and programmer. The user views and interacts with an animation specified by the visualizer. The underlying animation system is designed and implemented by developers. Finally, the programmer is the implementer of the visualized algorithm.

Our motivation for the development of this system was twofold – two different problems were addressed. First driving force behind our motivation - Ministry of science, education and sport in

Croatia has introduced official specification for pseudocode [15] with allowed statements, operators and functions as well as 1:1 mapping to conventional programming languages. With this specification pseudocode became the official language in programming exercises for high school, state graduation exam, and entrance exam for most colleges as well as for national competition in informatics for primary and high school students. Despite this fact, as far as we know, no one provided parser or interpreter for such specified pseudocode nor anyone developed environment for learning pseudocode (kind of integrated development environment) in which students would be able to test their programming skills. As second motivation driver we had heterogeneous group of freshmen students attending "Artificial Intelligence" course. They had finished very different high schools and their general programming skills varied a lot (some of them were not familiar with any conventional programming language at all). What they did have in common was – they all had prior knowledge about pseudocode. Within the course they were expected to master some basic algorithms related to artificial intelligence like breath first search, depth first search, limited depth first search and a like. Although most of the students passed the course exam we have noticed that they were missing this conceptual link / connection between pseudocode and algorithm behavior. They were able to write algorithm pseudocode and to explain algorithm behavior but they weren't able to connect line of pseudocode with specific algorithm routine. In other words, most of them were not able to answer questions like - how it would reflect on algorithm behavior if this line of code were different?

At that point we realized that it would be of great help if we could develop a system that will be able to visualize appropriate algorithms purely by interpreting pseudocode.

2. RELATED WORK

Algorithm visualization history can be divided in two phases [22] – systems that came before the rise of Sun's Java programming language and wide content sharing on Internet and system that came after. Systems developed in first phase mostly came packaged with pre-generated AV's but allowed educators and students the freedom to implement other AV's using special purpose scripting languages or by annotating real programming language. Since widespread use of Java, systems have moved away from authoring toolkits towards suites of "canned" AV's and they are mostly distributed as operating system and environment independent collections of AV's. Balsa (Brown Algorithm Simulator and Animator) [1] is considered as the first major interactive software visualization system. Balsa was used extensively in the Brown University Workstation Project as an educational tool for teach fundamental computer science concepts using program-generated animations. Another recognized system of the early years of algorithm animation is Tango (Transition-based Animation Generation) [25] developed by John Stasko at Georgia Tech. Tango was one of the first systems supporting smooth animation. In subsequent years number of animation systems has risen steadily. These systems were much different from each other according to certain characteristics and implemented features.

Taxonomy of software visualization [17] introduced the categorization by which systems were categorized by: visualization specification style (animation creation approach), visualization specification technique (specifying connection between visualization and algorithm source code) and animation creation effortlessness (how much time and effort is needed to create algorithm animation). In original taxonomy visualization specification style was measured using terms like hand-coded, library, and automatic. Since that taxonomy is bit outdated alternative categorization was introduced in [20] and refined in [9]:

- Topic-Specific Animation - animations built specifically for some topic and often they are coming in form of stand-alone animations instead of algorithm animation systems.

- Direct Manipulation - In direct manipulation [26], the animation is specified by manipulating graphical objects. Good example of AV systems using direct manipulation to generate animations is MatrixPro [10].

- API-based Generation - API-based generation involves method invocations using a special visualization application programmer's interface (API). Perhaps most popular system using this approach is JHAVE [14].

- Scripting-based Generation - animations are described using some intermediate format, usually a textual format. The expressiveness of those scripting-like languages for describing animation is strictly limited to animation purposes. Methods, variables, loops and such stuff are usually not supported. Good example of such system is Animal [21].

- Declarative Visualization –visualization is specified by defining mapping from a given program state to graphical representations. It uses abstract mathematical expressions which can result in complex visual representations. A good example of this approach is the ALPHA language [3].

- Code Interpretation - Some animation systems offer a direct visualization of algorithms from the underlying code. This could be achieved by relying on debugger used to retrieve the current state, by preprocessing the underlying source code or by interpreting source code "as is". Example of system using code interpretation for animation generation is Jeliot 3 [12] – used to visualize execution of Java programs. Main strength of code interpretation-based animation systems are effortlessness and tight connection between the source code and its visualization. However, code interpretation approach has some weaknesses also.

While creating algorithm visualization one of most important tasks is to specify connection between visualization and algorithm source code. By visualization specific techniques systems can be categorized as follows [11]:

- Event driven approach consists of identifying interesting events and annotating the algorithmic code with calls to suitable visualization routines. The interesting event approach was pioneered by Balsa [1] and has been used in many algorithm animation systems including Tango [25].

- State driven approach consists of specifying mapping between program and visualization states, usually constructed by the visualizer before program execution. Good example of this approach is its early adopter Pavane [19].

- Visual programming makes programs easier to specify by letting users create programs manipulating program elements graphically rather than by specifying them textually. Example of this approach can be found in Dance [24].

- Automatic Animation – although being simplest way to specify an animation from the algorithm developer point of view, automatic algorithm animation is extremely difficult task. Perhaps the most popular system which is producing animation automatically (from source code) is Jeliot [12]. This approach was more often used for visualizing program execution rather than visualizing algorithms because algorithm visualization requires animation on much higher level of abstraction (more conceptual level) which is extremely hard to achieve with automatic animation approach.

As it's already pointed out, time and effort needed to learn and create algorithm visualizations are one of the key reasons why AV technology is still not widely used by computer science educators. Animation creation effortlessness is subjective matter and includes many factors. One characteristic that has a great influence on the effort required is the ability to use the system on-the-fly. With possibility to create animation on-the-fly lecturer is able to show different use cases, to answer to students "what-if" questions and to show same animation multiple times with different input sets which is not possible with predefined animations.

3. DEVELOPED SYSTEM

To make algorithm animation creation process as effortless as possible we decided to make our system interpretation based in a way that it will be able to produce animations automatically just by interpreting pseudocode "as is". Introducing the approach of automatic interesting events detection we managed to avoid annotating the source code and by interpreting unmodified source code still end up with visualization at a sufficiently high level of abstraction to be educationally effective for students. For the sake of simplicity we have decided to make first version of the system

course-specific and start with smaller set of search algorithms performing on tree (depth first search, breadth first search, depth limited search, etc.). Developed system is Web-based application consisting solely of frontend component and as such, together with pseudocode parser and interpreter, is completely written using frontend technologies (JavaScript, HTML and ExtJS).

3.1 Pseudocode

As already mentioned, ministry of science, education and sport in Croatia has introduced official specification for pseudocode [15]

with allowed statements, operators and functions as well as 1:1 mapping to conventional programming languages. This fact gave us the opportunity to develop a system in which students will be able to write an algorithm in pseudocode and see its visualization without the need for prior knowledge of any conventional programming languages. Writing algorithms in pseudocode allows students to concentrate on algorithm basic concepts rather than thinking about algorithm implementation in specific programming language. To meet the needs of this system we have extended this pseudocode specification by adding definition for functions, function calls, arrays, structures, few new keywords, few built-in functions (like print – to print something to the console), etc. For such specified pseudocode we have developed parser and interpreter. We have also leveraged the fact that pseudocode specification includes 1:1 mapping to some conventional languages (Pascal, C/C++, Python) and as proof of concept we have developed converter that is capable of converting pseudocode to Python language. We chose Python because it leaves us the possibility to embed Online Python Tutor (Embeddable Web-Based visualization of Python programs) [5] in our system and thus make our system capable of visualizing program execution.

3.2 System design

System has two modes of operation – *edit* and *animation* mode. While in edit mode, system allows user to write/edit algorithm and to create structure on which algorithm will perform. Once that is done, by clicking button *run* system goes to animation mode. In animation mode user is allowed to navigate through algorithm animation while most other components of the user interface become disabled (read-only). User interface of the system in animation mode is shown in Figure 1.

In the part of the figure numbered 1 there is code editor for pseudocode with some useful features like live pseudocode syntax check, syntax highlighting, code folding, etc. When system is in edit mode, in code editor users can write their own program/algorithm or choose one of the available algorithms. At any time, users can switch to Python tab and see their pseudocode converted to Python programming language. When system is in

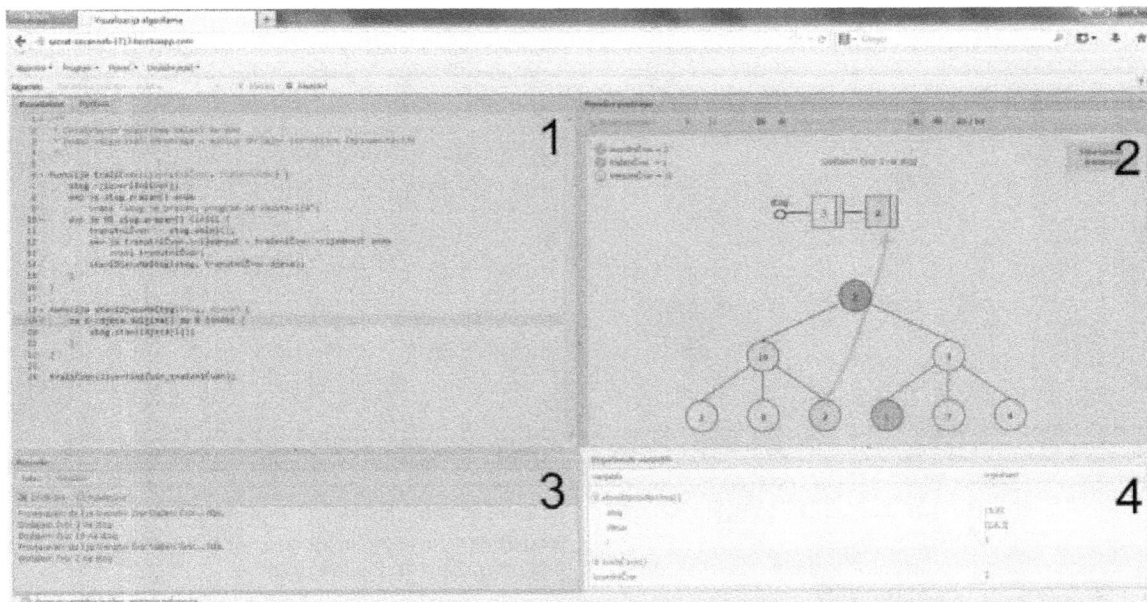

Figure 1. Developed system user interface (system in animation mode)

animation mode code editor becomes read-only and reflects code execution in a way that it highlights the line that is currently being executed.

Part numbered 2 contains visualization area. When system is in edit mode, visualization area is used to create tree structure on which selected algorithm will perform. The root node is created automatically with default value set to "…". When we point the cursor over the node, node value becomes editable and it can be easily changed just by entering new value. Also, we can easily add child to the node just by double clicking on it. All those actions (add child, remove child, etc.) are also available through the context menu when we right click the node. Context menu contains two additional options – "Mark as source node" and "Mark as target node" as an input to the search algorithm – which node we are searching for and where to start. There is also possibility to create random tree (with random number of nodes and random values) just by clicking "Generate random tree" button. Once the system is in animation mode it's no longer possible to change the tree structure. At this point navigation bar becomes enabled and we can navigate through animation step by step by clicking forward and backward buttons or we can achieve smooth navigation by clicking autoplay button. At any time smooth animation can paused and we can continue navigation using forward and backward buttons. There is also a slider for faster navigation through animation steps. In the top right corner of this section there is a label named "how to create a tree?" when system is in edit mode and "how to use animation?" when system is in animation mode. By pointing cursor over that label we will get detailed instructions of how to create a tree or how to use an animation.

In the part numbered 3 there is a console containing program / algorithm output (for example messages outputted with *print* built-in function) and animation accompanying explanatory messages (for example "comparing two nodes"). Besides output, there is also an *error* tab containing all potential errors from parsing and interpreting written pseudocode.

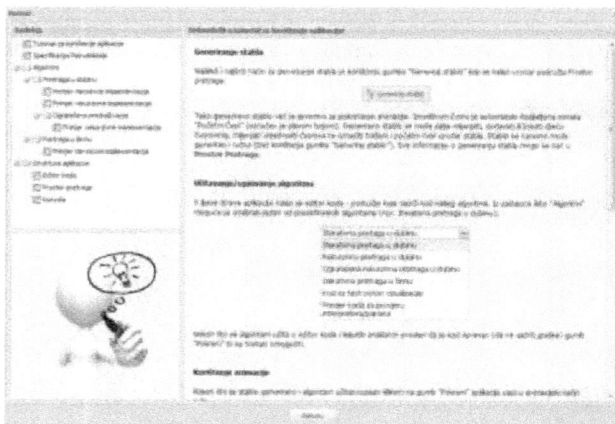

Figure 2. Help section of the system

In the part numbered 4 we can see execution stack and observe variable values at any point of algorithm animation or program execution. Variable values, as well as the highlighted line of code in code editor, are synchronized with animation and changes accordingly by navigating through animation using navigation bar.

There is also a help section containing detailed description of provided algorithms, tutorial for system usage, specification of pseudocode extension and a like. Help section is shown on the Figure 2.

3.3 Automatic detection of interesting events

We are pairing each node in the tree with accompanying object in memory which we have called *animation object*. While interpreting pseudocode our interpreter detects every access to animation object and then, if access is characterized as interesting event, some visualization routines are triggered. Regarding algorithms for searching within the tree structure, accesses that we have characterized as interesting events are: accessing animation object (reading value property of animation object), comparing values of two animation objects, assigning value to animation object, pushing animation object to queue structure (array) and removing animation object from queue structure. For some other types of algorithms different interesting events could be specified. For example if we want to visualize some sorting algorithm then swapping two elements should be detected and characterized as interesting event. Within this work we have we considered only the algorithms for tree searching, tree as the only structure that algorithms are performed on and tree node as the only type of animated object. If we ever decide to extend this system to support visualization of other type of algorithms (for example sorting algorithms) then we should introduce array as new structure that sorting algorithms will perform on. We will have to introduce array member as new type of animation object and to specify which events should be characterized as interesting events when sorting algorithm is performing on array. This process could be automated to some extent in the way that the system itself determines which events to consider as interesting events depending on which structure algorithm is performing on (for example if algorithm is performing on array than system can conclude that comparing value of two members or swapping position of two members should be considered as an interesting event). On the other hand, we can let the user to decide which events are interesting events in context of specific algorithm animation.

3.4 Visualization generation

Regarding visualization specification style developed system is using code interpretation approach. The vast majority of other systems that use this approach annotates source code in a way that they injects calls to visualization routines in places that are considered interesting events to achieve visualization at a sufficiently high level of abstraction. Thanks to ability to automatically recognize interesting events our system is capable of producing algorithm animation automatically and visualizing algorithms on high level of abstraction by interpreting unmodified source code. Using code interpretation approach makes visualization generation as effortless as possible and provides tight connection between the source code and its visualization. Every change in source code is automatically reflected on algorithm visualization which improves user understanding of how algorithm works. Animation is created in parallel with the interpretation of the source code and when the interpreter has finished animation is ready and divided into a certain number of steps. Animation step is created when interesting event is recognized and after any line of source code. For creating algorithm animations we have used JSAV (The JavaScript Algorithm Visualization Library) [8]. By accompanying animation with appropriate explanatory messages and updating of variable values at every step we intended to improve user's understanding of the algorithm.

4. EVALUATION OF THE SYSTEM

We have conducted preliminary evaluation of our system on the students taking the course of artificial intelligence. The students (n=23) had short introduction to system during which we showed them how they can solve the problem of "Missionaries & Cannibals" using our system. After this short introduction, students were asked to solve "Travelling Salesman" problem in a similar way. 13 out of 23 of them solved the task correctly and web-based questionnaire based on [2] that they have filled out upon the completion of the exam shows that they are general quite happy with the system and believe that system will help them in understanding the algorithms. Original questionnaire contains 12 questions from which we have extracted 7. Results of the conducted survey are shown in Figure 3. As future work, we plan to conduct a long term evaluation of this approach.

5. CONCLUSIONS AND FUTURE WORK

Our primary goal was to develop an algorithm animation system which will be able to animate algorithm execution purely by interpreting pseudocode at a sufficiently high level of abstraction to be useful for students in understanding of the algorithms. Although there already exists similar systems that are capable of creating visualizations from pseudocode (e.g. [18]), our system differs in a fact that it creates visualizations of algorithms, not low level animations of program execution. Another thing that distinguishes our system from others is the fact that pseudocode used in our system is strictly defined and externally dictated.

We believe the system that we have developed could be considered as more than just system for algorithm visualization. Within the scope of this work we managed to achieve following goals:

- We have extended formal pseudocode specification, parser and interpreter for such specified pseudocode as well as converter which is able to convert pseudocode to Python.

- Our system is web based, education oriented, cross-browser compatible (platform independent)

- Since animation creation process is automatic in our system, it's truly effortless for both - lecturers and students. They can be considered as system consumers because visualizer role is avoided since the system is interpreting code "as is".

- Our system encourages students to be highly engaged. Besides direct engagement with visualization itself (stepping through animation, changing input set / visualization elements), in our system learners are able to change target software (algorithm) which is visualized or even write their own algorithms and visualize them - which is an aspect of engagement that merits greater explicit consideration in the context of educational visualization [23].

- By accompanying animation with explanatory messages, highlighting currently executing pseudocode line and providing possibility to inspect variable values at any step our system is capable of producing visualization that hopefully will enhance learning and help students mastering algorithms basic concepts.

- Our system can be also used as kind of integrated development environment for anyone who wants to test their skills and learn to program in pseudocode. In editor supporting features like pseudocode live syntax check, syntax highlighting, code folding, etc. users are able to write their programs, execute them, see console output and in debugging manner inspect variable values, see execution stack and observe code execution line by line.

- Thanks to the possibility of converting pseudocode to Python, with relatively little effort it would be possible to embed Online Python Tutor [5] into our system and see visualization of program execution which would make our system fully featured program execution visualization system and visual debugger.

- Our system contains comprehensive documentation with detailed description about included algorithms, pseudocode extension, system usage tutorial and a like.

So far, our system contains only front-end component and doesn't require internet connection to work properly. One of the plans for the future development is introducing back-end component with database after which we will be able to implement features like: Let user to write and save his own algorithm, save created structures on which algorithm performs (just trees so far), exercises with automatic assessment, feedback form to measure the level of users satisfaction, etc. Regarding scope, at this point developed system can be considered as course-specific system (supports visualization of searching algorithms from artificial intelligence). As future work, we have a plan to extend its application area to domain specific (to

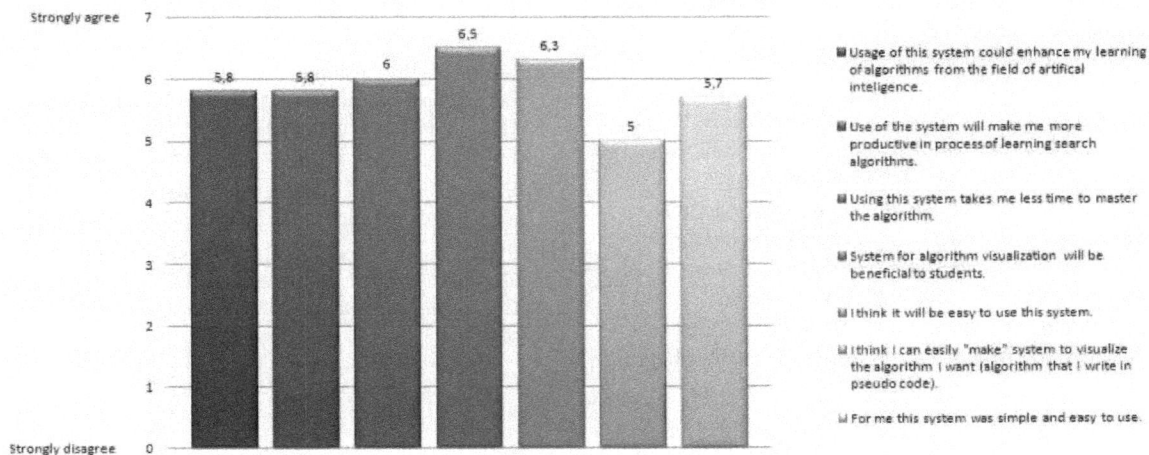

Figure 3. Results of the survey regarding usage of developed system

allow visualization of other types of algorithms like sorting algorithms, etc.). Also, as next step we intend to provide the converters which will be able to convert pseudo code to C/C++ and Pascal.

6. REFERENCES

[1] Brown, M.H., and Sedgewick, R. 1984. A system for algorithm animation. In *Proceedings of the 11th annual conference on Computer graphics and interactive techniques*, SIGGRAPH'84, pages 177–186. ACM Press.

[2] Davis, F. D. 1989. Perceived Usefulness, Perceived Ease of Use, and User Acceptance of Information Technology. MIS Quarterly, 13:3, 319-340.

[3] Demetrescu, C., and Finocchi, I. 2001. Smooth animation of algorithms in a declarative framework. *Journal of Visual Languages and Computing*, 12(3):253–281.

[4] From CS0 to advanced CS courses. In *Proceedings of the 34th SIGCSE technical symposium on Computer science education*, SIGCSE'03, 162–166, Reno, Navada, USA.

[5] Guo, P.J. 2013. Online Python Tutor: Embeddable Web-Based Program Visualization for CS Education. In *Proceeding of the 44th ACM technical symposium on Computer science education*. Pages 579-584. ACM New York, NY, USA.

[6] Hansen, S.R., Narayanan, N.H., and Schrimpsher, D. 2000. Helping learners visualize and comprehend algorithms. *Interactive Multimedia Electronic Journal of Computer-Enhanced Learning* 1.

[7] Ihantola, P., Karavirta, V., Korhonen A., and Nikander, J. 2005. Taxonomy of effortless creation of algorithm visualizations. In *Proceedings of the 2005 International workshop on Computing Education Research (ICER)*, pages 123–133, New York, NY, USA.

[8] Karavirta V., Shaffer, C.A. 2013. JSAV: the JavaScript algorithm visualization library. In *Proceedings of the 18th ACM conference on Innovation and technology in computer science education*, pp. 159–164, New York, NY, USA.

[9] Karavirta, V. 2007. Facilitating Algorithm Animation Creation and Adoption in Education. Licentiate's thesis, Helsinki University of Technology.

[10] Karavirta, V., Korhonen, A., Malmi L., and Stålnacke K. 2004. MatrixPro - A tool for on-the-fly demonstration of data structures and algorithms. *In Proceedings of the Third Program Visualization Workshop*, pages 26–33, The University of Warwick, UK.

[11] Kerren, A., and Stasko, J.T. 2001. Algorithm animation. In *Stephan Diehl, editor, Software Visualization: International Seminar*, pages 1–15, Dagstuhl, Germany. Springer.

[12] Moreno, A., Myller, N., Sutinen, E., and Ben-Ari, M. 2004. Visualizing programs with Jeliot 3. In *Proceedings of the International Working Conference on Advanced Visual Interfaces*, pages 373 – 376, Gallipoli (Lecce), Italy.

[13] Naps T.,L., Rößling G., Almstrum V., Dann W., Fleischer R., Hundhausen C., Korhonen A., Malmi L., McNally M.,

Rodgers S., and Velázquez-Iturbide J.A. 2003. Exploring the role of visualization and engagement in computer science education. SIGCSE Bulletin, 35(2):131– 152, June.

[14] Naps, T.L., Eagan, J.R., and Norton, L.L. 2000. JHAVE – An Environment to Actively Engage Students in Web-Based Algorithm Visualizations. In *Proceedings of the 31st SIGCSE Technical Symposium on Computer Science Education*, pages 109–113, Austin, TX.

[15] Official pseudocode for Computer Basics. Available on https://www.infokup.hr/content/downloads/Infokup-Osnove-informatike-Pseudo-kod-katalog.pdf (accessed on 15.02.2013).

[16] Price, B., Baecker, R., and Small, I. 1998. An Introduction to Software Visualization. In Stasko, J., Domingue, J., Brown, M.H., and Price, B.A., editors, Software Visualization, chapter 1, pages 3–27. MIT Press.

[17] Price, B.A., Baecker, R.M., and Small, I.S. 1993. A principled taxonomy of software visualization. *Journal of Visual Languages & Computing*, 4(3):211 - 266.

[18] Rajala T., Laakso M.-J., Kaila E. and Salakoski T. 2007. VILLE – A Language-Independent Program Visualization Tool. In *Proceedings of the Seventh Baltic Sea Conference on Computing Education Research* - Vol 88.page 151-159.

[19] Roman, G.C., Cox, K.C., Wilcox, C.D., Plun, J.Y. 1992. Pavane: A system for declarative visualization of concurrent computations. *Journal of Visual Languages and Computing*, 3(2):161–193.

[20] Rößling, G. 2002. Animal-Farm: An Extensible Framework for Algorithm Visualization. Phd thesis, University of Siegen, Germany.

[21] Rößling, G., and Freisleben, B. 2000. Program visualization using AnimalScript. In *Proceedings of the First Program Visualization Workshop*, pages 41–52, University of Joensuu, Finland.

[22] Shaffer, C.A., Cooper, M., and Edwards, S.H. 2007. Algorithm visualization: a report on the state of the field. In *Proceedings of the 38th SIGCSE technical symposium on Computer Science Education*, SIGCSE'07, pages 150–154, New York, NY, USA, ACM Press.

[23] Sorva J., Karavirta V., and Malmi L. 2013. A review of generic program visualization systems for introductory programming education. *ACM Transactions on Computing Education (TOCE)*. New York, USA.

[24] Stasko, J. 1998. Building Software Visualizations through Direct Manipulation and Demonstration. In Stasko J., Domingue, J., Brown, M.H., and Price, B.A., editors, Software Visualization, ch. 14, pages 187–203. MIT Press.

[25] Stasko, J.T. 1990. TANGO: A framework and system for algorithm animation. *IEEE Computer*, 23(9):27–39.

[26] Stasko, J.T. 1991. Using direct manipulation to build algorithm animations by demonstration. *In Proceedings of Conference on Human Factors and Computing Systems*, pages 307–314, New Orleans, Louisiana.

Selective Hiding for Improved Algorithmic Visualization

Zoltan Katai
Sapientia University
Târgu-Mureş/Corunca, şoseaua Sighişoarei 1C. Romania.
+40 727 370 346
katai_zoltan@ms.sapientia.ro

ABSTRACT

In order to benefit most from algorithm visualization (AV) technology students have to be meaningfully involved in the algorithm visualisation process. This may imply that they are invited to predict and implement (using an interactive visual learning environment) the operation-sequence of the studied algorithm. In such learning environments users become active players in the AV process. Students are invited to process algorithms (in terms of their high-level operations) created to be processed by computers. The study we have performed reveals latent deficiencies such AV systems might have. Compared to humans, computers are blind in many ways. Visualizing information that has extra meanings for human viewers can obstruct them in following strict computer algorithms. Research results show that wisely applied hiding may result in more effective algorithm visualization due to its higher epistemic fidelity.

Categories and Subject Descriptors

K.3.2 [**Computers and Education**]: Computer and Information Science Education – *computer science education.*

Keywords

Algorithm visualization, Interactive learning environments, Constructivist approach, Epistemic fidelity.

1. INTRODUCTION

Computer algorithms are inherently abstract entities. Since they lack any tangible real-world representation it is quite difficult to teach and learn them. As Turing [17] stated: "One's object is then to have a clear mental picture of the state of the machine at each moment in the computation. This object can only be achieved with a struggle." Graphical representation of an expert's "clear mental picture" of the algorithm has become the most common method of illustrating how algorithms work. According to a recent survey "while many good algorithm visualizations are available, the need for more and higher quality visualizations continues" [15,16].

The term 'algorithm visualization' (AV) refers to the graphical illustration of computer algorithms in terms of their high-level operations, usually for the purpose of enhancing students' understanding of the algorithms' procedural behavior.

ITICSE'14, June 21–25, 2014, Uppsala, Sweden.
Copyright © 2014 ACM 978-1-4503-2833-3/14/06...$15.00.
http://dx.doi.org/10.1145/2591708.2591734

Algorithm visualization technology usually includes video or computer-based animations that visually illustrate computer algorithms in action [15,16]. A recent meta-analysis comparing instructional animation with static pictures confirmed the educational effectiveness of representational animations especially when procedural-motor knowledge had to be assimilated [5].

In addition, several studies conclude that AVs foster effective learning when students are actively involved in the visualization instead of passively viewing it [7]. For example, students should be invited to run the animation for several inputs observing the input variant/invariant characteristics of the studied algorithm. A genuinely active involvement may provide learners with the opportunity to have control over the algorithm animation process, even orchestrating it [11]. This implies that learners are invited to play the algorithm processing role of computers.

Compared to humans, computers are blind in many ways. An AV system may visualize information that has extra meanings for learners. In such enriched learning environments learners may find it difficult to follow a strict computer algorithm. For example, sorting algorithm visualisations usually expose the number-sequence to be sorted. Since learners see the numbers, they implicitly realise if two elements are in right order or not, and may skip the explicit comparison operation of the computer algorithm.

In this paper we investigate this phenomenon and suggest solutions to avoid potential side-effects of substituting "blind computers" with "not blind humans" in AV learning environments.

2. THEORETICAL FRAMEWORK

Theories of Epistemic Fidelity and Cognitive Constructivism provide the theoretical framework for this study. Wenger [18] defined the epistemic fidelity of a representation as the degree to which an external representation of a phenomenon reflects the expert's model of this phenomenon. Epistemic Fidelity theory has its origin in representationalist epistemology [14], which assumes that objects can be represented in the mind by symbolic models, and these "images" are the basis for human reasoning and action (Knowledge representation assumption). According to Hundhausen [6], other assumptions of the epistemic fidelity view are:

- Knowledge flow assumption: (1) Transmitter's knowledge is encoded in a graphical representation; (2) Graphical representation is decoded by receiver. In terms of AV: knowledge is seen to flow from teacher to AV to student through the conduit of the visual medium.

- Graphical medium effectiveness assumption: Graphical representations are effective tools for presenting mental models. They have the potential to support representations that closely match the source mental model at an appropriate level of abstraction (eliminating unnecessary detail).

• Epistemic Fidelity Assumption: High-epistemic-fidelity encoding promotes efficient decoding.

Hand in hand with IT advances and based on the epistemic premise that more encoded information results in more decoded information, AV researchers have developed more and more sophisticated AV software tools. On the other hand, recent research results have revealed other factors, in addition to epistemic fidelity, contributing to successful knowledge transmission. One of them is the learner's level of attention: heightened learner attention results in more robust and efficient decoding [10]. In addition, heightened attention can be fostered by increasing the learner's level of involvement. Students' active engagement in the learning process is even more important from the perspective of Cognitive Constructivism theory.

According to the Cognitive Constructivism theory, meaningful learning involves active knowledge structure construction [2]. Students filter and interpret (based on their prior knowledge) any new information and this process results in progressively reconstructed conceptual schemes [3]. Active knowledge construction implies the active use of new information by applying it to new situations [12]. The role of technology is not simply to transmit knowledge, but to support the knowledge construction process. Accordingly, in order to benefit most from AV technology (no matter how high the level of its epistemic fidelity) students have to be meaningfully involved in the algorithm visualisation process [7]. For example, environments which engage students in so-called interactive prediction may promote more effective learning [4].

Interactive prediction basically means that animation process is interrupted and the viewer is invited to predict what the visualisation will next show about the algorithm. This feature can be implemented in several ways:

• Students can be invited to orally predict what would happen at pre-defined breakpoints in the visualisation process. According to Byrne, Catrambone and Stasko [1], these "interventions" in AV process led to significantly better post-test results.

• In the Korhonen and Malmi [9] study students had to manually trace the execution of algorithms. In addition, in some key points of the algorithm, students were invited to record (using a graphical editor) their answers to questions about the current state of the data structure (and they received immediate feedback about their responses). The authors reported excellent results with their AV system.

• Naps, Eagan and Norton [13] also reported anecdotal success with the incorporation of stop-and-think questions into their AV system. They found that forcing students to answer the questions, registering their responses for grading purposes, and giving them immediate feedback could result in more effective learning.

• On the other hand Jarc, Feldman and Heller [8] reported opposite results. The AV system they developed presents students with algorithm animations in two modes: (1) "Show Me" (students passively watch the animation, trying to learn the behaviour of the studied algorithm); (2) "I'll Try" (Students

are engaged with interactive prediction questions). Surprisingly, the group that used the interactive prediction feature of the AV system performed worse (but not significantly) than the group that did not use it.

Possible enhancing/diminishing factors contributing to above results are:

• Immediate feedback students receive after they have answered the questions can reset confused ones' perception of the algorithm back to the track intended by the teacher [13].

• Instead of thinking thoroughly on the questions, students (especially weaker ones) may tend to view interactive prediction as a guessing game [8].

In this paper we present further factors that could increase/diminish effectiveness of AV systems that include interactive prediction.

3. STUDENT ORCHESTRATED COMPUTER ALGORITHMS

A special case of interactive prediction is when students have to orchestrate the studied algorithm. They are invited to predict and even "perform" (for a given input; using an interactive visual learning environment) the entire step-sequence of the algorithm. Features like immediate feedback, possibility to try-again and help-button (available at each step of the algorithm) can guarantee that all students will be able to complete their task. The primary goal of the orchestrating process is not to assess but to enhance or refine students' understanding about the studied algorithm. Obviously, this "You are in Charge" phase of the learning process should be preceded by "Preparation" phases (teacher explanation; watching the animated algorithm) when students are initiated on and familiarized with the strategy the algorithm is built on. A possible scenario could be: "Listen to It" (to be initiated on) + "Watch It" (to become familiar with) + "Try It" (to assimilate it).

In such learning environments (especially during "Try It" phases) users become active players of the AV process. If an AV system has this feature, then the concept of epistemic fidelity acquires new connotations. "Not blind users" are invited to process algorithms (in terms of their high-level operations) created to be processed by "blind computers". Effective AV systems should support users in identifying with the computer. From this perspective, high epistemic fidelity implies that at each state of the algorithm animation process users are not more informed (they do not see more), than the computer would be. For example, as we mentioned above, almost all computer algorithms include comparison operations (depending on how the compared values relate to each other the computer chooses between parallel scenarios to be followed). If the AV software shows the values to be compared, students may perform the comparison in their mind, implicitly (without realizing it). As a result they may skip the explicit comparison operation of the algorithm. On the other hand, by hiding the values to be compared, AV designers can force students to explicitly perform the comparison operation (as part of animation process). After this students are informed about the result of comparison by the AV software.

We have proposed to investigate the following questions:

• Could it happen that information that might have extra meanings for human viewers obstructs them in following strict computer algorithms?

• Can wisely applied hiding result in more effective algorithm visualization?

4. METHOD

Sorting algorithms are probably the most directly perceived computer algorithms by IT users. Sorting a list is a common operation in many fields of work and is one of the most fundamental problems in computer science. Bubble-sort is a popular introductory sorting algorithm that works by repeatedly stepping through the list to be sorted, comparing each pair of neighboring elements and swapping them if they are in the wrong order. The pass through the list is repeated until no swaps are needed, which indicates that the list is sorted. The algorithm can be easily optimized by observing that:

• The i-th pass is guaranteed to put the i-th largest element into its final place.

• All elements after the last swap of the current pass are in the right order, and they do not need to be checked again in the next pass.

We developed an online e-learning environment (http://algo-rythmics.ms.sapientia.ro/) that enabled us to implement the following syllabus. Students were invited

• to watch an exciting illustration of bubble-sort algorithm as a folkdance choreography;

• to watch an expressive computer animation of the algorithm;

• to orchestrate the algorithm on a white/black-box sequence.

"Algorithm-dance" illustration: The number-sequence is personified by a dancer-sequence (dancers are wearing the corresponding number on their clothes). Proper dance-steps illustrate the two key-operations of the algorithms: (C)omparing/(S)wapping two neighbouring elements. The choreography closely follows the sorting strategy the bubble-sort algorithm applies to. To increase the epistemic fidelity of the visualization we added graphical elements to the video-recordings that emphasize that the number-sequence is stored in an array. (see Figure. 1)

Figure 1. Bubble-sort with Gyímesi Csángó folk dance.

Computer animation: The array that stores the numbers to be sorted is visualized as a white-box sequence (numbers are visible). Comparing / Swapping two elements is animated by proportionally-expanding / interchanging the corresponding boxes. Pairs of arrows direct the user's attention to the elements the current operation is applied to. Elements that have reached their final positions in the sorted sequence are re-coloured. (see Figure. 2)

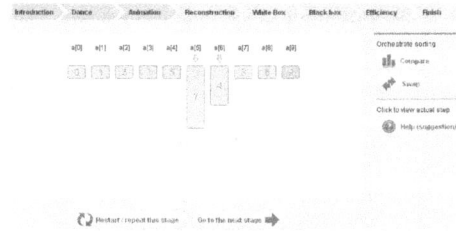

Figure 2. Animating the Bubble-sort algorithm.

White-box task: The user is invited to predict the "bubble-sort operation sequence" for a randomly generated number sequence stored in a white-array (numbers are visible). In order to implement the predicted next operation he/she has to click on the: 1. corresponding element-pair (parameters), 2. proper action button (compare/swap). Possible immediate feedbacks (in this order):

• Wrong parameter number (WPN)

• Wrong parameters selected (WPS)

• Wrong action selected (WAS)

• The software animates the correctly predicted operation (by proportionally-expanding / interchanging the corresponding boxes)

To prevent a "getting-stuck experience" we implemented a help button to inform users about the next correct operation: compare/swap (a[i],a[i+1]).

Black-box task: The user has to perform the same task but on a random sequence stored in a "black-array" (numbers are hidden). After the user has selected correctly the next element-pair and pushed the proper operation button, the software applies the corresponding animation. Although the numbers are invisible, users can realise the result of the currently performed (and animated) comparison since the corresponding boxes are expanded proportionally to the values they are storing.

By inviting students to orchestrate the studied algorithm we managed to generate the so-called "not-blind learners processing blind-computer algorithms" phenomenon. We expected that students performing the white-box task might have problems with comparing operations. We anticipated that they might tend to

• skip the explicit comparing operation if the current element-pair had to be swapped;

• omit to deal with the next element-pair if these are in the right order.

Our particular research question was: Can the "comparison problem" (resulting from replacing blind-computers with not-blind learners) be diminished by hiding the numbers to be sorted (resulting in increased epistemic fidelity)?

4.1 Participants

We initially proposed to involve in the experiment (presented to the students as a mandatory testing) all the 161 first year (school year 2013-2014) undergraduate students enrolled in science oriented programmes (Computer sciences, Electrical engineering and Mechanical engineering). Since the group of our first year students is consistently heterogeneous (regarding their prior knowledge in programming), we organized a pre-test to create two statistically equivalent groups (experimental/control). One-hundred and fifty one students participated in the pre-test. They had to solve the following problems:

1. Elaborate an algorithm to determine the "minimax points" of a numerical input matrix. (To detect students with above average programming skills)

2. Elaborate an algorithm to compute the averages of the negative/positive elements of a numerical input sequence. (To detect students with average programming skills)

3. Imagine n jail-cells (1..n). Initially all cells are locked. A jailer traverses the cells n times. During his i-th (i=1..n) traverse he changes the status (locked/unlocked) of door j (j=1..n), if i divides j. The number of doors remaining unlocked after the jailer had finished his n-th traverse? (a) n=10; (b) n=1000; (c) give a formula for the general case. (To detect students without prior programming knowledge, but with promising algorithmic thinking)

We characterized students' programming skills as follows:

- "Above-average": task_1 ≥ 50%;
- "Average": task_1 < 50%, task_2 ≥ 50%;
- "Promising": task_1 < 50%, task_2 < 50%, task_3 ≥ 50%;
- "Others": task_1 < 50%, task_2 < 50%, task_3 < 50%.

Based on their pre-test results we allocated students into two groups:

- A: control group (76 members; average score: 4.06)
- B: experimental group (75 members; average score: 4.06)

Obviously, no significant differences were detected between groups A and B: p = 0.49 > 0.05 (independent samples t-test)

As usual, not everything went exactly as we had planned. Only 138 students participated to the e-learning experiment. Furthermore, fifteen of them had to be eliminated because they had not accomplished their white/black-box task. In addition, some students from group A forgot to indicate their group ID (at the registration) and the software assigned them implicitly to group B. In the end, we had a valid control group with 52 members (group vA), and an experimental one with 71 members (group vB). The average pre-test scores of these groups were 4.47 and 4.16, respectively. According to the independent sample t-test groups vA and vB could also be considered as statistically equivalent ones (p = 0.21 > 0.05). The "Above-average"/ "Average"/ "Promising"/ "Others" distributions in groups vA and vB were 12/11/8/19 and 14/16/12/29 students, respectively (At these sub-group levels also no significant differences were detected).

4.2 Procedure

We performed the experiment during the first week of school year 2013-2014 (in computer labs where all students had individual access to the online e-learning tool). After they had received their group-ID (A or B) students were asked to participate in the following three phase e-learning session:

1. "Listen to It": First two slides presented a brief definition of what a sorting algorithm means. Accordingly, students from both groups were informed that the algorithm was going to be danced, animated and user-orchestrated. They were made aware of the need to focus on the strategy and the ways that comparing and swapping operations are animated.

2. "Watch It": Students from both groups were invited to watch (1) the folk-dance illustration and (2) the computer animation of bubble-sort algorithm.

3. "Try It":

a) Students from group A had to orchestrate the algorithm on a random sequence stored in a white-array.

b) Students from group B had to orchestrate the algorithm on a random sequence stored in a black-array.

4.3 Results and discussion

The software registered the errors (and the type of errors) students had made, the amount of time they had spent with their task, and also counted their help requests. Based on the number of errors, group vB performed significantly better the group vA (see Table 1). At sub-group level the means and the p-values were: "Above-average" (5.21, 4.71: 0.43); "Average" (8.7, 3.2: 0.06); "Promising" (11.17, 4.16: **0.02**); "Others" (12.65, 8.2: 0,08).

We focused on the following types of errors:

1. Although the next element-pair to be dealt with was selected correctly, the operation to be applied on was chosen incorrectly: (a) S in place of C; (b) C in place of S;

2. Wrong element-pair was selected when the next operation had to be: (a) C; (b) S

(No significant differences were detected with respect to WPN)

Table 1. Comparative analysis of students' performance scores (groups vA and vB).

	Time /step	Help	Errors	WPN	WAS		WPS	
					C	S	C	S
vA	5.05	1.58	9.6	1.48	1.42	0.62	5.32	0.76
vB	4.15	1.19	5.56	1	0.52	0.47	2.53	1.02
p	**0.002**	0.34	**0.009**	0.1	**0.0002**	0.24	**0.006**	0.28

Type 1a errors indicated those moments when students performed directly the swapping operation without previously comparing the element-pair in case. Whenever they omitted to compare initially right ordered element-pairs, the software registered type 2a errors. Comparing groups vA and vB with regard to these four types of error we found that group vA had made significantly more type 1a and 2a errors than group vB. No significant differences were detected between groups with respect to type 1b and 2b errors.

As we mentioned above the primary goal of white/black-box tasks were to refine students' understanding of the studied algorithm. According to the constructivist view, immediate feedbacks students received (with respect to the errors they had made) could result in progressively reconstructed mental pictures of the algorithm. To detect initial misconceptions we have proposed to investigated how many students

- skipped the explicit comparing operation of the first element-pair that had to be swapped (first possible type 1a error);

- omitted to deal with the first element-pair that was in the right order (first possible type 2a error).

Significant differences were detected between groups. 30.77% of students belonging to group vA failed to avoid the first possible type 1a or 2a error. This percentage in the case of group vB was only 14.08%.

Interestingly, students belonging to group vA spent significantly more time with their tasks, than their colleagues from group vB (see Table 1). A possible explanation: since group vB was exposed to less distracting factors, they could stay focused on the sorting strategy.

It can also be noticed that students from both groups (especially weakly performing ones) failed to profit enough from the presence of the help button (see Table 1; Compare columns "Number of help request" and "Number of errors"). For example, four students who made more than 50 errors had zero help requests. They preferred guessing instead of pushing the help button. (No significant differences were detected between groups with regard to the number of help requests)

According to the above presented results, as we expected, students working on white-arrays had significantly more problems with comparing operations than those who had to sort invisible sequences. More specifically, students sorting visible sequences skipped significantly more frequently comparing operations than those working on a hidden sequence. A plausible explanation could be that students who saw the numbers performed the comparing operation in their mind, implicitly. Since students sorting black-arrays did not see the numbers, they were forced, in a same sense as blind computers are, to explicitly perform the comparing operations in order to find out if the corresponding element-pair had to, or did not have to be swapped.

Table 2. The state of array a[0..9] after each pass of bubble-sort algorithm.

	0	1	2	3	4	5	6	7	8	9
Initial sequence	3	0	1	8	7	2	5	4	6	9
After first pass	0	1	3	7	2	5	4	6	_8_	_9_
After second pass	0	1	3	2	5	4	6	_7_	8	9
After third pass	0	1	2	3	4	_5_	_6_	7	8	9
After forth pass	**_0_**	**_1_**	**_2_**	**_3_**	**_4_**	5	6	7	8	9

We have observed this phenomenon in other circumstances too. We posted the bubble-sort dance on youtube (more than 600.000 views were registered in two years). Table 2 shows the sequence after each pass (the elements are indexed from 0 to 9). After each pass dancers who reached their final position (at the end of the sorted list) turned back (bolded elements). Currently bolded

elements are underlined, too. In the first pass (0..9) the last swapping operation was swap(a[7],a[8]) (gray cells) and, consequently (according to the optimized version of the algorithm), both dancers 8 and 9 turned back. After the second pass (0..7), by chance, also two elements (6 and 7) were on their final places, but only one of them (number 7) in a proven way (last swapping was: swap(a[6],a[7])). Consequently, only dancer 7 turned back.

A typical question posted by many users was:

User1: *Why 6 vs 7 didn't turn back both, but 8 vs 9 and 5 vs 6 did?*

One of the users answered this question in the following way:

User2: *There is a memory of where the last exchange took place, so all values greater than the memory must be in the correct order or there would have been a change. For 6 and 7 there is no proof that they were already in order because the change took place on the last comparison, so the memory was only of the value in the highest index.*

Since user 1 saw that after the second pass numbers 6 and 7 had reached their final places, this tended to shorten the next pass by two elements. On the other hand, user 2 comprehended that a bubble-sort algorithm guided blind computer "cannot realize" (after the second pass) that cell a[6] stores the right number. Accordingly, misconceptions induced by the studied phenomenon can be observed even during illustration/animation phase.

From the perspective of epistemic fidelity theory these results can be interpreted as it follows:

- In computer algorithm visualization invisibility could contribute to higher epistemic fidelity and, consequently, more effective learning.

- Wisely applied hiding results in higher epistemic fidelity especially when learners are substituting computers in their algorithm processer role.

- High epistemic fidelity AV systems supports not blind learners in identifying with blind-computer.

We also observed that students working on black-arrays tended to skip swapping operations more frequently than those who had to sort white arrays (see Table 1). A possible reason could be that since numbers were invisible they did not realize that comparison did not imply swapping either (although only comparison was animated). It seems that black-box tasks required more "implementational focus". In addition, "black-box students" who had completely failed to catch the logic of the algorithm during "Watch it" phases, apparently had less chance to do this during the "Try it" phase. Among those who abandoned their orchestrating task 60% had faced a black-box task. Among those who complete their task, but made more than 50 errors (roughly equal to the number of steps the correct operation sequence had) 66% belonged to the "black-box group". Black-box tasks were especially useful for that majority who previously caught the logic of the algorithm, but needed to be helped in assimilating it from the perspective of a blind computer.

5. CONCLUSION

To teach and learn computer algorithms is a challenging educational task. In order to elaborate the algorithm, students have to condescend to the primitive level of the computer. Thinking only of those primitive operations computers can execute, they have to design the operation-sequence that, as executed, results in the solution to the problem to be solved. Interactive AV has become a common method to help students to assimilate computer algorithms.

Effective AVs can be powerful supplementary, complementary and alternative tools to written presentations or verbal descriptions [15]. On the other hand, as we have discussed above, AVs might have their own specific weak points (compared to written/verbal descriptions): too much visualized information can be harmful.

We developed a software-tool that, after a brief description of what a sorting algorithm means, generates (by applying sequenced multiple AVs) a three-phase learning experience. Phase 3 harmonizes with the constructivist approach to learning: learners become active participants of the AV experience. From the perspective of Epistemic Fidelity theory:

- During the first two phases we tried to increase epistemic fidelity by common methods:

    - Adding graphical elements to the video-recordings;

    - Dancers/elements that had reached their final positions "turned-back" / "were re-colored";

    - A pair of arrows direct user's attention to the elements the current operation is applied to;

    - Expressive animations for comparison/swapping operations (the way we animate comparison operation transmits the idea of weighing the number-pair to be compared by a balance).

- During black-box task we have proposed to increase epistemic fidelity in a new way: by applying invisibility.

While more research is needed to draw general conclusions in the studied topic (it is a limitation of this study that we investigated the proposed research questions only with respect to one specific sorting algorithm), the study we have performed reveals latent deficiencies that AV systems might have. Visualizing information that has extra meanings for human viewers can obstruct them in following strict computer algorithms. Research results show that wisely applied hiding may result in more effective algorithm visualization due to its higher epistemic fidelity. As a final conclusion: Effective AV systems support not blind learners in assimilating the algorithm processing role of blind-computers.

6. REFERENCES

[1] M. D. Byrne, R. Catrambone, and J. T. Stasko. *Do algorithm animations aid learning?* (Tech. Rep. No. GIT-GVU-96-18). Graphics, Visualization, and Usability Center, Georgia Institute of Technology, Atlanta, August 1996.

[2] S. Carey. *Conceptual change in childhood.* MIT Press, Cambridge, MA, 1985.

[3] R. Driver. Students' conceptions and the learning of science. *International Journal of Science Education*, 11(5):481–490, 1989.

[4] S. R. Hansen, N. H. Narayanan, and D. Schrimpsher. Helping learners visualize and comprehend algorithms. *Interactive Multimedia Electronic Journal of Computer-Enhanced Learning*, 2(1), April 2000.

[5] T. N. Hoffler and D. Leutner. Instructional animation versus static pictures: a meta-analysis. *Learning and Instruction*, 17(6):722–738, December 2007.

[6] C. D. Hundhausen. *Toward effective algorithm visualization artifacts: designing for participation and communication in an undergraduate algorithms course.* Department of Computer and Information Science, University of Oregon, http://eecs.wsu.edu, 1999. [Online; accessed January 3, 2014].

[7] C. Hundhausen, S. A. Douglas, and J. T. Stasko. A meta-study of algorithm visualization effectiveness. *Journal of Visual Languages and Computing*, 13(3):259–290, June 2002.

[8] D. J. Jarc, M. B. Feldman, and R. S. Heller. Assessing the benefits of interactive prediction using Web-based algorithm animation courseware. In *SIGCSE '00: Conference Proceedings*, pages 377–381. ACM Press, New York, March 2000.

[9] A. Korhonen and L. Malmi. Algorithm simulation with automatic assessment. In *5th Annual SIGCSE/SIGCUE Conference Proceedings*, pages 160–163. ACM Press, New York, July 2000.

[10] A. W. Lawrence. *Empirical studies of the value of algorithm animation in algorithm understanding.* Georgia Institute of Technology, Atlanta, http://www.dtic.mil, 1993. [Online; accessed January 3, 2014].

[11] R. E. Mayer and P. Chandler. When learning is just a click away: Does simple interaction foster deeper understanding of multimedia messages? *Journal of Educational Psychology*, 93(2):390–397, June 2001.

[12] R. H. Mayer. Designing instruction for constructivist learning. In *Instructional Design Theories and Models*, pages 141–160. Lawrence Erlbaum Associates, Mahwah, NJ, April 1999.

[13] L. Naps, J. Eagan, and L. Norton. JHAVÉ – An Environment to actively engage students in Web-based algorithm visualizations. In *SIGCSE '00: Conference Proceedings*, pages 109–113. ACM Press, New York, March 2000.

[14] A. Newell. Physical symbol systems. *Cognitive Science* 4(2):135–183, April 1980.

[15] C. Shaffer, M. Cooper, and S. Edwards. Algorithm visualization: a report on the state of the field. In *SIGCSE '07 Conference Proceedings*, pages 150–154. ACM Press, New York, 2007.

[16] C. Shaffer, M. L. Cooper, A. J. D. Alon, M. Akbar, M. Stewart, S. Ponce, S. H. Edwards. Algorithm visualization: the state of the field. *ACM Transactions on Computing Education*, 10(3):1–22, August 2010.

[17] A. M. Turing. Computing machinery and intelligence. *Mind*, 59(236):433–460, 1950.

[18] E. Wenger. *Artificial Intelligence and Tutoring Systems.* Morgan Kaufmann, Los Altos, CA, 1987.

Failure Rates in Introductory Programming Revisited

Christopher Watson
School of Engineering and
Computing Sciences
University of Durham
United Kingdom
christopher.watson@dur.ac.uk

Frederick W.B. Li
School of Engineering and
Computing Sciences
University of Durham
United Kingdom
frederick.li@dur.ac.uk

ABSTRACT

Whilst working on an upcoming meta-analysis that synthesized fifty years of research on predictors of programming performance, we made an interesting discovery. Despite several studies citing a motivation for research as the 'high failure rates of introductory programming courses', to date, the majority of available evidence on this phenomenon is at best anecdotal in nature, and only a single study by Bennedsen and Caspersen has attempted to determine a worldwide pass rate of introductory programming courses.

In this paper, we answer the call for further substantial evidence on the CS1 failure rate phenomenon, by performing a systematic review of introductory programming literature, and a statistical analysis on pass rate data extracted from relevant articles. Pass rates describing the outcomes of 161 CS1 courses that ran in 15 different countries, across 51 institutions were extracted and analysed. An almost identical mean worldwide pass rate of 67.7% was found. Moderator analysis revealed significant, but perhaps not substantial differences in pass rates based upon: grade level, country, and class size. However, pass rates were found not to have significantly differed over time, or based upon the programming language taught in the course. This paper serves as a motivation for researchers of introductory programming education, and provides much needed quantitative evidence on the potential difficulties and failure rates of this course.

Categories and Subject Descriptors

K3.2 [**Computer and Information Sciences Education**]:
Computer science education

General Terms

Measurement, Experimentation, Verification.

Keywords

Introductory Programming, CS1, Programming, Pass Rate, Failure Rate, Statistics

1. INTRODUCTION

The demand for skilled programmers is increasing on a global scale. Recent projections from the United States Bureau of Labour Statistics [11] suggests the growth of computing careers is set to continue through 2020, and that various computing skills will be in strong demand for the foreseeable future. To address these future labour demands, governments throughout the world are in the process of bringing programming into the classroom environment, so that students can be better prepared to work within a digital economy. From September 2014, UK schools will replace the Information and Communication Technology (ICT) course with Computing. Pupils aged 5-7 will be expected to understand "what algorithms are" and how to "create and debug simple programs". Ordinary classroom instructors are naturally concerned about the proposed changes. A recent poll showed that 74% of current ICT teachers do not believe they have the right skills to deliver the new computing curriculum, and fear that they do not have the time to learn the new skills required [5].

This is perhaps not surprising, as learning to program can be an incredibly difficult task, to the point where the phrases "failure rate" and "programming course" are almost synonymous [2]. For instance, [3] states: "*Substantial failure rates plague introductory programming courses the world over and have increased rather than decreased over the years*". Although high failure rates are an often cited motivation for research into programming education, only a single paper to date [2] has attempted to provide quantitative evidence to support this claim. This is problematic, and a lack of hard facts on the outcomes of introductory programming courses (henceforth called CS1) can have implications for both instructors and students. Instructors of failing CS1 courses may accept their shortcomings as "that's just the way programming courses are". Likewise potential students may be easily put off taking the course to start with, which will not help future labour demands to be satisfied.

In this paper, we expand the work of [2] by performing a systematic review of introductory programming literature, in an effort to statistically consolidate further quantitative evidence on the often cited worldwide high failure rates of programming courses. The contributions of this paper are:

1. Verify the findings of Bennedsen and Caspersen.

2. Demonstrate that failure rates in CS1 have not significantly improved over time.

3. Explore possible moderators of failure rates, including: country, grade level, language, and cohort size.

2. RELATED WORK

Although many researchers have cited high failure rates as an off the cuff motivation for CS1 research (e.g. [3, 8, 10]), only Bennedsen and Caspersen [2] have attempted to provide quantitative evidence on this phenomenon. Around 2005/6, [2] sent a short survey to the authors and panel participants of five CS educational conferences: Koli Calling '04, ICALT '04, ACEC '04, SIGCSE '05 and ITiCSE '05. The survey was designed to collect data on the outcomes of the CS1 courses at the respective researcher's institution. A total of 63 usable responses from researchers in 15 different countries were received, representing a response rate of 12.3%. The main findings of their study were:

1. A worldwide pass rate of CS1, estimated to be 67%, however large variations in the pass, fail, abort, and skip rates were reported.

2. Smaller classes (< 30 students) are suggested to have a higher pass rate than larger ones (82% vs 69%).

3. Colleges are suggested to have a higher pass rate than universities (88% vs 66%).

4. The pass rates would seem to be independent of the language taught (objects-orientated vs imperative).

However there were several limitations of the study which we attempt to address in this work. Firstly, the work of [2] provides a useful snapshot of the state of CS1 education, but only at a single point in time. A more interesting analysis would be to examine whether the pass rates of CS1 have improved over time, possibly in response to the introduction of more advanced pedagogical techniques and tools, such as game-based learning techniques [15], or improvements to the compilation feedback provided by novice IDE's [12].

Secondly, the authors acknowledge that their sample size may be insufficient to make generalized conclusions to CS1 courses worldwide. Only the outcomes of 63 courses taken from 62 different institutions were used, and it is perhaps interesting to consider why 87.7% of contacted authors failed to respond. One possibility is that the non-responding authors had higher failure rates than they wished to report, and therefore did not respond. This would mean that the worldwide pass rate of CS1 could be lower than [2] reported.

Thirdly, although researchers from 15 different countries responded, the sample of 63 responses was heavily dominated by institutions from the United States. 66% of responses came from US institutions, with the remaining 14 countries providing (mainly) 1-2 responses each. This limitation again makes generalization of the findings on CS1 pass rates to a worldwide scale difficult.

Fourthly, the findings were based upon a survey that was only sent to the authors at five conferences on CS education. This is a narrow target group, and inevitably omits a great deal of evidence on pass rates that remains unexplored, published in the proceedings of other conferences and journals. By exploring this additional source of data, a fuller picture on the worldwide outcomes of CS1 courses can be identified.

In short, there is still a need to further examine and analyse quantitative evidence on the outcomes of CS1 courses on a worldwide scale. This can only benefit the research community as a whole, as the more quantitative evidence that is available on CS1 outcomes, the more solid motivation can be used for further research into CS1 education.

3. RESEARCH DESIGN

Whilst the work of Bennedsen and Caspersen [2] was based upon surveying the authors of selected conference papers and performing a statistical analysis of the responses, our work is based upon performing a systematic review of the literature on CS1 education, and performing a statistical analysis of the data extracted from relevant articles.

3.1 Research Questions

To answer the call of [2] by expanding their work, our research questions were defined as follows:

1. What are the pass and failure rates of introductory programming courses? Are these high figures?

2. How do the pass and failure rates of introductory programming courses compare over time?

3. Are the pass and failure rates moderated by any of the following aspects of the teaching context:

   (a) Country
   (b) Programming language taught in the course
   (c) Size of the class
   (d) Grade level of the institution

3.2 Data Collection Method

The motivation for this work arose whilst we were working on an upcoming meta-analysis which synthesized fifty years of research on predictors of programming performance. As such a proportion of the data we have used for our analysis on the failure rates of CS1 was extracted from articles identified while we conducted the meta-analysis. Supplementary searches were then conducted to identify additional data.

3.2.1 Initial Search

In an attempt to identify every study that examined predictors of programming performance, a search of all articles published between the years 1960 - June 2013 was carried out. Initial electronic searches were made of the following databases, repositories, and websites: (1) ACM, (2) IEEE, (3) Science Direct, (4) Wiley Online, (5) Taylor & Francis, (6) JSTOR, (7) SAGE, (8) PsycNET, (9) EThOS, (10) ProQuest, (11) DART, (12) Trove. Following this, further general searches were made using (1) Google Scholar, (2) ISI Web of Knowledge, (3) ERIC, and a final search was conducted by manually screening the indexes of selected conference proceedings and journals for relevant studies.

Keywords were identified by two researchers. A boolean strategy using the operators AND and OR refined the searches ensured that an exhaustive search was conducted. Specifically the search criteria used was: (Predict OR Predictors OR Predicting OR Identifying OR Indicators OR Influence OR Factors OR Traits OR Tests OR Relationship) AND (Performance OR Aptitude OR Ability OR Success OR Training OR Achievement OR Outcomes OR Learning) AND (Programming OR Programming Course OR Introductory Programming OR CS1).

1378 articles were identified. After applying an inclusion screening based on abstract and full text content, a sample of 58 articles that examined predictors of programming performance remained. Only 12 of these articles provided quantitative data on the failure rates of their respective CS1 courses, and these were extracted for analysis in this study.

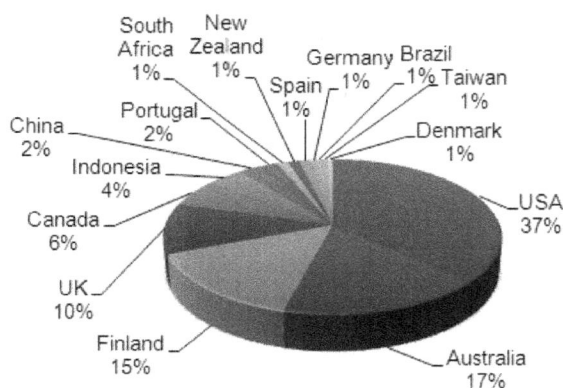

Figure 1: Geographical distribution of the outcomes

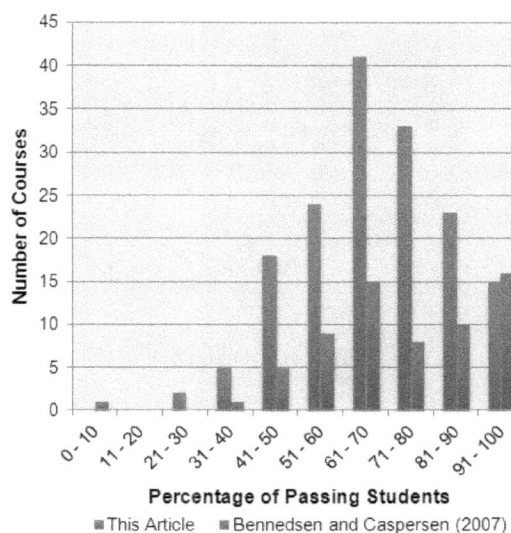

Figure 2: Pass rates of the 161 CS1 courses compared to the findings of Bennedsen and Caspersen.

3.2.2 Secondary Search

As our meta-analysis focused upon a narrow area of CS1 research (predictors), it was necessary to conduct supplementary searches to identify other articles that provided quantitative evidence on the pass rates of CS1. We believed that an abundance of such data would be available from articles that described interventions designed to improve the performance of CS1 students. As such, the initial search process was repeated, but with the following search criteria: (Pass Rate OR Failure Rate OR Success Rate OR Withdraw OR Completion OR Dropout OR Improving) AND (Programming OR Programming Course OR Introductory Programming OR CS1). This resulted in the identification of an additional 42 articles after screening that provided pass rate statistics of the CS1 courses at their institutions.

3.3 Description of the Sample

After verifying that the same failure rate had not been coded twice (e.g. reported in two articles), the resulting sample consisted of 54 articles: 37 conference, 11 journal, 3 theses, 2 unpublished, and 1 book chapter. The sample described the outcomes of 161 CS1 courses that ran between the years 1979-2013, although the majority of outcomes (80%) were for courses that ran from 2003 onwards. The outcomes included in this sample were from 51 different institutions, across 15 different countries. The geographical distribution of the outcomes used in this study are shown in Figure 1. To compare our sample to the one used by [2], our sample was less dominated by a single country. In the sample used by [2], 67% of outcomes were from US institutions whereas in our sample, 63% of outcomes came from 14 countries. US institutions contributed 37% of the outcomes, followed by Australia 17%, Finland 15%, and UK 10%.

4. RESULTS

4.1 Pass and Failure Rates of CS1

The first question addressed by this study was to determine the average pass rate of CS1 courses, and to verify whether or not the 67% pass rate found by Bennedsen and Caspersen [2] was accurate. Figure 2 shows a distribution of the 161 pass rates used in this study, alongside the pass rates reported by [2]. As can be seen from this figure, the pass rates used in this study followed a normal distribution (Shapiro Wilk test, $p > .05$). The proportions of each

pass range were similar to the ones reported by [2], with the modal pass range being 61-70%, and the majority of pass rates (61%) concentrated in the range of 50-80%. As can be seen, the pass rates varied considerably, ranging from a low of 23.1% to a high of 96%.

The mean CS1 pass rate found by this study was 67.7% (95% CI: 65.3% to 70.1%), which is practically identical to the 67% figure reported by [2]. Whilst it is debatable whether or not, a sample based on the outcomes of only 161 CS1 courses across 15 countries is representative of the worldwide state of CS1, when this finding is considered in conjunction with the similar result found by the independent [2] study, an average CS1 pass rate of 67% may be close to the mean figure across other countries.

The natural question which follows is what happens to the remaining 32.3% of students who do not pass? Disappointingly, individual breakdowns on the failure and withdraw rates of courses were difficult to come by, and only 36 fail rates were explicitly stated as such. Analysing this data only, a similar mean pass rate of 66.9%, and mean failure rate of 30.3% was found, with the remaining 2.8% presumably representing withdrawals and non-completions. Whilst these figures are comparable to the results on the complete sample, and we can state that 32.3% of students did not pass CS1, we cannot say what the exact reason for this was.

4.2 Pass and Failure Rates Over Time

The second question addressed by this study was to determine whether or not, the pass and failure rates of CS1 have changed over time. Grouping the 161 pass rates by the year in which the course was run, a one-way ANOVA was performed. There were no outliers in any of the groups, as assessed by the inspection of a box plot. The pass rates were normally distributed for each year, as assessed by Shapiro-Wilk test of normality ($p > .05$), and homogeneity of variances was confirmed by Levene's test ($p = .108$). A one-way ANOVA showed that there were no statistically significant differences in pass rates of CS1 for any of the years covered by this study, $F(21, 139) = .486$, $p = .971$.

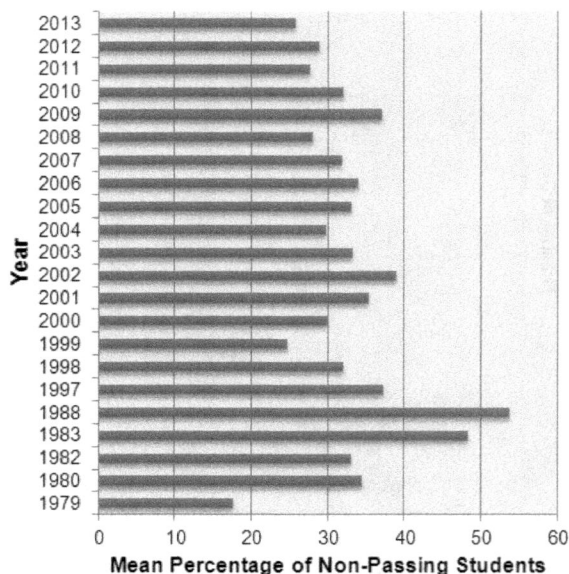

Figure 3: Non-passing students by course year.

As can be seen from Figure 3, the mean percentage of non-passing students has remained constant throughout the 2000's, and similar rates can be seen during the 1980's and 1990's. The percentage of non passing students by year ranged from 53.5% to 17.4%, and 67% of years covered by this study had a pass rate of between 67% and 75%. Given the increased amount of tools available to support CS1 students, it is interesting to see that there have been no significant improvements in the pass rates of CS1 over time.

4.3 Pass and Failure Rates by Moderators

The third question addressed by this study was to determine whether or not any aspects of the teaching context (country, programming language taught in the course, size of the class, grade level) moderated the overall pass rates.

4.3.1 Country

It is well known that educational practices and assessment criteria can vary across different continents. Therefore the first moderator we considered was whether or not the pass rates of CS1 differed by the country the course was taught in. Grouping the 161 pass rates by the 15 countries that were previously presented (Figure 1), a one-way ANOVA was performed. The previously stated assumptions were satisfied, and a Shapiro Wilk test confirmed the pass rates were normally distributed for all countries ($p > .05$), with the exception of Canada ($p < .05$). However as violations from normality do not substantially affect the type I error rate, and an ANOVA is considered relatively robust against this violation, we proceeded. Levene's test confirmed the homogeneity of variances ($p = .15$), and a one way ANOVA revealed significant differences in the pass rates of CS1 by country, $F(14, 146) = 4.58$, $p < .001$.

From Figure 4 it can be seen that the mean percentage of non-passing students varies considerably by country. Portugal was found to have the lowest mean pass rate ($\bar{\mu}_{pass} = 37.9\%$), followed by Germany ($\bar{\mu}_{pass} = 44.7\%$), and Brazil

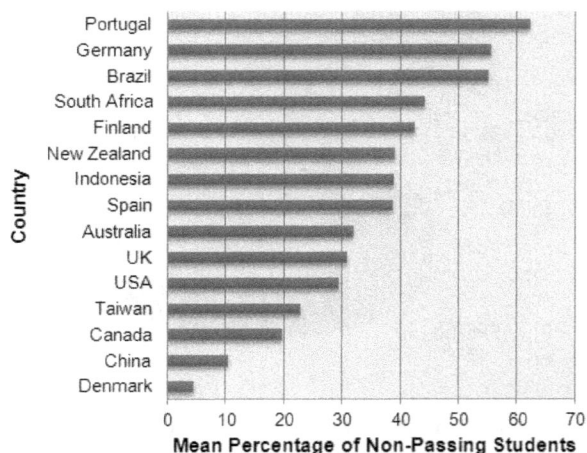

Figure 4: Non-passing students by country.

($\bar{\mu}_{pass} = 45\%$). But, these findings were based on a small sample, and cannot be generalized. In terms of the 4 countries which made 80% of the sample, Finland was found to have the lowest pass rate ($\bar{\mu}_{pass} = 57.7\%$) and the pass rates of the USA ($\bar{\mu}_{pass} = 70.9\%$), UK ($\bar{\mu}_{pass} = 69.3\%$), and Australia ($\bar{\mu}_{pass} = 68.3\%$) were not found to be statistically different. We hypothesized that on larger samples, the pass rates for each country would tend towards a similar range, as was the case with our largest 4 groups.

4.3.2 Programming Language

There has been much debate among CS educators as to which programming language should be taught to students first (e.g. adopting an objects-first or imperative first approach [4, 6]). We next examined whether or not the pass rates of CS1 differed by the programming language that was taught in the course. Pass rates were grouped into 9 categories, as follows: C (4.3%), Python (10.6%), C++ (6.8%), Java (46.6%), VB (1.9%), Fortran (1.9%), Novice (Scratch, Karel, 6.2%), Others (Standalone, 8.1%), and Not Stated (13.7%). An ANOVA was performed. The previous assumptions were satisfied, and a Shapiro Wilk test showed that the pass rates were normally distributed for all languages ($p > .05$), apart from Python ($p < .05$). The variances were heterogeneous (Levine's test, $p < .05$), and a Welch ANOVA showed no significant differences in the pass rates of CS1 by language, Welch's $F(8, 18.74) = 1.26$, $p = .31$.

In Figure 5 it can be seen that the mean percentage of non-passing students does not vary considerably by programming language. The percentage of passing students appears to be lower for C (61.1%) and C++ (56.2%) however the differences are not significantly different to the other languages whose pass rates are in the range 65% to 75%. This result is consistent with the work of [2] who also found no significant differences in pass rates based upon the language taught.

4.3.3 Class Size

As the size of a class has a natural impact on the level of support that a student receives, we explored it as a third moderator. Class size data was only available for 101 (62.7%) of the courses included in our sample. To verify previous work, we replicated the binary classification used by [2].

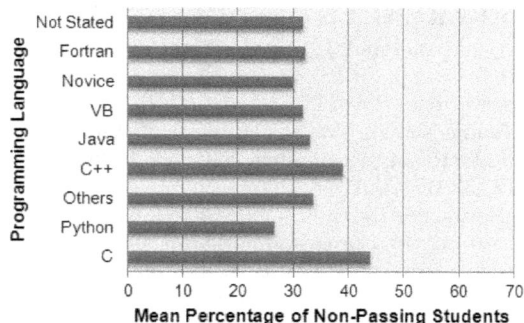

Figure 5: Non-passing students grouped by language

Classes were defined as small if they consisted of < 30 students, and large otherwise. A Shapiro Wilk test showed that the pass rates were normally distributed for both small and large classes ($p > .05$), and that variances were heterogeneous (Levine's test, $p < .05$). An ANOVA showed significant differences in the pass rates of CS1 by class size, Welch's $F(2, 27.23) = 6.78$, $p < .01$. The results on our sample for small classes ($\bar{\mu}_{pass} = 80.1\%$, $SD = 11.4$) and large classes ($\bar{\mu}_{pass} = 65.4\%$, $SD = 16.7$) confirm the findings of [2], who found higher CS1 pass rates for smaller classes, than larger classes (69% and 82% respectively).

4.3.4 Grade Level of Institution

Finally, we explored whether there were any significant differences between the pass rates of universities and other educational institutions (colleges, high school). Our sample consisted of 145 university courses and 16 from other institutions. An ANOVA was performed. A Shapiro Wilk test showed that the pass rates were normally distributed for Universities ($p > .05$), but not for other grade levels. Homogeneity of variances was confirmed by Levene's test ($p = .20$), and one-way ANOVA revealed significant differences in the pass rates of CS1 by grade level, $F(1, 159) = 11.62$, $p < .001$. The results on our sample for universities ($\bar{\mu}_{pass} =, 66.4\%$, $SD = 15.3$) and other grade levels ($\bar{\mu}_{pass} = 79.9\%$, $SD = 11.9$) confirm the findings of [2], who found the pass rates for universities to be lower than other institutions.

5. DISCUSSION

The findings of this study confirm the results of the small study conducted by Bennedsen and Caspersen [2]. As shown in Table 1, this study found an almost identical pass rate of CS1 courses of 67.7%, and comparable results were found based on course size, and institutional grade level.

The additional contributions of this study have been to show that CS1 pass rates vary by different countries, have not improved over time, and they are largely unaffected by the programming language taught in the course. The question which arises from these findings is that if external aspects of the teaching context do not have a substantial moderating effect on the pass rates of certain students enables them to acquire programming skills whilst others endlessly struggle? However, recent studies have suggested that despite over fifty years of research, we still do not know precisely which characteristics influence their ability to acquire programming

Table 1: Comparison of Results.

	This Study		Bennedsen [2]	
Pass Rate	Courses	Pass %	Courses	Pass %
Overall CS1	161	67.7	63	67
Colleges	16	79.9	12	88
Universities	145	66.4	50	66
Small Class	10	80.1	15	82
Large Class	91	65.4	48	69

skills [14] and possibly the programming behaviours of student may have the strongest influence on their performance [13], and in turn, the failure rates of CS1.

Until such characteristics can be identified, the implication from this study is that the best approach for teaching CS1 may be based upon small groups, and replacing traditional lectures with classroom based instruction. This ties in with research on small group teaching, and the use of pair programming to improve performance [9].

5.1 Are the Pass Rates of CS1 Low?

When considering the average pass rate found by this study, we share the sentiments of [2], in that 67.7% is not an *alarmingly* low pass rate. On the other hand, when considering this figure within the wider context of CS education, we have a different view. Enrolment and retention of CS majors are well known problems [1]. Within the UK for instance, statistics provided by the Higher Education Funding Council show that out of all STEM degrees, Computer Science is the only subject where enrolment has consistently declined between the academic years 2001/2002, and 2011/12. A decline in enrolment numbers from 67,896 to 45,158, or 33% [7]. Although showing improvement in recent years, the number of students studying American institutions has also declined to half that it was in 2000 [16].

Part of this decline may stem from the reputation of Computer Science, or to be precise CS1, of being a difficult course. As CS1 is usually one of the first subjects taught to students taking a CS degree, it forms a benchmark of their impressions of the entire discipline. If the pass rates of CS1 are perceived to be low, then attracting students will undoubtedly prove problematic.

On the other hand, if pass rates can be improved, then the reputation of CS1 will in turn be improved. This may lead to an increase in enrolment numbers, and possibly increased retention. Currently we have found in this study 3/10 students do not complete, or fail CS1. If an estimated 2 million students are currently enrolled worldwide in computing courses worldwide [2], then an improvement in the pass rate of only 5%, would lead to an additional 100,000 students graduating with the skills required to satisfy the future labour demands that were outlined at the start of this article. Therefore while we do not believe that a 67.7% pass rate is *alarmingly* low, we also believe that there is considerable potential for improvement.

5.2 Threats to Validity

Whilst the sample of outcomes used by this study was over double the size of the sample used by [2] (98 more outcomes), it is still debatable as to whether or not it is representative of CS1 courses on a global scale. [2] reported that in 1999, there were over one million students enrolled in computing courses across 72 different countries. In this paper, we were only able to identify outcomes from 15 different countries, which means that we lack data from the majority of the countries in the world. Only by collecting such data can our results be further validated to a worldwide scale. On the other hand, when considering the results in conjunction with the findings of [2], our findings are consistent, and therefore may be close to the actual results in the population.

The second threat to validity concerns the sources of the data used. Whilst [2] surveyed authors of selected conference papers and panel attendees directly via email, our data has come from a systematic review process. It is possible that the data used by [2] was already published in the articles that we have used in this study, in which case, 63 of our articles may represent data that has already been analysed by earlier work. However we believe this is unlikely, as 83% of our sample came from articles published during a different time period to the authors contacted by [2], and only 2 articles were included from the conferences that their authors were selected from. Also whilst [2] was based entirely on *grey* literature, ours was based entirely on published works. It is possible that our results may suffer from publication bias - as there may be a reluctance among authors and institutions to publish high failure rates, and the actual pass rate of CS1 may be lower than our study has indicated.

The final threat to validity concerns the assessment criteria of the individual courses that have been included in this study. Studies within the UK generally defined 'pass rate' as consisting of those students who had scored over 40% in the course. However, other studies defined pass rate as consisting of those students who had scored at least a 'C', and others defined pass rate as consisting of those students who had scored anything apart from an 'F'. Other studies did not supply details at all. Therefore this study unavoidably has to assume that a consistent notion of pass rate exists and holds valid across the different teaching contexts.

6. CONCLUSION

There is a tendency among CS1 researchers to generalize high failure rates as a motivation for work. In this paper, we answered the call of [2] for further substantial evidence on the fail rate phenomenon by performing a systematic review of introductory programming research, and a statistical analysis on the data extracted from relevant articles.

An almost identical mean worldwide pass rate of 67.7% was found. Moderator analysis revealed significant, but perhaps not substantial differences in pass rates based upon: grade level, country, and class size. However, pass rates were not found to have significantly differed over time, or based upon the language taught in the course. The question which follows from these findings is that if external aspects of the teaching context do not have a substantial moderating effect on the pass rates of CS1, then which internal characteristics of certain students enables them to acquire programming skills whilst others endlessly struggle?

The limitation of this study is the sample size. Whilst the sample was over double the size of the one used by [2], 161 pass rates is still a relatively low number. But as two independent studies have both found a mean CS1 pass rate of 67%, it is possible this is not too far away from the figure in the population (estimated 65.3% to 70.1%). Whilst we did not find the pass rate of CS1 to be alarmingly low, we do conclude that there remains scope for improvement.

7. REFERENCES

[1] T. Beaubouef and J. Mason. Why the high attrition rate for computer science students: some thoughts and observations. *SIGCSE Bulletin*, 37(2):103–106, 2005.

[2] J. Bennedsen and M. E. Caspersen. Failure rates in introductory programming. *SIGCSE Bulletin*, 39(2):32–36, 2007.

[3] R. Bornat, S. Dehnadi, and . Simon. Mental models, consistency and programming aptitude. In *Proc. Australasian Computing Education*, pages 53–61, 2008.

[4] K. B. Bruce. Controversy on how to teach cs 1: a discussion on the sigcse-members mailing list. *SIGCSE Bulletin*, 37(2):111–117, 2005.

[5] D. Crookes. Educators call for reform in how programming is taught in schools, 2013. Retrieved Nov. 19, 2013 from *http://ind.pn/1evOJgl*.

[6] A. Ehlert and C. Schulte. Comparison of oop first and oop later: first results regarding the role of comfort level. In *Proc. ITiCSE*, pages 108–112. ACM, 2010.

[7] Higher Education Funding Council. Data about demand and supply in higher education subjects, 2013. Retrieved Jan. 5, 2013 from *http://bit.ly/19WRiLi*.

[8] T. Jenkins. On the difficulty of learning to program. In *Proceedings of the 3rd Annual Conference of the LTSN Centre for Information and Computer Sciences*, volume 4, pages 53–58, 2002.

[9] C. McDowell, L. Werner, H. E. Bullock, and J. Fernald. Pair programming improves student retention, confidence, and program quality. *Communications of the ACM*, 49(8):90–95, 2006.

[10] A. J. Mendes, L. Paquete, A. Cardoso, and A. Gomes. Increasing student commitment in introductory programming learning. In *Proc. Frontiers in Education*, pages 1–6. IEEE, 2012.

[11] US Bureau of Labor Statistics. Computer and information technology occupations, 2013. Retrieved Nov. 19, 2013 from *http://1.usa.gov/1a63neI*.

[12] C. Watson, F. W. Li, and J. L. Godwin. Bluefix: using crowd-sourced feedback to support programming students in error diagnosis and repair. In *Proc. ICWL*, pages 228–239. Springer, 2012.

[13] C. Watson, F. W. Li, and J. L. Godwin. Predicting performance in an introductory programming course by logging and analyzing student programming behavior. In *Proc. ICALT*, pages 319–323. IEEE, 2013.

[14] C. Watson, F. W. Li, and J. L. Godwin. No tests required: comparing traditional and dynamic predictors of programming success. In *Proc. SIGCSE*, pages 469–474. ACM, 2014.

[15] C. Watson, F. W. Li, and R. W. Lau. Learning programming languages through corrective feedback and concept visualisation. In *Proc. ICWL*, pages 11–20. Springer, 2011.

[16] S. Zweben. Computing degree and enrollment trends. *Computing Research Association*, 2011.

APPENDIX

Due to space limitation, and to serve as a starting point for future researchers, a list of articles that were used in the analysis of this study have been made available in the following document: http://bit.ly/1iJdBSz

Effect of a 2-week Scratch Intervention in CS1 on Learners with Varying Prior Knowledge

Shitanshu Mishra
IDP in Educational Technology
Indian Institute of Technology Bombay
Mumbai, India
shitanshu@iitb.ac.in

Sudeesh Balan
IDP in Educational Technology
Indian Institute of Technology Bombay
Mumbai, India
sudbalan@gmail.com

Sridhar Iyer
Department of CSE
Indian Institute of Technology Bombay
Mumbai, India
sri@iitb.ac.in

Sahana Murthy
IDP in Educational Technology
Indian Institute of Technology Bombay
Mumbai, India
sahanamurthy@iitb.ac.in

ABSTRACT

A large CS1 class often needs to provide scaffolding for novices while keeping advanced learners engaged. Scratch has been shown to be suitable to address a diverse set of requirements. In this study, we determine whether a 2-week Scratch intervention in a CS1 course is useful from two perspectives: i) as a scaffold for novices to learn basic programming concepts and transition to C++, and ii) as a tool for advanced learners to remain engaged and do challenging work. We conducted a field study of 332 first-year undergraduate engineering students, two-thirds of whom were novices. We analyzed student performance on exams and Scratch projects. We administered a survey to determine student perceptions on the usefulness of Scratch. Some key findings of our study are: (i) Novices were able to catch-up to advanced learners in Scratch questions of the type 'Predict the output' and 'Debug the program', (ii) Projects by advanced learners reached 80% of the complexity of 'most loved projects' on the Scratch website, and (iii) 69% of students perceived Scratch to be useful for learning programming concepts and transitioning to C++.

Categories and Subject Descriptors

K.3.2 Computer Science Education.

Keywords

CS1; scratch intervention; novice learners; advance learners;

1. INTRODUCTION

In typical Indian universities, there is a single programming course for all freshmen engineering students, with the main programming language taught in the course being C++ or Java. Students come with widely varied programming experience, ranging from those with zero prior exposure, to those already competing in programming contests. Thus, novices get daunted because they have to simultaneously learn both new constructs and syntax, while advanced learners tend to get bored when

basic concepts are being taught. Instructors face a dual challenge: (i) quickly equip novices with basic programming concepts and skills so that they can keep up with the main learning outcomes of the course, (ii) keep the advanced learners engaged. Hence we need a solution that addresses both these problems. In this study, we examine the suitability of a 2-week Scratch curriculum as a solution for both novices and advanced learners, in a large CS1 course. Scratch has been found to facilitate the learning of programming and computer science concepts [11]. It has been shown to have: a "low floor" (easy to get started with); "high ceiling" (complex projects can be built); and "wide walls" (can address variety of topics and themes) [13], especially at the middle school level, with some attempts to use it in a CS1 course at the college-level [20]. It has been recommended for novice programmers for its ease of use, as well as for advanced programmers for its facility to build complex projects [9].

Motivated by the potential of Scratch to address such diverse needs, the research goal of this study is to investigate the impact of a short intervention of Scratch in a large, academically diverse, college-level CS1 course on C++ programming. Most Scratch studies (except 2 or 3 such as Malan's [20]) are done in middle school while ours is at the college level. We determine the effectiveness of Scratch from two perspectives: i) as a scaffold for novices to learn basic programming concepts and transition to C++, and ii) as a tool for advanced learners to remain engaged with content. Our research questions (RQ) are:

RQ1: How much have novices learnt, in terms of: (a) basic programming concepts and (b) how much were they able to transition to C++?

RQ2. What are the benefits of Scratch to advanced learners?

RQ3: How useful do students perceive Scratch to their learning of programming concepts and their engagement?

We conducted a field study of implementing Scratch in a large CS1 class to answer the above research questions. Our treatment consisted of two weeks of Scratch instruction that included four lectures, three labs and a project. Our research was conducted in-situ, instead of controlled lab experiments, as we were interested in determining the effects of deploying Scratch as a short-term intervention in a regular university classroom setting, wherein the rest of the course was taught using C++. We used a mixed-methods research design to answer the research questions (RQs). We categorized students as novices or advanced learners based on their responses to a questionnaire on prior programming background, which was administered in the first week of the semester. Students' learning of programming concepts after instruction was assessed via questions on an in-semester quiz and mid-term exam (RQ1). Data from one other source was used to determine the extent of novice students' application of programming concepts and skills (RQ1). This source was a non-traditional assessment tool in which students were asked to generate questions in different CS1 topics. Another data source was Scratch projects done by students. These were analyzed via Scrape tool [6], to determine the complexity of projects created by advanced learners, which we used to infer the engagement of advanced learners (RQ2). Finally, we administered a survey questionnaire to determine students' perceptions of the usefulness of Scratch for their learning and engagement (RQ3).

Our results showed that novices were able to catch-up to advanced learners in Scratch questions of type – 'Predict the output' and 'Debug'. However, we found that novices did not perform comparably on questions where they had to write a program of a numerical nature (such as generating Fibonacci sequence or Pascal's triangle). In case of advanced topics that can be easily taught via Scratch - threads and graphics - both novices and advanced learners showed evidence of learning. Projects by advanced learners reached 83% of the complexity of the "Most-loved projects" on the Scratch website [15] indicating high engagement. Student perceptions from the survey confirmed that Scratch was beneficial in helping them learn basic programming concepts and transitioning to C++, with 69% agreement. The most frequently cited benefit of Scratch was that it helped students overcome the barrier to start programming, which is a key insight regarding the usefulness of Scratch for students' affective component. The survey also showed that Scratch projects helped keep students engaged with the content.

2. THEORY AND RELATED WORK

In this section, we first discuss the theoretical basis for using Scratch (Section 2.1), from the perspective of reducing cognitive load and scaffolding for novices, and balancing skill versus challenge for advanced learners. We then focus on prior work on the use of Scratch in college-level courses (Section 2.2).

2.1 Theoretical basis for using Scratch

Students without any prior exposure to programming need to simultaneously learn the techniques to solve a problem, and the use of a programming language as a tool to solve the problem. These multiple demands on working memory could lead to cognitive overload [19] for a novice programmer. This prevents novice students from learning computer science concepts and has been reported to be a major problem in CS education [5]. One approach to reducing cognitive load has been the use of visual programming environments [1] that allow students to assemble code snippets using a drag-and-drop interface. Scratch is one language having such an environment.

A Scratch intervention can thus be considered as a scaffold for novice students. Scaffolding is a temporary support provided by an instructor to assist learners for dual purposes [12]: i) in completing a task that they otherwise would not be able to accomplish, and, ii) in enabling students to learn from that experience so that they are prepared to perform similar tasks in the future. Our Scratch intervention makes use of both functions of scaffolding by helping novice programmers to conceptually solve a problem without having to focus on the details of syntax,

and to apply these programming concepts when they later transition to writing programs in C++.

Advanced learners, on the other hand, need a sufficiently challenging set of learning materials so that they remain engaged with the content. From the perspective of Flow Theory [4], students become and remain engaged in learning when there is equilibrium between the challenge level of the activity and the learner's personal skill. A high-school study has reported students to have experienced higher engagement when the perceived level of challenge and their skills were high and in balance with each other [17]. We exploit the 'high ceiling' feature of Scratch [13] to provide advanced learners with activities commensurate with their skill level.

2.2 Scratch in CS0/CS1

Scratch is a visual programming environment that provides various 'blocks' of programming constructs, such as statements, conditions, loops, operators, variables, and so on. These can be dragged and dropped onto a 'stage' area in 'stacks' that can be then executed. A detailed account of the features and capabilities of Scratch can be found in [8] and [13].

Scratch was designed to promote 'technological fluency' [13] among young learners. It enables users to create media rich 'projects' (Scratch programs) such as animation, music videos and games. In terms of programming, Scratch has been shown to be useful to learn concepts such as loops and conditionals [8].

Though majority of Scratch users are at the middle and high-school levels, Scratch has been used in a few formal courses at the college level [20]. In [9], Scratch was used in a CS1 course for a short period (1-2 weeks) before transitioning to more advanced programming constructs in Java. Students were first introduced to basic programming constructs using Scratch. They created Scratch projects with multiple stacks as part of the assignments. The study reported overall positive findings of student perceptions. In a different implementation for at-risk students [14], Scratch was deployed in a semester-long CS0 course to improve the retention and performance of students. Survey and performance data indicated that the CS0-Scratch course was effective in preparing students for the next level CS1 course. Our study includes both learning data and perception data.

We found that there are several other programming tools and techniques to help novices learn programming [16]. Some are visual programming environments, such as Alice [3] and JPie [18]. Others allow students to visualize the control flow of a program [7] and create mental models [10]. However, some researchers have commented that these tools either have a high learning curve for first-time programmers, or are restrictive as compared to Scratch [9]. Hence we did not explore the use of these tools for our intervention.

3. COURSE IMPLEMENTATION

The setting for our study was a large enrollment CS1 class of 450 first year undergraduate students, across various engineering disciplines, excluding CS majors; the student characteristics are described in Section 4.1. The goal of the CS1 course was to teach programming concepts and C++ skills. The course was conducted over 14 weeks in Spring 2013, using lectures and labs. Our Scratch intervention was limited to the first two weeks of lecture and three weeks of lab. The details are as follows:

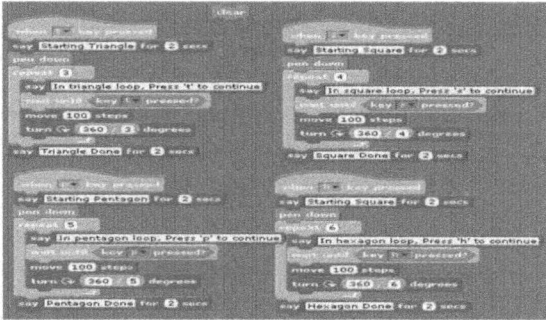

Figure 1: Example program -'predict the output' activity

- *Lecture*: The blocks on motion, control, sensing, operators, and variables, were discussed in detail, with lesser emphasis on the blocks on looks, sounds and pen. Additional attention was given to the advanced constructs such as lists (arrays) and event handling (broadcast-receive). The lectures had an active learning structure. For example, the program shown in Figure 1 was used in the second week. Students were required to make predictions to answer questions like "What will happen if keys *s* and *t* are pressed simultaneously?"

- *Lab*: The lab activities depended on the lecture contents of the previous week. The students worked in pairs. The first lab got students familiar with the Scratch environment, by getting them to run and modify a given program. The second lab required them to play a game of space-invaders, already implemented in Scratch, do a code walk-through, and then modify the code for altering a given behavior of the game. The third lab had students use the single step mode to observe threads interleaving, debug programs, and also work on their projects as described below. Activities from the fourth lab onwards were using C++.

- *Project*: In parallel with labs two to four, the student pairs also worked on building a game for their Scratch project, which they demonstrated to the TA at the start of lab five. A description of the projects is given in Section 4.2.2 and their analysis is presented in Section 5.2.

- *Question Generation*: In lab five, each student pair was asked to generate two questions that other students could practice on. A description of this activity is in Section 4.2.3 and the corresponding analysis is presented in Section 5.1.

- *Assessment*: One quiz (1-hour written exam) and one midterm had Scratch questions, to test students' conceptual understanding along traditional lines. Midterm had C++ questions also, which were used to address RQ1b.

This intervention meets our requirements as: 1) Scaffolding for novices was achieved by the gradual ramp-up of the concepts in the two weeks of lecture, followed by applying the concepts in the labs. 2) Engagement for advanced learners was achieved by having the project start in the second week, and giving students the freedom to decide the nature and complexity of their project. The only incentive for performance was that the top few projects were to be showcased as the 'Hall of Fame'.

4. STUDY METHODOLOGY

We used a mixed methods design and triangulated our data with multiple types of measurements for each research question. We describe the data collection instruments and the analyses in Section 4.2. Now, we first describe our sample and how we categorized students into 'novices' and 'advanced learners'.

4.1 Sample

There were 450 students registered for the class (395 male, 55 female). All were first year students majoring in different branches of engineering. Students who were admitted to our institute were among the highest ranked in an extremely competitive exam testing analytical skills in mathematics, physics and chemistry (they were all among the top 1000 out of 500000 students). Hence all students in the study can be considered as equivalent in all respects, except prior exposure to programming.

To determine prior programming background, we conducted a survey in the first week of the semester. Students had to respond to a series of questions on their familiarity with computers and programming experience. Those who had opted for programming electives in Grades 10 or 12, or had done programming outside of school, were classified as 'advanced learners'. Others were classified as 'novices.' 332 students completed the above survey, hence only those students were considered in the sample. We found 217 students were novices, and 115 were advanced learners. 10 advanced learners had participated in programming contests.

4.2 Data collection tools and analysis

4.2.1. Quiz and mid-term exam question scores

Scores from the quiz (4th week) and the mid-term (6th week) were used to determine students' acquisition of basic programming concepts (RQ1). The quiz contained four questions, all of which were based on Scratch, while the mid-term exam contained three questions, of which one was based on Scratch and the others on C++. There was a mix of conceptual and programming question types, including: 'predict the output', 'debug the program', as well as 'write a program'. These were typical CS1 questions. For example, a program for BubbleSort with erroneous array initialization and loop conditions was given and students were required to debug the program. In another question, they were required to write a program to output the Fibonacci series. We did not analyze scores from tests after the mid-term exam since the topics in the latter half of the semester were not related to the Scratch intervention.

Analysis

We analyzed novice learners' performance on the above questions and examined the scores in each category of questions. We have also used scores of advanced learners as a benchmark to estimate the absolute learning gain for Novices (RQ1).

4.2.2 Scratch projects

At the end of the second week, students were asked to work on a Scratch project in teams of two. They were expected to exercise their creativity and also demonstrate their learning, by writing games using multiple scripts and blocks. Students worked on their projects for a period of two weeks during their labs but were free to work outside of lab hours also. Projects were graded by lab TAs and exceptionally good projects (with large number of sprites, having complex interactions and emulating real-world functionality) were hosted on the course website as 'Hall of Fame' entries.

Analysis

We analyzed the Scratch projects using the Scrape visualization tool [6]. The Scrape tool provides a record of the programming constructs used in each project, such as, variables, sprites, stacks and blocks. We analyzed the frequency of use of different constructs by advanced learners and students whose projects were showcased in the Hall of Fame. We used the reference of

Table 1: Scores on exam questions of different types in Scratch and C++ (Maximum Marks for each question: 10)

	Novice Average (SD)			Advanced Average (SD)		
	Predict output	**Debug a program**	**Write a program**	**Predict output**	**Debug a program**	**Write a program**
Scratch	Ques.1 - 7.5 (3.4) Ques.2 - 7.2 (2.2)	Ques.3 - 6.9 (3.5) Ques.4 - 4.6 (4.5)	Ques.5- 3.4 (3.3) Ques.6 - 2.8 (3.5)	Ques.1 - 8.2 (3.0) Ques.2 - 7.6 (1.9)	Ques.3 - 8.1 (3.0) Ques.4 - 5.4 (4.2)	Ques.5 - 6.8 (3.2) Ques.6 - 5.8 (3.9)
C++	NA	Ques.7 - 7.1 (4.3) Ques.8 - 5.4 (3.7)	Ques.9 - 6.4 (2.9)	NA	Ques.7 - 9.2 (2.3) Ques.8 - 7.8 (2.8)	Ques.9 - 9.1 (1.9)

average frequency distribution of constructs used in the 'Most-loved' projects [15], as an estimate of 'high ceiling' [13], while examining the performance of our advanced learners (RQ2).

4.2.3. Question-generation by students
In the 5th lab, students did a question-generation exercise. Each pair of students was asked to generate two questions, pertaining to the topics covered so far, which could be given as practice questions for the next lab-batch. They were free to set either a programming problem or a conceptual question, and had to submit detailed answers to their generated questions. They were given only one open-ended guideline "The questions should be challenging but should not be too difficult for the students in the next batch to complete in the lab". We used the question-generation exercise as an independent measure to examine the extent of application of programming concepts, and hence of students' learning of the concepts (RQ1).

Analysis
We analyzed each question generated on the basis of the programming concepts targeted by it. These concepts were chosen from computational thinking concepts described in [2], and include: Sequence, Loops, Threads, Events, Conditionals, Operators, Variables, and Arrays.

4.2.4. Survey questionnaire
We created a survey to address RQ3: How useful do students perceive Scratch to their learning of programming concepts and their engagement? The survey had five questions, the first three of which were on a Strongly Agree to Strongly Disagree Likert scale. **Q1** was on whether students perceive Scratch useful for learning programming concepts; **Q2** was to determine students' perception of the usefulness of Scratch to transition to C++; **Q3** asked students if they enjoyed programming with Scratch; the last two questions were open-ended. In **Q4**, students were asked to write the main benefit they found in using Scratch, and in **Q5** they were asked for the most frustrating aspect in using Scratch.

Analysis
Quantitative analysis of first three questions gives the measure of students' engagement and their perception about usefulness of Scratch for their learning. Open ended - Questions 4 and 5 were analysed using content analysis technique to examine the advantages-disadvantages of Scratch as perceived by students.

5. RESULTS
Recall that our goals were to explore use of Scratch as : i) a scaffold for novices to learn basic programming concepts and transition to C++, and ii) a tool for advanced learners to remain engaged and do challenging work. Section 5.1 gives the results corresponding to goal 1 which relates to RQ1 and RQ3. Section 5.2 gives the results corresponding to goal 2 which corresponds to RQ2 and RQ3.

5.1 Learning of Programming concepts by Novices
5.1.1 Acquisition of programming concepts and transitioning to C++: Exam scores
Table 1 shows exam scores of novices and advanced students in different types of questions in Scratch and C++. An independent sample t-test shows that novices were able to catch-up to advanced learners in Scratch questions of type – 'Predict the output' and 'Debug'. Novices were not able to catch-up in C++ 'Debug' questions, perhaps because they did not get adequate time to get familiar with the syntax; the test was conducted within 3 weeks after the transition. Novices were not able to catch-up in any 'Write a program' question, which is somewhat to be expected (RQ1).

The correlation analysis between midterm scores in the Scratch with midterm scores in C++ indicated a moderate positive linear relationship. In addition to this, 65% of the students who did well (score higher than 1 SD above mean) in Scratch in the midterm exam, also did well in the C++.

5.1.2 Application of Programming Concepts: Question-Generation
Table 2 shows the number of student-pairs who generated questions involving various programming concepts. We labeled a pair as 'advanced' if at least one of them was an advanced learner as per 'prior programming background' survey. The presence of a concept in a question generated by students indicates that they have learnt and applied that concept.

Table 2: Concepts addressed in Question-generation activity

Concepts	Questions generated by novices (% questions in which this concept is addressed) total no. of questions =84 *Note: % questions generated by **advanced** learners are given in ( )*
Sequence	92 (90)
Loops	65 (83)
Threads	10 (5)
Events	11 (5)
Conditionals	61 (66)
Operators	94 (83)
Data	95 (93)
Arrays	10 (24)

We note that for concepts of sequence, data and conditionals, the percentage of questions generated by novices was comparable to that of advanced learners. Moreover, since all students submitted solutions to their generated questions, it shows that students are not only addressing different programming concepts but are also comfortable in solving questions requiring these concepts.

5.1.3 Student Perception of Learning

We show a summary of responses to the first two Likert-scale items (Questions 1, 2) on the student perception survey. To simplify the presentation, we have combined responses in the Strongly Agree and Agree categories as Positive, and the Strongly Disagree and Disagree as Negative. The neutral responses to the Likert items were left as is. These are shown in Table 3 (Total number of responses=337).

Table 3: Summary of survey responses – Learning

Item	Positive (%)	Neutral (%)	Negative (%)
Scratch is useful for learning programming concepts.	70	18	12
It is useful for beginners to learn Scratch before moving on to C++.	69	15	16

The results show that a majority of students perceived Scratch to be useful for learning basic concepts as well as for transitioning to C++ (RQ2).

5.2 Engagement of Advanced Learners

5.2.1 Application of Programming Concepts: Scratch Projects

We were able to obtain 93 projects for analysis. In 35 out of 93, one or both members of the team had not taken the 'prior programming background' survey conducted in the first week (See section 4.1). Hence we could not classify these projects as belonging to novice or advanced learners. Of the remaining 58 projects, any team that had both novices was classified as a 'novice' project, while any team with at least one advanced learner was classified as an 'advanced' project. This resulted in 18 'novice' projects and 40 advanced projects. 13 out of the 40 advanced projects qualified as Hall-of-fame entries, so for analysis we split the advanced category into 27 'advanced' and 13 'Hall-of-fame'.

There was a variety of games in the projects. Some of the most frequent types of games were "shooting games", "maze based games", "batting games", and "car racing games". Six games were multi-player and thirty nine were single player games; forty were found to be single-level games while five had multiple level options. Each game was tested and found to be acceptable in terms of usability. First, we counted the number programming constructs used in novice, advanced and Hall-of-fame. These are shown in Table 4, along with corresponding numbers for 'Most-loved' projects from Scratch website [15], for reference. From Table 4, we note that advanced projects use on an average 67% constructs as the most-loved projects, while Hall-of-fame projects use 105% of constructs compared to Most-loved projects. If we combine the results of all advanced learners in our course, i.e., advanced and Hall-of-fame, we find that their constructs usage is 80% that of Most-loved projects.

Thus, our advanced learners are able to achieve results comparable to the Most-loved projects, even in a period of only three weeks. It should be noted that the reward for the Scratch project was just 5 marks, and even with this meagre reward students generated complex projects. This shows that they were indeed engaged.

Table 4: Average number of occurrences of programming constructs used in Scratch projects

Programming Constructs	'Novice' projects (N=18)	'Advanced' projects (N=27)	Hall-of-fame projects (N=13)	'Most loved games' (N=10)
Variables	5	9	12	9
Sprites	14	30	35	35
Stacks	38	77	131	101
Control	111	230	417	454
Motion	51	83	147	129
Operator	38	92	147	197
Sensing	32	63	117	75
Other blocks	38	117	177	403
Total	**327**	**701**	**1183**	**1403**

5.2.2 Student Perception of Engagement

The summary of responses corresponding to the Question 3 of the student perception survey questionnaire is shown in Table 5. (Total number of responses=337).

Table 5: Summary of survey responses - Engagement

Item	Positive (%)	Neutral (%)	Negative (%)
Enjoyed programming with Scratch.	65	15	20

As evident from Table 5, a majority of students perceived the experience of Scratch programming to be positive. This shows that Scratch has positively affected students' engagement.

6. DISCUSSION

We first examined if the Scratch intervention was effective in novices' acquisition of basic programming concepts and in their transition to C++ (RQ1). From the analysis of scores on exam questions, we find evidence of learning basic programming concepts. However, the performance of novice students was comparable to that of advanced learners only on Scratch questions of types: Predict output of a program, and debug a program. In typical questions of write a program, novices lag behind advanced learners. This is to be expected as only six weeks had elapsed in the course. The gap persists in scores on C++ questions. So from the perspective of achievement on traditional exams, we conclude that our Scratch intervention was only a qualified success.

When we analyze students' learning (RQ1) in terms of how well they apply programming concepts in the question-generation activity, we find that novices have a high 'catch-up' with advanced learners. In this non-traditional assessments, we see that i) novices indeed show strong evidence of application of programming concepts and ii) the performance of novices is often comparable to that of advanced students.

Student perception data from the survey strongly support that Scratch was useful for the learning of basic concepts of novices and that it helped them transition to C++ (RQ3).

The effectiveness of Scratch for advanced learners (RQ2) is clearly seen from the performance of advanced learners on Scratch projects, and is corroborated by survey data. The Scratch project creation activity pushed advanced students towards a high boundary in terms of the extent of their application of programming concepts. We see this as evidence of students' engagement with the content and conclude that Scratch was an appropriate choice to address this instructional goal.

Open-ended responses in the survey data (Q4) support this point: students have said that "[I am] thrilled to be able to code complex games" and "[coding] games helped increase my interest, […], there was lot of room for experimentation." Responses to the first open-ended question in the survey data identified some major benefits. In addition to the cognitive aspect of the benefit of Scratch to learn programming concepts and skills, nearly a third of the responses addressed the affective benefit of using Scratch to begin programming. Several students commented that Scratch "helped improve confidence" and "removed fear of programming." Majority also commented that Scratch "helped in understanding C++", indicating its usefulness in transitioning to C++. Other benefits were the ease of programming threads and graphics, syntax-free visual environment and the fun element in using Scratch. On the contrary, responses to the second open ended question (Q5) brought out some disadvantages of using Scratch such as cumbersome features of the IDE and the limitation of the language capability of Scratch.

As mentioned in Section 1, our findings are subject to validity threats due to the field-study setting in which they were conducted. The biggest threat is the lack of control while interpreting exam scores. Since we could not compare the performance of our students with a group that did not get the Scratch intervention, it is possible that the learning we observe through exam performance could have been due to reasons other than the 2-week Scratch intervention. To offset this issue we used a combination of different data collection sources and different analysis approaches – qualitative and quantitative. We triangulated our findings from exam scores with several other sources. The variety of assessment instruments we used gave us different views into our research questions, and we were able to infer learning and engagement from several perspectives.

7. CONCLUSION

We conclude that an intervention of two weeks of Scratch lectures, along with three labs and a project is useful for learning basic programming concepts at CS1 level, addressing diversity by scaffolding for novices, engagement for advanced learners. However, this specific intervention of Scratch has limited usefulness in helping novices to catch up with advanced learners in typical programming exam questions.

Even though the original motivation for our study was to address the needs of the diverse academic population in an Indian university, our results are useful for: a) CS0/CS1 instructors looking for a solution to help students with no programming background from getting daunted by syntax and concepts, and, b) for engaging college students with prior programming exposure with building complex programs and exercising creative expression in programming.

8. REFERENCES

[1] Blackwell, A.F. 1996. Metacognitive Theories of Visual Programming: What do we think we are doing?. *Visual Languages, 1996. Proceedings*. IEEE Symposium on, Cambridge, Pages 240-246.

[2] Brennan, K., Resnick, M. 2012. New frameworks for studying and assessing the development of computational thinking. *In Proceedings of the 2012 annual meeting of the American Educational Research Association* (Vancouver, Canada).

[3] Carnegie Mellon University. Alicev2.0. www.alice.org.

[4] Csikszentmihalyi, M. 1997. Finding flow: The psychology of engagement with everyday life. Basic Books.

[5] Gray, S., Clair, S. C., James, R., Mead, J. Graduated exposure to programming concepts using fading worked examples. 2007. *ICER '07 Proceedings of the third international workshop on Computing education research.* Georgia, ACM, Pages 99-110.

[6] Home of Scrape. River Sound Media. happyanalyzing.com

[7] Jeliot3.Program Visualization tool. cs.joensuu.fi/jeliot/

[8] Lifelong Kindergarten, MIT Media Lab. Scratchweblogs. http://media.mit.edu/llk/scratch/.

[9] Malan, D. J., & Leitner, H. H. 2007. Scratch for budding computer scientists. ACM SIGCSE Bulletin, 39(1), 223-227.

[10] Margulieux, L. E., Guzdial, M., Catrambone, R. 2012. Subgoal-labeled instructional material improves performance and transfer in learning to develop mobile applications. In *Proceedings of the ninth annual international conference on International computing education research* (pp. 71-78). ACM.

[11] Meerbaum-Salant, O., Armoni, M., and Ben-Ari, M. M. 2010. Learning computer science concepts with scratch. In *Proceedings of the Sixth international workshop on Computing education research* (pp. 69-76). ACM.

[12] Reiser, Brian J. 2004. Scaffolding complex learning: The mechanisms of structuring and problematizing student work. *Journal of the Learning Sciences*: 13(3), 273-304.

[13] Resnick, M., Maloney, J., Monroy-Hernández, A., Rusk, N., Eastmond, E., Brennan, K., and Kafai, Y. 2009. Scratch: programming for all. Communications of the ACM, 52(11), 60-67.

[14] Rizvi, M., Humphries, T., Major, D., Jones, M., and Lauzun, H. 2011. A CS0 course using scratch. Journal of Computing Sciences in Colleges, 26(3), 19-27.

[15] Scratch projects: scratch.mit.edu/tagged/toploved/game

[16] Sheard, J., Simon, S., Hamilton, M., Lonnberg, J. Analysis of Research into the Teaching and Learning of Programming. 2009. *ICER '09 Proceedings of the fifth international workshop on Computing education research workshop.* (California). ACM, Pages 93-104.

[17] Shernoff, D. J., Csikszentmihalyi, M., Shneider, B., and Shernoff, E. S. 2003. Student engagement in high school classrooms from the perspective of flow theory. School Psychology Quarterly, 18(2), 158-176.

[18] The JPie project. www.jpie.cse.wustl.edu/

[19] Van Merrienboer, J. J., & Sweller, J. 2005. Cognitive load theory and complex learning: Recent developments and future directions. Educational psychology review, 17(2), 147-177.

[20] Wolz, U., Leitner, H. H., Malan, D. J., and Maloney, J. 2009. Starting with Scratch in CS1. Proceedings - 40th *ACM technical symposium on CS education*, Tennessee, ACM, pp 2-3.

Think-Pair-Share in a Large CS1 Class: Does Learning Really Happen?

Aditi Kothiyal
Inter-Disciplinary Program in
Educational Technology
IIT Bombay, India
aditi.kothiyal@iitb.ac.in

Sahana Murthy
Inter-Disciplinary Program in
Educational Technology
IIT Bombay, India
sahanamurthy@iitb.ac.in

Sridhar Iyer
Department of Computer Science
and Engineering
IIT Bombay, India
sri@iitb.ac.in

ABSTRACT

Think-pair-share (TPS) is a classroom active learning strategy in which students work on activities, first individually, then in pairs and finally as the whole class. TPS allows students to express their reasoning, reflect on their understanding and obtain prompt feedback on their learning. While TPS is recommended to foster classroom engagement and learning, there is a lack of research based evidence in computer science education on the benefits of TPS for learning. In this study, we investigate the learning effectiveness of TPS in a CS1 course. We performed a quasi-experimental study and found that students who learned via TPS performed significantly better on a post-test than students who learned the same concept via lecture. We also conducted a survey and focus group interviews to understand student perceptions of learning with TPS. The majority of students agreed that TPS activities helped improve their conceptual understanding. From an instructor's point of view, TPS was useful to address the challenges of a large class, such as students tuning out or getting distracted and was easy to implement even in a large class.

Categories and Subject Descriptors

K.3.2 [Computers and Education]

Keywords

CS1, large class, active learning, think-pair-share, experimental study, effectiveness, learning.

1. INTRODUCTION

CS1 is an introductory programming course at many universities. Typical goals of a CS1 course are conceptual understanding of programming constructs, code tracing to predict the output, debugging and modifying code, and finally writing the program itself [7]. At our institute, CS1 is mandatory for freshman engineering students of all disciplines. It is a large class (450 students) with diversity in terms of student prior exposure to programming and motivation. Hence an instructor faces the challenge of ensuring that students across these variations are engaged and learning effectively.

Active learning techniques are known to enhance student engagement and improve student learning [13]. The choice of the active learning technique to be used for a class or a topic depends

ITICSE '14, June 21–25, 2014, Uppsala, Sweden.
Copyright 2014 ACM 978-1-4503-2833-3/14/06 $15.00.
http://dx.doi.org/10.1145/2591708.2591739 .

upon the corresponding instructional goals. For CS1 we need an active learning technique that is easily implementable in a large classroom setting and can be used for the goals stated above. Think-Pair-Share (TPS) [9], [10] is one such active learning technique. TPS is a structured co-operative strategy implemented in three phases as follows: 1) Think: The instructor poses a question and students think and write their answer to it, 2) Pair: Students work in pairs on an extension of the task posed in the Think phase and 3) Share: Students share their solutions and engage in a class-wide discussion, moderated by the instructor.

TPS has several known benefits of small group cooperative learning, such as engaging students with the content, the instructor and each other [1] [3], development of higher order thinking skills [4], and opportunity for formative assessment [2]. Despite the benefits of TPS, it has not been researched and evaluated in computer science education (CSE) for evidence of student learning. In a related paper [5], we provided evidence that TPS results in high student engagement in a large CS1 class. In this paper, we present a two group experiment showing that TPS results in effective learning. In addition we also offer guidelines on how to design TPS activities that not only meet the CS1 instructional goals but also are easy to implement in a large class.

Our broad research goal was to study the effects of TPS activities on the conceptual understanding and application of CS1 concepts in a large enrolment class. Our specific research questions (RQs) were:

1) Do TPS activities lead to increased conceptual understanding and application of CS1 concepts?
2) What are the students' perceptions of learning with TPS?
3) What are the instructor's perceptions of teaching with TPS?

We performed a control group experiment to answer RQ1, surveyed students and conducted focus group interviews to answer RQ2 and used instructor class logs to answer RQ3. We found that students in the experimental group who learned a concept via TPS performed significantly better on the post-test than students in the control group who learned the same concept via an interactive lecture. Further, in the perception survey, a majority of the students agreed that they would not have learned as much from the lectures had there been no TPS activities, and that the tasks in each of the phases helped conceptual understanding. Instructor perception confirmed that many benefits of TPS activities, such as getting students to engage deeply with the content, continue to hold even in a large CS1 classroom setting.

2. BACKGROUND AND RELATED WORK

Active learning comprises research-based instructional strategies in which students engage with the content in a deeper way than just listening to lecture or copying notes. They express their thinking and reasoning by writing, speaking, drawing diagrams, and problem-solving [1][13]. Characteristics of active learning methods are that students often work in small groups, are engaged in tasks emphasizing qualitative reasoning and conceptual thinking, and receive rapid feedback [13].

Active learning methods researched in CSE include pair programming (PP) [12], [14] peer instruction [15], [16], just-in-time teaching [11], process oriented guided inquiry learning [6] and inverted classroom [8]. PP [12], [14] is a collaborative technique in which two students work together in the lab to solve open programming problems like design, development and testing [18]. It has been shown that PP improves student retention and confidence [12] and quality of programs produced [18]. A method for large classes that been extensively researched in CSE is Peer Instruction (PI) [15]. In PI, students work on multiple choice questions aimed at improving conceptual understanding and qualitative reasoning [15]. It has been shown that students learning via PI have higher grades in the CS0 course than equivalent students learning via a traditional lecture [16].

An active learning strategy that has not received significant attention in the CSER community is Think-Pair-Share (TPS). TPS and PI have some common features. In both methods students initially think about the problem posed by the instructor individually and commit to an answer, the difference being that students record a written answer in TPS and vote on their choice in PI. Students then discuss in pairs or groups. In TPS, this discussion can involve a checking of each others' answers, as well as working together to solve the next part of the problem; while in PI, the discussion is mostly focused on the students' votes. The final Share phase in TPS can be compared to the Whole-class discussion recommended in PI [19]. In this phase, TPS involves discussion of multiple solutions and their pros and cons, while PI focuses on students' reasoning for various answers. Both methods can be used to address the goals of conceptual understanding. In addition, TPS allows the posing of open-ended problems such as writing programs, which is not possible with PI.

TPS is based upon several key ideas that have been shown to be effective for learning, including active learning [13] and cooperative learning [4]. TPS has been shown to be a good classroom formative assessment technique [2][17]. Since grouping is done informally, the constraint on movement and requirement of teaching assistants, typical of large classes, is overcome. While there have been some studies to establish the effectiveness of TPS for learning in domains like psychology [2][17], there are fewer studies evaluating the effectiveness of TPS in the learning of computer science and other STEM disciplines. As we showed in a related paper, >80% of students were engaged and on-task in each phase of the TPS [5].

3. COURSE DESIGN
3.1 Course Goals and Challenges
The specific instructional goals of our CS1 class were to teach our freshman engineering class programming concepts and skills, i.e., conceptual understanding of programming constructs, analysis of a program to predict the output and debug/modify code, developing programming logic to solve a specific problem, writing pseudo code and finally writing the program itself.

All classes were taught by the same instructor. Challenges that the instructor had to deal with included: large number of students

(450); large diversity in prior exposure, ranging from students who had never used a computer to those who were fluent in C++ programming; and stadium style seating with fixed chairs and tables, leading to constraint on student movement and grouping for collaborative learning. The challenge was to keep students engaged with the content, the instructor, and with each other, despite these constraints.

3.2 General Course Implementation Details
The CS1 course was conducted over 14 weeks in Spring 2013. The topics covered were control structures such as conditionals, iteration, functions and recursion, data structures such as arrays, matrices, strings and queues, object-oriented structures such as classes and the concept of inheritance. In the first two weeks of the course, Scratch was used to introduce basic programming constructs; the rest of the course was taught via C++.

Students were from varied engineering disciplines but not CS majors. They were divided into two sections for lectures. Each section had two 90-minute interactive lectures per week, in which instructor lecturing was interspersed liberally with instructor and student questions, open discussions, student activities and program demos. The course did not have recitations and problem solving activities were included into the lecture itself. The course also consisted of a 2-hour lab per week, which consisted of programming exercises designed to give students practice in the application of the skills and concepts learned in the lectures.

3.3 Instructional Method: Think-Pair-Share
Problems addressing goals of tracing, modifying and writing code can have multiple valid solutions. As instructors, we want students to not only be able to devise a solution to the problem, but also analyze the pros and cons of various solutions. Hence we need a format of active learning that: (i) gets students vested in the problem by getting them to first devise their own idea of the solution, (ii) prevents students from feeling daunted with the task by allowing them to work with each other, and (iii) affords discussion of pros and cons of multiple solutions. The three phases in TPS offer a natural fit to meet these requirements. Most lectures had two TPS activities on average.

Think phase. The instructor presented the task, and students worked individually on the task for about two minutes and wrote their answers in their notebooks. For example, the instructor presented the following question (Also see Table 1).
"Predict the output of the following program:
```
int main() {
    int A[4], *p;
    for (int i = 0; i < 4; i++) A[i] = i;
    p = &A[0];
    cout << *p << " " << *(p +=2) << *(p+1) + *(p-1) <<
endl; }"
```
Pair phase. The instructor gave a task related to or extended from the Think phase question. In the above example the task was, "Check your neighbor's solution and determine if it is the same as yours. If not, discuss and come up with a solution that you both agree on." The students worked with their neighbors to complete the task in three to five minutes. The instructor walked along the aisles, encouraging discussion and answering queries.

Share phase. The instructor led a class-wide discussion related to the tasks in the Think and Pair phases. In the above example, the instructor elicited a few responses, and then executed the program to show the output. He then asked students to propose modifications in the code that could result in the other responses that came up. Students followed the discussion to verify their solution and discuss 'what-if' scenarios. This phase was open-ended, lasting from three to ten minutes depending on the depth of the discussion. At an appropriate point, the instructor transitioned from this phase into the next topic.

During the first TPS activity of the semester, the instructor described the structure of the activity to the students and what was expected of them. Thereafter, we found that the problem statement was sufficient to cue the students to the task. For the first few activities, the instructor explicitly encouraged the students to write their responses during the Think phase. In subsequent activities the students did not need any prompts for any of the phases.

3.4 Creation of TPS activities

Once it was decided to use TPS in the course, the instructor piloted a few TPS activities in the class and observed students' behavior along with an external observer. Their observations led to the following design principles for TPS activities which were employed throughout the rest of the semester:

1. Each phase of think-pair-share should be meaningful in solving the problem. That is, the problem must contain parts that require individual thinking and writing, the Pair phase deliverable should require two students to work together, and the Share phase activity should merit a class-wide discussion.
2. The Think and Pair phases should have precise deliverables to ensure that the ensuing Share phase discussion is focused towards the answer for the original problem.
3. The phases should be logically connected. Students should use the output of one phase in next phase.
4. Sufficient time should be planned for each phase. Too little time can cause frustration among students and too much time can lead to boredom.

TPS can be used for a variety of learning outcomes. Depending on how the phases of the activity are designed, TPS can be used to improve students' ability to analyze a given program, write programs for the given tasks or acquire conceptual knowledge of programming constructs. A summary of the structure of the TPS activities for various learning outcomes is shown in Table 1.

Table 1: Examples TPS activities

Instructional goals	Think Pair Share	Example as shown in the slide to students
Conceptual understanding	*Think* Students write down the answer to the given question *Pair* Students (i) Identify parts of the answer that they have missed out. (ii) Discuss their answers; do pros-cons analysis if there are multiple solutions. *Share* Instructor discusses (i) What are all the essential parts in the answer? (ii) Pros-cons of various solutions given by students	"Consider an unsorted array of N elements. Think: Write the pseudo code for sorting the array Pair: Discuss your answer with your neighbor, do pros and cons analysis of your algorithms Share: Follow instructor led discussion of your solutions and others." *This led to a discussion of various sorting algorithms.

Code tracing: Predict the output; Debug/modify the given code	*Think* Students determine and write down the answer.
	Pair Students (i) check each others' solution (ii) discuss changes in code needed to get others' solutions
	Share Instructor (i) executes the program and shows the output (ii) discusses a few modifications based on student answers.
		"Predict the output of the following program:
		  int a = 1, b = 2, c = 3;
		  int* p, int* q;
		  p = &a; q = &b;
		  c = *p; p = q;
		  *p = 13;
		  cout << a << b << c << endl;
		  cout << *p << *q << endl;"
		Think: Draw the memory arrangement and predict output.
		Pair: Check your neighbor's solution. If you don't agree, discuss and come up with a solution that you both agree upon.
		Share: See demo of above code and modified versions."
		*The example for the outcome "Debug/modify" is similar

Develop programming logic for a problem: Write program.	*Think* Students write down the pseudo-code. *Pair* Students (i) identify missing pieces in each others' solutions (ii) write the program. *Share* Instructor (i) shows one possible solution. (ii) Discusses a few representative student solutions.	"Recall your program to reverse a 4 digit number. Extend your solution to arbitrary integers. Think: Write the pseudo-code individually. Pair: Write the C++ code with a partner. Share: Compare your solution with demo10-reverseNum-mod1.cpp"
Design a solution: Write pseudo-code	*Think* Students write down the different parts (structures and functions) of the solution *Pair* Students discuss the pseudo-code for other structures and functions that are required *Share* Instructor discusses a few representative solutions.	"Design a taxi scheduling service for an airport as follows: (i) When a driver arrives, his ID is entered in an array (ii) When a customer arrives the earliest waiting driver is assigned Think: What structures and variables are required? Pair: Discuss the pseudo-code for the functions that are required. Share: Follow instructor led discussion of your solutions and others."

4. RESEARCH METHODOLOGY

4.1 Learning outcome measurement

To answer RQ1, "Do TPS activities lead to increased conceptual understanding and application of CS1 concepts?" we conducted a two group pre-post quasi-experimental study to determine the effectiveness of TPS activities over interactive lecture.

Sample. One of the two sections was randomly assigned as the experimental group (263 students), which received a TPS treatment, and the other as control group (184 students), which received a regular interactive lecture. The equivalence of both the groups was established on the basis of a pre-test which had 5 questions testing students' understanding of prerequisite concepts. The results of a Mann-Whitney U test between the pre-test scores of the experimental group ($M_{expt}=16.3$, $SD=5.6$), and the control group ($M_{control}=16.7$, $SD=6.7$) showed no significant difference (Mann Whitney U = 20440, $p=0.574$).

Procedure. The concept chosen for the experiment was the interleaving of multiple threads in the CPU. This concept is new to both novices and advanced learners, so their prior knowledge does not play a role. The instructor chose to use Scratch to explain threads because it is a visual programming environment in which multi-threading is very easy to implement. In both the groups the instructor first explained the concept of multiple threads and thread synchronization via an interactive lecture. Next the instructor presented a problem on interleaving of threads.

"Consider three threads as shown below.

Thread A	Thread B	Thread C
When Run flag clicked, Say "Thread A start"; Repeat 2 times • Move 10 steps; Say "Thread A done"	When Run flag clicked Say "Thread B start"; Turn 90 degrees; Broadcast "event"; Say "Thread B done";	When I receive "event", Glide to (0,0).

Assume that: (i) 'When' and 'Say' statements result in 2 assembly instructions, (ii) Loop initialization, increment and condition check, each results in 1 assembly instruction, and (iii) all other statements result in 3 assembly instructions. Also assume that: (a) all assembly instructions are atomic and take the same amount of time, (b) CPU time-slice is sufficient for 3 assembly instructions. What are the possible interleaved execution sequences?"

In the control group, the instructor explained the solution as a worked example while students followed along and asked questions. In the experimental group, the problem was presented as the following TPS activity:

"Think: Write one possible interleaved execution sequence.
Pair: Check your neighbours' solution. If it is the same as yours, come up with a second interleaved execution sequence.
Share: Instructor explains one possible solution and discusses alternate solutions."

Post-test. The post-test consisted of a single question (this was sufficient because it covered the entire concept that was taught using the TPS activity) on thread interleaving similar to the one above. It was included as the last part of the quiz that students took in the class following the above problem-solving activity. The post-test question was graded out of a maximum score of 4.

4.2 Student perception survey and focus group

To answer RQ2 "What are students' perceptions of learning with TPS?" we administered a survey to all students. The instrument had questions on student engagement and learning. All questions were on a 5-point Likert scale (strongly disagree, disagree, neutral, agree, and strongly agree). The questions relevant to the learning construct were:

Q1. Thinking about the problem and writing the solution during the think phase helped me learn CS1 concepts.

Q2. Discussing my solution with my partner during the pair phase helped me learn CS1 concepts.

Q3. Listening to other students' solutions and discussion during the share phase helped me learn CS1 concepts.

Q4. I would not have learned as much from the lecture if there had been no think-pair-share activities.

In addition, at the end of the course, we conducted four focus group interviews with 8-10 students in each group. The interviews lasted 30 minutes each and were conducted by an external observer. The interviews were audio recorded, transcribed and analyzed using the content analysis technique.

4.2 Instructor perception data

To answer RQ3, "What are the instructors' perceptions of teaching with TPS?" we have two sources of data. The instructor maintained detailed logs of the class. In addition, an external observer, who attended all classes, maintained notes of classroom observations.

5. RESULTS

5.1 TPS activity leads to increased conceptual understanding

250 students in the experimental group and 169 students in the control group took the post test. The distribution of scores was not Normal, hence we used Mann-Whitney U-test to compare means of the two groups, the results of which are shown in Table 2.

Table 2: Analysis of post test scores of experiment

Experimental Mean (SD)	Control Mean (SD)	p-value	Difference significant at p=0.05
1.91 (1.65)	0.88 (1.38)	0.00	Yes

We find that there was a statistically significant difference between the post-test scores of the two groups, with the experimental group (TPS) performing significantly better than the control group (interactive lecture). Further, Cohen's effect size ($d = .67$) suggests a moderate to high practical significance.

This experimental study was conducted in one class during which the applicability of TPS for the learning outcome of conceptual understanding was tested. In the interest of fairness to students we did not repeat the study in any further classes. For the remainder of the semester, both the sections were taught using interactive lectures interspersed with TPS activities for maximum learning in both sections. In Table 3, we present the scores of a problem from a course exam which was based on concepts taught to both groups using TPS. We find that there is no significant difference between the group means when both learnt via the same method. This result continues to hold for all exam problems throughout the semester. Table 3 also shows the final exam scores of students, where we find no significant difference between the groups. These results together indicate that it was the introduction of the TPS activity which caused the significant difference between the post test scores of the two groups.

Table 3: Comparing groups when taught via the same method

	Experimental Group Mean (SD)	Control Group Mean (SD)	p-value	Difference significant at 0.05?
Problem taught via TPS (out of 4)	3.66 (1.69)	3.43 (2.07)	0.848	No
Final exam (out of 100)	64.08 (23.7)	66.48 (23.44)	0.18	No

To understand these results better we classified the students based on their pre-test scores into 3 categories, low (<40%), medium (40-70%) and high (>70%) achievers. We similarly classified them based on their post-test scores to low (0), medium (1 or 2) and high (3 or 4) achievers. We determined the percentage of students who transitioned from category A pre-test to category B post-test by counting the number of students who were in category A pre-test and category B post-test. This enabled us to develop an empirical model of the students' learning in each group as shown in Figures 1 & 2.

Our first observation is that while nearly two-thirds of the control group got zero on the post-test problem a majority of the students in the experimental group scored three marks or higher. Next we observe that in the experimental group 61% of high achievers remain high achievers, while a significant percentage of medium (37%) and low achievers (30%) move into a higher achievement category. In the control group, however, 79% of high achievers moved into low or medium achievement categories and small percentages of medium (14%) and low (18%) achievers moved into higher achievement categories. This demonstrates that the TPS activity enabled students of all categories in the experimental group to perform better on the post-test as compared to the students in the control group.

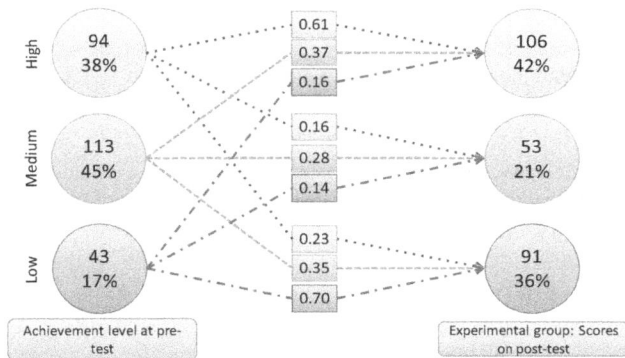

Figure 1: Transition diagram of experimental group

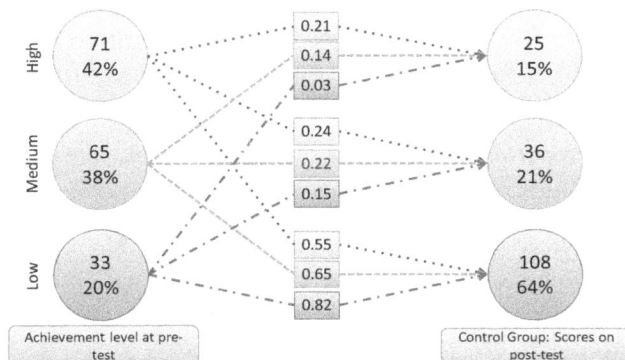

Figure 2: Transition diagram of control group

5.2 Students perceive TPS useful for learning

We received 336 valid responses to the student perception survey. The summary of student responses is presented in the Table 4.

Table 4: Student perception of learning with TPS

	Strongly Agree + Agree (%)	Neutral (%)	Strongly Disagree + Disagree (%)
Q1	72	21	7
Q2	67	24	9
Q3	73	21	6
Q4	58	29	13

These results show that a majority of the students perceived each stage of the TPS activities to be useful for learning CS1 concepts. A majority of the students also felt that they learned better from an interactive lecture interspersed with TPS activities than an interactive lecture only. Transcripts of the focus group interviews were coded, categorized and classified to identify student perceptions regarding learning with TPS and confirm the survey results. In the interest of space, we are not reporting all the results of the content analysis and only a few illustrative quotes below.

"The think and pair parts were equally important. Unless we think on our own, we won't get to know at what level we are. When we were made to think on certain questions we realize that these are some places we get stuck. We discuss those things with our partner, we realize that he overcame this problem in a certain manner and then we may come up with better solutions.."

"In a class of 240 you can come with 4 or 5 different solutions. [...] In that half an hour [of TPS] we are able to learn five methods of solving a problem and pros and cons of each method. That's more that you can learn in an hour."

Finally, the overall percentage of the end of semester course evaluation conducted by our institution was 85%, which is comparable to the top courses at our institution.

5.3 Instructor finds TPS engaging for all students

The instructor's perceptions of the benefits and challenges of teaching with TPS were as follows:

1) TPS is useful to address the challenges of students tuning out, getting distracted or going off-task. When specific deliverables were given in each stage of the activities, students were on-task. For this to happen, the activities must be interesting and balance student ability and challenge. Such activities ensured that the problem of boredom and frustration was resolved.

2) The activities were easy to implement even under the constraint of fixed seats. Students naturally turned to their classmates on their left and right, formed informal groups and discussed their solutions.

3) The activities easily scale to large numbers. The Think and Pair phases are distributed among the students and so do not pose a challenge to the instructor. The Share phase can be a bottleneck, but the instructor did not find it so because many solutions turned out to be similar and so only the first instance of each type of solution needed to be discussed.

4) TPS mitigates problems due to diversity of prior knowledge. Since seating and pairing are random, learners without prior knowledge often get benefits of one-on-one tutoring. Learners with prior knowledge of a given topic are engaged due to discussion with peers or tutoring.

5) There is increased participation by everyone, not just the vocal students. Since everyone has worked on the problems individually and in small groups, everyone has something to contribute to the share phase and so gets involved.

6) The entire class gets the benefits of multiple and unusual solutions because the instructor explicitly invited sharing of those solutions which were different from what had already been discussed.

6. DISCUSSION AND CONCLUSION

Our first research question "Do TPS activities lead to increased conceptual understanding and application of CS1 concepts?" was answered by the results of the quasi-experimental study which showed that the group who learned a concept via a TPS-activity performed significantly better (with a moderate to high effect size) than the group which learned the same concept from an interactive lecture. Further, the transition diagrams show that a majority of students in the experimental group transitioned into equal or higher performance level from pre to post test. In the control group however, students moved into lower performance levels.

One concern of such an experimental study is student motivation. Even though we established group equivalence on the basis of a pre-test, this was a mandatory course for all freshmen. Hence it is possible that the students who were new to programming were more enthusiastic about the course than others and so learned better. However since we chose the concept of threads using Scratch as the target concept for the study, it was a new concept to all students, and we expect that all students had the same motivation to learn this concept. Another concern is instructor bias. While it is possible that the subtle changes of instructor behavior between the two methods can impact student learning, the instructor made every effort to ensure that the interactive lecture was engaging. In addition the end-of-semester evaluations (84% vs. 86%) show that the two sections did not perceive differences in instructor behavior.

Results of the second research question "What are students' perception of learning from TPS?" showed that a majority of students approved of a TPS-based classroom environment, and they would not have been able to learn CS1 as well had they not performed the TPS activities. The results of our final research question "What are the instructor's perceptions of teaching with TPS?" have shown that the instructor perceives TPS i) to be an effective technique that engages all students of varying levels, and ii) is easy to implement even in a large class.

Think-Pair-Share has been known to be an effective strategy for improving learning outcomes in various disciplines [2][17]. Our study has reconfirmed this finding in a CS1 large class. The main takeaway for instructors is that rather than framing a question as an open discussion to the whole class, creating a TPS activity is more effective. One reason is that the TPS activity ensures that students are vested in the outcome in each phase leading up to the discussion. The structured phases focus the discussion and ensure that it is more fruitful than an open discussion which typically tends to be dominated by the vocal students. The three phase structure also ensures that there is some part of the activity to keep different students engaged, thus addressing the issue of diversity of achievement levels. The guidelines and examples we provide in Table 1 help an instructor operationalize TPS for a programming course. This paper thus provides another effective active learning technique for CS instructors of large classes.

7. REFERENCES

[1] Bonwell, C. C., and Eison, J. A. Active learning: Creating excitement in the classroom. Washington, DC: School of Education and Human Development, George Washington University, 1991.

[2] Butler, A., Phillmann, K. and Smart, L. Active learning within a lecture: Assessing the impact of short, in-class writing exercises. *Teaching of Psychology*, 28 (4), 257-259.

[3] Cooper, J. L. and Robinson, P. Getting Started: Informal Small-Group Strategies in Large Classes. *New Directions for Teaching and Learning*, 81.

[4] Kagan, S. The structural approach to cooperative learning. *Educational Leadership*, 47(4), 12-15.

[5] Kothiyal, A., Majumdar, R., Murthy, S. and Iyer, S. "Effect of Think-Pair-Share in a large CS1 class: 83% sustained engagement", In *Proc. 9th Int. Comp. Edu. Research Workshop*, August 12-14, 2013, San Diego, USA.

[6] Kussmaul, C. Process oriented guided inquiry learning (POGIL) for computer science. in *Proc. 43rd ACM Tech. Symp. on Comp. Sci. Edu.*, pp. 373-378.

[7] Lee, C. B. Experience report: CS1 in MATLAB for non-majors, with media computation and peer instruction. In *Proc. 44th ACM Tech. Symp. on Comp. Sci. Edu*, pp. 35-40.

[8] Lockwood, K. and Esselstein, R. The inverted classroom and the CS curriculum. In *Proc. 44th ACM Tech. Symp. on Comp. Sci. Edu*, pp. 113-118.

[9] Lyman, F. The responsive classroom discussion. in Anderson, A. S. ed. *Mainstreaming Digest*, College Park, MD: University of Maryland College of Education, 1981.

[10] Lyman, F. Think-Pair-Share: An expanding teaching technique, *MAA-CIE Cooperative News*, v. 1, pp 1-2.

[11] Martinez, A. Using JITT in a database course. In *Proc. 43rd ACM Tech. Symp. on Comp. Sci. Edu*, pp. 367-372.

[12] McDowell, C., Werner, L., Bullock, H. E. and Fernald, J. Pair programming improves student retention, confidence, and program quality. *Comm. of the ACM*, 49(8), 90-95.

[13] Meltzer, D. E. and Thornton, R. Resource Letter ALIP–1: Active-Learning Instruction in Physics, *Am. J. Phys.*, 80, 6.

[14] Nosek, J. T. The case for collaborative programming. *Comm. of the ACM*, 41.3 pp. 105-108.

[15] Porter, L., Lee, C. B., Simon, B., and Zingaro, D. Peer instruction: do students really learn from peer discussion in computing? In *Proc. 7th Int. Workshop on Computing Edu. Research*, pp. 45-52.

[16] Simon, B., Parris, J., and Spacco, J. How we teach impacts student learning: Peer instruction vs. lecture in CS0. In Proc. *44th ACM Tech. Symp. on Comp. Sci. Edu*, pp. 41-46.

[17] Vreven, D. and McFadden S. An Empirical Assessment of Cooperative Groups in Large, Time-compressed, Introductory Courses. *Innov. High Edu*, 32, 85–92.

[18] Williams, L., Kessler, R. R., Cunningham, W. and Jeffries, R. Strengthening the case for pair programming. *Software, IEEE*, 17(4), 19-25

[19] http://www.cwsei.ubc.ca/resources/files/Clicker_guide_CWSEI_CU-SEI.pdf

Assessing Computational Learning in K-12

Shuchi Grover
Graduate School of Education
Stanford University
Stanford, CA 94305
shuchig@stanford.edu

Stephen Cooper
Computer Science Department
Stanford University
Stanford, CA 94305
coopers@stanford.edu

Roy Pea
Graduate School of Education/
H-STAR Institute
Stanford University
Stanford, CA 94305
roypea@stanford.edu

ABSTRACT

As computing curricula continue to make their way into K-12 schools, the issue of assessing student learning of computational concepts remains a thorny one. This paper describes the multiple forms of assessments used in a 6-week middle school curriculum with the goal of capturing a holistic view of student learning. A key aspect of this research is the use of instruments developed and shared in prior research. Included among these were several questions used in an Israeli nationwide exam to test middle school student learning of programming in Scratch. This paper reports on the use of the curriculum in two studies conducted in a public US middle school classroom, and compares performances of these students with those reported by the Israeli Ministry of Education in their large-scale study. It also argues for multiple modes of assessment of computational learning in K-12 settings.

Categories and Subject Descriptors

K.3.2 [**Computers and Education**]: Computer and Information Science Education - *Computer Science Education, Curriculum*

General Terms

Design, Experimentation, Human Factors.

Keywords

Computational Thinking, Computer Science Education, Computing education, assessment, K-12 curriculum development.

1. INTRODUCTION

Computational Thinking (CT) is recognized as a necessary skill for today's generation of learners [26]. A consensus has been building around the view that all K-12 children must learn CT [10] and be offered experiences with computer science. Several recent efforts are underway among researchers and educators working in concert with organizations such as CSTA and NSF to define guidelines for–and designs of K-12 (especially high school)–curricula. Many of these introductory experiences are being designed in the context of programming in block-based environments such as Scratch, Alice, and MIT App Inventor. Despite the many efforts aimed at tackling the issue of CT assessment [12,17,25], there are several challenges for assessing the learning of computational concepts and constructs in these programming environments.

Without attention to rigorous assessment, CT can have little hope of making its way successfully into K–12 school education settings at scale [9]. Our work on assessment of computational thinking is inspired by–and builds on–noteworthy efforts described in the next section that have attended to assessment of computational learning (CL) [6] in the context of Scratch and Alice. It also draws on recent work on deeper learning and the need to build and assess core disciplinary knowledge and students' ability to transfer conceptual learning, in addition to interpersonal and intrapersonal abilities [20].

2. RELATED WORK
2.1 Assessment of Computational Learning

In the context of block-based programming, there have been few studies devoted specifically to assessing foundational CT concepts like algorithmic thinking, repetition and selection in the algorithmic flow of control (loops and condition?al logic). Among these are a series of investigations in the context of game programming in Alice with middle school students within school and afterschool settings [25]. These studies were conducted with the aim of providing motivating experiences in computing contexts to empower students from underrepresented communities. The Alice "Fairy Assessment" requires students to code parts of a predesigned program to accomplish specific tasks. By having students modify or add methods to existing code, the researchers assessed student understanding of algorithms, abstraction and code. This assessment is Alice-based and requires subjective and time-consuming grading, a challenge for assessing student code.

Brennan & Resnick [5] highlight issues related to assessment of CT, especially with grading student-created programs. They underscore the need for multiple means of assessment. Student-created artifacts while "rich, concrete and contextualized" and a necessary tool for assessing students, do not tell the whole story of student understanding. They lack elements of process and are often misleading indicators of student understanding [21]. Though student projects point to apparent fluency as evidenced by the existence of certain computational constructs in the code, probing deeper through questions may reveal a different story. When asked about how parts of their code work, students' descriptions often reveal significant conceptual gaps, as they cannot explain how their code works. It is salient to note a similar observation in [25] where the authors discuss "students' partial understanding of someone else's code" in their analysis of the results of student performance on the Fairy Assessment mentioned above. This problem may occur when students work in pairs or when the learning environment allows for students to seek and give help, or copy and paste code. Assessing student projects is also subjective and time-consuming, especially with a large student population.

There is a need for more objective assessment instruments to illuminate student understanding of specific computing concepts and other CT skills such as debugging, code-tracing, problem decomposition and pattern generalization. Cooper [18] created a multiple-choice instrument for measuring learning of Alice programming concepts, but it has not been used to measure student learning in K-12 education. Lewis' online Scratch course for middle school [14] also uses such "quizzes".

It is also important that students learn—and be assessed on—the vocabulary of computing. Analogous to the benefits seen in developing and using academic vocabulary in science and math [13], fostering deeper computational learning and an affinity for CS includes building a language of the domain to aid thinking about and communicating computational ideas more effectively and learn the shared vocabulary of the discipline and its community of people.

This belief is seen in studies conducted in Israel involving systematic assessments of students' conceptual vocabulary and CL in the course of a semester-long class for introducing computer science concepts to 9th graders [17]. Their work also tackles aforementioned issues related to relying on student-created artifacts for assessing CL. They used pre-, interim and post-tests designed to assess CT through a combination of Bloom's modified taxonomy as well as the SOLO taxonomy [3]. They tested students on CT terms, and also required them to solve problems related to a pre-designed Scratch programming task. These were done on paper in response to scripts presented in the test and through additions to existing code in Scratch in response to question prompts. The tests were thus more objective and able to assess a student's use of appropriate computational constructs in a pinpointed way. Ben-Ari generously shared the instruments with the lead author via an email exchange.

2.2 Large-scale Efforts

A few large-scale efforts to roll out introductory computing curricula at the middle school level include useful ideas for assessment. Prominent among these are the UK national effort [23] and the Israel Ministry of Education's Science and Technology Excellence Program including a national curriculum and exam [27]. The UK curriculum includes objective exercises using Scratch code, Scratch programming assignments and a final project of the student's choosing. We have used all three modes of assessment in our curriculum as well.

It is the use of multiple-choice assessments and attendant rubrics to measure learning in the Israeli effort [28] that make their work particularly pertinent. Their national exam comprises 9 questions (with roughly 30 sub-questions). Arguably such multiple-choice measures are easier to implement in a large-scale setting than open-ended student projects. Similar to previous work done in Israel [17], they use Bloom's taxonomy to classify the questions and inferences that can be drawn about the appropriate learning level of the associated computing concepts. The assessment tool was used to measure not only student learning but to evaluate the curriculum that the Ministry hopes to evolve based on results. This highlights a critical, but often-ignored purpose of assessment— *leveraging assessments to improve a curriculum so as to better meet learning goals.*

With the stated focus on deeper learning of computational concepts, our research draws on all these ideas of multiple assessment mechanisms or a "system of assessments" [7] to assess to deeper learning in a computing context. We thus designed a curriculum with structured formative and summative assessment instruments in addition to programming assignments and open-ended projects in Scratch. By reusing assessment instruments from prior efforts, we also test their use in new settings. For example, we employ many of the same questions used in the Israel national exam, and their grading rubrics. Beyond using these assessments to measure student learning in a holistic way, our design-based research effort also used them to refine our curriculum over two iterations. The following sections describe our iterative efforts involving our introductory CS course for middle school using Scratch that not only employed several types of formative and summative assessments based in Scratch, but also included novel assessments that measured learners' ability to transfer those skills to a text-based programming context. The latter are described in [11]. We describe the assessments used, and in the results and discussion section, provide a comparative report between the results from Israel and ours. We comment on what we believe makes our effort distinct from prior studies.

3. METHODOLOGY

This section describes design-based research involving two studies of a six-week middle school module, titled *"Foundations for Advancing Computational Thinking" (FACT)*. The module was designed to include elements aimed at building awareness of computing as a discipline while promoting engagement with foundational computational concepts such as algorithmic flow of control comprising sequence, looping constructs, and conditional logic. The goal of the research was to study multiple and novel mechanisms for assessing learning of these core computational concepts, and helping to refine the curriculum.

3.1 Curriculum Design

As a short, introductory module, we believed students would be well served with material focused on the most basic CT topics. Our module focused on systematic processing of information, structured problem decomposition, algorithmic notions of flow of control including selection and repetition (i.e. conditional logic and iterative thinking) along with some learner engagement with abstractions and pattern generalizations as well as debugging. The organization of the 6-week module is shown in Table 1. Each topic mapped roughly to a week of course contact time.

The curriculum adopted the following approaches in its design:
- Builds on the rich body of prior research involving children and novice programmers to guide the pedagogy and assessments for the content being taught. These include: using worked examples for conceptual learning [24], using pseudo-code [4], teaching reading/code-tracing [15], and using frequent multiple-choice "quizzes" to push student understanding and reinforce concepts learned [9];
- Makes explicit the foundational ideas of computer science and computational thinking [16];
- Uses academic language to explain concepts in terms of the vocabulary of the computer science domain [13]; and
- Promotes active, constructivist learning in Scratch through several hands-on activities and assignments.

Table 1: Topics covered in 6-week FACT Intro CS module

Unit 1	Computing is Everywhere! / Algorithms / Programs
Unit 2	Serial execution; Problem solving, task breakdown, solution as precise sequence of instructions
Unit 3	Iterative/repetitive flow of control: Loops
Unit 4	Data and variables
Unit 5	Boolean Logic & Advanced Loops
Unit 6	Selective flow of control: Conditional thinking

3.1.1 Design of Formative Assessment of CL

Formative assessment was integrated throughout the course as multiple-choice quizzes, designed to give learners encouraging feedback and explanations. Many quizzes included small snippets of Scratch code on which questions were based. These were similar to those used in existing curricula [14,23]. These assessments aimed to help learners develop familiarity with code tracing and the ability to understand an algorithm in Scratch or in pseudo-code [4,15]. Figure 1 shows three sample quiz questions. Correct answers to quiz questions were accompanied by explanations. Some formative assessments also involved presenting jumbled blocks in Scratch required for a program (akin to Parson's puzzles), and having students snap them in correct order [19].

The curriculum placed a heavy emphasis on learning by doing in Scratch. In addition to open-ended time to dabble in Scratch, there were specific assignments that built on the concepts taught in the preceding lecture(s). Sample assignments include making a "spirograph" (using nested loops); a polygon generator depending on a size and shape specified by the user (employing user inputs and variables); "4-quadrant art" which colors the screen in different colors depending on the position of the cat (using conditionals with compound Boolean conditions); 2-paddle pong (using conditionals within repeat-until loops); "guess my number" game (which uses all the constructs taught through the course). *The assignments were manually graded based on rubrics provided to students.* Students had the freedom to design specific elements of their artifacts or add to them.

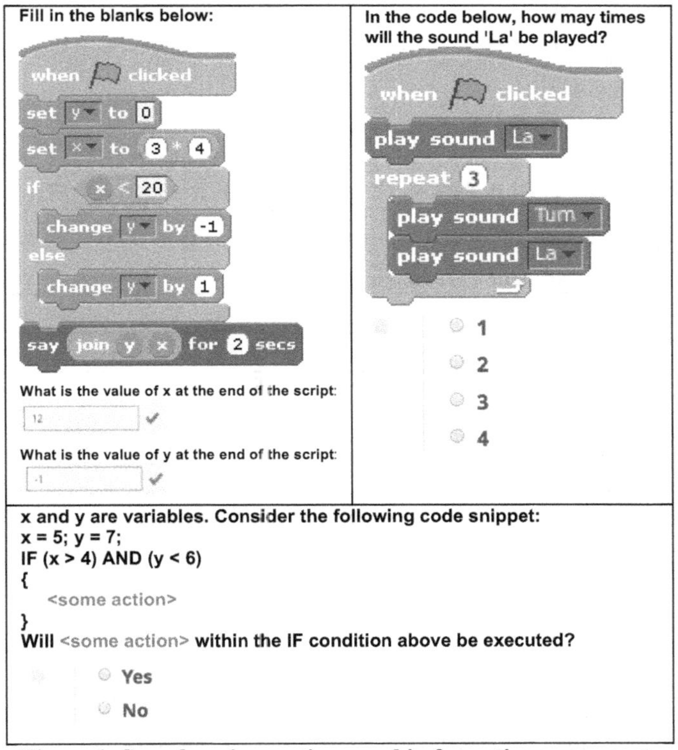

Figure 1: Sample quiz questions used in formative assessments

3.1.2 Design of Summative Assessments of CL

The pre- and post-test instruments borrowed from earlier work in Israel [17,28], both of which used the Scratch environment. The Israeli national curriculum [28], like ours, focuses on task decomposition, sequences, loops and conditionals as the foundational building blocks of algorithmic thinking. This made it

convenient to reuse questions from their exam. We incorporated questions 2, 4, 5, 7, 8 and 9 from their national exam [28]. We did not incorporate the other three questions since we did not get access to details on those questions prior to our study's launch. In addition to the six questions from the national exam, we required students to provide definitions of key computational terms such as *algorithm*, *variable*, *initialization*, *conditional*, *Boolean variable*, and *loop*. These were borrowed from [17] as were some additional questions to test student understanding of algorithms written in pseudo-code. We also included questions that used snippets of basic Scratch code to test if students could identify the core constructs in them as used in [8]. Lastly, we added a few questions of our own to assess code-tracing and debugging skills in snippets of code that used more advanced looping and conditional logic, as shown in Figure 2.

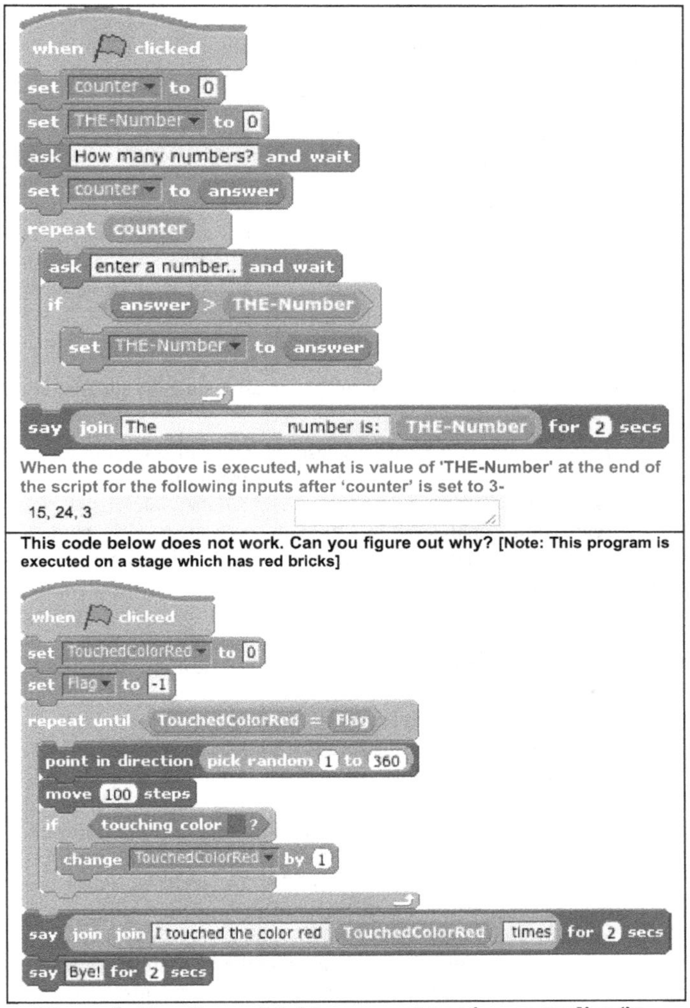

Figure 2: Questions added to our post-test in our studies (in addition to questions from Israel)

3.2 Study and Data Measures

3.2.1 Participants & Procedures

For Study 1, the FACT module was taught for six weeks in April-May, 2013 in a public middle school classroom in Northern California. The student sample comprised 26 children from 7th and 8th grade (21 boys and 5 girls, mean age: ~13 years) enrolled in a semester-long "Computers" elective class. The course was taught face-to-face in a computer lab (lectures and demonstrations in Scratch), with the units on conditionals and Boolean logic offered online in the form of short videos. The online units were done as a pilot to get student feedback ahead of online deployment of the entire module.

For Study 2, the FACT curriculum was taught in Sept-Oct, 2013 in the same middle school as Study 1, but with a new cohort of students in the "Computers" elective class (20 boys, 8 girls, mean age: 12.3 years). Study 2 involved the use of a completely online version of the course deployed on the Stanford OpenEdX online platform. The lectures and Scratch demonstrations in this version of FACT were in the form of short Khan Academy-style videos ranging between 1-6 minutes in length. Some changes were made to the assignments and duration for which certain concepts were taught based on our experiences, student performance, and student feedback from Study 1. For example, we devoted more time to loops and variables; more projects involving games and art were incorporated; and a more formal final project requirement was added with student interviews based on the project. The quizzes described in section 3.1.1 used automated grading and feedback in OpenEdX in Study 2. In Study 1 these were administered through Schoology, a learning management system used by the school, which also allowed for auto-grading and feedback. In both studies, the class met for 55 minutes four times per week. The lead researcher on this effort was also the curriculum developer and teacher for the FACT module. An independent researcher assisted with subjective grading.

3.2.2 Data Measures

In both studies, data were captured for assessing the curriculum and student learning:

- *Prior Experience Survey*: These gathered information about students' prior experiences in computational activities, especially programming [1]. This data was used for regression analyses to explain variances in student performance that are beyond of the scope of this paper.
- *Pre-Test*: This measured prior knowledge of computational concepts, including questions on the definitions of computing terms, student understanding of serial execution of algorithms presented in English, and questions that tested student knowledge of Scratch and programming in general. These were borrowed from [8,17].
- *Post-Test*: This measured student knowledge of computational concepts, the ability to read and decipher code or pseudo-code, and to debug a piece of code. The focus of these tasks was on algorithmic flow of control: sequence, loops, and conditionals. As described in 3.1.2, the post-test included questions from [8,17,28] as well as those we created. The pretest was a subset of the post-test as it seemed unreasonable to give children a large number of problems on skills and content completely alien and new to most students.
- *Quizzes*: Although not used to "test" students, data on student performance in these formative assessments were gathered as indicators for monitoring student progress and capturing conceptual targets of difficulty.
- *Scratch Assignments:* These were given throughout the course and graded according to a rubric.
- *Final Scratch Projects & Student Interviews (only in Study 2):* Students used the final project-guiding document used in the UK curriculum [23] for planning and reflecting on their project. Students were interviewed on their final projects. Transcription and analysis of these is yet to completed.

Additional instruments such as a *"Preparation of Future Learning"* [22] test designed to assess transfer of learning to a text-based programming language [11] are outside the scope of this paper. The Results section focuses on the post-test in which questions from the Israel national exam were used and additional questions akin to them designed for an online test. The open-ended summative assessments that included student-created games as well as interviews with students in keeping with the ideas of holistic assessment discussed earlier are not discussed in this paper.

4. RESULTS

Figure 3 shows the pre-post test scores (both averaged out of 100) in Studies 1 and 2. All the points are above the 45-degree line, indicating that all students had higher averages on the post-test than the pre-test. Statistical tests t-tests on the difference of the mean learning gains revealed that the learning gain in Study 2 was significantly higher than that in Study 1. Table 1 shows the test scores by gender, which suggests that girls in this sample performed significantly better than boys, although there were no significant differences by age or grade.

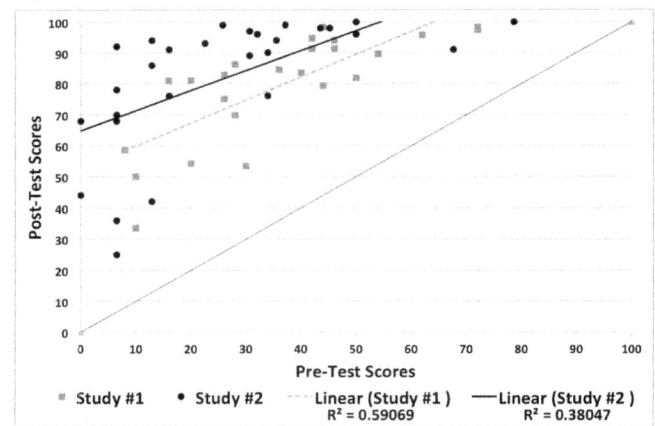

Figure 3: Pre-Post test average scores in Study #1 & Study #2

Table 1: Student Test Outcomes by Gender

	Mean (SE)		p-value
By Gender	Male (n = 40)	Female (n = 12)	
Pre-Test	29.9 (3.3)	38.4 (4.8)	0.20
Post-Test	77.1 (3.2)	89.7 (2.5)	0.04*

Note: p-values for the Pre-Test and Post-test come from a t-test of equality of means across samples with unequal variance. Given the non-normal distribution of the Post-test, the Mann-Whitney (Wilcoxon) rank sum test was also used and the p-value in that test was 0.07 for Post-test scores by gender.

Figure 5 shows student performance in the 6 questions containing 22 sub-questions that were re-used from the 2012 Israel national exam. It compares student performance for the 54 participants in our two studies with that of the 4082 students in Israel [28]. We found the difference in performance on all questions not statistically significant except in Question 9 in which our students performed significantly better than the Israel students scoring an average of almost 70% as compared to their 57%. We discuss this in more detail in Section 4.1. The Israel study report broke down the assessment measures according to **thinking skills** based on a modified version of Bloom's taxonomy as comprising Remembering & Understanding, Applying & Analyzing, and

Evaluating & Creating. The figures for the 2012 Israel Exam were 82%, 78% & 64% respectively for these three categories. Those corresponding figures for our students were 83%, 85% and 74%, however it is *important to note that a fair comparison cannot be made as the calculations in the former were made based on the whole exam comprising 9 questions; and ours are based only on the 6 (out of those 9) questions that we used.*

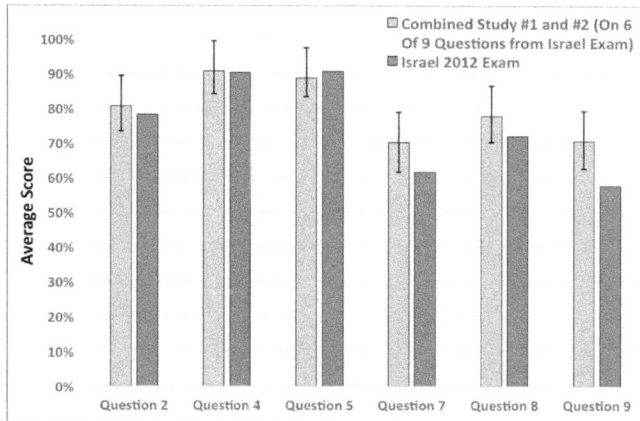

Figure 4: Comparison of Student Performance in Study #1 & #2 vs. 2012 Israel results (on 6 of 9 questions)

Additionally questions in the Israeli study were categorized according to **topics taught**, classified as serial execution (8%), conditionals (30%), Forever/Forever-If (12%) and For Loops (50%). The numbers in parentheses represent the percentage of the exam grade that was associated with that topic. The Israeli students' scores across the whole exam on the four topics was reported to be 87%, 85%, 89% & 64% respectively. We could not calculate corresponding figures for these as we were missing some questions, however the breakdown of *our entire exam* by topics taught is seen in Table 2 below.

Table 2: Post-Test Scores Breakdown by CS Topics Taught

	Mean (SD)
Overall Score	80.6 (19.2)
By CS Topic	
Vocabulary	72.9 (20.6)
Serial Execution	94.1 (17.6)
Conditionals	84.7 (19.6)
Loops	75.7 (24.1)

4.1 Discussion of Results

Based on results shown above, our students seemed to learn well for both Study 1 and 2 iterations of the 6-week FACT module. Based on student performance on the post-test in Study 1, we altered some strategies in Study 2- devoting more teaching time to certain topics, and a few different examples and programming assignments. This clearly helped as the student performance in the post-test in Study 2 improved.

Regarding the comparison of our students' performance following FACT on the same questions given to the students in Israel in 2012 following their national curriculum, it is worth noting the following distinctions in the research contexts. The Israel results were based on a sample of 4,082 7th grade students, while both of our research studies included both 7th and 8th grade students, comprising a total of 54 students. The Israel nationwide exam was given following a yearlong Introductory CS class. According to information provided by Zur Bargury to the lead author, the class was held for 2 hours a week for a school year, a total of 60 hours.

The results shared here from our studies are from the post-test taken after roughly 24 hours over 6 weeks of learning with the FACT module. While we have demographic and other data, there is no such data available to us on the Israel students. In the Israel study, students taking this class were selected from within their schools as those "who excelled in their age group." In our studies, students were in the elective class based on stated interest or a counselor placing them in this elective; it was not seen as a part of the core curriculum or connected to official testing.

Despite these differences in the Israeli context from ours, most results were statistically no different. The only difference that warrants comment is that our students' performance in both Study 1 and Study 2 on Question 9 were significantly better than those of students in Israel. This was the only question that did not have multiple choice answers provided but required students to fill in 10 blanks in a Scratch script and involved the highest level of thinking, "Evaluating and Creating" in Bloom's taxonomy. Our students' success on this question may be due to a curricular focus on deeper understanding of concepts as well as practice in tracing existing code and reading/writing pseudo-code. Not having more details on the curriculum used in Israel, we are hesitant to comment on what may have affected the result in their case.

5. CONCLUSIONS & FUTURE WORK

Although student results on the post-test are encouraging overall, we hope to get a more holistic view of student learning, especially for children who did not perform as well on the test. To this end we are currently coding student interviews and grading final projects from Study 2. Preliminary results suggest that decontextualized assessment measures requiring reading abilities to understand written questions may not favor the English Language Learners in the student population. The projects and interview shows evidence of understanding of computational concepts even among low performers in the post-test, in addition to the obvious increased confidence and engagement levels when describing their own projects in contrast to discussing a question from the post-test, where they appear to get confused about some aspects of questions that appear ambiguous to them.

It is noteworthy that efforts to improve the instruction and Scratch assignments in Study 2 following Study 1 resulted in learning gains in Study 2 despite using an all-online version of FACT. We attribute the success of the FACT curriculum, especially on advanced questions like #9 of the Israel exam, to a good balance between explanation, demonstration of worked examples, use of pseudo-code, regular assessments that required children to trace (read) Scratch script and answer questions based on them, and several hands-on assignments in Scratch. However, future research is required to tease apart the productive conditions of the learning environment. Though unguided or minimally guided instructional approaches are popular among teachers employing easy-to-use environments like Scratch, we were guided by the argument that these approaches are less effective and less efficient than instructional approaches that place a strong emphasis on guidance of the student learning process [16]. A curriculum such as the one proposed in this research aims to help students see deeper structures in their computational artifacts and assess this learning via appropriate assessments.

A salient finding from our reuse of questions from the Israel exam is that student performance seems to be remarkably similar despite the distinctions between our research contexts, and the curriculum, location, student population as well as sample size taking the Israel National Exam. Perhaps more interesting is that both efforts are being used in part to hone a CS curriculum. Given that two completely unrelated curricula taught across the world to two very disparate groups of students presented such similar results suggests that the ease or difficulty that students face in learning certain computational concepts transcends teaching methods and materials, and are perhaps a function of age and cognitive maturity more than anything else.

A significant contribution of our research is the demonstration of the use of multiple forms of assessment in a structured introductory CS curriculum in a K-12 setting. Neither multiple-choice questions nor open-ended projects alone tell the whole story of student understanding. It would be unwise to ignore learner agency, motivation, creative expression and design thinking that students bring to projects of their own choosing [2]. This is especially critical when one of the stated goals of introducing CS is to inspire children to pursue this discipline and broaden the CS pipeline. However, it would be equally imprudent to not include objective measures that can be scaled and assess students' understanding of core computational concepts as well as associated skills such as debugging and code-tracing.

Perhaps the most noteworthy aspect of this effort is the reuse of assessment ideas and instruments from prior and ongoing efforts in different parts of the world *to build a cumulative knowledge base of a learning science for computational thinking*. This is especially pertinent as our individual nations move concurrently but separately towards a shared goal of building a computationally literate generation of learners. Leveraging the efforts of others and testing curricular instruments in new settings helps validate ideas and move the field forward.

6. REFERENCES

[1] Barron, B. 2004. Learning ecologies for technological fluency: Gender and experience differences. *Journal of Educational Computing Research*, 31(1), 1-36.

[2] Barron B. & Daring-Hammond, L. (2008). How can we teach for meaningful learning? In Daring-Hammond, L., Barron, B., Pearson, P. D., Schoenfeld, A. H., Stage, E. K., Zimmerman, T. D., Cervetti, G. N., & Tilson, J. L. 2008. *Powerful learning: What we know about teaching for understanding*. Jossey-Bass

[3] Biggs, J. B., & Collis, K. F. 1982. *Evaluating the quality of learning*. New York: Academic Press.

[4] Bornat, R. 1987. *Programming from first principles*. Prentice Hall International.

[5] Brennan, K., & Resnick, M. 2012. New frameworks for studying and assessing the development of computational thinking. *Paper presented at AERA 2012, Vancouver, Canada.*

[6] Cooper, S., Pérez, L. C., & Rainey, D. 2010. K-12 computational learning. *Communications of the ACM, 53*(11), 27-29.

[7] Conley, D. T., & Darling-Hammond, L. (2013). Creating Systems of Assessment for Deeper Learning.

[8] Ericson, B., & McKlin, T. 2012. Effective and sustainable computing summer camps. *Proceedings of the 43rd ACM technical symposium on CS Education*, 289-294.

[9] Glass, A. L., & Sinha, N. 2013. Multiple-Choice Questioning Is an Efficient Instructional Methodology That May Be Widely Implemented in Academic Courses to Improve Exam Performance. *Current Directions in Psychological Science, 22*(6), 471-477.

[10] Grover, S. & Pea, R. 2013. Computational Thinking in K–12 A review of the state of the field. *Educational Researcher, 42*(1), 38-43.

[11] Grover, S., Pea, R. & Cooper, S. (2014). Expansive Framing and Preparation for Future Learning in Middle-School Computer Science. In Proceedings of the 11th International Conference of the Learning Sciences (2014), Boulder, CO

[12] Ioannidou, A., Repenning, A., & Webb, D. C. 2009. AgentCubes: Incremental 3D end-user development. *Journal of Visual Languages & Computing, 20*(4), 236-251.

[13] Lemke, J.L. (1990). *Talking science: Language, learning and values*. Westport, CT: Ablex Publishing.

[14] Lewis, C. M. (2011). Is pair programming more effective than other forms of collaboration for young students? *Computer Science Education, 21*(2), 105-134.

[15] Lopez, M., Whalley, J., Robbins, P., & Lister, R. 2008. Relationships between reading, tracing and writing skills in introductory programming. *Proceedings of the 4th International Workshop on Computing Education Research*, 101-112.

[16] Mayer, R. E. (2004). Should there be a three-strikes rule against pure discovery learning?. *American Psychologist, 59*(1), 14.

[17] Meerbaum-Salant, O., Armoni, M., & Ben-Ari, M., 2010. Learning computer science concepts with Scratch. *Proceedings of the Sixth International Workshop on Computing Education Research (ICER '10)*, 69-76.

[18] Moskal, B., Lurie, D., & Cooper, S. 2004. Evaluating the effectiveness of a new instructional approach. *ACM SIGCSE Bulletin, 36*(1), 75-79.

[19] Parsons, D. & Haden, P. 2006. Parson's programming puzzles: a fun and effective learning tool for first programming courses. *Proceedings of the 8th Australasian Conference on Computing Education-Volume 52*, 157-163.

[20] Pellegrino, J. W., & Hilton, M. L. (Eds.). (2013). *Education for life and work: Developing transferable knowledge and skills in the 21st century*. National Academies Press.

[21] Piech, C., Sahami, M., Koller, D., Cooper, S. & Blikstein, P. 2012. Modeling how students learn to program. *Proceedings of the 43rd ACM technical symposium on Computer Science Education*, 153-160.

[22] Schwartz, D. L. & Martin, T. (2004). Inventing to prepare for future learning: The hidden efficiency of encouraging original student production in statistics instruction. *Cognition and Instruction, 22(2)*, 129-184.

[23] Scott, J. 2013. The royal society of edinburgh/British computer society computer science exemplification project. *Proceedings of ITiCSE'13*, 313-315.

[24] Sweller, J., & Cooper, G. A. 1985. The use of worked examples as a substitute for problem solving in learning algebra. *Cognition and Instruction, 2*(1), 59-89.

[25] Werner, L., Denner, J., Campe, S., & Kawamoto, D. C. 2012. The Fairy Performance Assessment: Measuring Computational Thinking in Middle School. *Proceedings of the 43rd ACM Technical Symposium on Computer Science Education*, 215-220.

[26] Wing, J. 2006. Computational Thinking. *Communications of the ACM, 49*(3), 33-36.

[27] Zur Bargury, I. 2012. A new Curriculum for Junior-High in Computer Science. *Proceedings of ITiCSE'12*, 204-208, Haifa, Israel.

[28] Zur Bargury, I., Pârv, B. & Lanzberg, D. 2013. A Nationwide Exam as a Tool for Improving a New Curriculum. *Proceedings of ITiCSE'13*, 267-272. Canterbury, England, UK.

Engaging High School Students Using Chatbots

Luciana Benotti
Logic, Interaction and
Intelligent Systems Group
FAMAF, Universidad Nacional
de Córdoba/CONICET
Ciudad Universitaria,
Córdoba, Argentina
benotti@famaf.unc.edu.ar

María Cecilia Martínez
Facultad de Filosofía y
Humanidades
Universidad Nacional de
Córdoba/CONICET
Ciudad Universitaria,
Córdoba, Argentina
cecimart@gmail.com

Fernando Schapachnik
Fundación Dr. Manuel
Sadosky and
Depto. de Computación,
FCEyN, UBA
Buenos Aires, Argentina
fschapachnik@
fundacionsadosky.org.ar

ABSTRACT

Chatbots have been used in different scenarios for getting people interested in CS for decades. However, their potential for teaching basic concepts and their engaging effect has not been measured. In this paper we present a software platform called Chatbot designed to foster engagement while teaching basic CS concepts such as variables, conditionals and finite state automata, among others. We carried out two experiences using Chatbot and the well known platform Alice: 1) an online nation-wide competition, and 2) an in-class 15-lesson pilot course in 2 high schools. Data shows that retention and girl interest are higher with Chatbot than with Alice, indicating student engagement.

Categories and Subject Descriptors

K.3.2 [**Computer and Information Science Education**]: Computer science education

General Terms

Education

Keywords

Computer science K-12 outreach, chatbot, experimental evaluation, engagement, gender

1. INTRODUCTION

Argentinean universities graduate only 3500 Computer Science (CS) students a year (compared to 10000 in Law and 15000 on Economics) while the national industry needs to hire twice that amount. Part of the problem is that CS is not taught at K-12 level. This lack of early CS education influences career choices as students may not be selecting CS simply because they do not know what CS is [6]. We found through student surveys that although more than 90% of

our Argentinean K-12 students use computers as consumers, most of them believe that programming means "installing programs".

This context is not unique to Argentina, many developed countries share the same problem (e.g., [27, 13, 1]). The industry and the government are tackling this problem with several initiatives. One of them is a programming contest based on the well-known tool Alice [8, 9] called Dale Aceptar, described in Section 3.2, that despite having attracted more than 27000 students, faces the issue of low female participation and low retention rates. In an effort to improve these issues, the Sadosky Foundation,[1] the institution running the competition, partnered with the Universidad Nacional de Córdoba to develop Chatbot.

This article documents the findings of that experience and makes the following main contributions:

• We present the educational tool Chatbot which is an open source software that hides the complexity of chatbot programming. It provides a simple interface that helps students learn basic Computer Science concepts such as variables, conditionals, and finite state automata, among others.
• We propose a pedagogical strategy to increase student engagement by using it in a specific way: a gamified, inquiry oriented, structured task where students program a chatbot and get automated progress feedback. It is gamified as a mystery game called "Alibi".
• We develop a 15-lesson pilot classroom learning experience and report on the engagement and difficulties encountered by K-12 students while learning basic CS concepts using Chatbot and Alice in both the classroom and the online contest Dale Aceptar.

The rest of the article is organized as follows. It describes the Chatbot platform (Section 3) and both the outcome of its introduction in the Dale Aceptar contest and in a pilot study specially designed to test it in a classroom environment (Section 4). Before that, Section 2 surveys previous work in the area of engaging K-12 students in CS learning. Some final remarks and future research agenda conclude the article in Section 5.

ITICSE'14, June 21–25, 2014, Uppsala, Sweden.
Copyright 2014 ACM 978-1-4503-2833-3/14/06 ...$15.00.
http://dx.doi.org/10.1145/2591708.2591728.

[1]The Manuel Sadosky Foundation is a public/private institution whose goal is to promote stronger interaction between ICT industry and the scientific-technological system. Its Chairman is the Minister of Science, and the Vice-chairmen are the chairmen of the most important ICT chambers of the country.

2. PREVIOUS WORK

The typical K-12 student in Argentina almost never encounters CS topics during its school years. Computer Science is just not taught at school, not even as an optional course. The curriculum in Argentina focuses on ICT training classes rather than CS content. In these courses, computing entails little more than learning how to use a word processor, a spreadsheet or create an online blog. Students often get bored in their ICT classes and outperform their own teachers. This context is not unique to Argentina, many developed countries share the same problem [27, 1, 13, 5]. There are some exceptions such as Israel, among others, where CS has been taught at high schools for many years now [28].

The need to interest more K-12 students in CS has been addressed by government institutions, companies, universities and teachers around the world. The work is extensive and varied and we we will not be able to make a complete survey here. We just comment on some representative examples. Many excellent initiatives have bloomed, like Alice [8, 10], CS Unplugged [2], the Computer Science Teachers Association and Code.org, just to mention a few. As a result, several outreach programs exist that are interested in how to best enthuse more students. Many activities and different approaches to teaching CS are being evaluated. Doran et al [12] developed and tested a curriculum for video-game design and evaluated its impact on student engagement and performance in other fields, such as Math and English.Other studies concentrate in analyzing teachers' opinions [26, 5].

Despite advances in the last decades, it is still a matter of debate how to interest students, and specially girls, in CS. Moreover, there is no consensus on what CS concepts should be included in the school curriculum (e.g., [1, 14, 22, 7]). Documenting experiences of teaching CS in high school will contribute to the discussion of what and how CS concepts could be taught at high school in order to keep the students interested.

There has been much research on how to foster interest in CS by teaching how to program 3D video-games. Alice [8, 9] is a pioneer in this regard whose engagement potential has been thoroughly investigated. Such research lead to the development of Alice Story Telling [16] that was specially designed to interest girls in CS. In Section 4 we compare Chatbot with Alice.

Chatbots have been used in different scenarios for getting people interested in CS for decades. In most cases chatbots are used as tutoring systems [17, 11]. Several programming clubs have proposed the programming of chatbots as a method for interesting their students in computer science. Shaw [25] used chatbot programming to teach computing principles in introductory CS courses. Keegan et al [15] presented Turi, a chatbot software for secondary and primary schools. Bigham et al [4] used low level chatbot programming to inspire blind high school students to pursue Computer Science. Bigham et al study showed that this was a successful tool in spite of technical difficulties such as the fact that the produced chatbots could not connect to the more used social networks. In spite of their repeated use, to the best of our knowledge, the potential of chatbot programming for teaching basic CS concepts and its engaging effect has not been measured. In this paper we not only evaluate the engagement shown by students with no previous interest in CS but we also compare it to animations and video game programming with Alice. For this study, engagement means student cognitive investment on learning and completing the task. The main indicators for engagement are amount of student participation (task completion and attendance), intensity of concentration, enthusiasm, and expressed interest [20].

3. CHATBOT

Chatbot is an educational software tool whose design goal is to motivate students to learn basic CS concepts through the construction of chat automata. It has a mode of operation where it can connect to social networks (such as Gtalk and Facebook) and reply to chat conversations automatically. The chatbots can be programmed to answer in different ways depending on who it is talking to, what the person is saying, which topic they talked about before, etc.

By programming their chatbots, students learn basic CS concepts such as variables, conditionals, finite automata, recursion, randomness, regular expressions, among others. Chatbot can also be used to explore more advanced concepts such as the Turing test and Natural Language Processing concepts (e.g. lemmatization and syntactic analysis). Chatbot is open source and is available at `bit.ly/1iglAf6` .

3.1 Teaching Basic CS Concepts with Chatbot

In this section we illustrate how Chatbot can be used to teach the basic Computer Science concepts of **variables** and **conditionals**.

Chatbots are programmed in Chatbot by writing sets of **(pattern, effect)** pairs. The chatbot responds with the *effect* when the *pattern* matches the stimulus received by the chatbot. Patterns are simple regular expressions that may include wildcards and variables, and effects may include variables and conditionals (among more advanced structures) as illustrated in Figure 1.

In this example the chatbot programmed is the suspect of a murder who is talking to the leading detective. The following dialogue is given to the students and they are asked to implement a single (pattern, effect) pair to program a chatbot that can answer like this suspect.

> *Detective: Do you think that the cook is the murderer?*
> *Suspect: it's possible that the cook did it*
> *Detective: or the photographer is the murderer?*
> *Suspect: no, I am sure he didn't do it*
> *Detective: what if the gardener is the murderer?*
> *Suspect: it's possible that the gardener did it*

A possible correct answer to the exercise is shown in Figure 1. In the figure the pattern includes the wildcard * that can match any number of words and the variable [person] that stores the value of the word that comes right before the phrase *"is the murderer?"*. The effect is a conditional expression that, depending on the value of the variable [person], may give two different answers (one of them uses the content of the variable).

Pattern: * [person] is the murderer?
Effect: {**if** [person] = photographer}
              no, I am sure he didn't do it
              {**else**} it's possible that the [person] did it

Figure 1: Sample (pattern, effect) pair that uses variables, wildcards and conditionals in Chatbot.

3.2 Open-Online Contest for Teenagers

Dale Aceptar (Spanish for "just hit OK" but also "go with it") is a free online competition organized by the Sadosky Foundation (www.daleaceptar.gob.ar). Based on Alice, it is performed annually with the aim of interesting more students into pursuing CS-related careers. The competition is atypical, in the sense of being aimed at students with no prior background in programming, who sign in because they see the commercials on national TV and feel like having fun, win a prize or both. While they participate, students are also exposed to short pieces of information about CS and its advantages as a career choice.

The site offers 23 short-video lessons on Alice, going from the basics up to building a turn-taking, timer-based game. Multiple fora provide support for Q&A. The competition has attracted more than 27000 students along its three editions.

Besides proposing working with Alice, the 2013 edition added a "gamified" alternative: students could participate in "Alibi", a murder story based on Chatbot. Five funny suspects, a corpse and a detective are left alone in a mountain. The detective keeps a log book with his findings and speculations, which is weekly made available to participants along with an interrogation questionnaire from the detective for each suspect. Participants download the file and are supposed to program their Chatbot so that it answers the questions properly (a structured task). Chatbot confesses guilt if it cannot find a matching rule, and flags an answer as incorrect if there is a rule but the output does not match the (encrypted) regular expression that the questionnaire file has for identifying correct answers. Students must keep their bot from confessing but also from flagging answers as incorrect. Based on how well the bot answers a score is calculated. It reaches 100% if all questions are answered properly. A jury of experts then picks winners among the top ranked bots, which must be programmed using concepts such as variables and finite state automata. As in the case of Alice students are supposed to learn by watching the five online Chatbot tutorial videos and using the support fora.

Figure 2: "Alibi" suspects lining up for questioning.

3.3 Comparative Pilot Study at High School

At the same time "Alibi" was launched we conducted a pilot study using both Chatbot and Alice in two public high schools in the city of Córdoba (Argentina) through a 15-lecture course. The expectation was to compare Alice and Chatbot without the bias of self-learning that Dale Aceptar has. We also wanted to know how students from diverse and specially poor context, with no previous interest on CS, engage in programming using Chatbot.

Introducing Chatbot in the context of public high schools also promoted the platform dissemination. We agree with Pears [23] that researchers often spend a great amount of

time developing a teaching tool, but very little effort disseminating its use. Tools need customization and pedagogical work before other educational institutions can adopt them.

The Alice course was designed to teach students how to program animations and the Chatbot course was designed to teach students to program chatbots that played the role of a suspect in a short version of "Alibi". Tutors visited the schools once a week to teach Alice in the first place and Chatbot in the second. The rationale was presenting students with a platform that could develop a familiar product such as animations first, and then move to less known products such as chatbots. It is possible, though, that if we had started with Chatbot, our results would have been different.

The lesson design for teaching both Alice and Chatbot followed a discovery based approach [24]. All lessons had four different segments. 1) Motivational. Aimed at interesting and challenging students to create the need to use some CS concept. In this segment, we presented students with a short challenge, such as moving an object in Alice in a particular way or reproducing a short dialogue in Chatbot. 2) Short lecture. Which consisted in a brief introduction to a CS concept that can solve the problem. E.g., conditionals. Intentionally, the tutor does not solve the problem leaving room for student discovery. 3) Exploration and production. Students explore the platform combining the right concepts that solve the challenge. The purpose of the segment is exposing students to experimentation for gaining understanding [21]. 4) Show and assess. In the last part of each lesson students share their progress on their animations or chatbots with other students. Student construction, presentation and evaluation of their products seems to improve learning computer programming [19].[2]

The pilot course was attended by 47 students, the average age was 15.4 years old. 55% of the students were female and 45% were male. Students from both schools had similar socio-economical situations: most students came from impoverish families. The course was mandatory and taught during school hours, however students were not evaluated and did not get extra credits for the course. All students completed the evaluation survey of the course, whose results are reported in Section 4.2.

An assistant made classroom observations and both tutor and assistant filled in post observations notes after each lesson. Both the assistant and the tutors had previously designed the lesson plans. In addition, students were given a pre-test, mid-test (when Alice module concluded) and a post-test at the end of the Chatbot module. We triangulated qualitative and qualitative data to increase the validity of the study and to better describe our findings adding a pedagogical dimension [3].

4. FINDINGS

In this section we report the outcomes of both introducing Chatbot in Dale Aceptar and the comparative pilot study in high schools.

4.1 Open-On line Contest for Teenagers

Besides the issue of lack of female participation, we also wanted to address engagement: although many students sign

---

[2]Chatbot offers the obtained score and incorrect question flags as a self evaluation mode that provides students with feedback on the quality of their rules.

| | Alice | | | Chatbot | | |
	Start	End	%End	Start	End	%End
Female	1022	16	1.57%	337	27	8.01%
Male	7480	93	1.24%	1117	75	6.71%
%Female	12%	15%		23%	26%	
Total	8502	109	1.28%	1454	102	7.01%

Table 1: Comparison of 2013 participants that registered (Start) vs those that uploaded their work to the competition web page (End).

in, only a few are self-motivated enough to complete the task of designing a game or animation and participate until the end of the competition. Although it is well-known that retention rates are low in online courses [18], a specific note about retaining teenagers in that setting is in order.

As argued in [20], in the classroom engagement is the product of three main factors, 1) the need for personal competence (which varies among socio-economic status) 2) the types of tasks students are required to do (mechanic, fun, authentic), and 3) the school environment (support, care, fairness, academic status). Positive school and classroom environment include teachers providing personal support to avoid frustration when difficulties arise, and caring about students as individuals in a context where academic expectations are clear and school success is promoted for all.

How does that work in the online world? What do you do to retain students, who have not logged in to your site for a while, so that they can come back? How do you reach out proactively to offer help? Some years ago, the email address provided when registering would have been the way, being a communication channel that was independent of whether the user visited back the site or not. Nowadays teenagers do not use email. They communicate through Facebook, and that platform, partly to avoid spam, do not allow sites ("fanpages" in Facebook jargon) to initiate communications, so a good part of retention tools are lost. We believe that this lack of strategies to reach back to students that had not logged in for a while explains the small percentage of participants that stayed in the competition long enough to present some finalized work piece ("End" column in Table 1).

As can be seen in Table 1, more people decided to participate with Alice than with Chatbot (8502 vs 1454). We attribute the difference to the fact that most teenagers do not know what a chatbot is while Alice was presented as a tool to program video games and animations, two concepts very familiar to them.

Two interesting observations can be made from Table 1. First, although Dale Aceptar attracts mainly male students (partly because the prize of the competition is a gaming console), the percentage of female registration is twice higher with Chatbot (23%) than with Alice (12%), this difference is statistically significant (Chi-square test, p=0.01). We do not know what motivations students have for choosing one platform over another, but similar female preferences were seen in the classroom (see next Section), and the evidence collected there points into the direction of highlighting a gamified task such as "Alibi" that requires the use of language and dialogue, as valuable to increase girls interest. Second, despite the challenges for retention in online courses, engagement, as measured by number of students who completed their work in the competition, reaches 7.01% in Chatbot while only 1.28% in Alice, this difference is statistically

significant (Chi-square test, p=0.01). We believe that the difference might be attributable to "Alibi" providing both a more structured task, with more clearly defined goals and periodic updates, in a platform such as Chatbot that provides feedback in the form of a score, as opposed to the more open and unstructured task of designing and creating video games or animations.

4.2 Comparative Pilot Study at High School

We conducted a pilot study in high schools to collect more detailed information on students behaviour using both tools, to learn about how students use Chatbot in the classroom and to analyze its potential to engage students in programming. After the pilot classroom course we applied a post-test to the students asking the following questions that provided us with indicators of student engagement. All questions are based on a scale ranging from 0 (meaning "not at all") to 10 (meaning "very much").

C1) How **interesting** was learning Chatbot for you?
C2) Do you want to **learn more** using Chatbot?
C3) How **easy** was learning Chatbot for you?
A1) How **interesting** was learning Alice for you?
A2) Do you want to **learn more** using Alice?
A3) How **easy** was learning Alice for you?

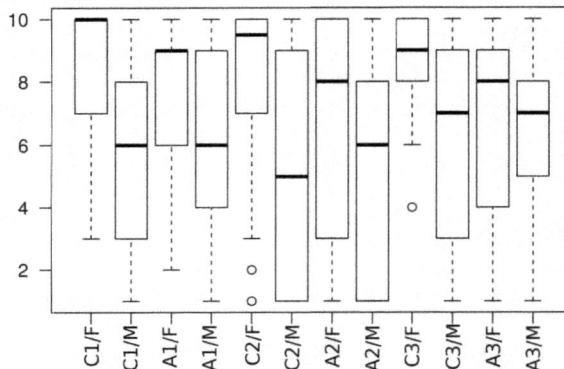

Figure 3: Results of engagement indicators obtained in the high school pilot study, by gender.

In Figure 3 we show a box plot of the results obtained in the post-test. Girls' self-reported interest was higher than boys' both for Chatbot and Alice. However, the difference is statistically significant for Chatbot (Chi-square test, p=0.01) but not for Alice. Girls' interest with Chatbot had a median value of 10 over 10 and girls' interest with Alice had a median value of 9 over 10. After finishing the course, girls want to learn more using Chatbot (median 9.5) while half of the boys don't (median 5), the difference is statistically significant (Chi-square test, p=0.01). In terms of easiness, the differences are not statistically significant, neither by gender, nor by tool. However, one can observe more variation in Chatbot for boys and Alice for girls than vice versa.

4.2.1 Interest with Alice and Chatbot

To increase the validity of our study we triangulated self reported student data with tutors perceptions documented in post lesson observations. While the tutors reported that

Platform	"Interesting"	"Fun"	"Engaged"
Chatbot	5	6	10
Alice	5	0	8

Table 2: Frequency of keyword appearance in post-lesson observations.

most lessons were engaging for students, upon a closer examination of their discourses we discovered subtle, but yet interesting differences, which mirror the findings on the items C1 and A1, students self reported interest.

In general, according to our tutors and research assistants, Chatbot resulted more engaging for our students. When describing the attitude of students working on their lesson they used the words "engaged", "interested" and "fun", all indicators of engagement according to Newmann [20]. Table 2 shows the number of times each word was repeated in the post lesson observations. Tutors seemed to observe that students have "fun" more often in Chatbot than in Alice. Also, the word "hook" appears more often in Chatbot. One possible explanation is that programming with Chatbot was part of playing the game "Alibi". As with the online experience, we believe the "gamification" of the task could have provided a source of fun. For example, based on post lesson reflections, one lesson included collective testing of some interesting pre-made chatbots (the psychologist and a chatbot that chats about his birthday). As those worked well, students showed interest in seeing how they were programmed. After that segment of the lesson, "Alibi" was presented. Students got hook into the characters, and all of them preferred to start creating their own "Alibi" chatbot instead of trying to build one of the topic of their choice.

4.2.2 Explaining "Easiness"

The second emerging theme in the qualitative analysis was that most CS concepts tackled either with Alice or Chatbot resulted "easy" for the majority of the students. Tutors and assistants reported in their observations that students learned "easily", solved most the challenges and discovered new rules or instructions to develop their products. For example one reflection mentioned: "*I asked them to write something that required a conditional and gave the class time to find the right tool to solve the problem. In particular, one of the students found the option 'create a conditional rule' and solved the challenge.*" Other classroom observations considered for this theme reported that students could solve challenges "rapidly". Tutors observed that students easily understood and applied conditionals.

However, some concepts did result harder for our students. As an example, in the Chatbot module, in one school, the tutor reported students had difficulties understanding finite state automata, despite eventually being able to apply it into their chatbots.

One finding emerging from the analysis of classroom observations is that some concepts students can discover or learn more intuitively than others. For example, variables and conditionals were intuitive concepts that students discovered when exploring the platform. Some other concepts, such as dummy objects in Alice and finite state automata in Chatbot seemed to require much more thought, practice and analysis. In spite of this, students reported that they found both platforms easy to learn.

5. CONCLUSIONS

In this article we document an experience on using the well-known educational tool Alice and Chatbot, a chatbot programming platform, both in an online competition and in classroom environments. The purpose of creating the tool was increasing student retention and engagement, specially in girls, while teaching basic CS concepts, both as a way of promoting interest towards CS-related careers and contributing to the increasingly important discussion of what CS concepts should be taught at school and how they should be approached.

We found that most indicators of engagement (task completion, participation, enthusiasm and self reported interest) increased when using Chatbot in comparison to Alice. With some differences between girls and boys, in the online experience, task completion and participation rates grew by a factor of 5 on Chatbot vs Alice. In the in-classroom pilot course, girls' self-reported interest was much higher than boys' as was their willingness to learn more using Chatbot.

The data seems to align well with previous reports stating that girls engage more in verbal oriented activities such as developing chatbots. Our mix has other ingredients as well: besides having a platform in common, both the online and classroom experience were structured in the format of a game called "Alibi" (gamification). Teaching materials such as the questionnaires, online videos and Chatbot immediate feedback, as well as the discovery-based lesson, were carefully designed to promote student engagement. We believe that more structured tasks and immediate feedback are important, and future work should include collecting evidences to prove or disprove their significance as individual drivers of engagement.

For instance, work with Alice could also be made more structured, focusing on building a particular type of game instead of each student choosing their favorite, and requiring to follow some sort of schedule where each week a particular aspect of the game is tackled, providing feedback to students on the quality of what they are doing. Last issue is key: providing support and feedback on the their programming can be done in class, while an online contest would need an immense amount of resources to provide the same level of support and feedback.

The difference on engagement could be due to the fact that the programming concepts covered are not exactly the same. For instance, Alice has data types, methods and parameters, which are key to CS and somehow harder to understand. If the difference in engagement could be attributed to Chatbot being somehow "incomplete", a teaching strategy could be depicted for girls: start with more engaging albeit "incomplete" tools, get them to the "want to learn more" state (Figure 3) and only then move to more powerful platforms.

Despite the scholarly interest of researching the separate significance of each of the these separate variables (platform and teaching approach), we highlight their combined value, and future agenda includes digging deeply into integral approaches on how to best enthuse and engage students in CS.

6. ACKNOWLEDGMENTS

This work was partially supported by grants ANPCyT-PICT-2008-306, ANPCyT-PICT-2010-688, ANPCyT-PICT-2012-712, the FP7-PEOPLE-2011-IRSES Project MEALS, two Google RISE awards, and grants by the Argentinean

Ministry of Science, Technology and Productive Innovation's Manuel Sadosky Foundation. The authors wish to thank the teams at Universidad Nacional de Córdoba and the Manuel Sadosky Foundation for their support and collaboration.

7. REFERENCES

[1] T. Bell, P. Andreae, and L. Lambert. Computer science in New Zealand high schools. In *Proceedings of the Twelfth Australasian Conference on Computing Education - Volume 103*, pages 15–22, 2010.

[2] T. Bell, P. Curzon, Q. Cutts, V. Dagiene, and B. Haberman. Introducing students to computer science with programmes that don't emphasise programming. In *Proceedings of the 16th ACM annual joint conference on innovation and technology in computer science education*, pages 391–391, 2011.

[3] A. Berglund, M. Daniels, and A. Pears. Qualitative research projects in computing education research: An overview. In *Proceedings of the 8th Australasian Conference on Computing Education - Volume 52*, pages 25–33, 2006.

[4] J. P. Bigham, M. B. Aller, J. T. Brudvik, J. O. Leung, L. A. Yazzolino, and R. E. Ladner. Inspiring blind high school students to pursue computer science with instant messaging chatbots. In *Proceedings of the 39th SIGCSE Technical Symposium on Computer Science Education*, pages 449–453, 2008.

[5] J. Black, J. Brodie, P. Curzon, C. Myketiak, P. W. McOwan, and L. R. Meagher. Making computing interesting to school students: Teachers' perspectives. In *Proceedings of the 18th ACM Conference on Innovation and Technology in Computer Science Education*, pages 255–260, 2013.

[6] L. Carter. Why students with an apparent aptitude for computer science don't choose to major in computer science. *SIGCSE Bulletin*, 38(1):27–31, 2006.

[7] Computing at School Working Group. *Computer Science: A Curriculum for Schools*. Computing at School Working Group, 2012.

[8] S. Cooper, W. Dann, and R. Pausch. Teaching objects-first in introductory computer science. In *Proceedings of the 34th SIGCSE Technical Symposium on Computer Science Education*, pages 191–195, 2003.

[9] W. Dann, S. Cooper, and D. Slater. Alice 3.1 (abstract only). In *Proceeding of the 44th ACM Technical Symposium on Computer Science Education*, pages 757–757, 2013.

[10] W. Dann, D. Cosgrove, D. Slater, D. Culyba, and S. Cooper. Mediated transfer: Alice 3 to java. In *Proceedings of the 43rd ACM Technical Symposium on Computer Science Education*, pages 141–146, 2012.

[11] O. V. Deryugina. Chatterbots. *Scientific Technical Information Processing*, 37(2):143–147, Apr. 2010.

[12] K. Doran, A. Boyce, S. Finkelstein, and T. Barnes. Outreach for improved student performance: A game design and development curriculum. In *Proceedings of the 17th ACM Annual Conference on Innovation and Technology in Computer Science Education*, pages 209–214, 2012.

[13] S. Furber. Shut down or restart? The way forward for computing in UK schools. Technical report, The Royal Society, London, 2012.

[14] O. Hazzan, J. Gal-Ezer, and L. Blum. A model for high school computer science education: The four key elements that make it! *SIGCSE Bulletin*, 40(1):281–285, 2008.

[15] M. Keegan, R. D. Boyle, and H. M. Dee. Turi: Chatbot software for schools in the turing centenary. In *Proceedings of the 7th Workshop in Primary and Secondary Computing Education*, pages 153–154, 2012.

[16] C. Kelleher and R. Pausch. Using storytelling to motivate programming. *ACM Communications*, 50(7):58–64, July 2007.

[17] A. Kerly, P. Hall, and S. Bull. Bringing chatbots into education: Towards natural language negotiation of open learner models. *Knowledge Based Systems*, 20(2):177–185, Mar. 2007.

[18] D. Koller, A. Ng, C. Do, and Z. Chen. Retention and intention in massive open online courses: In depth. *Educause Review*, 2013.

[19] T. L. Naps, G. Rössling, V. Almstrum, W. Dann, R. Fleischer, C. Hundhausen, A. Korhonen, L. Malmi, M. McNally, S. Rodger, and J. A. Velázquez-Iturbide. Exploring the role of visualization and engagement in computer science education. *SIGCSE Bull.*, 35(2):131–152, 2002.

[20] F. Newmann. *Student Engagement and Achievement in American Secondary Schools*. Teachers College Press, 1234 Amsterdam Avenue, New York, 1992.

[21] J. O'Kelly and J. P. Gibson. Robocode & problem-based learning: A non-prescriptive approach to teaching programming. *SIGCSE Bull.*, 38(3):217–221, 2006.

[22] H. Park, S. Khan, and S. Petrina. Ict in science education: A quasi-experimental study of achievement, attitudes toward science, and career aspirations of korean middle school students. *International Journal of Science Education*, 31(8):993–1012, 2009.

[23] A. Pears, S. Seidman, L. Malmi, L. Mannila, E. Adams, J. Bennedsen, M. Devlin, and J. Paterson. A survey of literature on the teaching of introductory programming. *SIGCSE Bull.*, 39(4):204–223, 2007.

[24] M. J. Prince and R. M. Felder. Inductive teaching and learning methods: Definitions, comparisons, and research bases. *Journal of Engineering Education*, 95(2):123–138, 2006.

[25] A. Shaw. Using chatbots to teach socially intelligent computing principles in introductory computer science courses. In *Proceedings of the IEEE 2012 Ninth International Conference on Information Technology*, pages 850–851, 2012.

[26] M. M. Voyles, S. M. Haller, and T. V. Fossum. Teacher responses to student gender differences. In *Proceedings of the 12th Annual SIGCSE Conference on Innovation and Technology in Computer Science Education*, pages 226–230, 2007.

[27] C. Wilson. *Running the Empty: Failure to Teach K-12 Computer Science in the Digital Age*. Association for Computing Machinery, 2010.

[28] I. Zur Bargury. A new curriculum for junior-high in computer science. In *Proceedings of the 17th ACM Annual Conference on Innovation and Technology in Computer Science Education*, pages 204–208, 2012.

Serious Toys: Three Years of Teaching Computer Science Concepts in K-12 Classrooms

Yvon Feaster[†], Farha Ali[‡], Jiannan Zhai[†], and Jason O. Hallstrom[†]
[†]School of Computing, Clemson University, Clemson SC 29634-0974 USA
[‡]Department of Mathematics and Computing, Lander University, Greenwood, SC 29649-2099 USA
yfeaste@clemson.edu, fali@lander.edu, jzhai@clemson.edu, jasonoh@cs.clemson.edu

ABSTRACT

Computational thinking represents a collection of structured problem solving skills that cross-cut educational disciplines. There is significant future value in introducing these skills as early as practical in students' academic careers. Over the past three years, we have developed, piloted, and evaluated a series of K-12 outreach modules designed to introduce fundamental computing concepts. We piloted two modules with more than 340 students, and evaluation results show that the modules are having a positive impact. We combined the two previously piloted modules with a newly developed module and piloted the combined program with over 170 students. Evaluation results again show that the combination is having a positive impact. In this paper, we summarize the program, discuss our experiences piloting it, and summarize key evaluation results. Our hope is to engender discussion and adoption of the materials at other institutions.

Categories and Subject Descriptors

K.3.2 [**Computers and Education**]: Computer and Information Science Education—*Computer Science education, Curriculum*

General Terms

Experimentation, Human Factors

Keywords

Binary numbers; networks; protocols; algorithms; sensor networks; outreach; K-12 curriculum; experimental evaluation

1. INTRODUCTION

For more than three decades, the third grade has been recognized as a milestone year in gauging students' future academic success. Reading comprehension has been a focal point. A recent national study commissioned by the Annie E. Casey Foundation [14, 17] reports that students who lag behind in reading performance at the end of the third grade are four times less likely to earn a high school

ITICSE'14, June 21 - 25, 2014, Uppsala, Sweden
Copyright 2014 ACM 978-1-4503-2833-3/14/06 ...$15.00
http://dx.doi.org/10.1145/2591708.2591732 .

diploma. Those with the lowest reading performance are six times less likely to earn a diploma. The explanation for this trend is simple: Third grade marks a transition from "learning to read to reading to learn". Reading comprehension skills are assumed in subsequent grades, and independent learning outside of the classroom is emphasized.

We posit a corollary between reading comprehension skills and computational thinking skills. As early as kindergarten, many students begin to use computers in their classrooms. As they progress to more advanced grades, computers become essential tools to facilitate learning. But the importance of computing does not end there; computing is more than learning to use a computer. Computational thinking represents a discipline of structured problem solving, encompassing skills that are broadly useful to students throughout their academic careers [24]. As the academic challenges students encounter become progressively more complex, students who possess strong computational thinking skills are likely to outperform those who do not. It is safe to assume that there is a "pivot year", similar to the reading comprehension scenario, where these skills become essential to more advanced learning. While there is no evidence available to identify the particular year when this occurs, it would be prudent to introduce computational thinking as early as practical in the K-12 curriculum.

Unfortunately, in the United States, computing curriculum is virtually nonexistent in the K-12 system [23]. To address this deficiency, we have developed a series of curriculum modules to introduce K-12 students to computing concepts using embedded computing manipulatives, or "serious toys". The instruction style is designed to simultaneously engage visual, auditory, and kinesthetic learners through lectures, visual demonstrations, and hands-on activities. The first module introduces the fundamentals of the binary number system. The second is focused on networks, protocols, and algorithms. The third centers on sensors, sensor networks, and their significance in today's high-tech society. Although the modules are designed to enable incremental, independent adoption, together they form a coherent thread of instruction.

We have piloted the first two curriculum components and supporting toys in a variety of contexts over the past three years, reaching more than 340 students. The third is new; it will be individually piloted in the current semester. Evaluation results for the first two modules show that they are having a positive impact, both in terms of content understanding and attitudes toward the discipline [8, 9]. We made minor modifications to the first two modules, added the third module, and piloted the combined program with over 170 students. Evaluation results indicate the combined program is having a positive impact. In this paper, we summarize the outreach program, discuss our experiences piloting it, and summarize key evaluation results.

2. RELATED WORK

We first review efforts to teach the binary number system. Sarkar et al. [21, 22] describe a variety of kinesthetic activities designed to introduce students to computer organization based on the PIC microcontroller, as well as the importance of binary numbers in computing. Their activities differ from ours in that student interaction involves writing a desktop program to turn on a display of light emitting diodes (LEDs). Further, their work does not cover arithmetic. Sakala et al. [20] describe a software tool to teach the binary number system, with a focus on conversion from decimal to binary. We rely on a physical manipulative. Goldschmidt et al. [12] describe how to count in binary using rhythm in physical education. Similiar to this group, we use lectures and activities to teach alternative number systems. CS Unplugged [5] uses games to teach computer science concepts. The binary games focus on counting with binary and relating the importance of binary to computer science. Our module also considers the importance of binary in computing, along with converting binary numbers and performing arithmetic.

Next, we review efforts related to teaching networks, protocols, and algorithms. CS Unplugged [5] includes an activity that requires students to complete a task by following instructions given by their peers. This activity emphasizes the importance of developing step-by-step instructions for computers to follow. Another activity, *Muddy City–Minimal Spanning Trees*, introduces the fundamentals of networking concepts. Each of these modules involves playing games, whereas our modules rely on instruction aided by physical computing manipulatives. Computing Science Inside [4] offers modules designed to teach basic networking and algorithm concepts. Their curriculum focuses on the importance of protocols and algorithms for proper computer network operation. Although many of the concepts are similar to ours, our approach relies on hands-on activities with an embedded device, rather than paper and pencil exercises. Resnick et al. [18] discuss four digital manipulatives used in K-12 outreach. These include LEGO Programmable Bricks, Programmable Beads, BitBall, and Thinking Tags. Participants are tasked with writing programs to control the actuators on the manipulatives. Our goal is to teach specific networking concepts, while at the same time allowing students to play, explore, and ask questions.

Finally, we review efforts to teach basic concepts of sensors and sensor networks. Saad et al. [13,19] discuss a three-year project comprising a series of workshops and summer camps for 90 teachers and 120 students. The curriculum covers concepts such as data acquisition, trasmission, and analysis, as well as an introduction to web development. This program differs from our work in that their curriculum is web-based, whereas ours is taught in the classroom and includes hands-on activities. Baker et al. [1] discuss the development of a series of curriculum modules for teachers to use to teach middle school students engineering and technology concepts. One of the modules uses LEGO Mindstorm® NXT robots to teach students about touch sensors, light sensors, and RFID

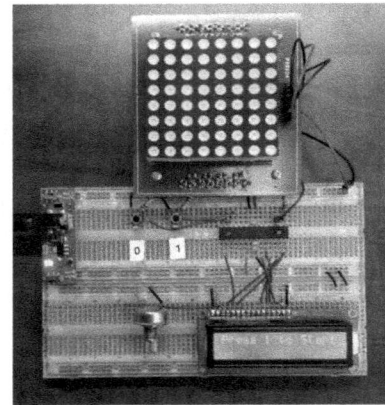

Figure 1: Binary Toy

sensors. This work concentrates on the application of sensors, whereas we concentrate on how sensors work. Dabney et al. [6] use the sensors on a smartphone to introduce programming through mobile application development. Again, this program focuses on creating applications that use sensors, whereas our program teaches how sensors work and how to create networks of sensors.

3. PROGRAM

In this section, we describe the three curriculum modules and summarize the combined program. The first two modules and preliminary evaluation results are reported in [8,9]. Each module spans two 60 minute sessions, depending on participants' class schedule. The first session includes a lecture facilitated by a series of questions and demonstrations designed to engage students. The second provides hands-on activities using the toys, designed to reinforce the specific concepts being taught.

3.1 Binary Number System Module

Understanding the binary number system is fundamental to computer science. Although it is often one of the first concepts taught in many CS1 courses, binary is largely perceived as not being fun to teach or learn. We have developed a module to teach the binary number system that is both informative and fun.

3.1.1 Toy Architecture

The embedded toy, shown in Figure 1, has all the necessary components of a basic computer – an input device, an output device, and two processors. The input device consists of two tactile buttons. The output device consists of an 8x8 LED display and an LCD screen. An ATMega168 and an ATMega8515 provide processing for the embedded toy. The tactile buttons are connected to the ATMega168 microcontroller. When a button is pressed, the change is detected and the information transmitted to the ATMega8515, which drives the display.

3.1.2 Day One: Lecture

We begin with a basic review of the base-10 number system. Using ten fingers, we illustrate that base-10 can represent 9 objects before a new digit column is added. We further illustrate that ten groups of ten objects requires a third column to be added, and so on. Using this same setup, but with only two fingers, we ask students how high they could count before needing to add a new column, based on an approach described in [11]. Next, we introduce the process of converting a decimal number to binary through item grouping. We then give students several small numbers to convert using the grouping method. We explain that while using this form of conversion is interesting and easy, it is not feasible to use with larger numbers. We then teach students how to convert decimal numbers to binary by dividing by 2, drawing parallels between conversion using the grouping method and conversion by division. Next, we teach students the process of adding and subtracting binary numbers. To provide additional practice, we provide students with various conversion, addition, and subtraction problems, inviting volunteers to complete the problems on the board. We conclude with a discussion of the importance of binary numbers in computer science.

3.1.3 Day Two: Activity

We begin the second day with a review of the previous day's lecture, and then introduce the embedded toy. Students are divided into groups of two or three and tasked with several conversion, addition, and subtraction problems. They are asked to verify their work using the embedded toy. Once the students demonstrate competence using the toy, we provide a worksheet with various problems and randomly choose a problem from the worksheet for each group to complete. The first group to complete the assigned problem correctly is rewarded with candy.

The toy consists of an 8x8 LED matrix and an LCD screen, shown in Figure 1. To verify their answers to the assigned problems, students must enter the binary representation of the decimal numbers in the first two rows of the LED matrix, using the tactile buttons labeled "1" and "0". After each operand has been entered, students enter the desired mathematical operation; '11' represents addition, and '10' represents subtraction. Upon entering the expected answer, the device displays the correct answer on the adjacent line, allowing students to verify their solution. The LCD screen provides step-by-step instructions, as well as a message concerning the correctness of the answers entered.

3.2 Networks, Protocols, and Algorithm

Networks have been essential to society for thousands of years. The human body is a network of organs. The mail service, connecting people worldwide, has roots dating back to 2400 B.C., when the Egyptian Pharaohs deployed a network of couriers to deliver written communications [10]. Today, the mere mention of a network brings to mind computers, the Internet, and a range of social networks. Recognizing the importance of networks in our society, networks, protocols, and algorithms are fundamental topics.

3.2.1 Toy Architecture

The serious toy is a small computer built on stackable printed circuit boards, inspired by the MoteStack design [7]. It consists of three layers: power, control, and sensing, as shown in Figure 2. **The power (bottom) layer** is used to provide power and interconnectivity to the toy. To allow devices to be connected, forming a network, each device has four sets of headers, female for power and data, and male for ground. **The control (middle) layer** uses an ATMega168 microcontroller to run the network protocols and algorithms, providing computation support to the toy. Three LEDs (red, green and yellow) are used to display the current status of the toy. **The sensor (top) layer** is used to collect data

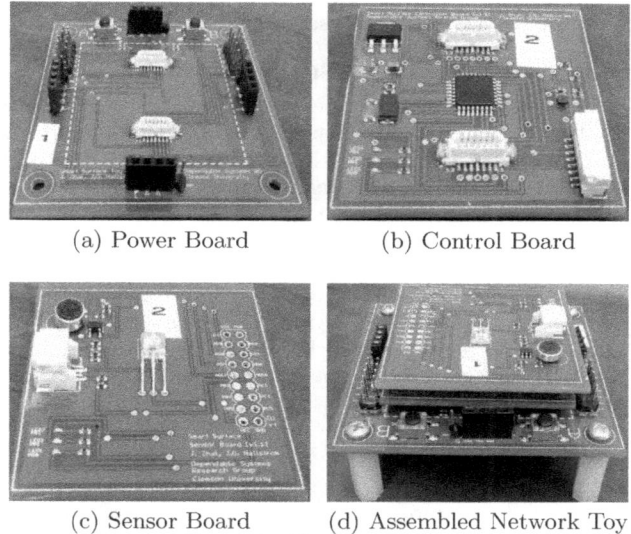

(a) Power Board   (b) Control Board

(c) Sensor Board   (d) Assembled Network Toy

Figure 2: Network Toy

that will be transmitted through the established network. It consists of a galvanic skin response sensor, a broad spectrum photosensor, and a microphone.

3.2.2 Day One: Lecture

We start our lecture by asking students to name a familiar network. The answers range from the Internet to families. We then ask students about the criteria they used to identify these networks. Student responses typically convey the idea that a network is formed when a group of entities communicate with each other. We use their responses to discuss the importance of communication and the communication medium in a network. Next, we discuss how the Internet works by first showing an example of how mail is forwarded from a sender to a receiver, explaining the role of post offices and discussing mail forwarding criteria. We then substitute post offices with routers and explain that the Internet works in a similar fashion. Continuing the above analogy, using first the postal service, then the Internet, we discuss the definition of a protocol and an algorithm, as well as their importance in computing. The last portion of our lecture involves a discussion of centralized and distributed networks. We discuss the benefits and problems associated with each approach and conclude by inviting questions.

3.2.3 Day Two: Activities

The second day begins with a review of the previous day's lecture. We divide the students into two groups. Each group participates in two activities designed to reinforce the concepts discussed in the lecture. In the first activity, students are given a set of embedded devices and jumpers, instructed how to connect the devices, and tasked with forming a network. We explain that the toys are communicating with each other using a wired medium and are following a protocol created specifically for this network. The activity provides several teaching opportunities and invokes a wave of questions from students. The second activity demonstrates the importance of providing clear step-by-step instructions in an algorithm. First, a student is designated as a "robot" and blindfolded. Next, a maze is created using desks and chairs. The remaining students are then tasked with defining three tasks the robot can perform – step, turn left, and turn right. Taking turns, the students guide the robot, using only the defined instructions, through the maze.

3.3 Sensors and Sensor Networks

The use of sensors has become pervasive. Virtually all appliances in our homes, business, and schools are equipped with one or more sensors. Networks of sensors are used in a wide variety of applications, spanning home and medical monitoring [2], military applications [15], and environmental management [7]. Just as the human body is a network of organs, it is also a network of sensors. To name a few, the human eye reacts to light, the ear to vibrations, and the nose to vapors. Observing the value of sensors in computing, and building on the Networks, Protocols, and Algorithms module, we chose the concept of sensors and sensor networks for the topic of this module.

3.3.1 Sensor Network Architecture

Our sensor system is designed to collect, transmit, and display data. Sensors made by the students are connected to a set of MoteStacks, which read voltage changes corresponding to changes in environmental parameters. To transmit data, each MoteStack is equipped with a GPRS-enabled cellular board, allowing students to deploy their sensors in either indoor or outdoor environments. The collected data is transmitted to our data center using the cellular network. The data center processes and saves the received data in a database. Sensor observations collected from different sensors are identified by unique IDs assigned to the sensors. A customized website is used to retrieve the saved data from the database and display the data in the form of graphs. Each group of students can track the data collected from their sensors by selecting their sensor ID on the website.

3.3.2 Day One

We begin by asking students to identify familiar sensors, and then discuss their responses. We ask students to consider simple sensors in the human body – eyes, ears, nose. This discussion leads to the question of what sensors are used for – namely, to detect change. Using two common sensors as examples, temperature and motion, we examine the basics of how sensors work, discussing questions that arise from students. We demonstrate the value of sensors to society by discussing several applications – in agriculture, water conservation, and automotives. We provide a short demonstration of a motion sensor that activates a piezo buzzer when motion is detected, a demonstration of a galvanic skin response sensor, and conclude by assisting students in making a simple soil moisture sensor from plaster of paris, nails, and a straw, as adapted from [3].

3.3.3 Day Two

Day two begins with completing and testing each of the soil moisture sensors by connecting the probes of a multimeter to the nails in the sensor, inserting the sensor in a cup of dry soil, slowly adding water, and observing the change in resistance on the multimeter. The next step involves connecting each sensor to a MoteStack, inserting the sensor probe in various degrees of moist soil, and observing the readings using our web-based application. This exercise provides the opportunity to discuss i) how the MoteStacks collect data, ii) how data is transmitted to the data center, and iii) how data is retrieved and displayed by the website. Weather permitting, this exercise takes place outdoors; otherwise, containers of soil are provided for use in the classroom. This activity provides a natural opportunity to review the information taught in the Networks, Protocols, and Algorithms module.

3.4 Combined Program

The modules are designed to be adopted independently, or combined to form a coherent thread of instruction. Depending on participants' class schedule, the combined program spans 8-10 days. Local middle school class periods are shorter than local high school class periods – 40 minutes for middle schoolers, and 70 minutes for high schoolers.

We begin with the Binary Number System module, followed by the Networks, Protocols, and Algorithms module, and finally, the Sensors and Sensor Networks module. On the first day of the program, we introduce ourselves and administer the pre-evaluation instruments described in Section 5. The last day of the program begins with a short review of each module, a discussion on careers in CS, and administration of the post-evaluation instruments. Finally, students are given a final hands-on opportunity to play with, explore, and ask questions about the "serious toys".

4. PILOT GROUPS

We piloted the combined modules with six groups from a local middle school, and one group from a local high school.

4.1 Local Middle School

The participating middle school is the largest in the state, with approximately 1,350 students. During 2013, the middle school achieved an overall rank of "Good", indicating that its performance exceeds the standards for the state's "2020 Performance Vision". The vision states that by "2020, all students will graduate with the knowledge and skills necessary to compete successfully in the global economy, participate in a democratic society, and contribute positively as members of families and communities" [16]. The pilot group consisted of two classes each from the sixth, seventh, and eighth grades. The pilot group was chosen from a technology exploratory course. The two sixth grade classes were participants in an "Introduction to Careers" study, where students explore careers in STEM fields. The remaining seventh and eighth grade pilot groups were participants in "Gateway to Technology", which provides an introduction to various topics in engineering, including robotics, 3D modeling, and other topics.

4.2 Local High School

The participating high school is one unit within a K-12 charter school system, a nonprofit public school system operating within the local public school district. The participating school qualifies as a Title 1 school, with a high percentage of at-risk students. The school system has approximately 800 students, with 95% of the students living in poverty. The pilot group consisted of eighth, ninth, and tenth grade students chosen from a geometry course.

5. EVALUATION

The combined modules were piloted with the local middle and high schools during the fall of 2013. The evaluation instruments consisted of pre- and post-surveys, pre- and post-quizzes, and supplemental quizzes introduced after the completion of each module.

Survey Statements	6A pre	6A post	6B pre	6B post	7A pre	7A post	7B pre	7B post	8A pre	8A post	8B pre	8B post	HS pre	HS post
S1	—	3.14	—	3.65	—	4.46	—	3.83	—	3.8	—	3.45	—	4.44
S2	3	2.81	2.94	3.06	4.21	4.29	3.67	3.71	2.85	3.65	2.95	3.85	3.31	3.94
S3	3.14	**4.76**	2.88	4	3.67	4.17	1.91	**4.30**	2.3	**4.45**	2.8	**4.6**	2.5	**5.31**
S4	2.41	**4.52**	2.41	**4.06**	3	**4.3**	1.96	**4.5**	2.05	**4.5**	2.5	**4.5**	2.31	**5.31**
S5	2.91	**4.52**	3.29	**4.35**	3.417	**4.67**	3	**4.46**	2.6	**4.45**	3.1	**4.65**	2.88	**5.44**
S6	3.33	**4.48**	3.83	4.5	3.83	**4.58**	3.58	4.04	2.52	**4.8**	2.9	**4.95**	3	**5.19**
S7	4	4.38	3.77	4.65	4.04	4.67	3.25	**4.46**	2.95	**4.7**	3.19	**4.75**	3.13	**5.19**
S8	3.62	**4.95**	3.81	**4.94**	4.04	4.67	3.71	4.13	3	**4.3**	3.	**4.75**	3.12	**5.19**
Quiz	43.6	**67.5**	38.6	**83.3**	43.7	54.8	43.3	**64.**	43.5	**76.8**	41.7	**75.**	55.2	**91.7**

Table 1: Local Middle and High School Pre-/Post-Survey and Quiz Results

Listing 1 (Pre-/Post-Survey Statements):

1. I would like to attend more outreach programs related to CS.
2. I might be interested in majoring in Computer Science in college.
3. I think I understand the importance of binary numbers in CS.
4. I think I understand the concept of a binary numbering system.
5. I think I know the definitions of a network, a protocol, and an algorithm.
6. I think I understand the importance of networks, protocols, and algorithms in CS.
7. I Think I understand the importance of sensors and sensor networks in CS.
8. I think I understand what sensors are used for.

Listing 1: Pre-/Post-Survey Statements

Participants	6A	6B	7A	7B	8A	8B	Total
First Day	23	22	26	29	29	26	155
Last Day	21	17	24	24	20	20	126
Special Consid.	3	2	3	4	6	2	20

Table 2: Middle School Participation Information

Module	6A	6B	7A	7B	8A	8B	HS
Binary	57	63	60	64	74	62	79
Network	83	62	68	66	76	73	79
Sensors	53	51	48	63	56	55	58
Revised Sensor	67	57	59	80	70	61	90

Table 3: Supplemental Quiz Averages

The survey was designed to determine student attitudes toward CS, and students' self-efficacy with respect to their understanding of the material covered. It consisted of Likert-style statements, shown in Listing 1. Students were asked to rate their level of agreement by choosing from *strongly disagree, disagree, moderately disagree, moderately agree, agree, and strongly agree*, weighted from 1-6, with 1 being *strongly disagree*. All quizzes consisted of true/false and multiple choice questions designed to evaluate student understanding of the material covered. The pre- and post-quiz consisted of 8 questions, 3 pertaining to The Binary Number System module, 3 pertaining to the Network, Protocols, and Algorithms module, and 2 pertaining to the Sensors and Sensor Networks module. The additional quizzes administered after the completion of each module consisted of 6-8 questions specific to the module.

Table 1 summarizes the results of a statistical analysis of students' pre- and post-survey responses, as well as the pre- and post-quiz scores. The first column of the table refers to the statements found in Listing 1. The second, fourth, sixth, eighth, tenth, and twelfth columns list the average scores for the pre-survey and quiz for the middle school pilot groups. The third, fifth, seventh, ninth, eleventh, and thirteenth columns list the average scores for the middle school post-survey and quiz. Column fourteen lists the average scores for the pre-survey and quiz for the high school pilot group, and column fifteen lists the post-survey and quiz averages. The post averages shown in bold represent statistically significant increases between the pre- and post-survey and quiz responses. To determine statistical significance, a two sample F-test was performed to determine if the variance was equal. Depending on the variance determination, the appropriate t-test was performed to determine if the changes between the pre- and post data sets were significant (p-value = 5%). Survey statements 1 and 2 measure student attitudes toward CS. The remaining six statements measure students' self-efficacy with respect to their understanding of the material covered.

5.1 Local Middle School

The middle school classes are referred to by their grade and class section; e.g., 6A refers to sixth grade, section A. Table 2 shows that 155 participants completed the pre-survey and quiz, and 126 participants completed the post-survey and quiz. Survey and quiz results were only considered if participants completed both pre and post instruments. Table 2 also indicates that there were 20 participants identified by the school as needing special learning considerations. The evaluation process was anonymous; therefore, these students received no additional help completing the pre- and post-survey, the pre- and post-quiz, or the supplemental content quizzes.

Interest in Computer Science. Statement 1 concerns the outreach program and could not be answered until completion of the program; only post-survey data was considered. As shown in Table 1, the average scores were mostly positive, ranging from 3.14 to 4.46, with a median of 4 (moderately agree) or above for all groups except 6A. Statement 2, designed to gauge student interest in CS as a career choice, indicated an increase for all groups except 6A; none of the changes were significant, however.

Content Understanding. Three evaluation instruments were used to gauge students' content understanding. First, pre- and post-surveys measured student self-efficacy with respect to their understanding of the material. Table 1 shows that statements 3-8 indicated an increase in content understanding across all groups, with 78% (28 out of 36) of the average scores being statistically significant. Pre- and post-quiz averages were used to measure content understanding.

The post-quiz averages increased across all groups, with 83% (5 out of 6) of the average scores being statistically significant. Finally, table 3 summarizes the average scores across the six groups. Table 3 shows that most of the supplemental quiz averages for the Sensors and Sensor Networks were lower than the Binary Number System and the Networks, Protocols, and Algorithms supplemental quiz averages. Further investigation revealed that there were two questions on the Sensors and Sensor Networks supplemental content quizzes that most of the students answered incorrectly. It was determined that these questions were ambiguous; therefore the averages were re-calculated excluding these two questions. As shown in Table 3, the scores increased on average, across the six groups, by 11 points. Considering that approximately 13% of the students participating on the first day of the pilot had special learning needs, we believe the average scores, across all groups, are mostly positive.

5.2 Local High School

The high school pilot class, HS, had a total of 17 students, with 16 completing both the pre- and post- surveys and the quiz: 2 eighth, 11 ninth, and 3 tenth grade student participants.

Interest in Computer Science. Post-survey data was only considered for statement 1. Table 1 shows that students, on average, would like to participate in more CS outreach. Though not statistically significant, their interest in CS increased. The post average for statement 2 was 3.9 (median score of 4). A closer examination of the data indicated 10 out of 16 students' post responses were 4 or higher, compared to 8 out of 16 pre responses. This is an indication of an increase in student interest in majoring in CS in college.

Content Understanding. Similar evaluation instruments were used to gauge student content understanding. Table 1 shows that post-survey statements 3-8 indicated a statistically significant increase in students' self-efficacy with respect to their understanding of the material taught. The pre- and post-quiz averages also indicated a statistically significant increase. Finally, as shown in Table 3, the average scores for the quizzes administered after the completion of each module indicated students understood the material taught. As with the middle school pilot groups, most of the HS students incorrectly answered one or both of the two ambiguous questions on the sensor quiz. Again, these questions were discarded, increasing the average score by 38%.

6. CONCLUSION

The lack of K-12 computing curriculum in the United States during a time when computer technology is becoming increasingly important across disciplines is troubling. Recognizing this deficit, we have developed a series of curriculum modules that use "serious toys", embedded computing manipulatives, to introduce K-12 students to computing concepts. The modules include visual demonstrations, lectures, and hands-on activities to engage students of all learning styles. We have summarized each module, discussed the combined program, and presented evaluation results from two pilots of the combined program with more than 170 students. The evaluation results from the combined pilots are largely positive.

Although the results of the attitudinal statements pertaining to CS as a career mostly increased, the average scores are slightly less than 4, indicating disagreement. We are exploring enhancements to the modules that may increase students' interest in computer science as a career. We acknowledge, however, the difficulty associated with achieving attitudinal shifts without prolonged student engagement.

Acknowledgments

This work was supported by the National Science Foundation through awards CNS-0745846 and DUE-1022941. Yvon Feaster is an NSF Graduate Research Fellow, DGE-0751278.

7. REFERENCES

[1] J. Baker et al. Application of Wireless Technology in K-12 STEM Outreach Programs in Middle Schools. In *APSURSI, 2010 IEEE*, pages 1–4, 2010.

[2] D. Basu et al. Wireless Sensor Network Based Smart Home: Sensor Selection, Deployment and Monitoring. In *SAS, IEEE*, pages 49–54, Feb 2013.

[3] G. Branwyn. No-cost soil moisture sensor. makezine.com/2009/03/04/nocost-soil-moisture-sensor/. (*last access*).

[4] CS Inside. csi.dcs.gla.ac.uk/index.php. (*last access*).

[5] CS Unplugged. www.csunplugged.org. (*last access*).

[6] M. Dabney et al. No Sensor Left Behind: Enriching Computing Education with Mobile Devices. SIGCSE '13, pages 627–632, New York, NY, USA, 2013. ACM.

[7] G. Eidson et al. The south carolina digital watershed: End to end support for real time management of water resources. *IJDSN*, 2010, 2010.

[8] Y. Feaster et al. Serious Toys: Teaching The Binary Number System. ITiCSE '12, pages 262–267, New York, NY, USA, 2012.

[9] Y. Feaster and others. Serious Toys II: Teaching Networks, Protocols, and Algorithms. ITiCSE '13, pages 273–278, New York, NY, USA, 2013. ACM.

[10] C. Federal Internet Law and Policy An Educational Project. Postal Service. http://www.cybertelecom.org/notes/usps.htm, 2013. (*last access*).

[11] R. Garlikov. The socratic method teaching by asking instead of by telling. www.garlikov.com, 2011. (*last access*).

[12] D. Goldschmidt et al. An interdisciplinary approach to injecting computer science into the K-12 classroom. *Journal of Computing Sciences in Colleges*, 26(6):78–85, 2011.

[13] L. He et al. Information Technology Education for K-12 Students and Teachers: From Sensor Network to Comprehensive and Customized Web Interaction. SIGITE '08, pages 65–70, New York, NY, USA, 2008. ACM.

[14] D. Hernandez et al. Double Jeopardy How Third-Grade Reading Skills and Poverty Influence High School Graduation. www.aecf.org. (*last access*).

[15] K. Kumar. IMCC protocol in heterogeneous wireless sensor network for high quality data transmission in military applications. In *1st International Conference on Parallel Distributed and Grid Computing (PDGC)*, pages 339–343, October 2010.

[16] G. Middle School. 2011 report card. gms.pickens.k12.cs.us/. (*last access*).

[17] A. Paul. Why Third Grade Is So Important: The Matthew Effect. ideas.time.com/2012/09/26/why-third-grade-is-so-important-the-matthew-effect.

[18] M. Resnick et al. Digital manipulatives: New toys to think with. In *CHI*, pages 281–287, 1998.

[19] A. Saad et al. Ossabest: A Comprehensive ITEST Project for Middle and High School Teachers and Students. SIGITE '08, pages 71–76, New York, NY, USA, 2008. ACM.

[20] L. Sakala et al. The use of expert systems has improved students learning in zimbabwe. *Journal of Sustainable Development in Africa*, 12(3):1–13, 2010.

[21] N. Sarka and T. Craig. Teaching computer hardware and organisation using pic-based projects. *IJEEE*, 43(2):150–312, 2006.

[22] N. Sarka and T. Craig. A low-cost pic unit for teaching computer hardware fundamentals to undergraduates. *inroads - The SIGCSE Bulletin*, 39(2):88–91, 2007.

[23] C. Wilson et al. Running on Eempty: The Failure to Teach k-12 Computer Science in the Ddigital Age. www.acm.org. (*last access*).

[24] J. M. Wing. Computational thinking. *Commun. ACM*, 49(3):33–35, Mar. 2006.

The Magic of Algorithm Design and Analysis

Teaching Algorithmic Skills using Magic Card Tricks

João F. Ferreira
School of Computing   HASLab/INESC TEC
Teesside University   Universidade do Minho
Middlesbrough, UK   Braga, Portugal
joao@joaoff.com

Alexandra Mendes
Faculty of Arts
York St John University
York, UK
a.mendes@yorksj.ac.uk

ABSTRACT

We describe our experience using magic card tricks to teach algorithmic skills to first-year Computer Science undergraduates. We illustrate our approach with a detailed discussion on a card trick that is typically presented as a test to the psychic abilities of an audience. We use the trick to discuss concepts like problem decomposition, pre- and post-conditions, and invariants. We discuss pedagogical issues and analyse feedback collected from students. The feedback has been very positive and encouraging.

Categories and Subject Descriptors

K.3.2 [**Computers and Education**]: Computers and Information Science Education—*Computer science education*; F.1.0 [**Computation by abstract devices**]: General

Keywords

Algorithms; Algorithmic Problem Solving; Invariants; Pre/Post-conditions; Hoare Triples; Magic Card Tricks; Puzzles and Games

1. INTRODUCTION

There is a growing number of educators who advocate the use of recreational problems and so-called "unplugged" activities to teach computer science concepts [2, 4, 12]. We have ourselves been using "unplugged" activities for a few years to teach algorithmic problem solving at undergraduate level [7, 8]. Recently, inspired by the engaging work done in the project cs4fn [4, 5, 13, 14], we incorporated magic card tricks into our activities.

In this paper, we describe our experience using magic card tricks to teach algorithmic skills to first-year Computer Science (CS) undergraduates. Our main contribution is to show how more formality can be added to the presentation of card tricks so that they can be presented at university level (this was suggested as future work in [4]). We enrich the contribution by including some pedagogical comments and by discussing feedback provided by the students.

We start in Section 2, where we discuss in detail a card trick that is typically presented as a test to the psychic abilities of an audience. The trick was taken from [14], a booklet on magic tricks that

has been used to demonstrate computer science concepts to school students. After we describe the trick, we present a detailed explanation of why it works, highlighting the algorithmic techniques used along the way. In Section 3 we discuss some pedagogical considerations that make the teaching of algorithmic skills using card tricks more effective. We have collected feedback from first-year CS undergraduates who attended a learning session based on the trick. We analyse the feedback in Section 4. In Section 5 we present related work and we conclude the paper in Section 6, where we also discuss some of the next steps.

2. ALGORITHMIC CARD TRICKS

Algorithmic card tricks (also called self-working tricks) are tricks that do not involve any hidden mechanisms like rigged decks or double lifts. In other words, if the spectator replicates the *visible* steps performed by the magician, the same (surprising) result will be achieved. Essentially, we can describe algorithmic card tricks as algorithms that manipulate cards. We believe that card tricks are excellent vehicles to teach important algorithmic skills, because:

- Students think about the underlying algorithms on a more abstract level, ignoring implementation and computer language details;

- The kinaesthetic and interactive nature of manipulating cards helps students visualise the algorithms: they can quickly verify properties and test new hypotheses using the cards;

- Students learn that algorithmic problem solving applies to areas outside computer science;

- The recreational nature of card tricks promotes student engagement;

- Card tricks can be used to illustrate important concepts like loops and invariants, assertions, and problem decomposition.

2.1 Example: are you psychic?

In this section, we present a card trick whose analysis and proof of correctness is non-trivial. The trick is typically presented as a test to the psychic abilities of an audience. We analyse the underlying algorithm and show how the card trick can be used to practise problem decomposition and the identification of pre- and post-conditions. The correctness of the algorithm is proved by identifying and formulating two invariants. To describe the trick, we follow the explanation found in [14] (but we include more graphical aids).

2.1.1 Description of the card trick

We start by getting five pairs of cards out of the pack. Any five pairs can be used, but for simplicity, let us choose the five pairs 2♥ 2♠, 3♥ 3♠, 4♥ 4♠, 5♥ 5♠, and 6♥ 6♠.

Next, set the cards up in one ordered pile as shown in Figure 1. Show the pile to the audience and explain that the trick is about to start.

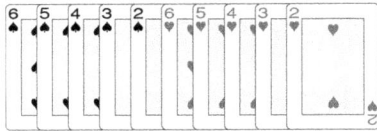

Figure 1: Five pairs of cards as one ordered pile.

To facilitate the explanation of the trick, we explain how to perform it with the faces of the cards up. *However, when performing the trick, the faces should be down!*

Spread the cards in your hand and have the audience point to any card. Split the pack at that point and place the top pile at the bottom of the pack. Repeat this until the audience is happy the cards are well mixed. For example, if the audience points to the four of hearts shown in the left image of Figure 2, the resulting deck is the one on the right image.

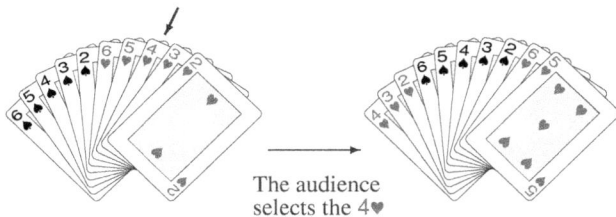

The audience selects the 4♥

Figure 2: Mix the cards until the audience is happy, by cutting the pack at the point selected by the audience.

When the audience is happy the cards are well mixed, deal the top five cards, one at a time, into a pile on the table, thereby reversing their order. Place the remaining undealt cards in a second pile beside them. By putting this second pile straight down you have kept their order the same. For example, from the deck shown in the right image of Figure 2, we get the two piles shown in Figure 3. Please note that the card 5♥ is the top card in the right deck shown in Figure 2. (Remember that when performing the trick, the cards should have their faces down.)

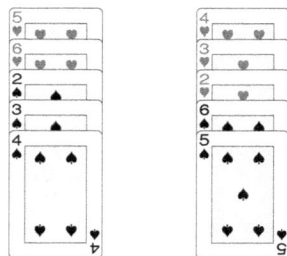

Figure 3: Division into two piles. The left pile contains the top 5 cards of the right deck shown in Figure 2, in reverse order. The right pile contains the remaining cards, in the original order.

Explain to the audience that as there are 5 cards in each pile you will give them 4 chances to use their psychic powers. They can have 4 swaps. A swap involves taking the top card on one of the piles and placing it on the bottom of the same pile. Explain that they can, for example, do all 4 swaps on one pile, 2 on each, or 3 on one and 1 on the other. It is their choice, remembering that their aim is to be left with two matching cards. For example, if the audience chooses to perform 3 swaps on the left pile of Figure 3 and 1 swap on the right pile of Figure 3, the resulting piles are the ones shown in Figure 4.

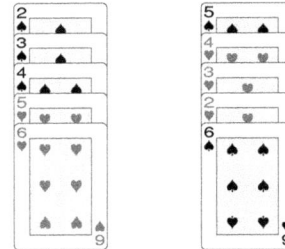

Figure 4: Resulting piles if the audience chooses to perform 3 swaps on the left pile of Figure 3 and 1 swap on the right pile of Figure 3.

Once the 4 swaps are made, remove the top card on each pile and place them aside (with their faces down!). Point out that it does not matter what they are as they are being discarded. Now there are 4 cards in each pile, as shown in Figure 5.

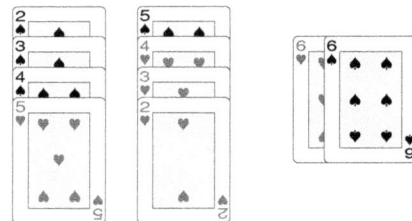

Figure 5: After the top card on each pile is removed, we are left with two piles of 4 cards. We place the two removed cards aside.

At this point, offer the spectator 3 swaps in total, and once the swaps are done remove the top two cards from the piles. There are now three cards left in each pile, so give them two swaps this time, and again remove the top card from both piles. This leaves two cards in each pile. This is their final chance to get it right. Tell the audience that one swap is left, and one card can make all the difference. They choose their swap, and the top two cards from each pile are discarded. Now it is time to reveal the final two single cards left on the table. **They match!** The audience chose freely how to mix the cards and which cards to eliminate, so it was their secret psychic powers that came through to ensure a match at the end. Give their jaw time to drop, then dramatically reveal that all the pairs of cards they removed match in value too.

2.1.2 Discussion and analysis of the trick

This trick can be used to discuss the specification of algorithms (via Hoare triples), the identification of pre- and post-conditions, problem decomposition, and the identification and formulation of invariants [8]. It also provides a good example to discuss the concept of *proof of correctness*, because students are very keen on understanding why the trick works.

In what follows, we explain our approach when presenting the analysis of the trick to first-year CS undergraduates.

Formal specification and abstraction. The first step in the analysis of the algorithm is to specify what it does. Using a *Hoare triple*, a high-level specification can be written as:

{ 10 cards: 2♥ 3♥ 4♥ 5♥ 6♥ 2♠ 3♠ 4♠ 5♠ 6♠ }

perform card trick

{ 1 pair: pile1 = N ∧ pile2 = N

where N is the number on a card }

In the description of the trick we referred to both piles as "left" and "right". Here, we name them pile1 and pile2. The expression "pile1=N ∧ pile2=N" means that pile1 and pile2 both contain one card with the number N; we use the conjunction operator ∧ to denote "and". The expressions between curly brackets correspond to assertions. An expression of the form { P } S { Q } where P and Q are predicates and S is a program statement (i.e., an algorithm) is called a *Hoare triple*. It means that if P is true before the execution of the statement S, execution of S is guaranteed to terminate in a state where property Q is true. We are stating that when we start the trick with the 10 cards 2♥ 3♥ 4♥ 5♥ 6♥ 2♠ 3♠ 4♠ 5♠ 6♠ we are always guaranteed to terminate with 1 pair of cards with the same number.

An important algorithmic skill is the avoidance of unnecessary detail, so we start by observing that the suits of the cards are irrelevant and the trick works with any five pairs. We can thus abstract from the specific cards used and be more general by introducing variable names to represent arbitrary cards:

{ 10 cards: $ABCDE\,ABCDE$ }

perform card trick

{ 1 pair: pile1 = N ∧ pile2 = N

where N is the number on a card }

There are many (and possibly better) choices for expressing the pre- and the post-condition. The one we use was tested and works well with first-year CS undergraduates.

Problem decomposition. Now that we have a high-level specification, a reasonable step is to decompose the problem into simpler components. The algorithm can be decomposed into three main parts: the "shuffling" process, where the audience chooses how to mix the cards; the division into two different piles; and finally, the part where multiple swaps are performed. We can express this decomposition as follows:

{ 10 cards: $ABCDE\,ABCDE$ }

shuffle

{ ? };

divide into two piles

{ ? };

perform swaps

{ 1 pair: pile1 = N ∧ pile2 = N

where N is the number on a card }

The goal now is to characterise the assertions marked with "?". We investigate each part separately.

The specification and decomposition of the problem are obtained through an interactive discussion with the entire classroom. For the remaining steps of the analysis, the students work together in small groups.

Shuffling step. In the first part of the algorithm, we ask the audience to point to any card and we split the pack at that point, placing the top pile at the bottom of the pack. We repeat this until the audience is happy the cards are well mixed. Figure 2 shows how the initial pack changes when the audience selects the four of hearts. The figure also shows that the cards are indeed mixed, that is, the order of the cards changes. However, there is a key property being maintained by this mixing process: *the top five cards match the bottom five cards*. In other words, the sequence of numbers corresponding to the top five cards is the same as the sequence of numbers corresponding to the bottom five cards. This can be easily observed in the right image of Figure 2, where the top five cards are 5♥ 6♥ 2♠ 3♠ 4♠ and the bottom five cards are 5♠ 6♠ 2♥ 3♥ 4♥.

This property is also satisfied by the initial configuration (shown in the left image of Figure 2). Since the mixing process corresponds to a finite sequence of rotations, the property will clearly be maintained. In other words, it does not matter how many times the pack is rotated, the top five cards will always match the bottom five cards.

We can thus conclude that an invariant of the mixing process is: *the top five cards match the bottom five cards*. A simple way to specify this invariant is as follows:

{ 10 cards: *the top five cards match the bottom five cards* }

shuffle

{ 10 cards: *the top five cards match the bottom five cards* }

We can avoid the use of natural language and be more consistent with the pre-condition written above, by introducing five new variables A', B', C', D', E':

{ 10 cards: $ABCDE\,ABCDE$ }

shuffle

{ 10 cards: $A'B'C'D'E'\,A'B'C'D'E'$ }

The introduction of new variables is necessary because we do not know what will be the first card in the sequence; nevertheless, we are certain that the top five cards will match the bottom five.

Creating two piles. When the audience is happy the cards are well mixed, we deal the top five cards, one at a time, into a pile on the table, thereby reversing their order. We then place the remaining undealt cards in a second pile beside them. By putting this second pile straight down we keep their order the same. For example, from the deck shown in the right image of Figure 2, we get the two piles shown in Figure 3. It is easy to see that these piles are reverses of each other. A simple way to specify this is:

{ 10 cards: $A'B'C'D'E'\,A'B'C'D'E'$ }

divide into two piles

{ 10 cards: pile1 = $E'D'C'B'A'$ ∧ pile2 = $A'B'C'D'E'$ }

A more compact and formal way of writing the post-condition is as follows:

{ 10 cards: $A'B'C'D'E'\,A'B'C'D'E'$ }

divide into two piles

{ 10 cards: pile1[k] = pile2[$4-k$], for $0 \le k \le 4$ }

The expression pile1[k] denotes the kth card of pile1. We start counting at 0, so pile1[0] corresponds to the top card of pile1. Using this notation and naming the piles in Figure 3 as pile1 and pile2, we observe, for example, that pile1[0]=**4**=pile2[4 − 0] and pile1[4]=**5**=pile2[4 − 4].

Performing swaps. The last step of the algorithm consists of an iterative process, where a number of swaps are done and the size of the two piles is reduced until the piles only have one card each. We start with two piles of the same size (that are reverses of each other) and we keep reducing the size of both piles by 1. Initially, in the first iteration, each pile contains 5 cards, so the audience has to perform 4 swaps. One card is removed from each pile, meaning that in the second iteration each pile contains 4 cards and the audience has to perform 3 swaps. More generally, if at a given iteration each pile contains n cards, the audience has to perform $n-1$ swaps. This can be modelled more precisely (but still at a high-level) as follows:

$\{$ 10 cards: pile1[k] = pile2[4−k], for $0 \leq k \leq 4$ $\}$

    swaps := 4 ;

    do swaps ≥ 1 $\rightarrow$

        Ask for number j where $0 \leq j \leq$ *swaps* ;

        Swap j cards in pile1 ;

        Swap *swaps−j* cards in pile2 ;

        Remove the top card from each pile ;

        swaps := *swaps−*1

    od

$\{$ 1 pair: pile1 = N $\wedge$ pile2 = N

where N is the number on a card $\}$

We write *do swaps* $\geq 1 \rightarrow$ $\cdots$ *od* to express a loop that executes while *swaps* ≥ 1. So, the loop terminates (and the trick ends) when no more swaps can be performed. Let us focus now on the step where cards are swapped. The step "*Swap j cards in* pile1" puts the card pile1[j] at the top of pile1, without affecting the relative order of the other cards. Similarly, the step "*Swap swaps−j cards in* pile2" puts the card pile2[*swaps−j*] at the top of pile2, without affecting the relative order of the other cards. As a result, after the swaps, the top cards on pile1 and pile2 are, respectively, pile1[j] and pile2[*swaps−j*]. We can easily observe this in the transition from Figure 3 to Figure 4. In Figure 3, we have pile1[3] = 6♥ and pile2[1] = **6♠**. The two piles shown in Figure 4 are formed after the audience chooses to perform 3 swaps on the left pile (pile1) of Figure 3 and 1 swap on the right pile (pile2) of Figure 3. We can see that the cards 6♥ and 6♠ are now at the top; moreover, the relative order of the other cards is maintained.

Given that the initial value of *swaps* is 4, we conclude from the pre-condition that pile1[j] = pile2[*swaps−j*]. As a result, after the swaps are performed the top cards of both piles form a pair. So, after the step "*Remove the top card from each pile*", a pair is removed and the resulting piles are reverses of each other. This means that an invariant of the loop is the property that the piles are reverses of each other. Given that the value of *swaps* is decreased, we can formulate the invariant as

pile1[k] = pile2[*swaps−k*], for $0 \leq k \leq$ *swaps* .

As discussed before, the invariant is valid initially when each pile contains 5 cards. We have just discussed that the invariant is valid after each iteration, when the size of each pile decreases by 1. Therefore, the invariant will be valid on termination when each pile contains 1 card. So, on termination we will have two piles with one card each that are reverses of each other. This means that the two remaining cards must match! More formally, we observe that the final value of *swaps* is 0, so we can conclude immediately from the invariant that pile1[0] = pile2[0].

Further discussion. The formulation of the last step can be simplified by not introducing the variable *swaps*, because *swaps* can be determined by the number of cards in the piles. However, when presenting the trick, we feel that the introduction of variable *swaps* facilitates discussion; it also provides the opportunity to discuss program transformation: we often ask the students how can we rewrite the algorithm without using that variable.

As mentioned above, we target first-year CS undergraduates. For that reason, we avoid formalisms that students are not familiar with. If we were teaching more advanced students, we could use modular arithmetic to express the key properties of the algorithm and write more formal proofs of correctness.

3. PEDAGOGICAL COMMENTS

Although, in our experience, the recreational nature of card tricks naturally promotes student engagement, learning sessions still need to be planned considering psychological constraints on learning. In particular, sessions are more effective acknowledging that a) the attention of students is typically maintained for about 10 to 15 minutes, after which learning drops off rapidly; b) a change of activity every 15 minutes restores performance almost to the original level; and c) a period of consolidation at the end of the session greatly enhances retention [3].

We observed that the introduction of group work in the sessions on magic tricks contributes to their effectiveness. It is known that group work promotes active involvement and deep learning, mainly because it increases the amount of time that students spend thinking about conceptual ideas [16], encouraging discussion and negotiation of ideas and meaning. As stated in [17], "*having to achieve practical outcomes as a group can lead to more understanding of processes due to having to plan explicitly, articulate and agree the next steps forward*". Moreover, an important aspect of group work is that *reflective aspects are sharpened because students readily identify each other's learning in a way they do not with top-down teacher-directed learning* [3]. As part of a formal peer-review system, one of the sessions where we present the card trick described in the previous section was observed by another academic member of staff. In her written comments, the observer confirmed that engagement was positive: "*Good student involvement and engagement from the start [...]*" and "*From where I was sitting (at the back) all students appeared engaged in the task*".

The observer also wrote that "*students responded well to questions*". Our sessions are normally structured around questions (e.g., it is very common to start the discussion with the question "How can we specify this algorithm?" or "How can we decompose the problem into simpler and smaller problems?"). As [16] suggests, this gives the students the opportunity to exercise responsible choice in the method and content of study. Moreover, because often students suggest multiple correct ways of tackling the problem, they decide which path to follow; this gives them ownership of the learning process. Normally, the questions that we ask are *convergent*, i.e., there is a correct (or "best") answer in mind and students are steered towards that answer. This promotes *social construction of knowledge*, where learners *contribute and agree on the structure as it emerges* [3].

4. EVALUATION

We have collected feedback from students to gain a better understanding of their opinion about the use of card tricks for teaching algorithmic skills. As part of a first-year undergraduate module on algorithms and data structures offered at Teesside University, we delivered a one-hour session on the card trick presented in Section 2. All the students enrolled in the module are studying for a BSc in Computer Science. Forty (40) students attended the session. They had the opportunity to work in small groups of two or three students. Each group had one deck of playing cards to replicate the trick.

The feedback was collected through an online, voluntary questionnaire that was completed by 23 students, in their own time outside the classroom. The questionnaire was made of six compulsory and three optional questions. Table 1 shows the first six questions and the average of the results on a Likert scale from 1 to 5, where 1 corresponds to *Strongly Disagree* and 5 corresponds to *Strongly Agree*.

The feedback is positive for all questions: the lowest average score is over 4.2 and the overall average score is a very encouraging 4.4. For questions 1, 4, and 6 there were no negative answers. This clearly suggests that students enjoyed the session and that they would like to have more sessions where card tricks are used to illustrate algorithmic concepts. It is also interesting to see that students found the use of real playing cards helpful to understand the algorithm. For questions 2 and 3, only one student disagreed with the statements. Another student disagreed with the statement in question 5. All other feedback for questions 2, 3, and 5 was either neutral or positive indicating that, although there is still room for improvement, the vast majority of students found the use of a card trick engaging, motivating, and a good way to learn and practise algorithmic skills. It is interesting to note that no student "Strongly disagreed" with any of the statements.

These results are encouraging and a good indication that card tricks are a good vehicle to teach important algorithmic skills.

The remaining three optional questions were more general:

1. *What did you like about this session? (If anything)*
   (19 answers) Several students indicated the interactivity of the session as one of the highlights: "*I enjoyed the interaction, by using objects to explain algorithms*". Some students indicated that the session was entertaining and unique: "*The uniqueness of the session. Nothing else done in this interesting manner*". Being able to "visualise" the algorithm through the card trick seems to be appreciated by several students. One student wrote "*Much more easier as I was able to see exactly how it worked instead of thinking how it worked and trying to get my head around previous tasks*". Other answers regarding the visual aspect of the session included "*The engagement within the lecture, and particularly the visualisation in which helped me understand the algorithm a lot better [sic]*", and "*I like the way that I could see the algorithm working*". Another student wrote "*I liked how well the use of the card trick was explained as the lecturer went through the steps clearly while demonstrating it in a practical way*". One student answered that he liked "*Everything*". In addition, feedback indicates that card tricks can benefit students with certain learning difficulties: "*I liked how I could visually engage with the lecture, having an auditory learning difficulty sometimes affects my ability to fully engage with new material so having a visual aid and something I could use with my hands helped me a lot*".

2. *What did you dislike about this session? (If anything)*
   (10 answers) 7 answers did not point out anything wrong with the session, most answering "*Nothing*" or "*N/A*". One of these 7 students wrote "*I didn't dislike anything really, it helped me understand algorithms a lot more*". One student indicated that it "*Would be nice if there were more cards*"; we cannot be certain, but the student was possibly indicating that each student should be given one deck cards (instead of one deck per group). One considered the session "*a bit fast-paced*". Another one wrote an answer unrelated with the content of the session.

3. *Please provide any further comments or suggestions that can be used for improving this session. (If any)*
   (5 answers) Two students indicated that more hands-on demonstrations could be included in future sessions. One of these students wrote "*More hands on as it makes it easier to understand the problem much quicker*". The other one stated that other puzzles used throughout the module could also be demonstrated in a similar visual way. Another student wrote "*I wouldn't just use card tricks. Keeping things different and interesting seems to help motivate people in my opinion*". Two students did not provide suggestions, answering "*None*" and "*N/A*".

Overall the feedback was very positive and clearly the session was a positive experience for the students. All suggestions for improvement include a more frequent use of similar approaches to teaching.

5. RELATED WORK

The current leading work in this area is the cs4fn project [5], whose goal is to enthuse school students about computer science and teach advanced computing ideas. The project consists of a free magazine, live interactive shows and a popular webzine. More details about their work with card tricks can be found in the booklets [13, 14] and in the papers [4, 5]. The work presented in this paper was developed after attending a cs4fn presentation where the card trick "Are you psychic?" was shown. We enjoyed it so much that we decided to add more formality to the presentation of the trick and test it with our first-year undergraduate students. We also extended the presentation to include other algorithmic concepts, such as pre- and post-conditions and problem decomposition. In [4], the authors write that their "target audience has been school students but the approach, with more formality added, could also be used to illustrate theory to university students too. We leave this as further work.". Our work contributes towards this suggestion.

Other related work includes the CS Unplugged project [2], who were pioneers in using magic to teach computing and algorithms. In [11], a trick for demonstrating binary numbers is shown and in [9, 10] a variety of tricks are used to demonstrate topics that include algorithms, modular arithmetic, and binary encoding.

A related line of work is the use of recreational problems to teach computer science. In [12], for example, the authors advocate a wider use of recreational problems in teaching design and analysis of algorithms. In [6], the authors introduce a sample syllabus and course material for engineering and computer science, using a puzzle-based learning approach; the main book on this approach is [15]. In [1], the author presents a problem-based approach to algorithmic problem solving, where all the problems have a recreational flavour. A similar approach is followed in [8], where principles and techniques of algorithmic problem solving are exemplified using recreational problems.

Table 1: Questions and scores

#	Question	Score
1	I enjoyed the session on "The Algorithmics of Card Tricks" (Lecture 11), where we analysed the algorithm behind a card trick	4.52
2	The use of a card trick improved my engagement during the lecture	4.43
3	I think that card tricks are a good way to learn and practise algorithmic skills	4.43
4	I would like to have more sessions where card tricks are used to illustrate concepts on algorithm design and analysis	4.30
5	The use of a card trick made me feel more motivated and interested in learning more algorithmic skills	4.26
6	Using real playing cards to simulate the card trick helped me understand better the underlying algorithm	4.43

6. CONCLUSION

Magic card tricks can be used to illustrate important algorithmic skills. We have shown how we use a specific card trick to teach first-year CS undergraduates concepts like problem decomposition, pre- and post-conditions, and invariants. We have discussed some pedagogical issues and we have analysed feedback collected from students.

We started this project inspired by the excellent work reported in [4], where the authors write that their "target audience has been school students but the approach, with more formality added, could also be used to illustrate theory to university students too. We leave this as further work.". Our work contributes towards their suggestion and the feedback that we collected suggests that card tricks can indeed be used to teach algorithmic concepts at first-year undergraduate level.

We intend to further develop the work shown here by adapting more tricks to teach first-year undergraduates. We also plan to test a more formal approach with rigorous mathematical proofs with students at a more advanced level. In both cases, we will perform more evaluation on whether students truly understand Hoare triples, and pre- and post-conditions.

ACKNOWLEDGEMENTS

We would like to thank all the students who provided feedback. We are also grateful to Eudes Diemoz for his encouragement and to the anonymous referees for their valuable comments.

REFERENCES

[1] Roland Backhouse. *Algorithmic Problem Solving*. John Wiley & Sons Ltd., 2010.

[2] Tim Bell, Ian H. Witten, and Mike Fellows. *Computer Science Unplugged*. 2010. Available at http://csunplugged.org. Last accessed: 17 Mar 2014.

[3] John Biggs and Catherine Tang. *Teaching for Quality Learning at University: What the Student does (Society for Research Into Higher Education)*. Open University Press, 4th edition, 2011.

[4] Paul Curzon and Peter McOwan. Teaching formal methods using magic tricks. In *"Fun with formal methods" at the 25th International Conference on Computer Aided Verification (CAV 2013)*, St Petersburg, Russia, July 2013.

[5] Paul Curzon and Peter W. McOwan. Engaging with computer science through magic shows. In *Proceedings of the 13th Annual Conference on Innovation and Technology in Computer Science Education*, ITiCSE '08, pages 179–183, New York, NY, USA, 2008. ACM.

[6] Nickolas Falkner, Raja Sooriamurthi, and Zbigniew Michalewicz. Puzzle-based learning for engineering and computer science. *Computer*, 43(4):20–28, 2010.

[7] João F. Ferreira, Alexandra Mendes, Alcino Cunha, Carlos Baquero, Paulo Silva, L.S. Barbosa, and J.N. Oliveira. Logic training through algorithmic problem solving. In *Tools for Teaching Logic*, volume 6680 of *Lecture Notes in Computer Science*, pages 62–69. Springer Berlin Heidelberg, 2011.

[8] João F. Ferreira. *Principles and Applications of Algorithmic Problem Solving*. PhD thesis, School of Computer Science, University of Nottingham, 2010.

[9] Daniel D. Garcia and David Ginat. Demystifying computing with magic. In *Proceedings of the 43rd ACM Technical Symposium on Computer Science Education*, SIGCSE '12, pages 83–84, New York, NY, USA, 2012. ACM.

[10] Daniel D. Garcia and David Ginat. Demystifying computing with magic, continued. In *Proceedings of the 44th ACM Technical Symposium on Computer Science Education*, SIGCSE '13, pages 207–208, New York, NY, USA, 2013. ACM.

[11] Gerald Kruse. "Magic numbers" approach to introducing binary number representation in CS0. *SIGCSE Bull.*, 35(3):272–272, 2003.

[12] Anany Levitin and Mary-Angela Papalaskari. Using puzzles in teaching algorithms. *SIGCSE Bull.*, 34(1):292–296, 2002.

[13] P. W. McOwan and P. Curzon. *The Magic of Computer Science*. 2008. Available from: http://www.cs4fn.org/magic/downloads/cs4fnmagicbook1.pdf. Last accessed: 17 Mar 2014.

[14] P. W. McOwan, P. Curzon, and J. Black. *The Magic of Computer Science II: Now we have your attention*. 2009. Available from: http://www.cs4fn.org/magic/downloads/cs4fnmagicbook2.pdf. Last accessed: 17 Mar 2014.

[15] Z. Michalewicz and M. Michalewicz. *Puzzle-based Learning: Introduction to Critical Thinking, Mathematics, and Problem Solving*. Hybrid Publishers, 1st edition, 2008.

[16] Paul Ramsden. *Learning to Teach in Higher Education*. Routledge, 2nd edition, 2003.

[17] Alison Shreeve, Shân Wareing, and Linda Drew. *Teaching for Quality Learning at University: What the Student does (Society for Research Into Higher Education)*, chapter Key aspects of teaching and learning in the visual arts. In [3], 4th edition, 2011.

A Method to Prove Query Lower Bounds

Jagadish M
Dept. of Computer Science and Engg.
Indian Institute of Technology Bombay
Mumbai 400076, India
jagadish@cse.iitb.ac.in

Sridhar Iyer
Dept. of Computer Science and Engg.
Indian Institute of Technology Bombay
Mumbai 400076, India
sri@iitb.ac.in

ABSTRACT

The query-model or decision-tree model is a computational model in which the algorithm has to solve a given problem by making a sequence of queries which have 'Yes' or 'No' answers. A large class of algorithms can be described on this model and we can also prove non-trivial lower bounds for many problems on this model.

Many lower bounds on the query-model are proved using a technique called adversary argument. In CS courses, a common example used to illustrate the adversary argument is the following problem: Suppose there is an unweighted graph G with n vertices represented by an adjacency matrix. We want to test if the graph is connected. How many entries in the adjacency matrix do we have to probe in order to test if the graph has this property (property being 'connectivity')? Each probe is considered as a query.

Since the adjacency matrix has only n^2 entries, $O(n^2)$ queries are sufficient. It is also known that $\Omega(n^2)$ queries are necessary. Proving this lower bound is more difficult and is done using the adversary argument.

In literature, we find that lower bound proofs of this problem rely too much on 'connectivity' property and do not generalize well. When the property being tested is changed, the proof changes significantly. Our contribution is a method that gives a systematic way of proving lower bounds for problems involving testing of many graph-properties. We did a pilot experiment and found that students were able to understand and apply our method.

Categories and Subject Descriptors

K.3.2 [**Computers and Education**]: Computer and Information Science Education

General Terms

Algorithms

Keywords

Query complexity, Lower bounds, Adversary arguments

1. INTRODUCTION

A major focus of computer science is on design and analysis of provably efficient algorithms. Once we have designed a correct algorithm for a problem, a natural question to ask is: 'Is this the best possible algorithm for this problem?'. The only way to know the answer for certain is to *prove* that no better algorithm exists. On the Turing-machine computational model, this question is very difficult to answer and very little is known. So researchers have been studying the question of proving the optimality of an algorithm on simpler models of computation. One such model that is widely studied is the 'query model' (also known as decision-tree model).

Query Model. In this model, the algorithm is not given the input directly. The algorithm has to output the answer by asking queries specified by the problem. The efficiency of the algorithm is measured by the number of queries it takes in the worst case. The query-model is popular because a large class of algorithms can be implemented on this model. Hence, proving optimality of an algorithm on the query model proves its optimality within a large class of algorithms. For example, consider the problem of sorting n numbers in an array. All comparison-based algorithms like Quicksort, Mergesort, Heapsort, etc. can be implemented as query algorithms where a query corresponds to a comparison between a pair of elements from the array.

Query Complexity. In the query model, we are concerned only with the number of queries asked by the algorithm and any other computation it may do is irrelevant. The *cost* of an algorithm that solves a problem P is the number of queries the algorithm takes in the worst case to solve P. The cost of an algorithm can usually be expressed as a function of the input size n. We say algorithm A is better than algorithm B if there exists a constant c_o such that the cost of algorithm A is less than B for every problem instance of size $n > c_0$. The *query complexity* of a problem P is the cost of the best algorithm that solves P. We denote the query complexity of the problem of size n by $T(n)$. Query complexity is a property of the problem and cost is a property of an algorithm.

Given below are four examples of query-model problems. We will refer to all of them later, but our method is applicable only to problems similar to the CONNECTIVITY problem.

Formal descriptions of the first three problems can be found in [3], [2] and [5], respectively.

Problem E1. SORTING. Given an array A of n numbers, sort the elements in the array using only comparison queries. A comparison query is of the type, 'Is $A[i]$ smaller or bigger than $A[j]$?'.

Problem E2. ELEMENT DISTINCTNESS. Given an array A of n numbers, find if all the numbers are distinct, using only comparison and equality queries. An equality query is of the type, 'Is $A[i]$ equal to $A[j]$?'.

Problem E3. 3-SUM. Given an array A of n numbers, find if there exists three numbers in the array, say a, b and c, such that $a+b+c = 0$, using only linear-equation queries. A linear-equation query is of the type, 'Is $3A[1]+2A[3]-A[6] > 0$?'.

Problem E4. CONNECTIVITY. Suppose there is a graph $G = (V, E)$ with n vertices. We know the vertex set V of the graph but not the edge set E. Vertices are labelled from 1 to n. For any two vertices, a and b with $a, b \in V$, we are allowed to ask the following query: 'Is (a, b) an edge in G?'. If G is given by an adjacency matrix, this query is equivalent to probing the entry at the ath row and bth column of the adjacency matrix of G. What is the query complexity of determining if the graph is connected?

If the objective of the problem is to determine whether an input satisfies a given property or not, then we call such a problem as 'property-testing' problem. A property-testing problem has exactly two possible answers: 'True' or 'False'. For example, problems E2, E3 and E4 are property-testing problems.

Tight lower bounds.[1] We call a lower bound tight if it asymptotically matches an upper bound of $T(n)$. We are interested in obtaining tight asymptotic bounds on $T(n)$ for problems involving testing of graph-properties (similar to Prob. E4).

Overview. There are four main techniques for proving query lower bounds. The four problems E1-E4 are generally used as examples to illustrate each technique (Sec. 2). However, our focus is only on proving lower bounds for testing graph properties. The known methods for proving lower bounds for this kind of problems are ad-hoc in nature and rely on problem-specific observations. Our main contribution is a method that gives a more systematic way of proving lower bounds (Sec. 5). In Sec. 6, we show that our approach works for many problems within the scope. We did a pilot experiment and observed that students are able to understand and apply our method (Sec. 7).

2. RELATED WORK

We review known methods for proving query lower bounds and provide context for our work.

Information-theoretic proof. An explanation of this method can be found in Chapter 8 of [3]. The main assertion of the proof is the following:

Fact. If a problem P has M possible outputs and the input to the problem can be accessed only via 'Yes/No' queries, then $\log_2 M$ is a query lower bound for P.

---

[1]Most of the terminology we use is standard. Definitions of algorithmic terms and graph theoretic terms can be found in [8] and [10], respectively.

In other words, $\log_2 M$ is the minimum number of queries any correct algorithm must ask, in the worst case. For example, in the sorting problem, if the input consists of n numbers, then there are $n!$ possible outputs. Each output corresponds to a different ordering of n numbers. So we can claim that the lower bound for sorting problem is $\log_2 n! = \Omega(n \log n)$.

However, this method is not useful for property-testing problems. In a property-testing problem, there are only two outputs: 'True' or 'False'. The information-theoretic proof only gives a trivial lower bound of one ($\log_2 2 = 1$).

Algebraic Methods. In 1983, Ben-Or gave an algebraic technique that proves a tight $\Omega(n \log n)$ lower bound for ELEMENT-DISTINCTNESS problem. His technique, in one stroke, proves non-trivial lower bounds for twelve different problems [2]. But problems E3 and E4 are not amenable to this technique.

Reduction. Reduction is another way of proving lower bounds. At undergrad-level, reduction is often taught in the context of NP-hardness. If we want to show that problem H is NP-hard, we do so by proving that some known NP-hard problem (like SAT) reduces to H in polynomial time. Query lower bounds can also be proved in a similar vein. Suppose we know that a problem R has query complexity of $\Omega(g(n))$ on a certain computation model, we can show that another problem S has query complexity $\Omega(g(n))$ on the same model by reducing problem R to S in $o(g(n))$ time. For example, we know that finding the convex hull of a set of n points takes $\Omega(n \log n)$ operations because the sorting problem reduces to it (Prob. 33.3-2 in [3]).

The 3-SUM problem is known to have a query complexity of $\Theta(n^2)$ [5]. The lower bound proof of 3-SUM does not result in any general technique. But the strength of 3-SUM lies in the fact that this problem is an excellent candidate problem for proving lower bounds by reductions. Several problems in computational geometry have been shown to be as hard as 3-SUM [6]. But a lower bound for Prob. E4 cannot be proved by reduction either.

Adversary Arguments. What can we do if none of the above three methods work? We take recourse to proving by 'first principles', commonly known as proving by *adversary argument*. Recall that a lower bound of $g(n)$ for a problem P means that any *correct* algorithm must make at least $g(n)$ queries to solve P. So if we show that any algorithm that makes strictly less than $g(n)$ queries must be incorrect, then we have proved a lower bound of $\Omega(g(n))$ for the problem. Imagine that the queries asked by the algorithm are answered by an adversary. The adversary's objective is to maximize the number of queries that the algorithm asks and the algorithm's objective is to minimize the number of queries. If an adversary can force any correct algorithm to ask at least $g(n)$ queries, then $g(n)$ is a lower bound on the query complexity of the problem. It is necessary to understand the format of adversary arguments in order to follow the proofs in this paper. Introduction to adversary method can be found in [4] or [9]. Two proofs that give *exact* lower bounds for Prob. E4 can be found in [4] and [1]. Both the proofs are based on adversary arguments. However, these proofs do not generalize easily to other graph properties. In the next section, we give a different proof for this problem using an adversary argument. Though our proof gives only an asymptotic tight lower bound, it generalizes easily to other graph properties.

3. ADVERSARY ARGUMENT REVISITED

Terminology

Notation. Throughout the text, the notation $G = (V, E)$ refers to an undirected unweighted graph G with n vertices, where V is the vertex set and E is the edge set. We may assume that the vertices are labeled from 1 to n. We denote a complete graph having r vertices by K_r.

Definition. If there is no edge present between a pair of vertices u and v in a graph, we say (u, v) is a *non-edge* in the graph.

3.1 Testing Connectivity

Problem E4. We are given access to a graph $G = (V, E)$ via queries of the form 'Is (a, b) an edge in G?'. We know the vertex set V but not the edge set. Prove that it takes at least $\Omega(n^2)$ queries in the worst case to determine if G is connected.

Proof: We prove that any correct algorithm must take at least $n^2/4$ queries. For contradiction's sake, let us assume that there is a correct algorithm $\mathcal{A}$ that makes less than $n^2/4$ queries. We first describe the adversary's strategy for answering queries asked by the algorithm and then give the analysis.

Let G_1 be the graph made of two complete subgraphs A and B, such that A has nodes labelled from 1 to $n/2$ and B has nodes labelled from $n/2 + 1$ to n (Fig. 1 (a)). Note that graph G_1 has the same vertex set V as G.

Adversary's Strategy. The adversary first picks the graph G_1 tentatively as input (in its mind) and answers the queries posed by the algorithm as follows:

> When the algorithm asks 'Is (a, b) an edge in G?', the adversary says 'Yes' if (a, b) is an edge in G_1 and 'No' if (a, b) is a non-edge in G_1.

The adversary also keeps track of all the queries asked by the algorithm.

Analysis. Consider the moment when all the queries are made and $\mathcal{A}$ has declared whether G is connected or not. By our assumption, $\mathcal{A}$ has made less than $n^2/4$ queries. Since there are $n^2/4$ non-edges in G_1, there exists some pair of vertices (say (i, j)) such that:

- Pair (i, j) is a non-edge in G_1.
- $\mathcal{A}$ did not ask the query 'Is (i, j) an edge in G?'

Let G_2 be the graph obtained by replacing the non-edge (i, j) in G_1 by an edge (Fig. 1 (b)). G_1 is not connected but G_2 is connected. But both the graphs are consistent with all the answers the adversary has given. The adversary can prove that algorithm $\mathcal{A}$ is wrong as follows:

If the algorithm outputs 'True. G is connected', the adversary 'reveals' that $G = G_1$ and shows that the algorithm is wrong. If the algorithm outputs 'False. G is not connected', the adversary reveals that $G = G_2$ and again proves the algorithm wrong.

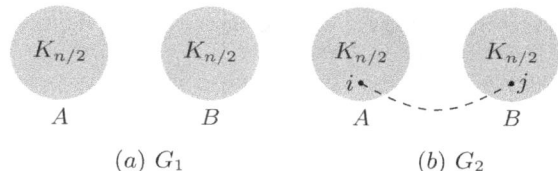

Figure 1. (a) G_1 is the graph the adversary tentatively keeps as input in its mind. Every pair of vertices (p, q) with $p \in A$ and $q \in B$ in a non-edge in G_1. So G_1 has $n^2/4$ non-edges. (b) G_2 is the graph obtained by replacing the non-edge (i, j) in G_1 with an edge. G_2 is connected but G_1 is not. Since (i, j) was not queried by the algorithm, both G_1 and G_2 could have been possible inputs to the problem.

So regardless of what the algorithm outputs, the adversary can always contradict the algorithm. Hence, every correct algorithm must make at least $n^2/4$ queries.

□

4. SCOPE OF PROBLEMS

Our method is applicable to problems of the following kind.

GENERIC-PROBLEM. There is a graph $G = (V, E)$ to which we do not have direct access. We know the vertex set but not the edge set. There are n vertices in G and we may assume that they are labelled from 1 to n. We are allowed to ask queries of the type 'Is (a, b) an edge in the graph G?', where $a, b \in V$. The problem is to find if G has a given property $\mathcal{P}$ by asking such queries.

4.1 Our approach

In order to prove a lower bound for the GENERIC-PROBLEM, when property $\mathcal{P}$ is specified explicitly, we do the following:

- Construct a critical graph G for property $\mathcal{P}$ which has many non-edges. We will define a critical graph shortly.

- Apply Theorem 5.1 which says that existence of a critical graph with many non-edges implies a lower bound for the problem.

5. MAIN THEOREM

Definition. Given a property $\mathcal{P}$, a graph G_c is said to be *critical* with respect to the property if the following two conditions are met.

(C1) G_c does not have the property $\mathcal{P}$.

(C2) Replacing any non-edge in G_c by an edge endows the graph with property $\mathcal{P}$.

For example, if the property is 'Connectivity', then the graph shown in Fig. 1 (a) is an example of a critical graph.

We will now prove our main result using ideas very similar to the proof of CONNECTIVITY problem (Sec. 3.1).

Theorem 5.1. *Suppose G_c is a critical graph for the property $\mathcal{P}$. If G_c has n vertices and x non-edges, then x is a query lower bound for the GENERIC-PROBLEM.*

Proof: We show that any correct algorithm must make at least x queries in the worst case. We prove by contradiction. Assume that there is some algorithm $\mathcal{A}$ that solves the GENERIC-PROBLEM by making strictly less than x queries.

We first give an adversary's strategy for answering queries by $\mathcal{A}$ and then give the analysis.

Adversary's Strategy. The adversary first constructs the graph G_c (in its mind) and answers the queries posed by the algorithm as follows: When the algorithm asks 'Is (a, b) an edge in G?', the adversary says 'Yes' if (a, b) is an edge in G_c and 'No' if (a, b) is a non-edge in G_c.

Analysis. Consider the moment when all the queries are made and $\mathcal{A}$ has declared whether G has the property $\mathcal{P}$ or not. By our assumption, $\mathcal{A}$ has made less than x queries. Since there are x non-edges in G_c, there exists some pair of vertices (say (i, j)) such that:

- Pair (i, j) is a non-edge in G_c.

- $\mathcal{A}$ did not ask the query 'Is (i, j) an edge in G?'

By our definition of critical graph, we have the following:

- Graph G_c does not have property $\mathcal{P}$.

- Suppose G'_c is a graph which is same as G_c except that the non-edge (i, j) in G_c is replaced by an edge in G'_c. So G'_c has exactly one more edge than G_c. More importantly, G'_c has the property $\mathcal{P}$, since G_c was a critical graph.

Either G_c or G'_c could have been the input graph for the problem since they are consistent with all the answers the adversary has given. But one graph has the property and the other one does not. Hence, whatever answer the algorithm outputs, the adversary can prove the algorithm wrong. Hence, any algorithm that makes less than x queries must be incorrect. □

Now we turn to the applications of this theorem.

6. APPLICATIONS

We prove lower bounds for many common graph properties by constructing a critical graph for each property. It turns out that all the problems we consider have a lower bound of $\Omega(n^2)$, which proves that the bounds are asymptotically tight.

For each problem, we describe how to construct a critical graph with $\Omega(n^2)$ number of non-edges. The lower bound follows from Theorem 5.1.

Here is a handy fact about the number of non-edges in a graph.

Lemma 6.1. *A graph with n vertices and m edges has x non-edges, where $x = \binom{n}{2} - m$.*

Proof: There are $\binom{n}{2}$ pairs of vertices in a graph. Between every pair of vertices, either there is an edge or a non-edge. If m is the number of edges and x is the number of non-edges we have $x + m = \binom{n}{2}$. □

6.1 Triangle Detection

A graph G is said to have a *triangle* if K_3 is a subgraph of G.

Problem P1. Given access to $G = (V, E)$ via queries of the form 'Is (a, b) an edge in G?' determine if G has a triangle.

Construction of G_c. A rooted star tree with the root node as 1 (Fig.2). In other words, G_c is a graph where we connect node 1 to every other node. There are exactly $m = n - 1$ edges in G_c.

It is easy to verify that G_c satisfies both the conditions of a critical graph.
(C1) G_c does not have triangle.
(C2) Replacing any non-edge in G_c, induces a triangle involving node 1.

No. of non-edges in G_c: $x = \binom{n}{2} - m = \Omega(n^2)$.

By Theorem 5.1, any algorithm must make at least $\Omega(n^2)$ queries. Since this step is same for all problems, in subsequent examples, we only describe the construction of the critical graph.

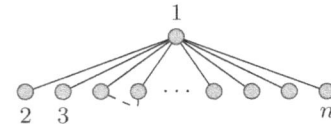

Figure 2. A critical graph for 'has a triangle' property. Node 1 is connected to every other node. The non-edges are between nodes $2, ...n$.

6.2 Hamiltonian Path

Problem P3. Given access to a graph $G = (V, E)$ via queries of the form 'Is (a, b) an edge in G?' determine if G has a Hamiltonian path.

Construction of G_c. We build two complete subgraphs A and B of equal size such that A has nodes labelled from 1 to $n/2$ and B has nodes labelled from $n/2 + 1$ to n (Fig. 3).

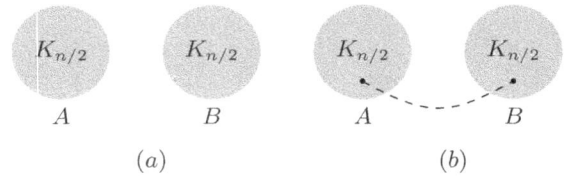

Figure 3. (a) A critical graph G_c for Hamiltonian property. G_c does not have a Hamiltonian path since it is disconnected. (b) Replacing any non-edge by an edge induces a Hamiltonian path.

6.3 Perfect Matching

Problem P3. A graph G is said to have a *perfect matching* if there exists a pairing of all nodes in G, such that every node is contained in exactly one pair and each pair has an edge between them. A necessary (but not sufficient) condition for G to have a perfect matching is that n must be an even number. Given access to $G = (V, E)$ via queries of the form 'Is (a, b) an edge in G?' determine if G has a perfect matching. Assume that n is even.

Construction of G_c. Since n is an even number, assume that $n = 2s$. If s is an odd number, we construct two complete subgraphs A and B such that A has nodes from the set $\{1, .., s\}$ and B has nodes from the set $\{s + 1, .., n\}$. If s is an even number, we construct two complete graphs A and B such that A has nodes in the set $\{1, .., s - 1\}$ and B

has nodes in the set $\{s, .., n\}$ (Fig. 4). Basically, we want to ensure that both A and B have odd number of nodes.

No. of non-edges is s^2, when s is odd and $s^2 - 1$ when s is even. Hence, number of non-edges $x \approx n^2/4$.

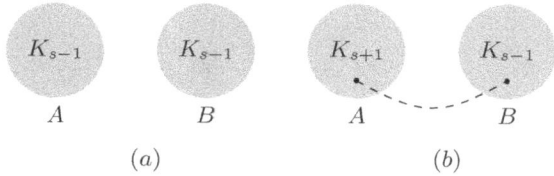

Figure 4. (a) Critical graph G_c for 'perfect matching' property when s is even. Graph G_c does not have a perfect matching since A and B have odd number of vertices. (b) If we replace any non-edge by a edge then it is easy to verify that the graph obtained has a perfect matching.

6.4 Non-Bipartite Detection

Problem P4. Given access to $G = (V, E)$ via queries of the form 'Is (a, b) an edge in G?' determine if G is non-bipartite.

Construction of G_c. G_c is a complete bipartite graph with two partitions A and B. where partition A has nodes labelled from 1 to $n/2$ and B has nodes labelled from $n/2+1$ to n. So G_c has $m = n^2/4$ edges (Fig. 5). No. of non-edges in G_c: $x = \binom{n}{2} - m \approx n^2/4$.

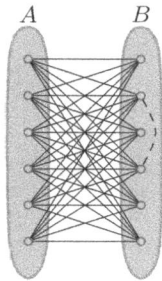

Figure 5. A critical graph for the property of 'Non-bipartiteness'. G_c is bipartite but adding replacing any non-edge by an edge makes in non-bipartite.

6.5 Cycle Detection

Problem P5. Given access to $G = (V, E)$ via queries of the form 'Is (a, b) an edge in G?' determine if G has a cycle.

Construction of G_c. A critical graph for 'has a cycle' property is a path containing all nodes. Hence G_c has exactly $n - 1$ edges (Fig. 6). No. of non-edges: $x = \Omega(n^2)$.

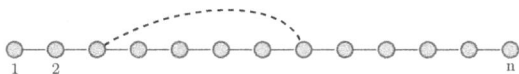

Figure 6. Critical graph G_c for 'has a cycle' property. Replacing any non-edge by an edge induces a cycle.

6.6 Degree-Three node

Problem P6. Given access to $G = (V, E)$ via queries of the form 'Is (a, b) an edge in G?' determine if G has a node whose degree is three.

Construction of G_c. A critical graph for property 'has a degree-3 node' is a cycle containing all nodes. Hence G_c has exactly n edges (Fig. 7). No. of non-edges: $x = \binom{n}{2} - n = \Omega(n^2)$.

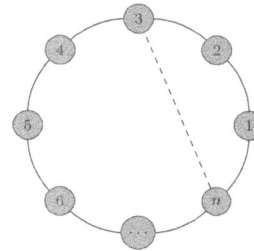

Figure 7. Critical graph G_c for 'has a degree-3 node' property. G_c has all nodes of degree two but replacing any non-edge by an edge gives a degree-3 node.

The method also works for other graph properties like planarity, two-connectedness, etc. but we have omitted these examples.

7. TEACHABILITY

We did a pilot experiment with five CS graduate students to see if they could apply our method to derive query lower bounds. We report our findings in this section.

Design. One of the authors of the paper had one-on-one interview-type session with each student. Prior to the start of the session, we made sure that the student understood the basic concepts and definitions related to query computational model. A session lasted for 2-4 hours and was divided into three phases. In the first phase, the students understood the format of adversary arguments. In the second phase, the student attempted to solve the CONNECTIVITY problem (Prob. E4) for one hour. Our objective was to allow the students to try the problem on their own so that we could identify the common approaches taken to solve the problem. The student was encouraged to think aloud during this time. If he persisted in a wrong approach for more than ten minutes, the author alerted the student to the mistake and let him continue. At the end of one hour, regardless of how the student performed, the author gave the solution to the problem along with an explanation of the method as described in Sections 3-5. In the third phase, the student attempted to derive lower bounds for the list of problems given in Sec. 6, without any help. We describe observations made in each phase below.

7.1 Phase I: Adversary Argument Explained

In the first phase, the students got familiar with the adversary argument. Two students who said they were familiar with adversary arguments were quizzed on the topic with a couple of questions. The other three students found it easy to follow the adversary argument through examples like 'n-Card Monte' and '20-questions', given in [4] and [9], respectively. Some students took more time than others to understand the format of the proof, which accounted for the variability in the duration the sessions.

7.2 Phase II: Teaching

We list common failed approaches taken while solving the CONNECTIVITY problem.

Failed approach F_1. Students find it hard to let go of the algorithm and think like an adversary. They often prove lower bounds assuming that the algorithm works in a certain way. For example, four out of five students gave the answer along the following lines: "Every vertex has $n - 1$ possible incident edges. When the algorithm asks $n - 1$ queries for a vertex, the adversary answers with a 'Yes' only for the last incident edge." The flaw in this reasoning is the assumption made about the algorithm's behavior. The algorithm need not ask queries in an orderly manner. The lower bound has to work for *any* algorithm, not just the one that probes vertex-by-vertex.

Failed approach F_2. All the students tried for exact bounds which is harder than proving asymptotic bounds. Even when the students were reminded that only asymptotic lower bound is sufficient, they could not figure out a way to make use of the relaxed constraint.

Failed approach F_3. Three students came up with the correct adversary strategy, but failed to do the analysis. The strategy was: The adversary always says 'No' unless saying so *definitely* disconnects the graph. This strategy is intuitive and is also correct, but unfortunately none of them were not able to prove that it works. The correct analysis of this strategy is given in [1].

7.3 Phase III: Testing

In Table 1, we give the time taken by each student to construct the correct critical graph. Some students gave different (correct) critical graphs than the ones we have given. For example, for 'Triangle' property two students gave complete bipartite graph as the answer. Similarly, for 'Cycle' property all the students gave 'any spanning tree' as the answer. As it can be seen from Table 1, most students were able to construct critical graphs quickly. We observed that three students who were not familiar with adversary arguments did equally well as the other two students. We did not anticipate this but it seems reasonable in hindsight. After all, the main reason why our method is helpful is because it shifts the focus from designing an adversary strategy to finding one critical graph. So prior knowledge of adversary arguments did not matter as much. In the words of a student, "Instead of thinking about how the queries must be answered, I just have to look for the right graph, which seems easier to do".

8. CONCLUDING REMARKS

Remark 1. An alternate approach to proving lower bounds for graph-properties can be found in [7]. However, this proof method is beyond the scope of most CS courses since it relies on deep ideas in topology.

Remark 2. There is a lacuna in most traditional textbooks when discussing lower bounds. We suspect that this is because much work on this topic has been done only in the last two decades. But lower bounds as a topic in complexity theory has gained a lot of importance in the last few years. In support of this claim, we would like to point out that the recent book by Arora and Barak titled 'Computational

Phase	Topic	Students				
		S_1	S_2	S_3	S_4	S_5
I	Adv.	Yes	Yes	No	No	No
II	E4	F_2	$F_{1,2,3}$	$F_{1,2}$	$F_{1,2,3}$	$F_{1,2,3}$
III	P1	8m	10m	-	9m	-
	P2	5m	5m	9m	6m	6m
	P3	8m	-	-	10m	9m
	P4	1m	2m	4m	2m	2m
	P5	1m	2m	2m	1m	2m
	P6	1m	1m	1m	1m	1m

Table 1. Summary of data from the experiment. Phase I: 'Yes' means that the student already knew the adversary method. Phase II: Subscripts in F refer to the failed approaches taken by the student as discussed in Sec. 7.2. Phase III: Numbers give the time taken by the student to answer. A - against a problem means that the student was not able to answer that problem within 15 minutes.

Complexity: A Modern Approach' [1] has one-third of the book devoted exclusively to lower bounds!

9. REFERENCES

[1] S. Arora and B. Barak. *Computational complexity: a modern approach.* Cambridge University Press, 2009.

[2] M. Ben Or. Lower bounds for algebraic computation trees. In *Proceedings of the fifteenth annual ACM Symposium on Theory of Computing (STOC)*, pages 80–86. ACM, 1983.

[3] T. H. Cormen, C. E. Leiserson, R. L. Rivest, and C. Stein. *Introduction to Algorithms.* The MIT Press, 2nd edition, 2001.

[4] J. Erickson. http://goo.gl/0z36dz. Last Accessed Jan 10, 2014.

[5] J. Erickson et al. Lower bounds for linear satisfiability problems. *Chicago Journal of Theoretical Computer Science*, 8:1999, 1999.

[6] A. Gajentaan and M. H. Overmars. On a class of $o(n^2)$ problems in computational geometry. *Computational geometry*, 5(3):165–185, 1995.

[7] J. Kahn, M. Saks, and D. Sturtevant. A topological approach to evasiveness. *Combinatorica*, 4(4):297–306, 1984.

[8] J. Kleinberg and E. Tardos. *Algorithm Design.* Addison Wesley, second edition, 2006.

[9] Sally A. Goldman and Kenneth J. Goldman. Adversary Lower Bound Technique. http://goldman.cse.wustl.edu/crc2007/handouts/adv-lb.pdf. Last Accessed Jan 10, 2014.

[10] D. B. West. *Introduction to Graph Theory.* Prentice Hall, 2 edition, September 2000.

Problem-Solving Using the Extremality Principle

Jagadish M
Dept. of Computer Science and Engg.
Indian Institute of Technology Bombay
Mumbai 400076, India
jagadish@cse.iitb.ac.in

Sridhar Iyer
Dept. of Computer Science and Engg.
Indian Institute of Technology Bombay
Mumbai 400076, India
sri@iitb.ac.in

ABSTRACT

The extremality principle is one of the commonly used problem solving strategies. It involves looking at the extremal cases of a problem in order to obtain insight about the general structure. Though the principle is widely known, its use in designing algorithms is rarely discussed in CS literature. We present a methodology based on the extremality principle that is useful in solving a wide variety of algorithmic problems. We illustrate the effectiveness of the methodology by deriving solutions to three difficult problems. We believe that the key steps involved in our methodology can be taught to students as individual drills. We have anecdotal evidence for the teachability of the method.

Categories and Subject Descriptors

K.3.2 [**Computers and Education**]: Computer and Information Science Education

General Terms

Algorithms

Keywords

Problem-solving, Extremality

1. INTRODUCTION

The extremality principle is a problem-solving strategy that involves studying objects with extreme properties in order to reason about more general objects. Although the principle is intuitive and well-known, its application to a specific problem can be difficult. There are many books on problem-solving that illustrate the use of extremality principle in solving mathematical problems ([2], [6]). These books typically contain several topic-specific problems that train students in identifying situations where extremality can be useful. However, the current texts on extremality principle focus mostly on math topics like geometry, number theory and combinatorics.

In computer science, extremality is discussed only in the context of greedy algorithms. A greedy algorithm makes a local choice at each step that is extremal in some sense. We show that the principle can be used in more general ways. We have devised a problem-solving methodology based on the extremality principle, which we call WISE, that can be used to solve a wide range of problems. WISE stands for "Weaken-Identify-Solve-Extend". For the purpose of illustration, we derive solutions to three hard problems using this methodology. The ideas in our technique are well-known to experts who probably apply them implicitly. Our contribution is to operationalize the extremal principle into a methodology that can be directly taught to students.

2. SOURCE OF DIFFICULTY

In this section, we explain why the extremality principle is too general to be useful directly and how WISE addressees some of the key difficulties. The main difficulty arises due to the multiple ways in which instances can be represented.

Choice of representation of instances. In many cases a single instance can be represented in multiple ways. The extreme values of the instance in one representation may be unrelated to extreme values in another representation. For example, let us take the case of numbers. A number is often represented in decimal notation. However, we could also represent it using a different base system or express each number by their prime factorization. For example, the number 15 can be represented as 1111 in base 2 system or as 3x5 in factorized notation. So the numbers 15, 31, 63 do not seem to be extremal when considered in decimal or factorized representation ($3 \cdot 5, 31, 3 \cdot 3 \cdot 7$), but are extremal when represented in binary (1111,11111,111111). We illustrate the use of representation by an example.

Problem. Consider the program given below. For a given value of n, what is the value of p upon termination of the program?

```
int main(){
        int n; int p=0;
        cin >> n;
        while(n > 0){
            if( n%2 == 1 ) p++;
            n = n/2;
        }
        cout << p << endl;
        return 0;
}
```

Sol. Let us inspect the behavior of the program for small values of n.

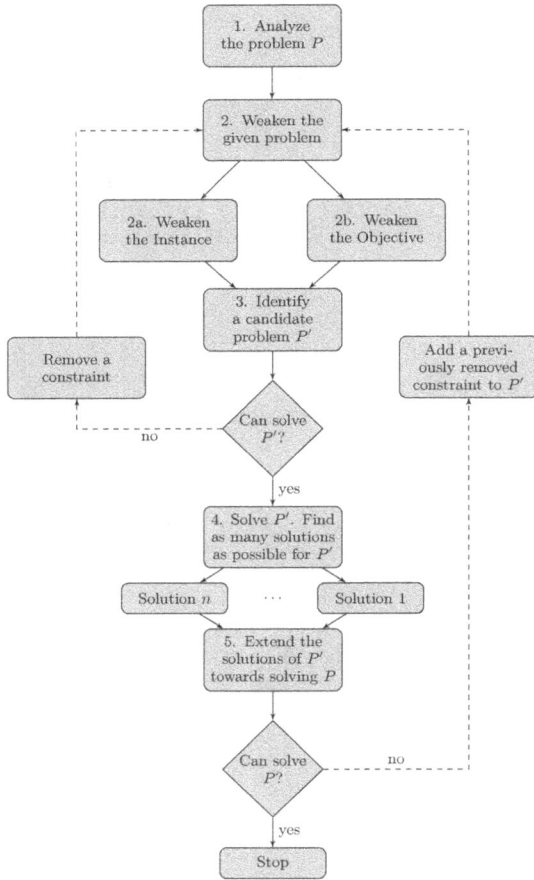

Figure 1. The WISE methodology based on extremality principle. (WISE is short for "Weaken-Identify-Solve-Extend")

n	1	2	3	4	5	7	10	15
p	1	1	2	1	2	3	2	4

It is difficult to find the relationship between **n** and **p** from the above table. However, if we switch the represention of **n** from decimal to binary the relationship becomes obvious.

n	01	10	11	100	101	111	1001	1111
p	1	1	2	1	2	3	2	4

It is now easy to see what the program does: At each iteration of the loop, **p** is incremented if the last bit of **n** is 1. Variable **n** is also right shifted by one bit at each iteration. Hence, when the program terminates, the value of **p** contains the number of 1 bits in the binary representation of original value of **n**.

The key to solving the above problem was to find the right representation for numbers. The importance of representation is mentioned in [5] in the context of 'transform and conquer' technique. It plays an important role in our methodology in finding extremal instances.

3. METHODOLOGY

We describe the steps involved in the WISE methodology. We elaborate the steps that are shown in Fig. 1.

The first step of the method is to identify the instances, constraints and the objective of the problem.

Instances and constraints in the problem are easy to identify by looking at the *nouns phrases* and *verb phrases* in the problem description, respectively.

For each instance, we select a *representation* and list their *properties*. For example, a graph can be represented either as an adjacency matrix or adjacency list. Graphs have properties like maximum degree of a vertex, diameter, connectivity, etc. The properties may depend on the choice of representation. A property can be intrinsic to an instance or depend on the choice of representation. For example, diameter is a property that is intrinsic to a tree, but height is a property that is applicable only if the tree is represented as a rooted tree. Table 1 shows representations and properties of common instances we encounter in algorithmic problems.

Instance	Properties (Representation)
Number	Value, Parity, Sign, Number of prime factors, Number of digits (Decimal), Numbers of bits (Binary).
Lines	Length and Slope.
Array	Length, Values, Number of inversions, etc.
Tree	Maximum degree of vertex, Number of leaves, Diameter, Height (Rooted tree).
Graph	Number of edges, Diameter, Connectivity, Regularity, Planarity, Bipartiteness, Number of cycles, Chromatic number, Girth, Number of overlapping back-edges (DFS Tree) Height (BFS Tree).

Table 1. Common instances and their properties.

Step 2 *Weaken the given problem*

If the problem is hard to solve, we look for a problem that is simpler to solve first. This is one of the most common problem-solving techniques [6]. We describe two common ways of weakening.

Weaken the instances. The most common way to simplify the problem is to retain the objective but restrict the instances to a particular type. In this section, we discuss ways to weaken the instances.

Extremal instances are those which optimize a function on properties subject to some constraints. Due to the number of ways in which we can combine properties, there are several extremal instances one can derive. We list some simple extremal examples in Table 2 that are useful in many problems. Solving the problem on a simple extremal instance usually gives a clue to what other extremal instances might be interesting to consider.

Emergent Properties. Interaction between instances can give rise to new properties which we call as *emergent* properties. For example, a pair of lines can have an *intersection point* which is not a property of either of the lines. Interaction could occur between multiple instances of the same kind or different ones. Since instances could interact in many ways, there could be a large number of emergent properties.

Weaken the objective. In this step, we identify the objective and relax the constraints of the problem. The common way to do this is to relax the individual properties of

Instance	Extremal function	Constraints	Extremal Instance
Number	Min. the number of prime factors	-	Numbers of the form p^n where p is prime
	Min. the number of 1s in bits	-	`10000,01000,00001, etc.`
Lines	Maximize or Minimize slope	-	Horizontal and Vertical lines
Array	Number of values	-	Array consisting of only 1s and 0s
Tree	Minimize the number of leaves	-	Path
	Minimize height	-	Star graph
	Minimize height	Max. degree is three	Complete binary tree
Graph	Maximize number of edges	-	Complete graph
	Minimize number of edges	Preserving connectivity	Tree

Table 2. Examples of extremal objects.

the constraints or operations. It is well known that simplifying constraints by itself can lead to insight [3]. Combining this with extremality makes it more powerful.

Step 3 Identify a candidate problem P'

Once we have a list of weaker problems, we identify all the trivial problems that can be easily solved. Usually, many of these problems do not give much insight. So we need to pick a candidate problem that gives some insight into original problem. The candidate problem is the *simplest non-trivial* problem to which we do not have a solution. If the candidate problem itself is too hard then we go back to Step 2 by and weaken it further. By repeated application of weakening the problem or objective, we obtain a candidate problem P' that retains some aspects of the original problem but is easy enough to be solved. Since the problem can be weakened in several ways, we usually end up with multiple candidate problems. We choose to pursue one candidate problem at a time.

Step 4 Solving the candidate problem P'

In this step, we can apply any of the commonly available techniques like greedy, divide-and-conquer, dynamic programming, etc. to solve P'. It usually helps to solve the candidate problem in multiple ways. Solutions differ in their strengths and weaknesses and may give different insights into the problem.

Step 5 Extend the solutions

We use each solution of the candidate problem to get insight into the original problem. One of the common ways of doing this is to first see if the solution applies to near-extremal instances *i.e.* extremal instances which are slightly perturbed. For example, we can try to extend a solution on prime numbers to numbers with two prime factors. Most often this extension gives an idea that works for arbitrary numbers. Similarly, we may try to extend a solution that works for a path to trees with only two paths. The solution to two paths may generalize to trees with fixed number of leaves and then to general trees.

However, if the solution does not extend to a general case then we add the difficult case to the candidate problem, go back to Step 1 and tackle it as a new problem.

4. ILLUSTRATIVE EXAMPLE I: COINS IN A ROW

We apply the WISE methodology to a problem that appears in the book "Mathematical Puzzles: A Connoisseurs Collection" by Peter Winkler [7]. The book is a collection of hard and interesting puzzles. This is the first of the three problems with which we illustrate the effectiveness of WISE.

Problem. COINS IN A ROW. On a table is a row of fifty coins of various denominations. Alice picks a coin from one of the ends and puts it in her pocket; then Bob chooses a coin from one of the (remaining) ends, and the alternation continues until Bob pockets the last coin. Prove that Alice can play so as to guarantee collecting as much money as Bob.

Step 1 Analyze the problem

We identify the instances, constraints and the objective of the problem. Noun phrases in the problem description usually correspond to instances and verb phrases to constraints and objectives. The cue phrases in the problem are shown in italics below.

Objective Find a strategy for Alice to *collect more money* than Bob.

Constraint Coins must be *picked alternatively* from both ends.

Instances *Coins* and a *sequence* of fifty coins.

Emergent Property. Since the game is deterministic, for any sequence of coins S, there is a unique value which denotes the maximum amount Alice can collect on S, assuming that both Alice and Bob choose optimally. Let *profit* denote the difference between Alice's amount and Bob's amount for a given sequence of coins. Note that profit is an emergent property of the sequence.

Step 2 Weakening

Weaken the instance. One way to weaken the input sequence is to restrict the values of coins to 1s and 0s. Zeroes and ones are extremal because they are the smallest two non-negative values. A sequence of all zeroes or all ones is also extremal, but this makes the problem trivial.

Weaken the objective. There are many options to relax the objective or constraints: Can Alice pick the largest coin always? Can Alice force Bob to pick a particular coin? Can Alice collect at least half the amount as Bob?

Step 3 Identify a candidate problem

Candidate problem. Given a sequence consisting only zeroes and ones, find a strategy for Alice to maximize her profit.

Step 4 Solving a candidate problem

This is the step in which extremality is most useful. We would like to identify problem-specific extremal instances of the candidate problem which can be used to get some insight into the problem.

Here is an extremal instance based on the emergent property profit: *Which configuration consisting of 1s and 0s gives the* maximum profit *for Alice?* The instance is not hard to construct since at each turn Alice should be able to pick 1 but not Bob:

0 1 0 1 0 1 0 1 0 1 0 1 0 1 0 1 0 1

In the above example it is easy to see that Alice can pick all the 1s and Bob gets zero. So the gain for this sequence is maximum over all sequences of the same length.

If 1s and 0s appear in alternate positions, Alice can always pick all the 1s.

o e o e o e o e o e o e o e o e
0 1 0 1 0 1 0 1 0 1 0 1 0 1 0 1

In general, Alice can pick all the numbers that are in positions of the same parity, regardless of the values of the coins (Key Idea). Notice how we made this observation simply by solving the *right* extremal problem: that of alternate ones and zeroes.

Step 5   Extend the Solutions

Near extremal instance: Alternate 1s and 0s except for one position. Alice can win by collecting 1s if x is less than the number of ones. Otherwise, she can win by collecting x. By generalizing this idea, we see that Alice has a winning strategy: Alice first sums up all the coins in even positions and all the coins in odd positions. Then, she will pick up all coins of the same parity that gives her a larger sum.

o e o e o e o e o e o e o e
0 1 0 1 x 1 0 1 0 1 0 1 0 1 0 1

Sol. Alice either picks all the numbers in even positions or odd positions (whichever is greater).

5.   EXAMPLE II: GRID MINIMUM

This problem is taken from the textbook by Klienberg-Tardos [4]. The authors mention that problems in each chapter appear roughly in increasing order of difficulty. GRID MINIMUM is the last problem in the chapter on divide-and-conquer technique.

Problem. Let G be an $n \times n$ grid graph. Each node v in G is labelled by a real number x_v; you may assume that all these labels are distinct. A node v of G is called a *local minimum* if the label x_v is less than the label x_w for all nodes w that are joined to v by an edge. You are given the grid graph G, but the labelling is only specified in the following *implicit* way; for each node v, you can determine the value x_v by *probing* the node v. Show how to find a local minimum of G using only $O(n)$ probes to the nodes of G. (Note that G has n^2 nodes.)

Step 1   Analyze the problem

We first identify the instances of the problem.

- Instances in the problem: Grid graph with values.
- Extremal instances
  - An $1 \times n$ grid graph (extremality in structure.)
  - A grid graph with only one node that is a local minimum (extremality in values.)

Step 2a   Weakening the instance

Let us consider the extremal instance when the grid graph is of size $1 \times n$. This means the graph is just a path.

Step 3   Identify a candidate problem

The candidate problem is as follows: What is the least number of queries in which we can find a local minimum on a path?

Step 4   Solving the candidate problem

Suppose we probe the middle node m and find its value to be 5 (say). If this node is the local minimum, then its neighbors must be larger than 5.

To check if the node m is a local minimum, we compare its value with its adjacent nodes. If m is smaller than both the neighbors, then we are done; otherwise we do the following:

Without loss of generality, assume that the right node is smaller than the middle node. Observe that the node with the smallest value in the right half (outlined) of the path must be a local minimum, so the right half of the path contains at least one local minimum. With one probe, we can reduce the size of the path by half. We can find a local minimum in at most $O(\log n)$ probes by recursing.

Step 5   Extend the solutions

Can we generalize the above idea to a $2 \times n$ size grid?

Suppose, we probe the middle nodes of the $2 \times n$ grid and find that one of them is a local minimum, then we are done.

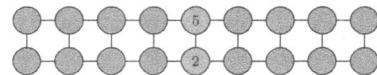

Otherwise, it means that each middle node is adjacent to a node that has smaller value. Consider the case when both the smaller adjacent nodes are on the same side of the middle nodes (say right side as shown below). In this case, we know that there exists a local minimum in the right half of the gird (outlined portion), due to the same reason as above: the smallest valued node in the right half is definitely a local minimum. Hence, the same idea that we used for a path extends to this case. We can recurse on the right half of the grid since it is assured to contain a local minimum.

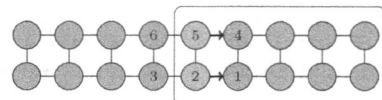

However, this idea does not extend to the case when the smaller adjacent nodes are in opposite directions (as shown in Fig. 2). This case is perplexing because we do not know if we can discard the right half or the left half of the grid (if at all we can discard). Let us add this difficulty and consider it as our next candidate problem.

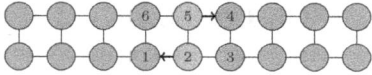

Figure 2. Should we recurse on the left half or the right?

Step 3 *Identify a candidate problem*

Candidate Problem 2: *Given a grid graph of size $2 \times n$ and the values of middle nodes and their neighbors, determine which half of the grid contains a local minimum.*

Step 4 *Solving the candidate problem*

We consider the difficult case when the smaller neighbors of middle nodes are on the opposite sides as given in Fig. 2.

Instead of approaching this problem directly, we use extremality to get some insight. Our instance is a $2 \times n$ grid. An extremal instance of a grid may be a grid with *only one* local minimum. Is it possible to extend the grid shown in Fig. 2 such that it has only one local minimum?

Note that if a node is not a local minimum, then one of its neighbors has a smaller value than itself. We can use this fact and complete the grid in Fig.2 with values such that it has only one local minimum. One such extremal case is shown in Fig. 3, where node 1 is the only local minimum.

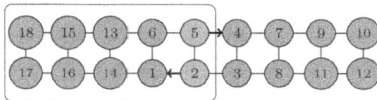

Figure 3. Node 1 is the only local minimum.

Note that the local minimum has appeared on the *left side* of the grid graph. We observe that no matter how we try to fill up the values for the remaining nodes in Fig.2, we always end up with a local minimum on the left side of grid graph. So in some sense, the middle node 2 seems to have more influence than middle node 5.

Key Fact. Node 2 is the minimum node among the middle nodes 2 and 5.

Here is the reason why the local minimum always appears on the left side of the grid graph shown in Fig.2: Suppose node 1 is a local minimum, then we are done. Otherwise, let node l be the minimum valued node in the left half of the graph (outlined portion in Fig. 3). Note that node l is less than *all* the nodes in the left half of the grid graph including the middle nodes 2 and 5. Therefore, node l is a local minimum. So in either case, we get a local minimum on the left side of the grid graph.

Using the above observation, we can now answer candidate problem 2. Suppose we are given a $2 \times n$ grid with middle nodes a and b. Without loss of generality, assume $v_a < v_b$. Let x be the neighbor of node a with $v_x < v_a$. Then there always exists a local minimum in that half of the grid graph that contains node x.

Step 5 *Extend the solutions*

The solution to the $2 \times n$ grid gives enough insight to solve the original problem. We give a divide-and-conquer algorithm below:

Sol. Given an $n \times n$ grid, we probe all middle nodes and check if one of the middle nodes is a local minimum. If this is true, then we are done. Otherwise, we find the minimum valued node among the middle nodes (call this minimum valued node m). Since m is not a local minimum, there exits a node x, either to m's right or left such that $v_x < v_m$. Let G' be the half of the grid than contains v_x. G' is a $n \times n/2$ grid. Apply the probing procedure again to G' and partition it into two halves. Let G'' be the half that contains the local minimum. Recurse on G''. This is the divide-step of the algorithm that uses only $3n/2$ probes and reduces the problem into an instance of size $n/2 \times n/2$. The associated recurrence relation is

$$T(n) = T(n/2) + 3n/2$$

which implies that the algorithm runs in linear time.

6. EXAMPLE III: BEADS

This problem was posed in a regional ACM-ICPC competition that was held in the authors' institute. None of teams were able to solve it during the competition. We consider the problem to be hard since most teams that take part in ACM-ICPC are competent in common algorithm techniques.

Problem. You are given a circular necklace containing n beads. Each bead maybe black or white. You have to rearrange the beads so that beads of the same color occur consecutively. The only operation allowed is to cut the necklace at any point, remove some number of beads from both ends and put them back in any order, and join the cut ends. The cost of this operation is the number of beads removed. Any number of such operations can be used. You have to find a sequence of such operations with minimum total cost for a given initial distribution of beads. For example, if the initial string is `wbwbwb`, this can be done by a single operation of cost 4. Design a linear-time algorithm for this problem. (Problem due to Ajit Diwan.)

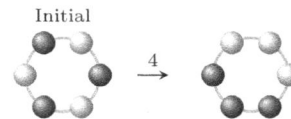

Step 1 *Analyze the Problem*

- Instances in the problem: Necklace.

- Property of the necklace: Number of misplaced beads.

Step 2a *Weakening the instance*

To simplify we use an array of beads instead of a circular necklace.

Extremal instance. Consider the problem on an array of beads with only one misplaced bead.

Step 2b *Weakening the objective*

Can we solve the problem if we allow the cut-and-join operation to be performed only *once*?

Step 3   Identify a candidate problem

Candidate Problem: Given an array of beads with one misplaced bead find the minimum cost by which we can sort the beads using one cut-and-join operation.

Step 4   Solving the candidate problem

Def. Let a maximal contiguous sequence of same colored beads be called a streak.

Observe that it is possible to solve this instance with cost of 8. But how can we prove that this is the minimum cost?

What if there exists a cut-and-join operation in the middle that achieves smaller cost? This not possible since the *untouched portion* of the array must be streak. If there are misplaced beads in the untouched portion, they will continue to remain so after the operations.

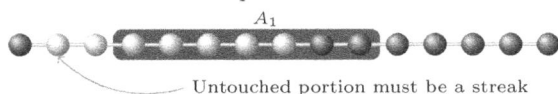

Untouched portion must be a streak

Step 5   Extend the solutions

In general, the untouched portions of the array must be streaks. Further, there cannot be a streak of a different color in between two streaks of the same color as this would also result in misplaced beads after the operation.

Adding a difficulty

Candidate Problem 2: Given an array of beads with one misplaced bead find the minimum cost by which we can sort the beads using *two* cut-and-join operations.

Would the minimum cost of operation remain 8, if we allowed two cut-and operations? Would it be possible to achieve lower cost by using two smaller operations?

Suppose A_1 and A_2 are two operations. The cost of these operations would be $|A_1 + A_2|$ which is more than 8 if the operations overlap. Hence, it is not useful to have to consecutive overlapping operations.

This idea coupled with the idea above gives enough information to resolve the problem.

Sol. Suppose the initial configuration of beads is represented by an array $A[1..n]$. The cut-and-join operation can be seen as rearranging a sub-array $A[i..j]$ while paying a cost of $j - i + 1$, allowing the sub-array to wrap around.

Suppose $A_1, A_2, \ldots, A_n$ is an optimal sequence of cut-and-joins. If A_i and A_{i+1} overlap or are next to each other they can be combined into one cut-and-join operation without increasing the cost. So there exits an optimal sequence in which A_is are separated from one another by streaks. Each A_i has at least one black bead and one white bead. There cannot be more than two A_is since this would result in two streaks of the same color after rearrangement. Since our goal is to get one streak of each color, the optimal strategy is to leave the maximum streak of white beads and maximum streak of black beads untouched and use (at most) two cut-and-join operations to rearrange the rest of the beads. This can be done in $O(n)$ time.

7. DISCUSSION ON TEACHABILITY

There are many more problems that can be solved using the WISE methodology. We have chosen to discuss three difficult problems as illustrations. The authors will be happy to share more examples upon request. Such illustrations can also be used for teaching WISE, through a cognitive apprenticeship model. The cognitive apprenticeship model is known to be a pedagogically sound way of teaching problem-solving [1].

We believe that the key steps involved in WISE can be taught to students as individual drills. The key steps involved in WISE are pervasive in all problem-solving techniques and not just limited to CS topics. Mastering these steps is likely to help the students in other areas too. These skills are not sufficiently emphasized in the current practice of teaching. For example, being able to formulate weaker problems is an important skill in any kind of problem-solving. However, there are hardly any questions in textbooks whose objective is to come up with a list of weaker problems for a given problem. Most instructors assume that this step will be implicitly done as part of solving a problem. In our preliminary experiments, we find that students tend to approach problems too directly and often get stuck in blind alleys.

WISE focuses on the method of inquiry rather than directly looking for a solution. This helps in the case of hard problems, when one cannot come up with the required insight directly. Often getting unstuck involves picking up a new line of approach. WISE does this by encouraging students to look at several simpler candidate problems and also gives explicit instructions for coming up with such problems. We have anecdotal evidence to show that the steps involved in WISE can be taught to students as individual drills. Based on our preliminary experiments, we find that students able to apply the first three steps of the WISE method but have difficulty in the 'Extend' step. In our future work, we plan to give guidelines to overcome this difficulty.

8. REFERENCES

[1] Vanessa P Dennen and Kerry J Burner. The cognitive apprenticeship model in educational practice. *Handbook of research on educational communications and technology*, pages 425–439, 2007.

[2] A. Engel. *Problem-solving strategies.* Springer, 1998.

[3] D. Ginat. Gaining algorithmic insight through simplifying constraints. *JCSE Online*, 2002.

[4] Jon Kleinberg and Éva Tardos. *Algorithm Design.* Addison Wesley, second edition, 2006.

[5] Anany Levitin and Mary-Angela Papalaskari. Using puzzles in teaching algorithms. In *Proceedings of the 33rd SIGCSE technical symposium on Computer science education*, SIGCSE '02, pages 292–296, New York, NY, USA, 2002. ACM.

[6] G. Polya. *How to Solve It - a New Aspect of Mathematical Method.* Princeton University Press, Princeton, 2 edition, 1957.

[7] Peter Winker. *Mathematical puzzles: a connoisseur's collection.* CRC Press, 2003.

MLSvisual: A Visualization Tool for Teaching Access Control Using Multi-Level Security

Man Wang
Department of Computer Science
Michigan Technological University
Houghton, MI
manw@mtu.edu

Steve Carr
Department of Computer Science
Western Michigan University
Kalamazoo, MI
steve.carr@wmich.edu

Jean Mayo,
Ching-Kuang Shene,
Chaoli Wang
Department of Computer Science
Michigan Technological University
Houghton, MI
{jmayo,shene,chaoliw}@mtu.edu

ABSTRACT

Information security continues to be a pressing issue for industry and government. Perhaps the two most fundamental mechanisms for controlling access to information are cryptography and access control systems. This paper presents MLSvisual, a tool that helps students learn the multi-level (Bell-LaPadula) access control model. MLSvisual allows students to create, explore, and modify an MLS policy through a graphical visualization system. A query system can be used by students to test their understanding of a given policy. Instructors can utilize a test function in the tool to assign an exercise or quiz, with answers sent to them via email. We also present the results of an evaluation of MLSvisual within a senior-level course on information security. This evaluation received positive feedback and showed that MLSviusal helped the understanding of the Bell-LaPadula model and enhanced the course. We believe that this user-level tool will help instructors to teach this material more effectively, and make teaching this material more practical in resource-constrained environments.

Categories and Subject Descriptors

k.3.2 [**Computers and Education**]: Computer and Information Science Education—*Computer science education, information systems education*

General Terms

Security, Access control model

Keywords

Security, visualization

ITiCSE'14, June 21–25, 2014, Uppsala, Sweden.
Copyright 2014 ACM 978-1-4503-2833-3/14/06 ...$15.00.
http://dx.doi.org/10.1145/2591708.2591730.

1. INTRODUCTION

Application of the principle of least privilege requires that a process be given access to only those resources necessary for it to complete its task. On modern systems, a very tight application of this principle can lead to a large (tens of thousands of rules) and complex access control policy that is challenging both to create and maintain.

This problem has been partially addressed through improved access control technology. Access control systems have evolved significantly over the last decade. A large part of the effort has been implementation of sophisticated security models, such as Multi-Level Security (MLS) [1, 2], Role-Based Access Control (RBAC) [7] and Type Enforcement (TE) [3]. These models abstract modern, common patterns of information access, and hence simplify policy development and administration.

Visualization has been applied to some access control models. Schweitzer, Collins, and Baird developed a visualization system to enable active learning about the Harrison, Ruzzo, Ullman and Take-Grant models of access control [11]. Hallyn and Kearns developed DTEEdit and DTEView for graphical analysis of DTE specifications [6]. DTEEdit and DTEView do not have pedagogical goals. Visualization and animation have also been applied in many areas of security education [4, 5, 8, 9, 10, 11, 12, 13, 14]. MLS is a fundamental access control model. To our knowledge, no visualization tool has been developed to help the teaching and learning of the model. This paper describes MLSvisual which aims to enhance the pedagogy of the MLS model. It allows students to create, modify, and analyze policies graphically. It also allows import and export of a human-readable text-based policy. To present and help explore the details, three graphical representations are used to illustrate a policy and an additional query subsystem is provided to answer some fundamental questions. Instructors may use a test module that requires students to answer questions about policies and then sends the answers via email. The system runs at the user-level and is not tied to the underlying file system. It currently supports Linux and MacOS. MLSvisual was tested in a senior-level course on computer security. The evaluation indicated that MLSviusal helped the understanding of the Bell-LaPadula model and enhanced the course.

The remainder of this paper is organized as follows: Section 2 provides the background of the computer security course where MLSviusal was evaluated, Section 3 presents our tool, Section 4 has a detailed study of our findings from student evaluation, and Section 5 has our conclusions.

2. COURSE INFORMATION

MLSvisual was used in a computer security course, CS4471 Computer Security, that was offered in the Department of Computer Science at Michigan Technological University. It is a senior level course that gives a basic introduction to topics in computer security. The access control component covers the Bell-LaPadula (BLP), Domain Type Enforcement (DTE), and Role-Based Access Control (RBAC) models. The course also covers secure coding in C, cryptography, key management, authentication, malicious logic, and intrusion detection.

Most students are computer science majors who take the course as an elective. The class in which the evaluation was conducted included seventeen CS majors, three Computer Systems Science majors (who are required to take the course), three Software Engineering majors, seven Computer Engineering majors, and three students from other majors including Electrical Engineering, Math and Communications, Cultures and Media.

Students were given paper and pencil exercises on the BLP model as part of the regular course homework. For this first use of MLSvisual, students were additionally given an extra credit assignment that required use of the tool. The problem was to evaluate a simple policy via a series of questions and then complete a test using the Test module. After the students had submitted their solutions to the extra credit assignment problem, the instructor distributed a survey to the class. Completion of the survey was voluntary.

3. SOFTWARE DESCRIPTION

MLSvisual is designed to facilitate the teaching as well as self-learning of Multi-Level Security using visualization. It implements the Bell-LaPadula model, where security levels are assigned to subjects (users and processes) and objects (files and directories). A security level (L, C) consists of a clearance L and a subset C of a comprehensive set of categories. A clearance such as "Secret" or "Top secret" represents the sensitivity of a subject or an object, and a set of categories indicates descriptive attributes such as "Documentary" or "States". Security levels are compared using the dominates relation $\geq$, where $(L_1, C_1) \geq (L_2, C_2)$ if and only if $L_1 \geq L_2$ (L_1 has a sensitivity higher than or equivalent to L_2, e.g., "Top Secret" $\geq$ "Secret") and $C_2 \subseteq C_1$. A subject can only read objects it dominates, and can only write to objects that dominate the subject. The dominates relation on the security levels forms a directed graph $G(V, E)$ where V contains a node for each security level (L, C) and there is an edge from the node for (L_1, C_1) to the node for (L_2, C_2) if and only if (L_2, C_2) dominates (L_1, C_1). Self-loops and edges inferred by transitivity that appear in a full digraph of the partial order are omitted to reduce clutter. Since two security levels can not dominate each other, $G(V, E)$ is a directed acyclic graph with the starting node dominating all the other nodes in V.

Figure 1 shows the user interface and visualization illustrating the relationship among security levels. The part with a white background is the drawing canvas. The red frame has all color coded clearances, and the blue frame has all cat-

egories indexed by numbers. Users may specify the clearance and categories of a security level by checking the buttons in these frames, and use the Add one node operation to draw the node for the security level on the canvas. The node will have the clearance color and the indices of its categories as its label.

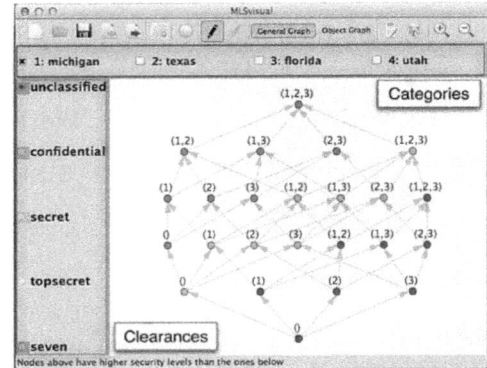

Figure 1: Main Window

MLSvisual supports the import and export of specification files (.mls) and visualization files (.mlsvis). A specification file contains a human-readable, text-based specification of components in an MLS policy, where clearances, categories, and the security levels of users and objects are designated. A visualization file stores the graph on the drawing canvas. A session may begin with loading a file of either type or building clearances and categories from scratch. The visualization focuses on the interpretation of the relationship among security levels and read and write permissions that subjects have towards objects. It includes three graphs: the Whole graph, the General graph and the Object graph. The Whole graph provides an automatically generated overview of the dominates relation among all security levels. The General graph allows users to gradually reveal the relations among security levels of interest. They may add nodes one by one or choose two existing nodes as end nodes and reveal the dominates relation between them using the Generate graph operation. The Object graph shows the security level assignment to objects. MLSvisual also has two modes: the Analysis mode and Edit mode. The Analysis mode allows the users to analyze properties of the policy they imported and helps the users better understand the BLP model. The Edit mode supports editing clearances and categories as well as the security level assignments to subjects and objects. This mode allows users to modify a policy and aims to help them design policies that fulfill specific security requirements. In addition, Specification and Exercise modules are provided for further exploration and design of MLS policies.

3.1 Visualization

The Whole graph $G_w(V_w, E_w)$ shows the directed graph described above of all security levels (Figure 4 (a)), where V_w contains all security levels and E_w contains the directed edges that represent the dominates relation. It starts with the node that dominates all the other nodes. The General graph $G_g(V_g, E_g)$ helps the users focus on the security levels and subjects of interest. (Figure 2). V_g is a subset of V_w, and E_g has the edges for the dominates relation among elements in V_g. The `Whole graph` and the `General graph` together provide both overall and partial views of the relationship among security levels so that a full understanding of a policy becomes easier.

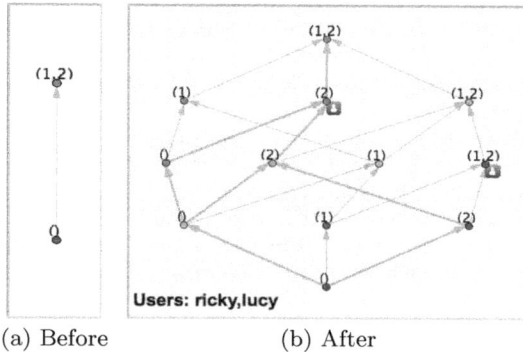

(a) Before   (b) After

Figure 2: General Graph Before And After Generate Graph Operation

The `Object graph` shows the security level assignment of objects. This graph has a number of concentric circles with the center being the root directory. The circles with increasing radii represent directories of increasing directory depth. The nodes in the graph are objects and the edges represent the membership of the directory (Figure 3). Each node is a rectangle with two colors. The left color indicates its clearance and the right one shows the category based on the color-category correspondence in the legend.

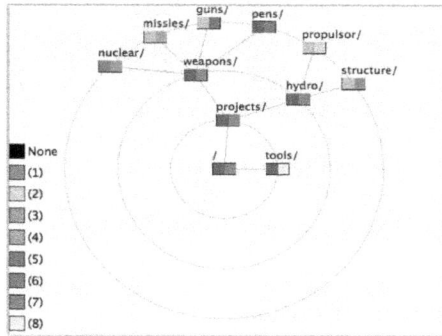

Figure 3: Object Graph

3.2 Analysis Mode

The `Analysis` mode is to facilitate the understanding of the relationship among security levels and permissions of subjects in the imported policy using the three graphs.

The `Whole graph` shows the relationship for all security levels. While a fine-grained policy may contain complicated and meaningful relationships, it also generates a cluttered graph. Hence, we use node grouping to reduce the clutter. If there are more than 15 nodes at one depth level in the graph, an expandable group node will replace the nodes with the same clearance at the same depth level and be labeled as the number of contained nodes. This group node can be replaced by the contained nodes when needed. Figure 4 (a) shows a `Whole graph` without grouping, while Figure 4 (b) has the same graph with grouping.

The `General graph` shows the relationship among some nodes in which users are interested. There are two methods

to draw the relationship: adding security level nodes one at a time and using the `Generate graph` operation. The first method draws an edge directly between nodes when they are related under the dominates relation. When a new node is added, the graph is updated. This helps students investigate when one node is reachable from another. Using the second method, a user designates two nodes and the tool generates the full directed graph between them. Nodes along all paths from the lower node to the upper node, as well as the edges between them, are generated. This is useful when investigating the reachability of the two given nodes, the possible paths and the involved security levels. It also avoids the overwhelming and repetitive operations of adding nodes. However, the first method still has its value when users are not interested in the detailed paths between nodes and prefer just knowing the reachability. Figure 2 (a) shows two nodes and their relationship. Applying the `Generate graph` operation to the same pair of nodes, Figure 2 (b) shows all the security levels in between. An icon by a node indicates there is a subject assigned to this security level. When the node (e.g., the red node with label (2) in Figure 2 (b)) is moused over, the subject's name appears at the lower left corner of the canvas, and its permissions to other security levels are shown in highlighted paths. These subjects can write to the nodes along the blue paths and can read the nodes along orange ones. By referring to the security levels of specific objects in the `Object graph`, it is easy to tell the permissions that subjects have towards objects.

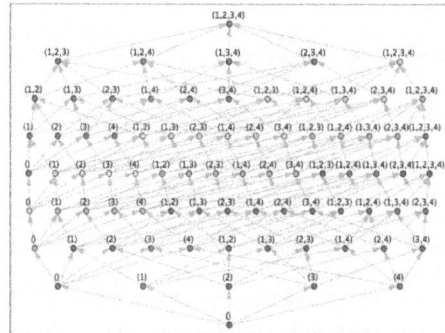

(a) Without Grouping

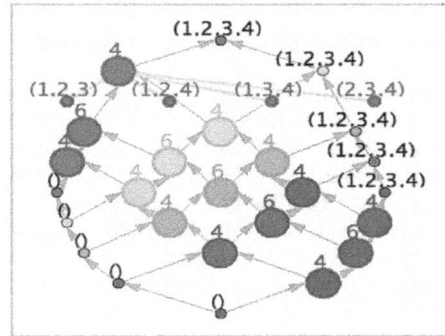

(b) With Grouping
Figure 4: Whole Graph

3.3 Edit Mode

MLSvisual starts with the `Edit mode` to create a policy. It can also be used to modify an existing policy. A policy contains four components: clearances, categories, security levels of users and security levels of objects. This mode provides four editing operations: `add/delete clearance`, `add/delete category`, `assign directory` (assigning security levels to objects) and `assign users` (assigning security levels to users in the operating system). One can move from the `Edit` mode to `Analysis` mode in the same session in order to evaluate policy changes.

3.4 Specification and Exercise Modules

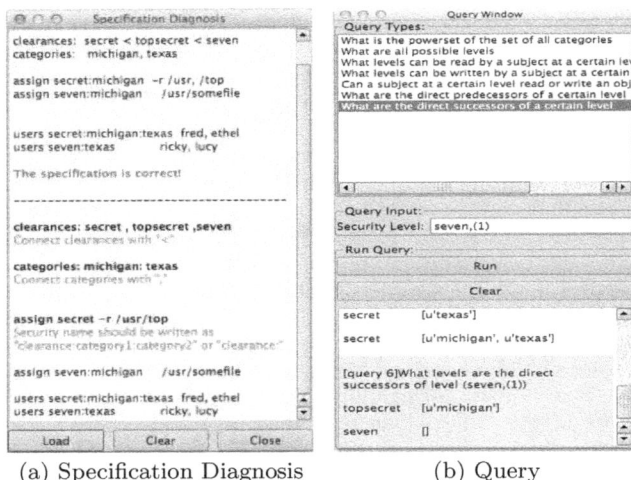

(a) Specification Diagnosis   (b) Query

Figure 5: Specification and Exercise Modules

Two more modules, `Specification` and `Exercise`, are provided to help the users understand the specification of an MLS policy and the BLP model. The `Specification` module has `Specification window` and `Specification diagnosis` components. The `Specification window` component generates a specification of the policy under consideration and is useful when a policy is being created graphically or the imported one is modified. The specification can be used as a guidance for writing correct specification files. The `Specification diagnosis` component is used to check the syntax of a `specification` file loaded in this module. If it is correct, confirmation of correctness will show up as the last line in green along with the original specification content in a pop-up window. Otherwise, information on how to correct the errors will be given under each problematic line (Figure 5 (a)).

The `Exercise` module consists of two components for self-evaluation: `Query` and `Test`. The `Query` component has seven questions (Figure 5(b)) to help the exploration of MLS policies. It provides answers to some frequently asked questions such as what are all sets of categories, what are the possible security levels and whether a specific subject has read or write permission to an object. The `Test` component provides a way to evaluate the understanding of clearance, category, relationships and permissions through 13 questions on policies in various scales. Users have to choose an answer to proceed to the next question. This can be used for in-class exercises or quizzes. Instructors will receive a student's answer, a grade on each question and overall grade via email. This component currently has an example set of questions covering the core aspects of the BLP model. Instructors may populate the test with their own questions by modifying an input text file.

4. EVALUATION

The `MLSvisual` evaluation consists of two components, 17 rating questions (Table 1) and 9 write-in comments. The first 14 questions (Q1-Q14) study the effects of `MLSvisual`. The choices are: 1:strongly disagree, 2:disagree, 3:neutral, 4:agree, and 5:strongly agree. Questions Q15, Q16 and Q17 study the use of `MLSvisual`. The choices for Q15 are 1:less than 5 mins, 2:5-10 mins, 3:10-15 mins, 4:15-30 mins and 5:more than 30 mins. The choices for Q16 are 1:once, 2:1-3 times, 3:3-5 times, 4:5-10 times and 5:more than 10 times. The choices for Q17 are 1:less than 5 mins, 2:5-15 mins, 3:15-30 mins, 4:30-60 mins and 5:more than 1 hour. We collected 22 valid forms. The distribution of majors is as follows: 10 in Computer Science, 6 in Computer Engineering, 3 in Computer Systems Science, 1 in Software Engineering, and 2 undeclared.

Table 1: Survey Questions

Q1	MLSvisual helped better understand BLP model
Q2	MLSvisual was helpful for my self-study
Q3	General graph's analysis mode showed the relationship between different security levels clearly
Q4	General graph's edit mode allowed easy creation and modification to policies
Q5	Object graph depicted files' security levels in a straightforward way
Q6	Whole graph helped better understand of policies
Q7	Representation and layout eased use of the tool
Q8	Colors helped understand BLP's information flow
Q9	Permissions of security levels are clearly depicted
Q10	The tool helped realize BLP's limitations
Q11	The tool helped learn Principle of Tranquility
Q12	Feel prepared to design policy after using the tool
Q13	The tool helped understand what wasn't understood
Q14	MLSvisual enhanced the course
Q15	How long did it take you to understand the BLP model by using the tool
Q16	How many times did you use the tool
Q17	How long did you use the tool in total

4.1 General Discussion

Table 2 shows the mean and standard deviation of each question. Feedback from participants was positive with an overall mean of 3.77 and standard deviation of 0.73. Q3 and Q8 received the highest scores of 4.2 and 4.3 with standard deviation 0.8 and 0.6, respectively. This indicates that the `General graph` showed the relationship among security levels clearly and that the use of colors helped students understand the BLP model. Q5 and Q11 received the lowest score 3.0. Q5 investigates whether the security levels of objects are straightforward in the `Object graph`. The low score may be because the `Object graph` and `General graph` were supposed to be used together. However, even if the security level assignment to the objects is visually presented, students probably treated them as separate and independent components, and hence Q5 received a neutral rating. Q11 received 3.0 because there is no direct visual presentation of this principle. Students have to edit a policy in several iterations to get hands-on experience of whether the strong or weak tranquility principle should be preserved. The `Edit mode` is designed for this purpose. The other questions received scores around 4.0. Hence, the general response to the tool was positive and participants considered that the tool helped them understand the concepts and enhanced the course. Of the three usage questions (Q15-Q17), Q17 had an average of 3.6, which indicated that students used the tool for 15 to 30 minutes. The average of Q15 was 2.9 which means that it took around 10-15 minutes for students to understand the BLP model using MLSvisual. The average of Q16 was 1.5 showing that students used the tool once or twice. Table 3 has the distribution of answers to these three questions. Q15 had 9%, 23% and 41% of students select Choice 1, Choice 2 and Choice 3, respectively. Thus, 73% of all students required less than 15 minutes to understand the BLP model. Since no student selected Choice 5, all of them understood the BLP model within 30 minutes. The answer distribution of Q16 indicated that 50% of all students used it only once while the rest used MLSvisual twice. For Q17, 87% of all students selected among Choice 1 to Choice 4, which means that 87% of all students spent less than one hour using the tool.

Table 2: Mean (μ) and Standard Deviation (σ)

	Q1	Q2	Q3	Q4	Q5	Q6	Q7	Q8	Q9
μ	4.0	3.8	4.2	4.1	3.0	3.7	3.7	4.3	3.8
σ	0.6	0.7	0.8	0.7	0.9	0.6	0.7	0.6	0.9

	Q10	Q11	Q12	Q13	Q14	Q15	Q16	Q17
μ	4.0	3.0	3.6	3.6	3.9	2.9	1.5	3.6
σ	0.7	0.9	0.6	0.8	0.5	0.9	0.5	1.0

Table 3: Usage Distribution

	Choice1	Choice2	Choice3	Choice4	Choice5
Q15	9%	23%	41%	27%	0
Q16	50%	50%	0	0	0
Q17	5%	9%	23%	50%	13%

We also looked at the correlations between each pair of questions from Q1 to Q14. The ratings of each question are loosely positively related with the highest correlations 0.65 for (Q3, Q10) and 0.64 for (Q7, Q8). The correlation between Q3 and Q10 suggested that those who considered the `Analysis mode` showed the relationship among security levels clearly (Q3) also tended to believe that MLSvisual helped them realize the BLP's limitations (Q10). For Q7 and Q8, those who considered the representation and layout made the use of MLSvisual easy (Q7) also might consider the color scheme helped them understand the information flow of the BLP model (Q8). There are some other pairs having correlations around 0.55. The correlations between (Q3, Q4) was 0.56, indicating that students who liked the `Analysis mode` of the `General graph` (Q3) also rated the `Edit mode` of the `General graph` (Q4) higher. The correlation 0.55 of (Q6, Q10) suggested that students who rated the `Whole graph` (Q6) higher might find it easier to realize the limitations of BLP model (Q10). The correlations between (Q1, Q13) and (Q2, Q13) were 0.52 and 0.55, respectively. This suggested that many students who felt that MLSvisual helped them understand what was not understood also tended to consider the tool helped self-study and a better understanding of the BLP model.

4.2 Statistical Analysis

We used MANOVA and ANOVA to investigate if the use of the tool may affect student ratings. The level of signif-

icance is $\alpha = 0.05$. The null hypothesis for this study is: the time spent on understanding the BLP model (Q15), the number of times using this tool (Q16), and the total time spent on this tool (Q17) did not affect the answers to the 14 questions (Q1-Q14). Based on the answers to Q15, we divided students into 3 groups. Group 1 had students who spent less than 10 minutes to understand the model. Group 2 spent 10 to 15 minutes, and group 3 spent more than 15 minutes. The p-value of a MANOVA Wilk's lambda test was 0.525, suggesting that there was no significant difference among these groups. To verify the result, we also used ANOVA to perform individual test against Q15, and found that Q5 vs. Q13 had the smallest p-values 0.051. Since it is still larger than the level of significance, we can not reject the null hypothesis.

Students were divided into two groups according to their responses to Q16. The first group had 11 students who used the tool only once. The second group had the other 11 students who used the tool twice. The p-value of a MANOVA Wilk's lambda test was 0.677, which indicated that the null hypothesis can not be rejected. ANOVA tests against Q16 showed that Q1 and Q12 had the two smallest p-values 0.062 and 0.070, respectively. Since they are still greater than the significance level, the null hypothesis can not be rejected.

For Q17, we divided students into 2 groups. The first group included 8 students who used the tool for less than 30 minutes while the other group of 14 students spent more than 30 minutes. The MANOVA Wilk's lambda test had a p-value of 0.332, and the null hypothesis can not be rejected. ANOVA tests against Q17 showed that the p-value for Q13 (0.0046) was the only one less than the significance level. The null hypothesis was rejected. Therefore, students who spent less than 30 minutes and the students who spent more than 30 minutes responded to Q13 differently. This happened because students used the tool after learning the BLP model in class. The parts they did not understand before were some challenging aspects. The different responses showed that many students were able to understand the challenging parts after spending enough time on the tool. Based on the findings, we have sufficient evidence to claim that the time students spent on the tool affects whether they could understand the parts that they did not understand before. But, in general, the use of the tool does not affect student rating when all questions are considered at the same time.

4.3 Student Comments

The set of 9 write-in questions was designed to gather suggestions from students for future improvement. The aspects we investigated are: whether the graph presentation is helpful, the `Specification diagnosis` module, the `Test module`, the use of colors and user interface, features to add and the software installation issues.

Student feedback was quite positive to the graph presentation. Some students said "*It clearly illustrated the lattice formed by the policy, and helped me see the relationship between levels*", "*The graph was very nice and definitely helped me understand the BLP model better*", "*The graph showed useful information with button to auto-generate*", and "*It worked perfectly as I imagined*". Therefore, we believe that the graph presentation did help students understand the BLP model better.

The comments on the `Specification diagnosis` model

were generally positive. Students mentioned that *"It was definitely useful"* and *"It was a nice addition to the visual"*. However, some students mentioned that they were not sure whether they had used the module. This is understandable since the extra credit assignment did not include the use of this module.

The `Test` module received positive feedback. Students mentioned that *"I was impressed by how well the software handled examples"* and *"The most populated object graph was nice"*. A suggestion *"It would be better if there were answers to the questions at the end of the test"* was also mentioned. Since instructors usually use the module as a quiz, the questions can be answered on demand in class.

All students were satisfied with the use of colors and the user interface. A student suggested that *"Queries should default to a pop-out window"*. Most of them did not think about additional features; however, one student indicated that *"Maybe a quick run down on the model and particular specification"*. No software installation problem was reported.

Students also provided some general comments for further improvement. They suggested adding tooltip to all buttons, having the larger default window size, and providing a version for 64-bit Linux since some of their systems were not 32-bit compatible and needed some packages installed before use.

In summary, we believe that `MLSvisual` effectively helped self-learning and in-class teaching of the MLS policies and BLP model. With the suggestions from the students, we will improve `MLSvisual` in the near future.

5. CONCLUSIONS

This paper discusses a visualization tool `MLSvisual` to facilitate the teaching and self-learning of the MLS access control model. Instructors may use the tool in class and read in policies while explaining the concepts and properties. Students who are interested in learning the model on their own or exploring the model further after class may use the tool to understand the model better. Students may also learn the design of an MLS policy and perform self-evaluations.

The evaluation showed that `MLSvisual` was helpful. In the grouping analysis, MANOVA tests found no difference in rating against student's use of the tool considering all questions at the same time while ANOVA tests showed that the time students spent on the tool affected whether they were able to understand the parts that challenged them before. As suggested in the feedback, we will improve the tool as follows: (1) include visual presentation of the principle of strong and weak tranquility, (2) provide a `Practice` component with answers to questions, and (3) add tooltip to the user interface.

`MLSvisual` is a part of larger development of security visualization tools supported by the National Science Foundation. Besides `MLSvisual`, `DTEvisual` for Domain Type Enforcement access control model has been developed. Visualization tools for Role-Based Access Control model and a large visualization framework for the combination and communication of all the visualization tools will be available in the future. The tool, user guide and demo video are accessible at the following link:

http://acv.cs.mtu.edu/mlsvisual.html

6. REFERENCES

[1] D. E. Bell and L. J. La Padula. Secure computer systems: Mathematical foundations. Technical Report MTR-2547, Vol 1, The MITRE Corporation, Bedford, MA, Nov. 1973.

[2] K. J. Biba. Integrity considerations for secure computer systems. MTR-3153, Rev. 1, The MITRE Corporation, Bedford, MA, Apr. 1977.

[3] W. E. Boebert and R. Y. Kain. A practical alternative to hierarchical integrity policies. In *Proceedings of National Computer Security Conference*, pages 18–27, Oct. 1985.

[4] J. R. Crandall, S. L. Gerhart, and J. G. Hogle. Driving home the buffer overflow problem: A training module for programmers and managers. In *Proceedings of National Colloquium for Information Systems Security Education*, June 2002.

[5] D. Ebeling and R. Santos. Public key infrastructure visualization. *The Journal of Computing Sciences in Colleges*, 23(1):247–254, Oct. 2007.

[6] S. Hallyn and P. Kearns. Tools to administer domain and type enforcement. In *Proceedings of USENIX Conference on System Administration*, pages 151–156, Dec. 2001.

[7] R. S. Sandhu, E. J. Coyne, H. L. Feinstein, and C. E. Youman. Role-based access control models. *IEEE Computer*, 20(2):38–47, 1996.

[8] D. Schweitzer and L. Baird. The design and use of interactive visualization applets for teaching ciphers. In *Proceedings of IEEE Workshop on Information Assurance*, pages 69–75, 2006.

[9] D. Schweitzer, L. Baird, M. Collins, W. Brown, and M. Sherman. Grasp: A visualization tool for teaching security protocols. In *Proceedings of National Colloquium for Information Systems Security Education*, pages 75–81, 2006.

[10] D. Schweitzer and W. Brown. Using visualization to teach security. *The Journal of Computing Sciences in Colleges*, 24(5):143–150, 2009.

[11] D. Schweitzer, M. Collins, and L. Baird. A visual approach to teaching formal access models in security. In *Proceedings of National Colloquium for Information Systems Security Education*, 2007.

[12] J. Tao, J. Ma, M. Keranen, J. Mayo, and C.-K. Shene. ECvisual: A Visualization Tool for Elliptic Curve Based Ciphers. In *Proceedings of ACM Technical Symposium on Computer Science Education*, pages 571–576, 2012.

[13] J. Tao, J. Ma, J. Mayo, C.-K. Shene, and M. Keranen. DESvisual: A Visualization Tool for the DES Cipher. *The Journal of Computing Sciences in Colleges*, 27(1):81–89, 2011.

[14] X. Yuan, Y. Qadah, J. Xu, H. Yu, R. Archer, and B. Chu. An animated learning tool for kerberos authentication architecture. *The Journal of Computing Sciences in Colleges*, 22(6):147–155, 2007.

Acknowledgements

This work was supported in part by the National Science Foundation under grants DUE-1140512, DUE-1245310 and IIS-1319363.

Empowering Faculty to Embed Security Topics into Computer Science Courses

Ambareen Siraj, Sheikh Ghafoor, Joshua Tower, Ada Haynes
Tennessee Technological University
Department of Computer Science
110 University Drive
Cookeville, TN 38505
{ASiraj, SGhafoor, JDtower21, AHaynes}@tntech.edu

ABSTRACT

Security illiteracy is a very common problem among Computer Science (CS) graduates entering the nation's digital workforce, which has contributed to a national cyber-infrastructure that could and should be more resilient to cyber-enemies than it is now. The Security Knitting Kit (SecKnitKit) project aims to improve security awareness, knowledge, and interest of undergraduate CS students by exposing them to computer security concepts and issues in their regular course of study. The project is developing, deploying, and disseminating a multi-faceted out-of-the-box instructional support system to empower non-security faculty. These are faculty who have no experience in teaching security but recognize the importance of security in today's world and want to broaden their teaching repertoire. This project enables them to weave relevant security topics traditional computer science courses seamlessly and effectively. The project is organized by the CS department at Tennessee Tech University (TTU) and supported by the National Science Foundation under grant DUE-1140864.

Categories and Subject Descriptors

K.3.2 [**Computer and Information Science Education**]: Computer science education

General Terms

Security, Experimentation

Keywords

Security, Security Education, ACM/IEEE-CS 2013 Curricula

1. INTRODUCTION

"At least some computer security instruction should be a prerequisite in participating in the information age" – Dr. C.Y. Irvine, Challenges in Computer Security Education," IEEE Software, Sept./Oct. 1997

Lack of information assurance (IA) and security in deployed computer software and in daily operational usage of software costs businesses and taxpayers severely every year. The CSI Computer Crime and Security Survey [3] reports that the average loss by an organization in 2009 was close to a quarter million dollars; and 60% of these financial losses were attributed to non-malicious actions by "insiders." These insiders are mostly end users and computer professionals with operational and developmental responsibilities. Examples include software engineers that leave exploitation opportunities for buffer overflow without proper input validation; application developers who do not implement access controls; and system users who do not ensure appropriate security configurations. Although it has become critical that "all" Computer Science (CS) students need to experience security training in traditional subject matters, at the least as threaded security topics, most higher education institutions do not have the faculty capacity to teach specialized security courses. The majority of institutions offering security courses at the undergraduate level offer them as standalone individual courses. In other words, security is treated in isolation. Since not mandatory in CS curriculum, many CS undergraduates can successfully achieve their degree without being exposed to any security courses during their course of study. Only 129 out of more than 4,000 higher education institutions in the United States are accredited by the government as National Centers of Academic Excellence in Information Assurance Education Programs (CAE/IAE) to specialize in computer security education [9]. With the absence of required security courses in traditional CS curriculum, the vast majority of graduates enter the digital workforce with no knowledge or basic understanding of information security – one of the essential skill sets for the 21st century. In addressing this concern, Information Assurance and Security (IAS) has been designated as a new knowledge area in the new ACM/IEEE-CS Curricula 2013 [1]. The guideline denotes that IAS "is added to the Body of Knowledge in recognition of the world's reliance on information technology and its critical role in computer science education". Also, for an academic institution to be accredited as CAE/IAE, one of the criteria that needs to be fulfilled is "Criteria 2: IA Treated as a Multidisciplinary Science" [8], which clearly states that the academic program under consideration must demonstrate that IA is not treated as a separate entity but is incorporated into existing courses and non-IA students are introduced to IA concepts. Since security concepts are not integrated into existing curriculum in the majority of institutions - the aspiration of accreditation remains beyond their reach. This leads to another key motivation behind this project, which is providing support for interested educational institutions to move closer towards CAE/IAE accreditation.

Since in today's world security consciousness has become an essential skill set and part of good citizenship [7], the primary goals of this project are:

- To improve security awareness, knowledge and interest of undergraduate computer science students by exposing them to computer security concepts and issues in their regular course of study *(student learning goal)*.
- To improve the security awareness and security teaching expertise for non-security faculty *(faculty expertise development goal)*.

- To promote the use of security integration strategy and materials in other institutions *(dissemination goal)*.

Security Knitting Kit (SecKnitKit): Integrating Security into Traditional Computer Science Courses" is a National Science Foundation supported project (DUE Award#-99999) that develops, deploys and disseminates a multi-faceted out-of-the-box instructional support system to empower non-security faculty (faculty whose primary teaching/research focus is not security) in CS to seamlessly and effectively weave security topics into traditional CS courses. The project is implemented by the CS department at Tennessee Tech University (TTU).

2. Related Work in Integrating Security into Traditional Courses

Primarily, there are three models of security education [11]: a security track; a single security course; and threading security topics into traditional CS courses.

Security specialization with a security track is used in the graduate curriculum and is intended to build and train cyber-warriors. The single security course approach is typically offered as an elective in the undergraduate curriculum. Not all institutions offer such dedicated courses because faculty expertise in this area is not always available and adding an extra security course to a full curriculum is very difficult. The unconventional third model, which addresses the problem of integrating security into CS curriculum, is the focus of this project.

Integrating security topics in the traditional CS curriculum is a well-recognized, challenging problem that has been the focus of many scholarly works [4,7,10,11,16-18]. Scholars have articulated this need, and in some cases shared ideas, observations, and recommendations, however, very few actual initiatives have been undertaken or implemented to solve this problem.

Graduate students at the University of Maryland, Baltimore County conducted a project where they proposed to create security modules for programming classes like CSI, CSII and data structures [12]. In Georgia State University, students are taught to consider information security through real world scenarios and relevant exercises within CSI [6].

Funded by NSF grant DUE-0817267, "Security Injections" is an ongoing collaborative project originating at Towson University [14], which integrates security topics into the undergraduate computing curriculum by developing and deploying online "security modules" for students to learn through self-study [13]. The CS courses that have been addressed with the development of security modules are primarily lower division courses with programming emphasis (CS0, CSI, CSII and CSIII). The Security Injections project emphasizes minimal intrusion and therefore promotes self-learning on the students' part without direct faculty involvement in teaching the material. Students are directed to the website by the faculty and are asked to read and learn the material themselves and to carry out assessment activities such as laboratory assignments, discussion questions, and security checklists. The only involvement mandated by the faculty is to administer security surveys before and after student exposure, direct students to the website or hand the material over to the students, and at the end take part in faculty surveys. In a workshop arranged by the Security Injections project, "getting faculty involved" was identified as one of the ways to improve the project's progress [15]. Another problem identified was that in some cases, students tended to skip materials that are online. Mostly geared at lower division programming courses, the project is being adopted by the Maryland Alliance for Information Security Assurance.

3. THE PROJECT OVERVIEW

The central themes surrounding the project objectives are student and faculty learning. The project creates and integrates relevant, adaptable, and extensible learning materials on security topics and teaching strategies for selected, required CS courses based on best practices in computer security education and pedagogy resulting in a multi-faceted instructional support system, which

- facilitates student learning in computer security by helping students understand "the big picture" and its relevancy with computer science education;
- offers ready-made instructional material to integrate security in traditional courses;
- is readily deliverable by faculty;
- is easily adaptable into CS curriculum; and
- is extendable to meet the need of the CS curriculum.

In this project, our learning model consists of assisting faculty in learning and acquiring new knowledge and skills, which will in turn, facilitate student learning (Figure 1). While the solid lines are the focus of this project, the dotted lines in the left are not.

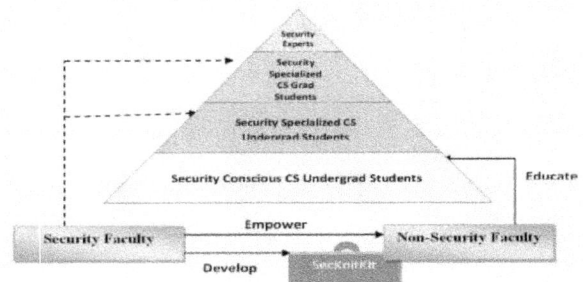

Figure 1: SecKnitKit Model

While our primary goal is to educate CS students better in security concepts, we believe that without active involvement of the faculty learning cannot be as effective as possible. However, as noted by Bransford in [2], it is difficult for faculty to undertake the rethinking of their subject matter and to take up the challenge of learning material out of their comfort zone. It is natural for faculty to feel vulnerable by taking on such risks. While we want to involve the faculty in the learning process, we certainly do not want to create an extra burden on an already overworked faculty workforce in higher education, especially in these days of resource limitations and budget cuts. Therefore there are primarily two aspects of our approach, as shown in Figure 2: SecKnitKit instructional support system and professional development workshops.

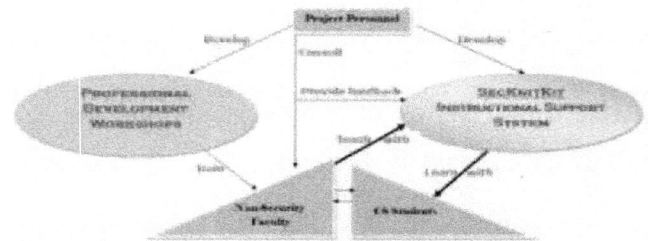

Figure 2: SecKnitKit Approach

3.1 SecKnitKit Instructional Support System

The SecKnitKit Instructional Support System is offered to any non-security faculty, allowing them to integrate relevant security topics into upper division courses as part of the course content as well as teach them about security issues with minimal effort on their part. We believe that the in-class experience is more effective than the out-of-class experience where students are left with the responsibility of sifting through materials on their own. Without over-burdening the faculty, we want to ensure that this teaching experience is as effortless as possible. The readily available instructional support system comes as a SecKnitKit toolkit (Figure 3) to be used by the faculty, which include the following:

o Instructional material in the forms of presentation slides and lecture notes where the material will include *(knowledge-centered components)*:

- Introduction, description of the topic, and its relevancy to the main course topic;
- Nature of the topic - whether it is a type of threat, attack,, vulnerability, or security mechanism:
  o If it is threat/attack/vulnerability, how to mitigate it;
  o If it is security mechanism, how to enforce it.

o Assessment material in the forms of *(formative and summative assessment compothounents)*:

- Discussion questions in assignments to engage in problem solving and critical thinking;
- Hands-on group active learning assignments to facilitate problem solving, active learning, critical thinking and collaborative learning (take home);
- Quizzes and exam questions (with answers);
- Surveys/feedback questionnaires (online).

The assessment-centered component facilitates improvement in teaching with formative assessments and assists in progress determination with summative assessments. While the knowledge centered components are delivered in class, most if not all, formative and summative assessments are designed to be online or out-of-class to save on class contact hours.

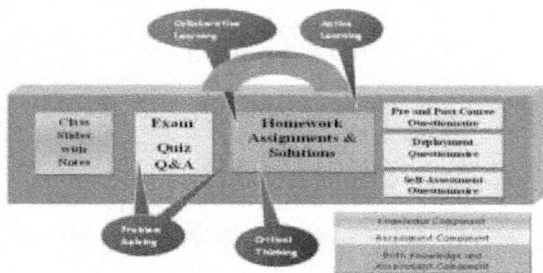

Figure 3: The SecKnitKit Toolkit

In this project, we concentrate on integrating security in four upper division courses that are common/typical in any ABET accredited CS curriculum (software engineering I, database management systems, operating systems and computer networks). With security included as integrated topics in these courses, all CS graduates will most likely experience some level of exposure to concepts of security. This also allows our modules to be adoptable to any other higher education institutions offering CS degrees. Other rationales are as follows:

- During the junior and senior years of undergraduate education, the students are more mature and have more experience, which helps them to better understand and realize the need and impact of security in all technological aspects of CS like software engineering, database management, operating systems and networks.
- Faculty who teach upper division courses are typically the ones who also teach graduate level courses and hence are more motivated and inclined to conduct research.

- For security topics related to lower division programming courses, the Security Injections project exists to offer aid to interested faculty.

For each of these courses, relevant security topics are identified using primarily Core Tier-1 IAS topics (absolutely essential topics) and some Core Tier-2 IAS topics (important foundational topics) identified in ACM/IEEE-CS CS2013 Body of Knowledge [1]; recommendations of experts in this field [4,7,10,11,16-18], computer science pedagogy, and consultation with faculty teaching these courses. The most significant challenge of content development was assessing what security material to integrate into traditional courses, considering the right balance of importance of material, relevance, and time to teach. Table 1 shows the topics in the SecKnitKit instructional modules and Table 2 shows the topics in the SecKnitKit active learning exercises.

Table 1. SecKnitKit Instructional Module Topics

Course	Threaded Security Concepts
ALL	Introduction to Security (basic concepts like threats, attacks, CIA model, defense-in-depth)
Software Engineering	Security risk management
	Security design principles
	Common programming errors with security implications
Operating Systems	Security design principles
	Common system management errors with security implications
	Access control
	Authentication
	Covert Channels
Database Management	Traditional security concerns in DB
	Security controls in DB
	Special security concerns in DB
Computer Networks	Security issues and controls in TCP
	Security issues and controls in IP

Table 2. SecKnitKit Active Learning Exercise Topics

Course	Security Concepts
Software Engineering	Buffer overflow attack
	Security problem with improper initialization
	Security problem with improper operand and insufficient random values
Operating Systems	Access control matrix in Windows
	Race condition
	Heap spraying
	Authentication in Unix
Database Management	SQL integrity control
	SQL access control
	Views
	SQL injection attack
Computer Networks	Man in the Middle attack with IP Spoofing
	Man in the Middle attack with ARP Poisoning
	Local cache poisoning
	Wireless security (secure and insecure configuration)
	Simple IP Spoofing

3.2 Faculty Professional Development Workshop for Non-Security Faculty

Professional development (PD) has been a well-established mechanism for enhancing educators' knowledge and skill with proven positive impacts. With the support of the SecKnitKit toolkit and effective training in adopting this approach, the learning curve for faculty was expected to be minimal and produce only a minor burden. A onetime professional development workshop for faculty was conducted midway through in the project cycle and this workshop was spilt into three parts:

- ❖ Security Awareness and Project Introduction: This was split into two components. In the first half, the faculty were introduced to the project, its goal, and the future plan. In the second half, they were introduced to current security landscape with basic concepts in IA and security, threats and protections.
- ❖ SecKnitKit Training: In the second one in the series, faculty were "walked through" the instructional and assessment materials for the courses. The instructional material was delivered in a lecture style and the faculty exercised the active learning material with guidance.
- ❖ Brain Storming: In the third, focus groups were formed for strategic discussion of issues or concerns such as:
  - o General security topics of interest relevant to the courses under consideration;
  - o Traditional topics in the course curriculum that can "potentially" be replaced with security topics.

It should be mentioned that since the security topics are added on to an already existing curriculum, some minor adjustments need to be made regarding the overall course structure. Careful consideration is given to the design of the integration such that total in-class delivery of security material does not exceed 1.5 to 2 lecture units of the host course. There are several alternatives to consider in the weeding out process. The traditional topics identified can be totally replaced (if appropriate), or condensed in content, and/or made available outside class through an online class portal. Throughout the workshop, local non-security faculty responsible for deploying SecKnitKit at TTU shared their experiences and insights gained by deploying SecKnitKit in TTU with the workshop participants and guided the participants in material walk throughs.

4. PROJECT IMPLEMENTATION – YEAR 1

We designed and developed the SecKnitKit toolkit during Fall of 2012. We deployed it at the TTU institutional level during Spring 2013 where we embedded security topics in four upper division courses that were taught by three faculty whose primary teaching expertise is not security. The training was conducted on a one-to-one basis.

We conducted a two day professional development workshop at the end of first academic year of the 2-year project (June 3-4, 2013) attended by 15 non-security faculty from other institutions who teach any of these courses: software engineering, operating systems, networks and database management systems. There was a call for participation and 12 out of approximately 50 applicants were carefully selected to be early adopters. They had no prior teaching experience in security, their curriculum did not offer any mandatory security courses and they had a definite interest in integrating security traditional CS courses. To defray the cost of travel, we received funding to provide each participant with a stipend of $1000.00 to attend the workshop. In addition, three faculty attended the program out of special interest without any travel reimbursement. Later two faculty from another institution volunteered to become additional early adopters.

5. PROJECT EVALUATION – YEAR 1

This year approximately 150 CS undergraduate students were exposed to SecKnitKit material through four courses at TTU in the Pilot deployment phase. These courses were Software Engineering II (CSC 4620), Operating Systems (CSC 4240), Computer Networks (CSC 4240), and Database Management Systems (CSC 4300). Pre and post surveys were administered to students and faculty associated with the courses. The purpose of these surveys was to gain preliminary data on the pilot of the SecKnitKit and related materials (including evaluation materials) before a wider dissemination to other institutions.

5.1 TTU Pilot Evaluation: Student

Overall, the results of this pilot have been very positive. However, we were able to identify some items to improve and some items that need further study. Each course was analyzed by conducting paired t-tests on the pre and post surveys of student responses. Responses were reported on a six-point scale reflecting interest and a five-point scale for awareness, knowledge and progress related to security topics. Missing data were eliminated by cases. The student survey results are reported for each course below. Due to space limitations, graphical representations of the results are not included here.

5.1.1 Results for Computer Networks

The Computer Networks course was the smallest of the four courses with only 8 students completing both the pre and post surveys. With only 8 students and only 7 degrees of freedom it was more difficult to get statistical significance between the pre and post surveys. Because of the small sample, only three variables showed statistically significant gains. The students reported significant gains on their awareness of the source of security incidents, the stand of the USA in security incidents as compared globally, and the number of computer security related jobs projected. Although generally students reported gains in knowledge in areas related to course material, (sometimes as much as a 1 point gain on a 6 point scale in the case of the abuse of ARP protocol for denial of service), due to the small sample size, these items were not statistically significant.

5.1.2 Results for Database Management Systems

The Database Management Systems course contained 43 matched pairs of student surveys. For this course, students reported significant gains in the awareness of security issues, knowledge gains in the course and reported progress in active learning and database opportunities. The students reported significant gains in awareness of the cost of security incidents, the source of security incidents, the impact of security incidents, the stand of the USA in security incidents as compared globally, and the number of computer related jobs. Students also reported significant gains in knowledge in each of the following areas: basic terms and terminology in security, threat categories, attack types, CIA model, defense in depth, security policy, traditional security concerns (CIA), security controls in DB schema, security controls with Views, and security controls in SQL. Students similarly reported significant progress on active learning and opportunities related to database security: identifying security problems in databases and how to address security in databases compared to typical previous classes. The one significant negative finding was students demonstrated less interest in learning more about security in general.

5.1.3 Results for Operating Systems

The Operating Systems class contained 22 matched pairs of students. Students reported a significant increase in awareness of the cost of security incidents. They reported a significant increase in knowledge of the basic terms and terminology in security, attack types, CIA model, Defense in depth, security policy, dangers of incorrect settings of process privileges, dangers of incorrect access control permissions, importance of memory protection, dangers of race conditions, importance of indivisibility, access control, authentication, use of shadow file for authentication, and covert channel detection and containment. They also reported significant progress in active learning opportunities related to network security, identifying potential security problems in networks, and how to address security in networks compared to previous classes. They demonstrated significant decrease in their agreement in security as an important issue and wanting to learn more about security in general. They were more likely to agree that they had had active learning opportunities related to network security.

5.1.4 Results for Software Engineering II

Software Engineering II had 16 matched pairs of students.. These students reported a significant improvement in their awareness of the cost of security incidents, the source of security incidents, the stand of the USA in security incidents as compared globally, and the number of computer security related jobs projected. They also reported the following knowledge gains: gain in knowledge in the basic terms and terminology in security, Threat categories, attack types, CIA model, defense in depth, security policy, threat modeling, risk assessment, risk mitigation, security engineering, security principles, dangers of improper configuration/initialization, dangers of buffer overflow, dangers of shared memory, dangers of poorly thought out error messages, and the importance of checking proper permissions. Students in the Software Engineering II class also reported significant progress in active learning opportunities related to computer security, identifying potential security problems, and how to think critically to improve computer security.

5.2 TTU Pilot Evaluation: Faculty

The faculty surveys for local deployment, due to the small sample size (4), were never meant to be statistically analyzed, but were meant to serve as a pilot for surveys to be administered to the larger group of faculty members in the next phase. Faculty feedback concerning SecKnitKit content in the 1st year is being taken into consideration for revising and improving for deployment in 2nd year. Also, as our motto was "minimal effort" for the non-security faculty to bring security concepts into classes, we sought feedback especially on faculty involvement and the following is the result.

- Preparation time for lectures: Approximately how much time was spent in preparing for security related lectures (not including active learning exercises), the average response was between 1 to 3 hours.
- Class time: Approximately how much time was spent in covering security topics in class the average response was between 90 to 120 minutes.
- Preparation for active learning and grading: Approximately how much time was spent in familiarizing/preparing with/for the active learning exercises?" and "Approximately how much time was spent in grading the active learning exercises, the average response was between 2 to 3 hours.

5.3 Faculty Professional Development Workshop Evaluation

The workshop was evaluated through a survey of participants. This survey included both quantitative and qualitative questions. By all indications, this workshop was successful in generating interest and awareness in non-security faculty to integrate security topics in their courses. Fifteen respondents from 13 institutions completed the workshop survey. The participants attending came from a wide range of institutions including R-1 schools such as the University of Wyoming and historically black schools such as Fisk University. Of the participants, 47% were female and 53% were male. Only 13% had a required security course for their majors. The number of years teaching computer science ranged from 1 to 30 years. Sixty percent had no computer security classes as an undergraduate while 40% had one computer security class as an undergraduate. While 73% had no computer security classes in graduate school, 7% had half a class, and 20% had one computer security class in graduate school. None of the participants had taught a computer security class previously.

All of the respondents found all of the sessions to be useful. All of the respondents also reported that the workshop provided an effective overview of the project and provided the information needed to implement the SecKnitKit All respondents similarly reported the workshop to be a good networking opportunity and indicated a willingness to share information about the workshop with other faculty members.

Similar to the students at Tennessee Tech, the faculty members across institutions participating in the workshop indicated that they had increased their awareness about computer security issues. The area with the lowest level of agreement was the area regarding awareness of funding in computer security where one faculty member slightly disagreed that the project had increased their awareness.

All aspects of the project seem to be key components in getting faculty members to incorporate computer security. The workshop seems to have accomplished its goals of providing the needed information about SecKnitKit to assist non-security faculty members in incorporating more issues related to security in their classes.

5.4 Summary of Findings and Retrospection

Overall, students reported significant gains in knowledge, awareness, and progress related to computer security in a wide variety of areas addressed by the SecKnitKit. These results are very encouraging. The primary purpose of this project is to raise awareness and importance of security in computing for CS students and faculty and the results indicate this has been successful. The one area in which the findings were not significant is the area of increasing student interest in computer security. A couple of possible explanations exist to explain why this may have occurred. First the scale for these questions was reversed from other questions on the survey. This may have confused some students. We have changed the scale of these questions for year 2 deployments so that positive and negative ratings are consistent on the survey. Another possible explanation is that most of the students in these upper division classes were seniors who likely have chosen their specific career path in CS before they were exposed to security. We have added some open-ended questions on the post survey for the current year to ask students to explain why they are (or not) interested in computer security careers and graduate studies.

Regardless, as mentioned before, indication of an increase in security awareness among CS undergraduates, and an increase in security knowledge among CS undergraduates in selected subject areas serves SecKnitKit's primary mission of raising security consciousness among CS graduates. This project has demonstrated that non-security faculty can successfully incorporate the SecKnitKit in non-security focused courses.

6. CONCLUSION

Security illiteracy is a very common problem among CS graduates entering the nation's digital workforce, which has contributed to a national cyber-infrastructure that could and should be more resilient to cyber-enemies. There is urgency in increasing the size of our security-aware workforce such that computing students enter the workforce with the knowledge needed to design and develop reliable systems - at the least –avoid poor development practices that often leave loopholes to exploit. This project focuses on integrating knowledge and understanding of security issues across multiple CS courses. Integrating the project requires active participation from the faculty; therefore faculty who do not teach security courses are provided support with adapting security topics into the existing curriculums and delivering learning material in a useful manner. It also provides an opportunity for fostering interest in security among non-security faculty, who may be motivated to become more involved in this area with teaching and/or research. The SecKnitKit toolkit is portable and accessible enough to facilitate the adoption at other higher education institutions.

We have institutionalized SecKnitKit at our university and have done it in a manner to continue even after funding ends. The successful deployment of the first phase of the project is providing innovative insights into the capabilities of threading security content into traditional CS courses. The project is in its second phase currently which involves working closely with the non TTU early adopter faculty in 13 institutions nationwide that are adopting SecKnitKit into upper division courses, using evaluation results and faculty feedback from Year 1 to improve SecKnitKit, continuing with deployment of SecKnitKit at TTU   and continuing with various activities to disseminate SecKnitKit material and model findings and experiences to the CS community. All SecKnitKit material that has been developed under this project (instructional, assessment, active learning) is accessible at the project website at www.secknitkit.org as per request.

7. ACKNOWLEDGMENTS

Our sincere gratitude goes to project senior personnel William Eberle and Mike Rogers for helping with institutional deployment of this project. We are thankful for their valuable feedback, guidance, and support. Special thanks go to Suzanne Henry and Valerie Nash for ensuring compliance with TTU policies and procedures. Last but not least, we acknowledge and appreciate all the workshop attendees/early adopters, whose interest, time, and effort is instrumental in the success of this project.

8. REFERENCES

[1] ACM/IEEE-CS Joint Task Force on Computing Curricula. 2013. Computer Science Curricula 2013. ACM Press and IEEE Computer Society Press. http://ai.stanford.edu/users/sahami/CS2013/final-draft/CS2013-final-report.pdf

[2] Bransford, J. D., Brown, A. L. and Cocking, R. R. *How People Learn: Brain, Mind, Experience, and School.* National Academy Press, Washington, D.C., 1999.

[3] Computer Security Institute. The 14th Annual CSI Computer Crime and Security Survey Report. Retrieved September 3, 2013 from http://gocsi.com/survey_2009.

[4] Irvine, C., Chin, S. and Frincke, D. Integrating Security into the Curriculum. *IEEE Computer, 31*(12). pp. 25-30.

[5] Irvine, C.E., Challenges in Computer Security Education. *IEEE Software,* Sept./Oct. 1997, pp. 110-111. Retrieved September 3, 2013 from http://www.dtic.mil/cgi-bin/GetTRDoc?AD=ADA484034&Location=U2&doc=GetTRDoc.pdf.

[6] Markham, S.A., Expanding Security Awareness in Introductory Computer Science Courses. in *Proceedings: Information Security Curriculum Development Conference,* (Kennesaw, GA, 2009).

[7] Mullins, P., Wynters, E., Wolfe, J., Calhoun, W., Oblitey, W., Fry, M. and Montante, R., Panel on Integrating Security Concepts into Existing Computer Courses. in *Proceedings of SIGCSE 2002,* (Covington, KN, 2002), ACM, pp. 365-366.

[8] National Security Agency and Central Security Service. 2012. National Centers of Academic Excellence in IA Education (CAE/IAE) Criteria for Measurement. Retrieved September 3, 2013 from http://www.nsa.gov/ia/academic_outreach/nat_cae/cae_iae_program_criteria.shtml

[9] National Security Agency and Central Security Service. 2013. National Centers of Academic Excellence. Retrieved September 3, 2013 from http://www.nsa.gov/ia/academic_outreach/nat_cae/index.shtml.

[10] Null, L. Integrating Security Across the Computer Science Curriculum. *Journal of Computing Sciences in Colleges,* 19(5). pp. 170-178.

[11] Perrone, L. F., Aburdene, M. and Meng, X., Approaches to Undergraduate Instruction in Computer Security. in *Proceedings of the American Society for Engineering Educational Annual Conference and Exhibition,* (2005), ASEE. Retrieved September 3, 2013 from http://www.ists.dartmouth.edu/library/116.pdf.

[12] Roberts, B., Cress, D. and Simmons, J. Towards a Security-Aware Undergraduate Computer Science Curriculum at UMBC. Retrieved September 3, 2013 from http://www.csee.umbc.edu/~cress1/ia/341-stuff/Questions-341-profs.doc

[13] Taylor, B., Kaza, S., Security Injections: Modules to Help Students Remember, Understand, and Apply Secure Coding Techniques. in *Proceedings of the 16th Annual Conference on Innovation and Technology in Computer Science,* (Darmstadt, Germany, 2011).

[14] Towson University. Security Injections. Retrieved September 3, 2013 from http://cis1.towson.edu/~cssecinj/.

[15] Towson University. Security Injections Workshop – January 2010. Retrieved September 3, 2013 from

[16] Vaughn, R., Application of Security to the Computing Science Classroom. in *Proceedings of the 31st SIGCSE Technical Symposium,* (Austin, TX, 2000), ACM, pp. 90-94.

[17] White, G. and Nordstrom, G., Security Across the Curriculum: Using Computer Security to Teach Computer Science Principles. in *Proceedings of the 19th National Information Systems Security Conference,* (Baltimore, MD, 1996), pp. 483-488.

[18] Yang, T. Computer Security and Impact on Computer Education. *Journal of Computing in Small Colleges,* 16(4). pp. 233-246.

Student Perceptions of the Acceptability of Various Code-Writing Practices

Simon
University of Newcastle, Australia

simon@newcastle.edu.au

Beth Cook
University of Newcastle, Australia

beth.cook@newcastle.edu.au

Judy Sheard
Monash University, Australia

judy.sheard@monash.edu

Angela Carbone
Monash University, Australia

angela.carbone@monash.edu

Chris Johnson
Australian National University

chris.johnson@anu.edu.au

ABSTRACT
This paper reports on research that used focus groups and a national online survey of computing students at Australian universities to investigate perceptions of acceptable academic practices in writing program code for assessment. The results indicate that computing students lack a comprehensive understanding of what constitutes acceptable academic practice with regard to writing program code. They are not clear on the need to reference code taken from other sources, or on how to do so. Where code from other sources is used, or inappropriate collaboration takes place between students, there appears to be a feeling that any academic misconduct is diminished or even nullified if the students subsequently work with the code to make it their own. These findings suggest a need for the development of standards that elucidate acceptable practices for computing, combined with ongoing education of computing students.

Categories and Subject Descriptors
K3.2 [**Computers and education**]: Computer and Information Science Education – *computer science education*

Keywords
Academic integrity, computing education, non-text-based assessment

1. INTRODUCTION
Academic integrity is often presented in terms of a straightforward choice: "to cheat or not to cheat" [9]. There is an assumption that students who cheat in any way do so knowingly and intentionally. This is undoubtedly true of some students, but the possibility must be considered that some students cheat unknowingly – particularly in a subject area such as computer programming, where the guidelines are not nearly as clear as they are for prose text [1]. Even when students have every intention of behaving with integrity in their computing assessments, do they know what that entails?

To help answer this question, we have conducted focus groups and a nationwide survey among Australian academics and students. In this paper we discuss our findings regarding student perceptions of whether particular practices are acceptable in the context of computing education.

2. BACKGROUND
Research into academic integrity explores such questions as students' understanding of the concept of plagiarism, the prevalence of and reasons for plagiarism, how plagiarism is detected, and how it is dealt with when discovered [1, 4, 7]. However, much of the research is focused on a limited view of plagiarism, a view that concerns prose text, quotation marks, paraphrasing, and related matters. In studies of academic integrity there is usually little or no reference to misconduct involving non-textual material such as computer code.

Computing education researchers [6, 10, 13] explain that the issues of academic integrity in computing education are markedly different from those in general education. A computer program bears very little resemblance to an essay; there might be different expectations regarding using the work of others; and there is certainly not the same clear convention for attributing that work when it is used. Therefore there is a case for research that deals with questions of academic integrity explicitly in the computing disciplines.

Sheard et al [12] surveyed undergraduate and postgraduate students in computing, asking them to indicate whether a number of practices were acceptable. Practices that the researchers considered unacceptable, but their survey respondents did not, include reusing one's own prior work (known variously as self-plagiarism or recycling), collaborating on an assignment intended to be the work of individual students, and copying the bulk of a friend's assignment but then doing a reasonable amount of additional work. Replicating the survey ten years later [11], they found that students had greater awareness of the unacceptability of a number of practices, but there were still some areas of concern.

ITiCSE'14, June 21-25, 2014, Uppsala, Sweden.
Copyright 2014 ACM 978-1-4503-2833-3/14/06...$15.00.
http://dx.doi.org/10.1145/2591708.2591755

Cosma and Joy [3] surveyed computing academics on four possible types of misconduct, and found a certain amount of equivocation: although a student might have inappropriately acquired some program code, the more work that the student must subsequently do on the code, the less likely it is to be considered misconduct. Several years later they surveyed computing students [8] to explore whether certain practices were seen as plagiarism. As with the work of Sheard et al [12], self-plagiarism was not seen as plagiarism, and there was no clear agreement regarding various forms of collaboration with other students.

Collusion – working with other students when required to work individually – is considered by some to be a form of plagiarism [8], whereas others consider it a different form of misconduct [13]. Regardless of this distinction, it does appear to be considered the most prevalent form of academic misconduct among computing students [5, 14], and a number of projects have focused on this aspect of misconduct. Dennis [5] conducted two surveys, one on collusion in programming and another on plagiarism in essays. Like other researchers [8, 12], she found that many students did not see a problem with working together on large parts of a program, so long as they then added their own individual contributions. Stepp and Simon [14] asked students to describe scenarios that entailed crossing the boundary of legitimate collaboration, and then found that there was very little student agreement on whether each of those scenarios was in fact misconduct.

Much of the research into reasons for misconduct [15] is based on the assumption that students know they are doing something wrong. When Joy et al [8] ask computing students 'is this plagiarism?', they are possibly sometimes getting purely semantic responses: a practice might not be considered plagiarism even though it might be considered wrong. We have therefore decided to focus on the question 'is this acceptable?' It is conceivable that one of the reasons students engage in academic misconduct is because they simply don't know they are doing anything wrong. For any educational resource, guideline or policy on plagiarism in the computing discipline to be effective, it must be based upon a sound understanding of computing students' views on the acceptability of various code-writing practices.

3. RESEARCH APPROACH

The research presented in this paper forms part of a broader project looking into academic integrity in non-text-based assessments. The project used a mixed methods approach that involved focus groups at three universities and a broad national online survey of students and academics who use non-text-based assessments in either computing or visual design. To ensure that relevant academics and students were aware of the survey, the researchers made contact with each university, established who would be the most appropriate people to pass on the information, and asked them to do so. As an incentive to complete the survey, participants were invited to enter a draw to win one of five tablets or comparable devices.

The survey elicited 1315 responses from academics and students who use non-text-based assessment items. Removal of incomplete and inappropriate responses left 990, of which 486 were from computing students. This paper focuses on the responses of those 486 computing students. The respondents were drawn from all 39 universities in Australia, but by no means evenly. It seem likely that the response rate at an institution relates to the extent to which students and academics

there were encouraged to complete the survey, as the highest response numbers came from the researchers' own universities.

The survey consisted of three main sections in addition to the usual demographic information. The first two sections used 14 parallel scenarios in essays and in computing to canvass perceptions of plagiarism and collusion and whether particular practices were considered to be acceptable. The third section examined opinions regarding academic integrity policies and their implementation in Australian universities, including techniques used by academics to deter plagiarism and collusion, and how breaches of academic integrity are detected and dealt with.

For each scenario, students were asked 'is this acceptable?', with only three responses possible: yes, unsure, and no.

The choice of a three-point response scale was quite deliberate. A five-point scale gives respondents more scope to hedge their bets: 'I think it might be acceptable, but I'm not sure, so I'll choose option 4'. In using just three points, we were effectively telling respondents not to guess, but to acknowledge if they don't know. Furthermore, in most research using five-point scales the analysis tends to consider the responses in three groups: 1 & 2, 3, 4 & 5. We simply chose to undertake this grouping before the survey rather than after it.

Three focus groups consisted of 12 students studying various computing degrees. While the focus groups preceded the survey, and were used to inform the survey design, quotations from the focus groups will here be used to illustrate and clarify the survey findings.

Focus group participants were not presented with explicit scenarios, as in the survey. First in the context of essays, and then in the context of computing assessments, they were asked more general questions, such as 'what is plagiarism?'; 'how serious is it?'; 'how would you avoid it?'; 'what is collusion?'; 'how serious is it?'; 'how would you avoid it?'

This paper presents the computing students' perceptions of acceptability in the 14 computing scenarios from the survey, clarified where appropriate by discussion from the focus groups.

4. FINDINGS

The focus group discussion provides some clues as to the issues confronting computing students in determining what constitutes acceptable academic practice. This section begins with some of the general observations arising from the focus group discussions. These are followed by the survey findings for the 14 computing scenarios, grouped into broad categories and supported where appropriate with quotations from the focus groups.

4.1 General Observations

In the first instance, students from all focus groups observed that defining plagiarism and collusion in computing is less clear-cut than in essays, and that students are not sufficiently informed about what is acceptable.

> 'I think there's such a grey area, it becomes hard to say what's plagiarism.' (FG3)

> 'If you look at the high standards they have for the essay-based stuff, the same probably applies to code, but we don't know to what extent.' (FG3)

The differences between essays and computing assessments were discussed at some length in the focus groups. Using code produced by others was perceived as a more complex situation than copying and pasting text into an essay because it involves manipulation and transformation of the code before it can be used in assessments. While some students were confident that using someone else's code without attribution was not acceptable, a number felt that unreferenced copying was justifiable if the code was changed sufficiently. The thrust of this argument related to the amount of effort required by the student to use the code successfully.

'…codes from different websites aren't going to work with each other. So you have to work twice as hard to get everything to work together which I think makes it yours because you've put that effort in to actually make everything interlock and work together.' (FG3)

'You still have to modify the things into your own work, into your code, to match up. The code from the internet will not work with your program' (FG1)

Students suggested that it was often neither possible nor desirable to write code from scratch and mentioned that academics frequently encourage them to reuse code. Students elaborated on situations where they thought it was legitimate to use code produced by others without the need for referencing, such as using open source code.

'…it's like open source, like everyone can use it, everyone can copy and paste it.' (FG2)

Mention of open source raises the confusion between, on the one hand, the legal considerations of copyright and licensing, and, on the other, the academic and professional consideration of acknowledging the contribution of others. This confusion was clearly evident in the focus groups, with many participants conflating academic integrity requirements with copyright requirements. One student suggested that professional standards should apply in both situations.

'[University assessments are] practice for when you can get a job so you should just have to understand and like work within the laws of copyright.' (FG3)

Another theme from the focus groups related to assessment as a vehicle for learning. Some students suggested that it is legitimate to use code written by others so long as they themselves understand how the code works.

'If we can dissect that code and like change things easily and we understand what's going on, then like how would that be plagiarism?" (FG3)

'Like if you understand it, then it's okay. But if you don't understand then it's not okay. But if you've taken a method then you're obviously understanding the method to know that it fits in your code' (FG1)

This perception may be reinforced by the academic practice of interviewing students after the code has been submitted, with the intent of deterring or detecting plagiarism by using the students' understanding of the code as a surrogate for actual authorship.

4.2 Using Code from External Sources

One of the main precepts of academic integrity is that when using the work or ideas of others one must correctly reference it. The survey included two scenarios involving the use of freely available code, the difference being whether the code is referenced. The following table shows the proportion of respondents replying no, unsure (represented as '?'), and yes to the question 'is this acceptable?'

Table 1: using and referencing external code

Scenario	Acceptable		
	No	?	Yes
Basing an assessment on code that is freely available from some source, such as the web, and referencing the source.	12%	15%	73%
Basing an assessment on code that is freely available from some source, such as the web, without referencing the source.	76%	14%	10%

In the context of essays, it is generally not only accepted but required that students include material from external sources, properly referenced. However, only 73% of our respondents think it acceptable to use external code and reference the source, with a further 15% unsure. This might reflect an understanding that a computing assessment is intended to show the student's own original work, whereas an essay is expected to build upon the work of others. On the other hand, 10% of students deemed it acceptable to use freely available code without referencing it.

Even assuming that they know that code from other sources should be referenced, focus group participants indicated that they had not been shown how to reference code.

'If you do have to do references I've noticed there's never a strict rule for them.' (FG3)

This observation is supported by the response to a question in another section of the survey. When asked how confident they were that they knew how to reference computer code, only 36% of students indicated confidence that they could reference code correctly. The problem is exacerbated by a lack of consistency in methods used to reference code; Gibson notes that acknowledging the use of code produced by others could range from a "vague and imprecise" statement through to precise details of the original code and a "difference file showing exactly the changes that were made" [6:57].

4.3 Paying for Code

Two scenarios were set to explore attitudes about paying for code. The vast majority of students thought that both scenarios were unacceptable.

Table 2: paying for code produced by others

Scenario	Acceptable		
	No	?	Yes
Paying another person to write the code and submitting it as one's own work.	95%	3%	2%
Purchasing code written by others to incorporate into one's own work.	85%	11%	4%

While these scenarios might at first glance appear comparable, the first suggests buying a complete product with no input from the student, while the second clearly implies that the student will still be doing some of the work.. It is worth noting that most of the difference in the unacceptability has shifted into the unsure response, not into the acceptable. When the student still has to do some of the work, some find the question of acceptability less clear-cut.

4.4   Using the Work of Other Students

Three scenarios explored different ways of using the work of other students in one's own work.

Table 3: using the work of other students

Scenario	Acceptable		
	No	?	Yes
Incorporating the work of another student without their permission.	94%	3%	2%
Borrowing another student's code and changing it so that it looks quite different.	81%	15%	4%
Borrowing an early draft of another student's work and developing it into one's own.	67%	22%	12%

Students overwhelmingly find it unacceptable to use the work of other students without their permission, a practice that could clearly be viewed as stealing. Participants in the focus groups were very definite about the unacceptability of this type of practice.

'You can't just sit back and do nothing and expect to get a good mark, just because your best friend has given you your assignment and you've changed a few variable names.' (FG3)

One student complained about the inequity of a particular situation where a student used the work of a high achiever to obtain high grades:

'...gets the same mark as the guy who was the first in our class. So the first guy in our class does all the work for him.' (FG2)

When it comes to using code from other students with their permission, a majority perceive this as unacceptable, but there is less certainty about this. The differences in acceptability between the second and third scenarios in this group indicate that more tolerance is shown for using another student's code when the situation involves further effort on the part of the student taking the code.

4.5   Reusing one's own Code

While reusing work submitted for a previous course is generally considered to be plagiarism [8] and explicitly breaches the academic integrity policies of some higher educational institutions, many students seem not to be aware of this (Table 4).

Reusing work from a previous assessment task did not arise in the student focus groups, so there are no comments to illuminate the survey response to this scenario.

Table 4: reusing code produced by oneself

Scenario	Acceptable		
	No	?	Yes
Basing an assessment largely on work that one wrote and submitted for a previous course, without acknowledging this.	58%	20%	22%

4.6   Getting Help to Debug Troublesome Code

A fundamental issue in computing courses is that errors in code prevent programs from running. Three scenarios were presented to students in an attempt to tease out the differences in perceptions of acceptability for different ways that students might seek help to fix problems with their code.

Table 5: getting help from others

Scenario	Acceptable		
	No	?	Yes
Posting troublesome code on a message board and asking for help with it.	23%	25%	52%
Showing troublesome code to another student and asking them for advice on how to fix it.	13%	19%	69%
Asking another student to take troublesome code and get it working.	60%	25%	15%

The differences in acceptability between the first and second scenarios show that asking a fellow student for advice was viewed as more acceptable than posting to a message board for assistance, a practice that is explicitly condoned in some courses [11, 12]. The levels of uncertainty for all of these practices indicate that many students are not clear about how and where they should be seeking assistance outside the classroom.

There is a marked distinction between the first two scenarios and the third, in which the other student is asked to actually get the troublesome code working: this clearly crosses the boundary, and is seen by most as unacceptable. However, in this, as well as the other scenarios, about a quarter of the respondents were unsure.

Comments from the student focus groups illuminate these positions and explain why students think it acceptable, or even essential, for them to gain some assistance when code does not function as intended. Assistance from online forums and friends may include advice on where errors are in the code, or on issues to consider, but would not extend to directly providing the solution.

'...they say this line isn't going to do this, it's going to do that' (FG1)

'...[they say] you should use this structure or this pattern, create these objects... that kind of thing' (FG2)

Online forums were also viewed as essential in instances where peers were not able to provide assistance. One focus group participant stated:

'He could ask everyone in the class and no one would have an idea about it. But if he goes online it's almost guaranteed that someone will know the answer.'(FG3)

The lower acceptability of online forums compared with asking friends might suggest a perception that online forums might sometimes provide complete solutions rather than constructive advice. One focus group participant commented:

'No the difference is, if you post your question online it will be their solution. And you're copying their solution. But when your friend is checking, he'll tell what's wrong and you have to change it yourself, so that's different.' (FG1)

While there was a majority view that asking another student to actually fix troublesome code was unacceptable, 40% of students were unsure or thought that it was acceptable. Some focus group participants explained the dilemma faced by students who were unable to get their code working:

'I feel like a lot of people would just not be able to submit assignments if they didn't go out and get help' (FG1)

'Especially like in coding, like if it just doesn't work and you're just stuck on one thing, you can't submit it' (FG1)

This sentiment supports the contention by Vogts [15] that novice programmers plagiarise source code due to their inability to master complex requirements quickly enough. Similarly, Stepp and Simon found that students frequently cited mitigating circumstances as a reason for unauthorised collaboration [14], and the mitigating circumstances included situations where students had exhausted their own resources to solve the problem.

4.7   Discussing Assessment Tasks

In situations where students are required to write an assignment on their own, getting help with troublesome code can clearly be seen as a form of collusion; however, there are other forms of possible collusion that might be expected to be less clear-cut. Three scenarios addressed three of these practices.

Table 6: discussing code with others

Scenario	Acceptable		
	No	?	Yes
Discussing with another student how to approach a task and what resources to use, then developing the solution independently.	3%	6%	91%
Discussing the detail of one's code with another student while working on it.	20%	23%	57%
Completing an assessment and then adding features that one noticed when looking at another student's work.	36%	32%	32%

Discussing the approach to the task and what resources to use, and then developing the solution independently, was clearly seen as acceptable. In the focus groups, too, there was general agreement that discussing the task was permissible:

'We work together to gather information but in the end you type it up yourself and you compile the information yourself, so I don't think that's plagiarism' (FG1)

Discussing the detail of one's code while working on it was seen as far less acceptable, and more students were unsure about this practice. The difference between these first two scenarios might reflect students' perception that their main effort and contribution in a code-writing assignment is in the actual implementation of the program rather than the idea of how the task should be approached.

For the third scenario, changing a completed assessment to incorporate features discovered by looking at the work of another student, opinions were divided almost equally among the three options. This indicates uncertainty among students as to where they may source their design ideas.

5.   DISCUSSION

While this paper reports just on the students' perceptions of what is acceptable, we did also gather data from computing academics, both in focus groups and in the survey. It is clear that some computing academics see nothing wrong with plagiarism and collusion as they are generally defined: that is, with using the work of others without acknowledging it. The authors of this paper take the alternative position that when using the work of others we should acknowledge it. We do not argue that everything should be created from scratch; just that due acknowledgement should be given when we use something that was done by somebody else. Failure to do this is generally considered within universities to be academic misconduct.

Why do computing students engage in academic misconduct? In many cases it could be because they don't know that what they are doing is not acceptable. In our study we found concerning levels of uncertainty for a number of scenarios that we presented to the students. Almost half of the scenarios had uncertainty levels of 20% or more.

Nearly a quarter of the survey respondents are not sure that it is acceptable to base an assessment on freely available code and to attribute that code with a reference. In an industry in which reuse is both prevalent and encouraged, this requires further examination. As academics, we are certainly expected to assess our students' individual capabilities; but if we do this by teaching our students that they must continually re-invent the wheel, we might be doing them a disservice.

Almost every scenario involving the use of code produced by others was considered unacceptable by a majority of the respondents. Nevertheless, when it comes to using code produced by others, there is evidence of some feeling that so long as one subsequently puts in work of one's own, the practice is acceptable and there is no need to reference the 'imported' code.

Nearly half of the respondents are unsure or think it acceptable to reuse, without reference, code that they have written for prior assessment items.

Programming novices are often insufficiently experienced to debug their own code. While they presumably all have access to academic assistance, such assistance is often not available when it is needed, and there is a clear acceptance of the practices of seeking assistance from fellow students and from online forums. It is tempting to suggest that further research is required to determine just how much assistance students would consider to be too much, but this would presumably vary greatly according to the student, the circumstances, and the proximity of the submission deadline, and therefore might not be so readily determined.

What is clear from our study is that we, as academics, cannot simply assume that students know what is acceptable: they need to be informed and educated. In a discipline in which collaboration is encouraged, in which students are urged to find ways to solve problems that they encounter, and in which code reuse is an accepted practice, we need to make it absolutely clear to them when the exigencies of assessment require any sort of departure from these practices.

Ideally, all computing academics would agree on a set of guidelines for the acceptable reuse of code and for referencing code that is reused. However, indications from the survey of academics by Cosma and Joy [3] are that this ideal is a long way from being realisable. The difficulty of producing a general set of guidelines is that there are differences in opinions about where to set boundaries for the amount of permissible code reuse and the level of help that can be provided, and this is compounded by the fact that different assessment items have different contexts and aims.

An alternative, at least in the short term, is for individual academics to make it clear to their own students where they perceive the boundaries to lie. Every assessment item should clearly specify the expectations regarding the code to be submitted: whether students may use code from whatever source they like, with no need to attribute it; whether they may use code from specified sources, with full attribution; or whether the code is expected to be entirely their own and created from scratch for the particular assessment item, notwithstanding that this might entail reinventing the wheel.

If students are permitted to use code from elsewhere and required to reference it, the means of referencing should be made clear to them. According to the survey, only 36% of students were confident that they could reference code correctly. In the focus groups, students indicated that they were not instructed adequately in how to reference code.

6. CONCLUSION

The authors of this paper have no wish to impose exactly the same requirements for code-writing on all students in all courses at all institutions. We clearly have our own opinions as to what is acceptable and what is not, and these opinions tend to align fairly well with generally accepted norms of academic integrity; but we acknowledge that other academics hold other opinions.

What we would like to see is a framework in which students undertaking any coding assessment are clearly informed as to what is acceptable and why. Informing the students is ultimately the responsibility of the person setting the assessment, but we believe that a suitable framework would both increase academics' awareness of the issues and the uncertainty, and make it easier for them to select and specify their own requirements.

Future investigations might aim to find a consensus on how to specify which practices are acceptable, both in general and for specific assessment tasks, for computing students in higher education. This could form the basis of a comprehensive educational package involving discipline-specific information and including detailed examples to clarify the specific practices that are acceptable for computing assessments.

7. ACKNOWLEDGEMENT

This work was funded by a grant from the Australian Government's Office for Learning and Teaching.

8. REFERENCES

[1] Carroll, J. (2002). A Handbook for Deterring Plagiarism in Higher Education. Oxford Centre for Staff and Learning Development, Oxford, UK.

[2] Chuda, D., P. Navrat, B. Kovacova and P. Humay (2012). The issue of (software) plagiarism: a student view. IEEE Transactions on Education 55(1): 22-28.

[3] Cosma, G. and M. Joy (2008). Towards a Definition of Source-Code Plagiarism. IEEE Transactions on Education 51(2): 195-200.

[4] Curtis, G.J. and R. Popal (2011). An examination of factors related to plagiarism and a five-year follow-up of plagiarism at an Australian university. International Journal for Educational Integrity 7(1): 30-42.

[5] Dennis, L. (2004). Student attitudes to plagiarism and collusion within computer science. International Plagiarism Conference 2004. www.plagiarismadvice.org/research-papers/category/2004, accessed 9 Jan 2014.

[6] Gibson, J.P. (2009). Software reuse and plagiarism: a code of practice. ITiCSE'09, Paris, France, 55-59.

[7] Gullifer, J. and G.A. Tyson (2010). Exploring university students' perception of plagiarism: a focus group study. Studies in Higher Education 35(4): 463-481.

[8] Joy, M.S., J.E. Sinclair, R. Boyatt, J.Y.-K. Uau, and G. Cosma (2013). Student perspectives on source-code plagiarism. International Journal for Educational Integrity, 9(1): 3-19.

[9] McCabe, D.L., L.K. Treviño, and K.D. Butterfield (2010). Cheating in academic institutions: a decade of research. Ethics & Behavior 11(3): 219-232.

[10] Riedesel, C.P., A.L. Clear, G.W. Cross, J.M. Hughes, Simon, and H.M. Walker (2012). Academic integrity policies in a computing education context. ITiCSE-WGR'12, 1-15.

[11] Sheard, J. and M. Dick (2011). Computing student practices of cheating and plagiarism: a decade of change. ITiCSE'11, Darmstadt, Germany, 233-237.

[12] Sheard, J., S. Markham, and M. Dick (2003). Investigating differences in cheating behaviours of IT undergraduate and graduate students: The maturity and motivation factors, Journal of Higher Education Research and Development 22: 91-108.

[13] Simon, B. Cook, J. Sheard, A. Carbone, and C. Johnson (2013). Academic integrity: differences between computing assessments and essays. 13th International Conference on Computing Education Research (Koli Calling 2013), Koli, Finland.

[14] Stepp, M. and B. Simon (2010). Introductory computing students' conceptions of illegal student-student collaboration. SIGCSE'10, Milwaukee, Wisconsin, USA, 295-299.

[15] Vogts, D. (2009). Plagiarising of source code by novice programmers a "cry for help"? 2009 Annual Research Conference of the South African Institute of Computer Scientists and Information Technologists, 141-149.

A Historical Examination of the Social Factors Affecting Female Participation in Computing

Elizabeth Patitsas, Michelle Craig and Steve Easterbrook
University of Toronto Department of Computer Science
Toronto, Ontario, Canada
patitsas, mcraig, sme@cs.toronto.edu

ABSTRACT

We present a history of female participation in North American CS, with a focus on the social forces involved. For educators to understand the status quo, and how to change it, we must understand the historical forces that have led us here. We begin with the female "computers" of the 19th century, then cover the rise of computing machines, establishment of CS, and a history of CS education with regard to gender. In our discussion of academic CS, we contemplate academic generations of female computer scientists and describe their differential experiences.

General Terms

Human factors

Keywords

Computer science education, women in CS, studies of CS

1. INTRODUCTION

Increasing the participation of women in computing is well-established as an important and difficult task in the CS education community [36, 15]. Much of why it is hard to increase the participation of women – and other underrepresented groups – is because social structures are complex, dynamic systems. We cannot reduce the matter down to a few issues that, if fixed, would change everything. For example, meta-reviews of diversity initiatives outside CS have found that historical trends must be considered when designing initiatives, since *"the disruption [of the status quo] is usually not complete, nor fully shared by everyone, leaving traces of the old gender order to co-exist with an emerging newer and more complex notion of gender at work.* [8]

This paper presents a historical sociology of female participation in North American computer science. By *historical sociology* we refer to an approach to history which focuses on the social and cultural developments, forces and trends. Existing histories of female participation in CS instead focus on individuals, such as Grace Hopper, Ada Lovelace and the ENIAC Girls (e.g. [25, 17, 40, 2]).

The histories of female computer scientists are fascinating, and useful for presenting examples of female role models in the field. However, a focus on individuals takes away much of the context: what was it like being a computer scientist at

that time? What was it like being a woman in society then? Understanding these social trends is important for changing a status quo where women continue to be underrepresented.

Not much has been written about the history of academic CS; most histories of computing focus on the technology, and end in the 70s (e.g. [12, 18]). For young CS educators, there is little detailed post-70s history. Our goal in this paper is to provide background information on what has happened with regard to female enrollments in CS since the 90s – which in turn requires us to look at what led to that point.

1.1 Background Information

1.1.1 Types of Barriers

As we discuss the barriers faced by women in CS and STEM careers, we find it useful to categorize these barriers into a 2x2 grid:

	Intentional	Unintentional
Institutional	*De jure* discrimination	*De facto* discrimination
Individual	Explicit sexism	Implicit sexism

Institutional vs. Individual. Is it a policy, such as restricting enrollment in CS, or a lack of maternity leave? Or is it the direct behaviour of individuals, such as sexual harassment or a prejudice against women?

Intentional vs. Unintentional. Policies created without considering the effects on women, and subconscious bias against women, are examples of unintentional barriers; sexual harassment and the explicit barring of women from studying CS in some countries are examples of intentional barriers.

2. A PRE-HISTORY OF WOMEN IN CS

2.1 Women as Computers: from the 1820s to the 1940s

2.1.1 19th Century and Early 20th Century

The 19th century marked the rise of women's colleges in the United States [42] as policies barring women from education were loosened. This came hand-in-hand with first-wave feminism, in which women fought *de jure* discriminatory practices in North American society. Women campaigning for access to higher education did so on an argument that it would "produce better wives and mothers". For women of privilege in American society, a basic understanding of science and math in turn became "necessary for motherhood".

It should be emphasized that this was a trend for white women of *privilege* – most women who studied science in the 19th century were the daughters of scientists and other intellectuals. Consider, for example, that Ada Lovelace was a countess in a family of mathematicians [25].

For the women scientists that emerged from these colleges, there were few job opportunities. Teaching at the women's colleges was the main possibility. Working as a "computer" was another possibility [42]. Women pursuing PhDs or faculty positions were expected to be single or "in no danger of marrying"; marriage meant resigning from the programme or their job [42]. As time progressed and society progressed, women in these positions began to feel they could be both wives and scientists – when they resisted the norm of resigning upon marriage, they were met with opposition: they were threatened and usually fired [42].

1870-1900 marked an era of slow infiltration: women began entering doctorate programmes at traditional (male) institutions in countries such as the US and Germany [42]. Most universities were hesitant to allow the women into the PhD programmes, but would instead admit them as "special students" and give them bachelor's degrees instead. Engineering schools, however, remained resistant to women [40, 42]. While by 1910 women were starting a presence in science at traditional institutions, there was no equality in employment, and jobs remained deeply "sex typed".

With the slow rise of women in science came the corresponding rise of "women's work" in science [42]. So-called women's jobs typically were "assistants" to scientists, or working as computers for larger groups. These women were systematically ignored in the larger scientific community, left out of lists of scientists, conferences, and histories [43]. Indeed, from 1911 onward there were overt efforts to reduce the numbers of women in science.

2.1.2 Women's Work

It should be emphasized that computation was considered "women's work" in the 19th and early 20th century. Looking at the history of the social sciences in this time, quantitative methods were considered "low" enough that women could do them – but qualitative methods required "the intellect of a man" [35]. The reversal of the status (and gendering) of quantitative vs. qualitative work in the social and biological sciences happened well into the 20th century (sometime between the 30s-50s) [35].

During the World Wars, women were stereotyped as better programmers: "programming requires lots of patience, persistence and a capacity [for] detail and those are trains that many girls have" [25]. This stereotype persisted into the 40s [17], and even as far as the 60s: a 1967 issue of *Cosmopolitan* featured Grace Hopper describing programming as "*[it's] just like planning a dinner*" [18].

2.1.3 The World Wars

By the 1920s, women in academia were still largely kept to the women's colleges [42]. The colleges, however, provided a place to organize campaigns for change. Women began fighting for access to education, using evidence from psychology and anthropology that women too were capable of science/math [42].

The 20s and 30s marked an expansion of government-employed scientists, who were assigned "women's work" (assistants, computers, etc) and were grossly underpaid and undervalued [42]. The World Wars increased the scope of "women's work" as labour shortages necessitated it. By 1938, the numbers of women working in scientific and technological roles for the US government had dramatically increased – despite overtly hostile job conditions [42]. Women were given lesser job titles such as "assistant" due to their gender [40]. And despite the large number of women working in tech, all of the leaders and managers were men [25].

Nevertheless, the women of this era remember it as a time of excitement [25]: it was a chance for them to be involved in something technical/scientific. And indeed, the World Wars also marked the birth of digital computing. Computing machines were devised in the UK for cryptographic purposes. These machines, and the hand computations done in the wars throughout the world, were commonly performed by women. ENIAC, arguably the first real computer, was announced in 1946. The plan to run the ENIAC was such: a male scientist would be the planner, deciding what was to be computed – and a low-rank, female "coder" would do the actual machine coding [18].

2.2 The Continual IT Labour Crisis: the 50s through 70s

For the men running computing labs, what was not anticipated was that the coding would actually be difficult [18]. As computers began being used for commercial purposes in the 50s, a labour shortage emerged. Computing in the 50s and 60s can be characterized by a large, shotgun approach to recruiting "good programmers" when little knowledge of what a "good programmer" was. Programming began to be seen as a "dark art" [18]. Due to the individuals who began programming at that time, programmers began to be seen as asocial [18] – kicking off a feedback loop that persists today.

Women continued to have a large presence in programming in the 50s. They contributed to the development of programming languages [25] and scientific computation [17]. But traditional gender roles in many way persisted. Women in the 50s still had to leave when they became pregnant [40]. And women hit what they dubbed the "glass ceiling": a collective barring from managerial and senior positions [17].

As computer programming rose in prominence, it became masculinized. Women were still allowed entry to the jobs due to the desperation for quality labour. However, lazy hiring practices that focused on spurious aptitude and personality tests hurt female participation in the industry [18].

Inconsistent professionalization efforts also hurt female participation by restricting what it meant to be a programmer. The men running the show did not intend to push women out of computing – instead, they simply did not consider how their hiring practices discriminated against women [18]. In short, *de facto* discrimination was the dominant driver of women out of computing.

3. WOMEN IN ACADEMIC CS

3.1 Early Days: 1960s and 70s

Computer programming stayed largely independent from academic computer science. In the 50s and 60s, CS was conducted through other departments, typically as a hobby or side-project [18]. The first CS classes were offered in the 60s, as the discipline struggled to assert itself [12]. By 1969, MIT had opened an undergraduate programme in CS – and the 70s marked the beginning of bachelor's degrees in CS offered typically through electrical engineering or mathematics [18]. It would not be until the 80s, though, that CS programmes moved into their own departments.

From the start, CS seemed like a "grab bag of various topics" related to computers and attempts to define the discipline were inconsistent [18]. Was CS about information? Analysis? Algorithms? No consistent narrative was established, though algorithms eventually became dominant.

It should be noted that the establishment of CS departments coincided with the sexual revolution in North America. While CS was opening its doors, women were asserting their rights – including those to work and study.

3.1.1 The First Generation: women who entered in the 60s/70s

As documented by Etzkowitz et al in a 1994 paper, women of different academic *generations* in STEM have had wildly different experiences in academia. In a study of 30 academic science departments in biology, chemistry, physics, CS, and electrical engineering in the United States, Etzkowitz found stark and sometimes conflicting differences between the women of different generations in these departments [20].

The First Generation of women in a given STEM department faces a very different environment than subsequent generations. Unlike today's undergraduates entering classrooms with women as minorities, these women often entered classrooms with *no other women* [20]. There were seldom other women in their field, and this continued into graduate school and faculty life. Such was the case for the majority of women who entered CS in the 60s and 70s – before CS was even an established discipline. Most came to CS via departments such as math, physics, electrical engineering, psychology, English, music, and linguistics [25].

One senior female scientist in Etzkowitz et al's study described her cohort as such: *"The ones who did [science] were really tough cookies. Now it's easier to get in. At one time it wasn't even acceptable to start. So if you started back then you were tough to begin with."*

In short, women with low self-efficacy simply did not go into that given STEM field. Only the strongest, the most focused and most ambitious stuck it out. And it led these women to expect that women had to be better than men in order to succeed [20]. Given the data that women today are subconsciously discriminated against with regard to job offers, postings, tenure applications, and collaborations (see [32, 49, 39]), it's not a surprising position to take – particularly when many of these biases were explicit and *conscious* when they began their careers. Women were underrecognized for their contributions [43], and when they were, they got "separate but not quite equal form[s] of recognition" [40].

With few other women around, these women worked in a culture which expected them to *"accept the strictures of a workplace organized on the assumption of a social and emotional support structure provided to the male scientist by an unpaid full-time housewife"* [20]. These women adopted lifestyles and approaches mimicking the traditional man, including a singular focus on research and career advancement [20]. Marriage and children were secondary, if done at all.

4. THE ESTABLISHMENT OF CS DEPARTMENTS: THE 80S AND 90S

4.1 The First Bubble: The 80s

The early 80s were also a boom-time for student enrollment in CS [47], which was linked to the rise of the personal computer. Personal computers had not been available until the late 70s; prior to then, CS was hence only pertinent to academia, military, and business.

However, by the late-80s, enrollments began dropping – and disproportionately so for women [41]. The decline was "largely the result of explicit steps taken by academic institutions to reduce CS enrollments when it became impossible to hire sufficient faculty to meet the demand." [41] Steps included adding new GPA requirements for entering CS programmes, requiring more prerequisites, and retooling first-year CS as a weeder course [41]. These actions disproportionately hurt not only female participation in the field, but participation of racial minorities as well [41]. These "non-traditional" students had disproportionately come to CS via non-traditional paths (such as via psychology or linguistics) and disproportionately lacked the prerequisites as a result. The retooling of first-year CS as a weeder course also resulted in a competitive atmosphere that deterred many women. Once again we see *de facto* discrimination pushing women out of computing.

4.2 Post-Bubble: The Early 90s

The situation for women worsened in the 90s. The personal computer led to further masculinization of computing [11]. Five reasons thought to have reduced female participation in the 90s were: the rise of video games, subsequent changes in stereotypes/perceptions of computing, the encouragement of boys to go into the field and not girls, an inhospitable social environment for women, and a lack of female role models [11].

The 90s appear to be when CS educators started worrying about female participation in CS. Before the drop in female enrollments in the late 80s, it had been fair to assume that reaching equal female participation in CS was simply a matter of time. Indeed, in the 80s and early 90s, CS was still seen as a "woman-friendly" science [20].

While women-in-CS initatives had existed in the 80s (e.g. The Anita Borg Institute was opened in 1987 [31]) – it was not until the 90s when they proliferated (e.g. The Committee on the Status of Women in Computing Research (CRA-W) was formed in 1991 [16], the Grace Hopper Celebration of Women in Computing was first held in 1994 [17]) and by the 00s they became "mainstream".

4.3 The Dot-Com Bubble: Late 90s

The birth of the World Wide Web in the 90s and its spread beyond academic/military use led to a second bubble in CS enrollments, known as the dot-com bubble. The hype of the dot-com bubble and the promise that a CS degree would lead to easy prosperity led to a resurgence in enrollments in the late 90s – particularly due to students who wanted to get rich quick. The dot-com bubble burst in 2000 – and enrollment with it a few years later [47]. Indeed, the NASDAQ has been found to be a predictor of CS enrollment at Stanford [37].

The boom-time in the late 90s and early 00s led to a return of strict enrollment controls and a spree of hiring more CS faculty [47]. Most of these new hires were relatively young, and of what we will refer to as the "Second Generation".

These boom-times also reduced the amount of service teaching: with CS programmes overburdened, CS departments had few resources and little motivation to teach non-CS students. At some universities, departments such as physics or math began offering their own CS classes to their own students – leading to CS becoming increasingly isolated from the other sciences – and from non-traditional students.

4.4 The Second Generation: women who entered in the 80s and 90s

Etzkowitz et al found that once women faculty were hired in a STEM department, *"it definitely changes the attitude of how male students react to women. They must take them seriously and this is positive"* [20]. Explicit sexist behaviour, such as public sexual joking and stereotyping decreased as a result [20]. Etzkowitz et al found there was a critical threshold at which women *in a department* begin to be treated more fairly, and blatant discrimination becomes uncommon. This appears to be at around 15% women.

The women entering this environment (in the 80s and 90s) had a different experience than the First Generation – who had had *no* female faculty when they were students[20]. The Second Generation was particularly eager about these First Generation female faculty. They had high expectations about these female faculty, and wanted to learn things from them such as *"how to dress, how to act at conferences, what to do when somebody is curt to you"* [20]. In a sense, some of these women saw the First Generation as their White Knights, to guide them through academia.

While the First Generation was preoccupied with simply getting on in a man's world, being a *woman* in a man's world was a preoccupation for the Second Generation [20]. These women were concerned about how many women there were in their programmes, hired as faculty, etc. Viewing science as only one part of their identity, these women also focused on how to balance career and family [20].

For Second Generation women, work-life balance was the key problem. Figuring out when to start a family, and seeking maternity and daycare support from their universities were priorities [20]. As noted already, many leave academia because they feel balancing both work and family care is untenable. However, more recent studies have found the decision making is complex: women who are more satisfied with their jobs are more likely to make having both academia and a family work. Women who feel they are discriminated against at work, and feel their promotion and tenure chances are unlikely, are more likely to leave the job to look after their families. [23] These women began most of the "women in science" type clubs, seeking to mitigate their feelings of isolation at work [20].

4.4.1 Conflict Between Generations

Etzkowitz et al observed that the different experiences between the first two Generations has led to a bifurcation of the women in their study's participating departments. When the Second Generation began most of the "women in science" clubs, some of the First Generation were leery of these organizations [20]. *"Fear of stigmatization led some [women] to deny the existence of gender-related obstacles. Calling attention to difficulties overcome could lead to countercharges of special privileges received"* – devaluing their hard-fought achievements that often took significantly more work than the achievements of their male colleagues [20].

Furthermore, *"frustrated by the emergence of women's issues, they regarded such concerns as indicative of a lack of commitment to science. They believed women's groups and programs [sic] to improve the condition of women harmed female scientists by making them appear 'different', and by implication less competent"* [20]. However, the sheer isolation, and blatant sexism experienced by the First Generation women led many of these First Generation women to support and lead diversity initiatives.

Advising was another source of inter-generational conflict. One female graduate student in the study reported that it was harder as an advisee of a senior woman, due to her advisor's "sink or swim" attitude. Many of the First Generation were harder on their female advisees, feeling they had to be to "prepare them to meet the higher standards they would be held to as women" [20].

5. AFTER THE DOT-COM BUBBLE

When the bubble burst, the "get-rich-quicker"s disappeared – and CS departments were left trying to get more "bums in seats". Enrollments did not recover again until the mid 00s – and have been on the rise since [47]. Indeed, recent reports paint enrollments at record numbers, even greater than the peak of the dot-com bubble [38].

Overall, a pattern of cyclical enrollment emerges. Boom times lead to more students, then more enrollment controls; bust times lead to more outreach. Bust times also result in disproportionately many women leaving the field, or not going in at all [47] – indeed, as of 2011, 18% of CS students are female [38].

5.1 The Third Generation: women who entered in the 00s/10s

The Etzkowitz et al paper was published 20 years ago, when the Second Generation was still growing. Women entering CS since the 00s have had a different experience of computing culture (arguably this has been true since the late 90s depending on the CS department). For the first author of this paper, who entered CS in 2007, approximately 20% of the CS faculty were women, predominantly women of the Second Generation. They have families and the Women in CS club was (and still is) highly visible and active, as is their delegation to Grace Hopper, as well as scholarship and research opportunities designed for women in CS.

The early 00s marked an era of focus on increasing female participation in CS. Margolis and Fisher's influential *Unlocking the Clubhouse* was published in 2002; this year also marked a SIGCSE bulletin special edition highlighting research on women in computing [26, 14]. For many (if not most) women of the Third Generation, their departments have made explicit efforts to improve the experience of women in their classrooms. The work by Margolis and Fisher, and others such as Joanne Cohoon, Maria Klawe, and Camp and Gurer, led to many departments working to remove *de facto* barriers for their female students. Follow-up studies at places that have implemented Margolis and Fisher-style recommendations have found a cultural shift that helps female students [9, 3].

And indeed, for female students entering CS in the 2000s and 2010s, there already exists a strong social network for women in computing. This network has been designed mostly by Second Generation women – and mostly around what the Second Generation women had wished they'd had when they entered the field. This is important as, again, people may take for granted the experiences of other generations.

For example, the findings we see in the 2002-era women-in-CS papers will discuss access to physical computers [26, 36]. For most women entering a CS classroom, computers have been ubiquitous for most of their life. Indeed, for these women, the Internet has been a world that girls use more heavily than boys [24]. Growing up, Third Generation girls performed equally well in science and math as boys. Finally, the Third Generation is far removed from the explicit sexism that the First Generation experienced.

5.1.1 Barriers for the Third Generation

Despite many improvements in the culture, female enrollment in CS hasn't significantly improved since hitting that 15% critical mass. Despite the uptick in the mid-80s, the numbers are now down to around 18%. Clearly, critical mass isn't enough on its own to get female participation to 50%. Concerningly, one issue affecting women in CS is backlash for the women-in-CS initiatives. Even in the Margolis and Fisher study era, female students have reported harassment along the lines of "you're only here because you're a girl" [36]. The stigma of receiving preferential treatment in science has been documented as decreasing self-efficacy for its recipients [52], decreasing the perceived competence of its recipients [30], and causing stereotype threat for its recipients [29, 48].

Implicit sexism appears to be the dominant barrier for women of the Third Generation. While *de facto* discrimination and explicit sexism (particularly sexual harassment) still occur, they are no longer predominant. The subtle biases that have been there from the beginning remain, such as:

- The CV of a woman applying to a STEM job is viewed as demonstrating less competence than the same CV with the name changed to a male name [39, 49].

- Conference abstracts with female authors are viewed as being of lower quality than if the abstracts are changed to have male authors [32].

- Articles written by women are cited less than those by men [50]. Women are less likely to be listed as either first or last author on a paper [53]. Similar disparities exist in funding [34] and earnings [45].

- Women are more likely to be promoted based on past accomplishments, whereas men are more likely to be promoted based on potential [6].
- Letters of references for female job candidates are more likely to use gendered wording ('warm', 'kind', etc) which in turn hurts a candidate's hireability [51].
- The language used in job postings has also been found to favour men: gendered wording is common, and women are less likely to apply for jobs using such wording [22]. An entire blog, "Tech Companies that Only Hire Men", which features job postings with gendered language in IT, has frequent entries [1].

With these implicit biases come other social-psychological barriers for women in CS, such as stereotype threat [33], tokenism [7], and benevolent sexism [28]. These subtle forms of sexism all continue to subtly push women out of CS through a "death of a thousand papercuts". Insidiously, many Third Generation women do not perceive any gender-based biases against them, and are unwilling to take action on what they consider a "problem of the past" [55].

6. DISCUSSION

In looking at how female participation in CS has changed over time in North America, we also gain some insight as to why female participation is different around the globe. CS is female-dominated or at gender-parity in places such as the Middle-East [27, 21], Eastern Europe [21], and South-East Asia [19]. A 1994 study by Barinaga set out to explain the cross-cultural differences in female participation in STEM. She found five positive factors, three of which are supported by the history of CS in North America [5]:

1. More women are present in countries with **recently developed science capabilities**. The academic culture is relatively unentrenched, and no "old boys network" has come to dominate. When CS was new, we saw more women in the field. This was true both in industry (female computers) and in academia (the 80s).

2. More women become scientists in a culture where **science is perceived as a low status career**. It is established in sociology that the lower the status and pay an occupation, the more likely it is that women will be found there [5]. When CS meant being a "computer" or a lowly "coder", women played these roles. When CS rose in prominence – such as during the 60s, and during dot-com boom, the percentage of women entering CS decreased.

3. For a given culture, if a woman of high class has higher social standing than a man of low class, we see more women in science. **Privilege** hence matters – and is linked not just to gender but also class and race. Women in CS are disproportionately from relatively affluent backgrounds [36]. Women of colour are disproportionately underrepresented. (Indeed, a weakness of this paper has been our focus on the history of *white* women in CS – more needs to be done to document the history of racial minorities in the field.)

While it is difficult to make CS "new" again, reducing the entrenched culture has proven benefits for attracting non-traditional students [9, 14]. It should also be noted that CS is not homogenous: fields such as gaming and security [46] lag behind with regard to female representation, and explicit sexism continues to be a problem.

What the history of women in CS shows is that this is probably best tackled one barrier at a time. The removal of *de jure* discriminatory policies allowed women to become "computers" and to attend engineering schools [40]. Such policies still exist in other countries, such as Iran, where women are barred from studying CS [44].

Once the First Generation of women arrived, explicit sexism was the next problem. When a critical threshold of women were present, explicit sexism decreased markedly in frequency. The change in culture produced the shift to the Second Generation, who focused on being both a woman *and* a scientist. *De facto* discriminatory policies have been the issue for these women, such as entrance requirements that disproportionately bar women from studying CS, and a culture that leads to social isolation for many women.

The Second Generation women have established a network of support for female students, from Grace Hopper to local women in CS clubs. While *de facto* discriminatory policies still exist, a larger problem facing the Third Generation are the subtle, social-psycological biases working against them.

Implicit sexism may be difficult to identify and fight, but it is possible [4]. Blind reviews in scientific journals, for example, lead to more women and minorities publishing [10]. Where possible, scholarships and research grants should use blind reviews. Social-psychological interventions have been found to reduce stereotype threat [54]. Changing the stereotypes about CS in popular media leads to women to have more interest in the field [13].

Meanwhile, enrollments in CS are now skyrocketing yet again: the 2012 Taulbee Survey found that CS enrollments have risen for the fifth straight year [38]. Facing packed classrooms and overburdened teaching resources, some CS departments are once again considering cutting interdisciplinary programmes and service courses. We hope that CS departments will maintain these initiatives, given their known benefit for women [14].

CS has come a long way since the day of female "computers", and progress has not been linear. Barriers remain, particularly for women of colour and women of lower class. Tackling these issues requires an understanding of all the forces at work – including our past.

7. REFERENCES

[1] Tech companies that only hire men, 2013.
[2] V. L. Almstrum, L. J. Barker, B. B. Owens, E. Adams, W. Aspray, N. B. Dale, W. Dann, A. Lawrence, and L. Schwartzman. Building a sense of history: Narratives and pathways of women computing educators. *SIGCSE Bull.*, 37(4):173–189, Dec. 2005.
[3] C. Alvarado and Z. Dodds. Women in CS: an evaluation of three promising practices. In *Proceedings of the 41st SIGCSE*, pages 57–61. ACM, 2010.
[4] M. R. Banaji and A. G. Greenwald. *Blind Spot: Hidden Biases of Good People*. Random House Digital, Inc., 2013.
[5] M. Barinaga. Surprises across the cultural divide. *Science*, 263(5152):1468–1470, 1994.
[6] J. Barsh and L. Yee. Unlocking the full potential of women in the US economy, 2011.
[7] Y. Benschop and H. Doorewaard. Covered by equality: the gender subtext of organizations. *Organization Studies*, 19(5):787–805, 1998.
[8] Y. Benschop, J. H. Mills, A. Mills, and J. Tienari. Editorial: Gendering change: The next step. *Gender, Work & Organization*, 19(1):1–9, 2012.
[9] L. Blum and C. Frieze. The evolving culture of computing: Similarity is the difference. *Frontiers: A J. of Women Studies*, 26(1):110–125, 2005.
[10] A. E. Budden, T. Tregenza, L. W. Aarssen, J. Koricheva, R. Leimu, and C. J. Lortie. Double-blind review favours increased representation of female authors. *Trends in eco. & evo.*, 23(1):4–6, 2008.

[11] T. Camp and D. Gurer. Women in computer science: where have we been and where are we going? In *Tech. & Soc.*, pages 242–244. IEEE, 1999.

[12] S. M. Campbell. *The Premise of Computer Science: Establishing Modern Computing at the University of Toronto (1945–1964)*. U. of Toronto, 2006.

[13] S. Cheryan, V. C. Plaut, C. Handron, and L. Hudson. The stereotypical computer scientist: Gendered media representations as a barrier to inclusion for women. *Sex roles*, pages 1–14, 2013.

[14] J. M. Cohoon. Recruiting and retaining women in undergraduate computing majors. *SIGCSE Bull.*, 34(2):48–52, June 2002.

[15] J. M. Cohoon and W. Aspray. A critical review of the research on women's participation in postsecondary computing education. *Women & info. tech.: Research on under-representation*, pages 137–79, 2006.

[16] CRA-W. About CRA-W.

[17] J. Currie Little. The role of women in the history of computing. In *Tech. & Soc.*, pages 202–205. IEEE, 1999.

[18] N. Ensmenger. *The computer boys take over: Computers, programmers, and the politics of technical expertise.* MIT Press, 2010.

[19] B. Ericson. Update from the NCWIT meetings, 2009.

[20] H. Etzkowitz, C. Kemelgor, M. Neuschatz, B. Uzzi, and J. Alonzo. The paradox of critical mass for women in science. *Science*, pages 51–51, 1994.

[21] V. Galpin. Women in computing around the world. *ACM SIGCSE Bulletin*, 34(2):94–100, 2002.

[22] D. Gaucher, J. Friesen, and A. C. Kay. Evidence that gendered wording in job advertisements exists and sustains gender inequality. *J. of personality and social psychology*, 101(1):109, 2011.

[23] J. L. Glass, S. Sassler, Y. Levitte, and K. M. Michelmore. What's so special about STEM? a comparison of women's retention in STEM and professional occupations. *Social Forces*, page sot092, 2013.

[24] E. F. Gross. Adolescent internet use: What we expect, what teens report. *J. of App. Dev. Psych.*, 25(6):633–649, 2004.

[25] D. Gurer. Pioneering women in computer science. *ACM SIGCSE Bulletin*, 34(2):175–180, 2002.

[26] D. Gurer and T. Camp. An ACM-W literature review on women in computing. *SIGCSE Bull.*, 34(2):121–127, June 2002.

[27] M. Guzdial. Women in CS in Qatar: It's complicated, 2010.

[28] M. D. Hammond, C. G. Sibley, and N. C. Overall. The allure of sexism: Psychological entitlement fosters women's endorsement of benevolent sexism over time. *Soc. Psych. and Personality Sci.*, page 1948550613506124, 2013.

[29] M. E. Heilman and V. B. Alcott. What I think you think of me: Women's reactions to being viewed as beneficiaries of preferential selection. *J. of App. Psych.*, 86(4):574, 2001.

[30] M. E. Heilman, C. J. Block, and P. Stathatos. The affirmative action stigma of incompetence: Effects of performance information ambiguity. *Acad. of Mgmnt. J.*, 40(3):603–625, 1997.

[31] A. B. Institute. About us.

[32] S. Knobloch-Westerwick, C. J. Glynn, and M. Huge. The matilda effect in science communication: An experiment on gender bias in publication quality perceptions and collaboration interest. *Sci. Comm.*, 2013.

[33] A. N. Kumar. A study of stereotype threat in computer science. ITiCSE '12, pages 273–278, New York, NY, USA, 2012. ACM.

[34] T. J. Ley and B. H. Hamilton. The gender gap in NIH grant applications. *Science*, 322(5907):1472–1474, 2008.

[35] K. Luker. *Salsa dancing into the social sciences: Research in an age of info-glut.* HUP, 2008.

[36] J. Margolis and A. Fisher. *Unlocking the clubhouse: Women in computing.* MIT press, 2003.

[37] A. McGettrick, E. Roberts, D. D. Garcia, and C. Stevenson. Rediscovering the passion, beauty, joy and awe: making computing fun again. SIGCSE '08, pages 217–218, New York, NY, USA, 2008. ACM.

[38] A. McGettrick and Y. Timanovsky. Digest of ACM educational activities. *ACM Inroads*, 3(2):24–27, 2012.

[39] C. A. Moss-Racusin, J. F. Dovidio, V. L. Brescoll, M. J. Graham, and J. Handelsman. Science faculty's subtle gender biases favor male students. *Proc. of the National Academy of Sci.*, 109(41):16474–16479, 2012.

[40] G. Reinish. A woman engineer's view of 50 years in the profession. In *Tech. & Soc.*, pages 219–222. IEEE, 1999.

[41] E. S. Roberts, M. Kassianidou, and L. Irani. Encouraging women in computer science. *ACM SIGCSE Bulletin*, 34(2):84–88, 2002.

[42] M. W. Rossiter. *Women scientists in America: Struggles and strategies to 1940*, volume 1. JHU Press, 1982.

[43] M. W. Rossiter. The matilda effect in science. *Soc. studies of sci.*, 23(2):325–341, 1993.

[44] F. Sahraei. Iranian university bans on women causes consternation, 2012.

[45] H. Shen. Mind the gender gap, 2013.

[46] R. Shumba, K. Ferguson-Boucher, E. Sweedyk, C. Taylor, G. Franklin, C. Turner, C. Sande, G. Acholonu, R. Bace, and L. Hall. Cybersecurity, women and minorities: Findings and recommendations from a preliminary investigation. In *ITiCSE Working Group Reports*, ITiCSE -WGR '13, pages 1–14, New York, NY, USA, 2013. ACM.

[47] J. Slonim, S. Scully, and M. McAllister. *Outlook on Enrolments in CS in Canadian Universities.* Info. and Commu. Tech. Council, 2008.

[48] C. M. Steele. A threat in the air: How stereotypes shape intellectual identity and performance. *American Psychologist*, 52(6):613–629, June 1997.

[49] R. E. Steinpreis, K. A. Anders, and D. Ritzke. The impact of gender on the review of the curricula vitae of job applicants and tenure candidates: A national empirical study. *Sex roles*, 41(7-8):509–528, 1999.

[50] C. R. Sugimoto. Global gender disparities in science, 2013.

[51] F. Trix and C. Psenka. Exploring the color of glass: Letters of recommendation for female and male medical faculty. *Discourse & Soc.*, 14(2):191–220, 2003.

[52] M. Van den Brink and L. Stobbe. The support paradox: Overcoming dilemmas in gender equality programs. *Scand. J. of Mgmnt.*, 2013.

[53] J. D. West, J. Jacquet, M. M. King, S. J. Correll, and C. T. Bergstrom. The role of gender in scholarly authorship. *arXiv:1211.1759*, 2012.

[54] D. S. Yeager and G. M. Walton. Social-psychological interventions in education. *Rev. of Ed. Research*, 81(2):267–301, 2011.

[55] M. Zuk and S. O'Rourke. Is biology just another pink-collar profession?, 2012.

Cultural Appropriation of Computational Thinking Acquisition Research: Seeding Fields of Diversity

Clarisse S. de Souza, Luciana C. Salgado, Carla F. Leitão, Martha M. Serra
Semiotic Engineering Research Group - Departamento de Informática, PUC-Rio
Rua Marquês de São Vicente 225
22451-900 Rio de Janeiro, RJ - Brazil
55 21 3527-1500 ext 4344 (voice)
{clarisse, lsalgado, cfaria, mserra}@inf.puc-rio.br

ABSTRACT

In this paper, we report the developments of a Computational Thinking Acquisition project carried out in pilot Brazilian schools. The project is a branch of a successful, more than a decade old project in the USA. We present and discuss the factors that led to specific cultural appropriation and diversification of the North American experience. In particular, we explain the kind of technology that has been developed in South America compared to the one developed and used in the USA, and propose that the lessons we have learned in the project's short history in Brazil can already seed the reflection of IT and Education researchers.

Categories and Subject Descriptors

K.3.2 Computer and Information Science Education

Keywords

Computational Thinking Acquisition, AgentSheets, Programming

1. INTRODUCTION

Computational Thinking Acquisition (CTA) has been increasingly valued in contemporary education. According to a large number of educators, the introduction of CTA in school curricula is a necessity in the 21st century, and for many reasons (motivational, cultural, economic and even socio-political). Taking the next step, however, leads into various debates and many shades of disagreements: *How* can this be effectively done? We should be neither surprised nor discouraged by this situation, for it manifests the variety and depth of diversity in human experience, to which education must necessarily attend.

Public policies in education are a challenge for all countries in the world. The so-called *developing* countries, however, face this challenge with additional difficulties brought about by the co-existence of extremes. On the one hand, these countries experience economic growth, with tangible social, cultural, scientific and technological advancements. On the other, they suffer the hardships of poverty and all of its consequences, given

that typically a substantial share of their population lives below the accepted threshold of civilized welfare and happiness. How can *public* policies in education reconcile the interests of such extremely different worlds? Ideally, the answer is to find mechanisms for the results and effects of economic growth to enfranchise the population living in the opposite extreme conditions.

In 2010 our research group started a CTA project affiliated to *Scalable Game Design* (SGD), a successful project [9] that accumulated more than a decade of experience in this area (counting previous projects) and was originated in the University of Colorado – Boulder (Computer Science and Education Departments, among others). Given the need for IT professionals in the Brazilian job market, as elsewhere, the development of computational thinking skills in middle and high school might not only represent an educational gain *per se*, but also an increase in job opportunities, especially for the poorer public schools' students.

This paper reports the developments of SGD in Brazil (SGD-Br) and discusses the factors that, according to the current state of our research, led to specific cultural appropriation and diversification of the North American experience in Brazil. In particular, we emphasize the kind of technology that has been developed in South America compared to the one developed and used in the USA, and propose that the lessons we have learned in the project's short history in Brazil can already seed the reflection of interested IT and Education researchers.

The paper is structured as follows. Section 2 provides information about the relevant parts of the Brazilian socio-economic and demographic context. Section 3 describes some characteristics of SGD-Br in terms of demography, research orientation and history. Section 4 presents and discusses the results of the first four years of research aiming at the creation of technology to support CTA activities in a widely diverse range of educational contexts. Finally, section 5 presents our concluding remarks about the significance of our results and the possibilities ahead of us.

2. SOME OF THE BRAZILIAN CONTEXT

Brazil is the 'B' in *BRICS*, "an economic grouping of five emerging markets comprising of Brazil, Russia, India, China and South Africa"[1]. The country's population is over 190 million people living in approximately 8.5 thousand square kilometers of

---

[1] http://beta2.statssa.gov.za/wp-content/uploads/2013/08/Mbalo_Brief_April_2013.pdf

land. World Bank data sources[2] indicate that, in 2010, the population density in Brazil, the United States and the European Union were, respectively, 20^+ people/km^2, 30^+ people/km^2 and 120^+ people/km^2.

While economic indicators suggest that Brazil is doing very well, the latest *Human Development Report* issued by UNDP in 2013[3] shows that the country ranks a 85th with a 0.73 Human Development Index. It is the second best HDI among *BRICS* (Russia's is 0.78)[4], but official statistics from the Brazilian government[5] display a most disturbing picture. More than 80% of the youth population (19 years of age) has failed to complete the cycle of basic education (lower and middle school). In 2013, studies carried out by an independent Brazilian NGO[6] concluded that only 26% of the whole country's population between ages 15 and 65 have reached the level of full functional literacy (very broadly, the ability to use reading, writing and counting abilities in order to participate fully in society and achieve one's goals as a citizen). Another 27%, according to the same studies, are quite plainly functionally illiterate (i.e. have no access to minimal levels of citizenship because they do not have fundamental reading, writing and counting skills to operate in contemporary society).

Technology-related indicators suggest that in spite of very poor educational opportunities, the Brazilian population has considerable access to (and makes considerable use of) ICT, especially the youth. A study carried out by the Brazilian Internet Steering Committee[7] reports that 47% of Brazilian youths (ages 9 to 16) access the Internet on a daily basis – 66% of these are high-income youths, 45% middle-income, and 17% low-income. Interestingly, there is relatively little difference between high- and middle-income youngsters when it comes to the second or third most frequent means of accessing the Internet. Personally-owned mobile phones are most frequently used by 25% of high-income adolescents and pre-adolescents (close third after 26% use of privately-owned personal computers) and 22% of middle-income. The most frequent point of access for both groups is a household computer (used by 60% of high-income and 33% of middle-income youths).

3. SCALABLE GAME DESIGN IN BRAZIL

The goal of the North American SGD is to "reinvent computer science in public schools by motivating & educating all students including women and underrepresented populations to learn about computer science through game design starting at middle school."[8] From a technological point of view, SGD uses its own game design environments, namely AgentSheets[9] and, more recently, its 3D online version called AgentCubes. Both are visual programming environments especially developed to support CTA. In both, learners can design and program games and simulations with extensively variable levels of complexity. Although their interface style suggests that AgentSheets and AgentCubes are software for children, very complex simulations can be built with them, requiring even professional programming skills from their creators. Thus, SGD technology supports truly *scalable* game and simulation design and development.

The project in Brazil started in March 2010, as a small-scale exploratory research initiative of a multi-disciplinary group of investigators. The aim was to chart the immediate challenges and opportunities for introducing CTA activities in public Brazilian schools. In view of striking cultural and socio-economic differences between Brazil and the United States, this group of researchers was aware that even if the SGD team counted many years of successful experience with a wide spectrum of partner schools, including some located in low-income communities in the State of Colorado, SGD-Br would not be a replication –and probably neither an application– of North American solutions. So, for both research groups, the excitement was precisely to meet the face of diversity and learn from it.

As is appropriate in such context, SGD-Br adopted a qualitative approach at this initial phase. We partnered with a public school (*School One*), whose headmaster, pedagogical coordinator and an expressive number of teachers welcomed the idea of running a pioneering 8-week CTA program with volunteer middle school students. The program, using AgentSheets, was carried out as an after-class activity led by a Geography teacher (for details see [2][3]). The highlights of this program were the following: (i) the goals and pedagogy of this activity were strongly influenced by established SGD knowledge; (ii) there was an emphasis on both the new game-based pedagogy that teachers of different subject matters (like Geography, for instance) could use to improve teaching-learning processes, and on the job market possibilities open to students who might develop an interest in Computer Science; and (iii) SGD-Br explicitly promoted the importance of ICT fluency for 21st century citizens to participate actively in an ever-increasing number of social processes.

In 2011, the success of the previous program in *School One* led us to run a second program with middle school students, this time coached by a Biology teacher. Once again, we followed SGD directives, this time devoting more attention to the *computational thinking patterns* used by SGD to evaluate progress in CTA [1]. SGD developed online technology with which computational thinking patterns used by learners in game programming projects can be automatically detected. This required, however, that more emphasis be placed in *teaching* such patterns. So, the 2011 program in *School One* paid closer attention to the learning of CT patterns such as 'collision' (when two game agents meet), 'absorption' (when one agent erases the other), 'transport' (when one agent *carries* another along as it moves about the game grid) and so on. As a result, the program took longer (12 weeks), but games produced by the students showed little structural difference compared to those produced in the previous year.

At this point, observations of class activities in 2010 and 2011, along with data collected in interviews with *School One*'s

[2]http://www.indexmundi.com/facts/indicators/EN.POP.DNST/co mpare.

[3]http://hdr.undp.org/sites/default/files/reports/14/hdr2013_en_com plete.pdf

[4]https://data.undp.org/dataset/Table-1-Human-Development-Index-and-its-components/wxub-qc5k

[5]http://conae2014.mec.gov.br/images/pdf/educacao_brasileira_ind icadores_e_desafios.pdf

[6]http://www.ipm.org.br/download/inf_resultados_inaf2011_ver_fi nal_diagramado_2.pdf

[7] http://www.cetic.br/publicacoes/2012/tic-kids-online-2012.pdf

[8]http://sgd.cs.colorado.edu/wiki/images/c/c7/One_Pager_CE21_C T4TC.pdf

[9] http://www.agentsheets.com/products/index.html

students and teachers showed that one of the major challenges for SGD-Br was to train and support school teachers continually. It was clear that introducing CTA in Brazilian schools could only scale up if we developed the means (including technology) to help teachers learn, appropriate and transform computational thinking knowledge in personally meaningful ways. This was a many-faceted multidisciplinary challenge involving strategic choices by our research group: what should we *focus* on?

The answer emerged from a small-scale study carried out with students from the 2010 program, one year after they had finished it [3]. We wanted to know what memories they had of the program, what value (if any) they saw in it, what knowledge they retained, and what they would like to do next (if anything) in game design. Among other things, we found out that participating students had important gaps in their learning, in spite of having produced nice game designs. The data collected in an interview and two program understanding and modification tasks suggested that students had *applied* game design patterns without grasping what they meant. The fact that the programming outcome was good encouraged them to move forward without seeking to clarify doubts or experiment other meaningful possibilities. At the same time, preparing teachers to support their students in such investigative activities required more teachers' training and preparation hours than we had been able to provide. So, the answer was to focus on developing support *technology* for CTA teaching and learning activities.

This was an important move towards the constitution of SGD-Br's distinctive profile when compared with the North American project. In 2012, we decided to involve two new partner schools in the project, each with a completely different profile from the other two. The initiative began with inviting teachers from a small set of considerably diverse schools for a 12-hour introductory CTA program with AgentSheets. Thirteen teachers participated in the program, three of which decided to begin teaching CTA to their students immediately. Two teachers –an Informatics and a Literature teacher– worked at a high-income private Brazilian school (*School Two*). The other teacher worked at an international (American) school in Brazil, teaching Media Arts and Informatics as an elective class.

By the end of 2012, there were three partner schools participating in the Scalable Game Design project in Brazil: one public (Brazilian) school, one private (Brazilian) school, and one international (American) school. The interest of having the latter as a partner was, of course, to be able to trace cultural aspects of North American education that might influence CTA pedagogy in the overall context of Scalable Game Design.

Class observations and interviews in all three schools informed the design of the subsequent versions of support technology for teaching and learning of computational thinking skills in a Brazilian context. This was essentially a live documentation Web system that stimulates *exploration* of and *reflection* upon game designs uploaded by learners [6][7]. As a result, in 2013 we concentrated on studying and understanding users' needs and perceptions with respect to PoliFacets[10].

2013 was *School One*'s first year of autonomous decisions regarding CTA-related activities. However, because of expiring employment contracts, three of four teachers with experience in

---

[10] http://www.serg.inf.puc-rio.br/polifacets/.

coaching CTA classes left. A new teacher was trained but up to now there have not been new CTA programs there.

School Two and *School Three*, however, intensified and diversified their activities, involving new students and teachers. *School Two*, like *School One* had done one year before, invited students from previous classes to help coach students of the subsequent year program. This was a greatly successful initiative, much appreciated by students (advanced and novices), teachers and parents. *School Three* experimented new forms of incorporating CTA in regular teaching activities of different subject matters. The results, further discussed in the next section, were also a great success in many respects.

SGD-Br activities in partner schools during 2013 were affected by two interventions. The first was the design, development and deployment of a fully functional Beta version of PoliFacets, aimed at providing an exploration and reflection environment for teachers and students interested in AgentSheets-based CTA. The second was a second, extensively reformulated, edition of our introductory CTA program for teachers. This time, we had a former teacher from *School One* lead the program for other teachers. As an enthusiast of PoliFacets, this teacher incorporated this technology in her teaching, which had some interesting effects, discussed in section 4. In **Table 1**, we summarize the main facts of SGD-Br from 2010 till 2013.

Table 1: SGD Br Facts

Partner Schools	Number of Teachers	Number of Students
School One 2010-2013 CTA Programs: 6	6 trained 5 conducted classes (1 Geography; 1 Biology; 3 Math)	72
School Two 2012 – 2013 CTA Programs: 5	5 trained 2 conducted classes (1 Informatics; 1 Literature)	33
School Three 2012 – 2013 CTA Programs: 5	8 trained 3 conducted classes (1 Media Arts; 1 Science; 1 Programming)	58

4. RESEARCH STRATEGY, METHODOLOGY AND RESULTS

The facts and history reported in the previous section are closely tied to our research strategy, methodology and results. Starting with the research strategy, let us go back to the Brazilian context briefly outlined in section 2. This is a country facing major social challenges, in particular with respect to education. Although we certainly share the basic concerns and motivations explicitly stated in the North American SGD mission –to reinvent Computer Science education in public schools– Brazil has a much deeper problem to solve in terms of public education, raising its *literacy* (in particular *functional literacy*) overall indicators. This is not only the government's and public policy makers' responsibility, but also –and importantly so– the responsibility of Brazilian society as a whole. Hence, if CTA can, at all, contribute to improve basic education levels in the country, all citizens should know this and be prepared to take action, for his/her own sake as well as that of the others.

This line of thought explains and justifies two of three distinctive strategic choices in SGD-Br. The first one is the notion that programming is an increasingly important means of self-expression and social participation in contemporary life. Therefore, programming languages can be used in similar ways as natural languages can, to communicate ideas, influence others' thoughts and behavior, disseminate values, and so on. The second is that although low-income students in public schools certainly experience greater needs and more severe hardship than higher-income ones, from private schools, all of them should learn how to use CTA in order to achieve social responsibility, in addition to improving their performance in science and math and being able to design and share their own computer games.

The third strategic choice is the decision to design and develop technology for exploration of and reflection upon computational thinking knowledge. This has sprung from data collected in several qualitative studies carried out throughout the last four years. Qualitative methodology privileges in-depth situated investigation with a small set of participants. It aims at articulating a rich interpretation emanating from empirical facts rather than testing existing hypotheses about them. Its role is therefore one of identifying, expressing and relating implicit *meanings* of insufficiently known (or plainly unknown) objects of study. A qualitative approach is especially well suited when researching previously unexplored complex questions such as the ones encountered in SGD-Br.

The overall cycle of research done with our partners follows a traditional qualitative path. We begin with a meaningful context of activity (a CTA program with teachers or students, a set of tasks to be achieved using a given set of proposed tools). We then observe how the activity develops, collecting empirical data with audio and video recordings, note taking and diaries. We also interview participants (teachers and students), using mainly open-ended questions that allow them to express their experience, perceptions and opinions more freely. Large volumes of collected data are then analyzed and triangulated. Speech is typically analyzed using discourse analysis techniques. Computer programs (games) are analyzed in terms of structure and meaning, based on syntactic, semantic and semiotic features manifest in program code and program execution. Moreover, given the outstanding role of computer technology itself in supporting the core of CTA activities, we also use existing usability and communicability evaluation techniques to sense how interaction with programming tools and environments may affect the learning process.

The results of such rich, cross-referenced sources of data and information allow us to gain increased knowledge about how we can contribute effectively (but by no means exclusively) to introduce CTA in Brazilian schools. For lack of space, we will present selected pieces of empirical data collected throughout four years of our research project, which explain what the Brazilian face of Scalable Game Design is and why it is so.

Our first study, in 2010, showed us how students expressed themselves using AgentSheets as a *language* [2]. The study compared verbal accounts of what participants *meant* to do with their games and the end result of their game design. A particularly powerful evidence that computer programming was rapidly appropriated and used as a rich means of expression came from one of the students, a 15-year old middle school boy, whose verbal account of what his game was about showed he had very poor mastery of the Portuguese language. Here is a short translated excerpt of his narrative:

"I begin with this guy, then I have to kill the hunters that are here and here. Then after he kills the last hunter he becomes this other guy here and he gets an armor."

Notice the switch in discourse from "I" to "he", the use of "guy" for naming different game characters, without any semantically significant vocabulary differentiation, and the use of "here and here" (deictic) to refer to different game setting regions whose names might have been easily provided (e.g. "on this tree", "in this part of the forest"). Another characteristic of this boy's narrative, even in such short passage, is the poorly articulated connection between sentences in the same paragraph. Discourse fragments follow one another, leaving it up to the hearer to make sense of what is happening in the game. Yet, the *computer* narrative produced by this boy was by far the richest of the group. His game setting was an elaborate structure of many agents, deployed in a cohesively designed space. Agents behaved consistently in response to the player's commands, and the game had even a second 'phase', whose programming the student was unable to complete due to lack of time and technical knowledge.

Along with other less impressive, but equally informative pieces of evidence, this encouraged us to invest more efforts in researching the connections between CTA and self-expression through programming. In a second study, we decided to probe the extent of students' apprehension and long-term retention of CT knowledge. The aim of the study was to detect CTA elements or dimensions that might be used to assess the learners' evolution in this new way of framing computer-programming skills. Remember that SGD in the USA was using computational thinking patterns to assess progress towards an improved understanding and mastery of computer science concepts and techniques (which is different from what we do in Brazil).

Findings of this second study (reported in [3]) showed that we needed to improve the means we offered to schools engaged in CTA programs. One year after having finished their introductory CTA program, learners gave us evidence of significant misconceptions and misunderstandings of how AgentSheets programming worked and what certain program elements meant. Quite importantly for us, when they used a set of program representations we had specifically put together for that study (not available as such in the AgentSheets programming environment), participants experienced sudden insights and new learning. One of them expressed his satisfaction and surprise like this:

"Oh! So, I have this [other] possibility to compose the background of the game… I built all of my background using agents, which sometimes caused me a lot of trouble."

Participants of the second study also manifested their desire to keep on learning. They were frustrated, because the introductory CTA program was not followed by a more advanced one. At the same time, in separate interviews, the teachers involved in CTA programs at *School One* were telling us that they needed more support and training than we had been able to give them. Their manifestation coincided with the fears experienced by other teachers in Brazilian schools, who feel unprepared to engage in teaching and learning activities with ICT [5].

By 2011, the conclusions we drew from evidence provided by study participants and school partners have contributed to shaping the distinctive profile of SGD-Br, in comparison with SGD in USA. Firstly, as a small although multidisciplinary group of researchers (coming from Computer Science, Psychology, Education and Linguistics), we are not in a position to address the complexity of all issues involved in introducing CTA in the curriculum of middle and high schools in Brazil at large. Secondly, in spite of the latter, we *are* in a position to make relevant technological contributions for a broader project, involving different stakeholders, such as public policy makers, professional teacher education specialists and others. Thirdly, the nature of our contribution should complement (rather than offer a new alternative for) existing learning environments for CTA, such as AgentSheets itself, Scratch[11], Alice[12], Greenfoot[13] and others. Evidence suggested that learners need technology to stimulate and support them in reflecting upon game programming, lest they may take the 'hacking approach' rather than a more *learned* perspective on programming. This is especially important in supporting teachers, who have a natural tendency (and need) to reflect on activities and skills that they will develop in class with their students. Finally, keeping with the 'think globally, act locally' motto promoted by ecologists, we should bring the multidisciplinary profile of our group of researchers to bear on the design of technology and ask ourselves *how* we could leverage literacy skills among students based on newly gained abilities to express themselves consistently, cohesively, effectively and efficiently using a highly structured *language* (or representation system). What else is literacy, after all?

Our response to such findings was the development of live documentation technology, PoliFacets, specifically designed to *deconstruct* game programs and highlight the various meaning and expression facets that concur to communicating the ideas and intentions embedded in games. For example, when a game player commands an agent to move around in a maze and eat dots along the way (as in Pacman), the sign of *eating* is that dots disappear when the agent comes next to them. This effect can be *programmed* in a number of ways, some better than others depending on whether the programmer is looking for clarity, execution speed, code reuse, or some other goal that he or she might have in mind (including that of getting the job done quickly, so that he or she can go do something else). In order to make learners aware of such facts and possibilities, teachers need a *reflective* tool, with which they can examine and compare different programming strategies. Such is, therefore, our design goal in PoliFacets [6][7].

The first version of our system was implemented and deployed in 2012. We immediately began to study the users' reaction to it, with a keen eye to if and how they interpreted the technology and thought about using it. An important piece of research was conducted with participants of the first Teachers Workshop carried out in mid-2012. The workshop strategy was to give them an introductory course on game programming with AgentSheets and then show them how they could use PoliFacets to explore expressive alternatives for communicating the same kinds of ideas incorporated in their games. For example, they could look at each others' programming strategies to find out new possibilities, and they could reflect about their own expressive choices and the effects each one of them brought about.

The data collected in this study was a collection of participants' games (in various incremental versions), their reaction during instructional workshop sessions, and their opinions and views as expressed in the answers to an open-ended questionnaire. Here are some examples of what they told us:

"I'm thinking of the countless possibilities that [AgentSheets] opens for working with my students" (Elementary School teacher)

[11] Scratch - http://scratch.mit.edu/

[12] Alice - http://www.alice.org/

[13] Greenfoot - http://www.greenfoot.org/

"I'm so excited! This is the feeling this tool [AgentSheets] brings out in me, because I can see almost unlimited possibilities of use by students and the benefits they can get from this learning." (High School IT teacher).

The fact that both pieces of evidence refer to AgentSheets, without mentioning PoliFacets is significant. The impact of the programming tool, at first encounter, was naturally stronger than that of the reflection-on-programming tool. Although, when specifically asked to tell what they thought of PoliFacets and five (out of 13) participants stressed the power of this tool in helping learners to understand in greater detail the computational concepts involved in programming with AgentSheets, we got a clear message from our first users. We were not communicating the value of our technology. This might be because we were mistaken this value or because our design did not bring out this value as users interacted with the system. We decided to probe the latter and start to redesign PoliFacets based on users' reactions.

In 2012 and 2013 we continued to observe classes and collect empirical evidence from teachers and students in partner schools. We were (positively) surprised, however, by one of the teachers in *School One*, a Math teacher coaching a group of students who had already followed an introductory program, and were now learning more advanced concepts. By her own initiative, this teacher elaborated a new pedagogy (compared to what she had used in previous CTA programs) where she began to talk about games looking at representations in PoliFacets. Her goal was to develop the students' ability to interpret programming code and project, in their minds, the effects caused during program execution. Of course, as a Math teacher, her interest in abstract reasoning and working with representations was highly pronounced. However, we saw other related evidence of technological discourse appropriation coming from a Literature teacher. He exposed his students to various game representations, in PoliFacets and AgentSheets, to discuss elements of digital narratives. In both classes, the Math and the Literature teachers', we saw evidence of students seeing programs as communication. One of the Math teacher's students commented about the game produced by an anonymous programmer and presented in PoliFacets:

"[Given his meaningless agents' names] this guy is writing the program for himself alone."

One of the Literature teacher's students designed a particularly significant game. This was a soccer match, where in reaction to more or less successful user attempts to score a goal a 'narrator' would produce sentences (popping up in balloons on screen) whose style was the same as that used by professional sports commentators on Brazilian TV and radio stations.

In 2013, we deployed the redesigned version of PoliFacets and tracked the users' reactions to and appropriation of it. We also used it in the second Teachers Workshop of SGD-Br. In order to see how the technology could be used by teachers in real contexts, we invited the Math teacher of *School One* to lead the workshop. One of the participants, who was then introduced to our CTA approach not only through AgentSheets but also through PoliFacets, taught a 3-month program in *School Three*. When interviewed about his experience and the tools he used, at the end of the program, he said:

"I think there should be a bridge between what is happening in the game's programming language and the user's language. Some

sort of connection [...] what we want to be happening in the game/simulation and not in the terms [of] commands."

Although the teacher did not speak of *literacy* and self-expression or communication of ideas through software programs, his awareness of what is actually at stake and what skills are required from learners is remarkable. In fact, he was talking about new connections that PoliFacets should explicitly do in order to improve the way it supports learning.

5. CONCLUDING REMARKS

In conclusion to this paper, we would like to go back to cultural appropriation and the diversification of research experienced by Scalable Game Design in Brazil. Our report shows how the seed of a successful project evolved differently in Brazil, compared to the grounds where it was first planted and cultivated. It also shows, we think, that diversification caused by contrasting cultural contexts can be beneficial not only to Brazilian researchers and Brazilian schools, but also for teachers from other cultures. Notice the piece of evidence presented at the end of the preceding section. The teacher that gave us the evidence is North American and *School Three* is an international American school operating in Brazil for many years. There are teachers and students from many different nationalities in *School Three*, and yet our *Brazilian* appropriation of SGD approach to CTA was welcomed and evolved by a North American teacher, working in a very similar educational context and orientation as those applicable to the original project, in the USA.

We highlight two contributions that, in our view, can be of interest and value to other researchers and practitioners involved in CTA (or even CS education, more broadly). One is the notion that we could, and perhaps should, attend to the need and opportunity of developing technology to *reflect* upon programming. One of the benefits we see in this –and in fact an item in our future work agenda– is the possibility to expand the scope of reflection beyond those pertaining to a single programming environment. We have, for example, already started to design an extension of PoliFacets that can deconstruct and create multiple representations for programs made with GreenFoot. The result of this expansion is the possibility of connecting and comparing program constructs in different programming languages, which provides the basis for a much richer and deeper learning experience in CTA or CSE contexts.

The second point we would like to highlight, which is related to (but not the same as) the previous one is the one about *new literacies*. It is now a common place to say that human communication is mediated by technology. This is used to justify the promotion of digital literacy (or computer literacy) in various forms. However, as Nadin suggests in a provocative book [8], our civilization is increasingly an *illiterate civilization* in the traditional sense. Larger and larger portions of social discourse, which we used to have to produce verbally or in writing in interpersonal contacts, is now automatically produced by machines, whose buttons we press expecting that they will 'do it for us'. We are, in fact, delegating much of our literate activity (again, in the *traditional* sense) to machines. However, there *are* literate people –the programmers of technology we use– who act on our behalf and extensively control the kinds of social interactions that we have with others. These people master *new literacies*, previously discussed by Gee [4] and Walsh [10]. We think that the cue to the nature and importance of educating youth in these new literacies was given to us by the student from *School One*, whose case we discussed in section 4. Viewing and *teaching* computer programming as a new literacy might, perhaps, bring new perspectives for researchers not only in Computer Science, but also in other disciplines. It might also show us that there are other roads to take towards functional literacy in contemporary society.

6. ACKNOWLEDGMENTS

We would like to thank CNPq and FAPERJ, the Brazilian agencies that support our research, and also the AMD Foundation, which has been the main sponsor of the Scalable Game Design Brasil project.

7. REFERENCES

[1] Basawapatna, A., Koh, K. H., Repenning, A., Webb, D., Marshall, K. 2011. Recognizing computational thinking patterns. In *Proceedings of the 42nd ACM technical symposium on Computer science education* (SIGCSE '11). ACM, New York, NY, USA, 245-250.

[2] De Souza, C.S, Garcia, A.C.B, Slaviero, C, Pinto, H, Repenning, A. 2011. Semiotic traces of computational thinking acquisition. In *Proceedings of the Third international conference on End-user development* (IS-EUD'11). Springer-Verlag, Berlin, Heidelberg, 155-170.

[3] Ferreira, J. de Souza, C. S, Salgado, L.C., Slaviero, C, Leitão, C. F., Moreira, F. 2012. Combining cognitive, semiotic and discourse analysis to explore the power of notations in visual programming. In *Proceedings of VL/HCC'2012*. Innsbruck, Austria.

[4] Gee, J. P.2003. What video games have to teach us about learning and literacy. *Comput. Entertain.* 1, 1 (October 2003), 20-20.

[5] Lopes, R. D., Ficheman, I. K., Martinazzo, A. A. G., Correa, A. G. D., Venâncio, V., Yin, H. T. & Biazon, L. C. 2010. O uso de computadores e da internet em escolas públicas de capitais brasileiras. In: Estudos & Pesquisas Educacionais, vol.1, Fundação Victor Civita, pp. 275-336.

[6] Mota, M., Monteiro, I., Ferreira, J.J., Slaviero, C., de Souza, C. 2013. On signifying the complexity of inter-agent relations in agentsheets games and simulations. In *Proceedings of the 31st ACM international conference on Design of communication* (SIGDOC '13). ACM, New York, NY, USA, 133-142.

[7] Mota, M., de Souza, C. S. Documentation comes to life in computational thinking acquisition with AgentSheets. In Proceedings of the XII Brazilian Symposium on Human Factors in Computing Systems (IHC '12), Porto Alegre, Brazil, Nov 05-08, 2012.

[8] Nadin, M. 1997. *The Civilization of Illiteracy*. Ebook published in The Gutenberg Project available online at http://www.gutenberg.org/ebooks/2481.

[9] Repenning, A. 2012. Programming goes back to school. Commun. ACM 55, 5 (May 2012), 38-40.

[10] Walsh, C. 2010. Systems-based literacy practices: digital games research, gameplay and design. Australian Journal of Language and Literacy, 33(1) pp. 24–4

Apps for Social Justice: Motivating Computer Science Learning with Design and Real-World Problem Solving

Sarah Van Wart
UC Berkeley School of Information
Berkeley, CA 94720
vanwars@ischool.berkeley.edu

Sepehr Vakil
UC Berkeley School of Education
Berkeley, CA 94720
sepehr@berkeley.edu

Tapan S. Parikh
UC Berkeley School of Information
Berkeley, CA 94720
parikh@ischool.berkeley.edu

ABSTRACT

In this paper, we describe a twelve-week *Apps for Social Justice* course that we taught at an after-school program. Students read social justice literature, identified local community needs, and went through a design process to create fully functional mobile applications to address these needs. Using Nasir and Hand's concept of practice-linked identities [13], we argue that an integrative approach to introducing computer science – where CS principles are used in pursuit of meaningful community goals – provides multiple opportunities for students to participate in software development while connecting these skills and dispositions to their own experiences and to larger social issues. Unlike a concepts-first approach, which introduces computer science ideas using small, often decontextualized examples, a practiced-based approach that builds on student experiences may foster a more motivating and meaningful learning environment.

Categories and Subject Descriptors

K.3.2 [**Computers and Education**]: Computer and Information Science Education–computer science education.

General Terms

Design, Human Factors

Keywords

App development, apprenticeship, social justice, HCI, computer education pipeline

1. INTRODUCTION

Computer Science (CS) careers offer many material and intellectual rewards, and yet women and low-income people of color are grossly under-represented in the field. This disparity can be seen starting in K-12. For instance, in 2011, only 19.2 percent of the Advanced Placement Computer Science (AP CS) test takers were female – "the lowest ratio of female-to-male test-taking rates of any of the offered Advanced Placement tests" [6]. Even more troubling, Jane Margolis reports that in California – home to

Silicon Valley and several of the nation's top computer science programs – although "underrepresented students of color make up a combined 49 percent of the high school student population, they account for only 9 percent of the AP computer science test takers (California Department of Education 2005; College Entrance Examination Board 2005)" [9]. Without a concerted effort to make computer science education more equitable, the field will remain stratified across gender and racial dimensions.

Computer Science has many of the same qualities as mathematics: both tend to attribute success in the domain to one's innate intelligence [7]; both serve a gatekeeping role in granting access to high-opportunity careers; both are critical tools in Science, Technology, Engineering, and Math (STEM) professions; both claim to teach abstract thinking and in particular mathematical/computational habits of mind [14][16]; and both have wide achievement gaps among groups [8][9]. Given these parallels, this paper draws from several equity-minded ideas in the mathematics education literature to explore how learning environments may be organized to provide more equitable opportunities for all students.

1.1 Equity in Mathematics Education

Danny Martin, a mathematics education scholar, asserts that "eliminating inequities in access, achievement, and persistence in mathematics is not an issue that can be separated from the larger contexts in which schools exist and in which students live" [10]. Many mathematics education scholars agree with this notion: that mathematics achievement disparities are embedded in larger, structural inequities. However, how these larger contexts might be addressed from within an educational setting is up for debate. Jo Boaler offers the notion of relational equity, which emphasizes the social opportunities provided to students to develop *equitable relations* with one another based on mutual respect, trust, and accountability [2]. She advocates for a classroom structure that focuses on *complex instruction*, a teaching method that aims to disrupt broader racial hierarchies from the inside out through the promotion of equitable classroom relations. A second perspective, articulated by González, Andrade, Civil, & Moll [12], questions the curricular choices that privilege certain types of knowledge over others in the standard mathematics curriculum. These scholars argue that by drawing from students' cultural Funds of Knowledge, a broader range of mathematical competencies can be valued in the classroom, which will in turn make mathematics more relevant and meaningful to minority students. A third perspective taken by Rico Gutstein [5] argues that mathematics should be used as a tool to directly critique the larger social and economic structures. This version of a social justice pedagogy applies statistics to real data sets to shed light on structural inequities in the "real world." Finally, Nasir and Hand [13], like Boaler, look to the ways in which learning environments are

ITICSE '14, June 21–25, 2014, Uppsala, Sweden
Copyright is held by the owner/author(s). Publication rights licensed to ACM.
ACM 978-1-4503-2833-3/14/06...$15.00
http://dx.doi.org/10.1145/2591708.2591751

structured to promote student engagement. Their study analyzes how opportunities for engagement differ across two settings – a high school basketball team and a mathematics classroom – focusing on three distinct aspects of these settings: 1) access to the domain, 2) opportunities to take on integral roles, and 3) opportunities for self-expression in the practice. Building on previous scholarship examining the importance of engagement for academic achievement, they argue that students develop practice-linked identities – or feelings of connection to an activity – through their experiences participating in the activity, and through the kinds of opportunities for engagement that the activity makes available to students.

Using Nasir and Hand's idea of practice-linked identities and incorporating Gutstein's notion of a social justice pedagogy, this paper examines how students engaged with computer science ideas as they designed and implemented a mobile app with relevance for their community. Using interview data, presentation transcripts, student project artifacts, and field notes from a case study in an after school program, we argue that such an approach can (1) give students access to the domain of computer science, (2) provide multiple and evolving ways in which students are able to demonstrate competency, and (3) allow students' to connect their own experiences and values to larger social issues.

2. BACKGROUND
In the spring of 2013, the first and second author co-taught a twelve-week *Apps for Social Justice* (mobile applications) course, which met once a week in the evening for two hours. The course was sponsored by OSMO – an after school STEM program in the San Francisco Bay Area that connects university mentors with low-income middle and high school students of color. OSMO provides a number of services for local youth and families, including weekly homework help sessions, a parent support group, and a variety of STEM enrichment classes.

Our research team provided instruction, technical support and mentoring to two student teams of middle- and high-school youth. The first student team – the focus of this paper – consisted of two female African-American high school students, Soraya and Mayra,[1] who were continuing work on an app idea that they had had formulated during the previous semester [15]. Soraya and Mayra's application, BAYP (Bay Area Youth Programs), was intended to support local teenagers' academic and extracurricular needs by helping teens to search for positive youth organizations. The second student team consisted of four students who were new to the program and were just beginning to devise their own mobile application idea.

Because Soraya and Mayra's team worked primarily on software implementation[2] (as compared to the brand new team's initial focus on ideation and design), Soraya and Mayra will be the focal point for this paper, so that we may highlight some of the ways in which the *Apps for Social Justice* course introduced the students to various computer science concepts. We highlight Soraya and Mayra's experiences to demonstrate *how* the course supported computer science learning. As we will show, Soraya and Mayra

made remarkable progress over the course of the twelve weeks, iterating on their initial design and implementing a functional Android application that could query and update a live database of local after school programs, which the students designed themselves (Figure 2). BAYP's various screens interacted with the database in different ways, showing program listings, detailed information pages, and maps of locations. Soraya and Mayra presented BAYP to family and friends at OSMO's year-end student showcase (Figure 1).

Both Soraya and Mayra were high achieving, college bound students who attended two different high schools and did not know each other before their enrollment in OSMO. Both students' parents were actively involved in their daughters' academics, and they regularly communicated with program mentors about their daughters' academic progress. Neither student had taken a computing course in school, but Soraya had participated in another out-of-school program, 'Technovation,' where she learned about App Inventor [11], the programming environment that was used to develop BAYP.

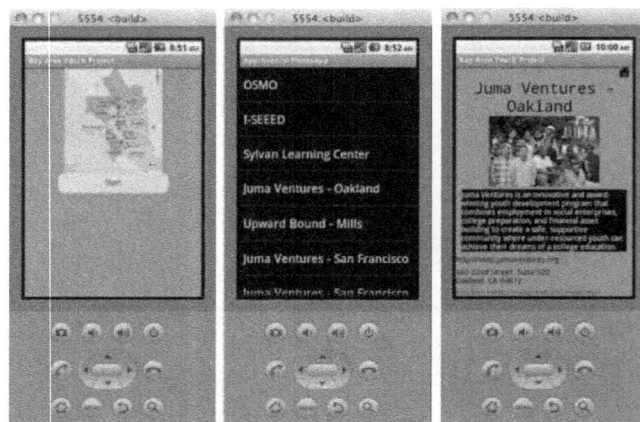

Figure 1: Screenshots of the BAYP mobile app, which allows users to browse for local, youth-oriented after school activities.

3. METHODS
During the twelve-week course the research team took field notes, documenting how Soraya and Mayra negotiated their responsibilities and worked together; engaged with social justice ideas as they proposed and refined their designs; used the various design and development tools; and applied various computer science principles to their app's functionality. We also recorded (video and audio) Soraya and Mayra's various practice presentations, as well as their final presentation to parents and community members, in order to capture how their official 'pitches' changed over time with respect to the social justice and computer science ideas they conveyed. In addition, we archived their weekly code iterations, prototypes and mock-ups during various stages of their design process, and their PowerPoint presentations. Finally, we interviewed Soraya and asked her to reflect on her experience in building BAYP, and how it might be relevant to her future academic pursuits. We were unable to interview Mayra, who was away at college.

4. FINDINGS
Because OSMO focuses primarily on teaching STEM, our research team was curious to explore how a more integrative learning environment – which engaged design thinking skills and a social justice orientation – might foster a more contextually

---

[1] The names of the study participants are all pseudonyms.
[2] In the previous semester, Soraya and Mayra had focused on ideation and design, and had taken several App Inventor tutorials. Thus, they were primed to begin implementing their ideas at the very beginning of the twelve weeks.

grounded approach for learning computer science. Using the BAYP project as an illustrative example, this paper will examine the learning environment in terms of (1) how it gave students access to the domain of computer science, (2) how it provided multiple ways in which students could demonstrate competency within the project, and (3) how it allowed students' to connect their own experiences and values to larger social issues.

4.1 Access to the Domain

Nasir and Hand define access to the domain as "the extent to which participants have the opportunity to learn both about the practice as a whole and about the specific tasks and sub-skills that make up domain knowledge" [13]. In the context of computer science, while the domain is limited by the Turing model of computation, CS has an ever-growing body of algorithms, design patterns, and best practices that can get quite sophisticated, and it therefore takes quite a while to become adept at using the tools of the language in meaningful ways. Thus, it is important to introduce learners to CS in ways that are intuitive and conceptually generative; incorporate diverse interests; and allow for some control over what is learned (and how fast).

4.1.1 Scoping the Domain

In the practice-oriented learning environment of app development, Soraya and Mayra had the ability to scope the computer science domain to only those concepts needed to build their proposed app's functionality. Together, they brainstormed various features of the BAYP app (which involved a Google map, a rating system, automatic notifications and alerts, categorization of activities by type, and the display of pertinent organizational information like price, hours, descriptions, a photo, etc.), and worked with mentors to translate their ideas to specific functional elements within the design. Hence, unlike a traditional introductory course which tends to focus on specific algorithmic concepts (variables, control structures, loops, etc.), Soraya and Mayra's context-driven list of design features drove the corresponding list of computer science topics: databases, HTTP, user interface design, loops, if/else statements, and event handlers. For example, consider the following transcript, which is an excerpt from a Q&A session immediately following Soraya and Mayra's final presentation:

1. S: "And we're not done yet...we're going to add tons more."
2. M: "Our future plan is, like, if you don't have like a...an Android or a smartphone, we're going to create an actual web page to find after school programs to put their kids in, and also we're thinking about (looks at Soraya)...Oh, we're thinking about partnering with schools and different after school programs that we have on this list to actually send notifications and updates to the app. And with the schools, we want to give it to the counselors or principals, so like if they see students who are like off-track, they can pull them in by showing them different after school programs. And we're also going to have a review page, saying if you guys like the app."
3. A1: "Like Yelp?"
4. Soraya and Mayra: "Yeah."

5. A1: "So, can you search...can you search by location?"
6. M: "Mmmmm. Not yet."
7. A1: "we believe you, we believe y'all will figure it out."
8. M: Smiles. "We'll figure it out."
9. S: "We want to do it by location, by, like, price..."

S = Soraya
M = Mayra
A1, A2 = Audience members

From the new set of enhancements that Soraya and Mayra listed above, we can now add HTML/CSS/JavaScript, SMTP (simple mail transfer protocol), SMS (text messaging), spatial querying, and a slightly more sophisticated database schema to their set of relevant CS domain knowledge. Hence, design continues to iteratively expand Soraya and Mayra's CS horizon, and because these concepts are motivated by genuine design needs, when it comes time to learn these skills, Soraya and Mayra will understand why they're important and what function they serve (discussed below). They also understood that this list need not be exhaustively tackled: although the SMS idea came up several times in design discussions before the final presentation, Soraya and Mayra ultimately decided not to pursue that avenue because it simply wasn't one of their top priorities, given all of the other features they wanted to implement. Thus, the creative process also allows students to not only enumerate the relevant computer science topics, but also to select which concepts to learn first. Though it was our role as mentors (instructors) to make suggestions and try to give Soraya and Mayra feedback regarding the technical complexity of their ideas, it was ultimately the students' responsibility to decide which concepts to learn.

4.1.2 A Needs-Driven Approach

Not only can a bottom-up needs assessment scope the domain, but it can also help to make the domain more intuitive. Consider the following excerpt, also taken from Soraya and Mayra's post-presentation Q&A session with the audience:

1. *A2:* "What are the starting options again [referring to the browsable categories of activities that users of the app could select]?"
2. *M:* "Let me show you the Fusion Table [uses the projector to display the Fusion Table onto the screen].... Wait, do you want to see, like, the..."
3. *A1:* "Like 'peer mentoring,' 'tutoring'...that?"
4. *A2:* "Yeah."
5. *S:* "So like, the categories now are 'peer mentoring,' 'tutoring,' 'employment,' 'science,' 'college prep,' 'math,' 'history,' 'social studies,' 'sports,' and 'music.' But we're going to be adding as time goes on to make this more [inaudible]."
6. *A1:* "And they're cross-listed, right? So OSMO's under science, math, and tutoring?"
7. *M:* "Right. Umm hmm. If you look at our Fusion Table [points to the Fusion Table on the screen], you can see that

Figure 2: The BAYP database, created using a Google Fusion Table

Organization Name	URL	Address	Categories	Verified
OSMO	http://www.oaklandscience	1625 Clay St. Suite 600, Oakland, California	Science, Math, Mentoring, Tutoring, College Prep	1
I-SEEED	http://www.facebook.com/I	1625 Clay St. Suite 600, Oakland, California	Social Studies, Academic Achievement, Science, Men...	1

we have a slot called category [referring to the column heading]. And under the categories...[she points to an organization record in the table, showing that each record has a comma-delimited list of categories underneath it (Figure 2)]."

8.   *A2:* "Oh, we see, they have multiple..."
9.   *A1:* "So when somebody goes and adds an organization..."
10. *M:* "We have to go in and verify it." [Points to the "Verified" column header]
11. *S:* "This is where we...it [the organization] would be up for a while, but we could always go back in and change it."
12. *A:* "That's smart."
13. *M:* "Over here, we have 1, 1, 0 [reading down the column]. That tells you if it's verified or not. And if it's not verified, we can go on here and delete it."

Soraya and Mayra had created their "youth programs" database using Google Fusion Tables [4], a web-based spreadsheet for organizing, storing and retrieving data (Figure 2). During the design process, Soraya and Mayra decided which attributes to collect (hours of operation, location, etc.) and an appropriate set of categories ("peer mentoring," "tutoring," "employment," etc.), and slowly populated their tabular repository of resources. Because Soraya and Mayra had designed this table by envisioning the kinds of questions that their users would ask the BAYP app (e.g.: "Show me all of the dance programs"), we conjecture that the task of learning how to query the database became more accessible. A *data-first* approach to learning – where students build their own databases and formulate questions and ideas about how this information might be used – could provide an alternate way to motivate CS learning and to make it more intuitive and relevant.

4.2 Multiple, Shifting Roles

Another benefit of embedding a CS curriculum within a design pedagogy is that the process requires many competencies: gaining a deep, contextualized understanding of the problem you are trying to solve; identifying your users and their potential needs; understanding constraints; conducting a 'social analysis'; communicating design ideas and advocating for them; and determining the precise features of the application. How will information be stored, updated and maintained? What will the screens look like? Who will have access to the app? How will users find what they need? Each of these needs and questions

requires a particular kind of expertise, which in turn provides many important roles to be filled in a design project. This closely parallels Nasir and Hand's notion of *integral roles*, which they define as "the extent to which participants are held accountable for particular tasks in a practice and are expected to become competent and even expert in a subset of activities that are essential to the practice." During the BAYP design and development process, Soraya and Mayra each took on and carried out multiple roles, building upon their existing competencies and gaining exposure to ways in which computer science learning could be applied to their own interests.

4.2.1 From Manager to Designer to Developer

Over the course of the twelve weeks we observed Mayra – who was initially unwilling to engage in some of the computer programming tasks – gradually become more interested in programming. Leading up to the study, she had taken on the role of the "marketing manager" [15], preferring to participate in the non-technical aspects of the project that involved writing, and creating presentations and graphics. However, as she and Soraya began to discuss the specific functionality of the app in detail, Mayra became interested in the more technical aspects of BAYP. For example, she began drafting technical sketches of the app (Figure 3a) to specify the information and options that would be presented to the user, and how each screen would look. From a CS perspective, this process: (1) scoped the many tasks that needed to be completed, serving as a to-do list; and (2) made a blueprint for each screen that precisely specified a discrete unit of work. When the research team introduced Mayra to Balsamiq [1], a drag-and-drop application prototyping tool that allows designers to create Android screens, she immediately began porting her sketches into the software, spending hours formalizing the BAYP design as she learned how to navigate the tool (Figure 3b). Without prompting, she explored how all of the different buttons, fonts, and widgets might represent her ideas, taking great care in her selection of colors and button positioning, and refining her design as she went. As her ideas transitioned from analog to digital, Mayra became interested in making her design "work" (so that clicking a button actually *did* something). When she realized that App Inventor also required skillful screen layouts, she became motivated to explore how button event handlers could be used to hide and show screen elements, and eventually learned to update the BAYP database using an event handler (Figure 3c).

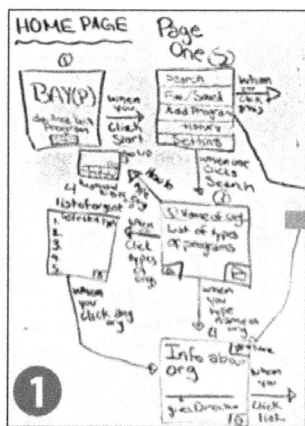

Figure 3a: Mayra's drawings   *Figure 3b: Mayra's Balsamiq mock-up*   *Figure 3c: Mayra's App Inventor layout*

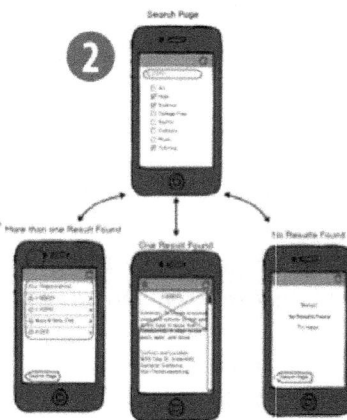

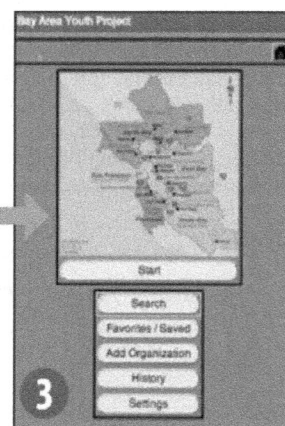

Hence, the design-based sequencing of activities and tools appears to be a critical element in making computer programming more relevant, familiar and interesting. Translating ideas into fine-tuned, screen-by-screen designs, a focus of Human Computer Interaction (HCI), is one way of motivating the learning of CS concepts. The *Exploring CS* project, developed by researchers from UCLA, adopts a similar HCI-focused approach in their introductory high school curriculum [3].

4.2.2 Broadening Student Visions of Computing

While Soraya seemed comfortable with the idea of using App Inventor from the beginning [15], when we interviewed her around six months after the final presentation, she appeared to have broadened her vision of the kinds of roles and expertise involved in computer science. At the beginning of the twelve weeks, she told us that she liked programming, but that she was more of an "English person" than a "math person." However, after the design process, she had expanded her notion of the kinds of skills and competencies needed to be an app developer:

1. [7:55] First author: "So we were just wondering at this point in time...and obviously it's going to evolve and stuff, where you see computing fitting in, or tech, or design, or business or..."
2. Soraya: "I feel like no matter what I do, some type of digital design or coding or some computing will be involved, just because I find it fun to do it. And like I do like to draw and write and stuff, so like I want to have kinda like that liberal arts feel in my interests, but yeah, I really like coding, and I feel like through technology, you can have your ideas reach more people, so that's kinda like what I want. Yeah. Whether it's like working at a startup or making my own app and trying to be one of those few really rich kids who makes it."
3. First author: "So do you think that when you go to [university name omitted] or wherever you go, you'll take another computer science course?"
4. Soraya: "Definitely. Like when I applied to [university name omitted], they have a school called Society, Technology, and Innovation I think. So that whole school is all about taking your ideas and like using technology to kind of like broaden them and put them out there and enhance them. So you like go into the community...it's kind of like what we're doing now, but like in college. So I'm like, 'that's awesome.'"

Soraya says that she will definitely continue coding – a shift from her earlier stance – and yet she specifically mentions that she wants to incorporate "liberal arts" into her notion of computing (turn 2), where she can draw, write (turn 2) and work with communities (turn 4). Hence, her liberal arts interests no longer appear to be at odds with her notion of computing. Soraya now sees her technology, writing, and community-oriented interests as compatible and mutually reinforcing, and sees technology as a way to achieve a diverse set of goals.[3]

This indicates that design, as it applies to problem solving in the world, might be a way to attract a wider range of students to the computing discipline. Secondly, it suggests that an app-centric as opposed to systems-centric curriculum might be an appealing way to introduce computer science ideas to novices. Finally, it suggests that an overemphasis on math skills as an indicator of

potential success in computer science may limit students' appreciation of computer science's relevance and potential.

4.3 Connecting to Student Experiences

A final way that a community-oriented design process promotes computer science engagement is by positioning students as local knowledge experts. This idea closely connects with Nasir and Hand's third tenet of an engaging learning environment: *opportunities to make a unique contribution and feel valued*, which they define as the way in which students can incorporate aspects of themselves into the practice. However, the *Apps for Social Justice* course expands on this idea by incorporating Gutstein's notion of a *social justice pedagogy*, which connects structural aspects of students' lives (including social, economic, and environmental factors) into the practice of app-building, thereby allowing students to situate their own experiences within a larger social context. In combining these two elements, Soraya and Mayra were able to (1) draw from their own local knowledge (which improved their design) while also (2) justifying why their app (and by extension their own experiences) mattered in a broader context.

4.3.1 Local Knowledge

Soraya and Mayra drew from their own experiences as participants in after school programs to create well-informed specifications which detailed how other youth would search for interesting programs, what information would be important to display, and why it mattered that students have access to afterschool programs in the first place. Though as technical mentors, we had expertise in software development, it was Soraya and Mayra's creativity, enthusiasm, and knowledge of their communities and peers that made their app relevant and valuable. Because of their deep connection to the design context, they were able to skillfully construct scenarios of young people and their search for direction and activity in Oakland.

4.3.2 The Role of Social Justice

While connecting the app to students' experiences leads to a more informed design, situating students' experiences within a broader social context gives the app legitimacy. In the following transcript, also taken from the final presentation, Soraya and Mayra connect the importance of afterschool programs not only to their own lives, but also to larger structural issues of government divestment in youth:

1. M: "BAYP also provides all different types of after school programs, not just educational ones. So let's say your daughter told you that she wanted to be a flute player. And her school doesn't have a music class anymore because the government's not funding it. You could find an after school program with BAYP that has different music classes. We created BAYP because we saw this problem and we kinda wanted to attack it and in the same way fix our community."
2. S: "We think BAYP will help because it will disrupt social stereotypes in the world and our community. It's like reinvesting back into the futures of our youth in our community. All the potential in Oakland as you can see through this program, Everyone needs to have access to that."
3. M: "It will also even the playing field for all ethnicities and races and genders. So let's say that a girl was told that she couldn't be a basketball player because only boys play basketball. Different after school programs can give her a different mindset saying that she can do this, because everybody can do whatever they put their minds to."

---

[3] We have recently learned that Soraya was awarded a four-year scholarship to a top computer science program.

Within this transcript, Soraya and Mayra argue that their app will play a role in addressing a variety of larger structural issues: government divestment in schools, social stereotypes, 'evening the playing field', racism, and sexism. However, rather than listing these issues indiscriminately, Soraya and Mayra relate them to their own personal experiences. By speaking to "all the potential in Oakland," they are able to assert with confidence that after school programs give access to important activities and "mindsets," and that their app is important.

Gutstein argues that in order to prepare young people to be leaders in the creation of a more equitable and just society, they must "understand, formulate, and address questions and develop analyses of their society" using the tools of mathematics [5]. From our experiences working with Soraya and Mayra, we believe that Computer Science is also a powerful tool with which to explore social issues because (1) the app development process can be easily geared toward addressing a community need, and (2) design provides an actionable way to study social inequities. Design has often been criticized as being overly "solution-oriented," without a sufficient understanding of the situated context of design problems and their potentially structural causes. Having a social justice and user-centered design orientation can mitigate this tendency by encouraging students to spend time investigating the underlying issues that justify their app, leading to better and more impactful designs.

5. CLOSING REMARKS

In this case study, we have tried to show how a more practice-oriented computer science learning environment (1) gave students access to the domain of computer science, (2) provided multiple and evolving ways in which students are able to demonstrate competency, and (3) allowed students' to connect their own experiences and values to larger social issues. This approach positioned students as local knowledge experts and gave students a way to apply their creativity and expertise to authentic community issues. It also helped to motivate computer science learning by giving students more agency in the concepts they chose to learn – specifically those that were most directly relevant to their goals.

We do not assume that our experiences working with Soraya and Mayra would be typical of any student team, given that Soraya and Mayra were already very hard working and motivated to begin with. Moreover, this activity took place in an out-of-school context, where students were self-selected, free to pursue their own interests without having to worry about performance or assessment, and could depend on the availability of dedicated, skilled mentors to guide their inquiry. That being said, we believe that a practice-oriented approach to learning computer science can provide students with an engaging and intuitive context for learning, which builds on student strengths. In future work, we hope to explore how such an approach might work in an in-school context, to examine what structures and support are needed to provide students with the skills and guidance they need to apply computer science to problems within their communities.

6. ACKNOWLEDGMENTS

We would like to thank the study participants, I-SEEED, and the Boys & Girls Clubs of Oakland (BGCO). In addition, this material is based in part upon work supported by the National Science Foundation under Grant Number IIS-1319849 as well as the Research in Cognition and Mathematics Education (RCME) pre-doctoral training grant.

7. REFERENCES

[1] Balsamiq: *http://balsamiq.com/*.

[2] Boaler, J. 2008. Promoting "relational equity"and high mathematics achievement through an innovative mixed-ability approach. *British Educational Research Journal*. 34, 2 (2008), 167–194.

[3] Goode, J. and Margolis, J. 2011. Exploring computer science: A case study of school reform. *ACM Transactions on Computing Education (TOCE)*. 11, 2 (2011), 12.

[4] Google Fusion Tables: *https://support.google.com/fusiontables/*.

[5] Gutstein, E. 2003. Teaching and learning mathematics for social justice in an urban, Latino school. *Journal for Research in Mathematics Education*. (2003), 37–73.

[6] Lewis, C. 2012. *Applications of Out-of-Domain Knowledge in Students' Reasoning about Computer Program State*.

[7] Lewis, C. 2007. Attitudes and beliefs about computer science among students and faculty. *ACM SIGCSE Bulletin*. 39, 2 (2007), 37–41.

[8] Lubienski, S.T. 2008. On" Gap Gazing" in Mathematics Education: The Need for Gaps Analyses. *Journal for Research in Mathematics Education*. (2008), 350–356.

[9] Margolis, J. 2008. Stuck in the Shallow End: Education, Race, and Computing. (Sep. 2008).

[10] Martin, D.B. 2003. Hidden assumptions and unaddressed questions in mathematics for all rhetoric. *The Mathematics Educator*. 13, 2 (2003), 7–21.

[11] MIT App Inventor: *http://appinventor.mit.edu/explore/*.

[12] Moll, L.C., Amanti, C., Neff, D. and Gonzalez, N. 1992. Funds of knowledge for teaching: Using a qualitative approach to connect homes and classrooms. *Theory into practice*. 31, 2 (1992), 132–141.

[13] Nasir, N.S. and Hand, V. 2008. From the court to the classroom: Opportunities for engagement, learning, and identity in basketball and classroom mathematics. *The Journal of the Learning Sciences*. 17, 2 (2008), 143–179.

[14] Schoenfeld, A.H. and Kilpatrick, J. 2008. Toward a theory of proficiency in teaching mathematics. *The international handbook of mathematics teacher education*. 2, (2008), 321–354.

[15] Vakil, S. 2014. A Critical Pedagogy Approach for Engaging Urban Youth in Mobile App Development in an After-School Program. *Equity & Excellence in Education*. 47, 1 (2014), 31–45.

[16] Wing, J.M. 2006. Computational thinking. *Communications of the ACM*. 49, 3 (2006), 33–35.

Things Coming Together:
Learning Experiences in a Software Studio

Julia Prior, Andrea Connor, John Leaney
Faculty of Engineering and Information Technology
University of Technology, Sydney
Sydney, Australia
julia.prior@uts.edu.au

ABSTRACT

We have evidence that the software studio provides learning that genuinely prepares students for professional practice. Learning that entails dealing with complex technical problems and tools. Learning that involves working effectively in groups. Learning that results in the building of students' self-confidence and the conviction that they can successfully deal with the challenges of modern software system development. Learning that allows the accomplishment of the more elusive professional competencies. In order for students to achieve this type of deep learning, they need time to immerse themselves in complex problems within a rich environment – such as the software studio. The studio also enables each student group to develop and succeed according to their needs, and in different ways.

The conclusions above arise from an ethnographic study in an undergraduate software studio prototype with two student groups and their mentors.

Categories and Subject Descriptors

K.3.2 [Computer and Information Science Education]: *Computer science education, Curriculum.*

General Terms

Design, Human Factors

Keywords

software engineering education; design practice; studio-based learning and instruction; ethnography; groups; graduate attributes; professional competencies.

ITICSE '14, June 21 - 25 2014, Uppsala, Sweden
Copyright 2014 ACM 978-1-4503-2833-3/14/06...$15.00.
http://dx.doi.org/10.1145/2591708.2591720

1. INTRODUCTION

Challenges in contemporary Information Technology higher education include: a significant mismatch between what employers perceive as important abilities and how universities prepare graduates for employment, particularly with regard to non-technical skills [16]; and the changing expectations and learning styles of students [1] [16].

One response to these challenges is to use studio-based learning, the classic approach in the creative arts. Over the last twenty years, the studio approach has gained traction in the ICT and Engineering disciplines because it offers a superior learning experience, especially in achieving practical skills [12] [6].

In the undergraduate ICT degrees at our university, one of our aims is to provide an industry-collaborative, reflective software learning and development environment for students [13]. This is in order to re-invigorate software education and make it more effective, vibrant and acceptable to students and industry. This entails moving a substantial portion of the current teaching objectives in some majors of the undergraduate IT and Engineering degrees into a Software Development Studio (SDS). The SDS will start mid-2014.

The SDS will be a component of every year of the degrees, with experiences and responsibilities increasing with each year. Institutionally, the studio will be a component of a course (subject), integrated with lectures, tutorials and laboratories. Educationally, the studio will be based on reflective practice, and developing software as design practice. It will incorporate the ideas of an iterative/agile approach to software development, using industrial tools and with students working in development roles appropriate to their stages of learning and experience. Grounding in professional practice will be provided by industry partners and mentors and industry projects.

Before our new studio-based approach becomes part of the way that software engineering and development is taught in our faculty, it was, and is, important that we explore, design, prototype and evaluate different aspects of the approach. This paper reports upon our prototyping.

1.1 Related Work

Empirical research to date demonstrates that students appreciate studios, and, that the studio's rich environment contributes to graduate attributes/professional competencies. The research methods used have included surveys, diary examination, structured interviews, action research and reflection.

With regard to students' appreciation of studios (where studios are compared to lectures, etc.), Carbone [5], Armarego [1], Hundhausen [15] [14] and Williams [19] all reported that students prefer the studio experience to the lecture/tutorial/laboratory format.

As for graduate attributes/professional competencies, Williams [19] found that "students overwhelmingly enjoy learning from their peers and believe that a collaborative environment better prepares them for the 'real world'."

Carbone [5] states that "Students found the studio precinct an inviting and comfortable place to learn despite some frustrations with IT-related problems. Students' comments indicate the teaching environment facilitated collaboration, and by the end of the year they began to see the course as being better integrated."

Cennamo [7] asserts that "students need to learn to iteratively generate and refine possible solutions to a design problem. Collaboration with others is essential to seeing the design problem in new and different ways, serving to both broaden solution possibilities and assist in idea refinement. Students need learn to communicate clearly by using the conventions of their discipline, in order to convey their design ideas and gain meaningful input from others."

Hundhausen et al's work [15] is notable in that they used what may be called a control group (which stayed in the lecture stream). Their results indicated that students' self-efficacy (empowerment, ability to control their situation), which may be extended to imply life long learning, increased with the studio group, and, *decreased* in the traditional stream group.

Daniels and Cajander have explored the issue of groups and collaboration over a number of years. In [9], they explore collaboration within and without groups, with the outcome of greater understanding between subgroups, and, a realisation by subgroups that greater collaboration would improve their work.

With regard to professional competencies, or graduate attributes, empirical work includes issues for students in evaluating competencies [4]; the issue of staff engagement [10] and the issues of success in developing competencies in students and assessing them [8].

2. RESEARCH APPROACH

Ethnography is seen as a method that allows a broad landscape to be developed, to find the (previously) unseen and unobserved, and may shed light upon the confusion mentioned. "The irony is that good ethnography requires the researcher to pursue the detours, and to become lost in the culture in order to learn the terrain" [11]. Previous empirical research has not used ethnography, and it seems appropriate to add ethnography to the research viewpoints from which to view studios.

Beyond the broad landscape, one of the things that we wanted to explore in the prototype was how the people worked together in a studio-type environment, as it was happening during the time that they were experiencing it. Bull et al, discovered that the studio is not as well defined as those who use the term may hope. "Our results suggest that there are many intertwined aspects that define studio education, but it is primarily the people and the culture that make a studio" [3].

As an experienced ethnographer, the second author was employed to lead the study. She was required to participate in all the weekly studio sessions, by 'being there', the most important aspect of fieldwork [11]. Her non-technical background gave her some distance from the participants (both students and mentors) and the process. This distance facilitated observations and the development of insights that someone more familiar with software development may have missed.

3. FIELDSITE AND SETUP

In the second semester of 2013, we ran a software studio prototype. We did this in an undergraduate second year core project subject, in which students work in assigned groups of 10, each with a project tutor, to design and develop a complete software system from scratch. The subject is regarded as being very challenging, by both students and staff, as it is the students' first full system development experience. The Agile Scrum approach is used and students have to practice version control, configuration management, different levels of testing etc. Prior to this semester, students have only done subjects that each focus on one, discrete aspect of software development, covering programming, requirements modelling, algorithms and data structures, interface design, database design and web systems.

All of the groups were given the same requirements: to develop a system to track feral animals for a state Wildlife and Parks department. The core of the system was a database to store details about sighted feral animals and registered users, with a web-based system to record and search for feral animals in various state parks and display analytics of the sightings. The web system needed to provide for user entry of sightings of particular feral animals, a search function for feral animals and an analytics function to visually display statistical and summary information on feral animals, and user account registration and management, The groups were allowed to choose whichever technologies they preferred – the studio prototype groups both chose to use MySQL and PHP for the development and Atlassian's Jira to manage the project.

Two groups enthusiastically volunteered to participate in the studio prototype, and so we had 20 students and 2 academic mentors (project tutors), one of whom is the first author of this paper.

There was also an industry mentor in the weekly studio sessions. His was a consultative role, and he answered students' queries on development issues as these came up and advised on contemporary development, particularly issues of architecture, scalability and usability. The two groups met together in same room with both academic mentors and the industry mentor once a week for two to three hours.

4. WHAT HAPPENED WAS …

In this section, a narrative of the studio prototype is presented. It is not a complete account of what happened in the studio over the semester; it is a distillation of the ethnographic record that focuses on particular aspects of the story. The events are given in chronological order to give the reader a sense of the temporal nature of the study and, especially, the changes that occurred over the semester. The names used in the narrative are pseudonyms.

4.1 Starting Off

The studio is a large trapezoid-shaped room, with tables with computers upon them, around the outside and in the centre of the room. There are no partitions, but the room shape allows a degree of separation. The two studio prototype groups are referred to as G1 and G2. Their first action was to elect leaders, Stephan (G1) and Neal (G2).

In the first studio session, the students performed an exercise called the Lego Scrum game, which is frequently used to introduce the Agile software development methodology. The students were given minimal instructions on how to go about the task, but they were told what was required: build a mini-town, with various components such as a house, a garage, roads, a sports stadium. There were also some constraints given such as colours, building functions and relative size of components. They were also told that the task had to be completed within a limited time. Each group was given a box of Lego blocks to use.

One of the groups, G1, immediately all sat down in a circle on the floor, and spread all their Lego blocks out in front of them to start. The group was very methodical and cooperative– they broke the tasks up, planned how to go about the building and allocated specific building tasks to each group member. This group finished in good time, with extra components built.

The other group, G2, stood around a table, with the box of Lego on top of it. They seemed to be rather overwhelmed by the assignment and went about the task in some confusion. There was not much discussion, and no planning or task allocation occurred. Two people tried to build the components while another two dug around in the Lego box and passed blocks to the two builders. The other members of the group just stood around and watched. This group was not finished by the end of the allocated time, and seemed very disheartened by their performance and the expectations imposed by the task.

The Lego Game was indicative of the first Sprint planning that the groups are required to do later in the session. G1 talked about the Scrum methodology and how to use it and implement it, as several group members were familiar with the approach and so they could get going with it immediately. This group were very confident in themselves, as well as with their understanding of the development process and how to use it. Most of the members of this group seem to be extrovert, self-confident personalities, and so the discussion was lively and they required little direction or prompting from the mentors.

G2 was a much quieter group whose members appeared more introverted than G1, and not at all confident about what they were required to do or their capacity to tackle the work. The Agile approach was totally new to all of them. This group focused on the technology that they wanted to use for the database, the programming language etc., rather than the Scrum methodology and its use as a process to understand the requirements and develop the software.

In the second week, G1 was still very focused and apparently organised, getting on with the work without much guidance. G2 needed significant direction, obtaining it from both their academic mentor and the industry mentor. Neal, the G2 group leader, was more confident than in the first week and, encouraged by the mentors, the group orientation started to change from listening to the mentors to listening to each other. At one point, Neal said to the group that collaboration is necessary and beneficial, and they should not be concerned... "those who are not strong can get better in the process."

A week later, G1 did not seem to have as much energy and focus as previously – one member, the communications leader, was unusually late, and the other members engaged and disengaged with the discussion at various times, looking at their own screens or moving out of the circle. Later in the session, the group worked together with some concentration on designing the database schema on the whiteboards, in two sub-groups, each on a different part of the schema. Their academic mentor was very pleased with their progress, stating to the ethnographer that they were ''exceeding expectations'' at that stage.

G2 had started to understand, implement and become comfortable with the Scrum process. They spent some time going over the approach again with their academic mentor, and the discussion seemed to be a breakthrough for the group. They started being methodical, with the whole group working out together which tasks they needed to do in the next Sprint and allocating them to specific group members. They used the class time to plan and organise the work, rather than to design or work on their software system They spent time outside class once or twice each week, to work together for a couple of hours.

Apart from the obvious use of technology in class, social media, especially Facebook, was used extensively by both groups to communicate about their work and the project.

4.2 Sprints and Leadership

A month into the semester, G1 still seemed more cohesive than G2, and indeed somewhat competitive with regard to G2. Both groups seemed to be in a similar place and doing much the same tasks in the studio session.

G2 could see "results" in terms of completing their allocated tasks and working as a group. There was a sense in the group that they might finally be on track and were able to envision the project in its various stages. Completing their first Sprint had given them momentum and a project plan through which to consider the next set of tasks.

The organisational tool of the Scrum Sprint seemed to helped both groups create a project plan. It also seemed to help Neal find his feet as the G2 group leader and as the coordinator of the Sprints and Backlogs week to week. His style was more understated than that of the other group leader, but he seemed to be more comfortable and grew into the leader's role with each passing week.

G1, which originally appeared the more cohesive, had its leader changed (to Hardeep) and a week later appeared to be undergoing another leader change. Wayne, one of the leadership contenders, acted as 'discussant' for the group, posing problems and suggesting possible directions for them to go in. [The ethnographer] was no longer sure if Hardeep was still the group leader as Wayne had assumed a central role.

4.3 The Hare and the Tortoise

It was the week before the mid-semester presentations, in which each group in the subject had to present their work to another group and their tutor for a peer review. G1 and G2 practiced their presentations in the studio session.

G1 was not ready at the beginning of the session, so G2 offered to present first. It was obvious that their efforts over the past few weeks had paid off in terms of group cohesion and understanding the Agile process – it had provided them with a structure to work within, and they had become deeply embedded in it and made significant progress. The group appeared fully prepared and acquitted themselves well, even if their presentation was a little unadventurous. As this was a simulation of the formal presentations, G1 left the room for a few minutes to put together some questions to ask the presenters, although 2 of them remained in the back of the studio and worked on their presentation. Neal, the G2 group leader, answered most of the questions. He came across as pleased and confident in answering the questions, and spoke about his group's work in a relaxed manner. He did not appear to be at all phased by any questions and one answer was that, yes, they are following the Scrum methodology very closely.

Overall, G1 seemed somewhat surprised by the quality of the presentation and work they had just seen.

G1 started their presentation in some disarray; it was clear that they were underprepared. Although their presentation perhaps better demonstrated the system requirements and how they responded to these, their slides were not complete, one of their presenters was missing and they finished in a bit of a muddle.

What struck [the ethnographer] most about the response from both groups was a level of generosity – no one was gloating or trying to point score off the other group. There was genuine curiosity and camaraderie on display, even if a sense of competition still hung in the atmosphere.

In discussing their presentation and progress later in the session, G1 decided to appoint a single ScrumMaster (Wayne) for the rest of the semester. Further, their mentor suggested that they needed to improve the level of communications within the group. One of the members, who was very tired, said to the ethnographer just before the session that working in groups was demanding, especially when most of their interactions were on Skype and via GoogleDocs. This was also when G1 found out that G2 had been meeting face-to-face every week outside class and decided to do the same.

4.4 The Invisible Boundary

It was mid-October. Both groups appeared relaxed. They knew they were nearing the end of the semester and had achieved goals in relation to setting up their systems. At this session they reported on the past weeks' achievements and plan for the final Sprint.

The mentors gave feedback to all the students together on the formal mid-semester presentations and discussion ensued. The G2 leader raised a problem that his group had with the presentation peer review. The reviewing group (non-studio group) marked very hard, whilst his group took a more measured and generous approach with the group that it reviewed. Perhaps this reflects the co-operative atmosphere and ethos that had been established in the studio setting over many weeks.

After more feedback and discussion in each group separately with their mentors about their presentations, and, the mentors' mid-semester assessment of their respective groups' work and progress, the groups worked on closing their previous Sprints and planning the final Sprints. At some point, Neal crossed over an invisible boundary and sat talking with members of G1, on G1's side of the room. This was the first time [the ethnographer had] seen him do this and it seemed like breaking a habitual, spatial division between the two groups, and, evidence of inter-group camaraderie, collaboration, and cooperation.

4.5 Doing Time

In the very last studio session for the semester, in the week after the final presentations to other groups in the subject, each studio group gave a detailed demonstration of their system to the rest of the studio - the first time everyone had seen 'step through' demonstrations of the entire system. Although the mentors asked probing questions about the system design, particularly with regard to the user interface and data management, the atmosphere was informal and relaxed, with some gentle teasing and laughter amongst all the students and the presenters from both groups.

After the two demonstrations, there was a class discussion about the subject as a whole, and more specifically, about the studio prototype – what the students found particularly helpful about the environment and approach and what was not very useful. One of the themes that came through very clearly was that the students felt strongly that they wanted more time working together in the studio, not just the 2-3 hours per week timetabled for the subject. Both groups of students had gradually learnt that working together face-to-face regularly and for extended periods was far more effective and productive than trying to get tasks done individually in their own time and then integrating these in class time.

5. FINDINGS

Two findings from this study are highlighted here. The first is the insight into group relations, both intra- and inter-group, and the changes in behaviour within and between the groups over the semester. The second is the holistic nature of the learning experience in the studio, which we call 'things coming together'.

5.1 Group Relations

Looking over the semester as a whole, some of the most significant changes occurred at a group level. We discuss these developments from two perspectives: within each of the groups, and between the groups.

5.1.1 Intra-Group Relations

Initial impressions suggested that G1 was cohesive, competent and collaborative from the beginning of the semester. In the Lego exercise, G2 showed little sense of how to organise, delegate, decision-make – in short, collaborate – in order to complete a task within a reasonable time. These early group impressions frame the perception, by the students themselves and the mentors, of each group in the coming weeks.

To start with, G2 had very little confidence, in their knowledge, skills or capacity to successfully deal with the challenges given by the project. Their inclination to focus on tools and technical details in the first two weeks may have been because they were unsure about the Scrum process and how to use it effectively. For the first couple of weeks, there was not much interaction amongst the group members in G2. Discussions were often oriented towards the mentors instead of each other. This changed as their knowledge, skills and confidence grew. Regular group meetings, in the studio and outside class to work together seems to have enabled the group to build relationships between the members, work things out more as a group, and to become familiar and comfortable with use of process. By the end of the semester they seemed to have achieved a harmonious yet determined ethos as a group. G2 cohered slowly and steadily over time – with the group leader growing into his leadership role. There are a few confident personalities in this group but they were not dominating, and none of them seemed interested in being the group leader at any stage. Once they started to gain an understanding of the methodology, this group stuck very closely to the Scrum approach and this helped them allocate roles, clarify workloads and establish group interactions that appeared to be equitable and inclusive.

G1 came across as super-confident, with a clear idea from the beginning of how to tackle the development challenges as a group. G1 had several members who were forthright, confident and willing to take on leadership positions. One individual worked as a de facto leader at various times in his role as communications leader. The group focused on system development, rather than the intricacies of implementing the process. From the start, they developed solutions quickly, individual tasks were allocated without much debate or coercion and these were completed relatively quickly. It seems, however, that their self-assurance and fast-paced approach meant that they were not as thorough as they might have been in understanding the requirements or considering alternate design solutions. Their mentor spent much of the studio time playing 'devil's advocate' and asking 'what if' questions, subtly reining them in to encourage them not to rush into decisions.

Further, ambivalence about and changes in the group leader role in the first half of the semester proved disruptive to their group functioning. It was also not clear how less self-assured members may have coped initially in a group where 5 (half) of the members had leadership personalities. The group had difficulty allocating roles, as well as ongoing concern over a group member who was not pulling his weight.

The wake-up call about their relative progress at the mock mid-semester presentations encouraged them to reflect on the way they were going about the work as a group. As a direct result of this, the group reorganised itself, allocated a ScrumMaster role to one specific person for the rest of the semester, separate to that of group leader, and started meeting and working together face-to-face regularly outside of class time. These strategies helped the group stabilise and smoothed their progress over the second part of the semester. They still appeared driven to succeed, but were less sure of themselves and perhaps more realistic.

Collaborative learning within each group

One of the most significant characteristics of a studio environment is collaborative learning, with students working out how to do things and to develop their own skills by learning together and from each other. This was very evident in the prototype.

The willingness of G2 to work slowly, methodically through the Scrum methodology and acquire confidence and competence in its use appeared to give them a solid foundation and enabled steady progress in system development. A sound, thorough understanding of the requirements, the Scrum process and various development tools were gained by a 'learning by doing' approach, More than this, together, the group had to figure out what they needed to know at each stage and how to use it effectively.

In G1, the group learnt about the Scrum approach from the three group members who already had experience in it, which meant the group got going quickly implementing a development process, and the other group members built up their own knowledge about Scrum from others' experience. Whatever else happened, it is clear that each group learnt how to operate effectively, but in very different ways; neither group's learning was better, just different.

5.1.2 Inter-Group Relations

The perception of how each group responded to the Lego exercise may have been a distraction. It set the groups up in a way that confirmed G1's view of itself as having the capacity, and then some, to cope with the semester project, which encouraged them to be somewhat gung-ho in their approach. G2 was left feeling overwhelmed and convinced that they did not know enough to deal with the challenges posed in the subject.

Initially there was some sense of rivalry and competition – particularly from G1, whose own self-perception was one of "having the edge" on G2.

A turning point in terms of shifting perceptions of both groups and the dynamic between them emerged during the mid-semester mock presentations. G1 appeared surprised by the standard of work done by and confidence of G2, leading to a re-assessment of their own work practices. This event changed the dynamic and the "assumed order of things" between both groups.

So, the interactions between the groups within the studio sessions effected changes in the way G1 went about their work and managed their intra-group relations, learning from what strategies they deemed successful for G2.

Collaborative learning across/between the groups

The co-operative atmosphere during the mock presentations was impressive. Each group appeared to be genuinely interested in the work of the other and afterwards this continued to permeate the environment.

Attitudes between the two groups changed, over the first half of the semester particularly, from competitive to a strong sense of camaraderie between the groups and across the studio as a whole, where the groups supported and encouraged one another.

Moreover, there was clear evidence of one group learning from the other when G1 made changes to their strategy as a direct consequence of finding out what had been effective for G2.

This section is about how the 2 groups worked and changed over the semester, but it is very important to recognise that this is not a comparison, or value judgement of the two groups' characters, behaviour and performance. It is simply a statement about how different groups function and flourish in different ways. Both groups ended up in a similar place – working together competently and effectively as a group, having designed and produced a good quality software system. But, the learning experiences and the changes that occurred in each group were very different.

This is a very significant finding in terms of the studio approach to learning software development. The studio environment allows each group to evolve, as they need to, given their specific member mix, with various backgrounds and experiences and preferred ways of working. This is in contrast to traditional teaching according to a syllabus, covering each topic regardless of where students are or what is their prior knowledge. Learning both technical skills and more on an as-needed basis throughout the project development process was made possible by the studio environment.

Much of what we learnt about the group relations, the behaviour within each of the groups and their interactions across groups can be considered to lead to the second finding. The changes in the group relations did not happen in a vacuum, but as part of the studio prototype experience as a whole. The import of this holistic experience is addressed in the following section.

5.2 Things Coming Together

One way of looking at the studio prototype is as a network which incorporates people, software tools, subject policies and procedures, a development methodology, processes, techniques, documents, practices and products [17][18]. This network is not static, nor is it pre-configured or already there. Rather, the relational and emerging nature of this type of network means that it is continuously and dynamically reconfigured over time. Star calls this network a web; she values "the ways in which knowledge is co-created by a web of people, symbols, machines and things" ([18] p.405).

So, we could consider the 'tangible' elements of this (studio) network to be the two groups' members, the three mentors, the system specification/requirements, the Scrum methodology, the development tools, the project management tools and communication tools. The 'intangible' elements include the intra-group relations and interactions, the inter-group relations, the relations and interactions of the mentors with the groups and individual members, and the relations of the groups and their members with the technical tangibles. All of these elements interconnect; dynamically providing a network or web in which software development knowledge and skills are co-created.

Perhaps the most challenging aspect of the project for the students was integrating their technical know-how, decision-making, and communications–verbal and written–at a systems level. Instead of being able to focus on a discrete thing such as a single program or a relatively simple data model, the students were required to deal with all the different aspects of the development experience at once. Although at specific times they could focus on a particular task or element, much of the time, their efforts were aimed at integrating things and working in a complex context.

The Lego exercise was something that needed to be done immediately, within a very limited time, and it was a contained problem, with very clear requirements and tasks. Very much like an assignment in a 'normal' subject. Using a methodology such as Scrum over a significant period of time to develop the effective use of a process by the whole group to design and build a particular software product of good quality was an entirely different proposition. Group functioning and relations had to be managed more thoughtfully, strategically and contingently. Ultimately, both groups were successful, but they went about the project in different ways and, notably, from different starting contexts.

Another significant factor is time – time for students to engage with a complex problem, time to build the group, time to build an effective solution. Time is the catalyst within a rich learning environment that allows students to immerse themselves and to deeply learn [2] as things come together.

6. CONCLUSION

In conclusion, we see evidence in this study that the studio provides a learning experience that genuinely prepares students for professional practice. Learning that entails dealing with complex technical problems and tools. Learning that involves working effectively in groups. Learning that results in the building of students' self-confidence and -conviction that they can successfully deal with the challenges of modern software system development. Learning that allows the accomplishment of the more elusive professional competencies

7. ACKNOWLEDGMENTS

Our sincere thanks to the studio prototype mentors and students and the subject co-ordinator. This research was made possible by Faculty and University teaching and learning grants.

8. REFERENCES

[1] J. Armarego and L. Fowler, Orienting students to studio learning, in *Proceedings of the 2005 ASEE/AAEE 4th Global Colloquium on Engineering Education*. Australasian Association for Engineering Education, 2005.

[2] J. Biggs and C. Tang, *Teaching for Quality Learning at University*, Fourth Edition. McGrawHill. 2011.

[3] C. Bull, J. Whittle and L. Cruickshank, Studios in software engineering education: towards an evaluable model, in *Proceedings of the 35th International Conference on Software Engineering (ICSE13)*, IEEE, 2013.

[4] Å Cajander, M Daniels and B von Konsky, Development of professional competencies in engineering education, in *Proceedings of the 41st ASEE/IEEE Frontiers in Education Conference*, IEEE, 2011.

[5] A. Carbone and J. Sheard, A studio-based teaching and learning model in IT: what do first year students think?, in *Proceedings of the 7th annual conference on Innovation and Technology in Computer Science Education*, 2002, pp. 213-217.

[6] A. Carter and C. Hundhausen, A review of studio-based learning in computer science, *Journal of Circuits, Systems, and Computer* (JCSC 27), October, 2011.

[7] K Cennamo, C Brandt, B Scott, S Douglas and M McGrath, Managing the complexity of design problems through studio-based learning, *Interdisciplinary Journal of Problem-based Learning*, vol. 5, Issue 2, 2011.

[8] M.Daniels, Developing and assessing professional competencies, *Acta Universitatis Upsaliensis, Digital Comprehensive Summaries of Uppsala Dissertations from the Faculty of Science and Technology 808*, 2011.

[9] M.Daniels and Å. Cajander, Experiences from using constructive controversy in an open-ended group project, in *Proceedings of the 40th ASEE/IEEE Frontiers in Education Conference*, IEEE, 2010.

[10] B. de la Harpe and A. Radloff, Developing graduate attributes for lifelong learning – how far have we got?, *Lifelong Learning Conference*, 2008.

[11] D. M. Fetterman, *Ethnography: Step-by-Step*. Third ed. Applied social research methods series, Vol. 17. Sage, 2010.

[12] D. Garlan, D. P. Gluch and J. E. Tomayko, Agents of change: educating software engineering leaders, *IEEE Computer*, November, 1997.

[13] O. Hazzan, The reflective practitioner perspective in software engineering education, *The Journal of Systems and Software*, 63, 2002.

[14] C. Hundhausen, A. Agrawal, D. Fairbrother and M. Trevisan, Integrating pedagogical code reviews into a CS 1 course: an empirical study, *SIGCSE'09*, Chattanooga, Tennessee, USA, 2009.

[15] C. Hundhausen, A. Agrawal, D. Fairbrother and M. Trevisan, Does studio-based instruction work in CS 1? An empirical comparison with a traditional approach, *SIGCSE '10*, Milwaukee, Wisconsin, USA, 2010.

[16] T. Koppi, P. Ogunbona, J. Armarego, P. Bailes, P. Hyland, T. McGill, F. Naghdy, G. Naghdy, C. Pilgrim and M. Roberts, Addressing ICT curriculum recommendations from surveys of academics, workplace graduates and employers, *OLT Final Report*. Wollongong: University of Wollongong, 2013.

[17] L. Suchman. *Human-Machine Reconfigurations: Plans and Situated Actions*, 2nd edition. Cambridge University Press, 2007.

[18] S. L. Star. The trojan door: organizations, work and the "open black box". *Systems Practice*, 5(4), 1992.

[19] L. Williams, L. Layman, K. M. Slaten, S. B. Berenson and C. Seaman, On the impact of a collaborative pedagogy on African American millennial students in software engineering, in *Proceedings of 29th International Conference on Software Engineering (ICSE'07)*, 2007.

Understanding Students' Preferences of Software Engineering Projects

Thérèse Smith   Swapna Gokhale   Robert McCartney

University of Connecticut
371 Fairfield Way
Storrs, Connecticut, USA
[tms08012,ssg,robert]@engr.uconn.edu

ABSTRACT

Students in a maintenance-centric, introductory software engineering course were expected to understand, analyze and extend an open source software project of their choice, selected from a limited set of prepared applications. Students fell into two groups: those who chose a project based on its perceived and estimated difficulty, and those who chose a project based on the appeal of the subject matter. Students in both groups, however, cited value for themselves in terms of enhanced learning experience, and for users in terms of increased benefit, as reasons for their selection. These insights into students' thinking can guide future efforts in selecting projects that can simultaneously support the learning objectives as well as motivate the students, not only in software engineering but also in broader computing courses.

Categories and Subject Descriptors

D.2.7 [**Software Engineering**]: Distribution, Maintenance, and Enhancement; K.3.2 [**Computers and Education**]: Computers and Information Science Education

Keywords

Software Engineering; Open Source; Student choice

1. RESEARCH QUESTION

Computing students who aspire to be software engineers must be able to comprehend and work with legacy code, which is challenging because such code may be poorly documented, ill structured, and/or lacking in human support. Therefore, to prepare students for industrial careers, we integrated Open Source Software (OSS) projects into a "maintenance-centric" software engineering (SE) course. Our objective was to impart skills and appreciation involved in understanding and evolving legacy software systems in the face of sparse documentation and minimal support.

We chose and prepared a set of ten open source Java and Eclipse applications and applets for this integration. The domains of these projects included outer space, music, home and family, natural languages, building architecture, epidemiology (humanitarian) and games. The students were presented with a description of these projects along with their suggested enhancements and were allowed to explore and experiment with them. Following a two-week period, the students were asked to name their top three choices for the one project with which they would practice comprehension, analysis, and evolution through the semester.

We wished for our projects not only to support our learning objectives, but also to foster the students' motivation. Therefore, we provided multiple projects to improve the likelihood that students with different motives for choosing computer science courses might nevertheless find projects that were well matched to their interests. This variety of projects available also offered the opportunity to investigate the factors that the students used in making a choice.

We assigned the students to tell us the basis for their selection. An analysis of their responses revealed that students generally fell into two disjoint groups; one group chose on the basis of perceived difficulty and the other based on the appeal of the subject matter. Students in both groups, however, cited value to themselves, users and other software engineers as a reason for their choice. We expect to use this understanding of what drives students' choice to guide and improve the efficiency of our otherwise labor intensive, iterative, and cumbersome project selection process [9]. Additionally, we hope that this understanding may transfer to other project-oriented courses in the computing curriculum.

The rest of the paper is organized as follows: Section 2 describes the course and OSS projects. Section 3 describes the analysis methodology. Section 4 presents and discusses our findings. Section 5 describes related work. Section 6 concludes the paper and identifies future directions.

2. THE COURSE AND PROJECTS

This section describes the SE course, its objectives, the chosen OSS projects and their integration.

2.1 Overview of the Course

Our SE course is offered to sophomores and juniors, who have taken a data structures course. Our students can write, test and debug small Java programs, use Eclipse, create UML class diagrams, and produce documentation. The lecture portion of the course covers SE principles and techniques, based on the text book by Ghezzi et al. [8]. These techniques are reinforced through practice on course projects. The objective of this project is for the students to comprehend and implement a feature enhancement to an existing open source software system. Students worked in pairs on the project, which incurred a significant amount of effort and constituted most of their grade.

We selected and prepared 10 open source projects for integration. The preparation involved debugging, compiling by finding missing dependencies, exercising with static and dynamic analysis tools [13], documenting the build process, writing a brief description of the features, identifying the list of potential enhancements, and installing on an instance of GitHub. Table 2 summarizes the domain, initial features and proposed enhancements for these projects. All projects except for Astrodynamics [1] were from Sourceforge [21].

A sequence of assignments was designed to help the students gain a good enough understanding of their respective projects to be able to implement and test their chosen enhancements. These assignments interleaved "reverse engineering" or comprehending the existing code with "forward engineering" or designing, planning and implementing their enhancements as in Table 1.

The first assignment, reproduced verbatim in Figure 1, was accompanied by a description of each project, including links to associated web sites, build and run instructions, a sampling of feature requests, and a screen shot. An example description of SweetHome project included in this assignment is shown in Figure 2. The assignment asked students to rank three projects and their respective enhancements and to explain what motivated their choices. Table 2 also lists the counts that each project was rated as first, second, and third by the students. In the table, the projects appear in order of decreasing collective student choice.

Table 1: Semester-long Project Assignments

#	Activity
1	Select a project and enhancement
2	Reverse engineer class diagrams
3	Plan class diagrams for enhancement
4	Uses case diagrams, for original functions and enhancement, emphasizing the change
5	Reverse engineer sequence diagrams
6	Plan sequence diagrams for enhancement
7	Implement and demonstrate enhancement

3. ANALYSIS METHODOLOGY

We loaded the students' text responses into Saturate [20] and analyzed them using a basic inductive qualitative analysis similar to that described by Braun and Clarke [4]. The process can be viewed as building a graph, where fragments of text are leaves, and each leaf also has a name, not usually unique. Nodes occasionally have more than one parent, and any number of children. Leaves are codes, and nodes one level up are categories, and those at the next level up are initial themes. Some initial themes are promoted to main themes, and others take a supporting role. These steps are as follows, with constant comparison applied in between each step [15].

Step 1: Assigning Codes The idea "unit of meaning" was relevant here and the groups of words that constituted a unit were determined by the research question. To highlight the meaning of our text fragments, we eliminated insignificant words, and then labeled the group of words with a

The semester-long project is to be completed in teams of two students. Choose your partner, preferably from within the same section. There are 10 projects, and each project is accompanied by a small selection of feature requests that were current as of this summer. You should read the summary of the projects and feature enhancements. In addition, you can explore the project and its domain using other resources available on the Internet. We hope that you'll find a subject area that interests you. After this exploration, each team should:

1. Identify three projects and a feature enhancement for each project. Rank your selection (project + feature enhancement) from first through third.

2. Explain your choices of the project and the enhancement. For example, the subject was interesting, the project design appeared good to work with, the feature enhancements looked interesting or not too daunting, you are planning ahead for a job interview where this project will be interesting to discuss, you have experience/knowledge in the domain or the application, it seems really fun, etc. Limit your response to 2-3 sentences per project.

3. For each project + feature enhancement pair, explain what you perceive to be the relation between the project and your chosen enhancement. For example, how does the software work now and the ability to change it so that the feature can be incorporated? Does it appear that the feature enhancement will change the project in an in-depth way? For example, choice of "skins" for displays appears to change "everything" but superficially from a code perspective. Changing a word processing program into a Kinect box adventure program would need a more in-depth modification. Alternatively, the change might appear to be localized. If the software has modes, for example, and the feature only applies to one mode, that suggests that the impact of the feature enhancement might be localized. Limit your response to 2-3 sentences per project-feature pair.

Figure 1: Assignment 1

name (a code) that captured the expressed meaning. We tried to reuse these codes when we saw a similar meaning expressed by another group of words. We then examined each code's content and wrote a memo to describe the concept shared among its phrases, and also differentiated it from other codes. We then reexamined each phrase in its original context to see whether it was an example of the code as defined. This process, referred to as "generating initial codes" aimed to condense the text while preserving its meaning [4].

Step 2: Creating Categories Having preliminary definitions of the codes, we intuited categories to group codes. The categories could be overlapping, i.e, a code could belong to more than one category. Using Saturate [20], we wrote a memo to describe the meanings by which we organized

Table 2: Summary Description and Popularity of OSS Projects

Project	Initial Features	Suggested Enhancements
Rapla (9, 5, 3)	Supports scheduling of resources such as rooms, projectors and people (with calendar), detects conflicts	Fixing the icon in the filter button, adding a missing confirmation dialog, and collapsing/expanding appointment GUI
Genealogy (2, 6, 5)	Recording and displaying family ancestry, both chart and tree views	Support for global locations, showing a tree view, opening all branches, incorporating a lunar calendar
TripleA (7, 0, 2)	Games, maps, supports play over computer networks	Better artificial intelligence, optional rules, better map editor, plug-in system to add new maps
SweetHome (3, 4, 1)	Select components, design and equip a house, and view it	Transparent walls, walls intersecting at angles other than right angles
MegaMek (1, 5, 2)	Complex war game with long, complicated forms for configuring armies and placing assets on maps	Incorporating additional geographic elements – working gates, and tunnels, and scattering of missiles that do not connect with their targets
Archimedes (1, 2, 5)	Computer-aided design for architects and building construction	Exit option on file menu, trim an ellipse, stretch graphic elements
Impro-Visor (2, 1, 3)	Musical notation at a professional level, lyrics to support improvisation performance	Display filename in window title bar, adding special chord symbol, getting accidentals (part of music notation) right
STEM (1, 1, 2)	Eclipse project on epidemiology, created and used temporal and spatial models of to study and potentially prevent the spread of infectious diseases	Mouse over tool tips, disease initializer to set compartments to specific values at every time step, assigning units explicitly to adjustable STEM parameters
AstroDynamics (0, 0, 2)	NASA program showing earth orbits and orbiting objects, Enabling calculation of new orbits, predicting of collision years	Constrained non-linear optimization, orbit estimation using Kalman filter methods, trajectory optimization
OmegaT (0, 1, 2)	Sophisticated tools for professional language translators, interpreters	Loading bilingual XLIFF documents, incorporating machine translation with Yandex

codes into categories, and differentiated between categories. In another backward check, each code was reviewed to see whether it meaningfully contributed to its category. This was another example of "constant comparison" [15].

Step 3: Axial Coding In this step, we took stock of our categories, in order to decide what might be promoted to main themes. Each category in turn was placed centrally on a hub and spoke-like diagram, and the spokes in the arrangement were labelled to find important relationships [22]. Axial coding provided another opportunity to review the definitions of the categories, and also a context for deciding which initial themes were the most significant.

Step 4: Thematic Analysis Combining the results of axial coding into a single diagram, where the more significant themes were represented in ovals, and remaining categories, depicted as rounded rectangles, were used to qualify and clarify. Consolidation of these relationships and reporting completed the basic inductive thematic analysis.

Step 5: Triangulation The qualitative analysis was triangulated with a quantitative method, counting the number of times projects appeared as first, second and third choices.

4. RESULTS AND DISCUSSION

In this section, we discuss the findings of applying thematic analysis from Section 3 to students' responses.

4.1 Themes and Relationships

Concepts in students' responses ranged from enjoyment, through cost-benefit (where they are balancing between how hard they might have to work, and what they hope to achieve), to how useful, and apparent the results of their work would be. Applying the first step produced codes, from which the following four main thoughts emerged, which were designated as categories to cluster the codes:

- **Subject Appeal:** A small number of students chose on the basis of appeal of the subject matter of the project, such as it was a game.

- **Value/benefit:** Students cared about the benefits of their work to themselves, to users, and other software engineers. Personal benefits included learning experiences and preparation for careers and coding challenges. The visibility and utility of their enhancements, to a broad audience, seemed to matter more.

- **Difficulty/ease:** Several students expressed the difficulty of implementing the enhancement as a primary factor in their choice.

- **Planning/estimation:** Some teams chose to plan the implementation, and attempted to estimate whether their skills would permit them to complete the work, and cited the consistency between skills and the expectations as a reason for their choice.

We summarize the prevalent codes for each category, sorted in an increasing order of the number of occurrences

SweetHome

This project provides a visualization of a home, from variable angles, and allows design and construction of the home, and selection and placement of furnishings for the home.

Websites connected with this project include:

- http://sourceforge.net/scm/?type=cvs&group_id =152568

  Feature requests can be seen at:

- http://sourceforge.net/tracker/?group_id=152568&atid =784668

Build Instructions:
Use Eclipse Juno for building.
Use Eclipse Indigo for creating class diagrams with Amateras.
Eclipse builds.

Run Instructions:
Select project SweetHome3D, run as application, from the list of "main"s, choose SweetHome3D - com.eteks.sweethome3d

Sampling of Feature Requests:
Wall transparency (for background images) Wall angle control
Resolution control (in pixels)
Scale (e.g., floor tiles are 1 foot square, rooms are 15 feet long)
Control of movement of objects
Users design and equip a house, selecting components, and view it.

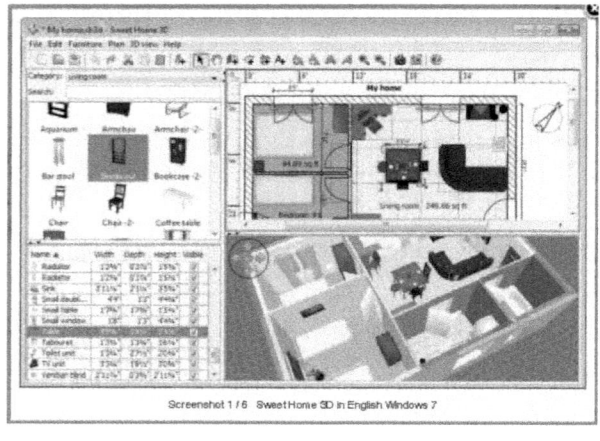

Figure 2: Description of Sweethome project

in Table 3. Codes in the planning and value-added categories denote examples of generating benefit, such as design freedom and flexibility for developers evolving the code.

In applying step three, we noted that the codes formed two non-overlapping clusters corresponding to two disjoint groups of students; one around how difficult the enhancements might be and another one around how enjoyable a

Table 3: Categories and Common Codes

Category	Code
Value-added (VA)	cost-benefit
	value of enhancement
Appeal (AP)	career associated
	valuable learning experience
	familiarity with concepts used
	software coding challenge
	subject appeal
	positive emotion
Planning (PL)	architectural consideration
	plan for implementation
Difficulty (DE)	not too demanding
	evaluating difficulty

project might be. Added value or benefit, however, was cited as a reason by teams in both groups. Therefore, on the basis of its relationships to other categories, the strongest category was value-added, so this was our main theme. Placing the common value-added theme in the center clarified the difference between the two groups. For students who chose for enjoyment, architecture evaluation was not an issue. The latter group, however, investigated the architecture and evaluated implementation strategies, before arriving at their choices. Thus, choosing on the basis of difficulty motivated useful work in these students, preparing the students to learn better methods for architecture exploration, interfacing, impact analysis and code generation. The planning/estimation category elaborated the difficulty category, and hence, emerged as a minor rather than a major theme. The summary and relationships between the themes is shown in Figure 3. A compact definition of themes appears in Table 4. Finally, the relationships corresponding to edges in Figure 3 are listed in Table 5.

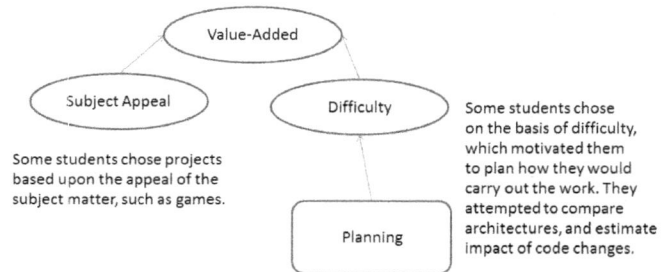

Figure 3: Themes, Major and Minor

4.2 Triangulation

Table 6 shows the most common codes (and their categories) for each of the top six projects. The two most frequent projects were selected because of the increased value that their enhancements would produce. Students cited anticipated difficulty as a secondary concern, followed by appeal. On the other hand, appeal was mentioned as a prominent feature for the third project, followed by value-added. Finally, the fourth most popular project was chosen with consideration of difficulty, and secondarily based on the value of modifications. Assessment of difficulty appeared in all but one of the projects. These counts support our findings that students cared about the value of their work more

Table 4: Definition of Themes

Theme	Definition
Value-added (VA)	Captures intent to create things of value. Students seemed to believe that it was easily possible to add value, they could factor fun into their selection.
Appeal (AP)	Satisfying subject area; games, astronomy, music, skills, usefulness, resume value, and humanitarian.
Difficulty (DE)	Estimation of how demanding specific enhancements might be.
Planning (PL)	Connected with the evaluation of difficulty, but is distinguished from it in exhibiting the way students think about approaching a project at this early stage. Architecture support for ease of completing the enhancements was mentioned.

Table 5: Relationships between Themes

Themes	Relationships
AP/VA	Value that their work on the project would produce was a significant component of appeal.
DE/VA	Combination of an achievable enhancement with anticipated value was an important element of satisfaction.
PL/DE	Planning as a means of estimating ease of implementation.

than entertainment. Already, our sophomores are cautious about the difficulty they might be taking on, except in the case of the better liked game.

4.3 Discussion

The project that appeared in the first, second and fourth places were chosen because they dealt with familiar concepts, were generally useful and had pleasant qualities. Games were third and fifth in popularity, ahead of the (building) architectural tool and a musical skills related program. The humanitarian program, which was extremely large and challenging, followed these.

Students considered familiarity in at least two ways, namely, a match between their conceptions and implementation of the project's features, and the size of the user community, which also imparted the sense of widespread benefits to the work. Thus, projects that addressed familiar needs with a big user base, like Rapla and Genealogy, were appreciated. Students considered value of their features: the capacity for holidays of multiple kinds, completeness of menu options, presence of user support, e.g., such as confirmation of deletion seen commonly and avoiding cognitive dissonance and distracting incompetence in games. Thus, we were shown that the majority of our sophomores are thinking about being productive of value, although they were primed to choose projects on the basis of domains or subject matter through project descriptions and homework assignments. Finally, this sense that the opportunity to be useful is so generally available that one could choose also on the basis of having fun was prevalent.

The importance of producing value, however, was tempered by a concern for the effort that might be involved in completing the enhancements. Choice motivated the students to explore the code and architecture to evaluate the difficulty of the implementation. This exploration provided them practice at examining code at an early stage of the course. That this beneficial work was undertaken to inform a choice, implies that providing a choice can implicitly support our objective of exercising code comprehension.

The students' reasons for choosing are consistent in the view of the idea of authenticity, as described by Shaffer and Resnick [19]. Authenticity involves learning that: (i) is personally meaningful; (ii) relates to the real-world outside of school; (iii) provides an opportunity to think in the modes of a particular discipline; and (iv) involves means of assessment reflective of the learning process. We chose projects that gave students an opportunity to think in the modes of software maintenance, and assessed them on assignments that mimicked the activities of maintainers. Open source is a part of the real-world outside of school. We saw that students described their choices while referring to what they found personally meaningful, namely, their ability to add value to a widely used application and/or an application about which they had opinions about its interactivity with users. The notion of authenticity thus embodies our aim to provide valuable instruction to the students and the students' desire to do something useful in the real world.

5. RELATED WORK

A project is a significant component of a Software Engineering (SE) course. It provides a context to reinforce the principles and techniques that students learn in the classroom. SE instructors may select projects based on many factors but primarily considering their suitability for the course objectives. Some selection criteria include appropriate complexity and outreach to under-represented students [2, 7, 11, 6, 16]. Some instructors mention the importance of student enjoyment of their projects [3]. Specific reasons why projects may appeal and motivate such as humanitarian, even to the level of career choice [7], real-world [12] and authenticity [19] are also noted. Examples of students choosing their own projects exist [10, 5, 18]; risks associated with such self selection include that it may be time consuming [14], and may require additional support [17]. Our literature survey, however, did not reveal a comprehensive inquiry into students' considerations in choosing projects, similar to the one reported in this paper.

6. CONCLUSIONS AND FUTURE WORK

This paper analyzed students' reasons for choosing projects in a maintenance-centric software engineering course, in which they were expected to comprehend and enhance an existing open source software system. The analysis revealed that students fell in two disjoint groups; one group choosing on the basis of their perception of difficulty, while the other one choosing based on the appeal of the domain or subject matter. Students in both of these groups were motivated by the sense of value that their enhancements would produce for users and by the possible learning experience.

Our future work involves incorporating these insights into a set of metrics for project selection not only for software engineering but for a broad range of computing courses. For

Table 6: Popular Projects with Codes and Categories

Category	Code	Rapla	Genealogy	TripleA	Sweethome	Megamek	Archimedes
VA	Value of enhancement	✓	✓	✓	✓		
DE	Evaluating difficulty	✓	✓		✓	✓	✓
	Not too demanding	✓				✓	✓
AP	Positive emotion	✓	✓	✓			
	Subject appeal		✓				
	Coding challenge				✓		

example, a set of measures to infer authenticity might include the number of downloads of the executable which could provide an estimate of the size of the user community and closely relate to the students' conceptions of value-added.

Acknowledgments

This material is based on work supported by the National Science Foundation under grant DUE-1044061. Any opinions, findings, and conclusions or recommendations expressed in this material are those of the authors and do not necessarily reflect those of the National Science Foundation.

7. REFERENCES

[1] http://opensource.gsfc.nasa.gov/projects/JAT/index.php.

[2] E. Allen, R. Cartwright, and B. Stoler. DrJava: A lightweight pedagogic environment for Java. *ACM SIGCSE Bulletin*, 34(1):137–141, 2002.

[3] J. Bayzick, B. Askins, S. Kalafut, and M. Spear. Reading mobile games throughout the curriculum. In *Proc. of the ACM Technical Symposium on Computer Science Education*, pages 209–214, 2013.

[4] V. Braun and V. Clarke. Using thematic analysis in psychology. *Qualitative Research in Psychology*, 3(2):77–101, 2006.

[5] V. A. Cicirello. Experiences with real projects for real clients course on software engineering at a liberal arts instituition. *The Journal of Computing Sciences in Colleges*, page 50, 2013.

[6] J. D. N. Dionisio, C. L. Dickson, S. E. August, P. Dorin, and R. Toal. An open source software culture in the undergraduate computer science curriculum. *ACM SIGCSE Bulletin*, 39(2):70–74, 2007.

[7] H. Ellis, R. A. Morelli, and G. W. Hislop. Support for educating software engineers through humanitarian open source projects. In *Proc. of Intl. Conf. on Software Engineering Education and Training Workshop*, pages 1–4, 2008.

[8] C. Ghezzi, M. Jazayeri, and D. Mandrioli. *Fundamentals of Software Engineering*. Pearson, Prentice Hall, 2003.

[9] S. Gokhale, T. Smith, and R. McCartney. Integrating open source software into software engineering curriculum: Challenges in selecting projects. In *Proc. of First Intl. Workshop on Software Engineering Education based on Real-World Experiences*, pages 9–12, Zurich, Switzerland, 2012.

[10] E. P. Katz. Software engineering practicum course experience. In *Proc. of Intl. Conf. on Software Engineering Education and Training*, pages 169–172, 2010.

[11] L. Layman, L. Williams, K. Slaten, S. Berenson, and M. Vouk. Addressing diverse needs through a balance of agile and plan-driven software development methodologies in the core software engineering course. *Intl. J. of Engineering Education*, 24(4):659, 2008.

[12] B. K. MacKellar, M. Sabin, and A. Tucker. Scaling a framework for client-driven open source software projects: A report from three schools. *The Journal of Computing Sciences in Colleges*, page 140, 2013.

[13] R. McCartney, S. Gokhale, and T. Smith. "Evaluating an early software engineering course with projects and tools from open source software". In *Proc. of the Intl. Conf. on Computing Education Research*, pages 5–10, Auckland, New Zealand, 2012.

[14] A. Meneely, L. Williams, and E. F. Gehringer. Rose: A repository of education-friendly open-source projects. *SIGCSE Bull.*, 40(3):7–11, June 2008.

[15] S. Merriam. *Qualitative Research, A Guide to Design and Implementation*. Jossey-Bass, 2009.

[16] M. Nordio, C. Ghezzi, B. Meyer, E. D. Nitto, G. Tamburrelli, J. Tschannen, N. Aguirre, and V. Kulkarni. Teaching software engineering using globally distributed projects: The DOSE course. In *Proc. of Collaborative Teaching of Globally Distributed Software Development-Community Building Workshop*, 2011.

[17] P. M. Papadopoulos, I. G. Stamelos, and A. Meiszner. Enhancing software engineering education through open source projects: Four years of students' perspectives. *Education and Information Technologies*, pages 1–17, 2012.

[18] V. P. Pauca and R. T. Guy. Mobile apps for the greater good: A socially relevant approach to software engineering. In *Proc. of the ACM Technical Symposium on Computer Science Education*, pages 535–540, 2012.

[19] D. W. Shaffer and M. Resnick. "Thick" authenticity: New media and authentic learning. *Journal of Interactive Learning Research*, 10(2):195–215, 1999.

[20] J. Sillito. Saturate. http://www.saturateapp.com/groups/1311319302.

[21] Sourceforge. Sourceforge.net: Find and develop open source software. http://sourceforge.net/.

[22] A. Strauss and J. Corbin. Grounded theory methodology. *Handbook of Qualitative Research*, pages 273–285, 1994.

Mobile Application Development Classes for the Mobile Era

Kelvin Sung
University of Washington Bothell
ksung@u.washington.edu

Arjmand Samuel
Microsoft Research Connections
arjmands@microsoft.com

ABSTRACT

There are many flavors of upper division[1] elective classes that cover subjects related to mobile technologies and application development. However, there is a general lack of publications discussing the philosophy, implementation, and results from these classes. When researching for a new upper division mobile application development elective class, based on our students' needs and state of the mobile technologies, we consulted the extensive online information, and drafted guidelines and desired learning outcomes. In the subsequent years, we implemented two versions of mobile application development classes based on the guidelines and learning outcomes. The first, focused on the development of practical mobile applications while the second studied design issues surrounding modern mobile applications and their development. Both classes are project based where students build mobile applications to demonstrate their understanding, and both classes were well received. This paper describes our efforts and the classes, summarizes the results from the classes, and discusses the merits of implementation vs. design based mobile application development classes.

Categories and Subject Descriptors

K.3.2 [**Computers and Education**]: Computer and Information Science Education – *computer science education.*

General Terms

Design, Experimentation

Keywords

Computer science education, Upper division, Elective, Mobile computing, Application development

1. INTRODUCTION

Founded in 1990, the University of Washington Bothell (UWB) campus is one of the newest and fastest growing public universities in the state of Washington. Initially designed to be an upper-division only campus serving place and time bound adult students, the campus has since grown to admit its first freshmen

class in 2006. In 2012 more than half of UWB incoming freshmen are first generation college students and 43% of the students receive financial aid.[2] Many of our students pursue their degrees with the main purpose of securing quality employment with the vibrant regional high-tech industry to improve their lives. Our courses are constantly under tension between students' desire for applicability that is suitable for near-term employability, and faculty's perspective of abstract conceptual contents that are important for life-long learning.

Our initial experience with mobile technology is in application development. As part of our efforts in generalizing the results from the Game-Themed Introductory Programming Project [30],[3] we investigated and developed location aware games on different mobile devices [29], e.g., music playing devices [15], and smart phones [12]. The needs for research students with appropriate mobile application development backgrounds, together with the significant student interests, motivated us in investigating a general upper division elective class in mobile computing.

Mobile computing as a field of study is relatively new, and depending on the specific definition,[4] can encompass a wide range of topics: ranging from security, to wireless and sensor technologies, to applications. Because of our areas of expertise in application development, our students' preparations and interests, the potentials for employment opportunities, and the fact that most of the major vendors provide and support free development environments, we have quickly focused our "mobile computing" course to be the study of mobile application development.

Though employment was one of the important motivations, with the proliferation and rapidly changing horizon of mobile platforms, it was decided right from the beginning that ours must be a course that is agnostic of specific vendor, programming language, or development environment. For this reason, instead of studying the suitability of existing technologies in supporting classroom teaching [9], we approached the course design by following the results from Gordon [10] where we began by laying out guidelines for the course design and identifying technology-independent learning outcomes. The underlying philosophy is that, while adhering to the listed guidelines, it should be possible to implement multiple versions of the same course to deliver similar student learning outcomes.

Over the past two years, we implemented two versions of our mobile application development class. The first version focused on application implementation where students learned about user interface design on small devices, programming with sensors, the importance of backend services and concentrated on developing practical and usable applications. The second version focused on application design where students learn about general issues

---

[1] In this paper, "*upper division students*" refer to Junior or Senior Computer Science majored students who have taken CS1, CS2, and data structures classes.

---

[2] http://www.uwb.edu/about/facts
[3] http://depts.washington.edu/cmmr/Research/XNA_Games
[4] http://en.wikipedia.org/wiki/Mobile_computing

related to mobile applications including security, power management, privacy, commerce etc. and concentrated on presenting research findings and prototype implementations. Both classes are well-received by the students with interesting final deliverables. This paper presents our experience with these classes from design, to implementation, and to results.

The next section contextualizes our classes by surveying existing mobile computing related classes. Section 3 presents our course design guideline; Section 4 describes the two classes; with the results from these classes being presented in Section 5. The paper concludes with a comparison of the two approaches to teaching mobile application development.

2. BACKGROUND

ACM curriculum[5] defines "Mobile Computing" to be a class that covers network and wireless technologies, and issues concerning mobile application development. While such a class is interesting and important, it does not align well with the strengths and needs of our students: with strong software development and algorithm foundation, and looking for skills and knowledge that are readily demonstrable for employment purposes. Balancing with faculty's objectives of concepts transferable and adaptable to the rapidly changing technologies and life-long learning skills, we set out searching for a curriculum that focuses on studying mobile application development and is agnostic to technology.

A simple Internet search reveals that there are numerous examples of upper division mobile computing related elective classes with multiple flavors. These classes range from e.g., survey of the field,[6] to integration with wireless communication,[7] or cloud computing.[8] Among these are ones that seem to specifically focus on mobile application development, e.g., CMSC628 at UMBC.[9] However, without firsthand communication and experience sharing with the faculty, it can be challenging to decipher the intended target student population, exact focus, and philosophy behind the classes. These examples serve as interesting references but in general are difficult to adapt from.

A survey of publications related to Computer Science education and mobile computing reveals three general categories of classes. The first category includes classes that use mobile devices and/or applications as tools for engaging students. For example, introducing technology to pre-college students with AppInventor[10] (e.g., [18, 32, 27, 6]), engaging students with interesting assignments on mobile devices [2, 24] or creative teaching tools [13], or using mobile computing as a vehicle for delivering other CS concepts (e.g., security [11], software engineering [25], Operating Systems [3], Human Computer Interface [19], or Database [22]). These are innovative usages of mobile computing in classes and are unrelated to our purpose.

The second category includes classes that teach mobile application development to students with no or minimum (CS1 and/or CS2) programming backgrounds. With little requirements in programming and no basic knowledge in data structures, these classes are typically targeted at engaging non-major students through mobile application development (e.g., AppInventor [1,

14, 33, 28] or mobile games based on simple libraries [4, 16, 17]), or at accomplishing other purposes (e.g., learning different programming languages [26]). These classes are not designed for students to understand issues surrounding mobile application development.

The third category includes classes that are upper division electives with prerequisites, i.e., data structures, and/or algorithm analysis, and with goals that are similar to those of our classes. Unfortunately, much of this work is based on specific vendors (e.g., Blackberry [20, 21]) or platforms (e.g., Android [8, 23]), where some of the results are not generally applicable for technology agnostic approach, e.g., resource references specific to Blackberry or best practices related to working with Android. However, the general discussions and experience shared, especially the brief but informative descriptions on results from Elon and Appalachian State [8], provided important insights that guided our approach, preparations, and the eventual structure for our courses. These will be detailed in the following sections,

Lastly, there are recent discussions on re-evaluating the entire CS education in the context of the fast changing, increasingly powerful, ubiquitous, and wildly popular mobile technologies [5, 31]. While the topics are important, for now they are relatively independent from a course that focuses on mobile application development.

3. COURSE DESIGN GUIDELINES

Our goal is to design an elective course in mobile computing that focuses on application development. As in all upper division elective classes, students taking such classes are expected to have concrete knowledge in discrete math and data structures. In contrast to simplifying mobile application development by layering higher level abstractions, e.g., Sofia for Android [7], or TouchDevelop [31], we expect students to self-learn vendor APIs. Together with the observations of the rapidly changing industry and constantly improving technologies, we have set the following guidelines for the design of our course.

- **Technology:** to ensure focusing on fundamental principles instead of skills that will become obsolete quickly, the course content must clearly present technologies and vendor hardware as mere vehicles for knowledge delivery.

- **Hands-on:** to be well-prepared for the future, students must be familiar with the existing APIs, the course must challenge students with all aspects of mobile application development: from frontend graphical user interface (GUI) and sensors to backend online services.

- **App Evaluation:** to adapt and develop apps for the future technologies, the course must provide a theoretical framework for students to evaluate future applications.

- **Research:** to remain current with the rapid changes, the course must guide students through self-discovery of knowledge in the mobile application domain.

- **Collaboration:** to develop interesting and useful apps, the course must facilitate students working collaboratively and in groups.

With these design guides, in the context of mobile applications, after taking the course students will be able to: discuss the evolution and trend; evaluate designs; evaluate existing and develop simple web-services; and mostly importantly design and

---

[5] http://www.acm.org//education/curricula/ComputerScience2008.pdf
[6] http://www.cs.columbia.edu/~nieh/teaching/e6998/
[7] http://www.cs.utexas.edu/users/ygz/395T/
[8] https://wiki.engr.illinois.edu/display/ece498hp2011spring/Home
[9] http://www.csee.umbc.edu/~nilanb/teaching/628/
[10] http://appinventor.mit.edu/

implement complete systems that are suitable for commercial distributions.

4. THE COURSES

Informed by best practices in teaching mobile computing [20], we began the solicitation for device donations early in the course development. We are fortunate to receive generous mobile phone donations from Microsoft Windows and Mobiles Teams. The content delivering vehicle is thus decided, the course will be based on Windows Phone and the C# programming language, and every student in our classes will have access to a device to program on.

4.1 Implementation Focused Class

In the first iteration of our course, we wanted to ensure students experience the entire mobile application development cycle. The delivery of a polished final application became the main theme. We followed the simple and yet elegant structure of starting the academic quarter with conventional lectures and assignments to orientate students, and turning the second half of the quarter into a student project-driven format [8]. We integrated additional components to adhere to our course design guidelines. Our course has four components, proceeding in sequence with some overlaps.

- **Phase I: Orientation**: guides students with discussions on history and evolution of mobile devices, development model for mobile devices, IDE, SDK, and very importantly, contrasts in different development environments. As a preparation for their final projects, each student research and present to the rest of the class, in 3 minutes, three of their favorite mobile apps.

- **Phase II: Hands on development:** discusses the Model-View-Controller model for GUI event driven programming, GUI issues specific to small devices, the often asynchronous programming interface with sensors, and web-service API models. There are three programming assignments, first two focused on device input and sensors, while the last assignment requires two or three person student-group building systems that work with sensors and multiple web-service APIs (e.g., check GPS, post to Facebook, and plot on map).

- **Phase III: Research:** this phase overlaps with both phase II and IV. During phase II, in between programming assignments, students in their final project groups are required to research on their favorite mobile related topics. The findings from each group are presented, in 10 minutes, during Phase IV.

- **Phase IV: Project and Evaluation:** the last phase begins at around mid-quarter (around sixth of the 10-week quarter). Students propose their final project, present UI design, implement concept prototypes, and go through alpha and beta user testing. The user testing are peer testing events where the entire class run/test each groups' final project, provide written and numeric evaluations.

The detailed results from this class will be discussed in the next section. Though popular and well-received, there were a few important shortcomings that were apparent: the workload was too heavy; students did not have time to understand and appreciate the important details of working with sensors (e.g., security or power management concerns), with the short five weeks schedule to deliver polished applications, though interesting and impressive, the final delivered apps tend to be conventional and lack in depth.

It was decided that we should reduce the intense hands-on programming requirements and provide students the opportunities for in-depth understanding and creativity. These observations led to the second iteration of the class that shifted the focus to mobile application design.

4.2 Design Focused Class

The goals of the course were to provide students with mobile application design knowledge which can be applied to any mobile platform; broaden student's perspective by immersing into the mobile eco-system comprising of sensors, power management, security and privacy, mobile cloud services, cross platform tools, commercial aspects of developing and selling apps, and future of mobile technologies; enable students to develop mobile apps applying above concepts in the form of hands-on projects on a chosen mobile platform (Windows Phone in this case), and encourage students to experiment with unique ideas and scenarios; and, encourage active learning by having students research and present topics of interest.

For the design focused class it was planned that students would not be given any structured instructions in the use of development tools for any mobile platform. The expectation was that students can use the available development tools and online training materials.

The topics covered during this course are as follows:

- What is mobile computing?
- Popular platforms (Android, iOS, Windows)
- Mobile Sensors
- Mobile app design - what works and what does not?
- Performance – tools and tricks
- Power management
- Cloud-enabled mobile computing
- Mobile security
- The cross platform movement
- The future: wearables, connected clothes, smart furniture

Two students were working on one self-chosen project. Students gave frequent updates in the form on in-class presentations. Students also wrote a weekly journal to document their progress in the form of an unstructured journal to be sent to the instructor over email. The goal of the journal was to provide a mechanism for accountability, and an opportunity of self-reflection.

Evaluation of this course was based on instructor grading of student presentations, and project presentations. The students also provided project feedback to each other informally, in the form of in class discussions, and formally in the form of peer reviewed presentations.

5. RESULTS

These two classes resulted in an interesting contrast on how to design a mobile application development class. On the one hand, the implementation focused class resulted in students gaining a high level of expertise in the use of development tools, and design and development of mobile applications which could very well be released to consumers. On the other hand, the design focused course enabled students to understand the theory behind mobile computing, and make design choices based on this theory. The following section reports some of the results, along with example projects.

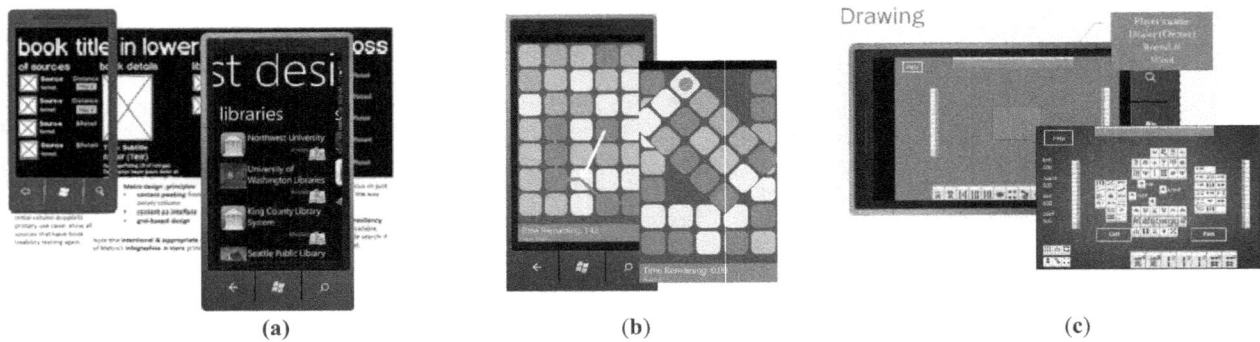

Figure 1: Projects from implementation focused class. (a) Phix the Bookfinder, (b) Joy Bubble, (c) Mobile Mahjong

5.1 Results: Implementation focused class

Figure 1 shows screen captures of three representative sample projects from the implementation focused (first offering) class. The three pairs of screen shots, each with UI design in the back and final delivered system in the front.

Though with different complexities, all projects satisfy the basic technical requirements: friendly application with backend online support.

(a) **Phix the Bookfinder** is an example of a project on the complex side in terms of the number of services involved: *Bing* service for zip code lookup, *GoogleBooks* for book information search, *WorldCat* service for locating libraries with the book that are near the user, and *Amazon* service for the option of purchasing the book.

(b) **Joy Bubble** is technically the simplest and yet ranking-wise (by students in class) the highest project. This is a *Match-3* type interactive game where players manipulate the on-screen squares to create patterns for earning points. The game allows players from physical vicinity to play against one another in fixed time periods. During user testing, the entire class would play against each other and go into frenzies towards the end of each play time period.

(c) **Mobile Mahjong** is a typical project where the backend service allows players to sign into a "table" and play against each other. Though the game requires four players per table, the backend logic supports non-trivial AI mode for tables with insufficient players.

Other final projects in class typical involve a few more backend services (e.g., maps, Facebook) but with slightly less polished frontend graphical user interface.

5.2 Results: Design focused class

Figure 2 shows examples of class projects:

(a) **Audio Feed:** An app for reading RSS feeds to be controlled entirely with speech commands.

(b) **Location based chat:** An app for chatting with friends from social networks who are in the physical vicinity.

(c) **Panic Alert:** An app to send out an SOS signal in case of an emergency based on movement of the phone in a preset pattern.

The above class projects have been selected based on the fact that each takes advantage of certain aspects of mobile computing in unique ways. Audio Feed experimented with voice activated control of a mobile app. The students had to understand the varying levels of noise a mobile device can be subject to. The students also had to make design choices between speech recognition engines available on the device and as cloud services. Location based chat allowed students to explore the modalities of location and to understand the choices to be made for location detection indoors and outdoors. Panic alert allowed students to understand the relationship between accelerometer and gyroscope so as to come up with a set of gestures which were repeatable and simple. Note that these, and other projects were selected, designed and scoped based on user feedback studies conducted by the students.

The students were encouraged to get feedback from friends and family. Some of the discussion topics in the class and over email include: choices between different UI designs; complexities of sensors on a mobile platform and how it can be used effectively; approaches to weave user feedback into the design of the app; and potentials of making money from the apps.

Figure 2: Projects from design focused class. (a) Audio Feed, (b) Location-based Chat, (c) Panic

While the chosen platform for the class projects was Windows Phone, throughout the course of the class, students were encouraged to explore other popular platforms. Towards the end of the class each student presented one favorite feature of platforms other than Windows Phone. Similarly students were also asked to research cross platform tools and present to the class for grade. Students presented topics such as Adobe Air, Unity3D, PhoneGap, XAMARIN, etc.

5.3 Discussions

Given that most of the students in both classes have never developed for any mobile devices, the research presentations and final deliverables do present a satisfactory learning outcome. The classes are successful.

Ironically, and somewhat painfully, after the first iteration of the class, the most informative feedback from our students pointed out the obvious, that without theoretical framework, students can simply pick up the "how-to" from online self-help, e.g.,

> "*while the course enabled me to learn mobile programming, it was not a stretch because I could learn the same by studying MSDN examples/code samples as well*"

Comments like the above, together with the observations that the sensor controls in the final projects lack sophistications in power management and privacy/security protection; and that the final projects tend to be conventional, e.g., text input, searches, web service displays; help motivated us to shift the focus from entirely application development to focus on design issues.

When comparing projects between the two classes, examples from Figure 1 appear to be more complex and better polished. Given that the implementation focused class dedicated much more time and efforts, e.g., peer testing, on the final app development, this observation comes as no surprise. However, notice that the projects from design focused classes involve more depth and sophistication, e.g., voice actuation, gesture based input, intelligent power management. These are precisely the motivations for this alternate approach.

In general, both of the classes are well-received by students where feedbacks are mostly positive commenting on the excitements and benefits of working with new and popular devices, e.g.,

> "*The opportunity to work with a new type of device with the limitation that came with it opened my eye to how important the fundamentals learned in previous classes are ...*"

Or

> "[this class is]... *good in its content, because of the content is so popular, I found an internship by showing them what I built* [in final project]"

In terms of being technology agnostic, in addition to the cross-platform research students carried out, we constantly remind them that the technology was but a vehicle. It is reassuring that while anecdotal, at least three of the students from the mobile computing classes secured mobile application development positions working on non-Windows Phone devices, HTC Android and iOS.

When evaluating against our design guidelines, it is clear that the two classes are on the opposite ends of the spectrum. In between heavy implementation focused with light design analysis, and design focused with light implementation, an appropriate class would depend greatly on the needs and strengths of the students.

We believe implementation focused classes are more suitable for students with less experience, perhaps junior or senior students, where the actual system implementation can improve students' coding maturity. A design focused class should be appropriate for more mature students, perhaps advanced senior or new graduate students, where equipped with matured coding experience the students can focus on understanding the design issues and self-learn the APIs for their final projects.

Course websites:
Implementation focused class: http://courses.washington.edu/css590/2012.Spring/
Designed focused class: http://courses.washington.edu/css545/

ACKNOWLEDGMENTS
Thanks to Microsoft Research, and Microsoft Windows Phone team for the Windows Phone donations and to our students for tolerating and working with us on experimenting different approaches to learning.

REFERENCES

[1] Khuloud Ahmad and Paul Gestwicki. Studio-based learning and app inventor for android in an introductory cs course for non-majors. In *ACM SIGCSE '13*, PP 287–292, 2013.

[2] Anthony Allevato and Stephen H. Edwards. Robolift: engaging cs2 students with testable, automatically evaluated android applications. In *ACM SIGCSE '12*, PP 547–552, 2012.

[3] Jeremy Andrus and Jason Nieh. Teaching operating systems using android. In *ACM SIGCSE '12*, PP 613–618, 2012.

[4] Jennifer Bayzick, Bradley Askins, Sharon Kalafut, and Michael Spear. Reading mobile games throughout the curriculum. In *ACM SIGCSE '13*, PP. 209–214, USA, 2013.

[5] Barry Burd, João Paulo Barros, Chris Johnson, Stan Kurkovsky, Arnold Rosenbloom, and Nikolai Tillman. Educating for mobile computing: addressing the new challenges. In *ITiCSE-WGR '12*, PP. 51–63, 2012.

[6] Matthew H. Dabney, Brian C. Dean, and Tom Rogers. No sensor left behind: enriching computing education with mobile devices. In *ACM SIGCSE '13*, PP. 627–632, 2013.

[7] Stephen H. Edwards and Anthony Allevato. Sofia: the simple open framework for inventive android applications. In *ITiCSE '13*, PP. 321–321, 2013.

[8] James B. Fenwick, Jr., Barry L. Kurtz, and Joel Hollingsworth. Teaching mobile computing and developing software to support computer science education. In *ACM SIGCSE '11*, PP. 589–594, 2011.

[9] Mark H. Goadrich and Michael P. Rogers. Smart smartphone development: ios versus android. In *ACM SIGCSE '11*, PP. 607–612, 2011.

[10] Aaron J. Gordon. Concepts for mobile programming. In *ITiCSE '13*, PP. 58–63, 2013.

[11] Minzhe Guo, Prabir Bhattacharya, Ming Yang, Kai Qian, and Li Yang. Learning mobile security with android security labware. In *ACM SIGCSE '13*, PP. 675–680, 2013.

[12] Ryan Hoaglan, Sidney Maxwell, Dmitry Ryzhkov, Kimberly Walker, and Kelvin Sung. Sammy's first day on campus. October 2010. Android phone game, search for "UWB" on Android Market Place to download for free.

[13] Wolfgang Hürst, Tobias Lauer, and Eveline Nold. A study of algorithm animations on mobile devices. In *ACM SIGCSE '07*, PP. 160–164, 2007.

[14] Stoney Jackson, Stan Kurkovsky, Eni Mustafaraj, and Lori Postner. Panel: mobile application development in computing curricula. In *ACM SIGCSE '13*, PP. 107–108, 2013.

[15] Shane Krolikowski, Scott McPherson, Aaron Amlag, and Kelvin Sung. Sammy library tour. March 2010. Microsoft Zune game available for checkout at UW1 receptionist desk.

[16] Stan Kurkovsky. Engaging students through mobile game development. In *ACM SIGCSE '09*, PP. 44–48, 2009.

[17] Stan Kurkovsky. Mobile computing and robotics in one course: why not? In *ITiCSE '13*, PP. 64–69, 2013.

[18] Jiangjiang Liu, Cheng-Hsien Lin, Phillip Potter, Ethan Philip Hasson, Zebulun David Barnett, and Michael Singleton. Going mobile with app inventor for android: a one-week computing workshop for k-12 teachers. In *ACM SIGCSE '13*, PP. 433–438, 2013.

[19] Susan Loveland. Human computer interaction that reaches beyond desktop applications. In *ACM SIGCSE '11*, PP. 595–600, 2011.

[20] Qusay H. Mahmoud. Best practices in teaching mobile application development. In *ITiCSE '11*, PP. 333–333, 2011.

[21] Qusay H. Mahmoud, Thanh Ngo, Razieh Niazi, Pawel Popowicz, Robert Sydoryshyn, Matthew Wilks, and Dave Dietz. An academic kit for integrating mobile devices into the cs curriculum. In *ITiCSE '09*, PP. 40–44, 2009.

[22] Qusay H. Mahmoud, Shaun Zanin, and Thanh Ngo. Integrating mobile storage into database systems courses. In *SIGITE '12*, PP. 165–170, 2012.

[23] Victor Matos and Rebecca Grasser. Building applications for the android os mobile platform: a primer and course materials. *J. Comput. Small Coll.*, 26:23–29, October 2010.

[24] Chris McDonald. A location prediction project on mobile devices. In *ITiCSE '13*, PP. 320–320, 2013.

[25] Victor Paul Pauca and Richard T. Guy. Mobile apps for the greater good: a socially relevant approach to software engineering. In *ACM SIGCSE '12*, PP. 535–540, 2012.

[26] Derek Riley. Using mobile phone programming to teach java and advanced programming to computer scientists. In *ACM SIGCSE '12*, PP. 541–546, 2012.

[27] Krishnendu Roy. App inventor for android: report from a summer camp. In *ACM SIGCSE '12*, PP. 283–288, 2012.

[28] Ellen Spertus, Mark L. Chang, Paul Gestwicki, and David Wolber. Novel approaches to cs 0 with app inventor for android. In *ACM SIGCSE '10*, PP. 325–326, 2010.

[29] Kelvin Sung, Kent Foster, and Stephanie Reimann. Mobile computing, smartphones, and existing computer science classes. In *SMACK 2011*, May 2011.

[30] Kelvin Sung, Michael Panitz, Cinnamon Hillyard, Robin Angotti, David Goldstein, and John Nordlinger. Game-Themed programming assignment modules: A pathway for gradual integration of gaming context into existing introductory programming courses. *IEEE Transactions on Education*, 54(3):416–427, August 2011.

[31] Nikolai Tillmann, Michal Moskal, Jonathan de Halleux, Manuel Fahndrich, Judith Bishop, Arjmand Samuel, and Tao Xie. The future of teaching programming is on mobile devices. In *ITiCSE '12*, PP. 156–161, 2012.

[32] Amber Wagner, Jeff Gray, Jonathan Corley, and David Wolber. Using app inventor in a k-12 summer camp. In *ACM SIGCSE '13*, PP. 621–626, 2013.

[33] David Wolber. App inventor and real-world motivation. In *ACM SIGCSE '11*, PP. 601–606, 2011.

A Teaching Model for Development of Sensor-Driven Mobile Applications

Hui Chen and Kostadin Damevski
Department of Mathematics and Computer Science
Virginia State University
Petersburg, Virginia 23806
{huichen,damevski}@acm.org

ABSTRACT

This paper concerns teaching computer science undergraduate students to develop sophisticated sensor-driven mobile applications, which students find interesting and motivating. Computer science students commonly adopt a trial-and-error application development process. However, indeterminacy inherent in sensor data makes the trial-and-error approach difficult, which frustrates students and impairs learning. In addition, the complexity of modern mobile devices' development environment and numerous APIs can further undo the motivating effect that these types of applications bring. To address these challenges, we propose a teaching model for sensor-driven mobile application development. The model features an application development process and a set of supporting tools and programs. The model provides a structured way for students to deal with the indeterminacy of sensor data and the complex development environments and results in a positive and supportive learning experience for the students. A case study of applying the model in an upper-level computer science elective course has shown it to be effective.

Categories and Subject Descriptors

K.3 [**Computer and Information Science Education**]: Computer science education

Keywords

Sensors-driven mobile applications, Teaching model

1. INTRODUCTION

The recent decade has witnessed the growth of smart phones and tablets (or mobile devices hereafter) integrating different types of sensors, such as location, motion, sound and video. Novel applications for these platforms are continuously emerging from the computing industry and the research community. Many of these applications are socially relevant and have the potential to improve our way of life.

ITICSE'14, June 21–25, 2014, Uppsala, Sweden.
Copyright 2014 ACM 978-1-4503-2833-3/14/06 ...$15.00.
http://dx.doi.org/10.1145/2591708.2591719.

For instance, by using a mobile device's microphone as a sound sensor, researchers have demonstrated the possibility to classify people's stress level and improve their well being [8]. Students are willing to spend more time in learning when they see the relevance of what they are learning in helping others and when they can apply it to impact their local community [4]. By teaching students to develop carefully selected sensor-driven mobile applications we can show that computer science is "social, relevant, important, and caring" [2].

The development process for these applications requires students to process and store streams of data, to deal with noise in data, to experiment and visualize data, and to construct predictive models using data. To be successful in developing such sensor-driven applications, students need to apply knowledge and skills learned from a variety of computer science courses (e.g., programming and operating systems), from mathematics courses (e.g., probability and statistics), and from other science courses, such as physics and chemistry. Such an integration of knowledge and skills from multiple courses helps students gain a comprehensive view of their computing curricula. Recent trends in computing are characterized by extracting knowledge from large amount of data [6]. The skills and the knowledge acquired from developing sensor-driven applications is also relevant to this trend.

The greatest difficulties to students in developing sensor-driven applications arise from two sources: (1) the indeterminacy of sensor data and (2) the complexity of the development environment and mobile platforms. Computer science students are often underprepared to appropriately prototype and test applications based on data collected from sensors, while the complexity of the development environment often confuses inexpert developers.

Our approach introduces sensor-driven application development during class projects in undergraduate computer science courses. This paper proposes a model to teach the development of sophisticated sensor-driven applications and mobile sensing techniques to computer science students. We also discuss the set of supporting tools for this model and perform a preliminary evaluation of the model in one of our courses.

2. RELATED WORK

Leveraging their attractiveness to students, many have explored using mobile devices as platforms to teach many subject areas within computer science, such as, programming, embedded software concepts, computer security, operating systems, software engineering, web development, mobile computing, and cyber-physical system (e.g., [5,9,9,10]).

One method that enhances students' learning is to increase their motivation. Mobile applications, in particular, socially relevant sensor-driven applications are attractive to students and can help increase students' motivation to learn [9]. Apple's iOS and Google's Android have become two leading mobile platforms in the market. The complexity of these development environments and the mobile platforms are challenging for novices. Development frameworks such as Android App Inventor [11] and Sofia Framework [7] are the results of efforts intended to make mobile development approachable to students.

Recently, mobile and participatory sensing have become an intensive subject of research [3]. Applications demonstrated in the research community are usually socially relevant and attractive, and much of such social relevancy and attractiveness of the applications is due to the sensing capability of the mobile devices. However, it remains rare to adopt recent research in mobile and participatory sensing in undergraduate computer science courses. Complementing prior approaches, ours is to teach computer science students the development of *sophisticated* sensor-driven mobile applications in a class project setting.

3. CHALLENGES IN CLASS PROJECT INSTRUCTION

We have observed two major challenges in teaching sensor-driven applications: indeterminacy in sensor data and complexity of development environment.

3.1 Indeterminacy in Sensor Data

Understanding sensors and processing sensor data are the core difference between developing sensor-driven mobile applications and general-purpose software development. When asked to develop such an application, students approach it in the usual way; they begin by reading documentation to understand the range of values for the specific sensor of interest and by discovering the ideal data stream produced by the sensor in various scenarios of interest. For instance, when using the accelerometer data to classify human activity, such as *standing still*, *walking*, or *running*, a student will usually reason that using the magnitude of the overall acceleration, which combines the acceleration produced by the sensor in each of the x, y, and z dimensions, is necessary to perform this classification. However, when the students implement the algorithm to perform the calculation based on these idealized expectations of the sensor data, they commonly encounter difficulties in producing a robust solution. In other words, their algorithm works only occasionally, as the sensor data sometimes behaves unexpectedly. For instance, as shown in Figure 1, sensor data typically demonstrates significant indeterminacy that arises from many sources, such as noise in the environment, such as our inability to create identical condition under which the observed sensor data is collected, e.g., one can never swing a mobile device the same when collecting accelerometer data[1]. Therefore, the students can never produce exactly the same data that they expected and based upon which they developed their algorithm. When this happens, students are unsure whether

[1] As Heraclitus famously states, "You could not step twice into the same river."

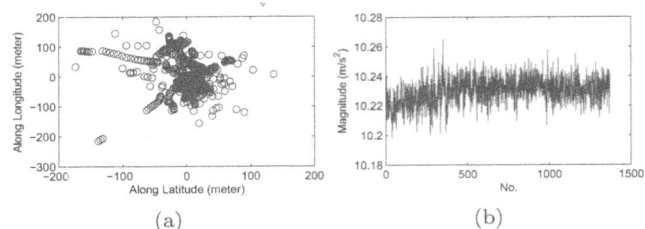

(a) (b)

Figure 1: Indeterminacy in location sensor and accelerometer data. Figure (a) shows the location sensor data collected when a mobile device is fixed at a location. The figure shows the displacement between each location reading and the average of the readings. The drifting of the location data is the result of multiple factors including multipath fading of GPS signals and GPS satellites' entering and leaving the reception range of the device. Figure (b) shows the magnitude of the accelerometer data when the device is also fixed at a location. Besides the noise in the data, it demonstrates also the drifting of the accelerometer data.

their reasoning is incorrect, their algorithm is faulty, or their implementation is buggy. Students often enter a state of confusion and their learning is impaired.

3.2 Complexity in Development Environment

The complexity of the environment commonly used to develop sensor-driven applications on mobile devices can become a serious distraction to students' learning. Popular development environments are built for professional developers and consist of a large number of advanced components: for instance, a typical Android development environment consists of Eclipse IDE, Android SDK, Android Virtual Device Emulator, and the Android platform. The complexity of learning such an environment can be a challenge to professional developers, and therefore it is not a surprise that the environment easily becomes a distraction to students who tend to spend more time in learning the environment than in developing algorithmic solutions to critical problems in the applications.

Learning actual mobile development environment, such as Android platform and Android SDK offer students marketable skills, which are important. However, the features of a particular mobile platform, such as the API specifics, are transient as the platform evolves quickly. In many computer science courses whose aim is at teaching students knowledge and skills that have a long-term effect, such as important cross-cutting concerns permeating in computing: concurrency, fault tolerance, debugging and testing methods, energy efficiency, as well as modeling and verification, the objective of teaching the development environment in addition to the named concerns can easily become overly ambitious and the learning can quickly frustrate students. This frustration would cancel any motivational effect that carefully selected sensor-driven applications initially bring to the students.

4. TEACHING MODEL

Considering the above challenges and the size and the complexity of the projects that students commonly undertake, we propose an teaching model that features a sensor-driven application *development process* and a set of *supporting tools and programs.*

The purpose of the proposed development process is twofold. First, we want to reduce the negative impact on learning caused by the sensor data indeterminacy (as discussed in Section 3.1). Second, we want to divide the application development task into a few sub-tasks with clearly defined objectives and gradually increased complexity, which form a gentle learning curve for the students and separates the main technical concerns in sensor-driven application from issues specific to a mobile development environment (as discussed in Section 3.2). Second, the supporting tools and programs provide scaffolding to students that will ease the development difficulties and create positive learning experiences. As indicated in [1], positive experiences and supportive environments are critical to learning effectiveness.

4.1 Application Development Process

As shown in Figure 2, sensor data drives the development process. The proposed application development process consists of three major phases, (1) sensor data collection and visualization, (2) application prototyping and prototype testing, and (3) sensor-driven mobile application development and testing.

4.1.1 Sensor Data Collection and Visualization

As an initial step, we require students to collect and annotate sensor data. For instance, for an application that classifies different human activities using accelerometer data, students conduct various experiments, such as standing still in different posture, walking with different pace and on different ground surface, and running at different speed, while collecting accelerometer data. The students annotate the data with the condition under which the data is collected, such as whether the user is standing still, walking, or running. Following this, the students are asked to provide an analysis of the data. As the beginning part of the analysis, we require students to visualize the collected sensor data.

Figure 3 is an example visualization of a set of annotated accelerometer data collected from students' experiments. By collecting and visualize the sensor data, e.g., as in Figure 3, a student can develop intuition, form heuristics, and develop a more robust algorithm, which would be difficult for students to obtain otherwise. For instance, a heuristic that the magnitude and the frequency of the spikes in the accelerometer data may be used to differentiate different human activities.

The collected sensor data should be stored on a non-volatile medium. For instance, the data can be stored as simple text files on a MicroSD card or transferred to a relational database on a remote server that is shared among the class. The aggregated sensor data will be used in subsequent phases (i.e., the prototyping phase or phase 2 and the application development phase or phase 3) to test the prototype and the developed application.

4.1.2 Prototyping and Prototype Testing

After analyzing the sensor data, students can proceed to develop a prototypical application on an ordinary computer, such as a desktop or laptop computer. In this stage, the students are not concerned with the different concurrency model of mobile platforms, or a large set of unfamiliar APIs, or an IDE that they have no experience of using. The focus here is solely on the *conceptual design* of the application on a familiar system.

We illustrate the method and the effectiveness of the prototyping using a *Phone Localization* app. The sophisticated but quite effective approach in [12] consists of a vehicle head controller and a mobile device whose location, i.e., on the driver's side or on the passenger's side in a vehicle, is to be determined by the application. Both the vehicle head controller and the device are equipped with Bluetooth interfaces. The device plays an audio file that contains a few sound beacons through the speakers of the vehicle via the head controller's Bluetooth interface. The mobile device records the sound, determines the arrivals of the sound beacons, calculates the difference between the beacon arrivals played in left speaker and those in right speaker, and determines whether the device is near the driver's seat or the passenger's seat. After the phone's location is discovered, interesting and socially-relevant safety features, such as disabling phone calls if the phone is used by the vehicle's driver, are possible.

The attempt to implement such a system directly on a mobile device can be very difficult as one has to deal with many APIs (such as those related to Bluetooth communication and audio) and concurrency issues (as the device needs to control both listening and playing). Audio data is many orders of magnitude larger than accelerometer or location sensor data. In addition, to process the audio data, we must use signal processing routines, such as Fast Fourier Transform, which are also computational expensive. A combination of all of these factors can put great stress on students.

Figure 5 shows the prototypical system using two laptop computers and a pair of computer speakers. The laptop computer that connects to the pair of speakers acts as the vehicle head controller and the other laptop computer the mobile device. The two laptop computers communicate with each other using a TCP connection via their Wi-Fi interfaces.

When working on the prototype, students do not need to be concerned with Bluetooth interface, unfamiliar APIs, and limited memory and processor power. The main focus of the students is on the conceptual design, i.e., the design of the signal processing flow and the detection of sound beacon arrivals. Since the students can examine intermediate results visually, as illustrated in Figure 4, the conceptual design on the prototypical system becomes intuitive and manageable.

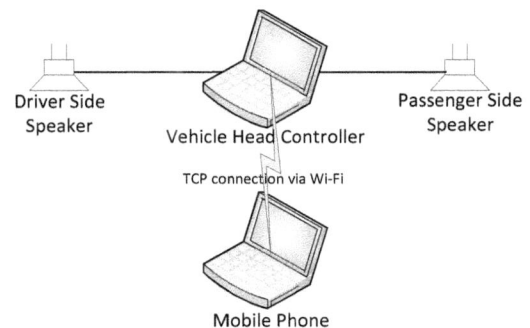

Figure 5: Prototype of the Phone Localization system using laptop computers and computer speakers.

The teaching model we propose requires the students to use the *sensor data collected in phase 1* to test the proto-

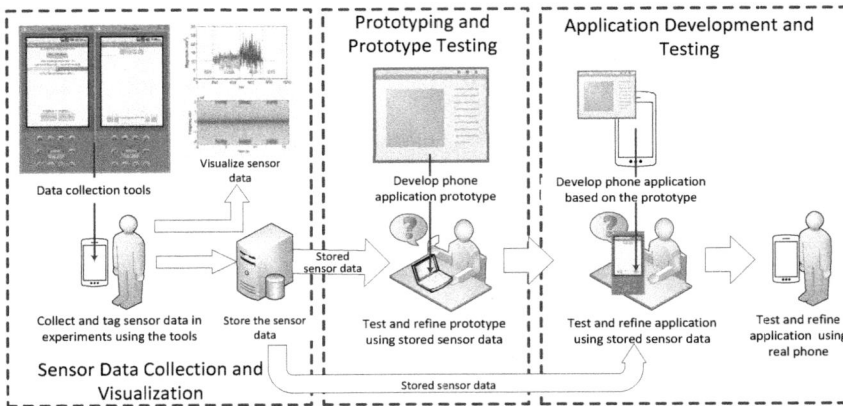

Figure 2: Instructional application development process

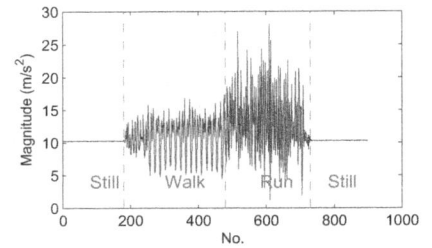

Figure 3: Magnitude of accelerometer data collected when a student is standing still, walking, running, and then returning to stand still.

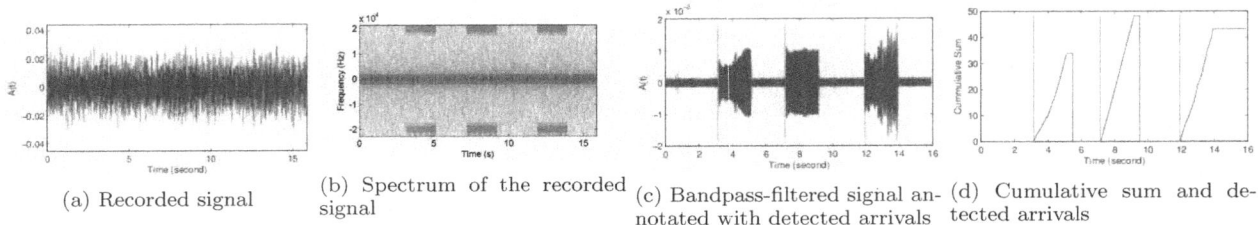

(a) Recorded signal

(b) Spectrum of the recorded signal

(c) Bandpass-filtered signal annotated with detected arrivals

(d) Cumulative sum and detected arrivals

Figure 4: Running result of a prototype in Matlab developed for the solution of the Phone Localization app. Figures 4(a) shows an example of recorded signals in the time domain. Figures 4(b) is its corresponding spectrum. In the recorded signal, localization beacons is invisible due to noise. However, the beacons is clearly visible in the spectrum. Figure 4(c) shows that the beacons become visible in the time domain after a bandpass filter is applied. Following the research in [12], a sequential change point algorithm using the cumulative sum of difference successfully determines the arrivals of the three sound beacons.

typical application. By using the *same set of data* that has been visualized and analyzed, students can verify whether their intuition and heuristics are correct.

4.1.3   Mobile Application Development and Testing

Only after the prototype is ready, the students start to port the prototype to a mobile device by converting this prototype to the mobile platform's target code.

Although the students now must deal with issues specific to the mobile platform and device, such as the user interface and interaction with the device, concurrency, etc., the core algorithms, such as the algorithm that classifies different human activities using accelerometer data and the algorithm that detects arrivals of sound beacons and calculates the location of a mobile devices using sound data, remain the same.

We also recommend that the students use *the same sensor data collected in phase 1* to test the application. Since the testing data is the same as that in phase 2, the mobile application should produce the same testing results or at least comparable results as those obtained in phase 2.

Although they are presented sequentially, the three phases should be *iterative*. For instance, if a student decides that testing sensor data is not sufficient during phase 2, the student should go back to phase 1 to collect more sensor data; when a student is developing an application on a mobile platform during phase 3 and becomes uncertain of the accuracy of the algorithm, the student can revisit phase 2.

After a complete pass of the development process, the student may run the application on the mobile devices to conduct tests using live sensor data. The students can reiterate the process to deal with the data indeterminacy and try out new algorithms. It is important for the students to learn to deal with indeterminacy in sensor data eventually. Without dealing with the indeterminacy in their applications, their applications may not be robust when executing on a real mobile device. Dealing with this indeterminacy often leads to completely different algorithms from those based on blind intuition and heuristics.

4.2   Supporting Tools and Programs

In each phase during the application development process, we provide the students with a set of software tools and programs. The supporting tools and programs reduce the students' cognitive load, make the learning curve gentle, and help make the challenging application development attainable with the students' effort, which ensures a positive learning experience to the students.

The supporting tools and programs are in four categories, (1) software tools for sensor data collection, (2) Matlab scripts for visualizing sensor data, (3) skeleton programs of the application prototype and the corresponding mobile application, and (4) mobile platform library supporting testing.

Students use the provided sensor data collection tools to conduct experiments and collect sensor data in phase 1. The data collection tools can be simple or complex. The instructor may not have to develop the tools if one already exists. For instance, for an application that uses a microphone as the sound sensor, we can advise students to use free recording software on ordinary computers or a free recording app from an App store on a mobile device and instruct the students to keep an associated journal on the condition under which the data is collected and to save the recorded sound clips as uncompressed Microsoft WAVE files without any alteration. For other type of sensors that ordinary computers generally do not have or with which on ordinary computers experiments are difficult to conduct (such as, collecting accelerometer data while running), we have developed simple Android programs that record different sensor data, such as, data from location and motion sensors and save the data as text files on the device's MicroSD card. The students can transfer the files to ordinary computers for visualization and analysis.

We recommend Matlab as the visualization tool and the language to build sensor-driven application prototypes in our classes. We always provide students with sample Matlab scripts to read and visualize the collected sensor data, for instance, a few Matlab scripts to load, play, filter, and graph recorded WAVE files. These scripts are typically short, consisting of a few lines of code. They allow the students who do not have prior experience with Matlab to learn a few necessary Matlab language constructs that they can use in phase 2.

In phases 2 and 3, we provide the students with skeleton programs of the prototype and the mobile application, respectively. The skeleton programs are not complete working programs. Using the skeleton programs as the starting point, the students must complete the Matlab prototype and the mobile applications. An instructor can control learning outcomes and learning curve by including or omitting selected functionality.

As we discussed before, we ask students to test their developed applications using the *same set of sensor data* collected in phase 1 and used for prototype testing in phase 2. To accomplish this, we provide the students with a simple Android library that reads sensor data from a file. The library allows the students to test sensor data specific algorithms on mobile devices using previously collected sensor data.

5. EVALUATION AND FEEDBACK

The teaching model is the result of our experience using smart phones to teach computer science subjects. First, the model should be applied in a class project that is aimed at developing a sophisticated sensor-driven application where the project is an integral component of the class. The instructor should clearly explain the goal of each of the three phases, demonstrate the tools and programs that are available for the students to use, and specify the outcomes that the instructor is expecting from the students.

Our most recent experience is to apply the model systematically in a computer networking class where a class project is an integral component. The application is a "Sound Communication" app inspired by [8]. The objective of the project is that by designing and implementing physical, data link, and application layer protocols, students deliver an application that allows two Android devices to transmit and receive digital data using sound as the wireless medium. This application shares the same sound sensor data processing component as the previously discussed *Phone Localization*

app. Additionally, the application must also segment received sound data and classify the sound segments into different groups each of which corresponds to a bit or a symbol (i.e., a bit sequence).

The instructor issued a pre-project survey and a post-project survey to the students. The pre-project survey's intent was to help understand students' profile, while the post-project survey's purpose was to assess whether the teaching model helped the students. The instructor also examined the project submission to assess whether the student completed each phase or the project, e.g., whether the application on two Android devices can transmit messages to and receive messages from each other using sound as a medium.

The result is summarized in Table 1. Among the 14 students in the class, 13 attempted the project. Among these 13 students, 12 returned the pre-project survey and 10 returned post-project survey. The *Response* column of the table records the number of students who gave a "Yes" answer to the assessment question out of the number of students who have a response.

Although most students have no or little experience in Matlab and Android, the students expressed positive feelings toward the teaching model as the majority indicates that they have attempted three phases and the phases are helpful. Although the majority completed phases 1, and 2, only 5 of 13 completed phase 3. Based on the instructor's observation, more students would have completed phase 3 given more time on the project.

Table 1: Assessment Results

Assessment Type	Question	Response
Pre-Project Survey	Took OS?	8 of 12
	Took Embedded Systems?	3 of 12
	Took Signal Processing?	1 of 12
	Knew Matlab?	5 of 12
	Knew C/C++?	11 of 12
	Knew Java?	8 of 12
	Have experience in Android programming?	4 of 12
Post-Project Survey	Phase 1 helpful?	10 of 10
	Phase 2 helpful?	10 of 10
	Phase 1 unnecessary?	0 of 10
	Phase 2 unnecessary?	0 of 10
	Phase 3 unnecessary?	1 of 10
	Phase 1 attempted?	10 of 10
	Phase 2 attempted?	10 of 10
	Phase 3 attempted?	10 of 10
	Project completed?	5 of 10
Instructor's Assessment	Student completed phase 1?	13 of 13
	Student completed phase 2?	11 of 13
	Student completed phase 3?	5 of 13

Considering the project's short duration (only 3 weeks) and its complexity, we believe that the teaching model contributed to the outcome and was effective. In particular, we observed that the development process allowed the instructor to insert at least two intermediate checkpoints during the course of the projects. The application development process and the scaffolding tools and programs provided the students with a gentler learning curve. Students were likely to have early success in phases 1 and 2, which helped them develop a belief that they are capable of identifying, organizing, initiating, and executing a course of action that will bring about a desired outcome. Such a belief, called "efficacy expectancies" [11] along with the social relevancy of the application, and the instructor's scaffolding support boosts students' motivation and improves learning. Future work includes broader assessment of the proposed model using more classes and larger numbers of students in order to confirm its validity.

6. CONCLUSION

It is challenging to use non-trivial mobile applications to teach computer science subjects. Students can focus their effort on learning language syntax, mobile platforms, and the platform APIs other than on learning the subjects. Students can get frustrated when navigating through the complex development environment and the large set of APIs. In particular, when the objective is to teach sensor-driven mobile application development, sensor data indeterminacy ubiquitously presented in sensor data can impairs students' learning as the indeterminacy reduce repeatability during debugging and testing.

We propose an teaching model that are characterized by a sensor-driven application development process and a set of supporting tools and programs. The development process consists of three phases, sensor data collection and visualization, application prototyping and prototype testing, and mobile application development and testing. With the supporting tools and programs, a student can select carefully a set of sensor data from early experiments and use the same set of sensor data during the later two phases, prototyping and application development. The teaching model thereby spares students from the confusion caused by the sensor data indeterminacy. In addition, the three-phase development process facilitates the separation of concerns allowing students to deal with different issues at different phases, which instills students' confidence, increases and retains students' motivation, and encourages students' learning of complex subjects and concepts. The result of our using the model in teaching appears to suggest that it should meet the design intention of the teaching model.

As suggested in [1], students must learn to assess the demands of the task, evaluate their own knowledge and skills, plan their approach, monitor their progress, and adjust their strategies as needed. The proposed teaching model allows instructors to provide feedback and assessment results to students during and at the end of each phase, which helps students frequently assess their project progress and adjust their strategies. Therefore, the teaching model helps students learn the important metacognitive skills critical for them to grow becoming life-long learners.

The tools and the course modules developed from this effort are available at http://sysnetgrp.net/cpsedu.

7. ACKNOWLEDGMENTS

The authors gratefully acknowledge support for this work from the U.S. National Science Foundation through award numbers 1044841 and 1040254.

8. REFERENCES

[1] S. A. Ambrose, M. W. Bridges, M. DiPietro, M. C. Lovett, and M. K. Norman. *How Learning Works: 7 Research-Based Principles for Smart Teaching.* Jossey-Bass, 1st edition, May 2010.

[2] M. Buckley. Viewpoint: Computing as social science. *Commun. ACM*, 52(4):29–30, Apr. 2009.

[3] J. Burke, D. Estrin, M. Hansen, A. Parker, N. Ramanathan, S. Reddy, and M. B. Srivastava. Participatory sensing. In *Workshop on World-Sensor-Web (WSW'06): Mobile Device Centric Sensor Networks and Applications*, pages 117–134, 2006.

[4] Committee on Developments in the Science of Learning with additional material from the Committee on Learning Research and Educational Practice, National Research Council. *How People Learn: Brain, Mind, Experience, and School: Expanded Edition.* The National Academies Press, 2000.

[5] K. Damevski, B. Altayeb, H. Chen, and D. Walter. Teaching cyber-physical systems to computer scientists via modeling and verification. In *Proceeding of the 44th ACM technical symposium on Computer science education*, SIGCSE '13, pages 567–572, New York, NY, USA, 2013. ACM.

[6] V. Dhar. Data science and prediction. *Commun. ACM*, 56(12):64–73, Dec. 2013.

[7] S. H. Edwards and A. Allevato. Sofia: the simple open framework for inventive android applications. In *Proceedings of the 18th ACM conference on Innovation and technology in computer science education*, ITiCSE '13, pages 321–321, New York, NY, USA, 2013. ACM.

[8] H. Lu, D. Frauendorfer, M. Rabbi, M. S. Mast, G. T. Chittaranjan, A. T. Campbell, D. Gatica-Perez, and T. Choudhury. Stresssense: Detecting stress in unconstrained acoustic environments using smartphones. In *Proceedings of the 2012 ACM Conference on Ubiquitous Computing*, UbiComp '12, pages 351–360, New York, NY, USA, 2012. ACM.

[9] V. P. Pauca and R. T. Guy. Mobile apps for the greater good: a socially relevant approach to software engineering. In *Proceedings of the 43rd ACM technical symposium on Computer Science Education*, SIGCSE '12, pages 535–540, New York, NY, USA, 2012. ACM.

[10] D. Riley. Using mobile phone programming to teach java and advanced programming to computer scientists. In *Proceedings of the 43rd ACM technical symposium on Computer Science Education*, SIGCSE '12, pages 541–546, New York, NY, USA, 2012. ACM.

[11] D. Wolber. App inventor and real-world motivation. In *Proceedings of the 42Nd ACM Technical Symposium on Computer Science Education*, SIGCSE '11, pages 601–606, New York, NY, USA, 2011. ACM.

[12] J. Yang, S. Sidhom, G. Chandrasekaran, T. Vu, H. Liu, N. Cecan, Y. Chen, M. Gruteser, and R. P. Martin. Sensing driver phone use with acoustic ranging through car speakers. *Mobile Computing, IEEE Transactions on*, 11(9):1426–1440, 2012.

Students' Performance on Programming-Related Tasks in an Informatics Contest in Finland, Sweden and Lithuania

Valentina Dagiene
Vilnius University
Vilnius, Lithuania
valentina.dagiene@mii.vu.lt

Linda Mannila
Åbo Akademi, Turku, Finland
Linköping Univ., Linköping,
Sweden
linda.mannila@abo.fi

Timo Poranen
University of Tampere
Tampere, Finland
timo.t.poranen@uta.fi

Lennart Rolandsson
Royal Institute of Technology
Stockholm, Sweden
lennartr@kth.se

Pär Söderhjelm
Lund University
Lund, Sweden
par.soderhjelm@teokem.lu.se

ABSTRACT

The ways in which informatics is covered in K-12 education vary among European countries. In Finland and Sweden, informatics is not included in the core curriculum, whereas, for example, in Lithuania, all students are exposed to some informatics concepts starting in the fifth grade. Bebras is an annually arranged international informatics contest for K-12 level, resulting in a large collection of data about contestants and their results. In this paper, we analyse contest data from the Finnish, Swedish and Lithuanian 2013 contests, focusing on students' performance on tasks related to algorithmic thinking. Our findings suggest that despite coming from different educational systems, students perform rather similarly on the tasks. The same tasks are difficult and the thinking behind picking an incorrect answer seems rather similar throughout the countries. The analysis also points out that there is a lack of easy questions – this needs to be fixed in order to not risk scaring students away.

Categories and Subject Descriptors

K.3.2 [**Computer and Information Science Education**]: Computer Science Education

General Terms

Algorithms, Performance

Keywords

Informatics Education, Contests, Algorithmic Thinking, Programming, Data Structures

1. INTRODUCTION

The lack of programming and computer science (from now on referred to as informatics) in K-12 education is increasingly recognized as a serious lack in the national curriculum of many countries [7]. While many European countries included informatics in their curricula as early as in the 1970s, many of these efforts were dropped for different reasons; often the change was due to insufficient awareness of the importance of informatics and the misunderstanding that using IT as a tool is all that needs to be taught. As a result, many students graduate from secondary school with quite a lot of experience from using computers and software, but little, if any, knowledge of the underlying principles.

Both digital literacy and informatics are essential components of a modern education. In today's world familiarity with programming and other informatics topics is as critical to all citizens as familiarity with traditional scientific disciplines was in the previous century. To be prepared for the jobs of the 21st century, students must not only be digitally literate but also understand key concepts of informatics. "All of today's students will go on to live a life heavily influenced by computing, and many will work in fields that involve or are influenced by computing. They must begin to work with algorithmic problem solving and computational methods and tools in K-12" [2]. This is also addressed in a recent report by the joint Informatics Europe & ACM Europe Working Group on Informatics Education, where one recommendation states that: 'all students should benefit from education in informatics as an independent scientific subject, studied both for its intrinsic intellectual and educational value and for its applications to other disciplines' [6]. The emphasis on informatics as a science as opposed to merely the use of IT as a tool can also help to promote a more equal gender balance in the field [1].

Recently, the development in two European countries in particular has received much attention: In Estonia, the Tiger Leap Foundation formed by the Ministry of Education launched the ProgeTiger program in 2012, aiming at teaching children informatics starting in the first grade [10]. Similarly, in the UK, a new national curriculum will come into force in fall 2014, where ICT has been replaced by a computing program covering both primary and secondary school [11].

In this paper we analyse students' results in the international Bebras informatics contest for three Baltic countries:

Finland, Sweden and Lithuania, where informatics is not included as a subject in the curriculum. The aim is to analyze how students manage with problems requiring algorithmic thinking, both in general and based on age and country.

2. BEBRAS - AN INTERNATIONAL K-12 INFORMATICS CONTEST

2.1 The Contest in a Nutshell

Several programming contests and olympiads [5, 8] are arranged globally on a regular basis. These are all aimed at talented children and as such not a suitable channel for introducing informatics to students at a larger scale. The idea of a contest in informatics that every child could take part in, and learn basic informatics concepts from, was proposed in Lithuania [4]. The contest was named Bebras ("beaver" in Lithuanian) and was arranged for the first time in 2004. Soon additional countries started participating in task preparation workshops and then also in organizing their own national contests. In 2013, over half a million students from 22 countries participated in the contest [3].

The Bebras contest addresses all primary, middle and upper secondary schools dividing pupils into five age groups: Mini (grades 3-4, age 8-10), Benjamin (grades 5-6, age 10-12), Cadet (grades 7-8, age 12-14), Junior (grades 9-10, age 14-16), and Senior (grades 11-12, age 16-18). In Finland and Sweden the contest is introduced one year earlier, hence the age groups there correspond to grades 2-3 (Mini), 4-5 (Benjamin), 6-7 (Cadet), 8-9 (Junior) and 10-12 (Senior).

The main goals of the Bebras contest are to raise all students' awareness of informatics and evoke interest in the field, as well as to motivate students to understand its fundamentals and become fluent with the technology, e.g. to be able to communicate with a machine. The contest should help children get interested in informatics and to stimulate thinking about contributions of informatics to science at the very early stage of their education. Since informatics is not a subject in its own right in many countries [7], this kind of contest might be one way, or even the only way, to introduce children to what informatics really is.

Finland organised its first national contest in 2010 and Sweden in 2012. The number of participants has increased in both countries from the beginning (1472 in Finland, 1625 in Sweden), and in 2013 there were 4434 participants from Finland and 1798 from Sweden. Participation numbers usually increase rapidly, sometimes even double on an annual basis, during the first years. Table 1 gives the participation statistics for different age groups in Finland, Sweden and Lithuania. Compared to Finland and Sweden, Lithuania has a very high participation rate: in 2013 over 25 000 students (0,9% of the population) participated in the contest.

As we can see, the participation rate for girls and boys is close to 50/50 for Mini, Benjamin and Cadet in all three countries. In Finland, the proportion of girls drops at Junior-level (69% boys, 31% girls), whereas in Lithuania the distribution stays more equal until Senior-level (68% boys, 32% girls). In Sweden, participation remains equal up to Senior-level, when there is a heavy drop in girl participation: not even one tenth of the participants is girls.

An additional detail worth noting is the decrease in number of participants for Seniors in Finland (from 1281 for Juniors to 170), whereas a similar drop cannot be seen for

neither Lithuania or Sweden. One can hence expect Finnish Seniors to represent a more selected group of pupils than what is the case for the other countries.

2.2 Contest Organization

Each country has free hands in implementing the national contest as long as it is arranged during the official contest week (second week of November). Most countries use web-applications for the contest. In Finland, an initial version of an online contest system was developed in 2009 [9]. Later the Finnish system has been further developed by Slovenia and Sweden. Lithuania has also developed its own contest management system with students/teachers/tasks database and assessment functions. Both the Finnish and the Lithuanian system make it possible to practice on contest questions from previous years before taking part in the actual contest.

The number of questions (usually between 15-21) varies depending on the age group and country. Students have fixed time to answer all questions: 45 minutes in Finland/Sweden and 55 minutes in Lithuania. The contest systems store students' name, gender, teacher's name, school data and used time in addition to answers; hence, the Bebras contest results in a collection of anonymised datasets depicting detailed information on gender, the time used, the chosen answer and the age-group.

The scoring system can also vary between countries. In Finland, Sweden and Lithuania, the same system is used: a correct answer gives full points, an incorrect one decreases points, and skipping a questions leaves the score unchanged. The number of points awarded also depends on the difficulty level of the task at hand (although this differentiation was not used in the following analysis).

Teachers are informed using the local contest website (www.majava-kilpailu.fi, www.bebras.se, www.bebras.lt) and through direct contacts from the organizers via email or other channels. The aim for all three countries is for Bebras to become a nation-wide contest and to convey the message "this is informatics" to teachers, so that they get a picture of what informatics is and what kind of content as well as problems are involved.

Prior to the contest, teachers register their school in the contest system, and receive instructions as well as contest keys for their students. The contest is open daily during the contest week, and teachers decide the time for when their classes take part in the contest. All participation takes place under teacher supervision.

2.3 Development of Bebras Tasks

Contest tasks are prepared during an annual international task workshop. The workshop produces a task pool, from which each country is obliged to choose tasks for their national contest. A majority of the contest tasks have to be from that pool, but countries are allowed to use a few of their own tasks or tasks from previous years. The workshop decides which tasks should be mandatory, e.g. must be used in all countries to make it possible to produce comparable results and to emphasise important educational goals (usually 2-3 tasks per age-group).

Contest tasks are divided into six categories [4] and each task is given a difficulty level (easy, medium, hard) that varies when used in different categories. Tasks are either multiple choice (four-choice questions with one correct an-

Table 1: Number of participants in Finland, Sweden and Lithuania in 2013

	Finland (X% boys, Y% girls)	Sweden (X% boys, Y% girls)	Lithuania (X% boys, Y% girls)
Mini	826 (52%, 48%)	262 (49%, 51%)	2 176 (55%, 45%)
Benjamin	852 (50%, 50%)	201 (56%, 44%)	7 022 (54%, 46%)
Cadet	1 294 (55%, 45%)	451 (55%, 45%)	6 550 (57%, 43%)
Junior	1 281 (69%, 31%)	413 (54%, 46%)	6 490 (60%, 40%)
Senior	170 (78%, 22%)	471 (91%, 9%)	3 671 (68%, 32%)
Total	4 423 (58%, 42%)	1 798 (63%, 37%)	25 909 (58%, 42%)

swer) or interactive (using drag-and-drop techniques, assembling constructions, picking items, writing, etc.).

2.4 Selection of Tasks for the 2013 Contest

Tasks for the 2013 contest were selected based on a process involving many researchers and teachers. In Finland and Sweden, the same tasks were used for all age groups. Lithuania has used the same task set as Germany/Austria/Switzerland/Netherlands for several years and for the contest in 2013 they also added a set of tasks used by Finland/Sweden (Lithuania offers the largest number of tasks in their contests, 18 for Mini and 21 for all others categories, whereas in Finland/Sweden there are 10 for Mini and 15 for the others). As a result there is a large overlap between the tasks included in the contest in Finland/Sweden and Lithuania.

As algorithms and programming are key concepts in informatics, and usually also the aspects missing in today's education, it is common practice for the contest to include a larger proportion of tasks related to algorithms and programming concepts than to e.g. tasks dealing with computer usage. This was also the case for the 2013 contest in Finland, Sweden and Lithuania. In Finland/Sweden the majority of tasks for all age groups were related to algorithmic thinking: 7 in Mini, 11 in Benjamin, 11 in Cadet, 12 in Junior, and 12 in Senior. Lithuania used all of these tasks and several additional tasks as well. All questions used are available on national contest websites and contest management systems.

In the following, we will provide some background information on what tasks were used in our analysis and the rationale for choosing these specific tasks.

3. ANALYSIS OF TASKS ON ALGORITHMS AND PROGRAMMING

3.1 Tasks of Specific Interest

All three countries used 27 tasks categorized as related to algorithmic thinking. Some tasks were used in two or three age groups. In our analysis we have focused on differences in performance between students based on age and country. After involved discussions on what tasks to analyse in order to cover as many algorithm/programming concepts as possible, we jointly selected a set of tasks of special interest. These tasks are listed in Table 2 together with brief descriptions. The data were anonymised by removing all personal and school related information prior to the analysis.

In order to give the reader an idea for how programming concepts are included in the Bebras contest, the complete wordings for two of the selected tasks are presented in Figures 1 and 2 respectively.

In the next section, we will present the results from studying the performance on the selected tasks by students of different age groups in the three countries.

Beavers discovered a piece of wood into which worms had made a system of tunnels and pits. A handy father used it to make a toy.

To start we put a marble in the middle. The goal is to get the marble out by turning the wheel to the left (L) and right (R). By each turn the marble either runs to the next pit or (at the end) out of the wheel.

By which of the following sequences will the marble reach the exit?

a) LRRLR   b) RLRLL   C) LRRLRL   D) LRRRRL

Figure 1: Complete wording of the task "Spinning Toy"

A long time ago in Japan, some Ninjas served the shogunate government. In case of emergency, they used smoke signals to communicate with each other.

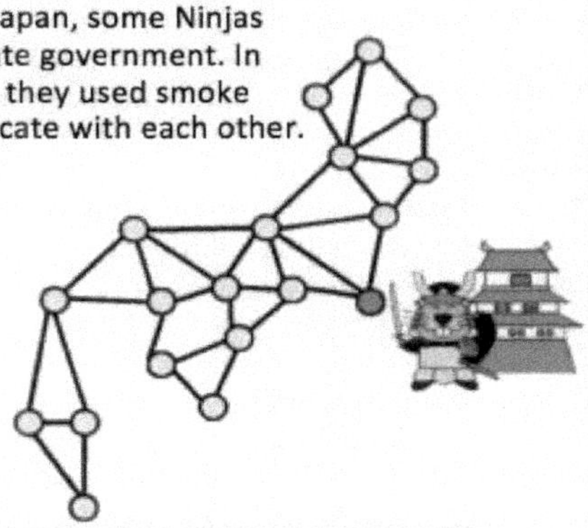

In the above figure, the red point is the location of the shogunate government. Each blue point is a location where a smoke signal should be lit. Also, two points are joined by a line if their smoke signals can be seen from each other. At every point, there are some Ninjas who stand on all day long. They fire a smoke when they see a signal from a point joined to theirs, just 1 minute after this signal was fired.

How much later will there be a signal lit at all points?

a) 4 minutes b) 5 minutes c) 6 minutes d) 8 minutes

Figure 2: Complete wording of the task "Signal fire"

Table 2: Selected tasks related to algorithms / programming concepts

Task name	Age group	Mandatory	What students can learn from the task
In the forest	Mini, Benjamin	no	finding a path; graph; tracing; finding a solution backwards
Zebra Tunnel	Benjamin	yes	to follow instructions; algorithm analysis; data structures: FIFO (queue) and LIFO (stack)
The highest tree	Benjamin, Cadet	no	search algorithm; local optimisation; global optimum
Spinning toy	Benjamin, Cadet, Junior, Senior	yes	binary tree representation; tree traversal; operations abstraction
Signal fire	Cadet, Junior, Senior	for Cadets	graphs; shortest path problem; breadth-first search
Necklace	Junior	yes	shortest path
Dice	Junior	yes	following a list of commands; procedure; imperative programming
Different paths	Junior	no	graphs; dynamic programming
River inspection	Junior, Senior	for Seniors	flow problem; planar directed graph; maximal cut; sweeping line
Visiting Friends	Senior	yes	top-down analysis; modulo operations; patterns
Apples in the basket	Senior	yes	patterns, invariants

4. RESULTS

4.1 Country-Specific General Performance

The average scores over the tasks common to all three countries are shown in Figure 3 (the same qualitative difference between Finland and Sweden was obtained when the average was taken over all tasks). Students in Sweden and Finland perform similarly, except in the Benjamin and Senior age groups, where the average score in Finland is ~40% and ~70% higher, respectively (measured over all tasks). The discrepancy among the Seniors can be explained by the different selection of participating students (cf. Section 2.1), whereas we see no obvious reason for the discrepancy among the Benjamins. One may speculate that the Finnish students' greater reading ability could have an impact in this age group, as problem texts are longer than in Mini and students are not yet perfect readers.

The students in Lithuania have similar scores as Sweden in Mini and Benjamin, but lower scores than both Sweden and Finland in the Cadet and Junior age-groups (and Senior, but there the different selection makes the comparison less useful). This is somewhat surprising, given that the Lithuanian students are in average one year older. One should, however, remember that the participation rate is much higher in Lithuania than in Finland and Sweden. Hence, although we do not have statistic evidence, we conjecture that the lower scores for Cadets and Juniors can be explained by Swedish and Finnish being biased towards academically stronger schools.

The average score on each task compared among the three countries is shown as a scatter plot in Figure 4 for Sweden vs Finland (all tasks) and Sweden vs Lithuania (common tasks). As can be seen from the diagram, the contest covers a whole spectrum of difficulties, from tasks that almost everyone solved to tasks that had a negative average score, i.e. worse results than if the cohort had answered randomly. It is clear that, apart from a few exceptions, the same tasks are difficult in the three countries.

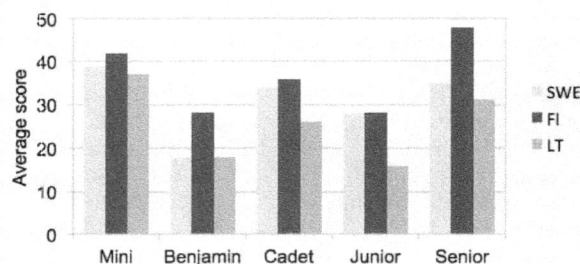

Figure 3: Average score for each age group and country calculated for the tasks common to all three countries. An average score of 100 means that all students solved all tasks correctly, whereas a score of 0 means that all students gave random answers on all tasks

4.2 Performance on Same Task in Different Age Groups

As mentioned above, some tasks are included in several age groups to make it possible to investigate how student understanding and performance change throughout the educational system. One such task in the contest is "Spinning toy", which – as shown in Table 2 – is included in Benjamin, Cadet, Junior and Senior. The average score on the task for boys and girls in the three countries are shown in the diagram in Figure 5.

As the diagram shows, the general trend is quite evident: performance improves with age. Whereas the results are overall quite similar for all countries, the diagram gives rise to some interesting questions: Why are Lithuanian girls performing substantially worse than the others starting at Cadet-level? Why is there no progression from Junior to Senior for Swedish boys? And are these findings merely related to the task at hand or do they indicate a more general

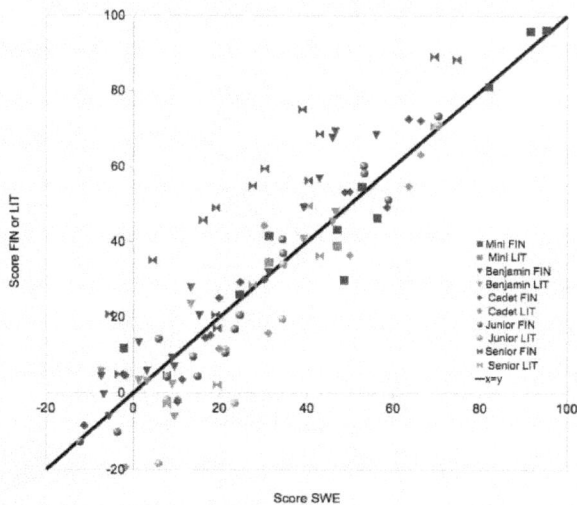

Figure 4: Scatter plot of the average score on each task for Sweden vs Finland (blue markers) and Sweden vs Lithuania (orange markers). An average score of 100 means that all students solved the task correctly, whereas a score of 0 means that all students gave random answers on the task

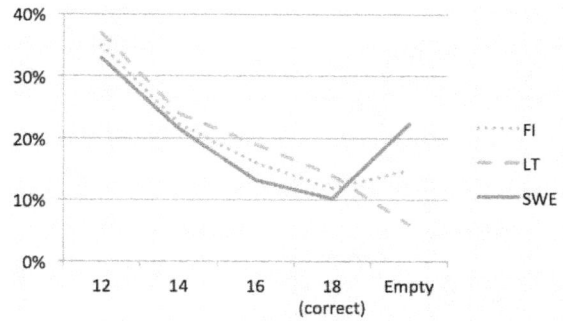

Figure 6: Distribution of answers given by Juniors in the "Different paths" task

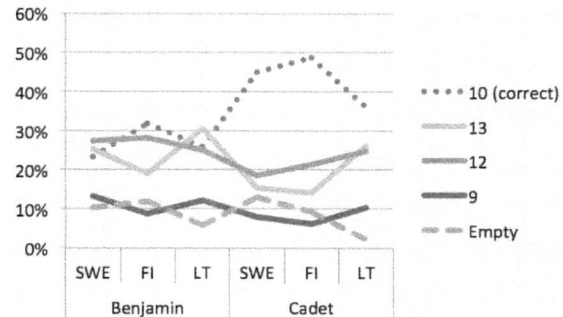

Figure 7: Distribution of answers to the "Highest tree" task for Benjamins and Cadets

trend for e.g. a certain type of tasks for given groups of students? These are examples of questions that merit further investigation and should be comprehensively discussed in our communities.

4.3 Dealing with incorrect answers

Besides looking at how well students do at giving correct answers, it is also interesting to look deeper into tasks where the most common answer is not the correct one. We chose three tasks related to graphs for this kind of analysis.

In the task "Different paths", the participants had to count the number of shortest paths between two points on a grid, in which some parts were inaccessible. As the diagram in Figure 6 indicates, all three incorrect answers were more common than the correct one. Students, however, seem to think rather alike in the three countries, as the proportions for the respective answers are quite similar.

In the task "Highest tree", the participants were given a description of a local search algorithm for finding the highest tree in a forest (always go to the highest tree you currently see) and were asked which tree the algorithm would find in a given example, where 13 is the global maximum but 10 is the local maximum found by the algorithm. In Figure 7, we see the chosen answers for two age groups. As the diagram shows, the task was rather tricky for Benjamins, whereas the proportion of students choosing the correct answer increased in the Cadet age group.

The diagram in Figure 8 shows the chosen answers for "Signal fire" for three age groups. This task appears to have been quite difficult throughout all age groups, with 6 min-

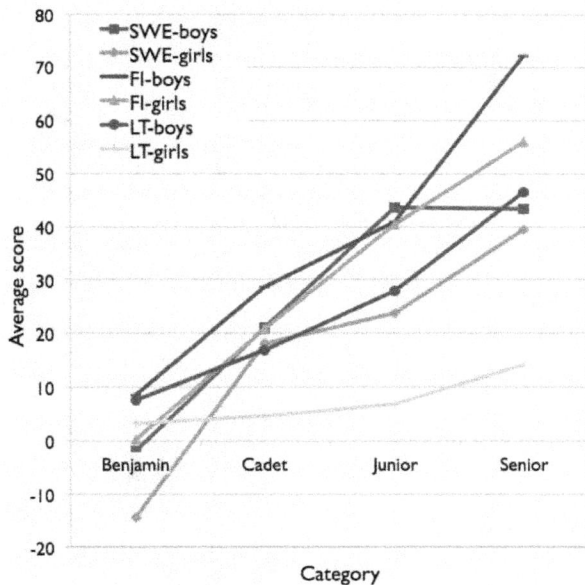

Figure 5: Diagram showing the performance of boys and girls on the task 'Spinning toy" included as a task in the contest for four age groups

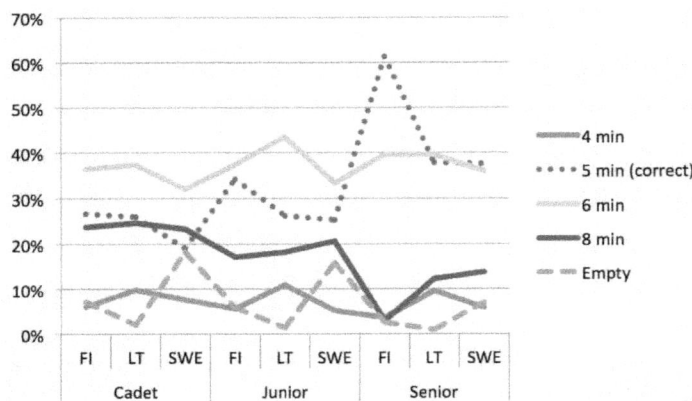

Figure 8: Distribution of answers in the "Signal fire" task for Cadets, Juniors and Seniors

utes being the most common answer (when the correct answer is 5 minutes). The only exception is Finnish Seniors, out of which more than 60% answered correctly. This can however be explained by the Finnish Seniors representing a selected group of students, as discussed in Section 2.1.

Students seem to struggle with abstract thinking: they should trace the graph mentally without real experimentation. Another difficulty can be to notice peculiarities of the graph and relying on what seems correct just by looking, whereas one should check by counting. The 8 minutes incorrect choice can be explained by students confusing the shortest path with the longest path.

5. DISCUSSION AND FUTURE WORK

An international contest like Bebras involves several countries, cultures and languages. Clearly, these are all factors that make it challenging to create unambiguous and clear tasks descriptions, which mean exactly the same in all languages and that are interpreted in precisely the same manner by all students.

In general, the task-wise scores are rather similar in the three countries (disregarding the Senior students of Finland). This is an interesting result, as it suggests that the average ability to solve a certain task is largely independent of the school system. However, Tomcsányi and Vaníček [12] noted that even small differences in translations, wording or pictures might affect the answers. Also, in some countries students are more willing to guess than in other countries; for example, in our comparison the students of Lithuania consistently gave fewer empty answers.

The results of analysing tasks where an incorrect answer is more common than the correct one also point out another similarity between students from different countries: not only is a certain task usually equally "difficult" in the three countries, but there is also a fairly constant fraction of students that thinks in the same way and therefore picks the same incorrect answer.

Our analysis has shown that, apart from the Mini category, there was a lack of easy tasks. This is problematic both for the contest itself (one risks scaring away students and teachers) and for the current analysis, because the results for the more difficult tasks contain more noise as a large fraction of the students might be merely guessing. Unfortu-

nately, it is not easy to estimate how difficult a task will be for a particular age group when developing the task [13].

The experience of doing this investigation, combining data from three countries, has given rise to many ideas on how to further develop the way in which tasks are created and translated. For instance, the translation process could be made more transparent, so that changes made to the task description during translation in some country immediately would be accessible for all other countries as well.

The large and multifaceted data collected in Bebras contests make it possible to analyze several interesting aspects related to e.g. students' understanding, difficulties and misconceptions based on different factors, such as age, gender and geographical location. In this paper, we have looked into some of these questions for a limited set of data, but many questions still remain unanswered. Some of these have already been mentioned in the paper (e.g. in Section 4.2). In addition, tasks where an incorrect answer is more common than the correct one merit further investigation – is the choice of an incorrect alternative associated with some commonly known misunderstandings? The gender aspect is also interesting - what would a detailed analysis of the performance of boys and girls tell us?

6. REFERENCES

[1] C. Ashcraft, E. Eger, and M. Friend. Girls in IT: The Facts. Technical report, National Center for Women & Information Technology (NCWIT), 2012.

[2] V. Barr and C. Stephenson. Bringing computational thinking to K-12: What is involved and what is the role of the computer science education community? *ACM Inroads*, 2(1):48–54, 2011.

[3] Bebras - International contest on informatics and computer fluency, 2013. http://www.bebras.org/.

[4] V. Dagiene. Information Technology Contests – Introduction to Computer Science in an Attractive Way. *Informatics in Education*, 5(1):37–46, 2006.

[5] V. Dagiene. Sustaining informatics education by contests. *LNCS*, 5941:1–12, 2010.

[6] W. Gander et al. Informatics education: Europe cannot afford to miss the boat. Technical report, Informatics Europe & ACM Europe Working Group on Informatics Education, 2013.

[7] V. Guerra, B. Kuhnt, and I. Blöchliger. Informatics at school - worldwide. Technical report, Universität Zürich, 2012.

[8] L. Hakulinen. Survey on Informatics Competitions: Developing Tasks. *Olympiads in Informatics*, 7:12–25, 2011.

[9] T. Poranen. Suomen ensimmäinen Majava-kilpailu. *Dimensio*, 1:32–33, 2011.

[10] ProgeTiger - Programming at schools and hobby clubs, 2012. http://www.tiigrihype.ee.

[11] Shut Down or Restart? The Way Forward for Computing in UK Schools, 2012. Royal Society report.

[12] P. Tomcsányi and J. Vaníček. International comparison of problems from an informatics contest. In *Proceedings of the Information and Communication Technology in Education*, pages 219–223, 2009.

[13] W. Van der Vegt. Predicting the difficulty level of a Bebras task. In *Olympiads in Informatics*, volume 7, pages 132–139, 2013.

Understanding Differences Among Coding Club Students

Antti-Jussi Lakanen, Ville Isomöttönen, Vesa Lappalainen
Department of Mathematical Information Technology
University of Jyväskylä, Finland
{antti-jussi.lakanen, ville.isomottonen, vesal}@jyu.fi

ABSTRACT

Scholars and instructors have been carrying out a multitude of actions to increase students' interest in computer science during the past years. Still, there is a need for knowledge on how these attempts develop student interest. In this qualitative study, we construct illustrative categories out of students who have attended our K-12 coding club and game programming summer course activities. We found four categories: *Inactivity, Lack of self-direction, Experimenting*, and *Professionalism*. We also briefly project this abstraction onto a four-phase model of interest development.

Categories and Subject Descriptors

K.3.2. [**Computers and education**]: Computers and Information Science Education—*Computer Science Education*

General Terms

Experimentation, Human Factors

Keywords

K-12; outreach; game programming; recruitment

1. INTRODUCTION

How to arouse interest in the computer science (CS) field is still a topical issue. CS educators and researchers worldwide have launched a number of initiatives to increase interest and enthuse youngsters about CS and computational thinking. On the one hand, appealing and easy-to-approach interfaces have been developed to attract novices and to lower the barrier to making first computer programs. On the other hand, continuous exposure or support may be necessary to re-engage students over and over again, and get them more interested in the subject [20]. Then, students may eventually begin to set challenges for themselves, redefining and exceeding demands of their work, thus leading to well-developed individual interest [11].

The Faculty of Information Technology at the University of Jyväskylä started an outreach program in 2009 to expose middle and high school students to CS and computational thinking, and to enthuse youngsters about CS through game programming. The program has included week-long programming courses in the summertime, coding club during school year, and collaboration courses with local area high schools. In this study, we focus on the coding club. More precisely, we continue our ongoing research project to understand student differences through categorization of study orientations. The present study focuses on constructing categories through a qualitative, inductive approach. We supplement the data collected in the coding club with the data collected from the summer courses on the same students, which gives us a better understanding of how student background influences interest development regarding CS and CS studies.

2. INTEREST DEVELOPMENT

We found that research on interest development theory supports the results of this study. Interest development has been studied across several disciplines, in particular in educational psychology, which we will address in the following paragraphs. Student interest has also been investigated in CS education research from several perspectives, with particular attention to recruiting students into the field, lowering dropout rates, and increasing attrition. We will briefly expand on this earlier research later in this section.

The importance of motivational aspects of education, arising from the genuine interest that "a person has identified himself with" [7], has been called for by educational theorists. Herbart and Dewey, among others, have "demanded to foster the development of lasting (educationally valuable) interests in school, which are seen as a supraordinate goal of education" [14] (see also, [7, 10]). Interest-triggered learning activities are alleged to yield better learning results and a higher degree of deep-level learning. According to Singh et al. [23], there is research evidence suggesting that interest, along with motivation, attitudes, and academic engagement (i.e. active involvement, commitment, and attention), seems to be a critical construct in learning. Interest also plays an important role in choosing a career: Interest has been found to have an influence on students' educational opportunities and the choices they make regarding their career options [13]. In particular, exposing children early to science correlates with choosing a science-related career [24]. It is important that this exposure happens in or before middle school years [18]. In this regard, teachers are an important factor, and are tasked with providing students more information about science subjects and their interest in science. To engender interest toward science, Xu et al [26] propose, for example, that teachers must show genuine interest in science to build the right atmoshpere in a classroom; they should also offer students multiple entry points to science, such as hands-on activities and access to technology.

The research literature thoroughly describes and explains the development and deepening of interest: see, e.g., model of domain learning [1], person-object theory of interest [14], and the model of constructive capriciousness [22]. One extensively cited model for interest development is a *four-phase model* discovered by Hidi and Renninger [11], who postulated the four levels of interest development: triggered situational interest, maintained situational interest, emerging individual interest, and well-developed individual interest. This four-phase model builds on several aspects of the approaches mentioned above and extends the level of granularity of the three-level model developed by Krapp [14].

We will return to the above viewpoints of the model regarding the present research in the Discussion section. We thus consider the above theoretical and empirical perspectives in science-related studies to be applicable to the field and the present study as CS often requires similar reasoning skills and logical abilities than mathematics and science [4].

Shernoff et al. [21] reports that CS as a school subject engages students at the same level as art studies. Furthermore, students report significantly higher interest and enjoyment scores during CS classes than other school subjects. Despite the engaging attributes and the ability to produce enjoyment as a school subject, the situation changes when transferring to high school and college: CS as a high school subject or major subject in college is sometimes experienced *decontextualized*, that is, students do not explicitly connect computing with usefulness, even though employment and the job world is highly *contextualized* [12]. In this regard, context is important to the human learning process, as it provides meaning and motivation for learners [6]. Guzdial [8] summarizes the literature concerning the usefulness of what students learn by stating that the students are less likely to give up if they understand the usefulness of what they are trying to learn.

Thus, there is a continuous need for tools that introduce CS to students with enough contextualization, so as to enthuse them to pursue CS and keep them motivated to complete their degrees (see also, [5]). The present study and our course concept is based on the idea that games may provide relevant context to CS. Computer games are a fruitful way of contextualizing computing education, as they incorporate many disciplines such as mathematics, artificial intelligence, and physics, as well as art and design, serving as a catalyst for arousing motivation for learning CS [9].

3. CODING CLUB AND SUMMER COURSES

Our coding club activity, which is the main context of the present study, is a continuation for the game programming summer courses that our faculty has been arranging since 2009 [17]. Since the beginning of the summer courses, there have been requests for follow-up courses. Earlier research indicates that continuous exposure or support is needed to engage a student over and over again, and to deepen or

Table 1: Students' participation activity. Please note that participation was recorded 6 times out of 9.

Times participated	1	2	3	4	5	6	Total
Number of students	17	5	5	13	5	6	51

Table 2: Contentual wishes for the coding club

I would like the coding club to include...	n	%
making a whole new game	31	61
continue making own game	25	49
more *C#*	20	39
new programming languages	17	33
info about faculty; studies, and research	13	25
more *XNA*	12	24
something else	2	4

broaden a student's well-developed individual interest for certain content [20]. Encouraged by these research findings, and due to the popular request, we started a coding club to gather old summer course attendees and new students once a month. During the first academic year, 2012–2013, the students improved games they had started during summer courses, began creating new games, and shared their ideas for the coding club activities. Examples of students' games can be found at `http://goo.gl/9Y9AFX`.

Our faculty arranged the coding club nine times during the year. As with our summer courses, girls were in the minority – only three girls attended the club. On six occasions, we kept record of the names of participants. Table 1 summarizes the participation activity of the students. It shows that 17 students attended the club once (most of them on the first time), and so on. The number of participants peaked in the first time with 51 students. After that, the number settled down to around 25–30. Taking into account that the club was arranged on weekends, the organizers considered that to be a successful number.

We also present here the frequencies of the answers to the multiple choice question concerning the students' wishes for the coding club activities, as given in Table 2. We observe, for example, that the students who wished to learn new programming languages mentioned Java, Python, C++, and C. As another example, many respondents wanted to learn arrays, sockets, and reading/writing to files with C# language. These frequencies were considered during the qualitative analysis presented in Section 5.

4. METHOD

This study complements our research project to discover student differences and categorizing students. In particular, we are interested in orientational and attitudinal aspects toward CS studies and computing education, as well as the characteristic demographic and other aspects of student background (e.g., age, earlier computing experiences, preconceptions in programming) that could be used to divide the student cohort into descriptive categories. In our previous study [17], using mixed methods research approaches [25], we found students taking a short summer course on game programming could be divided into five clusters. Regarding the whole research project, the present qualitative study builds on the previous mixed methods research. While the emphasis in our earlier study was on the analysis of the quantitative data, and the context was our summer courses, the present study relies on the qualitative data analysis, and the context is our coding club activity (see Section 3).

4.1 Data

There are two datasets in this study. Our first and primary dataset is the survey from the first day of the coding club. Fifty-one students filled out the questionnaire. The questions are listed below.

- What contentual wishes do you have for the coding club? (Multiple choice question with six options and a free text field.) (Q1)

- Have you done programming after the summer course, or done something else with programming? If yes, what? (Q2)

- Did the summer course inspire you to try out some new things related to programming that you had not done earlier? Describe freely. (Q3)

We also counted the number of times each student participated in the coding club during the school year. This information is counted in the primary dataset.

The primary dataset was supplemented with data from the summer courses that took place before the coding club began. In the summer courses, we collected detailed demographics and other background information[1]. This 'supplementary dataset' was used to enrich the primary dataset, and, on the other hand, was necessary to form a broader picture of students' responses to Q1–Q3. Please note that from the time a student took the summer course until the time of coding club could be quite long, in some cases many years. Also, some students have taken the summer course several times. These aspects are taken into account in the data analysis.

4.2 Analysis procedure

The main focus of the present study was to get a holistic view of each student's interest toward CS and CS studies, and its development. Therefore, we treated datasets as a whole — we wanted to get the "big picture", to see students both as individuals and as a cohort.

As for the data analysis procedure, we carefully examined all the research data, and interpreted an initial revision of the categories characterising student orientations. Thereafter we iteratively reviewed the data several times, and along with several adjustments made to the coding scheme, elaborated the emerging categorization. The analysis process resembles pattern coding in qualitative research, where regularities in the data are identified and finally low level themes form into higher level categorial scheme [19, pp. 67–69]. The first author made the initial categorization, after which the second author presented questions and pointed out his considerations. These observations were taken into account in the later iterations of the analysis.

---

[1]The complete questionnaires are available at `http://trac.cc.jyu.fi/projects/npo/about`

5. CONSTRUCTING THE CATEGORIES

Altogether, four student categories were identified: *Inactivity*, *Lack of self-direction*, *Experimenting*, and *Professionalism*. A fitting category for each student was identified during the process; each student was placed in exactly one category. We find this method to possess at least two benefits. First, this places students as individuals in the pivot of the interpretation of the results, while still retaining the level of abstraction produced by the categorization. Second, possibility to count the student distribution according to the categories concretizes the differences between the categories.

5.1 Category I: Inactivity (n=12)

The students in this category have had little or no earlier programming experience, and they appear not to experiment with programming or do "programming-related activities" (the term is described more broadly in [16]) on their spare time; only a few have taken (or will take) voluntary CS courses at school. The students' comments below illustrate the reluctance in working with programming independently.

> I have not remembered or felt up to starting [programming].

> I have not really done anything [after the summer course], but I think it will come back to me [once I start programming again].

However, this group seems to be three-fold. First, for some students, participating in a summer course or a coding club is a "visit" — they come once or maybe twice, but their level of effort or goal setting remains low. We assume that for those students, attending the coding club might be a nice way of spending one's time with an atmosphere filled with talk about games. The average number of attending times for the whole category was 3.1.

Second, the events can have a social bearing with a possibility to make new friends, despite whether or not a student finds programming itself an interesting topic. A few said they participated "because he was asked by a friend". Parents are another factor that influences students' attendance. In this group, the parents had a stronger influence on students' attendance than the other groups. We found earlier [16] that students who attend the course urged by their parents are more likely *not* to continue making games or other programming-related activities after the summer course.

Third, the inactivity between the first summer experience and the coding club is the other side of the coin. Even though the experiences vary, there are a number of students, who, regardless of the seeming inactivity, have shown a great interest toward CS studies *after* the coding club. For example, one student has started his university studies in our department, another student has completed some of our high school collaboration courses [15], and many students have expressed their interest in the field through surveys when participating in summer courses after the coding club events discussed here.

5.2 Category II: Lack of self-direction (n=16)

This was the biggest group that emerged from our analysis. Even though the students in Category I likely show the least interest toward taking an active role in learning programming, we argue that Category II was the most challenging one from the teacher's perspective. The reason for this may be a lack of competence or lack of interest in building knowledge in a self-directed manner. In other words, a student may take a voluntary course in middle school or high school, but the things learned in the classroom do not engender concrete actions outside the school (or scholastic) environment. In the coding club classroom situation, this can appear as reluctance to make game designs independently, write code, or do code refactoring herself.

Below are a few excerpts from students' answers to the survey on coding club.

> I have not done any programming after the summer course because I lost the note [that contained the web address for the IDE download page].

> To learn new programming tricks without instruction? How on earth could that be possible?

On the other hand, the lack of concrete actions outside the classroom environment may stem from inadequate skills in obtaining information and synthesis-making. Many students highlight that they have made efforts to start making code for a new game, for example, but have encountered challenges that have deflated this enthusiasm. These challenges may include not being able to download or install the tool set, not remembering the URL of the course web page, or more broadly, not believing in his/her own skills or lacking the ability to work out something independently. However, information acquisition and processing skills are important parts of the syllabi of the Finnish elementary and middle schools (grades 1 through 9), and are also demanded by the 21st Century Skills definition [2]. As teachers ourselves, we find the lack of these important skills worrisome, and we recommend that other instructors and decision-makers take this observation into account to improve on the situation.

With that said, we want to note, that the Category II students attend their first summer course with by far the least amount of prior programming experience. In that sense, the call for intensive teaching assistance is understandable.

As within Category I, we find some extremities inside Category II. When asked about the activities between summer courses and coding club, the majority say that they have been too busy to continue their games or start new programming projects. For these students, it seems quite obvious that working independently is not an option, due to lost URL address, for instance. The other point of view is that the students can be really dependent on the instruction and "expert confirmation," meaning that they feel unable to begin working on their own. This is illustrated by the second student quote above, which underlines high learner-control in instructional domain, yet a strong need for assistance in autodidactic domain (see, [3, p. 18]). That particular quote also illustrates another aspect of this group: programming as a collection of tricks that cannot be studied (and possibly self-studied), but *transferred* from person to person, reflects the general view of programming within the Category II student cohort. Surprisingly, this rather constrained view persists with many students, regardless of attending multiple courses.

One thing to note about Category II is that none of the students said that they came to the course urged by the parents. However, these students were still amongst the most inactive in terms of times participated: on average, a Category II student participated 2.7 times in the coding club events during the school year.

5.3 Category III: Experimenting (n=7)

A common denominator for the Category III students is that they have none or little (mostly none) experience prior to the first summer course visit, but have made small experiments or trials with programming, and have possibly succeeded in creating a functional program or a game, or have been to our high school collaboration courses. We find that the biggest difference compared to the students in Category II is that for the Category III students there has been a distinct "kick off"; this group's students have actually started to experiment with programming after taking a summer course, or, for instance, continued on some existing project. Modifying or further developing a game actually gives some indication about a student's motivation, since downloading and installing all the tools needed to compile the game was somewhat an effort with the tool set we used at the time. However, the students themselves are modest about their output, describing their efforts with words such as "little" and "random." On the question about activities between the summer course and the coding club, some students did not answer at all, or answered very briefly, and therefore it is difficult to interpret what they have really done after taking a summer course. Below are some examples of student comments.

> I have programmed some games occasionally, and [I attended] the course for high school students.

> I have done small projects with Java.

There exists only a little variation in the most previous future career plans of the Category III cohorts: six students gave 5 (on a five-step Likert scale, from 1 = strongly disagree, ..., 5 = strongly agree) on the question "are you interested in higher education STEM (science, technology, engineering, and mathematics) studies"; two students gave 3, making the average 4.5, which is a noticeable rise from the pre-survey's average, 3.5. However, some variation on the motives in attending can be found. For example, for some students attending the summer courses or the coding club may have become a habit over the years, and, for instance, attendance of friends can be very important. This is illustrated in the quote below picked from the summer course pre-survey.

> I've come to code <u>with my friends</u>. (Our emphasis.)

On average, the Category III students participated 3.8 times in the coding club events during the school year.

5.4 Category IV: Professionalism (n=9)

The Category IV may well stand out the most in a number of ways. This group consists of students, who have gathered a good deal of prior knowledge of programming. Besides this, they have experimented with different areas of programming, and their inclination toward CS shows in their awareness of terminology and names of technologies. They do not consider the summer course and their hobby to be solely about programming little games, rather they use the names of particular languages, e.g., C++, Java, Python, or specific topics of programming or algorithms, like A*, parallel programming, XNA or Windows Forms. Furthermore, they are the only ones who wish that the coding club

Table 3: Summarized view of the characteristics of each category.

Category I: Inactivity (n=12)	Category II: Lack of self-direction (n=16)
• Shows only little interest in trying "something new" in programming — neither in a self-directed way nor with instruction.	• Some interest toward CS topics arises, but the limited possibilities or the lack of competence prevents a deeper dive into programming activities in a self-directed manner.
• Attending a summer course may be influenced strongly by parents.	• Has little or no earlier programming experience. However, will take or have taken voluntary CS courses (or ICT courses) in high school.
• Scatters throughout the cohort regardless of the times attended a coding club.	

Category III: Experimenting (n=7)	Category IV: Professionalism (n=9)
• Has independently experimented with programming, or took voluntary courses in school; a distinct "take off" can be noticed. However, it remains unclear what kind of things he/she has done *exactly*.	• Though being among the youngest of the cohort, has somewhat clear plans for future career; expresses strong inclination toward STEM studies.
• Show strong interest in higher education and/or STEM subjects.	• Acquires knowledge on new techniques and concepts in spare-time, outside a formal classroom environment. Also actively participates the coding club activity.
• Participates in the summer more than once, and also is active participant in the coding club.	

included instruction on particular technologies, techniques and concepts, such as sockets, arrays, and making games for game consoles.

Inclination toward higher education studies in STEM fields is evident right from the first summer course pre-survey. All except one stated that they "agree or strongly agree" on the question about interest in studying in STEM fields. Moreover, those who gave 4 in pre-survey responded with 5 in later surveys. This indicates that the Category IV students already have a rather solid impression about their future plans. It is interesting to note that this mature mindset does not require more years of experience: The Category IV students were 13.9 years on average when they first attended our summer course, making them the youngest of this analysis; Category I students were 14.3 years, Category II students 14.4 years, and Category III students 14.5 years on average.

The students in the Category IV were the most active participants in the coding club: on average each participated 4.0 times during the school year.

5.5 Summarizing the analysis

Taken together, four categories emerged during the analysis. We found fundamental differences in the categories, as well as some similarities. With these categories, we focused on investigating and understanding, in a holistic manner, what *vantage points* arise through analyses of multiple data sets. In Table 3, we give a short, summarized view of the results and present the characteristics of each student category. Note that this is a simplified presentation of the study results in Chapter 5, and points out particularly the key differences found between the four categories.

6. DISCUSSION AND CONCLUSIONS

In this paper, we found four categories that characterized the orientations of K-12 summer programming course and coding club students (see summary in Table 3). We can project the discovered categories onto the four-phase model of interest development (see Section 2). We find that within the *Inactivity* category, students' *situational interest has been triggered*. It also seems that they were initially motivated by issues such as personal relevance due to the gaming context, and by external factors, like parents and friends. They have come to the coding club because they are "willing to explore" (see [20]). Within the *Lack of self-direction* category, situational interest is held and sustained through personal involvement, for example voluntary CS courses taken in school. The coding club and school courses provide external support for maintaining situational interest, yet the students fail to define tasks for themselves and generate questions about the content out of curiosity. It is clearly a challenge for us as educators to further promote emergence of individual interest as opposed to mere situational interest.

Within the *Experimenting* category, students begin to seek repeated re-engagement with CS topics and programming. Students may lack skills in information acquisition, and their *emerging individual interest* may still require external support, like engaging tasks and attending (beginner) summer courses multiple times. However, they are motivated to set challenges for themselves, and with the right support, possibly to redefine and exceed initially conceived task demands in their work. As for the *Professionalism* category, the positive feelings about learning CS, stored knowledge, valuing the opportunity to re-engage in programming and other CS tasks, and opting to pursue these tasks reflect *well-developed individual interest*. The students do not consider new tasks to be a burden, but take them as a positive challenge as "effort that feels effortles" [11] (see also [20]).

The results of this study can give instuctors a better awareness of the student cohort, help them plan their lessons, and take into account, for example, the issues related to students lacking self-direction. Also, the results imply that it is important to provide the students with the possibility to engage with CS at regular intervals, since for many students working independently outside the scholastic environment is challenging or impossible. With regular exposure (and proper support from experts), we argue, the students are more receptive to studying CS topics in later phases of their studies. This study supplements the results found in our earlier findings concerning student orientation and attitudinal aspects toward CS studies. In our future work, we will construct an overall picture of our research project where we combine the present results (qualitative study, four categories) with the results from our previous studies (quantitative study, five categories).

7. REFERENCES

[1] P. A. Alexander. A model of domain learning: Reinterpreting expertise as a multidimensional, multistage process. *Motivation, emotion, and cognition: Integrative perspectives on intellectual functioning and development*, pages 273–298, 2004.

[2] M. Binkley, O. Erstad, J. Herman, S. Raizen, M. Ripley, M. Miller-Ricci, and M. Rumble. Defining Twenty-First Century Skills. In P. Griffin, B. McGaw, and E. Care, editors, *Assessment and Teaching of 21st Century Skills*, pages 17–66. Springer Netherlands, 2012.

[3] P. C. Candy. *Self-Direction for Life-Long Learning: A Comprehensive Guide to Theory and Practice*. Jossey-Bass, San Franscisco, CA, 1991.

[4] D. E. Comer, D. Gries, M. C. Mulder, A. Tucker, A. J. Turner, and P. R. Young. Computing As a Discipline. *Commun. ACM*, 32(1):9–23, Jan. 1989.

[5] S. Cooper and S. Cunningham. Teaching computer science in context. *ACM Inroads*, 1(1):5–8, Mar. 2010.

[6] T. DeClue. A theory of attrition in computer science education which explores the effect of learning theory, gender, and context. *J. Comput. Sci. Coll.*, 24(5):115–121, May 2009.

[7] J. Dewey. *Interest and Effort in Education*. Riverside Press, Boston, New York, Chicago, 1913.

[8] M. Guzdial. Does contextualized computing education help? *ACM Inroads*, 1(4):4–6, Dec. 2010.

[9] M. Guzdial and E. Soloway. Teaching the Nintendo generation to program. *Commun. ACM*, 45(4):17–21, Apr. 2002.

[10] J. F. Herbart and D. Benner. *Systematische Pädagogik*. Klett-Cotta, 1986.

[11] S. Hidi and K. A. Renninger. The Four-Phase Model of Interest Development. *Educational Psychologist*, 41(2):111–127, June 2006.

[12] M. Knobelsdorf and C. Schulte. Computer science in context: Pathways to computer science. In *Proceedings of the Seventh Baltic Sea Conference on Computing Education Research - Volume 88*, Koli Calling '07, pages 65–76, Darlinghurst, Australia, Australia, 2007. Australian Computer Society, Inc.

[13] A. Krapp. 5 Interest and human development during adolescence: An educational-psychological approach. In J. Heckhausen, editor, *Motivational Psychology of Human Development*, volume 131 of *Advances in Psychology*, pages 109–128. North-Holland, 2000.

[14] A. Krapp. Structural and dynamic aspects of interest development: theoretical considerations from an ontogenetic perspective. *Learning and Instruction*, 12(4):383–409, 2002. Interest in Learning, Learning to be Interested.

[15] A. J. Lakanen and V. Isomöttönen. High school students' perspective to university CS1. In *Proceedings of the 18th ACM Conference on Innovation and Technology in Computer Science Education*, ITiCSE '13, pages 261–266, New York, NY, USA, 2013. ACM.

[16] A.-J. Lakanen, V. Isomöttönen, and V. Lappalainen. Life two years after a game programming course: Longitudinal viewpoints on K-12 outreach. In *Proceedings of the 43rd ACM technical symposium on Computer Science Education*, SIGCSE '12, pages 481–486, New York, NY, 2012. ACM.

[17] A.-J. Lakanen, V. Isomöttönen, and V. Lappalainen. Five years of game programming outreach: Understanding student differences. *Accepted to ACM SIGCSE '14*, 2014.

[18] A. V. Maltese and R. H. Tai. Eyeballs in the Fridge: Sources of early interest in science. *International Journal of Science Education*, 32(5):669–685, June 2009.

[19] M. B. Miles and A. M. Huberman. *Qualitative Data Analysis: A Sourcebook of New Methods*. Sage, Beverly Hills, CA, 1984.

[20] K. A. Renninger, W. Shumar, S. Barab, R. Kling, and J. Gray. The centrality of culture and community to participant learning at and with the math forum. *Designing for virtual communities in the service of learning*, pages 181–209, 2004.

[21] D. J. Shernoff, M. Csikszentmihalyi, B. Shneider, and E. S. Shernoff. Student engagement in high school classrooms from the perspective of flow theory. *School Psychology Quarterly*, 18(2):158–176, 2003.

[22] P. J. Silvia. Interest and interests: The psychology of constructive capriciousness. *Review of General Psychology*, 5(3):270–290, 2001.

[23] K. Singh, M. Granville, and S. Dika. Mathematics and Science Achievement: Effects of Motivation, Interest, and Academic Engagement. *The Journal of Educational Research*, 95(6):323–332, 2002.

[24] R. H. Tai, C. Qi Liu, A. V. Maltese, and X. Fan. Planning Early for Careers in Science. *Science*, 312(5777):1143–1144, 2006.

[25] C. Teddlie and A. Tashakkori. *Foundations of mixed methods research : integrating quantitative and qualitative approaches in the social and behavioral sciences*. SAGE, Los Angeles, 2009.

[26] J. Xu, L. T. Coats, and M. L. Davidson. Promoting Student Interest in Science: The Perspectives of Exemplary African American Teachers. *American Educational Research Journal*, 49(1):124–154, 2012.

Responses to Adaptive Feedback for Software Testing

Kevin Buffardi
Virginia Tech
2202 Kraft Drive
Blacksburg, VA 24060
+1 540-231-5723
kbuffardi@vt.edu

Stephen H. Edwards
Virginia Tech
2202 Kraft Drive
Blacksburg, VA 24060
+1 540-231-5723
edwards@cs.vt.edu

ABSTRACT

As students learn to program they also learn basic software development methods and techniques, but educators do not often directly assess students' development processes or evaluate their adherence to specific techniques. However, automated grading systems provide opportunities to evaluate students' programming and provide feedback while the student is still in the process of developing. Consequently, automated adaptive feedback may help reinforce effective techniques and processes.

This paper describes an adaptive feedback system that uses strategic reinforcement techniques to reward and encourage incremental software testing. By analyzing changes in students' code after they receive the system's reinforcement, we investigated students' responses to the presence and absence of rewards. We found that after receiving rewards, students respond with more test code in their subsequent submission.

Categories and Subject Descriptors

K.3.2 [**Computers and Education**]: Computer and Information Science Education; D.2.5 [**Software Engineering**]: Testing and Debugging.

Keywords

Adaptive feedback, behavioral change, operant conditioning, reinforcement, punishment, test-driven development (TDD), automated assessment, instructional technology.

1. INTRODUCTION

Computer science curricula include teaching students to adopt current techniques and methods for software development [1]. Nevertheless, since conventional programming assignments only evaluate the *product* of students' work, instructors are usually blind to students' adherence to the particular *processes*. Consequently, computer science education could benefit from tools that help characterize students' software development and encourage adherence to specific techniques.

For example, Test-Driven Development (TDD) is a technique, popularized by Agile development, that emphasizes an

incremental "test a little, code a little" approach [2]. Given its popularity, students could benefit from practicing its application. However, while some literature touts TDD's benefits, there is a consensus that some developers resist adoption and may require additional motivation to begin testing early within development [8]. To observe adherence to TDD in an academic setting, it is insufficient to evaluate students' software tests after completing an assignment. Instead, an incremental testing process can only be demonstrated by observing software development in process.

It is impractical for instructors to manually review every student's work often enough to understand their development processes. To the contrary, students may submit their code to automated grading systems that evaluate the code and provide prompt feedback. By allowing students to resubmit their work repeatedly for automated evaluation, the systems can record code revisions and provide adaptive feedback based on how well the students follow incremental testing patterns. Consequently, adaptive feedback systems can use rewards and other reinforcement mechanisms to encourage incremental testing.

Operant conditioning—as pioneered by notable psychologist, B.F. Skinner—is a well-established technique for promoting behavioral change through systematic reinforcement [15]. However, software development is a particularly complex behavior and will consequently be more difficult to change. Moreover, since the magnitude of the impact that TDD has on programming assignment outcomes is unknown, it may be difficult to observe long-term results of changes in software development behaviors. Instead, we initially concentrate on whether or not students demonstrate short-term behavioral responses to reinforcement mechanisms.

We developed an adaptive feedback system that observes students' software testing behaviors and provides reinforcement for incremental testing. After learning about TDD, students used the adaptive feedback system for programming assignments for a semester of a fundamental programming class. In this paper, we analyze changes in students' code after receiving automated feedback to evaluate their behavioral responses to incremental testing reinforcement.

In our experiment, after demonstrating improvements in their adherence to incremental testing approaches, students received hints for correcting flaws in their code as a reward. We investigated changes in the amount of test code in subsequent submissions and compared the responses after receiving rewards to those after no rewards. In other studies, we found no ultimate impact on the quality of students' final products [6][7]. However, this study found that after receiving rewards, subsequent submissions show increased concentration on testing.

2. RELATED WORK

Melnik and Maurer acknowledged that adopting Agile methods may be more challenging in an academic setting than it is in industry. Consequentially, they surveyed students' opinions of different aspects of eXtreme Programming (XP), including Test-Driven Development (TDD). They found generally positive views of all aspects of eXtreme Programming from 240 respondents, representing a variety of demographics with differing degrees of experience and exposure to XP [14]. In addition, they discovered a weak positive correlation between attitudes toward TDD and students' ages.

However, they also found that some students struggled to think with a test-first approach. They reasoned this difficulty may be due to TDD "almost like working backwards" by drawing attention to documenting design early through writing unit tests [11]. Similarly, Janzen and Saiedian compared the opinions and acceptance of TDD between novice and mature developers in computing courses. They found that mature developers are more willing to accept TDD. Furthermore, students were significantly more likely to choose to follow TDD in the future after having tried it [12].

To aide teaching TDD, Spacco and Pugh leveraged Marmoset [16], a rich submission and automated grading system. Students benefit from receiving prompt, online feedback including how their code performs against the tests. Despite the emphasis and prompt feedback on testing, Spacco and Pugh recognize that many students still favor a "test-late mentality of writing their implementation and then testing it at the very end" and call for a need to design incentives to motivate students to test early [17].

Positive reinforcement can be a powerful tool in motivating new behaviors. Schedules of reinforcement have shown to encourage target behaviors in both games and learning environments [13]. Linehan suggests a model for leveraging Applied Behavior Analysis to motivate target behaviors through a process of measuring performance, analyzing performance, presenting feedback, and defining a rewards schedule that coordinates with the target behavior. Likewise, we have the unique opportunity to measure, analyze, and use reinforcement and punishment to influence students' development processes.

To modify human behavior, operant conditioning usually depends on four mechanisms: stating the goal, tracking the behavior, rewarding target behavior with positive reinforcement, and discouraging deviations from the target behavior [15]. For example, providing rewards as incentives for demonstrating the target behavior provides positive reinforcement. Then, when the subject does not demonstrate the target behavior, the rewards can be removed (negative punishment) and the subject reprimanded (positive punishment).

Meanwhile, we have been teaching TDD in CS1 and CS2 courses. In a preliminary study of a five-year data set of snapshots of students' work, we found positive correlations between indicators of incremental testing and consequential outcomes. Specifically, we identified two measurements of quantity of testing average test statements per solution statements (TSSS) and average test methods per solution method (TMSM) with small but statistically significant correlations with functional correctness and test coverage. Similarly, average test coverage across all snapshots for an assignment was positively correlated with final functional correctness [5]. However, despite its advantages, we also witnessed some students who resisted adhering to TDD.

In a separate study, we investigated students' attitudes toward the test-first and incremental unit testing aspects of TDD [4]. Similar to reports in related literature, we discovered that students generally appreciated the value of testing but were apprehensive to adopt test-first habits. While students valued an incremental unit-testing approach, most students did not follow strict test-first procedures. Likewise, we identified a close relationship between students' perception of how helpful these aspects of TDD are and how likely they are to adhere to them.

This relationship is likely reciprocal in that expecting TDD to help should make students more likely to adhere; likewise, adhering to TDD should advocate students' appreciation of its benefits. However, most students reported that did not persistently write tests in small increments nor did they test first. For these reasons, we recognized a need to better understand students' development processes and investigate approaches to encouraging adherence to TDD.

3. METHOD
3.1 A Model for Adaptive Feedback

To observe students' development processes, it is necessary to gain insight into changes in their work over time. By using Web-CAT [9]—an automated grading system—to collect student submissions and provide rapid evaluation of their performance, students are encouraged to submit several versions of their work as they refine their assignments. Among other features, Web-CAT evaluates students' code on its correctness and coverage. Correctness is determined by the percent of instructor-provided tests (obscured from students) successfully passed by the student's solution. Coverage is determined by the amount of solution code evaluated by the students' own unit tests. Upon submitting their work, students promptly receive results of their correctness and coverage scores. Students may submit their work unlimited times, without penalty, until the assignment deadline.

Each time students submit and receive feedback, there are opportunities to assess their adherence to incremental testing methods and trigger interventions to encourage the desired behavior. Ideally, incremental testing would be demonstrated by maintaining high (at or near 100%) coverage while the correctness gradually increases. Consequently, we designed the system to reinforce this behavior and to correct students who deviate from it.

Our adaptive feedback system supplements Web-CAT's correctness and coverage assessment by monitoring progress from one submission to the next. Students receive positive reinforcement through images and brief messages acknowledging improvements in their solution and/or testing, as shown in **Figure 1**. When their submissions do not demonstrate improvement, the feedback encourages them to improve their testing by offering additional incentives. In particular, students receive hints about how to improve their solution as a reward for improving the thoroughness of their testing. **Figure 1** illustrates reinforcing feedback with two hints displayed.

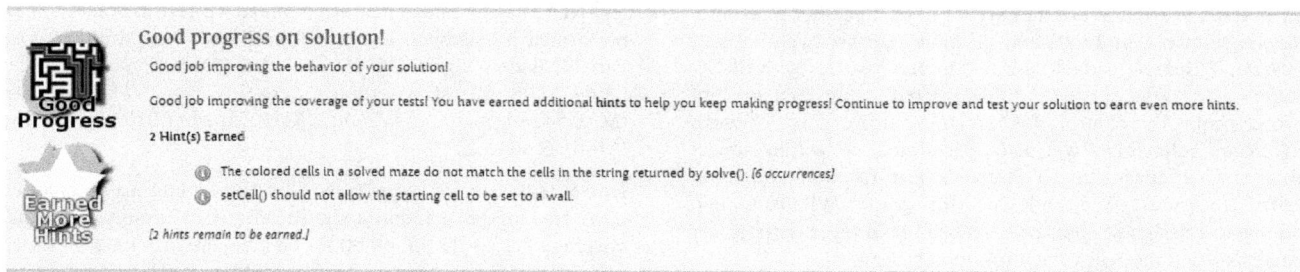

Figure 1. The Web-CAT plugin displays adaptive feedback with positive reinforcement and hints.

The system adaptively caters hints to help students correct problems with their solutions that are identified by failed instructor tests. Each instructor unit test includes a hint message to provide some guidance about why it failed. Closely related instructor tests may generate identical hint messages, but duplicates are combined and the collection of hints is sorted so precedence is given to hints with more occurrences.

Students earn their first hint from their first submission that demonstrates some progress on both the solution and testing with non-zero correctness and coverage scores. To earn additional hints on subsequent submissions, students have to meet a minimum threshold of coverage (initially $\geq 85\%$) to demonstrate they are testing their solution substantially. Given the minimum coverage is met, students can earn hints by either maintaining 100% coverage and making changes to their solution code, or by improving their coverage over the previous submissions. Following this model, students are required to begin testing in early submissions and continue to meet progressively higher coverage requirements as they progress.

If a student earns hints on sequential submissions, she may receive the same hints in both submissions' feedback. On its face, this approach may not seem to reward the student for earning hints. However, it allows the student to track the flaws in her assignment. For example, if a previously seen hint is replaced by a new hint, one may falsely conclude that the bug that generated the hint has been resolved. Instead, earned hints are only dismissed once their corresponding instructor test passes.

If students deviate from the incremental testing process, they do not receive hints on their submissions until they demonstrate sufficient coverage again. The system also controls for potential attempts to get additional hints by artificially manipulating measurements of progress. For example, the system records the highest correctness score achieved so far to prevent students from deleting or sabotaging their solution in one (worse) submission only to give the illusion of improvement by reverting to the previous (better) solution in the next submission.

3.2 Intervention Design

We integrated our adaptive feedback model into Web-CAT for students to submit their programming assignments. During the Spring 2013 academic semester, we introduced CS2 (Software Design and Data Structures) students to the adaptive feedback system. Of the 128 students who sat the final exam, 84 (66%) provided written consent to include their data in our analysis. Assignments included: (1) maintaining a list of digital photo metadata, (2) solving a maze with two-dimensional arrays, and (3) implementing both array- and link-based queues. In addition, students from each of the five sections of the course used different variations of the adaptive feedback system. Treatments included combinations of consistent or intermittent reinforcement and either with- or without- a visible goal for improving test coverage. The consistent reinforcement treatment rewarded students with hints every time they met the incremental testing criteria while intermittent reinforcement treatments only rewarded the students with hints at most once per hour or at random chance (after meeting the same criteria). The goal treatments either always showed the coverage threshold necessary to earn a hint or always obscured it. In a separate study, we analyzed the different treatments with inconclusive long-term outcomes [6][7]. However, in this study we concentrate on the immediate responses students demonstrate after receiving hints.

3.3 Evaluation

To observe students' short-term behavioral responses, we identified whether the feedback for each submission: received additional hints, maintained the same number of hints (but earned no additional hints), or received no hints. Accordingly, we inspected changes in students' work in their successive submissions. In particular, we considered the difference in the amount of code between the latter and former submissions. We recorded changes (Δ) in non-comment lines of code (NCLOC) for the solution and the tests independently. Likewise, we measured the change in test coverage as well as changes in the number of assertions in the students' test code.

Since the adaptive feedback system follows protocol for operant conditioning to encourage incremental testing, we suspected students to increase their testing efforts after receiving positive reinforcement. Specifically, we made the following hypotheses:

1. After receiving additional hints, students will be more likely to make any changes in their test code than after they do *not* receive additional hints.

2. After receiving additional hints, students will add significantly more test code than after they do *not* receive additional hints.

3. After receiving additional hints, students will add significantly more test assertions than after they do *not* receive additional hints.

4. After receiving additional hints, students will improve coverage significantly more than after they do *not* receive additional hints.

To address hypothesis 1, we first categorized types of change to test code. Adding new test methods constituted *major* changes, adding only new test NCLOC signified *moderate* changes, and any changes that did not require changing the number of test NCLOC were *minor* changes. Using chi-squared test, we compared the distribution of these types of change after receiving: *additional* hints, *same* hints, and *no* hints. To test hypothesis 2, we used a Wilcoxon signed-rank test to compare Δ test NCLOC in submissions after incidents of additional, same, and no hint reinforcement. To control for potential differences between individuals' behaviors, we also performed a within-subject analysis of variance using Friedman's test for non-parametric repeated measures. We followed the same Wilcoxon and Friedman test design to compare affects to the Δ test assertions for hypothesis 3 and the Δ coverage for hypothesis 4.

4. RESULTS

Across three programming assignments during the semester, we analyzed 3115 submissions. Since students' first submissions (170 out of 3115 submissions) to each assignment do not represent responses to the adaptive feedback intervention, their data was not included in comparing changes in code. 2169 (~74%) of the submissions followed submissions with *no* hints, while 524 (~18%) received the *same* number of hints and 252 (~9%) received *additional* hints. As described in the previous section, we categorized types of changes to test code as *minor* (1429, ~49%), *moderate* (856, ~29%), and *major* (650, ~22%). **Figure 2** illustrates the distribution of how *additional*, *same*, and *no* hint groups responded with *minor*, *moderate*, and *major* test changes.

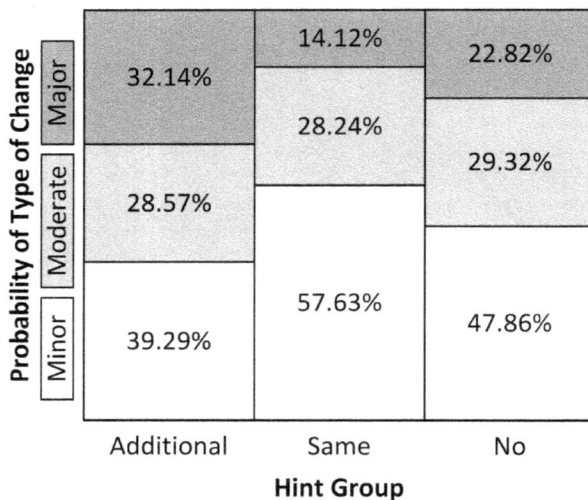

Figure 2. Probability of types of response to hints

We performed a chi-squared test to examine the relation between hint group and the type of change response. The relation between these variables was significant $X^2(4, N=2945)=41.45$, p<.0001 and there was no significant interaction with the subject variable $X^2(2, N=2945)=3.53$, p=.15. These results support hypothesis 1 that the greater likelihood of making major test changes after receiving additional hints is not due to chance.

We performed a Friedman test and found that the hint group variable had a significant effect on Δ test NCLOC F(2,1)=15.48, p<.0001. We used a Wilcoxon test to compare Δ test NCLOC between each pair of hint groups. We also used the Bonferroni correction to adjust the critical p value (α=0.0167) for multiple comparisons. The *additional hints* (M=9.52, sd=23.80) group responded with significantly greater Δ test NCLOC (p<.0001) than *same hints* (M=1.89, sd=18.51) and *no hints* (M=5.31, sd=17.59, p<.01). *No hints* responded with significantly greater Δ

test NCLOC (p<.0001) than *same hints*. To test hypothesis 3, we performed a Friedman test and found that while the hint group variable had no significant effect on Δ test assertions F(2,1)=7.79, p=.67. The Δ test assertions were low for *additional hints* (M=0.54, sd=3.26), *same hints* (M=0.35, sd=3.01), and *no hints* (M=0.36, sd=3.12).

However, we tested hypothesis 4 by performing a Friedman test on Δ coverage and found a significant effect of hint group on Δ coverage F(2,1)=13.39, p<.0001. To compare differences between each pair, we performed a Wilcoxon test (α=0.0167) and found that *additional hints* (M=0.03, sd=0.13) responded with greater Δ coverage (p<.0001) than *same hints* (M=-0.01, sd=0.05) but was not significantly greater than *no hints* (M=0.02, sd=0.11); moreover, *no hints* responded with greater Δ coverage (p<.0001) than *same hints*.

The initial statistical analysis provided support for hypotheses that students respond to *additional hints* as reinforcement with greater likelihood of adding test code and with greater amounts of test code. While tests did not support the hypotheses that test assertions would also increase, they did find that coverage increases. We also observed a recurring pattern across all the measurements where *additional hints* had the highest means while *some hints* had the lowest. Curious from this observation, we also investigated comparisons in other changes in students' code with post-hoc tests.

We performed a Wilcoxon test and found that after receiving *additional hints* (M=5.94, sd=23.44), students responded with greater (p<.01) Δ solution NCLOC than *same hints* (M=1.42, sd=13.81) and *no hints* (M=1.70, sd=17.09, p<.0001) while *no hints* approached significantly greater Δ solution NCLOC (p=.0293, α=0.0167). Similarly, we compared the elapsed time (in minutes) from the previous (intervention stimulus) to subsequent (response) submissions and found that *additional hints* (M=307.21, sd=1120.52) responded after more time (p<.0001) than *same hints* (M=111.45, sd=485.15) and *no hints* (M=227.73, sd=931.13). There was no significant difference (p=.07) between the elapsed time of *no hints* and *some hints*.

Consequently, we see that after *additional hints*, students produce more test code and more solution code but also take more time to do so. Therefore, it is possible that the additional code written was an artifact of taking more time than rather than as a response to positive reinforcement. Moreover, we found that elapsed time between submissions varied greatly. As a result, we categorized elapsed time by quartiles: *quick* included elapsed time under 3.47 minutes, *short* included longer elapsed time but within 8.85 minutes, *medium* included elapsed time greater than 8.85 but less than 31.93 minutes, and *long* included the remaining quartile of submissions with greater elapsed time. **Table 1** shows the Δ test NCLOC (with mean and standard deviation) for hint groups with subgroups for elapsed time.

Table 1. Change in test NCLOC by elapsed time

	Hint Group (M,sd)		
	Additional	**Same**	**No**
Quick	-0.15, 20.75	-0.28, 7.70	-0.16, 14.89
Short	2.67, 10.51	0.16, 11.28	3.23, 12.80
Medium	7.20, 15.06	3.58, 9.84	5.87, 11.66
Long	21.70, 33.34	5.12, 36.41	12.34, 24.87

We see that in *quick* resubmissions, the average Δ test NCLOC for each hint group is less than one line of code changed. That might be expected since the minimal time elapsed between submissions suggests that students gave little to no time to read the Web-CAT results before making small changes and resubmitting.

We performed Wilcoxon each-pairs comparisons between hint groups with each elapsed time interval independently. After *quick* time elapsed there is no significant difference between *additional hints* and *same hints* (p=.91) or *no hints* (p=.63) and no significant difference between *same hints* and *no hints* (p=.18). After *short* time elapsed, there is no significant difference between *additional hints* and *no hints* (p=.99) but approaches greater Δ test NCLOC than *same hints* (p=.04). *No hints* demonstrates significantly greater (p<.01) Δ test NCLOC than *same hints*. Likewise, after *medium* time elapsed, there is no significant difference between *additional hints* and *no hints* (p=.93) but approaches greater Δ test NCLOC than *same hints* (p=.04). *No hints* demonstrates significantly greater (p<.0001) Δ test NCLOC than *same hints*. After *long* time elapsed, *additional hints* has greater Δ test NCLOC than *no hints* (p<.01) and *same hints* (p<.0001) and *no hints* also has greater Δ test NCLOC than *some hints* (p<.0001).

One should also note that since the incidents of *additional* and *same hints* groups are considerably smaller when considering each interval independently (quick: n=33 and 134, short: n=70 and 154, medium: n=70 and 132, long: 79 and 104, respectively) so it is more difficult to find significant results. Nevertheless, we continue to observe a trend where *same hints* group responds with the fewest changes in their test code.

One possible explanation for most of the tests showing the greatest changes in test code after receiving *additional hints* is that students may be in a period of their development where they are mostly concentrating on testing. By improving their test coverage, they earn the additional hints and then may submit to observe their progress and then continue adding test code until they are satisfied with their test coverage. Such a pattern would suggest that receiving hints may have no influence on their behavior.

To investigate this case, looked exclusively at instances when students exhibit the target behavior (as identified by the adaptive feedback system) and compare their responses after being rewarded with new hints to those when no additional hints are received. Students may not receive additional hints despite earning them either because the system had no more hints to provide (because the student's solution did not have sufficient flaws) or because the reinforcement schedule treatment (described in section 3.2) withheld reinforcement on that particular submission. We identified these instances as *unacknowledged* (n=153, *no hints* shown despite earning some) or *unrewarded* (n=179, *some hints* shown but not *additional*, as earned) groups. By comparing these groups, we can observe the impact a hint reward has on students continuing the target behavior on subsequent submissions after exhibiting it for the previous submission.

We compared responses after *additional hints* to those after *unacknowledged* and *unrewarded* groups. While correcting the threshold for significance when making multiple comparisons (α=0.0167), we performed each-pairs comparison using the Wilcoxon test. We found that *additional hints* (M=9.52, sd=23.80) responded with significantly greater Δ test NCLOC

(p<.0001) than *unacknowledged* (M=1.57, sd=13.99, p<.0001) and *unrewarded* (M=0.55, sd=8.06) submissions. There was no significant difference (p=.36) between *unacknowledged* and *unrewarded* groups. In these cases, students exhibited similar behavior by initially satisfying the adaptive feedback system's criteria for incremental testing, but responded differently depending on whether or not they received additional hints.

5. DISCUSSION

The statistical analysis supported three hypotheses:

1. After receiving additional hints, students will be more likely to make any in their test code than after they do *not* receive additional hints.

2. After receiving additional hints, students will add significantly more test code than after they do *not* receive additional hints.

4. After receiving additional hints, students will improve coverage significantly more than after they do *not* receive additional hints.

while tests for one hypothesis was inconclusive:

3. After receiving additional hints, students will add significantly more test assertions than after they do not receive additional hints.

In general, the changes in the number of test assertions from one submission to the next were small (M=0.38, sd=3.11) so change in test code NCLOC (M=5.06, sd=18.45) offers more substantial alterations and consequently may be a better indicator of the short-term responses to adaptive feedback stimuli. While there are many factors that may influence changes students' code from one submission to the next, we found that after receiving rewards reinforcing incremental testing, their responses usually exhibited greater increases in test code. Even when comparing only submissions following demonstrations of incremental testing, those who received positive reinforcement responded by continuing to add more test code than those who did not receive rewards.

Likewise, when controlling for the amount of time elapsed between submission, we found that responses to receiving *additional* hints often increased test code more than those after receiving *no* hints. In turn, those receiving *no* hints often increased test code more than those who received hints, but no more than they had previously earned. Upon initial consideration, this pattern may seem counter-intuitive. To the contrary, the responses are consistent with principles of operant conditioning.

Receiving additional hints is an example of *positive reinforcement*—adding a stimulus that rewards a behavior and consequently increases the frequency of that behavior. Receiving no hints is an example of *negative punishment*—removing a pleasing stimulus (hints) to decrease the behavior. However, by neither adding nor removing hints, the behavior is neither incentivized nor discouraged. Consequently, receiving hints may encourage students to continue their incremental testing while removing hints may dissuade them from behaviors that do *not* exhibit incremental testing.

We considered that the insight provided by the contents within hints might have a greater impact on changes in students' test code than whether or not their behavior received reinforcement.

However, it should be noted that hints only describe flaws in the students' solution code. Students may be able to extrapolate missing test case(s) from a hint, but both hint selection and wording concentrate on students' solution code and disregard their test code (e.g. "*setCell() should not allow the starting cell to be set to a wall.*" for the maze solver assignment). Specific feedback on test coverage—both by line of code and as a percentage of all the code—is available regardless of whether a hint is provided.

More importantly, at the moment of the resubmission, those who responded to *additional* hint stimuli did not necessarily have greater insight from more hints. For example, a student who previously earned three hints and satisfied the criteria to earn a fourth—but did not because of the reinforcement strategy—would have seen more hints than another student who only just received his first new hint. If we consider every unique hint that a student had received for an assignment up until the stimuli response, responses to receiving additional hint (M=1.81, sd=1.25) had actually seen fewer hints (p<.0001) than those who earned an additional hint but did not receive one (M=2.30, sd=1.29).

Nevertheless, we should also acknowledge that the presence (or absence) of hints were not the only stimuli received upon submission to Web-CAT. Since Web-CAT is an automated grading system, it also provides indicators of the student's current score, along with some other analysis of their code. While hints appear to play a role in influencing students' immediate behavior, the scores that determine their grades also motivate them considerably [7]. Grade calculation for the programming assignments in our study included students' test coverage, but did not necessitate adherence to an incremental testing process.

6. CONCLUSION

In this study, students received rewards from an adaptive feedback system after exhibiting behaviors conducive to an incremental testing process. Rewards included social acknowledgement via digital "badges" and an encouraging message along with hints that guided students toward fixing flaws in their code. From 3115 submissions to the adaptive feedback system over the duration of an academic term, we analyzed changes in students' code from one submission to their subsequent submission.

We compared changes in test and solution non-comment lines of code (NCLOC), number of test assertions, and test coverage. Statistical analysis suggested that after receiving additional hints as rewards, students responded with significant increases in the amount of test code and coverage. Observations of increases in the amount of test code persisted when considering within-subject comparisons as well as when accounting for time elapsed between submissions and for behaviors exhibited before the previous submission.

Our findings are consistent with operant conditioning techniques of increasing target behavior with positive reinforcement and discouraging undesired behaviors with negative punishment. Meanwhile, lack of either overt reinforcement or punishment often resulted in fewer tests added than either positive reinforcement or negative punishment. Consequently, the study provides evidence for significant differences in short-term responses to rewards offered by adaptive feedback systems. However, despite invoking short-term responses, our

accompanying studies found no impact on long-term behavioral change nor final outcomes of software quality [6][7]. Future work is necessary to build upon the short-term effects of adaptive reinforcement to support the ambitious goal of affecting behavioral change on the complex task of as software development.

7. REFERENCES

[1] ABET (2013). "Criteria for Accrediting Computing Programs, 2013-2014." Retrieved May, 2014, from http://www.abet.org/

[2] Beck, K. (2003). Test-Driven Development by Example, Addison Wesley.

[3] Bhat, T. and N. Nagappan (2006). Evaluating the efficacy of test-driven development: industrial case studies. Proceedings of the 2006 ACM/IEEE international symposium on Empirical software engineering. Rio de Janeiro, Brazil, ACM: 356-363.

[4] Buffardi, K. and S. H. Edwards (2012). Exploring influences on student adherence to test-driven development. Proceedings of the 17th ACM annual conference on Innovation and technology in computer science education. Haifa, Israel, ACM: 105-110.

[5] Buffardi, K. and S. H. Edwards (2012). "Impacts of Teaching Test-Driven Development to Novice Programmers." International Journal of Information and Computer Science 1(6): 9.

[6] Buffardi, K. and S.H. Edwards. (2013) "Impacts of Adaptive Feedback on Teaching Test-Driven Development." Proc. of SIGCSE, Denver, Colorado.

[7] Buffardi, K. and S.H. Edwards. (2014) "A Formative Study of Influences on Student Testing Behaviors." Proc. of SIGCSE, Atlanta, Georgia.

[8] Canfora, G., A. Cimitile, et al. (2006). Evaluating advantages of test driven development: a controlled experiment with professionals. Proceedings of the 2006 ACM/IEEE international symposium on Empirical software engineering. Rio de Janeiro, Brazil, ACM: 364-371.

[9] Edwards, S. H. "Web-CAT." 2013, from https://web-cat.cs.vt.edu.

[10] Edwards, S. H. (2004). "Using software testing to move students from trial-and-error to reflection-in-action." SIGCSE Bull. 36(1): 26-30.

[11] Fraser, S., D. Astels, et al. (2003). Discipline and practices of TDD: (test driven development). Companion of the 18th annual ACM SIGPLAN conference on Object-oriented programming, systems, languages, and applications. Anaheim, CA, USA, ACM: 268-270.

[12] Janzen, D. S. and H. Saiedian (2007). A Leveled Examination of Test-Driven Development Acceptance. Proceedings of the 29th international conference on Software Engineering, IEEE Computer Society: 719-722.

[13] Linehan, C., B. Kirman, et al. (2011). Practical, appropriate, empirically-validated guidelines for designing educational games. Proceedings of the 2011 annual conference on Human factors in computing systems. Vancouver, BC, Canada, ACM.

[14] Melnik, G. and F. Maurer (2005). A cross-program investigation of students' perceptions of agile methods. Proceedings of the 27th international conference on Software engineering. St. Louis, MO, USA, ACM: 481-488.

[15] Pierce, W.D. and C. D. Cheney (2004). Behavior Analysis and Learning. Psychology Press.

[16] Spacco, J. "Marmoset." 2013, from http://marmoset.cs.umd.edu/.

[17] Spacco, J. and W. Pugh (2006). Helping students appreciate test-driven development (TDD). Companion to the 21st ACM SIGPLAN symposium on Object-oriented programming systems, languages, and applications. Portland, Oregon, USA, ACM: 907-913.

Do Student Programmers All Tend to Write the Same Software Tests?

Stephen H. Edwards and Zalia Shams
Department of Computer Science
Virginia Tech
2202 Kraft Drive, Blacksubrg, VA 24060 USA
+1-540-231-5723
{edwards, zalia18}@cs.vt.edu

ABSTRACT

While many educators have added software testing practices to their programming assignments, assessing the effectiveness of student-written tests using statement coverage or branch coverage has limitations. While researchers have begun investigating alternative approaches to assessing student-written tests, this paper reports on an investigation of the quality of student written tests in terms of the number of authentic, human-written defects those tests can detect. An experiment was conducted using 101 programs written for a CS2 data structures assignment where students implemented a queue two ways, using both an array-based and a link-based representation. Students were required to write their own software tests and graded in part on the branch coverage they achieved. Using techniques from prior work, we were able to approximate the number of bugs present in the collection of student solutions, and identify which of these were detected by each student-written test suite. The results indicate that, while students achieved an average branch coverage of 95.4% on their own solutions, their test suites were only able to detect an average of 13.6% of the faults present in the entire program population. Further, there was a high degree of similarity among 90% of the student test suites. Analysis of the suites suggest that students were following naïve, "happy path" testing, writing basic test cases covering mainstream expected behavior rather than writing tests designed to detect hidden bugs. These results suggest that educators should strive to reinforce test design techniques intended to find bugs, rather than simply confirming that features work as expected.

Categories and Subject Descriptors

K.3.2 [**Computers and Education**]: Computer and Information Science Education; D.2.5 [**Software Engineering**]: Testing and Debugging—testing tools.

General Terms

Experimentation, Verification.

Keywords

Software testing, automated assessment, automated grading, mutation testing, programming assignments, test coverage, test quality, happy path.

1. INTRODUCTION

Many educators have been adding software testing to their programming courses since the idea was first proposed over a dozen years ago [8][9]. Test-driven development [3], or at least using xUnit-style unit testing frameworks such as JUnit, are one approach. Automated assessment tools have grown to support assessing how well students test their own code [4].

More recently, however, some education researchers have begun investigating the quality of student-written tests, as well as techniques to evaluate this quality. By test quality—for a single test case, or an entire test suite—we mean its ability to detect bugs or faults in the software under construction. While most grading tools use some form of code coverage metric (e.g., statement coverage or branch coverage) to assess test thoroughness based on how much of the student's program is executed during testing, this metric may overestimate test quality. Aaltonen et al. [1] proposed mutation testing as an alternative metric, while Shams and Edwards investigated its feasibility for classroom use and compared its effectiveness to all-pairs testing [11].

This more recent work on alternative approaches to measuring test quality raises new questions, such as: How good are student-written tests at finding real bugs? And, how much variation is there in the software tests written by students? This paper presents a preliminary investigation of these questions in the context of CS2, in a classroom setting where students have already had almost two semesters of experience writing unit tests for their own code, and where they have been graded on the quality of their tests as measured by a combination of statement coverage and branch coverage. By applying the student-written tests to a large collection of naturally occurring (human-written) bugs, it was possible to determine how many of the bugs were detected by each student's tests. Although one might naively expect students who are independently writing tests to write a wide variety of tests, this small-scale experiment showed the opposite: there was a surprisingly large degree of similarity between the test suites written by different students, in terms of the bugs detected. Furthermore, while all student test suites found some bugs, overall, student-written test suites identified only 13.6% of the bugs under consideration, even though they achieved high branch coverage on their author's solution (95.4%). After analyzing the student-written tests, it appears that students were predominantly practicing *happy path testing*, where they exercised their code under typical-case scenarios without exploring situations likely to reveal bugs.

2. RELATED WORK

Among the automated assessment tools that have been created to process student-written programs, a number have the ability to grade student-written software tests as well—e.g., Web-CAT [3][4], ASSYST [7] and Marmoset [12]. These tools typically use some code coverage metric to measure the quality of student-written tests, such as statement coverage (the percentage of statements executed by the tests), or branch coverage (the percentage of control-flow branches executed). Web-CAT in particular uses a composite coverage metric that counts the number of methods, statements, and branches that have been executed by the student's tests, as a proportion of the total in the code.

Unfortunately, coverage metrics can overestimate test quality. Even if all branches in the solution are executed, some bugs may be invisible for the specific data values used in the tests. Alternatively, if the tests do not fully specify all the behavioral expectations, a bug may be executed but still go undetected. Usually, behavioral expectations in xUnit-style tests are expressed in the form of assertions about the program state that are checked after the code under test is executed—but the programmer may have written too few assertions, or assertions that are weaker than necessary. Finally, coverage metrics only check tests with respect to the code that was written, and do not take into account any code that is missing. When students overlook required behavior or fail to account for specific input cases and so write no code for those situations, code coverage measures do not reflect these omissions.

As a result of these limitations, Aaltonen et al. [1] compared coverage-based assessment against the use of mutation analysis, a stronger test adequacy criterion. Mutation analysis involves systematically injecting artificial defects into a program, then measuring how many of these changes are detected by a test suite. Mutation analysis was created as an artificial analog of the true task of any test suite: finding real bugs. A test suite that can detect a large percentage of the artificially injected defects is more likely to find bugs than a test suite that achieves a similar branch coverage percentage, for example.

Unfortunately, a number of obstacles make it impractical to apply mutation analysis for real-time feedback in the classroom. Shams and Edwards [11] proposed solutions for these obstacles and evaluated mutation analysis against an alternative, all-pairs testing, or running each student's test suite against all other students' solutions. This strategy, originally proposed by Goldwasser [6], is similar in principle to mutation analysis, but uses a pool of authentically occurring bugs (i.e., those written by other students trying to solve the same task) rather than artificially injected faults. Results from this experiment suggest that running students' tests against each other's solutions provides a better indication of the likelihood that a given test suite will find bugs than mutation analysis.

3. METHOD

To investigate the research questions in this paper, we conducted an experiment using student-written solutions and tests from the CS2 course at Virginia Tech in Spring 2011. This experiment focused on one data structures programming assignment where students implemented and tested two separate queue classes: one using an array-based representation and another using a linked chain of nodes. Students were required to provide full iteration support (including `remove()`), as well as proper implementations of `hashCode()`, `equals()`, and `toString()` for both representations.

3.1 Participants

101 students completed the assignment during the semester of the experiment, writing a total of 2155 individual test cases. All student tests were run against an instructor-provided reference solution to weed out tests that were invalid or only applicable to the student's personal design. This left a total of 2,001 individual test cases for analysis.

We chose a single assignment for evaluation for several reasons. First, even on this single assignment, the number of students involved is large enough to be representative of typical classroom results. Second, the complexity of the assignment allows for a wide variety of bugs to be written by students—in fact, every student solution contained at least one defect. Third, the assignment only requires basic testing knowledge common to many classroom situations. Fourth, this one assignment involves compiling and analyzing the results of over 200 thousand test case executions. As the result of using one assignment, the results should still be considered preliminary, however.

3.2 Identifying Student-Written Defects

The goal of this experiment is to evaluate the likelihood that a student-written test suite will discover any given bug, which we can call the suite's *bug-revealing capability*. Unfortunately, measuring this capability directly is both challenging and expensive in general.

Because of the size of the collection of programs, manual debugging and manual defect counting were cost-prohibitive. Instead, following the approach described by Edwards [2], we constructed a proxy for the set of bugs contained in the student programs. All student-written tests were combined into a single large test suite, along with the instructor-written reference tests for the assignment. This "master" test suite was then run against all student programs, collecting all results in a large matrix—one column per student program, and one row per test case. From this matrix, we could identify *equivalent test cases*, where every program that passed one test case also passed the other, and every program that failed one also failed the other. The master test suite could then be reduced by eliminating redundant test cases, keeping only one representative from each equivalent group.

After this reduction, all test cases in the master test suite were behaviorally distinguishable, in the sense that for any pair of test cases, there was at least one program that passed one test case in the pair but failed the other. This does not guarantee that the test suite is *orthogonal*, in the sense that test cases do not overlap or test the same behaviors. However, it does indicate that there is at least one bug that is uniquely detected by each test case. In other words, each test case differs from all others in the specific defect(s) that it detects—the sets of defects detected by any two test cases may overlap, but cannot be identical.

This master test suite is then a proxy for the set of all bugs contained in all of the student-written solutions produced for this assignment. While each individual test case in the suite may not necessarily represent a single defect, it does represent an "equivalence class" of defects, where all bugs in the equivalence class cause the corresponding test case to fail. Further, there may still be some bugs present in one remaining equivalence class—those that cannot be detected by any of the test cases in the master suite. However, for sufficiently large numbers of distinct test cases, and distinct bugs written in solutions, these equivalence classes proxied by each test case grow small, as does the number of bugs that are detected by no test case. Prior work indicates that test cases in a test suite created in this fashion are strongly correlated with the bugs revealed by manual means, justifying the use of this proxy approach [2].

Once the master suite is established, the number of test cases from the master suite that are failed by any given program is a strong estimate of the number of bugs present in the program. The frequency of the (equivalence class of) bug represented by a master suite test case can be determined by how many of the student programs fail that test case. Further, by comparing the tests in any given student-written test suite against the master suite, it is possible to tell which of the (equivalence classes of) bugs it can detect.

4. RESULTS

4.1 Bug-Revealing Capability

The master test suite produced for this experiment contained 112 distinct test cases, where each test case represents one (small) equivalence class of bugs that is uniquely identifiable. Every bug that is detectable by any test case written by any student (or the instructor) is represented in this set. On average, each student program passed 76.8% of the test cases in the master suite, with every student program containing at least one bug. Each student program failed an average of 26 test cases in the master suite. Across the 101 programs evaluated, this produced 2,486 individual faults that could potentially be detected by student-written tests. By using this master suite as a proxy for the observable bugs in the student solutions, it is possible to calculate which bugs are detectable by each individual student's test suite.

Figure 1 depicts all of the test cases in the master suite, arranged in order from easiest (most student programs passing) to hardest (most student programs failing). The test with the lowest failure rate was passed by all student programs but one, while the test with the highest failure rate was failed by 76.2% of student programs. Similarly, Figure 1 also allows one to visualize the frequency of the various bugs (or equivalence classes of bugs) represented by the test cases in the master suite.

By construction, every individual test case in each student test suite must *be equivalent to* one test case in the master suite, in the sense that the two test cases result in exactly the same pass/fail outcome on every program in the experiment. As a result, it is possible to count the total number of unique test cases (or equivalence classes of bugs) in the master suite that are included in a given student's test suite.

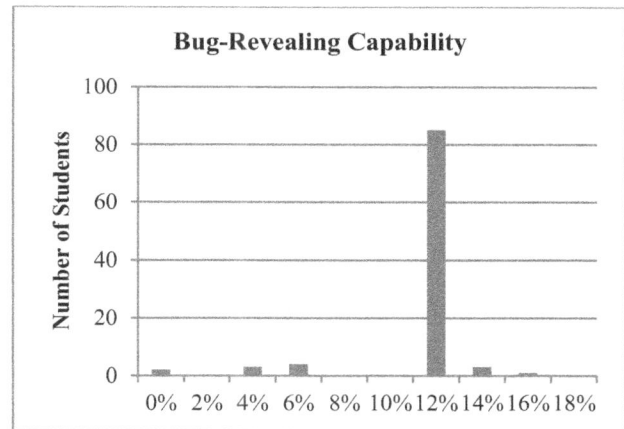

Figure 2: Distribution of test suite bug-revealing capabilities.

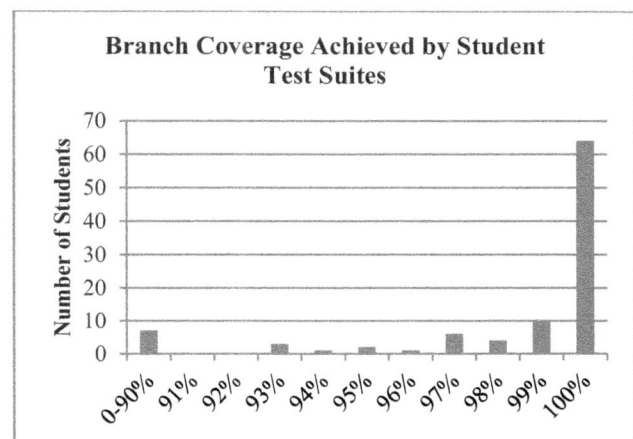

Figure 3: Distribution of branch coverage scores achieved by student-written test suites.

Further, from the master test suite's matrix of results we also know how many student programs failed each master suite test case—that is, how many student programs contained a corresponding bug from that equivalence class. Therefore, we can weight each test case in the master suite by its frequency of occurrence. By computing a weighted average over all master suite test cases that are duplicated within one student-written test suite, we can compute an approximation of the suite's bug-revealing capability—the probability that for any given bug that occurs in any of the student solutions, this suite will detect that bug.

Approximating the bug-revealing capability in this way produces sobering results. As shown in Figure 2, all student-written test suites had less than an 18% chance of detecting any given bug occurring in the population of programs being investigated. In other words, those test suites detected no more than 18% of the 2,486 observable failures across all programs in the experiment. Clearly, the majority of bugs present went undetected by the majority of student test suites. Surprisingly there is also a large spike in the bar representing scores from 12-14%. In fact, 86% of students had the same bug-revealing likelihood: 13.6%.

In comparison, Figure 3 shows the branch coverage scores achieved by the student-written test suites on their author's solution—that is, how many of the control-flow paths in the

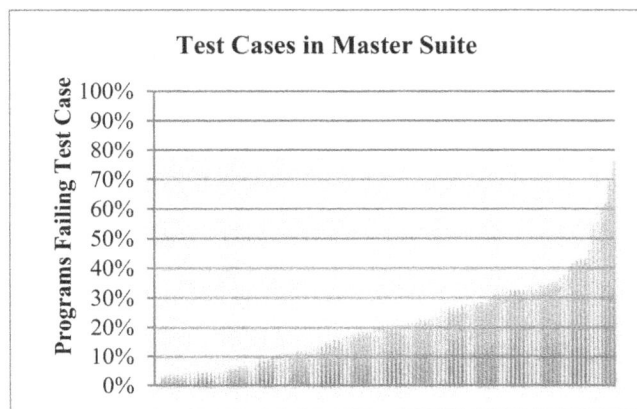

Figure 1: Master suite tests arranged in order of increasing failure rate.

student's code were exercised by the test suite. The average branch coverage was 95.4%, with nearly two-thirds of students (64.6%) achieving perfect 100% coverage of all branches in their solution. Clearly, students were able to write tests that exercised all of the code they wrote, even if these tests were less effective at finding real bugs.

4.2 Variation Among Students

As noted in Section 4.1, the master test suite contained just 112 distinct test cases, indicating a high rate of repetition among student test suites. Worse still, 68 (60.7%) of the final 112 test cases came from the instructor-written reference tests and were not represented in *any* student test suite. Thus, the equivalence classes of bugs represented by these test cases, including 1,338 (53.8%) of the observable failures, could not be detected by any student's test suite in principle. Only 44 (39.3%) of the 112 test cases in the master suite were found in any student-written test suites. This suggests strongly that, while students were writing tests, their test sets were missing a significant proportion of the bugs produced.

If we examine the numbers of test cases written by students, we see a similar pattern. Student test suites ranged in size from 6-23 test cases (s.d. = 3.3), with a mean value of 20 test cases per student. The mode was 21 test cases; 90 students produced test suites with *exactly 21 test cases*. Only one individual wrote more than this (23). It seems surprising that there would be so little variation among the student-written test suites.

Although some educators might at first suspect possible collusion on test case creation, an examination of the student work does not suggest this is the cause for such a high degree of structural similarity. Instead, this similarity appears to arise from the process students follow when writing software tests. At Virginia Tech, students are taught test-driven development during their first programming course. When they write JUnit tests for their assignments, they invariably begin a new test case for each method they write. Often, they end up with a one-to-one correspondence, where every method in their solution corresponds to one test case. While complex methods normally require many distinct tests, this one-to-one correspondence is appropriate for simple code, such as when students are learning in their first semester. While students are instructed to write multiple independent tests for more complex operations, they do not receive automated feedback on this aspect of their development practice. As a result, many students combine multiple scenarios for a single method under test into one test case, even though this leads to poorer test case design.

In the assignment used in this experiment, there were in fact 10 methods that students were required to implement. Further, they implemented these twice, once each for the two separate representations of the queue they had to produce. Figure 4 shows the frequencies of test case names used across all student test suites. Only 17 unique test case names appeared among the 2,001 test cases written by students. The top nine names shown in Figure 4 were used twice by approximately 95 students, typically once for their array-based queue and once for their linked representation. The next three were used once by approximately 94 students; one name refers to a feature that is only relevant for the array-based implementation, one refers to a feature that is only relevant for the linked implementation, and one refers to a feature that many students implemented once and reused in both implementations. These twelve names together (nine used twice) correspond nicely with the large proportion of students who wrote exactly 21 test cases.

Next, we undertook a behavioral analysis of the student-written tests to determine which test cases in the master test suite were most duplicated. Two test cases were extremely common, accounting for 28.2% of all student-written tests. These were the equivalent to the `testSize()` test cases in the master test suite for the array-based (18.8%) and linked (9.4%) queue representations. It is likely that these result from test cases written by students where the students only write assertions capturing their expectations about what happens to the size of the queue, without writing additional assertions to confirm the queue's contents, for example. Unfortunately, while these test cases made up a large proportion of the student-written tests, they were poor at finding bugs. Only 9 out of the 2,486 observable failures were detectable using test cases equivalent to these two.

The most commonly written student tests remaining were roughly

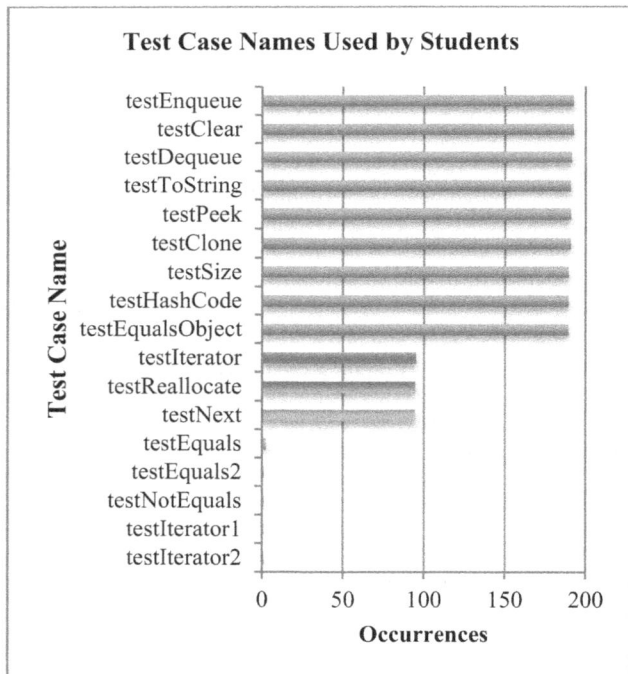

Figure 4: Student test suites use the same names.

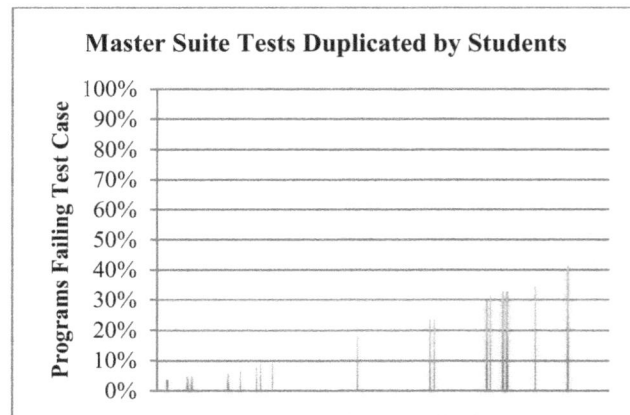

Figure 5: 17 test cases from the master suite accounted for nearly all tests written by students.

evenly distributed among fifteen other master suite test cases, each of which corresponded with the normal or expected-case behavior of one of the methods from the array-based queue implementation or the linked queue implementation. Figure 5 shows where these tests, together with the two `testSize()` tests, fell in the overall range of difficulty represented in the master suite (compare with Figure 1). Taken with the other results presented here, this presents a picture where students systematically write one test case per method, try to cover all of the branches present in that method, and confirm that the method works in the typical case.

Unfortunately, such tests are known to be relatively poor at finding bugs [10]. While professional programmers use strategies such as boundary value analysis, error guessing, and more to attempt to write test cases that have a better chance of finding significant errors, in this instance, there is no real evidence that students are following such strategies. While boundary value analysis and error guessing are explicitly taught to students in class, students are not explicitly graded on whether they practice these strategies and receive little classroom reinforcement. As a result, it appears that most students may not recognize the importance of these techniques.

Anecdotally, software testing professionals who train new software testers have reported to us observing the same pattern when programmers without training write software tests. They write what are colloquially known as *happy path tests*—test cases that exercise the mainstream, expected flow of events, where data is well behaved and errors do not occur.

One plausible explanation for the lack of variation observed among student-written tests is exactly this: that, as beginners, they are writing happy path tests that only check the mainstream conditions in corresponding methods, rather than writing tests that are strategically intended to reveal bugs.

These results clearly contrast from earlier experimental results published by the authors, where all student test suites were run against all student programs [5]. In that case, student test suites did find bugs in many student programs, leading to the conclusion that student test suites were effective at finding bugs. Further research [11] also indicated that running student tests against the code from other students was a more effective way to gauge test quality than using statement coverage or mutation analysis. However, in both of those cases, student test suites were rated based on whether they could find *any* bugs in a given student program. As long as at least one bug was found—no matter how easy or hard—a student program was judged to "fail" that test suite, and the test suite was judged to have detected (at least one) fault in that program. In this paper, however, we aren't just concerned with whether a test suite can find at least one bug—after all, all of the suites measured here were clearly able to find some bugs. Instead, here we are measuring the average probability that a test suite will detect any individual bug (which might be particularly easy to find, or particularly hard, and might occur in many student programs, or just a few). This involves counting which bugs were found and which were not, and then computing a weighted average based on the frequency of each individual bug. As a result, while earlier work found that student test suites do find bugs, the results presented here suggest that, while some bugs are consistently found by all or nearly all test suites, there are a larger proportion that go undetected by most suites entirely. In other words, while student-written test suites may be good at "finding at least one bug" in other student programs, they are much less effective at "finding most of the bugs".

5. SUMMARY AND CONCLUSIONS

Added software testing practices to programming assignments is a solid idea that has growing support. However, for this activity to be reinforced, it is necessary to assess students and give them feedback on how to improve. Existing grading tools largely use code coverage measures, such as statement coverage or branch coverage, to evaluate the strength of student-written tests. Unfortunately, these measures have limitations. Although other researchers are investigating the merits and applicability of alternative assessment strategies, here we have directly investigated the quality of student-written tests in terms of how many naturally occurring bugs those tests can detect.

In the CS2 experiment reported here, we created a master test suite where each unique test case could be used as a proxy for a (small) equivalence class of bugs that exhibited the same behavior. Using this master suite, we estimated the actual number of bugs present in each student solution, and identified which of these were detected by each student-written test suite. Student-written suites detected no more than 18% of the observable failures in the entire population of programs submitted for the assignment, indicating that they were poor at identifying large numbers of commonly occurring faults.

By examining the test suites themselves, a high degree of similarity was observed among the work of many different students, with 90% of student suites sharing major structural similarities. These similarities seemed to stem for the testing strategy used by the students, which was inspired by test-driven development. Students tended to write one test case per method, and to focus on testing the common/expected behavior instead of attempting to identify hidden bugs. Further, in some portion of the tests, students appeared to use simple assertions (testing the size of a queue) rather than more complex state-based assertions, lessening the effectiveness of their test cases. Further analysis of the suites suggest that students were following naïve, "happy path" testing, writing basic test cases covering mainstream expected behavior rather than writing tests designed to detect hidden bugs. These results suggest that educators should strive to reinforce test design techniques intended to find bugs, rather than simply confirming that features work as expected. Further, assessment approaches such as running all students' test suites against all other students' programs [5][6] might be a viable alternative for reinforcing the value of test design in the classroom.

REFERENCES

[1] K. Aaltonen, P. Ihantola, and O. Seppälä. 2010. Mutation analysis vs. code coverage in automated assessment of students' testing skills. In Proc. ACM Int'l Conf. on Object Oriented Prog. Sys. Languages and Applications Companion (SPLASH '10). ACM Press, pp. 153-160.

[2] S.H. Edwards. 2003. Improving student performance by evaluating how well students test their own programs. *Journal on Educational Resources in Computing*, 3(3): Article 1.

[3] S.H. Edwards. 2004. Using software testing to move students from trial-and-error to reflection-in-action. In *Proc. 35th SIGCSE Tech. Symp. Computer Science Education*. ACM Press, pp. 26-30.

[4] S.H. Edwards and M.A. Pérez-Quiñones. 2007. Experiences using test-driven development with an automated grader. *J. Comput. Small Coll.*, 22(3): 44-50. January 2007.

[5] S.H. Edwards, Z. Shams, M. Cogswell, and R.C. Senkbeil. 2012. Running students' software tests against each others' code: New life for an old "gimmick". In *Proc. 43rd ACM Tech. Symp. Computer Science Education.* ACM Press, pp. 221-226.

[6] M.H. Goldwasser. 2002. A gimmick to integrate software testing throughout the curriculum. In *Proc. 33rd SIGCSE Tech. Symp. Computer Science Education.* ACM Press, pp. 271-275.

[7] D. Jackson and M. Usher. 1997. Grading student programs using ASSYST. In *Proc. 28th SIGCSE Tech. Symp. Computer Science Education.* ACM Press, pp. 335-339.

[8] E.L. Jones. 2000. Software testing in the computer science curriculum—a holistic approach. In *Proc. Australasian Computing Education Conf.* ACM Press, pp. 153-157.

[9] E.L. Jones. 2001. Integrating testing into the curriculum—arsenic in small doses. In *Proc. 32nd SIGCSE Tech. Symp. Computer Science Education.* ACM Press, pp. 337-341.

[10] G.J. Myers, C. Sandler, and T. Badgett. 2011. *The Art of Software Testing, 3rd Ed.* Wiley.

[11] Z. Shams and S.H. Edwards. 2013. Toward practical mutation analysis for evaluating the quality of student-written software tests. In *Proc. 9th Ann. Int'l ACM Conf. Int'l Computing Education Research.* ACM Press, pp. 53-58.

[12] J. Spacco and W. Pugh. 2006. Helping students appreciate test-driven development (TDD). In *Companion to the 21st ACM SIGPLAN Symp. Object-oriented Prog. Sys, Languages, and Applications.* ACM Press, pp. 907-913.

QR Code Programming Tasks with Automated Assessment

Lasse Hakulinen
Dept. of Computer Science and Engineering
Aalto University
Espoo, Finland
lasse.hakulinen@aalto.fi

Lauri Malmi
Dept. of Computer Science and Engineering
Aalto University
Espoo, Finland
lauri.malmi@aalto.fi

ABSTRACT

In this paper, we present a novel method to support automated formative assessment of programming tasks. Whereas traditional automated assessment tools mainly apply textual comparison of test program output vs. model output, we present a method that applies graphical output in terms of QR (Quick Response) codes. In our approach, programming tasks are formulated in such a way that the correct output of the task is a QR code. The correctness of the solution can therefore be tested by scanning the QR code. Despite the simple form of the tasks, they can support automated assessment with instant feedback, multiple programming languages, and simple statistics of students' performance. In some cases, feedback about misconceptions can also be given automatically. Moreover, they fit well to game-like learning environments, because the output can be interpreted as an URL which can lead to new clues or puzzles in a game. This is very useful, for example, in alternate reality games.

Categories and Subject Descriptors

K.3.2 [**Computers and Education**]: Computer and Information Science Education—*Computer science education*

Keywords

QR code; Automated assessment; Programming task

1. INTRODUCTION

Testing for program correctness is an important concept in computer science education. Many tools have been developed to automatically test the correctness of programs and they are widely used in programming courses [1, 7]. However, learning programming is not restricted to courses with standard content but can take many forms from board games designed for children[1] to Massive Open Online Courses organized by universities. Therefore, different approaches for

---

[1] http://www.robotturtles.com/

testing the correctness of programming tasks are needed to suit the various ways to learn programming.

Most automated assessment tools test program correctness by comparing program output to teacher's model output in terms of textual comparison methods. Some tools that support functional languages also use direct comparison of list structures. While these are valid approaches, we decided to investigate the feasibility of another type of approach. The popularity of mobile devices and availability of methods for producing data that is easily readable by mobile devices open new possibilities for testing program correctness. Programming assignments can be formulated in such a way that the correctness of the solution can be assessed by scanning and interpreting the output with a camera.

Quick Response (QR) codes are two-dimensional matrix codes that can contain multiple times the amount of data than traditional 1D barcodes [2]. The data is encoded in the black and white pixels of the image and it is designed to be easily recognized using a computer vision. QR codes use Reed-Solomon error correction and therefore it is possible to restore the data even if parts of the code are not visible. The codes are gaining popularity and multiple applications with QR code scanners are freely available.

In our previous work [6], QR codes were used to provide access to puzzles in an educational alternate reality game. The game included puzzles requiring programming and other computer science skills. Some of the puzzles were chained so that the correct solution of a puzzle was a QR code containing a link to the next puzzle – a feature which many participants liked.

In this paper, we present how QR codes can be used in programming tasks to provide automated assessment. Automated assessment methods in programming education and typical use of QR codes are presented in Section 2. In Section 3, we describe a method for formulating programming tasks with QR code based automated assessment and give examples of such tasks. Discussion of the tasks is presented in Section 4 and conclusions in Section 5.

2. RELATED WORK

Automated assessment methods and tools are widely used in programming education to reduce human grading effort, as well as to provide instant feedback for students. Current tools can assess many different aspects of programs automatically. Assessing program correctness is probably the most important function. It is typically carried out by running student's program against teacher-defined test sets, and comparing the program output against the model output.

The model output can be generated dynamically with the aid of a model solution program, or it may be predefined by the teacher. Some string matching methods, like regular expressions, are commonly used in the comparison to handle variation in output formatting. For functional languages, some tools support direct comparison of program output that is presented as a list structure, e.g., [14]. For more information on automated assessment methods, the reader is encouraged to look at surveys by Ala-Mutka [1] and Ihantola et al. [7].

Many tools apply static analysis methods to evaluate and provide feedback on programming style, such as program layout and length of identifiers. Various software metrics can be used to evaluate the length and structural complexity of functions. Moreover, some tools check whether certain requested or forbidden syntactical structures or library functions have been used in the solutions. There are methods for evaluating program design and applied design patterns. Methods have been developed even for identifying whether certain algorithms have been used in the program code [18].

Dynamic analysis can be used to evaluate program efficiency by running the program with different input sizes and measuring the running time. Another dynamic method assesses the level of testing, that is, how well students have tested their programs before submitting them. For example, Web-CAT [4] requires students to submit their own test cases and thus encourages them to test their programs well themselves instead of using the automated assessment tool as a testing tool.

The previous methods focused on analysing program code and execution. Other types of automated assessment methods are being used in the context of simulation tasks. Algorithm simulation denotes a method, where students imitate how an algorithm manipulates a data structure by modifying a graphical presentation of the target data structure [8, 11]. The simulation operations can be logged and compared with the execution of an actual implemented algorithms to provide feedback for the students. The method allows also identifying some possible misconceptions [15]. Visual program simulation [17] is somewhat an analogous method, where students manipulate an abstract representation of program memory and imitate program execution step by step. As above, the simulation log can be analysed to provide feedback. Also some misconceptions can be identified [16].

From our point of view, we are interested in assessing program correctness. Textual comparison methods of program output vs. model output have the disadvantage that often simple formatting errors cause students to lose points. Especially in introductory programming, students may have hard time to see any meaning in such accuracy in the evaluation [9]. Although accuracy in program specification is a lesson to be learned, comparing and evaluating graphical output could be a more natural way to learn it.

2.1 Use of QR Codes

QR codes provide a way to represent data in a small area that is still easily automatically recognized with commodity hardware. It is easy to encode and decode QR codes and therefore they are used in many different contexts. A typical usage of QR codes is in advertising to provide access to additional material, to integrate traditional media with interactive media, and to engage users [3]. However, QR codes are used in educational contexts as well. Walsh [19] presents

an example where QR codes were used in library services to provide context appropriate information in an easily readable form. Hsin-Cheh et al. [10] used QR codes in outdoor education to provide additional material to the students.

New ways to take advantage of QR codes are also being invented. For example, Rouillard [13] introduced contextual QR codes that merge the public QR code with private information to provide data related to a particular context instead of showing the same content to everyone. They describe an example where, instead of generic "Hello World", a user can get a personalized greeting based on his or her private information that is processed during the QR code scan. Another example of creative use of QR codes is to use them to build a voting system where each scanning of QR code is recorded as a casted vote[2].

3. AUTOMATED ASSESSMENT WITH QR CODES

With the rise of smart mobile devices, we were interested in studying simple ways to provide automated assessment by taking advantage of mobile devices and their ability to scan QR codes. More specifically, we were interested in finding out if we can provide automated assessment with minimal infrastructure and still have support for multiple programming languages and misconceptions.

Many algorithmic problems can be converted to tasks that can be tested with a QR code scanner by giving the input as images and stating the problem in terms of manipulating the pixels in the input images. Therefore, the input images of each task must be designed in a way that the correct implementation of the algorithm produces the desired QR code. Testing of program correctness can then be done by scanning the produced image with a QR code scanner. If the scanner recognizes the image as a valid QR code, the message reveals that the task was done correctly.

In this study, we were interested to find out whether programming tasks with QR code based assessment can be formulated to fulfill the following criteria:

1. Automated assessment
2. Instant feedback
3. Programming language independence
4. Support for randomized input
5. Automatic monitoring of students' performance
6. Support for identifying misconceptions

In the following sections, we describe a set of different programming tasks that use QR codes for automated assessment.

3.1 Introductory Tasks

Programming tasks that take images as input and require students to manipulate the pixels of the images can be of many different levels of difficulty. For example, Guzdial [5] used this approach to teach introductory programming. Two example tasks using QR codes that are also suitable for introductory programming education are shown in Figure 1. Figure 1a shows the input for a task where the black and white colors of the pixels should be inversed. In Figure 1b, the rows of the input image should be shifted by N pixels where N is the number of the row. Both tasks result

---

[2]http://www.demoqracy.com/

in the image shown in Figure 1c when solved correctly. The tasks require students to be able to do basic manipulation of pixels and to use control structures such as loops.

(a) Inverse the colors of the pixels
(b) Shift each row by N pixels
(c) Correct output is a valid QR code

Figure 1: Simple programming tasks that produce a QR code as output when solved correctly.

3.2 Stable Sorting

Another example of a programming task with QR code assessment is shown in Figure 2. In the task, the pixels of the input image should be sorted based on the red component of the RGB value. However, only stable sorting algorithms produce the correct answer. The correct solution is an image containing a message encoded in a QR code. In addition, the input image can be made to resemble a custom picture.

(a) Input image
(b) Correct solution

Figure 2: Input and output images of the sorting task.

3.2.1 Producing Input Images

The input image for the task can be created by first assigning the red component of each pixel based on the solution QR code. Each block of pixels of the same color (black/white) should be given the same value of red. Then the pixel is made light or dark based on the correct QR code by assigning the green and blue components (small values for dark and values close to 255 for light). Some randomization can be applied to the green and blue values to enable a more appealing input image. Then, the pixels can be rearranged based on their darkness levels in order to make the input resemble the custom picture. The darkest pixel is positioned in a place of the darkest pixel in the custom picture and all the other pixels are positioned respectively.

To get the assignment to work only with stable algorithms, there must be pixels with same red component value that are not all dark or light. The image produced in the previous step is analyzed and all pixel pairs with adjacent red values that are already in correct order are assigned the same value of the red component.

It is not possible to produce an assignment where the use of an unstable algorithm would guarantee a certain output, because different algorithms handle elements with same key values differently. However, using any stable algorithm to solve this assignment produces the correct output shown in Figure 2b. Output of a solution created with a non-stable Selection sort is shown in Figure 3.

Figure 3: Pixels sorted with an unstable algorithm.

3.3 Boolean Algebra

Programming tasks involving Boolean algebra can naturally be designed so that they produce QR codes as output. Example tasks are shown in Table 1. The programming task consists of a Boolean sentence and input images. The assignment is to implement an algorithm that solves the sentence for each pixel of the input images. If the algorithm is implemented correctly, the image that it produces contains a valid QR code that congratulates for the correct solution. In addition, it is possible to create input images so that predefined misconceptions produce also valid QR codes with different messages. For example, the correct precedence of the first task is: A xor ((B and B) or C). A misconception where the precedence of the operations is ignored and the operations are calculated from left to right is recognized and produces the valid misconception QR code shown in Table 1. The QR code produced with the precedence misconception contains a hint about the mistake, saying: "Check precedences.". All the misconceptions of the example tasks are described in Table 2. Furthermore, by using more input images, it is possible to cover multiple misconceptions in one task.

Table 2: Misconceptions of tasks in Table 1.

id	Misconception description
1	The result of the sentence is calculated from left to right ignoring the precedences of the operators.
2	The functionality of OR and XOR is swapped.
3	Implication is done as b $\Rightarrow$ a instead of a $\Rightarrow$ b.
4	Same as in tasks 1 and 2.

3.3.1 Producing Input Images

Algorithm 1 represents an algorithm that can be used to automatically produce the tasks described before. The input for the algorithm consist of the boolean algebra sentence and the QR code of the correct solution. Optionally, the input can also have 1 to N misconceptions where the misconception sentence and the QR code containing the corresponding message are given to the algorithm.

Table 1: Boolean algebra tasks. Predefined misconceptions produce QR codes with a message addressing the misconception.

Id	Sentence	A	B	C	D	E	Correct	Misconception(s)
1	A xor B and B or C							
2	A xor B or C							
3	A ⇒ B and A xor C							
4	A xor B and B or C ⇒ D or E xor C							

Input: Boolean algebra expression and a QR code
containing the corresponding message for the
correct solution and each misconception
Result: Input images.
for *each pixel position in input images* **do**
    Find all combinations of input pixel colors that
    produce the correct pixel color for the solution
    image and the misconception images respectively;
    if *one or more input combinations exist* **then**
        choose a combination randomly and assign it to
        the input images;
    else
        print:"Unable to formulate task.";
        return *null*;
    end
    return *input images*;
end

Algorithm 1: Algorithm for producing Boolean algebra
programming tasks with a support for misconceptions.

3.4 Image Merging

Figure 4 shows two input images for a programming task
where the assignment is to form a QR code based on the
two pictures. The input images are created from a picture
consisting of black and white pixels (Figure 4c). Image 4a
is created by merging two adjacent pixels that are in the
same row in the original picture. If both of the pixels are
white, the corresponding pixel is white. If both of the pixels
are black, the corresponding pixel is black. If one is black
and one is white, the corresponding pixel is gray. Image 4b
is generated respectively, except taking each pair of pixels
from a column, not a row.

(a) Input 1   (b) Input 2   (c) Correct solution

Figure 4: Image merging task

To solve the assignment correctly, students need programming and problem solving skills. Generating the correct solution is not trivial since some of the information of the
original QR code is lost when creating the two input images. More specifically, when the both input images have
gray pixels, the colors of the corresponding pixels in the solution image are not known. However, the QR codes have
some error tolerance and randomly assigning colors to the
unknown pixels gives a valid QR code in reasonable time
with the input images shown in Figure 4.

3.5 Task Evaluation

In Section 3, we set criteria for the tasks with QR code
based assessment. All of the tasks described in this paper rely on the fact that the correct implementation of the
task produces a valid QR code containing a message stating
that the task was solved correctly. Therefore, all the tasks
have automated assessment of program correctness with the
help of a QR code scanner, and they also provide instant
feedback. Moreover, all the tasks have their input as images
and therefore they can be solved with any programming language.

The content of the output QR code is not fixed and therefore it is possible to formulate different task instances for
each student. For example, having a personalized message in
the solution QR code makes it possible for teachers to create
tasks with different input for each student. Furthermore, the
Stable sorting and the Boolean algebra tasks enable randomized input even if the solution QR codes contain the same
messages, because the input images can be customized for
each student.

Only the Boolean algebra tasks are able to support the
recognition of misconceptions. The input images for the
tasks can be created in such a way that a predefined misconception in the solution produces a valid QR code that
has a message concerning the misconception. As shown in
Table 2, it is also possible to include more than one misconception to a single problem statement. However, covering
more misconceptions requires longer sentences in order to
get more freedom to choose the input images.

It is possible to get basic statistics of students' performance by using URLs instead of plain text messages in the
output QR codes. The number of correct solutions can be
recorded by counting page hits to the corresponding web
page. Performance of individual students can be tracked by
giving each student a task instance with a unique URL.

4. DISCUSSION

There are several tools available for automated assessment of programming tasks. With the wide use of online learning environments and distance learning, there is a need for sophisticated tools that provide verbose feedback and guidance for the students. However, automated assessment can be done also with minimal need for infrastructure or dedicated tools. Many different programming assignments can be formed in such a way that the correct solution produces a valid QR code containing a textual message or a URL.

The example tasks described in this paper all fulfill the criteria 1-5 described in Section 3 to some extent. In addition, the tasks have different characteristics that might have an influence on their suitability in different educational settings. The Image merging task does not demand an implementation of any known algorithm. It requires students to understand the problem and create their own algorithm for it. Furthermore, the fact that some information of the correct solution is lost when producing the input images, requires students to come up with a method to overcome the obstacle. This kind of assignment would not be suitable at the early stages of programming education as the output of the task has missing information. However, it might be better suited as a puzzle where students have to come up with a solution to overcome the problem of missing data.

The Stable sorting assignment requires students to understand the difference between stable and unstable sorting algorithms and to implement a suitable solution. The possibility to use different recognizable input images makes it possible to create unique assignment instances for each student and may increase the appeal of the task.

Boolean algebra tasks are especially well suited for these kind of QR code tasks. The algorithm presented in Section 3 can be used to produce multiple Boolean algebra tasks. It is also possible to give students instant feedback about multiple misconceptions by designing the tasks in such a way that also known incorrect solutions produce valid QR codes.

All of the tasks described in this paper have their input and output as images. That makes it possible to use any programming language to solve the assignments. On the other hand, manipulating image files may bring unnecessary cognitive load for the students especially in the early stages of programming education. One option to overcome the issue is to provide students with base code for manipulating the image files so that they can concentrate on implementing the algorithms.

The use of QR codes for assessment might have some novelty value as such, but they also have other advantages. The solution has to be a valid QR code before the message is revealed. If the output would be plain text, in case of partially correct solution, the message would be more easily recognized and therefore students might be tempted to move to the next assignment without correcting remaining problems. This is an issue recognized by Kolikant and Mussai [9]. They studied students' conceptions of program correctness and found out that students rarely consider programs as incorrect, but instead think them as partially correct if the program fulfills some of the requirements correctly. They also state that the notion of partial correctness (as opposite of absolute *correct* or *incorrect*) is nurtured by the common policy of grading programs by the sum of points awarded for separate aspects of it. QR code based programming tasks enforce the students to improve the solution until they can produce completely correct QR code. As shown in Figure 3, "almost correct" solution produced an output that is not recognized by a QR code scanner. This way, by design, the programming assignment did not allow students to settle for a partially correct solution. Moreover, it is likely that students perceive this inherent accuracy requirement as a natural part of the problem, which is not necessarily the case if the output is in human readable form.

4.1 Purposes of Using QR Code Assessment

Many dedicated tools have been developed for automated assessment that provide more verbose feedback than QR code based tasks. Therefore, we do not suggest replacing automated assessment systems with QR code tasks in cases where it is reasonable to use more sophisticated and advanced tools. However, there are situations where simplistic programming tasks with QR codes could be more useful.

One possible purpose of using QR code programming tasks would be games and puzzle trails. Some of the tasks described in this paper (Simple shift, Stable sorting, and Image merge) were initially used in an alternate reality game (ARG) called *Stop Toilworn Diamond* [6]. The game had multiple puzzles that required skills from different areas of computer science. Some puzzles were formed in such a way that the correct output of a puzzle was a QR code containing a link to the next puzzle. The puzzles formed a path where the next puzzle was not available before the previous was correctly solved. The puzzles involving QR codes were received well by the players and many mentioned them in a positive light in the feedback collected after the game. One particular player commented a puzzle that had a QR code hidden in one of the RGB channels of an image like this: *"Not only was it an original way to hide information (the reward) it has in itself a *squee* reward when I finally got the QR codes to appear."*

One advantage of the QR code based tasks is the simple form of their input. Assignments can be distributed as images and with the tasks that use only few grayscale colors, the input can even be distributed as paper print. If needed, the input can be scanned and put into machine readable form with a reasonable effort. Alternate reality games often distribute puzzles in multiple imaginative ways and hide puzzle clues also in physical places. The ability to have programming puzzles with automated assessment distributed as paper prints would be a good fit for a computer science ARG. Furthermore, one key concept in ARGs is the *This Is Not A Game* (TINAG) aesthetic that emphasizes the fact that the game does not represent itself as a game but strives for a realistic experience [12]. In the light of the TINAG aesthetic, having players to register to an online system handling the assessment of programming puzzles would not be an option.

Beside games, solutions with QR codes that link to another task can be used in different forms of puzzle trails. Furthermore, puzzles with misconception recognition makes it possible to have adaptivity in the puzzle trail. An output produced with a predefined misconception can produce a QR code with a different URL. That link can direct the student to an additional webpage containing an extra task or information regarding the misconception in question.

QR code based assessment of programming tasks offers an option when more advanced tools for automated assessment are not available or suitable for the given purpose. They have advantages that make them especially suited for certain situations, such as alternate reality games. However, further research is needed on the suitability of such assignments in different forms of programming education.

5. CONCLUSIONS

In this paper, we introduced a method for formulating programming tasks that take advantage of QR codes in automated assessment of program correctness. The tasks take input as images and produce a valid QR code as output when solved correctly. The programming tasks were evaluated based on criteria set in Section 3. The tasks were able to provide support for automated assessment with instant feedback, randomized input, multiple programming languages, and monitoring of performance in the form of simple statistics. Furthermore, some of the tasks were also able to support predefined misconceptions and provide a QR code with different content in case a student had a misconception on the topic at hand.

QR code assignments can be used in alternate reality games and puzzle trails to provide automated assessment and distribution of programming puzzles without ruining the realistic setting of the game. Moreover, the ability to recognize misconceptions can be used to form an adaptive net of puzzles where a misconception directs the student to a different task than the correct solution. Finally, even the simple idea of "getting the code right and checking the result with a mobile phone" could have some novelty value for students.

Using QR codes as links to the subsequent tasks can be used to prevent students from stopping to work on an exercise when it is partially correct. The fact that the output has to be exactly correct for the QR code scanner to recognize the code encourages students in a natural way to continue improving the solution until it produces the correct answer.

Future work will focus on evaluating the use of assignments with QR code based assessment in programming education. We will also work on constructing more assignments covering different algorithmic programming tasks.

6. REFERENCES

[1] K. Ala-Mutka. A survey of automated assessment approaches for programming assignments. *Computer Science Education*, 15(2):83–102, 2005.

[2] A. Denso. Qr code essentials, 2011. http://www.nacs.org/LinkClick.aspx?fileticket=D1FpVAvvJuo%3D Accessed 10-January-2014.

[3] X. Dou and H. Li. Creative use of qr codes in consumer communication. *International Journal of Mobile Marketing*, 3(2), 2008.

[4] S. H. Edwards. Rethinking computer science education from a test-first perspective. In *Companion of the 18th annual ACM SIGPLAN conference on Object-oriented programming, systems, languages, and applications, Anaheim, California, USA, 26–30 October*, pages 148–155. ACM, New York, NY, USA, 2003.

[5] M. Guzdial. A media computation course for non-majors. *SIGCSE Bull.*, 35(3):104–108, June 2003.

[6] L. Hakulinen. Alternate reality games for computer science education. In *Proceedings of the 13th Koli Calling International Conference on Computing Education Research*, pages 43–50, New York, NY, USA, 2013. ACM.

[7] P. Ihantola, T. Ahoniemi, V. Karavirta, and O. Seppälä. Review of recent systems for automatic assessment of programming assignments. In *Proceedings of the 10th Koli Calling International Conference on Computing Education Research*, pages 86–93, New York, NY, USA, 2010. ACM.

[8] V. Karavirta and C. A. Shaffer. Jsav: the javascript algorithm visualization library. In *Proceedings of the 18th ACM conference on Innovation and technology in computer science education*, ITiCSE '13, pages 159–164, New York, NY, USA, 2013. ACM.

[9] Y. B.-D. Kolikant and M. Mussai. "so my program doesn't run!" definition, origins, and practical expressions of students' (mis)conceptions of correctness. *Computer Science Education*, 18(2):135–151, 2008.

[10] H.-C. Lai, C.-Y. Chang, L. Wen-Shiane, Y.-L. Fan, and Y.-T. Wu. The implementation of mobile learning in outdoor education: Application of qr codes. *British Journal of Educational Technology*, 44(2):E57–E62, 2013.

[11] L. Malmi, V. Karavirta, A. Korhonen, J. Nikander, O. Seppälä, and P. Silvasti. Visual algorithm simulation exercise system with automatic assessment: TRAKLA2. *Informatics in Education*, 3(2):267–288, 2004.

[12] J. McGonigal. This is not a game: Immersive aesthetics and collective play. In *Melbourne DAC 2003 Streamingworlds Conference Proceedings*. Citeseer, 2003.

[13] J. Rouillard. Contextual qr codes. In *The Third International Multi-Conference on Computing in the Global Information Technology (ICCGI)*, pages 50–55, 2008.

[14] R. Saikkonen, L. Malmi, and A. Korhonen. Fully automatic assessment of programming exercises. In *Proceedings of the 6th Annual SIGCSE/SIGCUE Conference on Innovation and Technology in Computer Science Education, ITiCSE'01*, pages 133–136, Canterbury, UK, 2001. ACM Press, New York.

[15] O. Seppälä, L. Malmi, and A. Korhonen. Observations on student misconceptions – a case study of the build-heap algorithm. *Computer Science Education*, 16(3):241–255, September 2006.

[16] T. Sirkiä and J. Sorva. Exploring programming misconceptions: An analysis of student mistakes in visual program simulation exercises. In *Proceedings of the 12th Koli Calling International Conference on Computing Education Research*, pages 19–28, New York, NY, USA, 2012. ACM.

[17] J. Sorva, J. Lönnberg, and L. Malmi. Students' ways of experiencing visual program simulation. *Computer Science Education*, 23(3):207–238, 2013.

[18] A. Taherkhani and L. Malmi. Beacon- and schema-based method for recognizing algorithms from students' source code. *Journal of Educational Data Mining*, 5(2):69–101, 2013.

[19] A. Walsh. Qr codes–using mobile phones to deliver library instruction and help at the point of need. *Journal of information literacy*, 4(1):55–65, 2010.

Intercultural Computer Science Education

Zoltan Katai
Sapientia University
Târgu-Mureş/Corunca, şoseaua Sighişoarei 1C. Romania.
+40 727 370 346
katai_zoltan@ms.sapientia.ro

ABSTRACT

The issues of Intercultural education (IcE) and Computer Science (CSE) education are of paramount importance in the twenty-first century. In this paper we describe a sweeping initiative to infuse cultural diversity in CSE through art-based pedagogical tools. We present an online e-learning environment that has the potential to equally promote both IcE and CSE. The folkdance choreographies we have created illustrate, on the one hand, basic CS concepts (six different sorting algorithms) and, on the other hand, the cultural diversity of Transylvania (Romania). Our "ALGO-RYTHMICS: science and art without ethnic borders" project also illustrates how the concept of 'unity-in-diversity' can be implemented in a science educational context: multicultural artistic performances promoting the cause of universal science. The study we performed revealed possible difficulties CS teachers may face when they are presenting scientific content in culturally diverse contexts (especially in regions with cultural tension). Research results revealed that students' culture related concepts and feelings may even influence the way they relate to the scientific content.

Categories and Subject Descriptors

K.3.2 [**Computers and Education**]: Computer and Information Science Education – *computer science education*.

Keywords

Computer Science Education; Algorithm Visualizations; Multicultural education; Intercultural education; Art and science; Multisensory education; Multimedia.

1. INTRODUCTION

Different words like 'multicultural' and 'intercultural' have been used to describe the changes that have been happening in modern society. These terms on the one hand describe a society in which different cultures live side by side, and on the other, express the conviction that we all become more enriched by coming into contact with and by experiencing other cultures. Furthermore, people of different cultures can and should be able to cooperate with, and learn from each other [18].

The last few decades have seen considerable efforts on the part of scholars and policy makers to embark on initiatives to acknowledge, accept, and value cultural diversity in place of the accustomed melting pot approach the objectives of which have been to assimilate minorities into the mainstream at the expense of their cultural identities. Cultural diversity has come to be seen as a promoter of tolerance and appreciation of difference [11]. According to a recent report of the Committee on Culture, Science and Education (C-CSE) [6], the Council of Europe Parliamentary Assembly recalls that education shall promote understanding, tolerance and friendship among nations and ethnic groups, and all forms of artistic expression are tools in intercultural education. Undoubtedly, the issues of inter- and multicultural education (IcE, McE) are of paramount importance in the twenty-first century [2].

Computer Science (CS) and Computer Science Education (CSE) are two key players in our modern society, often characterized as the Digital Era or Information Age. Computers play an increasing role in all fields of science. Computer programming skills constitute one of the core competencies that graduates from many disciplines are expected to possess [15].

Combining IcE with CSE is a challenging initiative, but arts could be a viable common denominator in this sense. With respect to the role of arts in IcE the C-CSE report states that music, art and dance can be effective tools in intercultural education [6]. On the other hand, for example, arts (dance, music, rhythm, theatrical role-playing) can promote such a multisensory learning environment that has potential to contribute to more effective CSE [14]. Recent research [20] has demonstrated that the human brain learns and operates optimally in environments in which information is integrated across multiple sensory modalities. Stevens and Goldberg [22] conclude that our brains desire multi-sensory input and that learning engages the whole body. Staley [21] emphasizes that senses not only reach our feelings, emotions and aesthetic sense, but our intellect as well.

According to [14], science combined with art could be a winning combination in educational contexts because: (1) it contributes to a balanced involvement of both sides (academic/artistic) of the brain in the classroom that could significantly improve the teaching-learning process; (2) it promotes various ways of learning that also enhance the educational process [12,13]. In recent years several papers have described works that combine science education with art. These initiatives can be categorized as follows: (1) professional art performances that use science as a thematic element (art dominates science) [1,4,17,23,25]; (2) professional art productions that illustrate abstract scientific models and phenomena (balanced presence of art and science)

[10,19]; (3) art-based methods for science education (science dominate art) [5,7,16,24]. The advantage of initiative (2) (the balanced presence of art and science) is that it can be exploited from both a scientific and artistic perspective.

In this paper we describe a sweeping initiative to infuse cultural diversity in CS education through art-based pedagogical tools. We proposed to design an online e-learning environment that has the potential to equally promote both IcE and CSE. The folkdance choreographies we created (in cooperation with a professional folk-dance institution) illustrate, on the one hand, basic CS concepts (six different sorting algorithms) and, on the other hand, the cultural diversity of Transylvania (Romania). Our "ALGO-RYTHMICS: science and art without ethnic borders" project also illustrates how the concept of 'unity-in-diversity' can be implemented in a science educational context: (1) multicultural artistic performances to promote the cause of universal science; (2) scientific content in an artistic framework.

From our previous research, we believe this initiative - with respect to Intercultural Computer Science Education (IcCSE) - is a pioneering project idea. Current literature lacks studies that address CSE from the perspective of IcE. In this study we propose to investigate whether students' ethnic background might influence (or perturb) their approach to the scientific content in terms of the cultural frame (context) in which it is presented.

2. METHOD

We designed our study taking into account that (according to the literature in this field) in order to be effective, science education must consider the cultural context of the society which provides its setting, and whose needs it exists to serve [26]. This is especially true for intercultural science education and also for IcCSE.

Transylvania is a pronouncedly multicultural part of Romania with several ethnic groups having coexisted in this region for centuries (Romanian, Hungarian, German, Gipsy, etc). The most important minority is the Hungarian one, and since (during its controversial history) Transylvania was often the scene of Romanian-Hungarian political tensions, this article refers to these two cultures as "opposite ones".

Educational institutions can be classified as mono-, bi- or multicultural ones. Promoting ICE in such a specific school environment, and in a neighborhood with similarly diverse cultural characteristics, may imply particular challenges to be taken in to account. Accordingly, the high schools selected for involvement in the experiment were: Schools_1 (Romanian mono-cultural institutions), Schools_2 (Hungarian mono-cultural institutions) and School_3 (bi-cultural institution with both Romanian and Hungarian educational programmes).

Our core research question was: How might the existing cultural concepts held by students (from mono- and bi-cultural institutions) affect their appreciation of sorting algorithms presented in a cultural context different to their own?

Romanian, Hungarian, German and Gipsy folk-dance choreographies were designed to illustrate six sorting algorithms. The number-sequence was represented by a corresponding dancer-sequence (dancers wore the corresponding number on their clothing). According to the specific characteristics of the selected algorithms, the dance choreographies included the following basic elements:

- Swapping two elements (all algorithms)

- Comparing two elements (all algorithms)

- Dividing the current sequence into two sub-sequences (quick-sort and merge-sort)

- Merging two neighbour sub-sequences (merge-sort)

The algorithm-dance associations were established by taking into account their common defining characteristics (insert-sort: with Romanian folk-dance, shell-sort: with Hungarian folk-dance, merge-sort: with German folk-dance, select-sort: with Gipsy folk-dance, bubble-sort: with "Csángó" folk-dance, quick-sort: with "Székely" folk-dance):

- Proper dance-steps were chosen for all key-operations of the algorithms.

- Each choreography has a dynamic intro simulating the mixing process of the numbers and ends with a vivid finale emphasizing the ordered character of the sequence. The central parts of the choreographies closely follow the corresponding sorting strategies.

- To increase the didactical impact of the sorting-dances, graphical elements (applied to the video-recordings) emphasize that number-sequence is stored in an array.

The balanced art-science collaboration was maintained by: (1) The choreographer promoting the artistic value of the dance-performances; (2) The CS teacher ensuring the clarity of the scientific message.

The e-learning environment we have developed (http://algo-rythmics.ms.sapientia.ro/) also incorporates algorithm animation and an automatic assessment system that allows students to learn from and correct errors in real time.

2.1 Participants

Ninety-six 9th grade novice computer science students participated in the experiment from three secondary education institutions: School_1 (31 Romanian students, group monoRO), School_2 (21 Hungarian students, group monoHU) School_3 (18 Romanian students, group biRO; 26 Hungarian students, group biHU). We performed the experiment after students had been introduced to programming, but before they had studied sorting algorithms. The concept of algorithm complexity (efficiency) was also introduced with respect to sorting algorithms. The age of the students was around 15 to 16 years. The percentage of female students was 27%.

2.2 Procedure

The experiment was conducted in computer labs where all students had individual access to the online e-learning tool. Before commencing the e-learning session, students were briefly introduced to, or reminded of, the concepts of algorithms and sorting algorithms. In addition, a brief overview of the e-learning session was presented to them. The students were asked to utilise a 7-point scale: (ranging from *strongly disagree … strongly agree*) and invited:

• to watch Selection-sort with GIPSY folk-dance; (see Figure 1)

• (item 1a) to respond to the sentence: "I liked this algorithm-dance show" (1: Strongly disagree … 7: Strongly agree);

• to watch Insertion-sort with ROMANIAN (region Bihor) folk-dance; (see Figure 2)

• (item 1b) to respond to the sentence: "I liked this algorithm-dance show" (1: Strongly disagree … 7: Strongly agree);

• to watch Bubble-sort with HUNGARIAN ("Gyimesi csángó") folk-dance; (see Figure 3)

• (item 1c) to respond to the sentence: "I liked this algorithm-dance show" (1: Strongly disagree … 7: Strongly agree);

• (item 2a) to answer the question: "Which algorithm performed the sorting-task most efficiently? GIPSY / ROMANIAN / HUNGARIAN";

• (item 2b) to answer the question: "Which algorithm performed the sorting-task most efficiently? BUBBLE-sort / SELECTION-sort / INSERTION-sort";

• (item 3) to choose the algorithm they found easiest to understand: "Selection-sort with GIPSY folk-dance / Insertion-sort with ROMANIAN folk-dance / Bubble-sort with HUNGARIAN folk-dance";

• to watch a bubble-sort algorithm animated on a white-box array (the numbers being visible); *all* students faced the bubble-sort algorithm, but without being informed of this fact; comparison / swapping of two elements was animated by proportionally-expanding / interchanging the corresponding boxes; a pair of arrows directed the user's attention to the elements the current operation was applied to; elements that had reached their final positions in the sorted sequence were re-colored) (see Figure 4);

• to orchestrate the bubble-sort algorithm on a randomly generated sequence stored in a white-box array; (at each step students had to choose the next operation to be executed and the elements the selected operation were to be applied to; the software informed them of the type of error they made (wrong parameters/operation) and they had the opportunity to correct their choice. We also provided them with help-buttons that informed them of the next operation to be performed);

• to orchestrate the algorithm on a randomly generated sequence stored in a black-box array (being informed about the results of the comparison operations); (see Figure 5)

Figure 1. Selection-sort with Gipsy folk-dance.

Figure 2. Insertion-sort with Romanian folk-dance.

Figure 3. Selection-sort with Hungarian folk-dance.

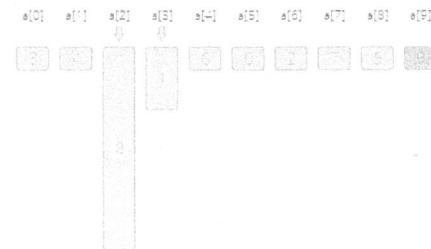

Figure 4. Animating Bubble-sort algorithm on a white-array.

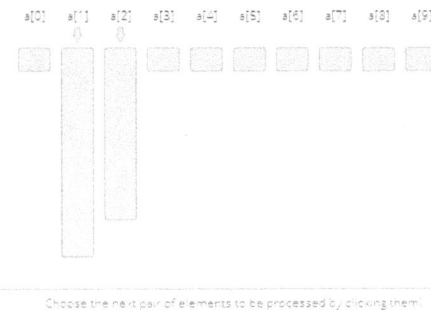

Figure 5. Orchestrating Bubble-sort algorithm on a black-array.

3. RESULTS AND DISCUSSION

Table 1 presents the means of students' response scores with respect to the three algorithm-dance shows. It can be seen that both Romanian (RO = monoRO + biRO) and Hungarian (HU = monoHU + biHU) students responded most favourably to the performance that represented their own culture. They showed the following preferences:

- Romanian students: 1) RO, 2) Gipsy, 3) HU;

- Hungarian students: 1) HU, 2) Gipsy, 3) RO;

Table 1. Response scores with respect to the algorithm-dance shows.

	Gipsy	Romanian	Hungarian
RO	5,24	5,65	5,16
HU	5,45	5,40	5,96
monoRO	5,23	5,55	5,58
monoHU	5,10	5,43	5,43
biRO	5,28	5,83	4,44
biHU	5,73	5,38	6,38

Comparing students' response scores with respect to their own and to the opposite culture (paired samples t-test), we found that Romanian (RO) students yielded a value of $p=0.09$ (not significant) and Hungarian (HU) students: $p=0.009$ (significant). No significant differences were detected between Romanian and Hungarian students' response to the Gipsy-dance performance.

Analyzing students' scores at group level, we observed that in the bi-cultural institution (School_3) both Romanian and Hungarian classes appreciated the performance that represented their own culture significantly more than the opposite one (biRO: $p=0.04$; biHU: $p=0.0003$). In the case of mono-cultural institutions we detected equality (School_2) or even a better (School_1) appreciation (not significantly) of the opposite culture.

More important are the results regarding algorithm efficiency when algorithms were identified by the corresponding culture (item 2a). We coded the students' choices as follow:

- 1: if they chose their "own folk-dance choreography" as the most efficient one;

- -1: if they chose the "opposite folk-dance choreography" as the most efficient one;

- 0: if they chose the "neutral folk-dance choreography" (Gipsy) as the most efficient one;

Again, while in the case of groups monoRO and monoHU the means were equal to zero (0: 11(own), 11(opposite), 9(neutral)) or near to zero (-0.04: 9(own), 10(opposite), 2(neutral)), these average values for the groups from the bi-cultural institution were 0.72 (biRO; 14(own), 1(opposite), 3(neutral)) and 0.42 (biHU; 16(own), 5(opposite), 5(neutral)). In the bi-cultural institution (School_3) significantly more students chose the algorithm that was presented in their own cultural context as "the best one", than in the mono-cultural ones (School_1 + School_2) ($p=0.006$; chi-

square test). At group level we observed the following results: 0.01 (monoRO–biRO), 0.1 (monoHU–biHU).

A comparative analysis of the answers to items 2a, 2b also revealed that students from School_3 were "too much focused" on the cultural aspects. In the case of groups biRO and biHU only 44.44% and 38.46% of members, respectively, chose the same algorithm when these were identified by culture/strategy (items 2a/2b). These percentages for the monoRO and monoHU groups were 64.52 and 61.9, respectively. By applying independent sample t-test we observed p values near to the limit of significance: 0.089 (biRO–monoRO), 0.057 (biHU–monoHU).

Applying the same (1,-1,0) coding to students' responses to item3, we observed quite similar results to those of item 2a:

- means near to zero for groups monoRO (-0.09: 11(own), 14(opposite), 6(neutral)) and monoHU (-0.04: 7(own), 8(opposite), 6(neutral));

- positive means for groups biRO (0.61: 12(own), 1(opposite), 5(neutral)) and biHU (0.19: 12(own), 7(opposite), 7(neutral));

- significant p value when we compared biRO+biHU with monoRO+monoHU (0.03).

- at group level: 0.01 (monoRO–biRO), 0.62 (monoHU–biHU).

A limitation of this study is that the students could be misled by the lengths of the video recordings (see Table 2).

Table 2. Some data about the operation sequences and the video recordings.

	Elementary operations (Comparing + Swapping)	Lengths of the whole dance performances (sec)	Lengths of the sorting processes (sec)
Insertion sort	37 (23+17)	4.04	2.25
Bubble sort	39 (26+13)	5.15	3.00
Selection sort	59 (45+14)	7.06	6.20

Comparing students' performance results (number of errors and help requests) with respect to their white- and black-box task (mono-bi; monoRO-biRO; monoHU-biHU; boys-girls) we did not find any significant differences.

4. CONCLUSIONS AND FUTURE WORK

Interestingly, Filpisan, Tomuletiu, Gyorgy and Moldovan [9] conducted a parallel research (independently) in a related topic in the same town from Transylvania, Romania. They implemented an intercultural educational project, addressing teenagers only in School_1 and School_2 (Lessons with intercultural concepts as the topic; Workshops on the subjects of: defining interculturality, culture profiles of Romanians and Hungarians, prejudices and discrimination). 100 ninth grade (four classes) Romanian and 100 ninth grade (four classes) Hungarian students were involved in the experiment. One of the purposes of the project was to give a "wake-up call" to teachers regarding the importance of "educating for interculturality". The authors conclude that one of the educational goals of Transylvanian educational institutions should be to prepare students as citizens of an extended multicultural society, such as the European Union or our globalized multicultural world. Our conclusions harmonize with this "wake-up call" too.

In this paper we have presented an online e-learning environment that is built on three central concepts of modern education: intercultural, multisensory and interdisciplinary education. As mentioned above, the software-tool we designed has the potential to equally promote both IcE and CSE. One of the key factors in this sense is the balanced art-science combination: a clear scientific message communicated through professional artistic performance.

The study we performed revealed possible difficulties CS teachers may face when they are presenting scientific content in culturally diverse contexts (especially in regions of cultural tension). Research results reveal that students' culture related concepts and feelings may even influence the way they relate to the scientific content. While we expected that students' responses would show higher appreciation of their own culture related dance-performance, it was surprising to notice that in the bi-cultural institution they made a similar choice regarding the most efficient algorithm.

Bennett distinguishes between ethnocentrism and ethnorelativism. Ethnocentric people do not have internalized perspectives emanating from other cultures and tend to value their own culture above everything else. Their early training in the home (and sometimes in the school) creates the habits of mind that characterise them. Conversely, ethnorelative people appreciate cultural perspectives other than their own, and recognize that particular cultures can only be understood within a cultural context [3].

According to our findings the bi-cultural character of an educational institution does not promote ethnorelativism implicitly. What is more, it can polarize differences. On the other hand, the mono-cultural character of an educational institution does not promote ethnocentrism implicitly either. Bennett describes a six-stage process that moves someone from ethnocentrism to ethnorelativism. Carefully designed IcCSE could have potential to become a promoter of this process.

Other topics that might be amenable to this approach:

- searching algorithms (linear/binary);

- parallel algorithms (for example: parallel merge/quick-sort);

- bicultural merge-sort (the two first level sub-sequences are personified by dancers from different cultures);

- sample algorithms that illustrate programming strategies like: greedy, backtracking, dynamic programming, etc.

We are planning to exploit the potential that lies in the e-learning environment that we have designed, to work out an effective intercultural CS teaching-learning-assessing strategy.

5. ACKNOWLEDGMENTS

The author wishes to acknowledge the help of Tóth László in developing the software-tool, and the support of Ignát Anna, Kondert Enikő, Osztián Erika and Kovács Barna in implementing the experiment. The author would like to thank Füzesi Albert, the choreographer of the Professional Art Institute "Muresul", for his artistic support.

6. REFERENCES

[1] M. Baldwin and R. Rivers. Dancing to the ideas of Einstein. *Physics World*, 18(5):16–17, May 2005.

[2] J. A. Banks and C. A. M. Banks. *Multicultural Education: Issues and Perspectives (4th ed.)*. John Wiley & Sons, New York, 2001.

[3] M. Bennett. Towards ethnorelativism: A developmental model of intercultural sensitivity. In: R. Paige (Ed.), *Education for the intercultural experience*, pages 27–71. Intercultural Press, Yarmouth, ME, 1993.

[4] J. Burg and K. Lüttringhaus. Entertaining with science, educating with dance. *Computers in Entertainment*, 4(2), April-June 2006.

[5] D. Chavey. Songs and the analysis of algorithms. In *27th SIGCSE Conference Proceedings*, pages 4–8. ACM, New York, June 1996.

[6] Council of Europe: Committee on Culture, Science and Education. *Cultural education: the promotion of cultural knowledge, creativity and intercultural understanding through education*. http://assembly.coe.int, 2009. [Online; accessed January 3, 2014].

[7] Eisenhower SCIMAST. The rhythm of mathematics. *Classroom Compass*, 4(2):1–8, Fall 1998.

[8] European Commission, Education, Audiovisual and Culture Executive Agency. *Arts and Cultural Education at School in Europe*. EACEA P9 Eurydice, http://eacea.ec.europa.eu, 2009. [Online; accessed January 3, 2014].

[9] M. Filpisan, A. E. Tomuletiu, M. Gyorgy, and T. Moldovan. Practical guide of intercultural education. *Procedia - Social and Behavioral Sciences*, 46:5523–5528, February 2012.

[10] P. A. Fishwick, S. Diehl, J. Prophet, and J. Lowgren. Perspectives in aesthetic computing. *Leonardo*, 38(2):133–141, April 2005.

[11] L. Galis. Merely academic diversity. *Journal of Higher Education*, 64(1):93–101, January-February 1993.

[12] H. Gardner. *Frames of mind*. Basic Books, New York, 1993.

[13] H. Gardner. *Intelligence reframed. Multiple intelligences for the 21st century*. Basic Books, New York, 2000.

[14] Z. Kátai and L. Toth. Technologically and artistically enhanced multi-sensory computer programming education.

Teaching and teacher education, 26(2):244–251, February 2010.

[15] K. M. Y. Law, V. C. S. Lee, and Y. T. Yu. Learning motivation in e-learning facilitated computer programming courses. *Computers & Education*, 55(1):218–228, August 2010.

[16] L. Moelwyn-Hughes. Dancing the words. *Animated: The community dance magazine*, Autumn 2003.

[17] S. Mtangi. Liz Lerman Exchange connects science and dance. *The Wesleyan Argus*, CXLI(26), February 2006.

[18] National Council for Curriculum and Assessment. *Intercultural Education in Primary Schools*. http://ncca.ie, 2005. [Online; accessed January 3, 2014].

[19] K. Schaffer, E. Stern, and S. Kim. *Math dance with Dr. Schaffer and Mr. Stern: Preliminary edition*. MovespeakSpin, Santa Cruz, CA, 2001.

[20] L. Shams and A. R. Seitz. Benefits of multisensory learning. *Trends in Cognitive Sciences*, 12(11):411–417, November 2008.

[21] J. D. Staley. Imagining the multisensory classroom. *Campus Technology*, June 2006.

[22] J. Stevens and D. Goldberg. *For the learners' sake: A practical guide to transform your classroom and school*. Zephyr Press, Tucson, AZ, 2001.

[23] New Zealand Institute of Mathematics & its Applications. *The dance of mathematics*. http://www.mathsreach.org, 2006. [Online; accessed January 3, 2014].

[24] H. Ward, C. Hewlett, J. Roden, and J. Foreman. *Teaching science in the primary classroom: A practical guide*. SAGE Publications Ltd, London, 2005.

[25] R. Wechsler. Computers and art: a dancer's perspective. *IEEE Technology and Society Magazine*, 16(3):7–14, Fall 1997.

[26] B. Wilson. The cultural contexts of science and mathematics education: Preparation of a bibliographic guide. *Studies in Science Education*, 8(1):27–44, 1981.

Course Development through Student-Faculty Collaboration: A Case Study

Dilan Ustek
Grinnell College
1115 Eighth Avenue
Grinnell, Iowa 50112 USA
+1 641-269-4208
ustekdil@grinnell.edu

Erik Opavsky
Grinnell College
1115 Eighth Avenue
Grinnell, Iowa 50112 USA
+1 641-269-4208
opavskye@grinnell.edu

Henry M. Walker
Grinnell College
Noyce Science Center
Grinnell, Iowa 50112 USA
+1 641-269-4208
walker@cs.grinell.edu

David Cowden
Inkling
153 Kesrney St.,Suite 400
San Francisco, CA USA
+1 415-975-4420
cowden@inkling.com

ABSTRACT

Traditionally, faculty plan and implement courses with students as the target audience, based upon educational goals and objectives. With today's interest in active learning, faculty try to anticipate activities that will resonate with students. This paper presents a different model that utilizes faculty-student collaboration for course development – in this case, creating an introductory C-based course on imperative problem solving with robots as an application theme.

Basing development on course goals and objectives, a faculty member works with a development team of undergraduate students to structure course content, prepare materials (e.g., readings, laboratory exercises, projects), and test each element of the course. In subsequent semesters, students taking the course provide feedback on all materials, the development team updates materials, and the refinement process iterates. The resulting course meets goals and objectives, provides wonderful motivation, and highlights creativity and intellectual challenge within computer science as well as syntax, semantics, and core technical skills.

This paper builds upon a previous report (SIGCSE 2013 Proceedings, pp. 27-32), by highlighting the course development process and providing data that assess course effectiveness. The resulting course has been identified as an "exemplar" by CS Curricula 2013 (pp. 454-455, 458-459), providing a strong second course in a three-course, multi-paradigm introductory sequence that emphasizes a lab-based approach with collaborative learning. Course materials at co-author Walker's home page.

Categories and Subject Descriptors

K.3.2 [**Computer and Education**]: Computer and Information Science Education – *computer science education, curriculum*

General Terms

Design, Experimentation, Languages.

Keywords

Robots, course materials, lab-based course, collaborative learning, modules

1. INTRODUCTION

This paper builds upon a previous report involving the use of robots within a lab-based context in order to teach an introductory CS2 course. In a previous paper [3], we detailed the technical process of preparing the robots and the development of a new curriculum for a CS2 course at Grinnell College⌐ . This paper begins by outlining relevant background for this course development. Section 2 then describes in some detail the novel faculty-student collaboration that allowed course development to proceed efficiently, and Section 3 presents results about the course thus far regarding our observations, test results, and student feedback. This information suggests that the method by which we added robotics to our introductory course resulted in an overall positive experience with no negative effects on students' performance, while positively affecting students' motivation. Finally, we detail possible next steps, conclusions, and acknowledgments.

1.1 Background

The project described in this paper, the development of a C-based and laboratory-intensive CS 2 course using robots, represents the integration of several on-going themes at Grinnell College and the wider computing community.

- *Multi-paradigm approach for introductory CS:* Since Spring 1997, introductory computer science at Grinnell College has followed a multi-paradigm approach: CS 1 introduces functional problem solving, supported by Scheme; CS 2 explores imperative problem solving and data structures, supported by C; and a third course studies object-oriented problem solving and algorithms, supported by Java. This type of breadth-first approach has been widely discussed, such as in [12].

- *Lab-based pedagogy:* Since Fall 1992, co-author Walker has followed a lab-based approach in introductory computer science courses. In the form used here, sometimes called a modified

- "inverted" or "flipped" classroom, a lecture during one class session might be followed by 2 or more lab sessions (e.g., in-class work might involve 30-35 labs during a semester). Details of this approach may be found in [18, 19].

- *Use of robots in introductory computing courses:* Many computing faculty have identified application themes for introductory courses. For example, Misra, Blank, and Kumar [14] and Heines, Greher, Ruthmann, and Reilly [7] have used music as a theme for learning computer science concepts. Summet [17] has described the use of robots with personal PC, and Kumar has written textbooks [10] (Python) and [11] (C++) to support Scribbler 2 robots in CS 1.

- *Experience with student-faculty collaborations:* For many years, Grinnell College has actively supported student-faculty collaborations. In a typical summer, 80-120 undergraduates may receive stipends and academic credits for on-campus independent projects related to faculty scholarship, and these collaborations may lead to posters, conference presentations, published papers, etc.

Within Grinnell's introductory sequence, CS 1 has utilized media scripting since the mid 2000s, resulting in increased enrollments attracting an increasingly diverse student population. Building upon this success, a natural next step was to consider robots as a possible application theme for CS 2. However, any revised course needed to fit within the existing curricular structure, and this raised several important constraints on a new or revised course:

- The course needed to focus upon imperative problem solving, data structures, data representation, and low-level memory allocation, based in C (not C++).

- The course had to cover the topics of the existing course (removing topic coverage would impact later courses).

- The course should be lab based (that format for active learning has been extremely successful for many years).

- The course should utilize robots whenever possible (as a means to maintain student motivation and interest).

With these constraints, course development faced several obstacles.

- With the need to focus on imperative problem solving, students likely would not have time to assemble robots from a kit. Thus, the robots needed to come fully assembled, and this led to the decision to utilize Scribbler 2 robots for this project. Details of the robot may be found at http://www.parallax.com/product/28136[16].

- Interfaces, software, and textbook support was available for the Scribbler 2 robots in both Python [10] and C++ [11], but no software library was directly available for Standard C.

- The use of Scribbler 2 robots could not be a simple add-on. During early experimentation with the Scribbler 2 robots, it became apparent that the introduction of robots into the coursework required a full-fledged re-thinking and re-writing of the entire curriculum to successfully combine the use of robots with laboratory readings, examples, exercises, and supporting examples.

Overall, the hope was to introduce robots as an application theme in CS 2, while maintaining the course's role within a multi-paradigm sequence and utilized a lab-based pedagogy.

1.2 Lab-based Pedagogy

At Grinnell College, introductory computer science courses have followed a lab-based format for about 20 years. The basic premise, now widely accepted among educators, is that lecture-based courses are not very effective. In contrast, a lab-based pedagogy encouraging pair programming actively engages students throughout a course.

Many studies indicate lecture format is largely ineffective. For example, see [2, 5, 13].

As an alternative to lecture, many science courses at Grinnell College have integrated lecture and lab into what is often called a "workshop" approach. For example, through the late 1980s and early 1990s, Grinnell mathematician, Eugene Herman, developed a lab-based approach for linear algebra, leading to complete a textbook and on-line laboratory exercises [6]. In Fall 1992, co-author Walker reorganized Grinnell's existing introductory course (then offered using Pascal) to this workshop style [18]. When the curriculum changed to a multi-paradigm approach. Stone and Walker rewrote CS1 to integrate functional problem solving and Scheme. Over the years, the same approach has been applied to introductory biology, physics, and psychology. In contemporary discussions of pedagogy, this approach is sometimes identified as a type of "inverted" or "flipped" classroom.

Students are expected to come to class prepared (e.g., having done the reading and composed any questions they might have). At the start of class, professors may address questions or anticipate common student difficulties, but too much lecture discourages students from coming to class prepared. For the remainder of the class period, students are divided into groups of two or three to work on a lab that asks for practical application of the concepts the students went over, building on previous labs to ensure organic growth of understanding. If the students run into trouble, either with being unable to fully grasp a concept and apply it or tracking down a persistent error in the code, students ask for help.

By expecting students to come to class familiar with the material, professors minimize time spent lecturing, and maximize time students are working on practical application of and engagement with the material. If a student or group of students runs into problems understanding a concept, someone is available to help them understand the material, paving the way for future success in the course. By conducting the entire course in this fashion, students are constantly engaged in using the material they are learning, and the instructor has a clear gauge of how the class is progressing both individually and as a group, allowing a quick response if many students seem to be having trouble with one of the concepts.

1.3 Educational Goals and Objectives

The development of a new CS 2 course using robots was guided by four high-level goals:

1. Cover the full range of topics on imperative problem solving, data structures, data representation, and C programming found in prior CS 2 courses.

2. Utilize robots in a meaningful way.

3. Boost interest in introductory computer science courses and encourage students to consider computer science as a major.

4. Increase excitement, motivation, and fun as part of the learning process.

The first goal was simple, clear, and key: convey the information presented in prior CS 2 courses in a new CS 2 course integrated with robots. The multiparadigm approach in Grinnell's curriculum involves an imperative problem solving course for CS2, taught using C. The topics covered in prior CS 2 courses included programming in C (functions and parameters, compiling, structures, syntax, semantics, et al.), usage of the Linux operating system (commands, bash scripts, and software development tools), imperative problem solving (assertions, invariants, top-down design, and common algorithms), data types (integers, floating point numbers, characters, strings), data structures (arrays, structs, linked lists, stacks, queues), data abstraction, and machine-level issues (data representation, pointers, and memory management). At the end of the semester, students should be able to perform basic system tasks using the terminal command line (e.g. move between file directories, create and open files, compile and run C programs), conceptualize solutions to problems using imperative methods of problem solving (e.g. be familiar with and able to explain common algorithms), write programs to implement data structures such as stacks and their attendant functions, identify the differences between data types such as integers, floating point numbers, and strings (as well as when to use each appropriately), and understand and use pointers in programs they write.

The second goal, and the primary motivation for a newly designed course, was the incorporation of robots in a meaningful way. Early experiments with robots converted previous labs to a robot context: for example, if a previous lab asked students to print the numbers 1 to 5, a new lab could ask students to beep once, twice, three times, four times and five times. However, quickly in the development process, the development team realized such simple applications of robots were generally dull and did not take good advantage of the available robots. Instead, students needed to be able to generate songs and/or duets through sound generators, access sensor data, utilize the sensors to impact robot behavior, and command the robots to perform interesting tasks.

The third goal resonates with nearly every computer science department: boost interest in beginning and continuing the study of computer science. Most students know that robots have played a variety of roles in popular culture, and robots have become popular in some formerly human-specific roles (e.g. Roomba © vacuum cleaners, robots performing surgical procedures, and robots that perform assembly-line manufacturing). Integrating robots into the CS 2 course had potential to provide some insights into these applications and to boost interest in continuing the study of computer science. At a small college, student numbers are generally small, and compiling meaningful statistics difficult. However, an important objective was to increase enrollments in CS 2 and later courses in some meaningful way.

The fourth goal, although difficult to measure, clearly supports the second and third goals: help students have fun with the practice of computer science. No matter how interestingly a text-based problem is phrased, contemporary students may find minimal motivation in receiving simple, text-based output. Rather, today's students generally prefer seeing something move, make noise, or otherwise manifest as a change in the physical environment. Robots have these tangible qualities and thus have great potential to engage students, help them have fun, motivate them to work through labs (even outside of class time), and talk to their friends about the "cool" things they were doing in a computer science class.

2. STUDENT-FACULTY COURSE DEVELOPMENT AND COLLABORATION

Since the new course using Scribbler 2 robots needed to provide appropriate coverage of both the imperative problem solving paradigm and C programming—as defined in the traditional, non-robot-based course, this development effort began with a basic list of required topics. In the early stages of this development, the instructor's naive expectation was that the new course could follow the same basic organization as the traditional one, and that previous laboratory exercises could be rewritten with minor effort to incorporate robots. Within a short time, however, the development team realized that a simple editing of past materials would

not take full advantage of the capabilities of the robots. This realization prompted a full reworking of the course and a reorganization of the course content.

Rather than follow an instructor-dictated development process, we took a different approach involving student-faculty collaboration. The student team consisted of four undergraduate students, who had taken the previous CS2 one to four semesters earlier. These students worked for a modest stipend and course credit for a summer. The instructor tabulated topics from the traditional course, reviewed ACM curricular guidelines, and provided experience with lab-based teaching. Students brought their recent learning experiences taking computer science courses, identified themes and applications that could excite students, and shared their experiences concerning potential obstacles they had with learning various topics. Together, the student-faculty team discussed how to could structure topics in a strategy that involved the robots.

The student team members experimented writing sample programs and examples that highlighted worthwhile elements of the robots or that they found interesting and motivating. The instructor and students identified groups of topics and activities that seemed to fit together naturally. Over time, brainstorming sessions helped identify an overall structure for the new course.

The result was a course that was divided into 8 modules (plus a mini-module on data representation) which are each one and a half to two weeks long. Each module contains an introductory day with some time for lecture and examples, followed by a series of readings, laboratory exercises to be done in class, and homework assignments to reinforce the material learned in the labs. Each module focuses on different topics (such as characters, strings, and I/O) and builds up to a small project utilizing the robots and stressing the topics covered in the module.

Once the course structure was determined, alternating teams of two students were assigned to work on each module. Students were responsible for the entire content of each module including the selection of readings from the textbook, example programs, labs for each class, the final project, and any supplemental information necessary to cover the selected materials. Students used the instructor's prior course offering as a framework and starting point when necessary and were also responsible for compiling the module web page. Throughout, the instructor offered guidance, suggested pedagogical considerations, and provided feedback to student-team suggestions. However, the student teams worked through the numerous details.

After one student pair completed drafting a module, the other pair of students worked through the module to check for errors and make sure the content was the appropriate length and difficulty for future students. The reviewing pair would then offer corrections, suggestions, and other feedback. After taking the feedback into consideration, the materials were revised and edited. The module was then polished and submitted to the instructor for final review. Once all the modules were finished, the instructor compiled them into the final course Web site.

Overall, full development of the course (planning, organizing, writing, reviewing, refining) filled a 10-week summer project, and complete materials were ready for the new course in the fall.

To promote further refinement, each laboratory exercise referenced a feedback form, and students taking the course in the fall were able to comment on every laboratory exercise throughout the course. Using this feedback as a base, the instructor worked with two student developers (both from the same initial team which developed the course) to review and refine all materials, particularly readings and laboratory exercises. Thus, student/faculty collaboration during the fall semester allowed thorough modifications and corrections to the materials throughout the semester and iteratively refine the course materials. In subsequent semesters, the instructor has continued to refine the materials, but feedback from students in the class suggests that we now have a well-refined course, as discussed in Section 4 below.

3. STATISTICS, RESULTS AND DISCUSSION

Since Grinnell College is a small school, and since computer science enrolls only a modest percentage of the undergraduate population within a liberal arts environment, evaluation of a course or pedagogical technique cannot utilize extensive statistical comparison of multiple student populations. However, even in a small setting, useful data may be obtained from at least three sources:

- Student performance between course offerings can be compared, when students answer identical final-exam questions.

- Students can fill out feedback surveys for each laboratory exercise in the new course.

- Students can provide high-level evaluative feedback through end-of-course evaluations that are part of the college's course-assessment practices. To evaluate reactions to the robot-based course, we reviewed end-of-course evaluations in depth for each of the first two semesters in which robots were used.

We have identified our four primary goals and objectives for this new course in section 2.3. The following comments summarize results obtained from these assessment vehicles for each of these high-level course goals.

1) Cover the full range of topics from prior CS 2 courses: To compare knowledge of imperative problem solving and C programming between the former non-robot course and the new robot-based course, five common questions appeared on the final exams of both courses. Questions were chosen that were not specifically related to examples from the course (e.g., no questions on applications previously discussed or on robots). Overall, a comparison of student answers indicated that, on average, the level of ability was the same. Students performed at an almost identical level on three questions. Students on one version of the course scored a little higher on one other question, but also scored a little lower on another. We concluded that the revision of the course met its target teaching imperative problem solving, data structures, and C, as well as providing students with the appropriate background for later courses.

2) Utilize robots in a meaningful way: Since completion of end-of-course evaluations and a feedback survey was a prerequisite for taking the final exam, these instruments were completed by 100% of students. The evaluations and survey asked whether the application to robots of skills taught in the course contributed towards the integration over the various topics of the course. 65% of the students said that the robots contributed to their understanding. One student said "It was a real world application of our code", which that student found motivating. Another student indicated that they benefited from the instant visual feedback that the robots provided. Most students also said that if they were to restart the course from the beginning, they would prefer for it to involve robots again.

However, some comments remark that "robots detracted from learning C in depth", and "I felt that solving problems with the robots distracted from more interesting aspects of program structure". These notions should be considered, since the robots are incorporated to maximize the benefits of their presence without detracting from other aspects of the course. In our surveys, these comments were not the norm and it was interesting to observe that the perception of a lack of depth was contrary to the actual evidence that student learning regarding C was at about the same level with both the non-robot and robot-based courses. One explanation for this sense of a lack of depth might be that the use of robots enhance interest and motivation and thus distracted some students from realizing the level to which they were learning.

3) Boost interest in computer science: One measure of student interest in a course or a major is number of enrollments and the number of majors. Of course, such numbers may reflect many factors, but student perceptions regarding a course likely are one important element.

A simple review of course enrollments in this CS 2 course shows a moderate increase in numbers over the past several semesters. An important component of this increase involves gender balance. Using Table 3, we analyzed the statistics over three or four semesters for the number of men and women participation for our multi-paradigm introductory sequence (CS 1 studies functional problem solving with Scheme and media scripting, CS 2 – reported here – studies imperative problem solving with C and robots, CS 3 studies object-oriented problem solving with Java).

Table 3: Recent Enrollments in Introductory Computer Science

Course	Semester	Women	Men	Total
CS 1	Fall, 2012	23 (41.1%)	33 (58.9%)	56
CS 1	Spring, 2013	15 (44.1%)	19 (55.9%)	34
CS 1	Fall, 2013	22(31.4%)	48(68.6%)	70
CS 2	Fall, 2012	4 (26.7%)	11 (73.3%)	15
CS 2	Spring, 2013	12 (41.4%)	17 (58.6%)	29
CS 2	Fall, 2013	15 (48.4%)	16 (51.6%)	31
CS 2	Spring, 2014	17(33.3%)	24(66.7%)	51
CS 3	Spring, 2013	8 (33%)	16 (67%)	24
CS 3	Fall, 2103	6(31.6%)	13(68.4%)	19
CS 3	Spring, 2014	13(59.1%)	9(40.9%)	22

Over time, the number of students has increased in each of these courses, although enrollments for a specific semester show moderate variation. Enrollments for all courses have increased over time, and a significant part of that increase has come from enrollments by women. In most sections of these courses, women comprise 30%-40% of the total enrollment – a substantially higher percentage that is reported elsewhere. Initial registration in CS 3 this coming spring shows 59% women . These numbers may be a result of students in CS 2 finding the robots different, motivational, and applicable to new and interest situations. The drop-out rate for individual courses at Grinnell is generally quite low, and this class is no exception with no observed difference from past offerings of the course.

4) Increase excitement, motivation, and fun as part of the learning process: The average of the three end-of-semester surveys showed that around 70% of the students who took *Imperative Problem-Solving and Data Structures* using the Scribbler robots said that the robots contributed to their understanding of the course material. Around 83% of the students said that the robots caused them to be excited and motivated about the material. One student said "Seeing my work come to life motivated me to complete the lab. They were certainly fun to work with." This feedback indicates that most students thought that working with robots made the class interesting and that the robots helped them in the process of the course.

Additionally, most of the students found the transition from problem-solving using robots to other forms of problem-solving to be easy. To consider this particular question carefully was vital because the supplemental problems did not involve robots, and the curriculum involved more and more non-robot-based problems as the course wound on. Further, 85% of the reporting students indicated that the transition from assignments with robots to assignments without robots was smooth. In order for this to have been the case, the robot-based segments of the course must have taught the concepts well; otherwise, the students would have struggled with the non-robot-based assignments later in the course.

Beyond the performance on exams, surveys, and evaluations, an additional observation seems appropriate. As already noted, Grinnell follows a multi-paradigm approach for its introductory courses, and the redesigned CS 2 course is a central part of this sequence. After review of materials, the ACM/IEEE-CS Joint Task Force on Computing Curricula has identified both the three-course multi-paradigm sequence in general and this new robot-based course as "exemplar" for the CS2013 Final Report [1, pp. pp. 454-455, 458-459]. This recognition suggests interest in both content and pedagogy.

Overall, the results given here seem quite positive. They show that students enjoyed having the robots in the course. In terms of academic knowledge, the exam results show that students have a similar understanding. We did not have to sacrifice academic knowledge in order to make the class more interesting and fun for the students. Robots provided a good motivation and a way to test and see the effects of their code in a hands-on environment. As a result, gender balance seems to be improving, and overall enrollments have increased.

4. POSSIBLE NEXT STEPS

Although this project have been quite successful in incorporating robots within a CS 2 course at Grinnell College and makes up a part of the exemplar introductory computer science curriculum, future work is needed to address limitations and to meet future needs.

In the short to moderate term, two activities require attention:

- The underlying infrastructure of the current course relies on a C++ framework. This prevents our work from being portable. For example, the installation of all the C++ libraries take 4.5 hours on a Mac. In order to overcome this problem, in Fall 2013 we started working on a Standard C library to support this course. However, this is not fully complete. Finishing the pictures part of this library and changing the labs and examples accordingly is the first step that will follow our work.

- The current modules and labs rely upon popular and well-written standard C textbooks. (Students can choose either [8] or [9] for their semester reading assignments.) However, the books do not discuss Scribbler 2 robots, so the current course requires a moderate level of supplemental materials. At present, much material is available, but students have to move among several sources, and the coverage of materials is uneven. To resolve this difficulty of resource materials, a moderate-range project involves the development of a full textbook, just as Deepak Kumar has developed books in Python [10] and C++ [11] for a somewhat more elementary audience.

In the moderate to long term, work will need to focus on continuing course refinement and the development of alternative application themes.

- Since computer science is a quickly evolving discipline, courses must be rewritten and revised to reflect the modern world of computing. The success of this project with student-faculty collaboration suggests that a similar team-based approach might be applied to other courses. Our experience demonstrates that this approach can draw upon an instructor's experience and teaching insights, distribute much work from the instructor to a student team, and improve material by taking students' perspectives into account.

- Although the use of robots provides significant motivation to many students, other application themes likely motivate other audiences. Further, the novelty of robots might wane if the same robot theme were used in multiple courses. Thus, it seems appropriate to consider lab-based materials for other application themes, such as image processing [4, 15], art and music (e.g., following [7, 14]).

Although the utilization of robots as an application theme for a CS 2 course on imperative problem solving with C has been quite successful, faculty should not become complacent. Rather faculty must find new and creative ways to make fine courses even better.

5. CONCLUSIONS

The robot-based course described in this paper covers most or all of the standard topics that appeared in the traditional predecessor course. Results on some common exam questions suggest that students in the new, robot-based course had achieved similar proficiency with imperative problem solving and C programming as students in the earlier course. The addition of experience and practice with the robots required a substantial reorganization and rethinking of topics, allowing new topics regarding robots to be added without reducing traditional content.

Students also reported that the range of robot-based laboratory exercises and applications provided good practice in sharpening their problem-solving skills, and students indicated they could apply their experience with robots to the solving of other types of problems.

The team-based approach, involving both students and a faculty member in a collaborative effort, provided an excellent framework for the development of a course. Collaborative planning, organization, review are essential. Multiple student groups working in parallel allowed the production and refinement of a massive amount of material (8 modules, 30-35 labs, 55 sample programs, dozens of Web pages) – all within the reasonable time frame of 10 weeks.

The course designers regularly needed to remind each other of the high-level goals of imperative problem solving. The robots could help in many ways, but the developers had to be careful not to get carried away with a tool or nifty detail. Rather the development team focused on the teaching of central topics and, when appropriate, how the robots could foster understanding. Although the application theme of robots often applied nicely, some topics (e.g. data representation and pointers) are hard to convey through the Scribblers, and we did not try to force use of the robots onto every possible topic.

Altogether, this student-faculty approach for course development yielded an effective course, in which Scribblers provide a unifyingtheme for the application of course topics, which promotes learning, generates excitement, and enhances problem-solving skills.

6. ACKNOWLEDGMENTS

Since the original development work on this project, several team members, including April O'Neill, have graduated. With logistics after graduation, April became a secondary contributor to this paper; she made substantial contributions to this overall effort!

We would like to thank Dr. John Stone for his help with technical problems and system administration help with the robots and the network. Additionally, we would like to thank again Mr. John Hoare at University of Tennessee at Knoxville who developed the MyroC++ library; his on-going advice and his responses to queries were extremely helpful at several key points. Finally, none of this work would have been possible without the funding provided by Grinnell College and the feedback of students from the Imperative Problem Solving and Data Structures courses who were helpful with the surveys.

7. REFERENCES

[1] ACM/IEEE-CS Joint Task Force on Computing Curricula. 2013. *Computer Science Curricula 2013*. ACM Press and IEEE Computer Society Press. DOI: http://dx.doi.org/10.1145/2534860

[2] Beck, L.L, and W. Chizhik, A. "An Experimental Study of Coopeative Learning in CS 1", *SIGCSE Bulletin inroads*, 40 (1), March 2008, pp. 205-209.

[3] Cowden, D., O'Neill, A., Opavsky, E., Ustek, D., and Walker, H. M., "A C-based introductory course using robots", Proceedings of the 43rd ACM Technical Symposium on Computer Science Education (SIGCSE 2012), March 2012, p. 27-32.

[4] Guzdial, M. and Ericson, B., *Introduction to Computing & Programming Algebra in Java(c) A Multimedia Approach*, Prentice Hall, 2007.

[5] Hake, R. R., "Interactive-engagement versus traditional methods: A six-thousand-student of mechanics test data for introductory physics", *American Journal of Physics*, 66 (1), January 1998, pp. 64-74.

[6] Herman, E. A, Pepe, M. D., and Moore, R. T., "Linear Algebra: Modules for Interactive Learning Using Maple", *The Linear Algebra Modules Project (LAMP)*, Addison-Wesley Publishing Company, 2000.

[7] Heines, J., Greher, G., Ruthmann, S., and Reilly, B., "Two Approaches to Interdisciplinary Computing+Music Courses", *Computer*, 44 (12), December 2011.

[8] Kernighan, B. W., and Ritchie, D. M., *The C Programming Language, Second Edition*, Prentice Hall, 1988.

[9] King, K. N., *C Programming: A Modern Approach, Second Edition*, W. W. Norton, 2008.

[10] Kumar, D., *Learning Computing with Robots*, Fall 2011. Textbook available at http://wiki.roboteducation.org/Learning_Computing_With_Robots_Using_Calico_Python_

[11] Kumar, D. (ed.), *Learning Computing With Robots in C++*, January 2011. Textbook available at http://web.eecs.utk.edu/~mclennan/Classes/102/LCRcpp/index.html

[12] Liberal Arts Computer Science Consortium, "A 2007 Model Curriculum for a liberal arts degree in computer science", *Journal on Educational Resources in Computing (JERIC)*, 7 (2), June 2007.

[13] McConnell, J. J., "Active and Cooperative Learning: Final Tips and Tricks", *SIGCSE Bulletin inroads*, Part I (Vol 37 (2), June 2005, pp. 27-30); Part II (Vol 37 (4), December 2005, pp. 34-38); Part III (Vol 38 (2), June 2006, pp. 24-28); Part IV (Vol 39 (4), December 2006, pp. 25-28).

[14] Misra, A., Blank, D., and Kumar, D., "A Music Context for Teaching Introductory Computing", ACM SIGCSE Bulletin/ITiCSE 2009, 41 (3), September 2009, 248-252 .

[15] Rebelsky, S. A, Davis, J., and Weinman, J. "Building Knowledge and Confidence with Mediascripting: A Successful Interdisciplinary Approach to CS1", Proceedings of the 44th ACM Technical Symposium on Computer Science Education (SIGCSE 2013), March 2013, p. 483-488.

[16] Scribbler 2 website: http://www.parallax.com/product/28136

[17] Summet, J., et al., "Personalizing CS1 with Robots", Proceedings of the 40th ACM Technical Symposium on Computer Science Education (SIGCSE 2009), March 2012, p. 433-437.

[18] Walker, H. M., "Collaborative learning: a case study for CS1 at Grinnell College and UT-Austin", Proceedings of the 28th ACM Technical Symposium on Computer Science Education (SIGCSE 1997), March 1997, p.209-213

[19] Walker, H. M., "A lab-based approach for introductory computing that emphasizes collaboration", Proceedings of the Computer Science Education Research Conference (CSERC '11), Heerlen, the Netherlands, pp. 21-31.

[20] Walker, H. M., Ustek, D., Opavsky, E.' O'Neill, A., Cowden, D., http://www.cs.grinnell.edu/~walker/courses/161.sp14/

Making Group Processes Explicit to Student: A Case of Justice

Ville Isomöttönen
Department of Mathematical Information Technology
University of Jyväskylä, Finland
ville.isomottonen@jyu.fi

ABSTRACT

This article considers student learning about group work in the context of project courses where student groups work under realistic expectations. Based on the literature, *justice* is explicated as a group work concept and regarded as a professional skill that can be practiced. Preliminary student feedback on teaching through continuous discussions on justice are presented together with teacher experiences.

Categories and Subject Descriptors

K.3.2. [**Computers and education**]: Computers and Information Science Education—*Computer Science Education*

General Terms

Human factors, Theory

Keywords

Project-based learning; group work skills; justice

1. INTRODUCTION

Project-based courses in computing have a decades-long history [31]. Numerous project course models have emerged, ranging from skill-oriented individual projects and integrative capstones to multicultural team projects, authentic customer projects, and student-led companies, to mention but a few.

This article is concerned with realistic course contexts where students work under real expectations, and usually under a time constraint. The learning goal of such courses has often been defined as a *realistic experience*, or, in a more specific form, project teachers state that projects accumulate student experience in the wide range of skills needed in the projects (e.g., [18, 17, 22]). Because realistic project courses give students a valuable experience of survival in a professionally authentic context, it is clear that it has been justifiable to define the main learning goal simply as an exposure to professional realism.

In this article, however, the main concern is how to promote learning at a conceptual level. The main motivating viewpoint is that a *realistic experience* does not necessarily indicate learning in the sense of meaning making but may just accumulate students' tacit knowledge. Meaning making here refers to the development of explicit conceptual understandings. For example, if students report that they learned teamwork skills [4], or teachers report that a course requiring group work adds to the students' teamwork consciousness [18], meaning making about group work has not necessarily occurred. Further, one could polemically state that a realistic experience and experience in certain skills can be gained without any formal university studies. From this perspective, to add value to the students' coursework in the higher education context, promoting learning at a conceptual level should receive attention when delivering professionally authentic experiences to students.

The following sections motivate and describe a project course setting where justice in group work was conceptualized to students as a learning goal. Student responses to this course setting are analyzed based on an end-of-course survey. Teaching experiences are also incorporated into the analysis, as autoethnographic accounts of the remembered successes and challenges.

2. RELATED WORK

Many studies on realistic project courses have described the students' overall learning goal roughly in the same way, as an exposure to a realistic experience, which also concerns group work (see [18, 17, 6, 10, 2, 22]). Fincher et al. [13] again defined project course models on the basis of actual practice at more than 50 organizations. This taxonomy included "a project with a real client." Also here, the educational goal was defined as giving students "a taste of the real world". Parker et al. [24] discussed their experiences generally in the context of real customer projects. In line with the above references, they observed that all of the student effort was easily expended on demanding project assignments, with the result that the students had no resources to holistically reflect on various project work issues.

The *exposure* to professional realism is arguably a condition highly important for students who are able to improve their self-confidence by surviving authentic projects. This condition, as observed here, is not to claim that reflectional learning through usual vehicles such as learning journals would not in any way occur in realistic courses. Rather, it is noted that under the conditions of processional realism in very authentic project courses, considerations on how disciplinary conceptualizations can be explicitly promoted as learning goals could merit more attention.

Learning about group work in realistic courses can also be examined from another perspective. Namely, in a large number of computing education articles, learning about group work is referred to in the context of self- and peer assessment (e.g., [27, 34, 28, 14, 29, 7, 26]). However, in assessment-related studies, the dominant concern is (understandably) the assessment of individual contributions correctly and fairly in the presence of complex group processes (e.g., [27, 34, 14, 29]). This challenge is typically addressed through survey-based tools that collect information about the quantity and quality of individuals' contributions. Here, students are asked to rank each other with numeric scores or with some other predefined attributes; numerous techniques are described in [34]. Surveying is reported to support learning, as it provides valuable feedback for the students, while scholars also report that students show anxiety when ranking their peers (e.g., [7, 26]).

Whether students will *independently* develop explicit understandings of their coursework through reflective tasks is also in question. In agreement with this question, the study by Sims-Knight et al. [28] hints that students' knowledge about team skills is not easily developed during projects, which they tested with a pretest and post test procedure. A need for interventions to increase critical awareness among students is found, for instance, in the study by Daniels [9, p. 75], who reports that they (educators) often "reacted to students not seeing their own part in problematic issues," an aspect agreed with in the present study.

Several other viewpoints in the above and other studies accord with the present study. Richards [26] highlights fairness as a crucial attribute in project-based courses. Clear [8] examined group situations through a diagnostic tool where peer evaluation forms were issued to students in a group session that required students to immediately discuss the results of the evaluations. In the present approach, discussional group sessions were adopted as the main pedagogic instrument throughout the course. Drake, Goldsmith, and Strachan [11] again describe an approach where teamwork is taught in conjunction with a simulation game. They incorporated expert lessons and self-reflective exercises to emphasize group issues to students. Their study indicates that emphasizing team issues in teaching activities causes students to ponder team issues when giving feedback on the course. However, the study does not report what the group processes emphasized to students actually were, and it speaks of how students were effectively *exposed* to team issues through a simulation game. Pieterse and Thompson [25] investigated two attributes that tend to hamper realistic teamwork: social loafers and diligent isolates. Their study indicates that academic disparity within a team creates circumstances where these problematic roles tend to emerge. In their study, these two attributes were incorporated as research attributes. The present approach explicates similar dimensions directly to students to be considered as a central learning goal throughout the course.

The teaching approach in the present study complements the above approaches in emphasizing that group processes are to be conceptually and constantly explicated to students in order to guarantee that students effectively derive conceptual tools instead of mere tacit knowledge from their group experience. The specific feature of this approach is seeing a

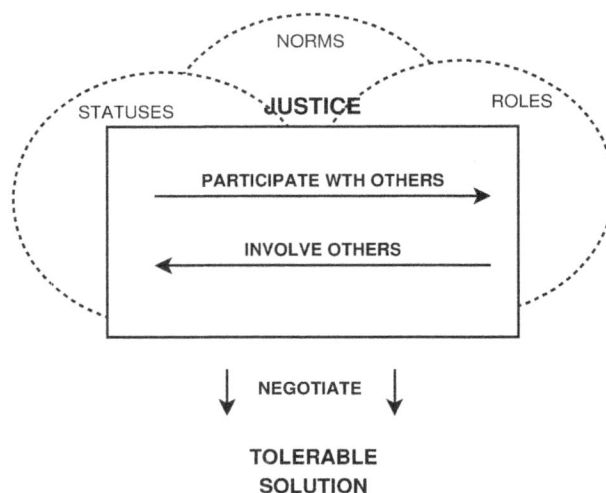

Figure 1: Justice conceptualized

conceptualization (here, justice) as a skill that can be practiced.

3. JUSTICE CONCEPTUALIZED

In the course studied here, basic group processes were explained to students according to a book by Brown [5], in particular through the concepts of statuses, roles, and norms therein. Then, a conceptualization sourced from the author's previous grounded theory project [15] was described to students as a model explicating justice in group work, as highlighted with a boldfaced line style in Figure 1.

This conceptualization on justice comprises two dimensions. On the one hand, the group member should "participate with others" actively, to avoid frustration on the part of other members due to unequal commitment. On the other hand, the group member needs to consider what his or her own participation indicates for the learning possibilities of other group members. Thus, while participating, the group member should concurrently consider the other, in a sense, opposite, dimension, here referred to as "involve others". The great practical challenge and a condition for enjoyable group work is that these dimensions should occur in a balanced way across group members. For justice to materialize, group members need to monitor their roles and keep negotiating a "tolerable solution". Thus, this conceptualization does not naively expect that all the members produce an outcome of the same size. Instead, it is advocated here as a pedagogically simple while integrative scheme to communicate about well-being in a group.

The concepts of status and role from Brown integrate straightforwardly with the present conceptualization on justice. The two dimensions of this conceptualization can be conceptually discussed through individuals' statuses and roles. On the other hand, the conceptualization on justice gives students an at-a-glance integrative view to consider their roles and statuses (read: learning possibilities in a group). Also the norms that emerge within a group relevantly underpin the concept of justice, as, for example, unspoken intra-group communication habits may affect how openly this sensitive issue can be dissected.

4. THE COURSE AND THE APPROACH

The project course under study is a 5-credit bachelor-level course, where student teams comprising 4–5 students each innovate and implement a software product under a selected topical theme. The course spans 12 weeks and is supervised by 2 teachers, one focusing mainly on issues in group work and software processes (the present author), and the other more on emerging technical questions. During the spring 2013 instance studied here, the course theme was Open Data.

Groups were teacher selected through a brief screening of the students' academic performances on their previous courses, using the principle of grouping students with fairly similar backgrounds. All groups were provided with a workroom to support independent group work. The course was started with a brief introduction to Open Data, which was followed by the starting lecture where group work topics were addressed. Thereafter, the student groups were required to work autonomously with one mandatory discussion session with the teachers each week. The required documentation included a synopsis on project management tasks and responsibilities and a synopsis describing the idea for the Open Data software product and its initial design. At the end of the course, each student was required to give a reflective report on the issues lectured at the beginning and discussed throughout the course.

The main pedagogic principle and the learning goal was to discuss students' work at a conceptual level. Selected group work conceptualizations (see Figure 1) lectured at the beginning were discussed in weekly sessions with the aim to prompt the students to think conceptually (theoretically) about their coursework. *Justice* in group work was the major and the connective topic. Students were informed about forthcoming sensitive discussions during the starting lecture. They were told that in this course these issues are considered to be skills that can be practiced and thus regarded as issues external from individuals' personalities. The course was graded with pass/fail, the pass requiring fair participation in the course activities. Frequent group discussions and the fact that students were required to keep track of their working hours enabled monitoring student activity.

On top of the weekly informal discussion sessions, two self-/peer evaluation rounds were carried out (on the sixth and ninth week). These were meant to guarantee that students really take time to reflect on their work in relation to group concepts. Similar to [8], students were issued with evaluation forms, and the results were openly discussed during the upcoming group discussion session of the week. In the remainder of this article, the routinely conducted weekly sessions are referred to as "group discussion sessions," and the two specific sessions summarizing the results of the self-/peer-evaluation rounds as "self-/peer evaluation sessions." In practice, both session types served the same purpose, with the latter incorporating the formal evaluation forms.

The above-described focus on thinking at a conceptual level indicated that the usual emphasis on learning goals in terms of development of skills related to various software process deliverables was to a great extent replaced with the advocation of conceptual knowledge. It should also be noted that the present study does not intend to investigate the effect of attributes such as grading or teaming on group work.

The teaching approach described above accords with recent educational discourse. The model of Integrated Ped-agogy, for instance, is based on accounts of expertise comprising four forms of knowledge: practical, theoretical, sociocultural, and self-regulative (e.g., [32, 33]). This model emphasizes the close integration of theoretical knowledge in practical learning settings, with reflection in terms of integrative thinking as the main learning medium. Su [30] again refers to a potentially inadequate mode in learning where students are simply expected to complete the work without deeper considerations of what is being learned and how it is learned during practical courses. In Mayer's [20] experience, students learn more effectively and their critical awareness is better generated when a constantly reinforced link exists between the conceptual level of analysis and empirical applications with everyday relevance. Yet another relevant mindset, being an education philosophy that the present author agrees with, is the social realism and its maxim "for knowledge", as put forward by Moore and others [23, 19]. Here, the conceptual level of knowledge is advocated such that the annoying dilemma between constructivist relativism and positivist absolutism is avoided. In brief, a possibility for professionally powerful objectifications is agreed with, while avoiding a naive association with positivism (fixed objectifications). This line of thinking draws on Bhaskar's critical realism [1] and scholars such as Bernstein.

5. THE STUDY

This section reports on a preliminary study. Instead of evaluating learning, the study presents aspects that emerged in terms of student reaction. The course participants had passed CS1 and CS2, and were in various stages in their bachelor studies. A research survey was answered by 21 out of 26 students, all of whom granted research permission on their answers. The questions address how the students responded to the course setting requiring them to explicitly attend to and discuss sensitive justice-related group issues:

- Q1 (Likert scale): Do you feel that you could grasp the topics lectured at the beginning?

- Q2 (Likert scale): Did you consider the lectured topics relevant?

- Q3 (open-ended): How did you feel about the self-/peer evaluation and group discussion sessions? tip: prompting, oppressive, etc.

- Q4 (open-ended): Did you experience the self-evaluations, self-/peer evaluation sessions, and group discussion sessions as useful for your learning?

The open-ended questions were analyzed using a pattern coding process of qualitative research [21]. In this process, the analyst extracts regularities in the data by observing similarities and differences, and yet potentially maps the resultant themes into higher level categories that provide a holistic and conclusive view of the results. As the data were relatively small, it did not seem relevant to group (or force) the themes into higher level categories, and neither were frequencies counted. Further, because it was observed that the students' answers to the open-ended questions (Q3 and Q4) overlap, the themes were not divided up according to these questions. Rather, the themes reported are emergent aspects across the study population (data). The themes are arranged from positive to negative student responses, which

Table 1: Students' general responses to the lecture. N=20/21 due to one student absence from the lecture.

Q1: Do you feel that you could grasp the topics lectured at the beginning?				
1=No	2	3	4	5=Yes
0	1	7	12	0

Q2: Did you consider the lectured topics relevant?				
1=No	2	3	4	5=Yes
0	3	6	9	2

is only for presentational reasons. Teaching experiences are incorporated as an autoethnographic [12] exposition from the same perspective as the survey questions above.

6. RESULTS

Students' responses to Likert scale questions Q1 and Q2 are displayed in Table 1, with the means Q1: 3.6, Q2: 3.5, and the modes Q1: 4, Q2: 4. These figures propose an overview of the student responses similar to one derived from the open-ended answers in the section below, that is, "valuable but challenging."

6.1 Themes extracted (Q3 & Q4)

"**A way to make it happen.**" Students commented that without the dedicated sessions, group issues would not have been discussed in their group, which, it is interpreted here, underlines the importance of external interventions. In another form, students reported that they received a confirmation on their group situation, and that potential dissenting opinions in their group might have otherwise remained unspoken. Students in groups consisting of friends commented that interventions helped clarify issues among friends.

"**Stimulative and useful for working life.**" Students experienced that they gained tools for the project and working life. Further, they reported that the constructive discussions helped in considering how to continue with the project, and were useful regarding learning about group work.

"**Liberating effect.**". While students felt nervous about discussions, they also experienced them as liberating. This liberating effect is considered here to be a highly pursuable outcome educationally, indicating that explicating justice to students and provoking them to constantly consider it during their group work can contribute to a sense of well-being in a group.

"**Nice, natural part of the course.**". Some students considered discussion sessions to be nice and refreshing, while some others explained that because the group topics were introduced at the beginning, the discussion sessions were a natural part of the course. Here, the extent to which making students aware of the sensitive topics beforehand contributes to how sensitive issues are experienced later on is considered to be an important research question. In this course, the justice-related topics were referred to as skills external from personalities already during the starting lecture. Some students also noted that they felt their feedback was addressed sensitively enough.

"**The effect of uncompromised realism.**" Students valued the supervision sessions because the sessions gave them a realistic picture of their progress. Serious discussions at a conceptual level, and insisting on the course deadline, appeared to make bachelor students aware of the simple fact that a reasonable outcome requires work. In this study, this rigidness pedagogically is referred to as "uncompromised realism."

"**Dramatic change in working style.**" One student reported that after the first few supervision sessions, working style in his group changed totally, which can be interpreted to be due to uncompromised realism. This attribute characterizes the tone that emerged during group discussion sessions throughout the course (see the next section).

"**Walking a tightrope between outspokenness and discretion.**" Students notice this communication challenge when considering justice in shared group sessions, which can be regarded as a positive learning outcome, that is, a skill that can be practiced after it is identified. Indicated by students' comments, this communication challenge was amplified by the short timescale of the course.

"**Justice accessible through informal dialogue.**" Some students commented that group discussion sessions were more useful than self-/peer evaluation sessions. Not all the students liked to consider their group situation formally by filling out evaluation forms about the progress of themselves and their peers, while they considered discussion situations less stressful through informal dialogue.

"**Predictability reduces stress.**". The students commented that foreseeing the issues that were likely to emerge in the discussions reduced the stress related to the discussions.

"**From *odd* to *useful*.**". Students commented that they felt the discussions odd at first but, during the course, understood their purpose and usefulness.

"**Unpleasant.**" Students commented that it was sometimes unpleasant to comment on peers or try to analyze themselves, which is in line with the literature in Section 2.

> [Student:] ...*On the other hand, I do not know anyone who would enjoy writing evaluations or consider them useful.*

However, for some students, the absence of effective group problems meant that no unpleasantness was experienced.

"**Difficulty of terminology.**" In line with the finding that students felt the group discussions odd at first, they reported on the difficulties in considering justice as a concept to be learned. In accord, some students reported on difficulties in interpreting self-evaluation questions and proposed the use of more comprehensible language.

"**Time wasted on meta-thinking.**" Some students did not develop an interest in considering group work conceptually during the course, as illustrated by this theme, which is a direct student quotation. In the same spirit, some students stated that the only benefit of the discussions was their project management-like role.

"**Uselessness due to dishonesty.**" Not all the students (groups) benefited from the self-/peer evaluation sessions. The reason reported by students is that they just could not be truly honest about their group situation.

"**Distracting awareness.**" One of the most interesting responses was that a student experienced the explication of group behavior as introducing a distracting awareness into group work:

> [Student:] ...*coding with peers turned into roles, statuses, and such calculating stuff. A bit in the*

same way the classes on the first language in the high school ruined the way I watch commercials...

6.2 Teaching experiences

Agreed by the student responses above, CS students appeared to experience dedicated sociology-related discussions on group work as odd. It was occasionally excessively difficult to induce students to participate openly, while their hesitation to openly discuss the topics led to cursory conversations with little value. If the students remained silent, only briefly commenting on our prompting questions, the discussion session became annoying for all. This course instance was the first time I personally introduced group issues to students in an in-depth manner, and I think I should have been more strict in insisting on analytic discussions at the beginning, to better communicate the intended norm of the course to the students. I also feel that the students were not accustomed to or prepared for thinking at a conceptual level in the present curriculum context, which was likely to make the conceptual discourse appear odd at first. Yet another related issue is that some of the most technically oriented students were almost impossible to persuade into the course topics and the mode of the discussions, a condition difficult to overcome during a single course.

One unexpected issue was that students really did not start working, by which I do not refer to the known confusion phase at the beginning of group projects, but to unrealistic expectations among the students, an aspect discussed by Daniels (see Section 2). One response to this challenge was the *uncompromised realism* already referred to above. One group, for instance, began to insist that I tell them what to write into a required synopsis document. I had given all the groups guidelines on the synopses and explained their purpose. I began to literally answer to this group that "I am not interested, this synopsis (decisions on project management activities and tasks) is for you." I also kept noting that without any set roles and tasks, the project usually makes very slow progress and is likely to fail. After a few weeks, this condition changed completely. This group began to work efficiently and independently, and the group finally completed a working software prototype well before the course deadline.

There were groups where some individuals took up tasks early, while at a group level, the issue of "not started working" applied to all groups. Not all the groups demonstrated a transformation to the degree described above. It seemed that while a student group could agree that they needed to improve their working style, this transformation already occurring in their dialogue was difficult to put into practice. The learner's previous conventions may be "a trap" that constrains transformation [3], which, in my view, might explain the slow change in the students' working style in the context where they agreed on the need for it.

I optimistically designed two rounds of self-/peer evaluations with questionnaires and follow-up discussions. However, as also reflected in the student data, it became obvious that the students were better reached through informal (ostensibly accidental) dialogue. This is in line with a research observation that students are willing to effectively ask for help through informal communication channels [16].

Insisting on discussions and the tone of the course, however, eventually paid of at least to a satisfactory extent. The majority of the students' end-of-course writings were surprisingly analytic about how their group situation evolved during the course. I found students commenting that this course made them think about themselves or provided something to think in general. Although there were a lot of observable challenges, the tone of the course eventually appeared to have a transformative impact on many students, which is an observation that merits a dedicated study in the future.

More generally, it is exactly the liberating effect, reported in the student data, that I hope to read in student responses during the future iterations of this course. I personally see justice in groups, whether student groups or whatever working life circumstances, substantively affecting our well-being, and then our willingness and effort to co-operate—an important academic topic.

7. CONCLUSION

This article reported experiences with a course where a conceptualization on justice in group work was regarded as a professional skill that can be practiced, providing a major learning goal for the course studied. In the student data, perhaps the most promising outcomes were the liberating effect of sensitive group discussions, and the fact that the students actually valued that they *had* to discuss group situations and project progress reflectively, as they came to know that this contributed to project progress, and increased their explicit awareness of group issues. Taking into consideration both the student views and teacher experiences, effective teaching and learning by focusing on relevant conceptualizations within a sensitive domain such as group work is a communication challenge for both sides. The teacher should be able to invite CS students to dialogue which they do not really expect in CS courses, yet should occur in a sensitive manner and with accessible language. The students should develop courage to bring to the foreground distracting issues in the presence of their peers.

The final conclusion is that there was a learning curve on the part of both students and teachers. While many expectations with the course model were validated by the feedback and experiences collected, this learning curve is far from trivial. From this perspective, a course of this kind could be placed in the early curriculum, and some aspects of the course could be iterated during later courses. Further, it is clear that justice encompasses only certain aspects of group work. Taking into account that fairness and the two dimensions in the present conceptualization on justice also emerge in the literature (e.g., [26, 25]), it should be fair to state that this theme is altogether relevant for realistic project courses.

8. REFERENCES

[1] R. Bhaskar. *A Realist Theory of Science*. Harvester Press, Sussex, UK, second edition, 1978.

[2] K. Bothe. Reverse engineering: The challenge of large-scale real-world educational projects. In *Software Engineering Education and Training. Proceedings. 14th Conference on*, pages 115–126, Los Alamitos, CA, 2001. IEEE Computer Society.

[3] D. Boud and D. Walker. *Barriers to Reflection on Experience*, pages 73–87. SRHE and Open University Press, 1993.

[4] J. Brown. Bloodshot eyes: Workload issues in computer science project courses. In *Software*

Engineering Conference. APSEC 2000. Proceedings. Seventh Asia-Pacific, pages 46–52. IEEE Computer Society, 2000.

[5] R. Brown. *Dynamics within and between Groups*. Basil Blackwell, Oxford, UK, 1988.

[6] K. Christensen and D. Rundus. The capstone senior design course: An initiative in partnering with industry. In *ASEE/IEEE Frontiers in Education, 33rd Annual*, pages S2B – 12–17 vol.3. IEEE, 2003.

[7] N. Clark, P. Davies, and R. Skeers. Self and peer assessment in software engineering projects. In *Proceedings of the 7th Australasian conference on Computing education - Volume 42*, ACE '05, pages 91–100, Darlinghurst, Australia, 2005. Australian Computer Society.

[8] T. Clear. A diagnostic technique for addressing group performance in capstone projects. *SIGCSE Bull.*, 34:196–196, June 2002.

[9] M. Daniels. *Developing and Assessing Professional Competencies: a Pipe Dream?* PhD thesis, Uppsala University, 2011.

[10] M. Daniels and L. Asplund. Full scale industrial project work, a one semester course. In *ASEE/IEEE Frontiers in Education Conference, 29th Annual*, pages 11B2/7–11B2/9. IEEE, 1999.

[11] R. Drake, G. Goldsmith, and R. Strachan. A novel approach to teaching teamwork. *Teaching in Higher Education*, 11(1):33–46, 2006.

[12] C. Ellis, T. E. Adams, and A. P. Bochner. Autoethnography: An overview [40 paragraphs]. *Forum Qualitative Sozialforschung / Forum: Qualitative Social Research*, 12(1), Art.10 2010.

[13] S. Fincher, M. Petre, and M. Clark, editors. *Computer Science Project Work: Principles and Pragmatics*. Springer-Verlag, London, 2001.

[14] J. Hayes, T. Lethbridge, and D. Port. Evaluating individual contribution toward group software engineering projects. In *Software Engineering, 2003. Proceedings. 25th International Conference on*, pages 622 – 627, 2003.

[15] V. Isomöttönen. Theorizing a one-semester real customer student software project course. In *Jyväskylä Studies in Computing*, volume 140. University of Jyväskylä, 2011. PhD Thesis.

[16] V. Isomöttönen, V. Tirronen, and M. Cochez. Issues with a course that emphasizes self-direction. In *Proceedings of the 18th ACM conference on Innovation and technology in computer science education*, ITiCSE '13, pages 111–116, New York, NY, 2013. ACM.

[17] C. Johansson and P. Molin. Maturity, motivation and effective learning in projects—benefits from using industrial clients. In *SEHE '95: Proceedings of the second international conference on Software engineering in higher education II*, pages 99–106, Billerica, MA, 1996. Computational Mechanics.

[18] P. J. Knoke. Medium size project model: Variations on a theme. In *Proceedings of the SEI Conference on Software Engineering Education*, pages 5–24, London, 1991. Springer-Verlag.

[19] K. Maton and R. Moore. *Introduction: Coalitions of the Mind*, pages 1–13. Continuum, London, 2010.

[20] J. Mayer. Teaching critical awareness in an introductory course. *Teaching Sociology*, 14(4):249–256, 1986.

[21] M. B. Miles and A. M. Huberman. *Qualitative Data Analysis: A Sourcebook of New Methods*. Sage, Beverly Hills, CA, 1984.

[22] M. Mochol and R. Tolksdorf. Praxis-oriented teaching via client-based software projects. In A. Pears and C. Schulte, editors, *9th Koli Calling: International Conference on Computing Education Research*, pages 31–34, Uppsala, Sweden, 2009. Uppsala University.

[23] R. Moore. For knowledge: Tradition, progressivism and progress in education—reconstructing the curriculum debate. *Cambridge Journal of Education*, 30(1):17–36, 2000.

[24] H. Parker, M. Holcombe, and A. Bell. Keeping our customers happy: Myths and management issues in "client-led" student software projects. *Computer Science Education*, 9(3):230–241, 1999.

[25] V. Pieterse and L. Thompson. Academic alignment to reduce the presence of 'social loafers' and 'diligent isolates' in student teams. *Teaching in Higher Education*, 15(4):355–367, 2010. doi:10.1080/13562517.2010.493346.

[26] D. Richards. Designing project-based courses with a focus on group formation and assessment. *Trans. Comput. Educ.*, 9(1):1–40, 2009.

[27] D. Sanders. Managing and evaluating students in a directed project course. In *Proceedings of the fifteenth SIGCSE technical symposium on Computer science education*, SIGSCE '84, pages 15–25, New York, NY, 1984. ACM.

[28] J. Sims-Knight, R. Upchurch, T. Powers, S. Haden, and R. Topciu. Teams in software engineering education. In *Frontiers in Education, 2002. FIE 2002. 32nd Annual*, volume 3, pages S3G–17 – S3G–22 vol.3, 2002.

[29] H. H. Smith and D. L. Smarkusky. Competency matrices for peer assessment of individuals in team projects. In *Proceedings of the 6th conference on Information technology education*, SIGITE '05, pages 155–162, New York, NY, 2005. ACM.

[30] Y.-H. Su. The constitution of agency in developing lifelong learning ability: The 'being' mode. *Higher Education*, 62(4):399–412, 2010. doi: 10.1007/s10734-010-9395-6.

[31] J. E. Tomayko. Forging a discipline: An outline history of software engineering education. *Annals of Software Engineering*, 6(1):3–18, 1998.

[32] P. Tynjälä. Perspectives into learning at the workplace. *Educational Research Review*, 3:130–154, 2008.

[33] P. Tynjälä and D. Gijbels. *Changing World: Changing Pedagogy*, pages 205–222. Springer Netherlands, 2012.

[34] D. E. Wilkins and P. B. Lawhead. Evaluating individuals in team projects. In *Proceedings of the thirty-first SIGCSE technical symposium on Computer science education*, SIGCSE '00, pages 172–175, New York, NY, 2000. ACM.

A Methodological Approach to Key Competencies in Informatics

Christina Dörge
FOM University of Applied Sciences
Mary-Somerville-Str. 3
28359 Bremen, Germany

Christina.doerge@fom-net.de

ABSTRACT

Competencies in informatics have traditionally been fixed, defined, and identified either normatively by groups of experts or as derivations from educational standards of one of various external fields. This paper presents a novel approach, which is methodologically driven by Qualitative Content Analysis (QCA). My goal was to derive key competencies in informatics from previously established educational approaches in informatics. First I consulted a number of textbooks on didactics in informatics and compiled a list of possible candidates for competencies. The list was used as a QCA category set, by which six different educational approaches were analyzed. Every time a new competency was identified, it was added to the category set and a new iteration of the analyzing process was commenced using the newly enhanced list of competencies. Since the material for the analysis consisted of research documents of existing educational approaches for school education, the result was a collection of competencies with the property of maximal prevalence across the range of educational concepts. A final refinement step identified those competencies which have connections to all of the four main categories of informatics, namely theoretical informatics, technical informatics, practical informatics, and applied informatics. These competencies were termed "Key Competencies in Informatics".

Categories and Subject Descriptors

K.3.2 [Computer and Information Science Education]: Computer science education

General Terms

Measurement, Documentation, Performance, Standardization, Theory, Verification.

Keywords

Competencies, key competencies, qualitative content analysis, methodology, didactics, education, educational approaches and concepts.

ITICSE'14, June 21–25, 2014, Uppsala, Sweden.
Copyright © 2014 ACM 978-1-4503-2833-3/14/06...$15.00.
http://dx.doi.org/10.1145/2591708.2591742

1. INTRODUCTION

In Germany, the subject of competence / competency has marked a development in education away from instructional content towards the person to be instructed. In the process, the focus of educational standards shifted from input-orientation to output-orientation. Today, the educational standards of the KMK (Kultusminister Konferenz, see http://www.kmk.org/) reflect this change and are therefore output-oriented. They concentrate on competencies and skills pupils are supposed to gain within a specified cycle of education.

In the 1970s, the debate on competencies experienced a revival. Researchers found that professional life had changed so profoundly that it seemed impossible to teach everything necessary to ensure a seamless transition from education to the challenges of working life. What were the missing ingredients which could help students to adapt to the ever-changing world of professional work? In 1974, the question was addressed by Dieter Mertens under the heading of Schlüsselqualifikationen (key qualifications). Mertens was then director of the Institut für Arbeitsmarkt und Berufsforschung (IAB) (= Institute for Labor Market and Employment Research) [32]. His paper initiated a discussion which is still alive today: How may humans be equipped with skills which will help them throughout their lifetime to adapt to constantly varying challenges?

What began as a discussion about key skills / key qualifications has now become one about key competencies. Some definitions for qualifications and competencies amount to the same, sometimes the same term is used to express different concepts and sometimes definitions have different levels of detail. Some scientists even speak of an inflationary use of terms [38]. Dörge's paper on the differences of the English and German speaking communities, published in the proceedings of the KCKS 2010 conference in Brisbane, Australia, examines the issue in detail [12].

To counter the abundance of terminology, the Bundesinstitut für Berufsbildung (BIBB) (= Federal Institute for Vocational Training) commissioned a study in the 1990s: The commissioned researchers created a list of terms titled key competencies. Over 600 were found in number [11]. A similar program was carried out within the English speaking research community by Allen [1].

Almost two decades later there is still no unified terminology concerning competencies. Researchers continue to add new concepts and terminology to an already heterogeneous field (see for example [33], p. 12). Some have asked whether "competency" is not simply a replacement term for other already established concept names, such as "education" ([20], p. 17).

Competency catalogues can be generated in different ways, e.g. normatively as the result of a debate among experts, or by derivation from an educational standard of a field external to informatics. Thus, the educational standards for computer science education in Germany are derived from the American educational standards for mathematics, as created by the National Council of Teachers of Mathematics (NCTM) ([14], p. 2).

In a normative process of creating competencies, it is likely that only competencies important to the experts compiling the list will appear in the result. Looking for a more objective way to ensure that no important competencies are left out, it may at first seem impossible to achieve a truly non-normative approach because even if multiple expert accounts are taken into consideration, there will be no guarantee for the outcome to be free of normative elements, since any results will still be based on normative sources. However, qualitative research methods can shed new light on the source material: If a qualitative analysis is applied to a large enough cross-section of the works of many experts, the outcome will be non-normative because only those competencies will persist in the analysis which have a potential to last over time.

Consequently, in my dissertation, I used a qualitative approach: First, from textbooks on the teaching of informatics, a list of competencies was compiled, which was subsequently used as a category set as required by Qualitative Content Analysis. Next, the category set was used to analyze a number of educational approaches to informatics education in Germany. Competencies permeating all approaches were considered particularly important and were named competencies in informatics. Finally, these were checked for relevance in all core areas of computer science (theoretical, practical, applied, and technical), positive results yielding key competencies in informatics.

In what follows I would like to give more insight into the details of my research concept. A list of the resulting key competencies can be found at the end of this paper.

2. QUALITATIVE CONTENT ANALYSIS

Qualitative Content Analysis (QCA) is a method used to analyze text documents. Even though QCA is a qualitative method, it has a quantitative aspect, as we will see in V.

According to Mayring, the advantages of QCA over other qualitative methods are ([30], [31]):

- "Rules of analysis": Step by step document analysis using a fixed set of rules.

- "Categories in the center of analysis": Categories are used for text interpretation. They may be specified by description, definition, or both.

- "Criteria of reliability and validity": Independent researchers can attempt to reproduce the analysis to validate the results (intercoder-reliability).

QCA offers a way of accessing the information needed by analyzing the source material in the following way:

- State the research question

- Build a category set from source material which is close to the research question (For our case: Compile a list of candidates for competencies from textbooks on the teaching of informatics.)

- Set the rules for the application of the category set. (For our case: Brief definitions of the competencies to look for.)

- Build a valuation scheme to be used to assign points to the content to be analyzed. (For our case: A weighted content analysis called "intensity analysis" [30], p. 15.)

- Select the source material for the analysis (for our case: six different educational approaches to informatics education) and process it.

- Look for potential extensions to the category set (for our case: new candidates for competencies). If successful, begin a new iteration of the analysis process.

For the QCA's results, see chapter 5 and 6.

3. CATEGORY DEVELOPMENT

The category set was generated from textbooks on the teaching of informatics by authors R. Baumann [3], P. Hubwieser [17], S. Schubert & A. Schwill [39], and L. Humbert [19]. While all of them are concerned with the teaching of computer science, each book puts different emphases on its subtopics and contents, coming to different conclusions about what should be taught in computer science classes.

Whenever an author labeled a learning goal or content as important, I assigned a competency. For example, from the attribute "is able to develop software", "software development competency" was created. The textbooks' respective passages were used to describe the entries of the category set in detail. Similar or overlapping skills were not conflated. For example, "assessment competency" can also be subsumed under "general scientific competency" or "action-enabling competency".

4. CONTENT ANALYSIS

The following educational approaches were used as the source material for the content analysis:

- **Hardware-Oriented Approach**: H.J. Forneck, [13], p. 104-109; P. Hubwieser, [17], p. 50-51; R. Gunzenhäuser & U. Lehnert, [15], p. 42-46.

- **Algorithm-Oriented Approach**: P. Hubwieser, [17], p. 51; H.J. Forneck, [13], p. 147-159; L.N. Landa, [26], p. 19-81 and p. 106-112; J. Bruhn, [7], p. 210-215.

- **Application-Oriented Approach**: B. Koerber, [23], p. 11-17; W. Arlt & B. Koerber, [2], p. 18-27; P. Hubwieser, [17]; H.J. Forneck, [13], p. 179-195 and p. 199-202; D. Riedel, [37], p. 36-41.

- **User-Oriented Approach**: P. Hubwieser, [17], p. 52; H.J. Forneck, [13], p. 244-249; Bund-Länder-Kommission für Bildungsplanung und Forschungsförderung (BLK), [10], p. 11-15; H. Kaiser, [21], p. 7, and [22], p. 4; R. Buhse, [9], p. 7-8; W. v. Lück, [41], p. 29-30.

- **Idea-Oriented Approach centered on Fundamental Ideas**: S. Schubert & A. Schwill, [39] and [40]; J.S. Bruner, [8]. – This approach was excluded during the content analysis. See below for explanation.

- **Information-Oriented Approach**: N. Breier, [4], p. 90-93; P. Hubwieser,, M. Broy and W. Brauer, [18], all pages; N. Breier and P. Hubwieser, [5], p. 31-42.

- **System-oriented Approach**: J. Magenheim, [28], all pages, and [29], p. 13-19.

Examples of newfound potential competencies not included in the original category set are creative thinking ([13], p. 146) and transfer capability ([27], p. 214, cited in [13]), which turned up in the analysis of the algorithm-oriented approach.

The idea-oriented approach was excluded from the evaluation since the concept of Fundamental Ideas (FI) (see [39], [40] and [8]) does not define any educational goals but provides a tool for analyzing educational goals instead. Also, as Hubwieser points out in [17], p. 82f, the Fundamental Ideas have been included in the information-centered approach.

5. QCA RESULTS AND REFINEMENTS

For the remaining six educational approaches the QCA's valuation scheme was set up as follows: A directly addressed competency was assigned two points. An indirectly addressed competency received one point. Half a point was given if, in fringe cases, I assumed that a competency was being addressed.

As a first refinement step, I excluded all competencies not mentioned in every educational approach. As a second refinement step, I excluded all competencies which are not of paramount importance to every part of computer science. To do this, I employed the common subdivision into applied, practical, technical and theoretical computer science, using Rechenberg's book ([36], p. 12). The remaining competencies I termed key competencies in informatics.

Table 1: Key Competencies in informatics

Points	Competencies
12	algorithmic thinking, genetic learning / historical competency, heuristic competence, problem-solving competency, software development competency, structured thinking, user skills, formal thinking
11	design competency, reflection competency
10.5	analytical thinking, assessment competency, methodological competency, model-building competency, linguistic competence (formal), systematic thinking, theoretical thinking
10	awareness of implications on society
9.5	mathematical competency, simulation competency
9	abstract thinking, general scientific competency, linguistic competence (natural)

It may not be surprising that problem-solving competency is among those that received the most points. Most computer science education experts have devoted extra shares in their textbooks for problem-solving (see e.g. [39], p. 103; [19], p. 166; [17], p. 68). Together with problem-solving competency appear algorithmic thinking, software development competency, formal thinking and several others. It can be assumed that these competencies have a

special place, playing a key role, among key competencies in informatics.

6. KEY COMPETENCIES IN INFORMATICS

The following definitions are based on the passages marked during the analyses of the educational approaches. The results are shown in alphabetical order. All of the following definitions should be thought of as pertaining to computer science in the context of general education in schools.

Abstract thinking includes the use of computer science as a semiotic system, character-processing machine, the deconstruction of computer science systems and the discussion of modeling approaches that have been gained by abstraction, reduction of complexity or formalization. Overall, computer science requires a high level of abstraction because it contains many abstract concepts. [13], [18], [28], [37]

Algorithmic thinking refers to the ability to solve problems using algorithmic methods (problem-solving process), as well as the use of algorithms (design process). The ability to detect the limits of algorithmization processes is also a part of this competence. [5], [13], [15], [23], [26], [28], [29], [37]

Analytical thinking includes analysis of problems, communication and action sequences, source code and software systems. [7], [9], [13], [26], [28], [29], [37]

Assessment competency includes the ability to critically assess possibilities, impossibilities and limits of computer science and its systems, to learn to make rational decisions and to understand the social impact of the use of information processing. Also included is evaluation of results, the ability to assess and analyze problems and the evaluation of communication processes. [2], [5], [9], [10], [13], [17], [23], [28]

Magenheim refers to this competency as being equipped to assess the natural, human, and social dimensions of socio-technical systems and hence of informatics systems (see [28], p.4).

Design competency includes the use of diagrams for the design of linear programs and key problems of software development. This competency is also used in design decisions and the development of plans for solving problems and handling tasks. [13], [17], [18], [28], [29]

Formal thinking includes the ability to explore and understand the laws and methods of problem-solving. This includes the abilities to decompose problems into sub-problems, to understand and modify predefined programs, development of quasi-algorithms, development of appropriate diagrams, and the ability to formalize and solve problems within models. Further aspects are formal logic, formal and technical analysis of informatics systems and the recognition of the relationship between knowledge, information and data. [5], [7], [10], [13], [15], [18], [26], [28], [29]

Genetic learning / historical competency include knowledge of the historical development of the subject of computer science and information processing and the ability to recognize social and historical implications. [4], [10], [13], [15], [29], [41]

Heuristic competency includes the ability to verify results, to develop appropriate problem solutions, the discussion of possible alternatives, to be able to make decisions rationally and to recognize the limits of information processing. Also included are the ability to assess the impact information and communication technologies and their applications have on society and the private sector. [9], [10], [13], [15], [17], [21], [26], [28], [37]

Awareness of implications on society includes the use of information and communication technologies and an understanding of the technical and social importance and impact of IT. It has social, cultural and psychological dimensions. [2], [10], [13], [15], [17], [22], [28]

Linguistic competence (formal) comprises knowledge of information theory, computer-based communication and computer languages. It also includes the ability to use linguistic means such as technical language and extensions of language (e.g. flowcharts). [4], [9] [13], [15], [17], [26], [28], [29]

Linguistic competence (natural) includes the ability to apply language elements such as precise formulation of steps towards a solution, language syntax, and the use of language to exchange messages. It also refers to knowledge about differences between natural and artificial languages and the resulting implications. [4], [9], [13], [28]

Mathematical competency involves the ability to deal with the mathematical and technical principles of data processing and the handling of various number systems (binary, decimal, octal). Also included are the skills and knowledge of school mathematics, such as addition, greatest common divisor, least common multiple, prime factorization, fractions, division algorithm, rule of three, calculation of interest, and logic on sets and propositions. [13], [15], [17], [26], [29]

Methodological competency includes the ability to apply skills such as algorithmic methods, structured problem-solving, methods of construction and deconstruction of informatics systems, comparison of problems and their solutions, and computer science-specific methods. [4], [5], [13], [18], [21], [23], [26], [28], [29], [41]

Model-building competency comprises the ability to construct and classify models, as well as modeling as a part of social action, including an understanding of functional relationships within technical systems (e.g. in the design phase of software development). [2], [5], [13], [17], [18], [29], [37]

Problem-solving competency includes problem analysis (such as generalization, comparison, and narrowing down of problems), problem-solving (such as solution design and step-by-step refinement) and methods of problem-solving (e.g. formulation, structuring, reflection and representation of problems). It also refers to the ability to grasp and appreciate problems in theory and practice. [4], [9], [10], [13], [15], [17], [23], [26], [28], [29], [37]

General scientific competency refers to a general overview of the field of computer science. This includes basic structures, concepts, and techniques of computer science, as well as specific computer science knowledge and its application (e.g. knowledge about use and control of information, use of computers as tools, sophisticated insight into professional scientific concepts and methods of computer science). Also included are abilities to analyze facts from other areas of knowledge. [2], [10], [22], [23], [28], [29]

Reflection competency refers to the possibilities and limitations of the elements of computer science. This includes discussion of possible alternatives and illuminating the consequences of solutions (which include social, scientific, professional and leisure aspects alike). [2], [5], [13], [15], [17], [18], [26], [41]

Simulation competency includes implementation and testing of products, feedback for software development and the use of simulation programs. [5], [13], [29], [41]

Software development competency includes elements of programming (e.g. stop command, jump instruction, program branching, output, loops, binary coding, data structures, flow of programming) as well as aspects and skills referring to the preparation and review of programming (e.g. creation of flowcharts, class hierarchies and sequence diagrams). [5], [10], [13], [15], [17], [21], [28], [29], [37], [41]

Structured thinking encompasses methods to identify and create structures in computer scientific contexts. Fields of application include problem-solving, programming, analysis of information, informatics and data processing systems, and handling of formal structures (sequences and characters / symbols). [2], [4], [5], [10], [13], [15], [17], [18], [22], [28], [29]

Systematic thinking refers to the ability to approach problems and solutions systematically. This includes a grasp of systemic relationships and system functionality. [13], [17], [26], [28]

Theoretical thinking involves the application of theoretical knowledge (e.g. finding a solution to a task, use of graphical methods, design of software products) and its prerequisites (e.g. theoretical foundations of computer science, important structural and functional principles to describe data processing systems). [2], [5], [13], [18], [21], [26], [28], [29], [37]

User skills include applications of information technologies, computer usage, advantages and disadvantages of user systems, programming environments, and basic knowledge of hardware and software. [2], [13], [15], [37], [41]

7. CONCLUSION

The goal of this paper was to show how key competencies in informatics can be derived without recourse to normative methods using Qualitative Content Analysis. Six educational approaches were analyzed to produce a list of competencies. After two further refinement steps we arrived at key competencies in informatics.

Because the method described ensures the property of maximal prevalence over the entire range of the source material, the resulting group of key competencies has a better claim to objectivity than its predecessors, which were either normatively constructed or derived from fields external to computer science.

The derived key competencies can be used to analyze existing course material with the aim of finding out which competencies are conveyed, or as a starting point for the development of competency models or educational standards.

8. REFERENCES

[1]   Allen, M.G. 1993. *A conceptual model of transferable personal skills*. University of Sheffield, Personal Skills Unit, Employment Department, Sheffield, 1993. (Cited in [16])

[2]   Arlt, W. and Koerber, B. 1981. Ziele und Inhalte des Informatikunterrichts. In: W. Arlt. *Informatik als Schulfach*.

Didaktische Handreichungen für das Schulfach Informatik. Datenverarbeitung/Informatik im Bildungsbereich. Bd. 4, Oldenbourg R. Verlag GmbH, Munich, pp. 18-27.

[3] Baumann, R. 1996. *Didaktik der Informatik*. Klett Verlag, 2nd. Edition, Stuttgart.

[4] Breier, N. 1994. Informatische Bildung als Teil der Allgemeinbildung. Log In Verlag, *Log In 14*: 5/6, pp. 90-93.

[5] Breier, N. and Hubwieser, P. 2002. An information-oriented approach to informatical education. In: *Informatics in Education*, Institute of Mathematics and Informatics, Vilnius, Vol. 1, pp. 31-42.

[6] Brosziewski, A. 2010. Von Bildung zu Kompetenz -- Semantische Verschiebungen in den Selbstbeschreibungen des Erziehungssystems. In: *Soziologie der Kompetenz*. Eds.: Thomas Kurtz and Michaela Pfadenhauer, VS Verlag für Sozialwissenschaften, Wiesbaden, pp. 119-134.

[7] Bruhn, J. 1971. Datenverarbeitung im Unterricht. In: *Der mathematische und naturwissenschaftliche Unterricht 24/4*, Ferd. Dümmler's Verlagsbuchhandlung, pp. 210-215.

[8] Bruner, J.S. 1960. *The process of education*. Cambridge Mass.

[9] Buhse, R. 1987. Lehrerfortbildung zur informationstechnischen Grundbildung auf breiter Front angelaufen. Log In Verlag, *Log In 7*, Heft 3, pp. 7-8.

[10] Bund-Länder-Kommission für Bildungsplanung und Forschungsförderung (BLK). *Gesamtkonzept für die informationstechnische Bildung*, Bonn.

[11] Didi, H.-J., Fay, E., Kloft, C. and Vogt, H. 1993. *Einschätzungen von Schlüsselqualifikationen aus psychologischer Perspektive. Bundesinstitut für Bildungsforschung*.

[12] Dörge, C. 2010. Competencies and skills: Filling old skins with new wine. In: *Key Competencies in the Knowledge Society 2010 (KCKS 2010)*, Brisbane, Australia, held as part of WCC 2010, Conference of the IFIP (IFIP AICT 324).

[13] Forneck, H.J. 1992. *Bildung im informationstechnischen Zeitalter – Untersuchung der fachdidaktischen Entwicklung der informationstechnischen Bildung*. Verlag Sauerländer, Aarau.

[14] Gesellschaft für Informatik (GI). Grundsätze und Standards für die Informatik in der Schule – Bildungsstandards Informatik für die Sekundarstufe I, Log In Verlag, *Log In, Issue 150/151*, 28. Jahrgang.

[15] Gunzenhäuser, R. and Lehnert, U. 1970. Informatik als Unterrichtsfach? Grundlagen, Technik und Einsatzmöglichkeiten der elektronischen Datenverarbeitung als zukünftiges Lehrgebiet an allgemeinbildenden Schulen. In: *Elektronische Datenverarbeitung in Schule und Ausbildung. Erfahrungen, Praxis, Planung in Deutschland*. U. Lehnert (Ed.), Oldenbourg, Munich, pp. 40-46.

[16] Holmes, L. 2000. *Questioning the skills agenda. In: Integrating Key skills in higher education – Employability, transferable skills and learning for life*. Kogan Page Limited, London. S. Fallows and C. Steven (Eds.), pp. 201-214.

[17] Hubwieser, P. 2000. *Didaktik der Informatik – Grundlagen, Konzepte, Beispiele*. Springer Verlag, Berlin, Heidelberg, New York.

[18] Hubwieser, P., Broy, M. and Brauer, W. 1996. A new approach to teaching information technologies: Shifting emphasis from technology to information. In: *Information Technology -- Supporting change through teacher education*. IFIP TC3 WG3.1/3.5 Joint working Conference. 30th June - 5th July 1996, Kiryat Anavim, Israel. D. Passey and B. Samways (Eds.) Chapman & Hall, London / Weinheim / New York / Tokyo / Melbourne / Madras, pp. 115-121.

[19] Humbert, L. 2006. *Didaktik der Informatik -- mit praxiserprobtem Unterrichtsmaterial*. Teubner Verlag, Wiesbaden.

[20] Jäger, P. 2001. *Der Erwerb von Kompetenzen als Konkretisierung der Schlüsselqualifikationen – eine Herausforderung an Schule und Unterricht*. Universität Passau.

[21] Kaiser, H. 1987. Informationstechnische Bildung an Berliner Gesamtschulen (Teil 1). Log In Verlag, *Log In 7*, Issue 1, pp. 6-8.

[22] Kaiser, H. 1987. Informationstechnische Bildung an Berliner Gesamtschulen (Teil 1). Log In Verlag, *Log In 7*, Issue 2, pp. 3-5.

[23] Koerber, B. 1981. Weshalb Informatik in der Schule? In: *Informatik als Schulfach. Didaktische Handreichungen für das Schulfach Informatik, Datenverarbeitung / Informatik im Bildungsbereich*, Bd. 4. W. Arlt (Ed.), München, pp. 11-17.

[24] Koerber, B. and Peters, I. R. 1993. Informatikunterricht und informationstechnische Grundbildung – ausgrenzen, abgrenzen oder integrieren? In: *Informatik als Schlüssel zur Qualifikation*. K. G. Troitzsch (Ed.), Springer-Verlag, Berlin / Heidelberg / New York, pp. 108-115.

[25] GI-Fachtagung 'Informatik und Schule 1993' Koblenz, 11. - 13. Oktober 1993.

[26] Landa, L.N. 1969. *Algorithmierung im Unterricht. Volk und Wissen*. Berlin Ost.

[27] Lehnert, U. 1973. Die Förderung der Entwicklung geistiger Fähigkeiten durch den Einsatz von Rechnern im Unterricht. In: *Zeitschrift für erziehungswissenschaftliche Forschung 7/4*, pp. 201-224. (Cited in [13].)

[28] Magenheim, J. 2001. Informatiksystem und Dekonstruktion als didaktische Kategorien – Theoretische Aspekte und unterrichtspraktische Implikationen einer systemorientieren Didaktik der Informatik. In: *informatica didacta, Zeitschrift für fachdidaktische Grundlagen der Informatik*, Vol. 3.

[29] Magenheim, J. 2003. Informatik Lernlabor – Systemorientierte Didaktik in der Praxis. In: *INFOS 2003*, pp. 13-21.

[30] Mayring, P. 2003. *Qualitative Inhaltsanalyse – Grundlagen und Techniken*. 8. Auflage, Beltz Verlag, Weinheim / Basel.

[31] Mayring, P. 2000. Qualitative Content Analysis. In: *Forum: Qualitative Social Research*. Vol. 1, No. 2, Art 20.

[32] Mertens, D. 1974. Schlüsselqualifikationen – Thesen zur Schulung für eine moderne Gesellschaft. In: *Mitteilungen aus der Arbeitsmarkt- und Berufsforschung*, Vol. 7, pp. 36-43.

[33] Müller, E. 2010. Einige Anmerkungen zur Begrifflichkeit Schlüsselqualifikation – Schlüsselkompetenz – Schlüsselbildung. In: *SQ Forum, Schlüsselqualifikationen in*

Lehre, Forschung und Praxis, Ausgabe 1/2010, Bochum, pp. 7-20.

[34] Mulder, F. and van Weert, T. 2001. IFIP/UNESCO's informatics curriculum framework 2000 for higher education. *SIGCSE Bull*, Vol. 33, Number 4, ACM, New York, NY, USA , pp. 31-33.

[35] Reetz, L. 2003. Zum Zusammenhang von Schlüsselqualifikationen – Kompetenzen – Bildung. In: *Reader Berufsorientierung AND Schule-Wirtschaft / Arbeitsleben.*

[36] Rechenberg, P. 1991. *Was ist Informatik? Eine allgemeinverständliche Einführung.* Hanser, München.

[37] Riedel, D. 1981. Ansätze einer Didaktik des Informatikunterrichts. In: *Informatik als Schulfach. Didaktische Handreichungen für das Schulfach Informatik.*

Datenverarbeitung / Informatik im Bildungsbereich, Bd. 4, W. Arlt (Ed.), München, pp. 36-41.

[38] Schaeper, H. and Bredis, K. 2004. *Kompetenzen von Hochschulabsolventinnen und Hochschulabsolventen, berufliche Anforderungen und Folgerungen für die Hochschulreform.* Hochschul-Informations-System (HIS), Hannover, 6/2004.

[39] Schubert, S. and Schwill, A. 2004. *Didaktik der Informatik. Spektrum Akademischer Verlag*, Heidelberg, Berlin.

[40] Schwill, A. 1993. Fundamentale Ideen der Informatik. In: *Zentralblatt für Didaktik der Mathematik 1*, Vol. 25, ZDM, pp. 20-31.

[41] van Lück, W. 1986. *Informations- und kommunikationstechnologische Grundbildung in Nordrhein-Westfalen.* Log In Verlag, Log In 6, Vol. 2, pp. 29-30.

Weaving Computing into all Middle School Disciplines *

Susan H. Rodger
Duke University
Durham, NC USA
rodger@cs.duke.edu

Dwayne Brown
Duke University
Durham, NC USA
dwayne.brown@duke.edu

Michael Hoyle
Duke University
Durham, NC USA
michael.a.hoyle@gmail.com

Daniel MacDonald
Duke University
Durham, NC USA
dkm12@duke.edu

Michael Marion
Duke University
Durham, NC USA
michael.marion@duke.edu

Elizabeth Onstwedder
Duke University
Durham, NC USA
eho@duke.edu

Bella Onwumbiko
Duke University
Durham, NC USA
beo3@duke.edu

Edwin Ward
Duke University
Durham, NC USA
emw35@duke.edu

ABSTRACT

In order to get students interested in computing, we teach middle school teachers of different disciplines programming with Alice and work with them on integrating computing into their discipline. Alice provides an interface for novices to create animations easily and quickly, which is attractive to and fun for students. We have been developing Alice curriculum materials for integrating computing into middle school disciplines for six years. Although our target audience is middle school, our materials are used by teachers from elementary school to introductory college level. This paper describes our newest curriculum materials for several disciplines developed by both us and our teachers. Our newest curriculum materials include tutorials, sample projects, and *challenges*, which are projects with missing pieces. We also discuss our recent outreach efforts with middle school students.

Categories and Subject Descriptors

K.3.2 [**Computing Milieux**]: Computers and Education-Computer and Information Science Education

General Terms

Human Factors

*The work of these authors are supported by the National Science Foundation grant DRL-1031351 and IBM Faculty Awards

Keywords

Alice, virtual worlds, K-12 education, middle school, introductory computer science

1. INTRODUCTION

Although middle school students use computers constantly throughout the day, the majority of them do not understand the meaning of computer science. Their exposure is likely not computational thinking or algorithmic problem solving, but instead using software such as word processors, presentation tools, and online course environments such as Moodle. A report in 2010 [1] produced by the Association of Computing Machinery (ACM) and the Computer Science Teachers Association (CSTA) stated that computer science education in the United States is at a crisis. While the digital age is transforming the world, U.S. K-12 education is not preparing students with the fundamental computer science knowledge to be prepared to take on jobs in the more computing-intense future. The NCWIT Scorecard [15] mentions that the U.S. Bureau of Labor Statistics predicts a total of 1.4 million computing-related jobs by 2018 and that one-third of them will be unfilled because not enough students are choosing computer science as a major.

There are several difficulties in moving toward teaching computer science in middle schools. One such difficulty is the lack of computer science standards. The CSTA and ACM have developed K-12 computer science standards (revised in 2011) [20] and a number of other documents that link their standards with other national standards. Another difficulty is teacher certification. Recently the CSTA has developed a document [13] about the lack of teacher certification for computer science in the U.S. showing a state by state report and many flaws in the existing teacher certification and licensure processes.

There are many efforts to increase the number of K-12 students exposed to computing such as the CS10K project [8], the new AP CS Principles Course [6], and a new effort with code.org [5] that has gotten millions of students trying an hour of programming by using their one-hour tutorials. Many projects target middle school including CS Unplugged [7], Alice [2] and, Scratch [19], and some projects are focused on a specific discipline such as integrating mathematics with computing at the K-12 level [4, 12].

This paper describes our efforts on integrating computing with all disciplines using the Alice programming language. There are many books on Alice programming including one by Dann and others [9], and papers describing Alice curriculum materials such as one on Alice projects for middle school disciplines [17]. There have been three Alice Symposiums with the most recent one in 2013 [3] that show many ways how people are using Alice from elementary school to college level. For example the paper [21] shows how students at a camp create Alice videos and then use green screens to splice in videos of the students into their Alice videos. There are studies that show Alice aids in learning computer science such as [14] that shows college students using Alice had improved performance in CS 1, retention and attitudes about computer science. In [22], they show that students in a middle school game-programming course demonstrated an understanding of a range of computer science concepts while using Alice to make games.

In this paper we describe the curriculum materials we have developed for learning Alice programming, and how we work with teachers on integrating computing with Alice into all middle school disciplines. Although there are a few middle schools that have programming courses [22, 23, 10], most middle schools in the United States do not have a programming course or room to create one, and most teachers have no programming experience. Efforts such as code.org are reaching millions of students for one-hour, but the teachers are not being trained to support those efforts. In our work we run professional development to teach middle school teachers in all disciplines with no knowledge of programming how to program with Alice and help them prepare lesson plans that integrate computing with their discipine. Our curriculum materials include tutorials, sample projects, and *challenges*, which are projects with missing pieces. We also discuss our recent outreach efforts with middle school students.

2. BACKGROUND AND WORKSHOPS

We have been teaching Alice at the college level at Duke University for over twelve years. About seven years ago we started teaching Alice to middle school students. After seeing their excitement with Alice we started teaching Alice to K-12 teachers and started developing curriculum materials for those teachers. We hold two-week workshops in the summer to teach the teachers programming with Alice and to work with them on developing lesson plans. The teachers are mostly middle school, with some also at the elementary level and the high school level (but not programming teachers). Our focus is on teaching beginners in different disciplines. Since 2008, we have taught Alice to over 200 K-12 teachers. Those teachers are from the disciplines language arts, history, science, math, english as a second language (ESL), foreign language, music, art, business, media and physical education. Our curriculum materials and the lesson plans the teachers develop at our workshop are all available for free at our website [11]. We have over 130 tutorials and example worlds and over 170 lesson plans developed by teachers attending our workshops that are available for free. Although our target is middle school, the materials are being used by teachers at all levels in K-12 and even some colleges. We use many of the materials at Duke University in a semester Alice course CompSci 94. According to Google Analytics, since September 2012 when we started tracking visitors we have had over 26,000 visits to our Alice materials website of which over 19,000 were unique visitors.

3. CURRICULUM MATERIALS

We have developed five types of Alice curriculum materials for students to use in learning Alice, and for teachers to use in supplementing their lesson plans. We have created beginner tutorials, topical tutorials, enhanced objects, challenges, and projects. We have created two documents available on our web site to show how our Alice materials map with the CSTA standards mentioned earlier and for our math materials with the Common Core Mathematics Standards [16] in the United States. Forty-five states have adopted the Common Core State Standards. Many of our tutorials list the standard on the tutorial.

3.1 Getting Started Tutorials

Our simplest tutorials are beginner or *getting started* tutorials. These tutorials are essential for a teacher in a different discipline to be able to teach basic programming concepts in a short period of time to students. We have nine beginner tutorials to chose from that range from short 15 minute tutorials to introduce Alice, to multipart four-hour tutorials that put together many concepts. Based on feedback from teachers attending our workshop and our own experience of teaching the teachers these tutorials, we recently created simpler versions of many of our beginner tutorials. For example, we converted a four-part tutorial with a princess and dragon theme into a shorter three-part tutorial with simpler parts. It is exciting to teach a dragon how to flap its wings elegantly if one has a lot of time, but using a simpler quick up and down motion on the main part of the wing gets the point across in a lot less time. Since our teachers are mainly discipline-specific teachers they need shorter tutorials. As another example, we created a shorter version of one of our one-hour tutorials by removing the multiple camera views, and created a separate tutorial on moving the camera that could be added on at a later time.

The majority of our tutorials are in .pdf format. Based on teacher feedback we created a new one-hour getting started tutorial that is in video format, divided into six videos. The tutorial is about a person on an island who uses a rowboat to escape a shark. Teachers said there are times when some of their students have 10 or 15 minutes free and they needed shorter videos. We also provide finished worlds of each part that can be used to start a new part if needed. We have started converting our other tutorials into videos.

3.2 Topical Tutorials

We created *topical tutorials* on either computer science topics or animation topics. Our computer science topics include tutorials on typical programming topics such as conditionals, loops, methods, functions, parameters, inheritance, variables, randomness, loops, and events. However we use different names for the tutorials such as "making decisions" for the tutorial on conditionals and "creating a fancier chicken" for the tutorial on inheritance. We have recently created new tutorials on lists and arrays.

Figure 1: Showing four camera views

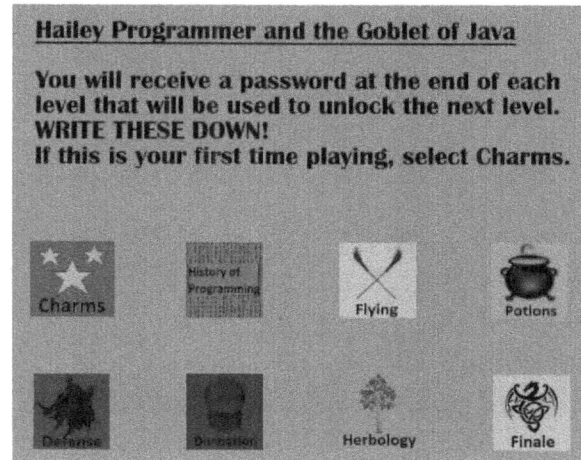

Figure 2: Start of Wizard Challenge

Our other topical tutorials are animation concepts. These cover topics such as moving the camera, changing scenes, adding in pictures, changing the texture of objects, and changing the lighting. With feedback from our teachers we modified previous tutorials. For example, we have a scene change tutorial that shows you how to setup an animation with three scenes, one in the dessert, one in the water and one on the moon, and how to fade to black and then fade in to another scene. We modified this tutorial to add a character and showed the teachers how to setup the location and orientation of the character in each scene, and then how to move the character between those set positions. We also created new animation tutorials requested by teachers. One of our new tutorials is on setting up multiple camera views that follow a particular person as they move through a world. Figure 1 shows four of the camera views that follow the girl as she walks along the road towards the igloo. First the camera is behind the girl, then looking from the side of the girl, then looking at the girl, and then is the girl's view. You can see the difference in her distance from the igloo as she walks towards it.

3.3 Helper Objects

We created *helper objects* to help teachers and students create an animation faster, instead of creating everything from scratch. The helper object is a 3D object that may be invisible and already has several functions and methods. We provide short tutorials that show how to use the functions and methods that come with the object and suggestions for possible modifications. A student can import the object into their world and start using the functions and methods. The first helper objects we created were for teachers to help them create quizzes. After importing a quiz object, the teacher can call a method with a question and answer passed in as arguments to parameters.

Based on requests from teachers we have created several new helper objects. We have a timer object that already comes with a start, pause and initialize method and displays the current number. The timer counts down from the starting value. We have a scorekeeper object that allows one to set a score, increment the score (by any amount) and decrement the score. This object could be used in a game or quiz. We have a fader object that fades out and fades into

scenes similar to our scene tutorial mentioned earlier, but this object comes with many of the methods already built.

3.4 Challenges

A challenge is an Alice world that is mostly built but contains missing pieces. Each challenge comes with a partially built Alice world and a handout describing the missing piece, the challenge! We expect students to know some basic programming before they do the challenge, such as our beginner tutorials, and some challenges may require additional topical tutorials. Most of the challenges are short so they can be completed as a short exercise in a class, another request from teachers. A challenge allows a student to focus on a particular topic and after implementing just that part have an interesting animation. Building the complete animation may take too long for them to do in class.

3.4.1 Wizard World Challenge

Our Wizard World challenge is our largest challenge world and is actually eight challenges in one world. It is a combination of math and programming challenges and the theme uses courses one might take in the school Hogwarts in the Harry Potter series by J.K. Rowling [18]. Our world is titled "Hailey Programmer and the Goblet of Java." The start of the animation shown in Figure 2 shows the eight levels for this game.

Here is how a general level works. When a level is clicked on, a method for that level runs and calls the method the student is suppose to modify. It then checks to see if the animation tasks were completed. If they were not, the student sees the animation does not work correctly and is given instructions and the name of the method they need to edit. Only the methods the student needs to edit are displayed at the top level. The program was designed with the code the student does not need to edit hidden away in folders. Additional tutorials are suggested before attempting some of the levels. The additional tutorials can be found on our website.

We describe the first level in detail which is a coding challenge. We will refer to the student in the animation as the "student" and the student completing the challenge as the "MS student". The MS student starts the animation and

Figure 3: Charms Class

the only level that does not have a password is the charms class, so they select it. This level focuses on basic code for moving and turning objects and the start of it is shown in Figure 3. The student in the animation is trying to use her magic wand to make the three objects rise and to turn the lion. She tries and nothing happens. The MS student is instructed to write code in the method world.charms to move and turn the objects. The MS student then stops the animation and edits the method world.charms This method has comments describing the tasks the MS student needs to complete. The MS student adds code and runs the Alice world again selecting the charms level. If the code is correct, the objects rise and turn and the MS student is rewarded with a password for the next level.

Level 2 is the History of Programming class and is also a coding challenge. In this level an instructor is talking at the front of the classroom while three students are watching and also playing pranks. The MS student needs to modify three sections of code in world.history to make an invisible object visible to reveal a message (changing a property), to make the teacher rise by the teacher's height (using a built-in function), and to make a chair bounce repeatedly (using a loop).

Level 3 is Flying class and is a math and programming challenge. The student must understand how a 2D coordinate system works. In the animation a picture of a coordinate plane is shown and the student has a broom. Their challenge is to fly to different coordinates on the grid by moving up, down, forward and backwards. For a sequence of coordinates, the MS student must add code to call functions for moving up, down, forward and/or backwards and pass the appropriate arguments for the number of units to move. For each new coordinate pair, the student with the broom must move from the current position to the new position. The first few coordinates are number locations such as to location (3,2), but then later coordinates use algebraic equations such as (2, 2x+1).

Level 4 is Potions class and is a math and programming challenge. Here students will add ingredients to a potion using the correct ratios and calling functions with arguments. Level 5 is Defense Against the Dark Arts class and focuses on geometry and programming. Here one will need to defend themselves by calculating distances such as the distance in a semicircle around a troll, or along the edge of a right

triangle. Level 6 is Divination class and focuses on drawing five cards to read their fortune and to calculate the odds of getting a royal flush. This level uses a list of cards. They would need to complete the list tutorial before attempting this challenge. Level 7 is Herbology. Students will use their knowledge of lists and population sampling to calculate the difference in height between the average height of a group of trees and the average height of a group of flowers. Students will need to know the concept of random sampling for this level. Level 8 is the final level. Students combine all the programming knowledge they have learned to save the golden dragon's egg from the giant troll to win the Tri-programmer Tournament.

3.4.2 Calculator Challenge

The calculator challenge started with a request from a math teacher attending our workshop for a calculator object. We forwarded the request to the Alice team and they made a calculator object with button parts. We then wrote the code to allow for one to enter numbers into the calculator and to display those numbers, and wrote functions for all the button operators. The calculator challenge provides our version of the calculator with the functions missing code. Before programming, the students can run the world and enter numbers but will see that buttons such as add do not work. Students then add the code for add, subtract, multiply, divide, square root and log to get the calculator to work. They can then create their own buttons for additional operators, make the button by creating an image and gluing the button onto the calculator, and then add a function for this button. One of the teachers attending a followup workshop showed us a calculator one of her students made who had added almost twice as many buttons and corresponding functions to his calculator.

3.4.3 Boat Racing Game Challenge

The Boat Racing Game is a game in which a student uses arrow keys to drive a boat through ten arches before the time is up. We have taken this game and built on several challenges, all that collect and analyze data. In one example challenge the arches move to random locations before the game starts and code has been added to collect in a list the distance traveled between pairs of arches. The student needs to then add code to use the data to calculate the total distance in order to calculate the average distance between pairs of arches. In another challenge, the student plays the game multiple times, saving each time in a list, and then computes the average time to complete the game.

3.4.4 Pythagorean Challenge

One challenge is to compute distances between objects placed on a 2-d coordinate system. The task is to move a character from his current location to other objects by computing the distance from their current location to the object they want to move to. To finish this challenge the student must modify one function to compute the distance between two points and to use the pythagorean theorem to compute this distance.

3.4.5 Science Challenge

An example of a science challenge for Biology is an Alice world on Punnett squares. Scientist use Punnett squares to predict the outcome of breeding experiments. In this

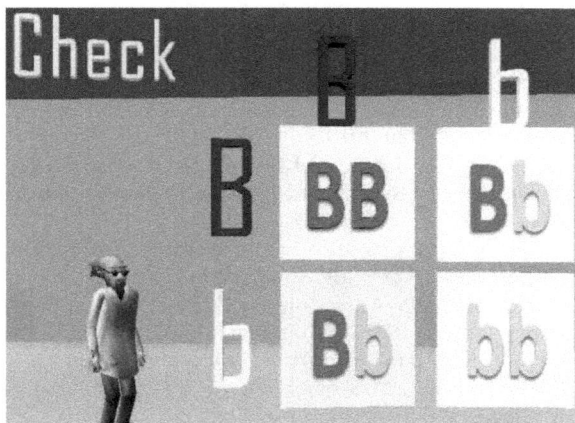

Figure 4: Calculating Punnett Squares

challenge the student has to create four events and complete a method to rotate between four images. When the completed world is run, the user is asked to compute the Punnett Squares for a problem, and they will click on four squares that each list four possible choices (images). For each square cycle through the four images until you find the correct answer as shown in Figure 4 in the top left square. Once correct, the student is then asked related probability questions.

3.5 Sample Projects

We have created over twenty sample project tutorials for a variety of disciplines that tell a story or play a game. The teachers wanted to see projects that put together in a cohesive story or game many of the topics they learned in the workshop. Projects are used heavily in middle school and are the most likely place for teachers to integrate computing. Instead of creating a poster, a power-point presentation or a model for a project, a student could create an Alice animation for a project. The animation could tell a story and also interactively ask quiz questions. Previous projects we created include a sample book report for a language arts class, a quiz on the sounds of different instruments for a music class, a cooking demo to make bread in spanish for a foreign language class. Here we describe some of the new project tutorials.

For science we describe two new projects. One is a tutorial for building an Asteroids game that is like the 1979 Atari classic video game. The user pilots a ship in space and uses the spacebar to shoot a laser at incoming asteroids. The goal is to hit all the astroids before one of them hits the ship. Another new science project is a tutorial that shows how to build an animation of the solar system. In this tutorial the student makes the planets by texturizing shapes and then programs the planets to move around the sun. The lighting is changed in the world to radiate from the sun.

A new project tutorial for a keyboarding class is a keyboard racing game with two characters on bikes who race to the finish line. One of the bikes only moves forward if letters that are displayed are correctly typed. The player is trying to beat the other bike which is moving steadily forward. This project comes with a starter world that already has all the objects you need in it.

3.6 Sample Worlds

We have created over 50 sample worlds to give students ideas on creating Alice worlds. The majority of the most recent sample worlds are for math topics.

Zombie soccer is an interactive world that gives math problems involving negative numbers. For a correct answer the soccer ball will score a goal and for an incorrect answer the zombie goalie will stop the ball. The instructions make it easy to alter the world to different levels of math. *Binary Game* is a game with penguins who have zeros or ones on their bellies. A decimal number is shown and the student has to click on the penguin to change the numbers on the penguin to compute the binary equivalent number. *Blaster* is an interactive game for shooting asteroids with numbers on them. In particular you want to only shoot the asteroids with the number that is the correct solution to a multiplication problem displayed. *Order of operations* is an interactive world in which an expression is displayed involving addition, subtraction, multiplication and division, and the student has to click on the operators in the order they should be calculated, and also has to give the result when applying each operation. After each operation the equation is simplified with the new result. *Fraction world* is an interactive world in which two fractions have an operator applied to them. The student is prompted to simplify the fractions first, and then to compute the answer, and finally simplify the answer if needed. *Bird graphing* allows a student to enter in a function in the code and then watch an animation of dots appearing on a graph to show the values of the function.

An example world for a keyboarding class is *Typing of the dead* game. Zombies with letters on their head come running towards you. They disappear if you type the letter displayed on their head before they get to you.

4. TEACHER LESSON PLANS

The teachers attending our workshops have created over 170 lesson plans that are available for use on our website. The lesson plans are categorized by discipline and within discipline by grade level. Each lesson plan has a title, the name of the teacher, the year it was created, a link to the lesson plan (usually in .pdf and .doc) and a link to the started and/or finished Alice world.

We give examples of two of the lesson plans from 2013. First, a history lesson for sixth graders on ancient Central America. The NC Standard is 6.TT.1, to use technology and other resources for the purpose of accessing, organizing, and sharing information. For this lesson the students will have already had one lesson with Alice and will first review some Alice and review the definition of civilizations. The students will then complete a short Alice tutorial to learn how to create billboards, sounds and 3D text in Alice. Students will view a short documentary and then research ancient civilizations in Central America. They will be given a sample Alice world to complete. They will fill in two scenes with billboards and information they obtained in their research.

Second we describe a lesson plan for a language arts class in 6th grade on fairy tales. Prior to class the students will read a collection of fairy tales and will have completed an Alice beginner tutorial. For this lesson, the students will analyze the fairy tales by identifying recurring themes. The teacher will show them an Alice world example of a fairy tale. The students will outline a story map for an original fairy tale including standard elements and fairy tale themes. Then the students will build an Alice world for their story.

5. OUTREACH

Although our focus is on teaching teachers Alice, we describe some of our outreach activities with students. In November 2012 we were invited by a teacher who took our summer workshop to visit his Middle School and we taught Alice to three sixth grade math classes, about 75 sixth graders total. Each class was about an hour long. We taught them a tutorial with a character on an island who jumps into a boat and rows away. Then we provided them with some of our sample Math worlds to play including the *Order of Operations* and the *Fraction World*. The students were clearly excited about using Alice. The volume level in the room dramatically went up when they added an event so they could control the boat with the arrow keys. In those classes where we finished earlier and the students had more free time with Alice, they added objects to the world and expanded the animation. They asked us questions on how to do certain actions.

In March 2013, we held two three-hour activity days for sixth graders on Alice, and had a total of 26 students attend one of the sessions, with a balance of gender. We taught the students Alice using the same tutorial as before (these students were from different schools than the school we visited earlier). After some free time, they ran the *Order of Operations* and *Fraction World*. Then they worked on the calculator challenge we described earlier. In a survey given at the end of the sessions, the majority of the students thought Alice was easy to use and noted that Alice helped them learn about programming. More than half of the students thought Alice would be fun and valuable to use in their classes for projects and presentations.

6. CONCLUSION

We have developed several types of Alice curriculum materials for integrating computing into several disciplines. We provide professional development for teachers in the summer to teach them Alice and to work with them in creating lesson plans. Our training provides them with confidence and the lesson plans they develop are ready to use. Our teachers are now giving Alice presentations and posters at conferences. One of our teachers developed a full Alice course using our materials and won Teacher of the Year at her school. Our materials and the teachers' lesson plans are available for free.

7. REFERENCES

[1] ACM and CSTA. Running on empty: The failure to teach k-12 computer science in the digital age, 2010. www.acm.org/Runningonempty/.

[2] Alice. website, 2014. Retrieved January 1, 2014 from http://alice.org.

[3] Alice Symposium June 2013. website, 2014. Retrieved January 1, 2014 from http://www.cs.duke.edu/csed/aliceSymposium2013.

[4] Bootstrap. website, 2014. Retrieved January 1, 2014 from http://www.bootstrapworld.org.

[5] Code.org. website, 2014. Retrieved January 1, 2014 from http://code.org.

[6] College Board. CS principles, 2014. Retrieved January 1, 2014 from http://csprinciples.org.

[7] Computer Science Unplugged. website, 2014. Retrieved January 1, 2014 from http://csunplugged.org.

[8] J. Cuny. Finding 10,000 teachers. In *CSTA Voice, 5, 6*, pages 1–2, Jan 2010.

[9] W. Dann, S. Cooper, and R. Pausch. *Learning to Program with Alice, Third Edition*. Pearson, Prentice Hall, 2011.

[10] C. Distler. Piloting alice in the upper school. In *The Proceedings of The Alice Symposium 2013*, 2013.

[11] Duke University Adventures in Alice Programming. website, 2014. Retrieved January 1, 2014 from http://www.cs.duke.edu/csed/alice/aliceInSchools.

[12] E. Freudenthal, M. Roy, A. Ogrey, T. Magoc, and A. Siegel. Mpct: Media propelled computational thinking. In *The Forty-first SIGCSE Technical Symposium on Computer Science Education*, pages 37–41, 2010.

[13] K. Lang, R. Galanos, J. Goode, D. Seehorn, and F. Trees. Bugs in the system: Computer science teacher certification in the u.s., 2013. CSTA Report.

[14] B. Moskal, D. Lurie, and S. Cooper. Evaluating the effectiveness of a new instructional approach. In *Thirty-Fifth SIGCSE Technical Symposium on Computer Science Education*, pages 75–9, 2004.

[15] National Center for Women & IT. Ncwit scorecard 2011: A report on the status of women in information technology, 2011.

[16] C. o. C. S. S. O. National Governors Association Center for Best Practices. Common core state standards math, 2010. National Governors Association Center for Best Practices, Council of Chief State School Officers, Washington D.C.

[17] S. Rodger, M. Dalis, C. Gadwal, J. Hayes, P. Li, L. Liang, F. Wolfe, and W. Zhang. Integrating computing into middle school disciplines through projects. In *The Forty-third SIGCSE Technical Symposium on Computer Science Education*, pages 421–426, 2012.

[18] J. K. Rowling. *Harry Potter and the Sorcerer's Stone*. Bloomsbury, 1997.

[19] Scratch. website, 2014. Retrieved January 1, 2014 from http://scratch.mit.edu.

[20] D. Seehorn, S. Carey, B. Fuschetto, I. Lee, D. Moix, D. O'Grady-Cunniff, B. Owens, C. Stephenson, and A. Verno. Csta k-12 computer science standards, revised 2011, 2011.

[21] J. Shanahan and D. Marghitu. Software engineering java k12 outreach course with alice and cloud computing. In *Proceedings of the 2013 Alice Symposium*, 2013.

[22] L. Werner, S. Campe, and J. Denner. Children learning computer science concepts via alice game-programming. In *The Forty-third SIGCSE Technical Symposium on Computer Science Education*, pages 427–432, 2012.

[23] L. Werner, J. Denner, et al. Pair programming for middle school students: Does friendship influence academic outcomes? In *The Forty-fourth SIGCSE Technical Symposium on Computer Science Education*, pages 421–426, 2013.

Early Validation of Computational Thinking Pattern Analysis

Kyu Han Koh
Department of Computer Science
University of Colorado at Boulder
Boulder, CO 80309
+1 303 492 1349
kohkh@colorado.edu

Hilarie Nickerson
Department of Computer Science
University of Colorado at Boulder
Boulder, CO 80309
+1 303 492 1349
hnickerson@colorado.edu

Ashok Basawapatna
AgentSheets Inc.
Boulder, CO 80301
+1 303 530 1773
ashok@agentsheets.com

Alexander Repenning
AgentSheets Inc.
Boulder, CO 80301
+1 303 530 1773
alex@agentsheets.com

ABSTRACT

End-user game design affords teachers a unique opportunity to integrate computational thinking concepts into their classrooms. However, it is not always apparent in game and simulation projects what computational thinking-related skills students have acquired. Computational Thinking Pattern Analysis (CTPA) enables teachers to visualize which of nine specific skills students have mastered in game design that can then be used to create simulations. CTPA has the potential to automatically recognize and calculate student computational thinking skills, as well as to map students' computational thinking skill progression, as they proceed through the curriculum. The current research furthers knowledge of CTPA by exploring its validity based on how its performance correlates to human grading of student games. Initial data from this validation study indicates that CTPA correlates well with human grading and that it can even be used to predict students' future achievement levels given their current skill progression, making CTPA a potentially invaluable computational thinking evaluation tool for teachers.

Categories and Subject Descriptors

K.3.2 [**Computers and Education**]: Computers and Information Science Education

General Terms

Measurement, Performance, Design, Experimentation

Keywords

Computational Thinking, Computational Thinking Assessment, Computational Thinking Pattern Analysis, Cyberlearning Infrastructure, End User Programming

1. INTRODUCTION

Since the 1990s there have been multiple efforts to fix the broken pipeline at the K-12 level in computer science education [1, 2, 3], and most of those efforts have focused on student motivation. The results indicate that these efforts have successfully increased student motivation in computer science. However, it is often not clear what educational benefits, if any, students receive from these motivational interventions. Part of the problem may stem from a lack of a proper instrument for measuring the knowledge students acquire through their activities in a class. Learning may be measured with existing tools such as grading rubrics, but these tools are extremely time consuming and have limited functionality with respect to assessing learning progress and providing ongoing feedback to students and teachers.

In this paper we present our early efforts to validate a method that we have developed for measuring concept learning in real time. Our technique is inspired by Latent Sematic Analysis (LSA) [4], in which calculations can be used to analyze the semantic meanings of a given context based on predefined subjects or phenomena. Theoretically, this idea can be applied to any domain in which low-level components are combined to form higher-level constructs, supporting analyses such as natural language processing and the examination of computer programs. Constrained environments, including those that make use of visual end-user programming, are especially suited to this kind of analysis. Therefore, this idea can be employed to build a learning assessment tool for computer science (CS) and/or computational thinking (CT) [5] education, where visual programming environments such as AgentSheets [6], Scratch [7], and Alice [8] are widely adopted.

The computer programming context used in our research is the construction of video games and science simulations. At the University of Colorado – Boulder we have four years of data from more than 20,000 students who created games and simulations using AgentSheets and its subsequent 3D version, AgentCubes [9]. Our analytical method, Computational Thinking Pattern Analysis (CTPA), examines the programmed rules of these student-created artifacts to unearth evidence of higher-level patterns that are found in such projects, which typically involve object interactions [10]. Computational Thinking Patterns (CTPs) are constructs students initially learn in game design that can be applied to creating simulations. Examples of CTPs include one agent tracking another agent, one agent absorbing another agent, and one agent creating another agent [11]. The presence of these semantically meaningful patterns indicates that students have grasped the concepts being taught and that they also have the ability to operationalize the concepts by creating programs. Therefore, CTPA can serve as a concept and skill learning assessment tool for CS/CT education.

The outcomes of CTPA can be used to provide valid and useful feedback to educators and learners in CS/CT education by measuring and tracking student learning outcomes. Student-created artifacts from educational programs around the United States and in several other countries have been analyzed by CTPA. These results have shown promising potential in providing educational feedback in the areas of learning transfer [12], learning trajectories [13], and programming divergence [14]. This kind of assessment in CS/CT education should be able to provide better individual feedback and faster learning assessments to students and teachers by measuring student skills and analyzing learning at the semantic level.

Overall, this research offers a partially-validated method to assess student learning skills and compute student learning outcomes. This type of method can be used to create authentic cyberlearning systems that will help large numbers of teachers and students to learn computational thinking. We envision that other investigators will be able to repurpose our calculation method for use in their own educational research contexts.

2. METHODOLOGY

Methodology for this research incorporates rubric-based grading of student projects from multiple classes, the Computational Thinking Pattern Analysis of these submissions, and skill progression calculation to measure learning performance.

2.1 Class Descriptions

The University of Colorado – Boulder Educational Game Design class is a course teaching undergraduate and graduate students to prototype and test educational games. The course has a fairly aggressive programming schedule in which each student builds a playable game every week. The course has three parts. In the first part students learn about computational thinking patterns [10] in the context of making four prescribed games ranging from simple 1980 arcade games such as Frogger to more contemporary games such as the Sims. The design and creation of a Sims-like game exposes students to computational thinking [5] concepts related to artificial intelligence such as collaborative diffusion [15] as well as psychological models such as Maslow's hierarchy of needs. In the second part students design four of their own games, but these games have to be educational. Evaluation includes peer assessment of engagement and the educational value of games. In the last part students work on their final educational game, receiving three weeks time to include more evaluation iterations. Students conduct game testing at a local middle school where they collect empirical evidence from game testers who have not been exposed to their designs.

The validation study presented here focuses on the prescribed games from the first part of the course. The validation process correlates scores produced by a human grader using a rubric with scores produced by Computational Thinking Pattern Analysis. We have correlated the human and machine scoring for individual games as well as for game clusters. This paper presents the correlation between CTPA-measured skills and human-graded

scores from the 2012 and 2013 classes graded by two different individuals. Additionally, the paper presents the inter-grader agreement for the 2012 class graded by two different human graders.

2.2 Computational Thinking Pattern Analysis

Computational Thinking Pattern Analysis (CTPA) is designed to evaluate the semantic meaning of the students' submitted games and simulations. The Latent Semantic Analysis [4] approach as applied in CTPA detects which computational thinking patterns (CTPs) are implemented in a given submission. CTPA looks for nine pre-defined canonical computational thinking patterns within a given game/simulation: user control, generation, absorption, collision, transportation, push, pull, diffusion, and hill climbing. These particular nine patterns are commonly found in video games and science simulations. In the future we could include more CT patterns in CTPA, but to date our research has focused on these nine.

2.2.1 Computational Thinking Patterns (CTP)

Computational thinking is a high-level concept that experts have still not been able to clearly define in a single sentence. We therefore conceptualized Computational Thinking Patterns within the game design context to help students and teachers understand how computational thinking can be practically utilized [10]. A Computational Thinking Pattern (CTP) is an abstract representation that can be easily found in game and simulation programming. For example, the Absorption CTP represents one agent removing another agent (e.g., big fish eats small fish in an ecosystem). In this way, each CTP represents one complete phenomenon or behavioral concept in a game or science simulation design.

Because Computational Thinking Patterns are high-level programming concepts, each pattern requires multiple rules and/or programming primitives to be implemented. For example, the following figure illustrates how the Absorption pattern is programmed using a single rule that contains one condition and one action.

Figure 1. The Absorption pattern implementation

To perform CTPA, a given AgentSheets project is converted such that the degree to which each CTP is present is expressed as a vector component. An AgentSheets project vector is calculated with the equation below, similar to that used in Latent Semantic Analysis [4] to describe semantic meaning [12].

$$\text{CTPA}\,(m) = \left[\frac{\sum_{i=1}^{n} u_i v_i}{\sqrt{\sum_{i=1}^{n} u_i^2} \sqrt{\sum_{i=1}^{n} v_i^2}} \right]_1^m$$

Equation 1. Computational Thinking Pattern Analysis

In this equation, m is the number of computational thinking patterns that are sought (currently nine). The calculated result of CTPA—CTPA (1) to CTPA (m)—can thus be represented as an m length vector. Also, n is the total number of different primitives (conditions and actions) that could possibly appear in any game/simulation (currently 39). Vectors u and v, both of length n, respectively describe the primitives that actually appear in a given game/simulation and in a canonical project that implements one of the m CT patterns.

2.2.2 Computational Thinking Pattern Analysis Graph

The Computational Thinking Pattern Analysis (CTPA) graph visualizes the semantic meaning and computational thinking patterns of the submitted games represented by the nine-dimensional vector calculated through CTPA. The computational thinking patterns implemented in each given game are depicted through this graphic (Figure 2).

This research implementation uses regular class curriculum and is assessed using official game tutorials provided by the Scalable Game Design project researchers and educators. In the case of Figure 2, the student CTPA (Brown in Figure 2) is overlaid with a graph of the tutorial CTPA (Green in Figure 2). Each CT pattern axis is aligned according its implementation difficulty level and its significance to the relationship between adjacent axes. For example, Generation, Absorption, and Collision usually happen in sequence or are highly relevant to each other.

This graphic analysis can work as a self-assessment tool and/or a learning path indicator through a semantic comparison of the submitted project to that specific submission's tutorial standard. In the absence of a comparative tutorial, standardized information can be programmed into the graphic analysis tool to serve as an appropriate comparison.

Computational Thinking Patterns

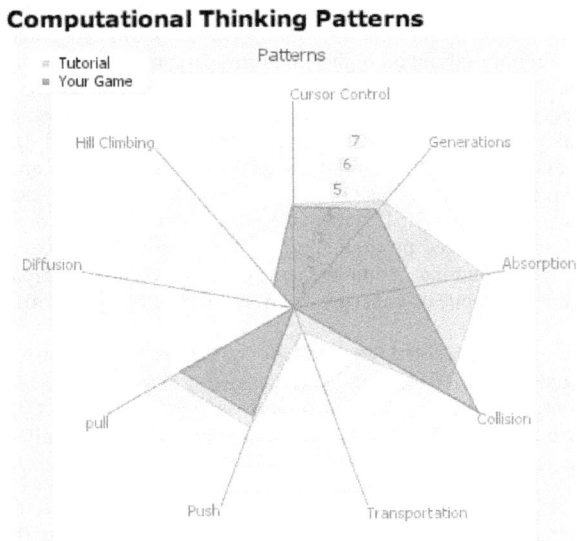

Figure 2. Computational Thinking Pattern Analysis Graph

2.3 Computational Thinking Skill Progression

While the semantic information from individual games/simulations provides useful insight into student learning development, the semantic analysis of individually created games or simulations could also provide an indication of a student's overall skill progress. Representing semantic meaning in measureable units to visually demonstrate student learning trends can benefit students and teachers directly. This approach could also indicate possible curriculum failings at a fundamental level.

The value of each axis on the CTPA Graph translates as the amount of implemented knowledge for a given computational thinking pattern within a game/simulation. The sum or average of these values is interpreted as the student's skill in designing the game/simulation. That is, the nine computational thinking patterns are target-learning categories. The score of each CT pattern in a tutorial represents that pattern's target-learning goal. Thus, the CTPA Graph illustrates how well students meet the target-learning goal in each assignment or group of assignments. Within the CTPA, a one-time assignment analysis is referred to as a Demonstrated Skill Score. Learning that takes place over time through several assignments is referred to as a Comprehensive Skill Score. Both Demonstrated and Comprehensive Skill Scores are calculated from the length (norm) of a vector of the nine computational thinking patterns reduced to one dimension (unit).

The Demonstrated and Comprehensive Skill Scores are calculated using the following equations.

$$\text{Demonstrated Skill Score }(n) = \frac{\sqrt{\sum_{i=1}^{n}(P_i)^2}}{\sqrt{n}}$$

Equation 2. Demonstrated Skill Score

$$\text{Comprehensive Skill Score }(m) = \frac{\sqrt{\sum_{i=1}^{n}[\max_{j=1}^{m}(P_{i,j})]^2}}{\sqrt{n}}$$

Equation 3. Comprehensive Skill Score

In these equations, P is a computational thinking pattern, n is the number of computational thinking patterns on the CTPA Graph, and m is the number of submitted assignments. The equations are derived from the formula for the length of a vector.

The Demonstrated Skill Score shows a student's programming skill as of when the game was submitted, while the Comprehensive Skill Score shows a student's progressed skill acquisition over time. Each Skill Score is the normalized size of the value on each axis of the CTPA Graph. For the Comprehensive Skill Score calculation, we make the following assumption to track students' skill progression: if there is a skill that a student has learned and demonstrated accurately at least once, then that skill is available for the student to use for the entire duration of the course even if it is not used again. In other words, a maximum value of any given game represents its creator's best achieved level in CT pattern implementation. Consequently the maximum value is selected in this equation.

3. RESULTS: ASSESSMENT VALIDATION

To gauge the value of CTPA as a Computational Thinking assessment tool, we conducted the early stages of concurrent validity and predictive validity evaluation using data from undergraduate and graduate students who took an Educational Game Design class in 2012 and 2013. For concurrent validity we compared student grades with CTPA-measured skills for four basic games: Frogger, Sokoban, Centipede, and the Sims. To assess predictive validity we computed students' comprehensive skill scores based on the four basic games and compared them to the demonstrated skill scores of their final projects.

3.1 2012 Class Concurrent Validity Results

For the 2012 class (19 students), we hired two graders for this research who were asked to provide grades based on the official grading rubric for each game. We also used CTPA to calculate a demonstrated skill score for each game.

Table 1. Four Basic Games and Spearman Rank Correlation Charts for the 2012 Class

Game	Spearman's Rank Correlation Coefficients
Frogger	0.246 (Spearman Correlation Coefficient)
Sokoban	0.705 (Spearman Correlation Coefficient)
Centipede	0.535 (Spearman Correlation Coefficient)
Sims	0.821 (Spearman Correlation Coefficient)

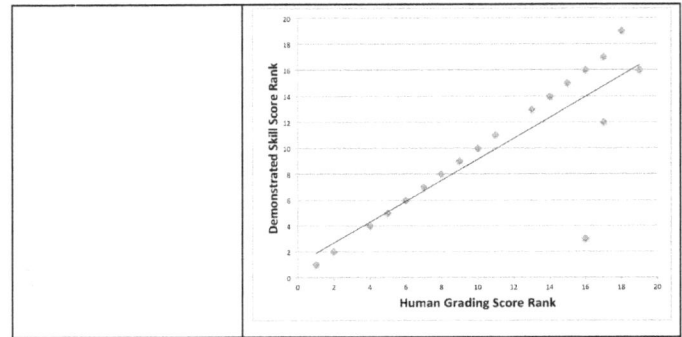

The human grades and the demonstrated skill scores are not normally distributed. Instead, they are skewed negatively. Therefore, we calculated Spearman's rank correlation coefficient to measure the statistical dependence between the CTPA-measured skills of students and the grades that they actually received.

3.1.1 Demonstrated Skill for Individual Games

As Table 1 shows, the Spearman rank correlation coefficients for three of the four basic games are high enough to demonstrate a correlation between human graded scores and CTPA-measured skills. These results indicate that CTPA is capable of measuring students' skills, and its measured results connect well with the human grades.

Although the originality and the design of the game were part of human grading, CTPA measures only programming skills. So for the tied scores, the person who received a higher grade in programming is ranked higher than the person who got a higher grade in originality and design. For example, there are two students who received 100 points where student A received 90 points for basic programming and 10 points for advanced design and student B received 80 points for basic programming and 20 points for advanced design. In this case, student A is ranked higher than student B. If students received exactly same scores for basic and advanced programming, then they are ranked based on their programming completeness (i.e., avoiding undeclared variables/methods or unnecessary programming components).

3.1.2 Comprehensive Skill Across Several Games

We also calculated students' comprehensive skill scores to reflect the correlation between the average student grades and CTPA-measured skill scores when students finished making all four basic games.

The Spearman rank correlation coefficient value between students' grades and their CTPA-measured skill scores is 0.415 (Figure 3). This number indicates a moderate level of positive correlation between students' grades and their CTPA-measured skill scores. Due to the small sample size, we verified its significance with critical values for the Spearman rank correlation coefficient. The critical value for N=19 with a significance level of 0.05 is 0.391, which is lower than the calculated correlation coefficient, 0.415. This calculation indicates that there is a 95% chance of the correlation being truly significant. This result offers another positive indication of the CTPA's validity as a programming assessment tool, suggesting that it would be usable in a real classroom situation.

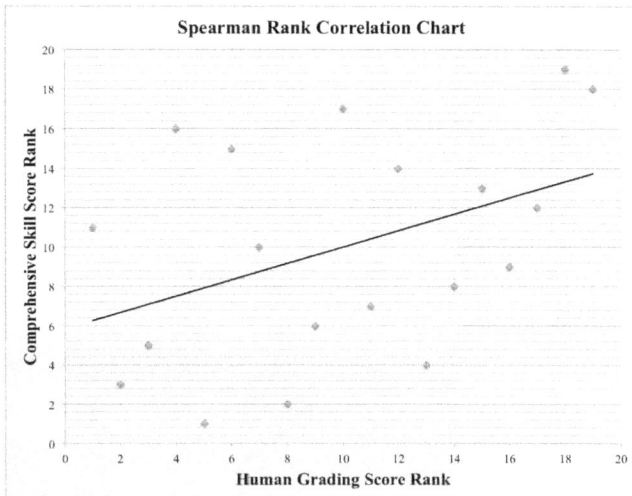

Figure 3. Spearman Rank Correlation Chart from 2012 Class

3.1.3 Inter-Rater Agreement

To check the inter-rater agreement between the two graders, we converted the original 1 to 100 scale scores to a letter grades from A to F. In a 1 to 100 scale score, there are 100 options for grades, and it was difficult to get high inter-rater agreement percentages since there were so many close scores but not exactly the same score (i.e. 93 vs. 95). We converted the scores above 90 to A, the scores above 80 to B, the scores above 70 to C, the scores above 60 to D, and the scores below 60 to F.

The inter-rater agreement percentage between the two graders was 95% on average for the four basic game grades.

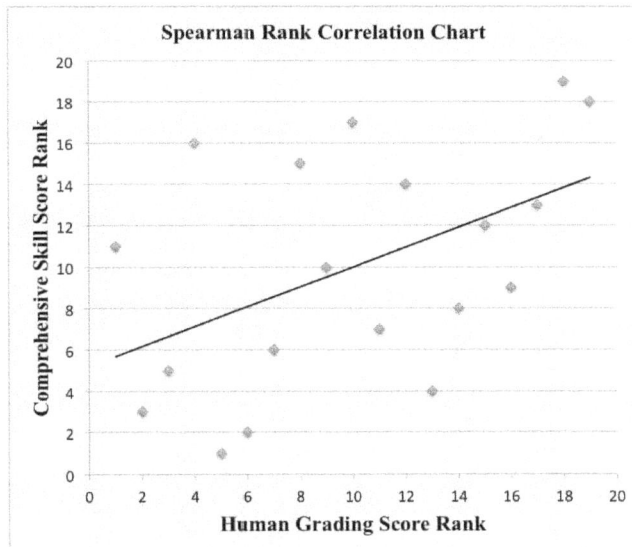

Figure 4. Spearman Rank Correlation Chart from 2013 Class

3.2 2013 Class Concurrent Validity Results

For the 2013 class (20 students), we hired one of the two graders who graded the 2012 class. The same rubric was provided for grading consistency. As for the 2012 class, the students' comprehensive skill scores were calculated as the basis for determining the correlation between average student grades and CTPA-measured skill scores when students finished making four basic games.

The Spearman's rank correlation coefficient value between students' grades and their CTPA-measured skills is 0.476 (Figure 4). This number indicates a moderate level of positive correlation between students' grades and their CTPA-measured skill scores. Due to the small sample size, we again verified its significance with critical values for the Spearman rank correlation coefficient. The critical value for N=20 with a significance level of 0.025 is 0.447, which is lower than the calculated correlation coefficient, 0.476. This calculation indicates that there is a 97.5% chance of the correlation being truly significant. This result illustrates CTPA-measured skill's reliability over two consecutive classes.

3.3 Predictive Validity Results

We then performed a predictive validity test to confirm CTPA's validity as a programming assessment tool. In contrast to the four basic games, the final project was graded based on originality, educational facts, engagement, and student presentation skills rather than programming skills. Thus, for predictive validity, it was not adequate to compare CTPA-measured student skills and student grades.

However, it is possible to use a pure programming comparison to predict students' future achievements based on their previous skills. In other words, if a student has shown high achievement through previous assignments, then s/he is expected to show high achievement in the final project, too. We therefore computed student CTPA-measured skills to show their correlation between pre-final projects and the final project. As Figure 5 illustrates, those who showed better performance through pre-final assignments tended to show better performance in the final project also. For the 2012 class, the Pearson correlation coefficient value between pre-final projects and the final project is 0.676, and there is a 99.5% chance of this correlation being truly significant. For a better correlation calculation, we excluded two students who missed more than three assignments and one student who didn't submit his final project.

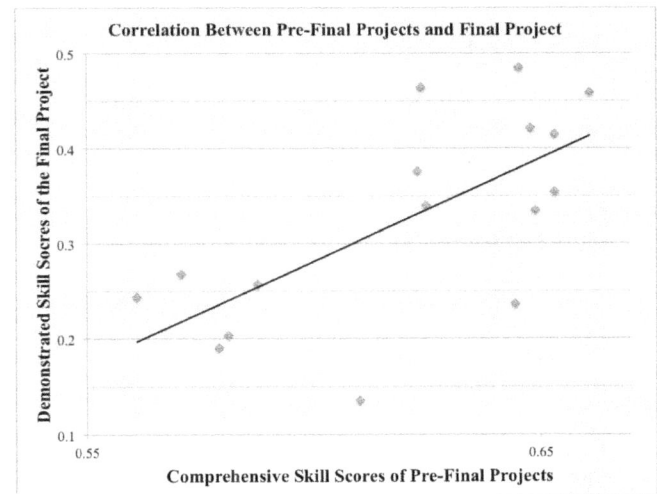

Figure 5. Predictive Validity Evaluation from 2012 Class

This high correlation between Skill scores from pre-final projects and the final project implies that CTPA is able to predict a student's future learning performance and skill trajectory. This capability of CTPA can be applied to build a cyberlearning infrastructure, including automated tutoring systems. For example, right now we are working on a system called REACT (Real time Evaluation and Assessment of Computational

Thinking) that provides the teacher with a dashboard to see what students are programming in real time using CTPA graphs and other visualizations. REACT provides teachers with a useful representation of class and individual progress, allowing them to make effective instructional decisions. The REACT system's feedback is based on CTPA-measured skill.

4. DISCUSSION

In this initial foray into CTPA validation, we found satisfactorily strong positive correlations between scores given by human graders and students' comprehensive skill scores calculated by CTPA, giving us confidence about proceeding with further validation activities. Several factors suggest that the correlations described here are lower than those we might expect to find during additional validation, including the small size of the samples. The current human grader scoring rubric includes both programming skill items, which are closely related to the characteristics examined through CTPA, and other, less related items. For example, the graders checked for the presence of expected computational thinking pattern implementation, and also looked for what users should experience while the game is played. Therefore, human graders are evaluating game design skill along with programming skill. A revised rubric with greater emphasis on programming would be expected to lead to higher correlations. Additionally, these samples include a large percentage of high-performing students, and we believe that we would see more accurate correlations using students having a greater range of skill levels. Overall, the early validation results for the CTPA are promising, though further exploration with a larger data set is warranted. Beyond demonstrating that CTPA and human grader performance are well correlated when assessing foundational games, we showed the predictive value of this analysis tool for assessing students' skill in designing their own games. We anticipate that it will be possible to use CTPA in the future to provide trustworthy educational feedback, especially given the consistency of the findings using data from two consecutive years.

5. ACKNOWLEDGMENTS

This work is supported by the National Science Foundation under Grant Numbers DLR-0833612 IIP-1345523, and IIP-0848962. Any opinions, findings, and conclusions or recommendations expressed in this material are those of the authors and do not necessarily reflect the views of the National Science Foundation.

6. REFERENCES

[1] Werner, L., Campe, S., Denner. J., Children learning computer science concepts via Alice game-programming. In *Proceedings of the 43rd ACM technical symposium on Computer Science Education* (SIGCSE '12). ACM, New York, NY, USA

[2] Koh, K. H., Repenning, A., Nickerson, H., Endo, Y., Motter, P., Will it stick? exploring the sustainability of computational thinking education through game design. In*Proceeding of the 44th ACM technical symposium on Computer science education* (SIGCSE '13). ACM, New York, NY, USA, 597-602.

[3] Maloney, J. H., Peppler, K., Kafai, Y., Resnick, M., Rusk, M., Programming by choice: urban youth learning programming with scratch. *SIGCSE Bull.* 40, 1 (March 2008), 367-371.

[4] Landauer, T. K., Foltz, P. W., Laham, D. Introduction to Latent Semantic Analysis. Discourse Processes, 25, 1998, 259-284

[5] Wing, J. M. 2006. Computational Thinking. Communications of the ACM, 49(3), pp. 33-35, March 2006.

[6] Repenning, A. 2000. AgentSheets®: an Interactive Simulation Environment with End-User Programmable Agents. *In Proceedings of Interaction 2000*, Tokyo, Japan, 2000.

[7] Resnick, M., Maloney, J., Monroy-Hernández, A., Rusk, N., Eastmond, E., Brennan, K., Millner, A, Rosenbaum, E., Silver, J., Silverman, B., and Kafai, Y. 2009. Scratch: programming for all. Commun. ACM 52, 11 (November 2009), 60-67.

[8] Werner, L., Denner, J., Bliesner, M., and Rex, P. 2009. Can middle-schoolers use Storytelling Alice to make games? results of a pilot study. *In Proceedings of the 4th International Conference on Foundations of Digital Games (FDG '09)*. ACM, New York, NY, USA, 207-214.

[9] Ioannidou, A., Repenning, A., Webb. D., AgentCubes: Incremental 3D end-user development. *J. Vis. Lang. Comput.* 20, 4 (August 2009), 236-251

[10] Ioannidou, A., Bennett, V., Repenning, A., Koh, K., Basawapatna, A. 2011. Computational Thinking Patterns. *In Proceedings of 2011 Annual Meeting of the American Educational Research Association (AERA) in the symposium "Merging Human Creativity and the Power of Technology: Computational Thinking in the K-12 Classroom"*. New Orleans, April 8-12, 2011

[11] Basawapatna, A., Koh, K. H., Repenning, A., Using Scalable Game Design To Teach Computer Science From Middle School to Graduate School, *ITiCSE '10: Annual Conference on Innovation and Technology in Computer Science Education*, Ankara, Turkey June 26-30, 2010.

[12] Koh, K. H., Basawapatna, A.,Bennett, V., Repenning, A. 2010. Towards the Automatic Recognition of Computational Thinking. *In Proceedings of IEEE International Symposium on Visual Languages and Human-Centric Computing 2010*, Leganés-Madrid, Spain, September 21-25, 2010

[13] Bennett, V., Koh, K. H., Repenning, A. Computing learning acquisition?, *IEEE International Symposium on Visual Languages and Human-Centric Computing* 2011, Pittsburgh, PA, USA, September 18-22, 2011

[14] Bennett, V., Koh, K. H., Repenning, A., Computing Creativity: Divergence in Computational Thinking, *ACM Special Interest Group on Computer Science Education Conference, (SIGCSE 2013)*, March 6-9, 2013, Denver, Colorado, USA

[15] Repenning, A., Excuse me, I need better AI! Employing Collaborative Diffusion to make Game AI Child's Play. *in Proceedings of the ACM SIGGRAPH Video Game Symposium*, (Boston, MA, 2006), ACM Press.

Guess My Object – An 'Objects First' Game on Objects' Behavior and Implementation with BlueJ

Axel W. Schmolitzky and Timo Göttel
Dept. of Informatics, University of Hamburg
22527 Hamburg, Germany
schmolitzky@acm.org, tgoettel@acm.org

ABSTRACT

Introductory programming education following the *Objects First* approach introduces the concepts of object-oriented programming early on. Objects with *state* (fields) and *behavior* (methods) that offer services to their clients (via their public *interface*) and hide the way these services are implemented (in their *implementation*) are the building blocks of any larger object system. These basic properties of objects are so crucial for understanding object-oriented programming (and later on object-oriented design) that diverse approaches to teaching them should be offered. In this paper we introduce *Guess My Object* (GMO) as a new approach to getting in contact with objects early that can complement existing teaching approaches. In essence, GMO is a way of using *BlueJ* for an interactive round-based game, each consisting of two stages, *behavior exploration* and *behavior implementation*.

Categories and Subject Descriptors

K.3.2 [**Computers and Education**]: Computer and Information Science Education—*Computer Science Education*

Keywords

CS1; Objects First; Gamification

1. INTRODUCTION

Introductory programming courses are challenging in many respects. Robins et al. [6] point out that students need to grasp several concepts and elements in parallel. Introductory courses often focus on teaching language constructs, but students rarely fail because they do not understand the concept of, say, a loop. Instead learners typically have problems in building mental models of the inner working of object systems, which is an important prerequisite for effectively making use of language constructs and applying them in problem solving.

Sorva [9] discusses these problems as well and introduces the term *notional machine* that denotes that students often see programming concepts, elements or paradigms as black boxes hindering them from creating a complete mental model. Sorva recommends to provide tools and approaches that allow students to explore notional machines in detail and inspect underlying processes and interactions.

In this paper we introduce a new approach to getting in contact with the objects of object-oriented programming that we call *Guess My Object* or GMO for short. GMO is not meant to replace existing approaches but merely to complement them. It is a game-based approach to exploring and imitating object behavior that allows students to individually adjust the speed and content complexity of their individual learning process.

The article is structured as follows: Initially, we present some backgrounds on our introductory programming course to convey understanding the intentions and the design of *Guess My Object*. In the main section we introduce the game mechanics of *Guess My Object*, depict an example game round and report on a pilot study with 12 participants playing *Guess My Object*. In the discussion we are primarily concerned with possible issues when increasing the number of participants and how to solve them while adhering to the core ideas of *Guess My Object*.

2. BACKGROUND: INTRODUCTORY PROGRAMMING EDUCATION

The introductory programming course *Software Development 1* (SD1) at the University of Hamburg is a mandatory course in the first semester of several B. Sc. degrees related to computer science and is also frequently chosen as a minor subject of students studying Math and Physics. This added up to more than 500 enrolled students in the the winter term 2013/2014 or about 3,000 students over the last eight years. From several surveys during these years we know that about a third of the participants had no prior knowledge of programming.

SD1 gives an introduction to object-oriented programming with Java. Introduced in 2005, the course has constantly been improved, based on evaluation results and our personal observations. The basic structure of the course - using an Objects First approach and lab classes with pair programming and very short feedback cycles - has not changed, though. SD1 is currently one of the best liked and most successful computer science courses at the University of Hamburg.

2.1 Objects First with BlueJ

Applying Objects First means that *objects* with their *behavior* and their *states* play a central role from the beginning of a course. The approach was described in a text book for the first time in 2003 by Barnes and Kölling, which is currently available in its fifth edition [1]. Instead of first introducing imperative foundations, such as statements, variables, expression and procedures with parameters, and later on adding object-orientation as an extension, the imperative concepts are embedded at the appropriate points in an object-centric approach. SD1 is strongly inspired by the approach of Barnes and Kölling, but deviates in several aspects from the book and its exercises.

One crucial aspect of this approach is the use of *BlueJ*, the interactive Java development environment. It allows interactive creation of instances of any class and calling any method of these instances. The core concepts of object-orientation become tangible this way. We had already used and embraced BlueJ before the introduction of SD1 in one of its ancestor courses.

2.2 Early Introduction of Interfaces

In SD1 we do not cover the Java programming language in full, instead we focus on the principles of *object-based programming*: classes allow an arbitrary number of instances that show some behavior (defined in their *methods*), which also depends upon their (internal) states (defined by their *fields*). Advanced topics, such as subtyping, inheritance with abstract classes, exception handling and packages, are postponed deliberately to the following course SD2 in the second semester. On the other hand, the language construct `interface` of Java is introduced quite early, in the middle of SD1, to allow discussion of the explicit description of class *interfaces* [8]. The concept of an interface is central to any kind of software development and can be illustrated well with the interfaces of (even small) objects.

2.3 Explicit Complexity Levels

Even though we focus on object-based programming, the number of topics in SD1 is still large. To give the students an orientation and to demonstrate the nature of programming as building on previously introduced concepts, we structure SD1 into four Complexity Levels. Higher Levels build upon previous Levels in the sense that concepts of prior Levels are mandatory for a proper understanding of the following Levels. For example, it is impossible to understand any collection implementation in the Java Collections Framework (Level 4) without a proper understanding of references and of iterations (both introduced on Level 2). Table 1 gives an overview of the Complexity Levels.

3. GUESS MY OBJECT

GMO is designed to be an additional offer to allow students to take different perspectives on core concepts of object orientation in a playful manner.

BlueJ allows saving projects without source code to prevent users from inspecting the implementation. This can be done by deleting the `.java` files in the project folder while keeping the `.class` files. To make the interface of the implementation available, the BlueJ editor has to be switched to documentation view before deleting the `.java` files. Subsequently, we call these BlueJ projects without source code *GMO projects*.

Each GMO game round is associated with a Complexity Level and consists of two stages: *behavior exploration* and *behavior implementation* (see Fig. 1). The individual progress (stages and rounds) of a player is directed interactively by a Game Master (SD1 tutor).

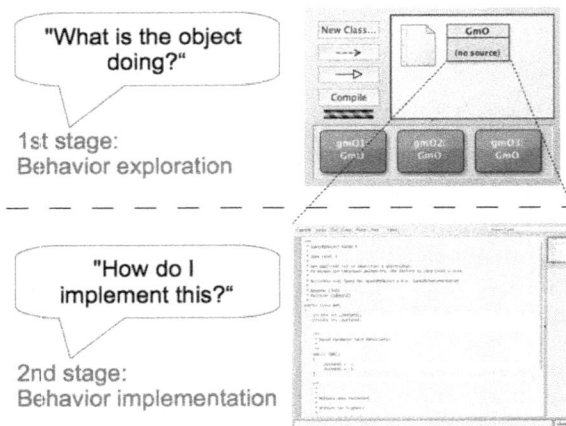

Figure 1: Motivational questions of a GMO round. In the first stage, the player interacts with objects (red boxes) in BlueJ in order to explore their behavior. In the second stage, a player rebuilds or rather implements this behavior using the BlueJ editor.

3.1 Behavior exploration

In the first stage the player gets a GMO project and explores the behavior of its classes by interactively creating objects, calling their methods, and observing the results of these calls. As soon as the player is confident to have a mental model of the behavior, she passes a textual description of it to the Game Master. The second stage is launched by the Game Master if the player's description is correct. The first stage has to be repeated if the description does not fit the behavior of the original implementation.

The player has to observe the following rules and hints in the first stage:

- The projects may only be explored using BlueJ.
- Players have to consider the hints and allowed ranges of values presented in the documentation of the methods (displayed in the BlueJ method call dialog).
- The *object inspector* of BlueJ must not be used because it may help to understand the object behavior without interacting with it.
- Each project has a complexity level assigned to it. The player can rely on the fact that only concepts introduced up to this level are used in the implementation to be guessed.
- Additional tools to explore a GMO project are forbidden. However, players may create clients to explore objects. In this connection, client code may use concepts of the next Complexity Level.

3.2 Behavior implementation

The player has to implement the discovered behavior in the second stage. This stage also comes with rules and hints:

Complexity Level	Core Idea	Concepts
1 (4 weeks)	"Simple Class, simple Objects"	class, object, method, parameter, field, variable, assignment, expression, conditional statement, primitive types
2 (3 weeks)	"Objects using Objects"	classes as types, references, strings, loops, recursions
3 (2 weeks)	"Interfaces with Interfaces"	black box test, test class, interface (Java keyword), consuming collections (of the JCF)
4 (5 weeks)	"Behind the Scenes of Collections"	arrays; implementing collections: array list, linked list, hashing; sorting

Table 1: The Complexity Levels of SD1

- The implementation is restricted to concepts of the currently assigned Complexity Level.
- Method names should describe the behavior of the methods well.
- The implementation has to comply with the coding conventions of SD1.

The implementation (a *BlueJ* project) is passed to the Game Master. Additionally, the player gives feedback on the perceived degree of difficulty of the current GMO round. The second stage has to be repeated if implementation is not correct. If found correct, the Game Master chooses a new GMO project based on the player's perceived degree of difficulty. In addition, the Game Master discusses the player's approach and attaches the original implementation to present differing potential approaches.

The course of events and interactions of GMO is presented in figure 2.

3.3 Rewarding environment

We consider GMO to be an interesting add-on for the regular structure of a programming course and we are aware that optional assignments not relevant for grading need further motivation. Therefore, we decided to add Gamification elements. Gamification is a fuzzy term that has diverse specifications and is often used in different scenarios with various intentions [3]. The underlying idea relevant for this paper is to augment or define tasks and activities with playful elements in small steps. Each accomplished task unlocks achievements that can be seen by other players. Denny [2] recently showed that achievements have a positive effect in educational contexts. Therefore, we decided to assign virtual badges (achievements) that reward task-related and exceptional activities. The Game Master provides a list containing possible achievements including the required activities. This allows us to introduce further incentives to advance the dynamics of the game, as for example "finish three GMO rounds in 72 hours". The players can check their achievements online and compare them to the performance of the other (anonymous) participants.

Additionally, by introducing a Game Master who interacts with the players, GMO allows for individual duration of rounds, degree of difficulty and fast feedback loops. Thereby, it individually allows for a momentum of success.

3.4 Guess My Object Example

A typical GMO project at Complexity Level 1 contains just one class. Our simple example class offers just the default constructor and one public method. In *behaviour exploration* the player must provide a string parameter when calling the method. She puts in "hello world" and receives the string "mjqqt btwqi" as a result. After some other calls, she suspects a Caesar cypher using the shift of 5. Hence, she writes an email to the Game Master about her assumption.

After receiving a confirming reply, she heads on to *behaviour implementation*, designing a Caesar shift that conforms with the current Complexity Level 2. Again, she passes her implementation to the Game Master, stating that she found the current round rather easy. The Game Master approves the implementation, provides his own implementation highlighting differing approaches, and starts the next round by offering a more challenging GMO project.

The Game Master updates the achievements of the player ("correct answer within 24 hours" and "five correct answers in a row"). A few hours later the player checks her achievements and is proud to be the first who has five correct answers in a row. Now, she also wants to be the first who gets the achievement "implementation of a supplemental test class for a GMO project".

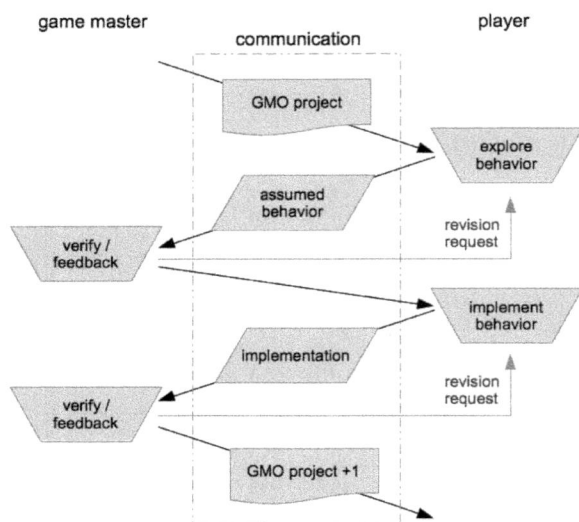

Figure 2: Activities of a GMO round as played in the pilot study.

3.5 Pilot Study

A pilot study on GMO was conducted in the winter term 2012/2013 in SD1 at the University of Hamburg. Students were invited to participate in the game by introducing the game concept and an example GMO round at the beginning of one of the lectures and presenting additional information in the online repository of the course. 12 (4 female) out of 14 interested persons actually took part in the pilot study (meaning that they finished at least two GMO rounds).

The participants could review their achievements at Class-Badges[1] and compare their performance with other (anonymous) participants. Furthermore, they could look up unfinished achievements (badges) to adapt further activities.

Remarkably, most players participated commendable: For example, nine out of twelve finished the first GMO round within 48 hours. The answers of 29 GMO rounds (out of a total of 39 played rounds) were correct straightaway. In case of mistakes or misconceptions, only one revision was needed respectively. Three participants did write additional test cases voluntarily.

Despite the small number of participants, the Game Master's workload was large because of many repetitive procedures and changes between applications (see table 2).

A good example of the Game Master's workload: many incorrect answers needed only little examination by the Game Master. However, each implementation had to be opened and compiled in *BlueJ* and proofread in detail in order to create only a generic short hint for the player to help her/him to find the right solution. Individual and detailed feedback became important because it allowed the Game Master to point to differences and specific features of the original and the player's implementations, e.g. focusing on object-oriented issues.

---

[1]http://classbadges.com/, last visited on May 7, 2014.

Additionally, some achievements considered timing or the amount of accomplished GMO rounds. This resulted in permanent examination of possibly unlocked achievements after a finished GMO round because of the individual course of events for each player.

The players were asked to fill out an online survey at the end of the term. Six participants finished the survey and gave very positive feedback. The individual and interactive elements of GMO were highly praised. Asked about reasons for ending GMO, all participants mentioned crunch times during exams. Asked about a potential semi-automatic environment supporting the Game Master, one participant was slightly concerned that this might affect players' motivation. Yet two participants were sure that this might even increase the dynamics of GMO. Four participants stated that they regularly checked their achievements at ClassBadges. Three of them were not familiar with achievement environments and used them to track their activities. The fourth was used to employing achievements to keep his motivation level high. He mentioned that he adapted his activities to gain more achievements.

4. DISCUSSION AND FUTURE WORK

GMO is an implementation of Mor's pedagogical pattern *GuessMyX* [5] which was originally aimed at math concepts. The pilot study showed that the adapted game mechanics of GMO can provide an additional aspect to introductory programming courses following the Objects First paradigm. It is a lightweight game that is based upon object interaction, exploration and implementation. By introducing a Game Master, the game can be easily adjusted to the speed and skill of each player. However, the pilot study highlighted that GMO might be sustained by building an environment that allows for semi-automatic communication processes between players and Game Master.

Semi-automatic processes may support the Game Master in focusing on individual answers by marking common mistakes or misconceptions before manual examination. Furthermore, a management of GMO projects and possible fits (levels of difficulty) for players may be helpful. Additionally, unlocking achievements should be managed by the environment itself by asking the Game Master for input on possible achievements only when needed. The players could submit their solutions via an online environment that allows standardized communication enhancing the game's interaction, developing categories of difficulties and promoting feedback.

Currently, the GMO rules do not allow using the object inspector of BlueJ. However, the inspector is often used during regular SD1 courses (or in Objects First approaches in general). We thus assume this rule easily to be the subject of unwanted and casual violations. Therefore, we prototyped a BlueJ patch that prevents opening of the object inspector in a GMO project. This patch could be integrated into BlueJ if its designers see enough value in it.

The participants of the pilot study were rather committed and skilled students. But we also see great potential in GMO for students who struggle with object-oriented programming. Therefore, it is important to embed GMO more naturally in the SD1 module. We plan to connect GMO elements and exercise activities by providing an extensive achievement environment that helps us to track more learning processes than just GMO activities. Furthermore, we will encourage students to cooperatively play GMO rounds

Activity	Application	Comment
Receiving solution of 1st stage	E-Mail client	
Giving feedback on mistakes/misconceptions	E-Mail client	Optional, as often as required
Receiving revised solution of 1st stage	E-Mail client	Optional, as often as required
Launching 2nd stage	E-Mail client	
Receiving solution of 2nd stage	E-Mail client	
Checking implementation	*BlueJ*	
Giving feedback on mistakes/misconceptions	E-Mail client	Optional, as often as required
Receiving revised solution of 2nd stage	E-Mail client	Optional, as often as required
Checking reimplementation	*BlueJ*	Optional, as often as required
Choosing next appropriate GMO project	OS / *BlueJ*	
Launching next GMO round	E-Mail client	
Checking achievements	*BlueJ* / E-Mail client	
Updating achievements	Web browser	

Table 2: Activities of the Game Master in a GMO game round for one player, done several times a day.

in tutorials. Accordingly, while we aim at large numbers of participants, we still wish to maintain the individual characteristics of GMO. We understand the successful peer review processes as presented by Hamer et al. [4] to be applicable, because in each round a subset of players will be assigned to the same GMO projects. Peer reviews could be done within such dynamically occurring subsets.

4.1 Portability of GMO

Although we present GMO as an 'Objects First' game on objects' behavior and implementation with BlueJ (respectively Java), we believe that the core concepts of GMO's game mechanics can easily be transferred to other object-oriented languages or editors. In this sense, AGUIA/J [7] appears to be worth a try. Yet, a rich command line interface, for instance, could work as well.

5. CONCLUSIONS

This paper presented the round-based game *Guess My Object* intended as a supplement for introductory programming education. It allows revisiting core concepts of object-oriented programming in a playful manner. Players have to explore the behavior of an 'anonymous' class first. After finding the right behavior, they have to implement it. A pilot study showed that the game mechanics of GMO are appropriate in the context of introductory programming education and were praised by the players. Currently, GMO is designed to be lead by a single Game Master who would have an immense workload if the numbers of participants increased (as intended). Therefore, we wish to develop an online environment that supports Game Master and players in their communication as well as game activities, while keeping individual feedback, pace and levels of difficulty.

6. ACKNOWLEDGEMENTS

GMO was designed and evaluated in a sub-project of a support program to augment university teaching funded by the German Federal Ministry of Education and Research (BMBF, 01PL12033).

7. REFERENCES

[1] D. J. Barnes and M. Kölling. *Objects First with Java: A Practical Introduction using BlueJ*. Pearson Education, 5th edition, 2012.

[2] P. Denny. The Effect of Virtual Achievements on Student Engagement. In *Proceedings of the SIGCHI Conference on Human Factors in Computing Systems*, CHI '13, p. 763–772, 2013. ACM.

[3] S. Deterding, D. Dixon, R. Khaled, and L. Nacke. From Game Design Elements to Gamefulness: Defining "Gamification". In *Proceedings of the 15th International Academic MindTrek Conference: Envisioning Future Media Environments*, MindTrek '11, p. 9–15, 2011. ACM.

[4] J. Hamer, H. C. Purchase, A. Luxton-Reilly, and J. Sheard. Tools for "Contributing Student Learning". In *Proceedings of the 2010 ITiCSE Working Group Reports*, ITiCSE-WGR '10, p. 1–14, 2010. ACM.

[5] Y. Mor. Guess My X and Other Patterns for Teaching and Learning Mathematics. In *Proceedings of the 13th European Conference on Pattern Languages of Programs (EuroPLoP '08)*, 2008.

[6] A. Robins, J. Rountree, and N. Rountree. Learning and Teaching Programming: A Review and Discussion. *Computer Science Education*, 13(2):137–172, 2003.

[7] A. L. Santos. AGUIA/J: A Tool for Interactive Experimentation of Objects. In *Proceedings of the 16th Annual Joint Conference on Innovation and Technology in Computer Science Education*, ITiCSE '11, p. 43–47, 2011. ACM.

[8] A. Schmolitzky. Teaching Inheritance Concepts with Java. In *Proceedings of the 4th International Symposium on Principles and Practice of Programming in Java (PPPJ '06)*, 2006. ACM.

[9] J. Sorva. Notional Machines and Introductory Programming Education. *Transactions on Computing Education*, 13(2):8:1–8:31, July 2013.

Game Programming for Improving Learning Experience

Raquel Hijón-Neira, Ángel Velázquez-Iturbide,
Celeste Pizarro-Romero
LITE Laboratory of Information Technologies in Education
Universidad Rey Juan Carlos
Móstoles, Madrid, Spain
(34) 914887379, 91664745, 914888125
{raquel.hijon, angel.velazquez, celeste.pizarro}@urjc.es

Luís Carriço
LaSIGE Large-Scale Informatics
System laboratory
University of Lisbon
Lisbon, Portugal
(35) 1 217500603
lmc@di.fc.ul.pt

ABSTRACT

In Computer Science Education there is a tendency to implement active learning paradigms where students are the focus of the educational process. An instantiation of these learning methods are gaming environments. We present ProGames, a system for learning programming skills through a leveled set of visually-attractive and interactive programming games in Greenfoot, categorized by student's likes offering them solutions to sets of problems that they really enjoy or like most. The system has been evaluated during the academic course 2012-13 in three Computer Science Degrees and our results indicate that using ProGames had a most positive influence in the students learning. Moreover, the subjective opinion of students reflects that they really enjoyed working with the system and increased the engagement with the course.

1. INTRODUCTION

The difficulty of learning abstract concepts, generally unknown to students, and the lack of systems proposing the unification between technical programming aspects and methods currently applied to foster the motivation of students, provoke a lack of interest, failure and, eventually, abandonment.

The main objective of ProGames, the system presented and discussed in this paper, is facilitating learning and foster motivation into the programming area. To this purpose, we propose a comprehensive set of programming games that are, in fact, sets of exercises arranged into categories that every student selects and completes according to his particular tastes. Therefore, there is a wide array of solutions to problems in environments attractive to students where they will presumably feel comfortable and capable, as they adapt the proposed games to their personal interests and progressively attempt more difficult tasks.

Once a given student has been categorized, he will begin his own path of learning ascending progressively through the levels of the chosen category. Moving to the next level is possible only after successfully completing all the tasks in the current one. In case of failure, the process must be repeated as many times as needed before users are allowed to proceed to the next level.

We selected and used the Greenfoot [1] development environment to provide visual interactive solutions to the programming exercises for two reasons: i) its target audience is the educative community, and, ii) it includes tools for developing outstanding visually-rich interactive applications.

We propose 4 categories or scenarios for the problems. Each category consists of 7 levels of contents. Therefore, a set of exercises is proposed for each category and its 7 levels. All in all, ProGames offers a total of 192 different exercises. Students working on a category will download the set of exercises for each level, to be executed in Greenfoot Programming Environment. Thus, they can visually execute the interactive exercise solution and understand it intuitively, playing with different inputs and observing the results. Then students are supposed to study in depth the programming code of the exercises, to understand it and become familiar with the various programming techniques used. After completing the set of exercises, the student must answer a specific test to check whether or not the concepts are clear. A successful test allows moving to the next (higher) level.

2. MOTIVATION, RELATED WORK, CONTRIBUTIONS

Greenfoot is a free Java game development environment that was designed for high school and undergraduate education. There is a textbook on introductory Computer Science with Greenfoot [1]. As Greenfoot uses Java, it gives the students a taste of a language currently used in introductory computer science courses.

We wanted to go a little bit further and create an application suitable to connect with the interest of the student, considering the comparison [2] of Alice, Greenfoot, Scratch and App Inventor and the conclusion that they share many goals, support rich graphics and sound and let users to create projects that connect to their interests. Alice and Greenfoot target older students than Scratch, introducing object-oriented programming and emphasize Java or Java concepts, preparing them for a more formal course in this language. Scratch targets younger users focusing on self-learning and emphasizes thinking ability. App Inventor targets a far wider audience interested in creating mobile applications in their smartphones. The four systems support a web community to share material and ideas for teaching and exploring.

In [3] Michael Kölling says "Greenfoot plays a little more of a teacher *Role. I guess Alice is somewhere in the middle. This very directly reflects the different stages of learning at the different age groups and shows, in fact, a common philosophy: Let them play first, let them achieve something, let them be creative, and then sneak the explanations in about what is going on when you're working with the system. That's why a sequence from Scratch to Greenfoot or from Alice to Greenfoot can work so well".*

Fincher and Utting [4] share this opinion about the target age groups and indicate their hope that using Greenfoot will reduce the gender imbalance in Computer Science, especially the under-representation of women at the more "technical" end of the discipline. They also point out that these systems manage to engaging and empowering the user.

An experience of teaching algorithms and computer programming with Greenfoot with first year students of Computer Science was reported on [5]. Here, a majority of students reached over 60% of success and their opinion about using Greenfoot was that they felt motivated and had fun solving the problems. These are essential factors for facilitating learning. A successful experience of teaching Object-Oriented Programming with Games was presented on [6].

Greenfoot also takes a motivational approach [4]. Learners will be interested in building (playing) games — but use a "real" programming language (Java). If learners learn programming rightly, they will learn well (and the job of the teacher—corporeal or environmental—is to present a carefully designed work the students can engage smoothly with).

3. ORGANIZATION, LEARNING AND ASSESSING THE PROGAMES SYSTEM

3.1 Organization of ProGames

To determine the student's preferences, we created an ad-hoc website to with a personal interest test based in the manual kuder-C [7]. This manual is applicable to teenagers and adults, so it perfectly fits the ProGames target audience. It offers an evaluation of interest of the subject on 10 different fields of interest with 168 questions on: open air, mechanical, calculus, scientific, persuasive, artistic, literary, musical, assistance and administrative. The results obtained by a subject reveal likings or preferences for a given type of activities. We have simplified it to the 4 more representative categories (selected from an evaluation of 20 randomly picked cs1 students in the analysis phase of the system) and only the 20 questions more suitable to select them. The selected categories are: 1- Open air: indicates preference for activities generally performed outdoors. 2- Artistic: indicates preference for creative works, generally dealing with (pleasing) works, such as drawing, colouring and attractive materials. 3- Assistance: indicates preference for activities that imply helping other people. 4- Calculus: indicates preference for numeric tasks and solving of mathematical problems.

The test gives the affinity percentage to the four categories and any student would work on the best qualified category. Of course, if desired, users can complete their learning choosing other categories, according with their preferences.

Each category in ProGames system includes seven levels of exercises with increasing difficulty (see table 1). Users first pick the category with mores similar tastes begins progressively with the adapted contents (lessons). Every set of seven lessons is followed by a set of exercises. The leading idea is that the student downloads the exercises and executes them in the Greenfoot programming environment. Thus, he can visually execute the exercise solution and, intuitively, understand it. Then, the student must study in depth the exercise code, understand it and learn the programming skills involved. Following this he will take a test on that level, as explained on section 3.3.

Table 1. Contents and Games for Category in ProGames

Timing	Contents of Programming Introduction Course	Number of Games for Category			
		Open Air	Artistic	Assistance	Calculus
Sep	1-Basic Programming Constructs	7	7	6	7
Sep	2-Structured Instructions	7	7	7	7
Oct	3- Sub Programming	8	7	7	7
Oct	4-Introduction to Recursion	7	6	6	7
Nov	5- Arrays and Algorithms with Arrays	7	7	7	7
Nov	6- Files and Records	7	7	7	7
Dec	7- Complex Data Types	6	7	7	6
	Total of Games for Category	49	48	47	48
	Total of Games in ProGames	192			

3.2 Learning with ProGames

Figure 1 shows Greenfoot's main window with a scenario that holds objects. A scenario will always have at least one world subclass, representing the actual world (the rectangular execution area) used, and one or more Actor subclasses (objects). Actors are those objects that are present in the world and exhibit behaviour to implement the scenario's objective (Scenarios are created by the teacher or instructor that implements the world and actor classes for a specific application. The idea is that the student faces an interesting framework that can be modified and extended to create even more interesting functionality).

Greenfoot displays the typical elements of a development environment: A source code editor (double-clicking a class opens a text editor, showing the class's Java source code); a compilation button; and execution control (below the world view are some execution controls that allow running, stop or single-stepping the scenario).

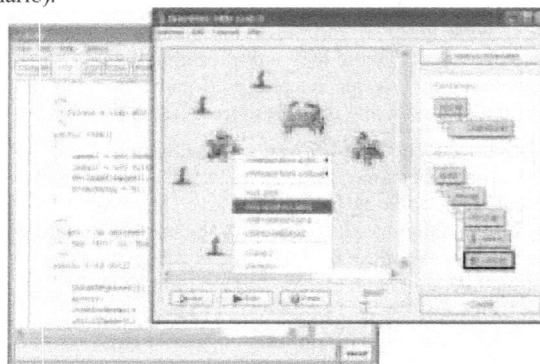

Figure 1. Example of Greenfoot Interface

Since this is an Introduction to Programming Course, we wanted to simplify the concepts of object orientation, so each game is planned on a single class and implemented on the *run* method.

The following subsections present four examples of one of the 192 games proposed on the ProGames System for each category and different levels.

3.2.1 Ordering Algorithms (Level 5) with the Planet Sorting Game for the Category Open Air

During their first semester of programming instruction, our students learn how to work with arrays and searching and sorting algorithms; for each algorithm a different interactive exercise exists in the collection and category. We use the Planet Sorting Game to make students understand and build the direct insertion algorithm for ordering arrays in the category Open Air. When executing this game, students firstly must enter the input data, in this case integer values for each of the planets, and then play the "Act" button and see how the planets get sorted following the steps of the algorithm. They can shift the speed bar, pause or reset the game or run it changing the input data (Figure 2 right).

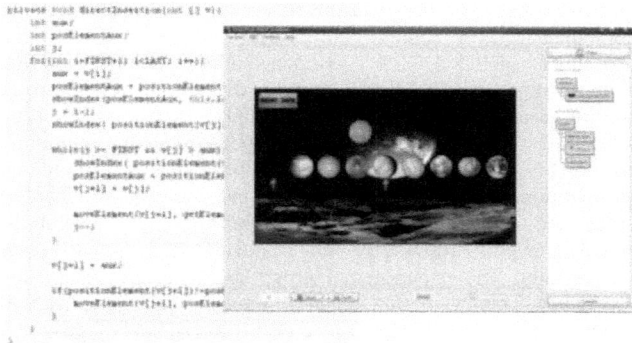

Figure 2. Algorithm Direct Insertion Interface (right) and source code (left) in the Greenfoot Planet Sorting Game in Category Open Air

After that, students would go on to the right panel, world classes, by right clicking on the *directinsertion* mouse right button; the program editor will show the source code for this exercise, which has been included in all cases on the *run()* method to facilitate students finding it without bothering them with object-oriented concepts that are not addressed in the first semester of the programming curriculum, which teaches the procedural paradigm (see Figure 2 left).

In this way, students can understand how the algorithm has been programmed, and will be asked a question about the code on the test to evaluate this level (5 - arrays and algorithms with arrays).

3.2.2 Basic Programming Constructs (Level 1) with the Ambulance Race for the Category Assistance

On this game (Figure 3) there is a simulation of an ambulance race, where the student will bet for one of the vehicles. The input data asked to the student will be the total amount for the race and the bet for each one of the ambulances. Then, the race will start.

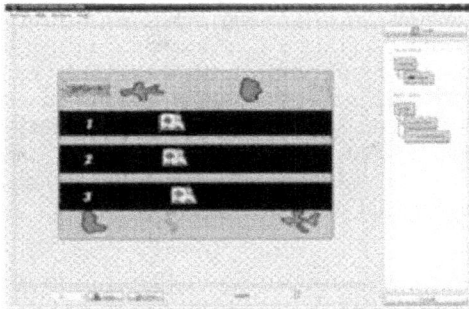

Figure 3. Ambulance Race (Level 1) in Category Assistance

Once ambulances arrive, the game will show the earnings on each bet and their arrival order. Students can play the game with other inputs, changing the speed, etc.

3.2.3 Subprograms (Level 3) with the Paper and Pencil Multiplications for the Category Calculus

The game (Figure 4) shows step by step how the multiplication would be made with pencil and paper. The input parameters asked are the multiplicand and the multiplier. Figure 4 illustrates the game being executed.

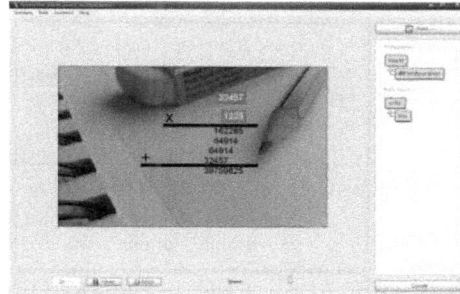

Figure 4. Multiplication (Level 5) in Category Calculus

3.2.4 Subprograms (Level 3) with the Caesar Cipher for the Category Artistic

This game performs a cryptographic method called Caesar Cipher (see Figure 5). The input parameters are: the cipher key, the letter to be encrypted and the letter to be decrypted. Cipher by this method consists on replacing the first letter of the alphabet for the nth letter, the second one for the (n+1) letter, the third one for the (n+2) letter and so on. Figure 5 shows and execution of the game.

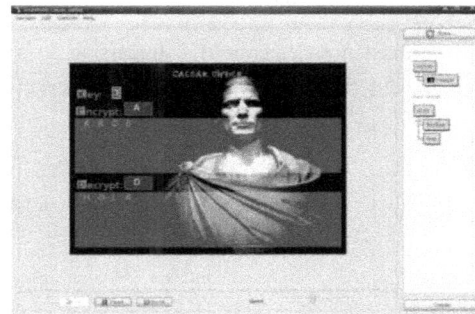

Figure 5. Caesar Cipher (Level 5) in Category Artistic

3.3 Assessing ProGames

The process envisaged for each level of content is that student must interact with each of its 6-8 games, executing it several times with different inputs and observing the results and, then, access the code, trying to understand how the interactive game has been prepared. When this phase is accomplished for all the games on that level, he must take a test. Once the test is answered successfully the student is allowed to proceed to the next level. Failure means repeating the process until the concepts are clear and answers right. We settle the step to the next level on 7/10.

We organized the ProGames system on a Moodle LMS, with several sections for each category. On the category there is a set of exercises for each level of content and their corresponding tests, which must be passed successfully before accessing the next (higher) level. Needless to say that any other hosting for the collection is also possible. Table 2 shows a few samples of games, questions and scoring rubrics used to assess learning.

Table 2. Games, level content and category and sample quiz questions

Game	Sample quiz question and scoring rubric
Calculus Category- L1 -Basic Programming Constructs	
Area Volume Cylinder- Calculates area and volume of a cylinder	From the following expression of the code for area= 2*Math.PI * r * h What data type should area be? Score: 1 double
Quadratic – Calculates de the second degree equation from the given values	Double p = a2 * pow + a1 * x + a0; Which order are operators evaluated? Score: 1 operators(*,/,%) have higher priority, first * operations and then + operations
Artistic Category- L2 -Structured Instructions	
Museum Noise- Calculates from different measures if average noise level is permitted	if(average > Noise.MAXIMUMLEVEL){ showResult("Harmful noise level!!!"); }else{ showResult("Acceptable noise level"); } When the instruction showResult("Acceptable noise level") will execute? Score: 1 only when variable average is equal or less than the constant
Alarms Paintbrush- two alarms are settled to remember to clean up the paintbrushes	while(divisor != 0){ int rest = dividend % divisor; dividend = divisor; divisor = rest; } Alarms code can be substituted for loop? Score:1 no
Assistance Category - L4- Recursion	
Hospital Waiting list- how many times a given name is repeated on the Hospital waiting list	private int accountName(int position, String name){ if(position == LAST){ return 0; }else{ if(this.list[position].equals(name)){ return 1+ accountName(++position, name); }else{ return accountName(++position, name); } } } Which is the recurrent case? Score: 1point for accountName(++position, name) is a recurrent case.
Open Air Category- L5- Arrays and Algorithms with Arrays	
Drinkable Water- 6 measures determine water drinkability	In the program it is used and array to store these values. Could this array modify its length on execution time? Score: 0.5 no Could this array content different data types? Score: 0.5 no
Temperatures Histogram-is printed with 10 intervals based on 30 temperature measures	In the program an array is created to store the 30 temperatures, by double [] temperatures = new double[NTEMP]; Which are the initial values of the array? Score: 1 it initializes to default values, since its data type is double, it is initialized to zero.

In addition to the content-based quizzes, the CS1 students also completed pre- and post- questionnaires that measured their knowledge in computing just before and after using ProGames. They also filled a subjective opinion questionnaire that measured students' self-reported interest, liking of the system, favorite level or category and so on.

4. EXPERIMENTATION
4.1 Participants and procedure
The sample of students belonged to 3 Degrees of the Rey Juan Carlos University of Madrid, Spain, Computer Science Degree, Computer Science – Mathematics Double Degree, and Computer Science – Business Administration Double Degree. The three degrees had the same teachers, course materials and schedules. ProGames has been tested in the first semester (from September 20th to December 20th) of the academic year 2012-2013. The experiment included 73 CS1 students of the 3 degrees of the course "Introduction to Programming", divided on two groups: a control group, formed by 29 students, and an experimental group with 44 students. The course included: basic programming constructs and structured instructions, sub-programming, introduction to recursion, arrays, files and records. The control group studied on more than 250 exercises with proposed solutions equally leveled (obviously not categorized) on paper, as traditionally. The experimental group did the same, but using ProGames. This evaluation consisted on a pre-test, taken right at the beginning of the experiment (September), and a post-test, taken right at the end (December). Both, pre-test and post-test were exactly the same. They consisted on 25 multiple-choice questions, with four possible answers for each question to eliminate randomly picked right answers. Correct answers added 100% of the grade and wrong responses subtracted 33% of the grade on that question. The use of the ProGames was an extracurricular activity, incentivized with the additional recognition of 1 ECTS credit when they passed with a grade of 7/10 all the tests of only one or two categories, 1.5 ECTS credits when have done the same with 3 categories and 2 ECTS credits when the 7/10 grade was reached for all the tests of the 4 categories.

4.2 Results
As this study aimed to evaluating whether or not using ProGames improves learning, analyses of results were oriented to firstly making a descriptive analysis of the presented data, and secondly, deduce whether or not there was significant improvement between pre-test and post-test of the evaluated variable on the three case study degrees. The analysis was performed with the SPSS 19 statistical package. The variables "object of study" taken are PRE-TEST and POST-TEST, where total mark is reflected – relating to 10 – obtained by the student on a test made by the teacher to evaluate student's understanding before and after using the ProGames system. First we did a descriptive analysis of results. Figure 6 displays boxplot diagrams for pre and post-test. Each box is delimited by the values Q1 (first quartile) and Q3 (third quartile). Each box encloses the corresponding 50% of cases, highlighting the median. The lowest and highest values of the diagram ends correspond to values which are not less than $Q1-1.5 \cdot (Q3-Q1)$ and not greater than $Q3+1.5 \cdot (Q3-Q1)$.

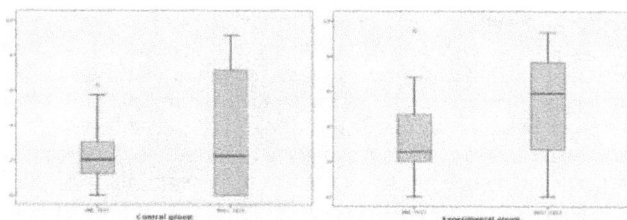

Figure 6. Boxplot for the control and experimental group on the phases pre-test and post-test

Therefore, we can observe that data in the control group maintain a central tendency around the same value of the median, which has suffered a slight variation in the pre-test and post-test phase. However, data dispersion is very great, and much greater in the post-test as compared with the previous phase. There is a slight asymmetry on both cases and some atypical values in the pre-test case. However, for the experimental group, a marked increase of the central values of the set of data is evident. The exact values will be commented afterwards with reference to Table 2. Data variability also increased, but it did less than in the control group, with a slight asymmetry in both cases. Table 2 shows the values for the median, mean and standard deviation of the test grades for the two sample groups. Including the median as a characteristic value makes sense for non-asymmetrical populations, as was the case, since its value is more representative than the mean.

These values support the previous assertions concerning Figure 6, since in the control group the mean presents a slight improvement (from 2.21 to 3.37) that is almost imperceptible in the median case. The standard deviation, however, increases on more than two points. On the contrary, the experimental group showed an obvious improvement (from 2.55 to 5.89 in the median case and from 3.17 to 5.13 in the mean), with data slightly more dispersed, as deduced from the slight increase of the standard deviation.

Table 2. Median, mean and standard deviation of the test grades for both groups.

	Control group (n=44)			Experimental group (n=29)		
	Median	Mean	Standard deviation	Median	Mean	Standard deviation
Pre-	2.02	2.21	1.49	2.55	3.17	2.32
Post-	2.25	3.37	3.39	5.89	5.13	2.92

The descriptive analysis gives a first idea of the sample distribution. Now, we offer a more detailed study comparing the results of the pre and post-test phases on both groups to elucidate if there was really any significant improvement.

Firstly, we studied the pre-test phase to deduce whether or not there were differences between the experimental and the control groups. Owing to the big size of the sample, we used the t-Student test for independent samples and concluded that there are not significant differences between them, with a significance p>0.05 (Table 3). Therefore, we can assume that both groups are homogeneous in the pre-test phase with respect to the variables object of the study, something necessary for obtaining relevant values from the posterior analysis.

However, we observed significant differences between both groups in the post-test phase, with a significance p= 0.009.

Table 3. Comparative study in pre-test phase using t-Student test with 0.05 significance level and p-value

(Control vs. Experimental)	t-Student test	p-value
Pre-test phase	-1.983	0.054
Post-test phase	-2.361	0.009

Table 4 shows the analysis of the pre-test *vs.* post-test phases:

- Control group: the big sample size allows using a parametric test to compare results of the pre-test and post-test phases, even although it is impossible to prove normality on the population (having obtained a p<0.01 using the Shapiro-Wilk test). Moreover, we found a significant correlation between both samples (r=-0.098, p=0.526). All this allowed using the t-Student test for paired samples. As differences between both groups are not significant, with a value p=0.051, we assume that there is no significant difference in this control group between the pre-test and post-test phases.

Table 4. Comparative study of pre-test vs. post-test phase using t-Student analysis

Pre-test vs. post-test phase	t-Student analysis	p-value
Control	t=-2.009	0.051
Experimental	t=-3.280	0.003

- Experimental group: again, we use a parametric test owing to the large number of elements on our sample, although we cannot suppose normality on the population (p<0.05). Furthermore, the presence of correlation between both phases (r=0.264, p=0.166) allows using again the t-Student test for paired samples. In this case, the differences between both groups are significant, with a p=0.003. Therefore, we conclude that there is significant difference in the experimental group between the pre-test and post-test phases.

To obtain additional information about the magnitude of the change in the experimental group, we calculated the effect size and differences (measured as change percentage) using the Cohen d statistical [8]. The obtained value (d=0.76) corresponds to a remarkable effect (Table 5). Additionally, the value of the change percentage (62%) indicates a huge increase.

Table 5. Sizes of effect and differences (change percentage) between pre- and post-test for the three variables studied

Pre-test vs. post-test phase	d	Differences (%)
Control	-	-
Experimental	0.76	62

The results of the present study indicate that using ProGames influenced positively the students' learning. We found significant differences in the grade that assesses knowledge before and after using ProGames on the experimental group, but not on the control group. We estimate the magnitude of this improvement as outstanding, counting a huge effect as a consequence of its use in the sample studied, with a very high improvement.

4.3 Acceptance by students

At the end of the evaluation, students were asked to fulfill an opinion questionnaire about self-reported interest, liking of the system, of levels and categories. According with their answers:

Taking into account the lesson analysis for categories, the first three lessons are more liked by students. From lesson 4 onwards, a higher percentage of students did 'not like much' the lessons; we think it is because the increased difficulty grade. On the contrary, almost 25% of students did not like lesson 7 in the Artistic category, which exercises must be improved in future versions. Lesson 3 in all categories (Subprogramming. Particularly) has been exceptionally well received. Particularly this lesson has had absolutely no dislikes in the calculus category.

On the categories analysis, Calculus, Assistance, and Artistic, were clearly preferred to Open Air, which was the last one that student completed. The category chosen on first place by male and female was Calculus. However, the percentage of female selecting (liking) the Assistance category on the second place is considerably higher than in any other category.

When, at the end of the evaluation, students were asked 'In general have you liked working with the ProGames system?' They answered favorable: quite much (48%), very much (25%), a little bit (20%) and not at all (8%).
They were asked to voluntarily and anonymously offer a comment about the experience. Here are some from the CS1 participants:

- "I really have enjoyed learning through ProGames".

- "I loved being able to edit the program on the games"

- "I have loved working on game programming"

- "Having such different scenarios prepared is so much fun!"

- "I have found my first choice category much more inspiring than my second choice one"

- "I loved the bubble sort game, it really made me understand the algorithm and how to code it"

- "I found very interesting the games on my category"

5. CONCLUSIONS AND FUTURE WORK
It was a challenge to think on a system for learning programming that fits the students' personal needs and likings, aimed to improving their learning process. Furthermore, it was our goal to offer the 192 leveled sample exercises in an interactive, visually attractive environment and through programming games. It was very important being able to offer the ProGames system to students in a LMS that nicely supported it. Finally, it was important for us to test the progress of students through their learning into the system, to analyze their interactions, and also to show them their personal progress, performance and comparison with their classmates. Those objectives have been fulfilled: (1) The categorization has been possible thanks to the development of a web system based on Kuder-C test of personal interests. (2) We adopted Greenfoot as the interactive, very attractive (to students) game-based programming environment for the development of the 192 programming exercises. (3) The LMS system proposed hosts the collection, Moodle, and the new module developed for it, Merlin-Know, with its virtual teacher that guides and motivates learning and show students their individual progress. As a whole, we feel very satisfied with the solution proposed.

The ProGames System has been tested on 3 Computer Science Degrees of Rey Juan Carlos University during the academic year 2012-2013. We are impressed by the conclusion of the statistical analysis of results. Besides, the students' analysis of interactions and their subjective opinion about the system were also very satisfactory and rewarding. Almost all exercises on almost all categories were very much enjoyed, successfully accomplished and accepted, leaving on them a most favorable opinion. The statistical results of the present study show that the use of ProGames influenced most positively the learning of students generating significant differences in the grade that assesses the knowledge before and after its use on the experimental group, that were not observed in the control group. The magnitude of this improvement is outstanding, and using ProGames in the three CS1 Degrees had a huge positive effect for the sample studied, with a very high improvement percentage in the experimental group.

Future experimental works with the ProGames system will be to determine the learning impact based on different categories. During the first semester of the academic course 2013-14 students assessing the system have been asked to use a different category of games than the one they liked on first place, a group of them was asked to use the second, another group the third and a fourth group the last one, keeping a control group that used the one they chose on first place. Although an in depth analysis of results has not been made yet for obvious reasons, we collected unfavorable remarks from students of the type: "*I feel bored of playing these games, I think I am going to quit*" from a girl student forced to use the forth category. This corroborates the findings that letting students play the type of games they actually like increases their engagement and therefore their performance on the course.

6. REFERENCES
[1] Kölling, M. 2010. The greenfoot programming environment. ACM Trans. Comput. Educ. 10, 4, Article 14 (November 2010), 21 pages.

[2] Sandoval-Reyes, S., Galicia-Galicia, P. & Gutierrez-Sanchez, I. (2011, November). Visual Learning Environments for Computer Programming. In Electronics, Robotics and Automotive Mechanics Conference (CERMA), 2011 IEEE (pp. 439-444). IEEE.

[3] Utting, I., Cooper, S., Kölling, M., Maloney, J. & Resnick, M. (2010). Alice, greenfoot, and scratch--a discussion. ACM Transactions on Computing Education (TOCE), 10(4), 17.

[4] Fincher, S. & Utting, I. (2010). Machines for thinking. ACM Transactions on Computing Education (TOCE), 10(4), 13.

[5] Doerschuk, P., Liu, J. & Mann, J. (2012, October). An INSPIRED Game Programming Academy for High School Students. In 2012 Frontiers in Education Conference Proceedings (pp. 1-6). IEEE.

[6] Begosso, L. C., Begosso, L. R., Gonçalves, E. M. & Gonçalves, J. R. (2012, October). An approach for teaching algorithms and computer programming using Greenfoot and Python. In 2012 Frontiers in Education Conference Proceedings (pp. 1-6). IEEE.

[7] Kuder, G. F. (1939). The Stability of Preference Items. Journal of Social Psychology, pages 41–50,

[8] Cohen, J. (1988). Statistical power analysis for the behavioural sciences (2nd ed.). Erlbaum: Hillsdale.

Assessment Process for a Simulation-based Training Environment in Global Software Development

Miguel J. Monasor
Lero, University of Limerick
Alarcos Research Group, University of Castilla-La Mancha
MiguelJ.Monasor @gmail.com

Aurora Vizcaíno
Alarcos Research Group, University of Castilla-La Mancha
+34 926 295300 ext. 6478
Aurora.Vizcaino @uclm.es

Mario Piattini
Alarcos Research Group, University of Castilla-La Mancha
+34 926 295300 ext. 3715
Mario.Piattini @uclm.es

John Noll
Lero, The Irish Software Engineering Research Centre, University of Limerick
+353-61-202956
John.Noll @lero.ie

Sarah Beecham
Lero, The Irish Software Engineering Research Centre, University of Limerick
+353-61-233769
Sarah.Beecham @lero.ie

ABSTRACT

Simulation has been applied in several Software Engineering fields, and is shown to be a useful method in industrial training. As part of our research work, we have used simulation to provide training in Global Software Development (GSD). We have developed a platform to strengthen GSD skills by simulating realistic settings in which learners interact with Virtual Agents of differing cultures. Thus, learners will experience multi-cultural problems and will develop specific GSD communication skills.

The development of these skills must, however, be accurately assessed, bearing in mind that the training is aimed at learners with different characteristics and skills. In this paper we present an assessment process based on educational theory adapted to our simulation-based training environment. Methods to minimize the instructors' effort and tailor the assessment to specific training needs are proposed. The assessment process has been evaluated by 34 potential users. Results indicate that the assessment method yields meaningful results and proof of learning. Also that automated assessment can be achieved with minimal intervention from the instructor. Though tailored for GSD, this method could be applied to other domains, in both industry and academia.

Categories and Subject Descriptors

K.3.2 [**Computer and Information Science Education**]: Computer science education;
I.6 [**Simulation and modeling**]: General

General Terms

Measurement, Design, Experimentation, Human Factors, Languages

Keywords

Assessment, Global Software Development, Training, Education, Simulation

1. INTRODUCTION

In recent years, Global Software Development (GSD) has introduced new challenges in the field of education. In order to develop software in a globally distributed team, practitioners can no longer rely on excellent technical skills. Soft skills such as the ability to collaborate and communicate effectively across a variety of geographic, cultural and linguistic settings has become equally important. Consequently, training in how to cope with cultural and linguistic differences is a recognized necessity [12].

In order to provide training in GSD skills, we have developed VENTURE (Virtual ENvironmenT for commUnication and collaboRativE training) [11], a simulation-based training environment that places learners in a realistic GSD scenario. In this setting, learners can hone required GSD skills in a systematic and guided manner by textually interacting with Virtual Agents (a Virtual Colleague and a Virtual Guide). Virtual Colleagues are characterized by a specific culture and play a role in the context of the problem. A Virtual Guide directs the interactions, corrects the learners and provides learners with feedback in real time. The feasibility of using VENTURE for cultural training purposes in GSD, was evaluated in our previous work [11], with encouraging results.

However, having proven that the concept has potential as a training tool, it is also important to independently assess the learning achieved through using the tool. There are several benefits to combining an assessment with the training. For example, the learners themselves will benefit from the assessment by having a feeling of achievement, and research shows that students are more motivated to learn when there is some 'proof' of learning [14]. Also, in the case of companies, managers will have a better view of the workforce as a whole, and will be able identify where individual strengths and weaknesses lie in communicating with different cultures and across different languages. This knowledge will help identify where further training is needed, and how best to use the available staff resources.

Fulfillment of the requirements to equip students with professional competences, can be hard to demonstrate in practice [7]. A good assessment must be valid, reliable and transparent, and must clearly outline the goalposts [13]. Assessment procedures can vary depending on the type of training, tools employed, training methodology, individuals involved or field of application [13]. Although lessons learned in creating GSD learning environments are reported [6], methods for GSD learning assessment is still an area in need of further research. Daniels [7] discovered that the assessment aspect in an international open-ended group project is strongly influenced by how competencies are supposed to be improved in a learning environment. The research question that guides this study is: "How can we assess GSD competencies in a simulation-based training environment?"

The objective of this paper is to present and evaluate the assessment process implemented in VENTURE in the field of GSD. Minimizing the instructors' effort and tailoring the assessment to specific training needs are also considered.

2. RELATED RESEARCH

The effectiveness of educational training environments has been assessed in different ways [9], [10]. Minimizing the instructors' workload is a common requirement in these systems, although not all aspects of assessment can be automated. As an example, a semi-automatic web-based assessment tool has been presented by Heo [9] with the aim to help instructors comment directly on students' submissions, provide students with access to this information, and measure their learning through quizzes.

Peer- and self-assessment is often used to track the learning process where instructors delegate the assessment responsibility to their students [4]. This type of assessment also plays a role in the motivation of the students by giving them goals to achieve and a means to follow their progress.

Assessment in Software Engineering education

Most of the current research in Software Engineering education is focused on the original Bloom's Taxonomy [5]. However Whalley et al. [16] suggests some deficiencies in the Bloom taxonomy when applying it to programming problems. The main difficulty with these approaches is assessing the students' improvement, as the scores are not linked to previous knowledge and skills. Some methods deal with this problem by assessing the students several times during the course [2]. The research in this field, therefore, shows the need to assess students before and after training in order to measure their progress.

Assessment in GSD training

Despite the lack of studies on assessment on the GSD field, Damian et al. [6] report on an experience of a GSD course conducted in collaboration with three universities. The course emphasized requirements management activities through synchronous computer-mediated relationships, incorporating metrics for assessing GSD skills in the fields of [6]: international teamwork, distributed project management, computer mediated communications and ambiguity/uncertainty. Authors applied these metrics (where different categories were weighted according to its importance), to produce a final score.

Assessment in multi-cultural training

In the related field of multicultural training, there are tools oriented towards providing training to multinational corporations and expatriates. Cross Cultural Adaptability Inventory (CCAI) [8] is an online tool that addresses learner's ability to adapt to any culture. By means of a 50 question test, it provides self-assessment covering four areas: emotional resilience, personal autonomy, flexibility/openness and perceptual acuity. A guide helps participants understand the implications of their scores and suggests actions that can help them strengthen their skills.

The Cultural Orientations Framework (COF) [15] is a framework to assess and compare cultures based on the following cultural dimensions: sense of power and responsibility, time management approaches, definitions of identity and purpose, organizational arrangements, notions of territory and boundaries, communication patterns, and modes of thinking.

In summary, the assessment methods reported in the literature are varied, and create a useful set of measures we can apply to our VENTURE training platform. For example, our assessment process should include self-assessment methods to identify

learners' improvement, and incorporate automatic assessment that take advantage of VENTURE's simulation capabilities. The next section explains how these assessments are applied in VENTURE.

3. LEARNING ENVIRONMENT

VENTURE [11] is based on an e-learning platform in which instructors can set up scenarios, upload teaching material, communicate with learners and monitor their progress. Learners can study theory online or/and attend classroom based classes, which are not always an option in industrial based teaching. A Chat Simulator (see Figure 1) allows learners to train on synchronous interactions. The learner's objective is to obtain as much information as possible from the Virtual Colleague within the time limit of the simulation. The Virtual Guide will provide learners with instant feedback during the interaction.

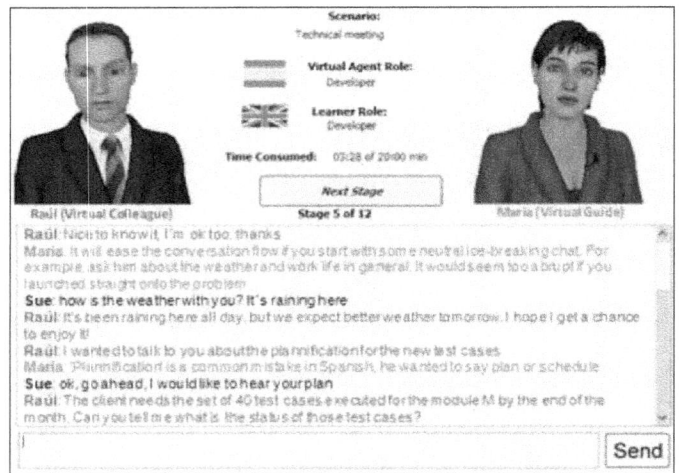

Figure 1. Chat simulator.

VENTURE's training objectives are to:

- provide knowledge of theory and best practices of GSD and teamwork in multicultural environments;
- expose learners to the multi-dimensional and multi-cultural nature of GSD through simulation;
- help students to acquire GSD skills and more specifically, cultural and linguistic skills;
- minimize the learners' and instructors' effort and coordination problems; and
- encourage students to engage through self- assessment.

4. ASSESSMENT OBJECTIVE

A key challenge for the VENTURE training platform is to objectively assess the level of learning achieved through this independent style of training. The aim of the assessment is twofold: to provide learners with advice on the skills they have and those they must improve, and to help the instructors to create training scenarios based on each learner's experience. More specific objectives are to:

O1. Identify skills in which the learner needs further training.

O2. Assess the learner's ability to put into practice or retrieve knowledge learned in training sessions.

O3. Monitor the learners' progress (knowledge and skills).

O4. Use unambiguous, systematic, reliable and objective assessment criteria.

O5. Promote knowledge construction.

O6. Minimize time and resources needed.

5. ASSESSMENT PROCESS

In order to achieve the objectives listed in Section 3, we have designed an assessment process for the simulated learning environment. This assessment incorporates concepts taken from assessment strategies found in the related literature, as discussed in Section 3. These fall into four kinds of assessment, presented here.

1. **Diagnostic assessment** determines a learner's starting level of knowledge and skills. The educator will determine the assignments for the learners based on this initial level. The scores earned in this assessment do not directly contribute towards the final grade of the learners, but provide a base-line measurement to act as proof of their advance at the end of the course or unit.

2. **Formative assessment** by means of simulation, learners can experiment with different ways to communicate, through feedback, asking questions and taking risks that they would not necessarily take in real settings. VENTURE provides feedback and direction to the learners so that they can improve their communication skills, which are assessed in real time.

3. **Summative assessment** measures the achievement relative to the course objectives; in our case the evaluation of artefacts and exams.

4. **Self assessment** by means of surveys and questionnaires is also used to allow learners to judge their own skills.

In order to achieve the Course Learning Objectives (CLOs), learners are assigned reflective tasks, learning from their successes and failures through provision of immediate feedback. The system gathers these reflections by automatically monitoring their advances and measuring their skills. Moreover, instructors can receive feedback from students and examine their self-assessments. The analysis of these reflections is used to examine whether learners achieved their goals. During the simulations, reflection is promoted by: explaining the consequences of certain actions, proposing alternatives or giving the learner the opportunity for finding alternatives, allowing learners to see the problem from various perspectives; and placing learners into different and varied contexts.

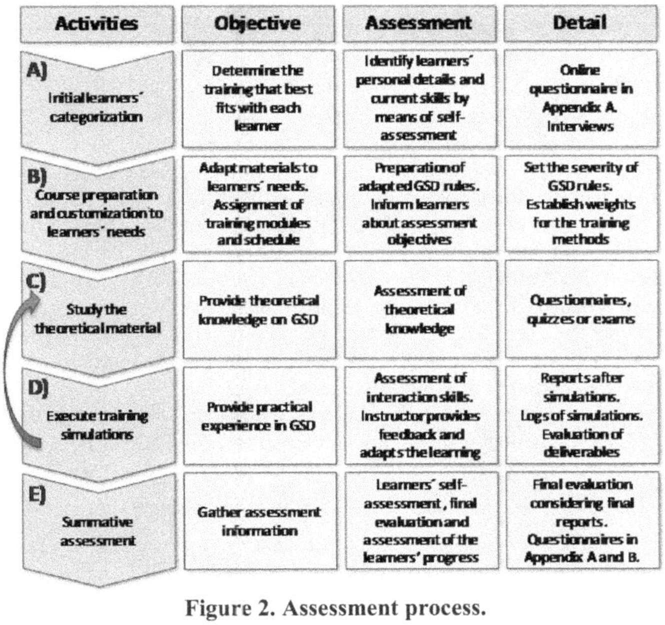

Activities	Objective	Assessment	Detail
A) Initial learners' categorization	Determine the training that best fits with each learner	Identify learners' personal details and current skills by means of self-assessment	Online questionnaire in Appendix A. Interviews
B) Course preparation and customization to learners' needs	Adapt materials to learners' needs. Assignment of training modules and schedule	Preparation of adapted GSD rules. Inform learners about assessment objectives	Set the severity of GSD rules. Establish weights for the training methods
C) Study the theoretical material	Provide theoretical knowledge on GSD	Assessment of theoretical knowledge	Questionnaires, quizzes or exams
D) Execute training simulations	Provide practical experience in GSD	Assessment of interaction skills. Instructor provides feedback and adapts the learning	Reports after simulations. Logs of simulations. Evaluation of deliverables
E) Summative assessment	Gather assessment information	Learners' self-assessment, final evaluation and assessment of the learners' progress	Final evaluation considering final reports. Questionnaires in Appendix A and B.

Figure 2. Assessment process.

The assessment process developed (shown in Figure 2), is described according to the following activities of the training process:

A) Initial learners' categorization (*diagnostic assessment*): Learners are assigned an initial predefined baseline questionnaire for identifying their current skills. Based on an online questionnaire, learners' culture and skills are determined. With these results, instructors can decide the training that best fits each learner's needs based on their skills and characteristics.

B) Course preparation and customization to learners' needs: In a further step, the kind of training that best fits each learner is determined and defined by the instructor. Instructors prepare the theoretical and training materials based on this categorization. Training modules are designed focusing on cultural dimensions and linguistic problems suited to each learner.

In case of specific needs, instructors can also adapt existing scenarios by customizing cultural, linguistic and GSD rules according to their individual training objectives.

C) Study the theoretical material: In VENTURE, the Teaching and Learning Activities (TLAs) consist of theoretical lessons and practical simulations. The cycle for learning theory and executing practical simulations is repeated with each lesson until completing the course scope. For each assignment learners must execute the associated training simulations (by chat or email) and submit their associated Assessment Tasks (ATs), basically answers to questionnaires. The information of their evaluation along with the information provided by the automatic reports generated by the simulators, will also serve to assess the learner (*formative assessment*).

D) Execute training simulations: After completing the different lessons, learners complete a questionnaire regarding concepts learned and they execute the training simulations. The instructor will monitor the accomplishment of each learning objective. This is achieved by reviewing the logs of the learner interactions with the chat and email simulators, which are stored in the system. These logs provide formatted and organized information about the rules that were fired and the context in which they were fired including the students' interaction. At the end of the simulation, prior to producing the report, the students can review any mistakes committed, one by one. After each lesson, learners receive the instructor's comments and future lessons can be adapted accordingly.

E) Proof of learning: The Course Intended Learning Outcomes (CILOs) are measured by means of a *summative assessment* which encompasses the different marks of the final reports of the simulations, questionnaires and exams. Each one of these ATs can be assessed by using different weights in the final score, according to the instructor's criteria.

Moreover, after completing each simulation, learners revisit and answer the same questionnaire that they answered at the start of the simulation. In this way GSD skills are quantified and compared with the results of the benchmark questionnaire. Learners are given an additional proof of learning questionnaire to quantify their improvement through measuring their perception on a 1-5 scale (*self-assessment*).

5.1 Self-assessment

Self-evaluation through reflection is promoted by means of questionnaires. Automating the self evaluation process provides learners and educators with a valuable mechanism for feedback, and a means to measure course progress online [3].

As VENTURE's design is aimed to minimize the training and assessment effort, the automation and ease of use of the assessment procedure is essential for its application in both universities and companies.

The first activity of the assessment process includes a self-assessment questionnaire where knowledge is checked relating to key aspects of effective work in GSD settings. In a similar vein, our initial baseline questionnaire will serve to categorize the learners at the first stage of the assessment process by considering not only multiculturalism, but also linguistic and GSD skills. This questionnaire gathers information about how well learners can perform in GSD skills. Learners will answer the questions in a 1-5 scale.

At a final stage of the process, after course completion, the questions answered at the start of the assessment are revisited. The objective is to evaluate the learners improvement at the end of the training process by comparing their knowledge at the beginning and at the end of the course.

Finally, at the end of the course, learners also fill in a proof of learning questionnaire, which serves to quantify how much they improved their GSD skills. The difference with the previous questionnaire is that in this case, learners are directly asked about their perceived improvement.

5.2 Automated assessment

The training scenarios comprise several cultural, linguistic and GSD rules. As an example, we can have cultural rules that fall into several categories such as use of direct/indirect speech, use of formal/informal language, uncertainty avoidance, etc. Each learner starts with a perfect score of 100, where, if no errors are made, throughout the interactions, their final score will be 100. However, each rule contained in the scenario is also defined by a severity mark, indicating the score that will be subtracted if the user fires such a rule. Therefore, the simulator can automatically assess the learners' performance when interacting with Virtual Agents. After the execution of a training scenario, an automatic assessment is presented in a report detailing learners' performance in the different areas trained (see Figure 3).

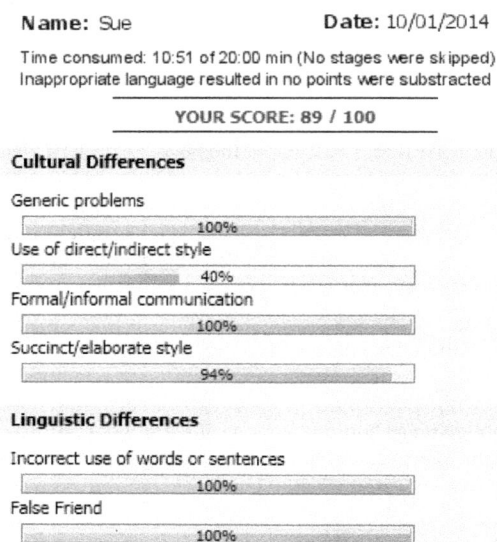

Name: Sue   **Date:** 10/01/2014

Time consumed: 10:51 of 20:00 min (No stages were skipped)
Inappropriate language resulted in no points were substracted

YOUR SCORE: 89 / 100

Cultural Differences

Generic problems
100%
Use of direct/indirect style
40%
Formal/informal communication
100%
Succinct/elaborate style
94%

Linguistic Differences

Incorrect use of words or sentences
100%
False Friend
100%

Figure 3. Automatically generated final report.

The final report includes information about the date and duration of the simulation, as well as the number of times that the user gets stuck during the simulation and has to skip a stage. The report also includes a final score and sectional results, detailing one by one the score obtained in each GSD skill that has been trained in the scenario. Use of inappropriate or offensive language during the simulation can also take points away of the final score.

The scores for each skill are calculated by taking into account the total number of learner's mistakes of a specific skill, considering the severity of the rules fired during the simulation.

By analyzing this report, learners will gain an insight of their progress. They can also examine the log of the conversation, in which the Virtual Guide provides them with feedback. Both, the information contained in the report and log of the conversation are stored in the database, so can also be inspected by the instructors.

6. EVALUATION

We conducted a field study to evaluate the assessment component of VENTURE. The objective was to determine whether the assessment effectively monitored the students' progress relating to the cultural, linguistic and GSD-related problems simulated by VENTURE.

A within-subjects design [1] was applied, in which comparisons are made between two or more results obtained from different circumstances involving the same participant. The experiment was conducted by individual participants in two sessions of up to an hour each. These sessions tested the same configuration of the tool with different training scenarios. The CLOs focused on improving participants' performance when interacting with people from Mexico (Scenario A) and from India (Scenario B). Participants played the role of onsite coordinators interacting with an onsite coordinator from Mexico and India respectively. Both training scenarios (Scenario A and Scenario B) provided training on similar skills, so that it was possible to compare the learning effects. The CILOs are related to raise cultural and linguistic awareness, use of appropriate communication styles, ways to avoid misunderstandings, conflicts resolution and negotiation.

Thirty-four participants representing ten different nationalities completed two scenarios and the associated surveys. The participants were potential users of VENTURE comprising 16 students, 12 researchers and six practitioners/researchers. Students represent the largest group and reflect the need to test VENTURE on the main target group. The following questionnaires were applied:

- *Baseline Questionnaire:* designed to collect the participant's demographic information and cultural background.
- *Pre Training Questionnaire:* including questions on the specific knowledge of what is taught on the course (i.e., their current knowledge of GSD issues; confidence levels in communicating with people from other cultures in the job).
- *Post Training Questionnaire:* whose objective was to check whether there was an improvement in the participant's knowledge. This included the same questions as the Pre Training questionnaire, but also gathered the participants' perception of their improvement.
- *Opinion Questionnaire:* this was conducted at the end of the experimental sessions and obtained information on how the students felt about their learning and assessment.

The following data was collected through the evaluation process:

- *Participant's opinion* of their learning and general experience with VENTURE (*Opinion Questionnaire*).
- *Participant's performance* via VENTURE's automatically generated logs and reports – where all mistakes logged.

- *Participant's learning* - a comparison of student's knowledge before and after training through pre and post questionnaires and comparative analysis of the automatic logs and reports generated in the different training sessions.

6.1 Procedure

The participants were split into two groups: G1 and G2. Both groups conducted the same tasks (as embedded in Scenario A and B) but in a different order (Evaluation G1, and Evaluation G2).

Both groups filled in the *Baseline questionnaire* as the first task. G1 then participated in Evaluation G1. Evaluation G1 executed **Scenario A** first followed by **Scenario B**. G1 filled in a *Pre Training Questionnaire* for *Scenario A*, after which *Scenario A* was executed, and finally a *Post Training Questionnaire* for *Scenario A* was filled in. After this, G1 participated in *Session B*, which consisted of filling in a *Pre Training Questionnaire* related to *Scenario B*, after which *Scenario B* was executed, and finally a *Post Training Questionnaire* on *Scenario B* was filled in.

The order of the sessions was different for G2, who participated in Evaluation G2, signifying that they executed **Scenario B** first, followed by **Scenario A**. After completing both sessions, both groups of participants (G1 and G2) completed the *Opinion Questionnaire*.

The reason for changing the order in which the two groups (G1 and G2) participated in the scenarios was to test whether there was any bias in the difficulty ratings of the two scenarios. For example, if all the participants who participated in Scenario A followed by Scenario B showed improvements, this might have been because Scenario A was more difficult than Scenario B; however, if Scenario A was always more difficult for the participant (independent of the order), it would not be possible to *compare* the two scenarios for any proof of learning.

6.2 Results

At an initial stage of the analysis it was observed that students received better automatic assessments scores in one of the scenarios than in the other regardless the execution order. After applying the Mann-Whitney U Test the values were obtained (U = 265.5, p=<0.001) showed that it is highly likely that this difference is not a random occurrence.

These results indicate that one scenario is more difficult than the other (as shown by consistently lower scores). This bias must be taken into account for the subsequent statistical analysis, as it will not be meaningful, from a statistical point of view, to compare all the automatic assessments across the two scenarios. However, each scenario includes the same number of rules of each type and on close inspection we observe that one of these rules was triggered in a similar way in each scenario. As there is no significant difference between scenarios (for this rule) it is possible to test whether any learning has occurred from one scenario to another using this dimension.

Based on this rule, the scores from the automatic assessment method served to detect an improvement in the participants' performance when they execute the second scenario (which can be either scenario A or B, depending on which order they executed the scenarios), after the experience of having executed the first one.

These results signify that the automated assessment is able to provide accurate information for drawing conclusions that are helpful for the instructors. These results also signify that the assessment can be used to compare the performance among the different students using the *same scenarios* instead of comparing

the performance of a student in different scenarios even if they are similarly designed.

By analysing the results from the pre and post questionnaires for each scenario, we observed that in both cases there is an improvement in the mean and the median of the answers provided. These differences were shown to be statistically significant by means of the Wilcoxon test applied to the pre and post questionnaires. Learning was observed in the three areas of knowledge tested: cultural differences, linguistic differences and understanding of GSD problems and concepts.

In order to check the accuracy of the assessment method, the participants' perceptions of their learning were requested at the end of the course by means of a new questionnaire. The answers served to validate that participant's perceptions were aligned with the results obtained with the automated assessment method.

6.2.1 Participant's perception

Analysis of responses given in the *Opinion Questionnaire* revealed that participants' perception about the use of VENTURE was positive, who found the training helpful, engaging and usable. The following questions were answered by the participants through a 1 to 5 likert scale: 1) The feedback provided facilitated learning, 2) I was aware of the learning outcomes at the beginning of the course, 3) The assessment information is easy to understand and interpret, 4) The reports helped me to understand the topics trained, 5) The scores I got seem fair, and 6) The assessment motivated me to improve my performance.

The analysis of the results shows that the median of the answers for each one of those questions was 4 out of 5, obtaining also an equal value for the mode, which is quite encouraging. Figure 4 shows the distribution of the answers for the first question, showing that students and researchers (main target users) are the most positive groups.

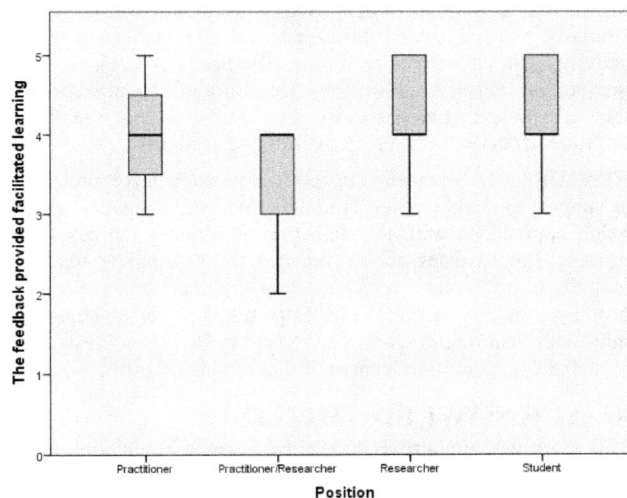

Figure 4. Perceptions of assessment method.

In addition to the quantitative analysis previously analyzed, the surveys also gave the participants the option of providing their opinion. The concept of a simulation-based platform with automated assessment was well received. Finally, after the analysis of the open ended responses of the *Opinion Questionnaire*, the inclusion of additional tutorials at the end of the simulation was suggested as a means to reinforce those points with which the student had more problems. In this respect, the inclusion of additional introductory material on the different cultures before initiating the simulation was also suggested as a means of reinforcing the process.

7. SUMMARY AND CONCLUSIONS

This paper presents a proposal of a systematic assessment process for a simulation-based training environment. The assessment process is shown to provide both the student and instructor with realistic measures of learning. Advantages of the assessment process are aligned with the objectives mentioned in Section 4:

- Guided adaptation to specific learning needs by automatically assessing the different GSD competences (O1).
- Provision of reliable and systematic assessment based on objective *rules* (O2, O4).
- Monitor learners' progress through logs and reports, minimizing time and resources (O3, O6).
- Promote knowledge construction by providing accurate feedback and assessment to the students (through Virtual Guide and reports) (O5).
- Independent training and minimum intervention from the instructors through the integration with VENTURE (O6).

The evaluation of the assessment process generated the following outcomes:

- The outcomes of the assessment were well valued by the participants.
- The interactions with the Virtual Agents were considered acceptable by the participants.
- Participants improved their knowledge and recognized having learnt from the experience.

The lessons learned will be used to increase the automation of the assessment without compromising the validity of the process as a whole. The information required for the analysis of the assessment was easy to access through the reports automatically generated by VENTURE. This indicates that the time and resources needed by instructors to validate VENTURE related assessments will be similarly reduced. Also the assessment and associated training activities can be adapted to the specific needs of learners, and to instructors' objectives. Moreover, the information gathered during the assessment process can be used to analyse where improvements can be made in the training scenarios.

VENTURE will be shortly applied in a Spanish university serving as support for a subject on Virtual Teams, and companies are also being approached with the objective of refining the assessment process. Future plans are to enhance the assessment reports to include tutorials that reinforce those points shown to cause problems to the learner. Ensuring students' engagement and improving learning outcomes are likely to be key success factors in the take up and effectiveness of the training platform.

8. ACKNOWLEDGMENTS

This work was supported, in part, by Science Foundation Ireland grant 10/CE/I1855 to Lero - the Irish Software Engineering Research Centre (www.lero.ie). It has also been funded by the GEODAS-BC project (Ministerio de Economía y Competitividad and Fondo Europeo de Desarrollo Regional FEDER, TIN2012-37493-C03-01). It is also supported by GLOBALIA (PEII11-0291-5274), Consejería de Educación y Ciencia, Junta de Comunidades de Castilla-La Mancha.

9. REFERENCES

1. Akar, E., Öztürk, E., Tunçer, B. and Wiethoff, M. Evaluation of a collaborative virtual learning environment. *Education + Training, 46* (6/7). 2004, 343 - 352.

2. Alaoutinen, S. and Smolander, K. Student self-assessment in a programming course using bloom's revised taxonomy *Proceedings of the fifteenth annual conference on Innovation and technology in computer science education*, ACM, Bilkent, Ankara, Turkey, 2010, 155-159.

3. Barzilay, O., Hazzan, O. and Yehudai, A. Evaluation of a software engineering course by reflection. *SIGCSE Bull., 41* (3). 2009, 273-277.

4. Black, P., Harrison, C., Lee, C., Marshall, B. and Wiliam, D. *Assessment for Learning: Putting it into Practice.* Open University Press, 2003.

5. Bloom, B.S. *Taxonomy of Educational Objectives Book 1: Cognitive Domain.* Addison-Wesley, 1984.

6. Damian, D., Hadwin, A. and Al-Ani, B., Instructional design and assessment strategies for teaching global software development: a framework. in *International Conference on Software Engineering (ICSE)*, (2006), ACM Press New York, NY, USA, 685-690.

7. Daniels, M. Developing and Assessing Professional Competencies: A Pipe Dream? ; Experiences from an Open-ended Group Project Learning Environment, Uppsala University, 2011, 107.

8. Davis, S.L. and Finney, S.J. Examining the psychometric properties of the Cross-Cultural Adaptability Inventory. *Educational and Psychological Measurement, 66.* 2006, 318-330.

9. Heo, M. A learning and assessment tool for web-based distributed education *Proceedings of the 4th conference on Information technology curriculum*, ACM, Lafayette, Indiana, USA, 2003, 151 - 154.

10. Huizinga, D.M. Identifying topics for instructional improvement through on-line tracking of programming assignments *Proceedings of the 6th annual conference on Innovation and technology in computer science education*, ACM, Canterbury, United Kingdom, 2001, 129-132.

11. Monasor, M.J., Vizcaíno, A. and Piattini, M. Cultural and linguistic problems in GSD: a simulator to train engineers in these issues. *Journal of Software Maintenance and Evolution: Research and Practice (Special Issue on Global Software Engineering), 24* (6). 2011, 707-717.

12. Monasor, M.J., Vizcaíno, A., Piattini, M. and Caballero, I. Preparing students and engineers for Global Software Development: A Systematic Review *International Conference on Global Software Development (ICGSE)*, IEEE Computer Society, Princeton, NJ, USA, 2010, 177-186.

13. O'Neill, G., Huntley-Moore, S. and Race, P. *Case Studies of Good Practices in Assessment of Student Learning in Higher Education.* AISHE, 2007.

14. Olina, Z. and Sullivan, H. Student self-evaluation, teacher evaluation, and learner performance. *Educational Technology Research and Development, 52* (3). 2004, 5-22.

15. Rosinski, P. *Coaching Across Cultures: New Tools for Leveraging National, Corporate, and Professional Differences.* Nicholas Brealey Publishing, 2003.

16. Whalley, J.L., Lister, R., Thompson, E., Clear, T., Robbins, P., Kumar, P.K.A. and Prasad, C. An Australasian study of reading and comprehension skills in novice programmers, using the bloom and SOLO taxonomies *Proceedings of the 8th Australasian Conference on Computing Education - Volume 52*, Australian Computer Society, Inc., Hobart, Australia, 2006.

Towards Identification and Classification of Core and Threshold Concepts in Methodology Education in Computing

Matti Tedre, Danny Brash, and
Sirkku Männikkö-Barbutiu
Department of Computer and Systems Sciences
Stockholm University
Sweden
matti|danny|sirkku@dsv.su.se

Johannes Cronjé
Faculty of Informatics and Design
Cape Peninsula University of Technology
South Africa
cronjej@cput.ac.za

ABSTRACT

Research methodology is a quintessential component of science, but methods differ greatly between sciences. In computing, methods are borrowed from many fields, which causes difficulties to methodology education in computing. In our methodology courses in computing, we have observed a number of core and threshold concepts that affect students' success. This essay describes a work in progress towards understanding those core and threshold concepts in methodology education in computing, classified along two dimensions. We classify methodological concepts in terms of standard elements of research design in students' projects in computing, and in terms of their centrality and difficulty. We present examples of three types of troublesome knowledge concerning methodology: the strangeness and complexity of methodological concepts, misimpressions from everyday experience, and reasonable but mistaken expectations.

Categories and Subject Descriptors

K.3.2 [**Computers and Education**]: Computer and Information Science Education—*computer science education, curriculum*

General Terms

Human Factors

Keywords

Methodology, Computer science education, Computing curricula, Threshold concepts, Troublesome knowledge

1. INTRODUCTION

Methodology is a quintessential component of scientific research and dictionary definitions of 'scientific' refer to methodologically sound, rigorous activities. As different kinds of

research employ different methods, methodology education differs between academic disciplines. In natural sciences students learn things like empirical laboratory work and statistical methods while in social sciences various qualitative and quantitative methods are part of the curriculum.

However, in computing, methodology has historically been an overlooked activity. Reviews of methodology in computing have pointed out deficiencies in many fields of computing, including information systems [31], computer science [23], and software engineering [33]. Some critics have argued that methodological terminology is sloppily used in computing [34]. In computing experimentation terminology is used differently from many other fields [28]. Others have argued that precautions against bias are often not taken [7, 8]. Yet others have argued that computing researchers just act like scientists but do not really do science [17].

The science of computing is so broad that different fields emphasize different kinds of research methodology education. In the field of information systems, which has social science methodology at its core, calls for stringent adherence to recognized research methodology can be found [10, 11]. Theoretical computer science employs deductive reasoning and analytical methods, although those are rarely explicitly described in research papers [10]. Human-computer interaction uses a variety of methods from various traditions, including behavioural sciences and social sciences. In systems development, engineering methods and techniques are common. In the recent years, methodological debates concerning system development has lead to an increased use of design science [15] as a methodological framework.

No quick improvement can be expected in research practice as long as methodology is not properly addressed in computing education. It has been argued that instead of methodology education, students learn methodological skills through mentoring and model learning—such as examining previous research reports [9]. Curricula guidelines in computing are thin on methodology courses. The ACM/IEEE curriculum report CC2001 [6] does not include a single course on methodology. Some of computing's field-specific curriculum guidelines—such as CS2008 (for computer science) and GSwE2009 (for software engineering)—offer little in terms of methodology. Other curricula—such as IS2010 for information systems and CE2004 for computer engineering—are more concerned with methodology education in their fields.

Education in computing fields is not just an academic issue. ICT has a great impact on the economy and functions of society, and when ICT systems fail, modern societies may grind to a halt. ICT's crucial role in industry and society creates various kinds of pressure towards university education in computing. Computing education has to balance between legislation regarding higher education, academic goals, and the needs of industry. In legislative terms, methodological knowledge and skills are, in many countries, decreed by the national agency for higher education. In our case, Sweden, methodological education is legislation-bound already on the B.Sc. degree level [26]. In terms of academic goals, computing education must prepare students for the possibility of following research careers, which puts more pressure on methodology education. In terms of industry, computing education must supply a skilled workforce—which is often research-intensive R&D (research and development) work.

This essay is based on the experiences of methodology educators from three universities: Cape Peninsula University of Technology, South Africa; Tumaini University, Tanzania; and Stockholm University, Sweden. The essay uses Stockholm University's computer science department, DSV, as an example. Typical of educational programs in computing, for 35 years after DSV was founded in 1966, methodology education did not exist as a curricular subject. The main focus of education and research at the department was artifact development. Over the years the department grew steadily in size and scope, encompassing an increasingly broad range of computing fields. That diversification encouraged the department to begin teaching research methodology in 2001, after which various initiatives have been introduced to improve the quality and quantity of methodology education.

Concerned with students' methodological understanding and skills, DSV initiated a department-wide initiative to improve methodology education. A number of courses were established on three levels—B.Sc., M.Sc., and Ph.D. level—and their coherence with the broader aims of education at the department was monitored. Emphasis of methodology in thesis grading was strengthened. A department-wide three-level quality control system for theses was introduced (supervisor, reviewer, and examiner). However, during the implementation of some changes we identified a number of troublesome concepts for students; concepts that were pivotal for understanding the topic but that were conceptually difficult, counter-intuitive, or alien to students [18]. Such threshold concepts need to be properly addressed because the learning of other concepts requires understanding of those threshold concepts [18, 20]. The issues with methodology education were, and are, complicated by the widely differing backgrounds of DSV's students: At the start of their studies some students have an extensive methodological training, while other students have very little.

This essay identifies troublesome concepts in methodology courses in computing, and proposes a distinction between core concepts [1] and threshold concepts [18, 20] in methodology courses in computing. This essay also presents examples of three sources of trouble concerning methodological concepts: misimpressions from everyday experience, the strangeness and complexity of methodological concepts, and reasonable but mistaken expectations [20]. The essay paves a way for further research and educational interventions concerning threshold concepts of methodology education in computing.

2. TROUBLESOME KNOWLEDGE

Threshold concepts and troublesome knowledge are topics of interest in educational research [19]. Perkins [20] discussed five kinds of "troublesome knowledge": ritual, inert, alien, tacit, and conceptually difficult knowledge. In computing education, many threshold concepts in methodology courses are conceptually difficult knowledge. Perkins wrote that difficulties with conceptually difficult knowledge may arise from misimpressions from everyday experience, the strangeness and complexity of scientific concepts, and reasonable but mistaken expectations. All those can be readily identified in methodology education in computing fields.

Some concepts in computing methodology education are muddied by misimpressions from everyday experience. Take, for instance, "hypothesis": The everyday use of the word "hypothesis" refers to a supposition or assumption, and the casual meaning of the word may carry to terms like "null hypothesis," which in methodology language should be testable and neutral. Similar, the casual meanings of terms like "factor", "random", and "significant" sometimes carry to research reports. Other concepts may appear strange and complex: Take ontological categories, for instance: The fact that 8 bits make a byte is a mind-dependent fact [29] may sound strange (how can a fact be mind-dependent?). Yet other concepts are confusing due to reasonable but mistaken expectations. Take, for instance, statistics in research: After a certain point in sample size, population has negligible effect on confidence—for example, statistically speaking, a random sample of 500 respondents is equally useful for the 150 thousand users of a specialized software product as it is for the 150 million users of a social networking website.

Equally difficult with some central methodological concepts might be what Meyer and Land [19] called each field's "ways of thinking and practicing" and what Perkins [20, p.42] called "epistemes"—"manners of justifying, explaining, solving problems, conducting enquiries, and designing and validating various kinds of products or outcomes". Epistemes are perhaps the main expected learning outcome of methodology courses, but much of the epistemes lie hidden beneath the surface of publications. Research reports provide the student only limited windows to epistemes of the field. Perkins [20, p.42] warned that without epistemes, students in science and mathematics may display ritualized routines instead of genuine disciplinary enquiry and problem solving. Insofar as knowledge is ritualized and tacit, learning how to conduct scientific work can be seen as a lonely rite de passage where little guidance aside from mentor-apprentice relationships is provided. However, as both the student body as well as computing as a discipline are becoming increasingly heterogeneous, there is an increasing need to introduce methodology, an essential element of disciplinary ways of thinking and practicing, into curricula, as well.

In computing, the context of knowledge creation is separated from the knowledge of justification. It is excessively difficult to learn the disciplinary ways of thinking and practicing from research reports, as they only present the context of justification. For example, similar to mathematics, in various theoretical branches of computing the research report presents a proof, but offers little insight on the actual process that led to the proof: Which heuristics were applied, what dead-ends were traversed, and in general, how exactly was the problem approached (see, e.g., [21]). In experiment-based branches of computing, few traces of the context of

	Knowledge and Understanding	Competence and Skills	Judgment and Approach
B.Sc. Degree	Students should ... • be aware of similar research problems that have been studied in recent years in the same domain. • understand what types of situations qualify for 'research problems,' on the basis of previous research.	Students should be able to ... • formulate a research problem in such a way that it deals with applied or theoretical problems that actually need solving and fill a gap of knowledge within the domain. • ground a research problem in scientific literature or justify a design problem.	Students should be able to ... • evaluate the degree of relevance of particular research problems for filling gaps in knowledge in a particular domain. • assess the ethical and societal dimensions of a chosen research problem.
M.Sc. Degree	Students should ... • understand similar research problems within a domain.	Students should be able to ... • distinguish and identify different types of problems, such as a lack of knowledge, artifacts, or processes that require improvement, a need for evaluation, or the need for development of new artifacts or processes.	Students should be able to ... • assess and discuss the implications of dealing with particular and varying research problems in varying circumstances and under changing conditions.

Table 1: Examples of Learning Objectives at DSV: Problem Description

discovery can be found from research reports: What really drove the researcher, what bad theories and bad hypotheses were filtered out, what guesses, intuitions, and approximations went into the model-building, and so forth. In engineering types of computing research, things like product specifications offer little information about exactly how and why did those specifications emerge. Methodology education should be able to open the black box of research reports and let students understand how knowledge is created.

3. CORE CONCEPTS

A major difficulty in methodology education in computing comes from the vast amount of new, conceptually difficult knowledge. Terminology is often dense, unrelated to other computing courses, and core concepts and threshold concepts can be hard to identify. In order to clarify the conceptual complexity, we present the core concepts and learning objectives for each state of a typical student research project. Different concepts are needed at different levels. This section outlines the vast amount of conceptually difficult knowledge, which methodology education in computing has to deliver, and which is often new to students. The section also uses those concepts to construct examples of learning objectives for a methodology course (Table 1 and Table 2).

Research Problem

Each research study in computing is a response to a problem, ranging from scholarly problems to evaluation problems to design and development problems [24]. Computing deals with a range of different kinds of problems, and different types of problems are rooted in different intellectual traditions [30]. Understanding what different kinds of problems entail is difficult as it stands, different kinds of problems each introduce their own sets of concepts, and they all point to different research trajectories. The problem statement plays a fundamental role by describing the rationale for research, grounding the study within a specific domain, and driving the research project. Table 1 presents example learning outcomes concerning research problem statements.

Core Concepts: Gap of knowledge, Research problem, Topic, Problem types, Literature review, Background

Aims, Objectives, and Questions

Proceeding from a research problem to research questions might not be conceptually challenging, but it introduces terminological complexity, and terminology should be in agreement throughout the project. A research aim, or purpose, when it exists, corresponds to the research problem, and is often expressed in verbs that define the type of research and resonate well with the problem type; verbs such as 'explore', 'describe', 'develop', and 'evaluate' [5]. Other common conceptualizations of research aims include exploratory, explanatory, descriptive, and emancipatory research [16, 32], or observation, description, prediction, and experimentation (e.g., [14, 22]). In some studies, particularly in evaluation and development, objectives present specific statements about how the research aim is going to be met, expressed in strong active verbs, such as 'classify', 'define', 'implement', and 'test' [27]. If aims, objectives, research questions, and subquestions are all present, they should form a tight fit. In some studies, such as some design research projects, there are no explicit questions but aims and objectives instead (cf. [15]), and sometimes research is defined through research acts [24, pp.32–34]. Table 2 presents example learning outcomes concerning research aims, objectives, and questions.

Core Concepts: Empirical research, Analytical / theoretical research, Desk study, Research acts, Question, Subquestion, Aim, Objective, Explanation, Demonstration, Evaluation, Description, Prediction, Exploration

Research design

The next sets of concepts arise from research designs, which vary between fields of science and between qualitative, quantitative, and mixed-methods types of research [4]. In exploratory types of research, designs are often descriptive, while in confirmatory types of research, experimental designs and correlational designs are common. Strategies of inquiry [4, pp.11–15] are common tools for a high-level overview and organization of research projects—and for improving alignment and congruence, which refers to how the parts of research study logically follow from each other and fit together. The different types of research design introduce a large number of complex but central concepts, which should be introduced from B.Sc. level upwards.

Core Concepts: Research design, Strategies of inquiry, Resource planning, Focus, Scope, Delimiters, Qualifiers, Hypothesis, Experiment, Independent and dependent variables, Construct, Category, Intervention, Control group, Experimental group, Survey, Phenomenology, Case study, Alignment, Congruence

Theoretical and conceptual frameworks

Theory can play various roles in research, but understanding those roles poses conceptual difficulties for students. In quantitative research, theories may provide, for instance, testable variables, models, or frameworks [4, Ch.3]. In qualitative research, theories may provide, for instance, a "vocab-

	Knowledge and Understanding	Competence and Skills	Judgment and Approach
B.Sc. Degree	Students should … • understand what constitutes a research question and how it is derived from, and related to, a research problem. • be familiar with different types of research questions.	Students should … • be able to search for and pinpoint relevant scientific literature to enable the formulation of research questions.	Students should … • be able to evaluate the potential implications of answering particular research questions for the researcher, for potential beneficiaries of research, and society in general.
M.Sc. Degree	Students should … • understand the feasibility of answering particular research questions. • understand the potential and expected scientific, technical, and social impacts of answering the research questions. • be familiar with the different types of answers that different types of research questions require, such as descriptions, explanations, artifacts, correlations, causal relations, comparisons, identification, and definition.	Students should be able to … • define aims of research, and derive measurable objectives that respond to the research aims. • refine and divide research questions into concrete, coherent, and researchable components that become subquestions. • formulate research questions in a variety of ways that allow the focus to be shifted towards different perspectives, depending on context and timing of the research as well as on different stakeholders.	Students should be able to … • evaluate the need for particular questions to be answered. • determine the limitations and utility of answering particular research questions.

Table 2: Examples of Learning Objectives: Research Aims, Objectives, and Questions

ulary" for phenomena and processes or a "lens" for interpreting results. Instead of a theoretical framework, many studies employ conceptual frameworks, both of which require properly done literature reviews [25]—although small-scale practice projects can rarely be literature driven. Theoretical frameworks are tightly interwoven with aims of research, as well as different philosophical assumptions, yet students can be very selective with some of those concepts [12, 29].

Core Concepts: Theoretical and conceptual framework, Ontology (e.g., mind-dependence, mind-independence), Epistemology (e.g., subjectivity, intersubjectivity), Model, Theory, Realism, Relativism, Postpositivism, Critical theory, Constructivism

Information needs and data collection instruments

Answering an empirical research question requires a properly executed collection of data that is of the right type and comes from the right source. Consequently, getting the data collection instruments right is crucial for a successful research project. Students often have preconceptions of terms 'research data' and 'methodology' due to widespread use of those terms. A number of concepts are related to data collection, and confusion is common between, for instance, primary and secondary data and qualitative and quantitative data. In empirical testing of computer systems, inputs, outputs, measuring instruments, parameters and databases are not always obvious and require specific attention. Simulation, emulation, and benchmarking are often used in experimental strategies for design research in computing [13].

Core Concepts: Data types, Data formats, Qualitative data, Quantitative data, Data collection method, Discrete, Continuous, Primary data, Secondary data, Demographic data, Computer-generated data, Questionnaire, Interview, Observation, Input, Output, Parameter, Simulation, Emulation, Benchmarking

Selection of information sources

Towards the end of the research project, retaining conceptual and terminological coherence becomes increasingly difficult. Depending on the type of research, a number of concepts are associated with sampling, selection of informants, or choice of data sources. In quantitative research 'randomness' is one of the more difficult concepts, as the term is often confused with its everyday meaning. In qualitative research, purposeful sampling strategies are often not described to the

extent they should be described—such as maximum variation, theory-based, or deviant case selection [3]. Data collection through social networks is notoriously problematic for traditional sampling terms. Laboratory and field testing of computer systems often lack proper description and justification of the setup, parameter choices, measured outputs and variables, and choice of competing systems [2, 7, 8].

Core Concepts: Selection of informants, Sampling strategies, Probability and nonprobability sampling, Sample, Population, Representative and purposeful sampling, Stratified and comprehensive sampling, Exploratory sample, Random / systematic / convenience sampling, Data saturation, Social networks, Automatic data collection, Log files

Research ethics

The relevant concepts of research ethics in methodology education range from those that should be introduced to students on their first year, like plagiarism, to those that are relevant much later in students' work, such as authorship in journal articles and conflicts of interest. Most importantly, those computing research studies that use human participants require proper permits and procedures.

Core Concepts: Research ethics, Informed consent, Data protection, Security, Anonymity, Research permits, Plagiarism, Authorship, Intellectual property, Conflicts of interest, Disclosure / non-disclosure

Data analysis and discussion

Analysis of data presents a set of concepts tightly interrelated with the previous sets, as well as a number of specific concepts. Qualitative and quantitative data and methods of analysis form a fourfold table, in which each quadrant introduces a specific set of concepts, principles, and processes [24]. Some of the harder concepts include, for instance, the distinction between correlation and causality, the differences between types of measurement (nominal, ordinal, interval, ratio), and the differences between reporting, analyzing, and discussing. The term "analysis" is sometimes used by students in its everyday use—meaning the provision of a detailed or complex opinion and reflection. That is, students may provide opinions instead of a rigorous, methodologically sound analysis.

Core Concepts: Data analysis method, Qualitative and quantitative analysis, Inference, Descriptive statistics, Inferential statistics, Transcript of data, Types of measurement,

	Basic concepts	Intermediate concepts	Advanced concepts
Research problem	Background, **Research problem***, Topic	Problem types, Systematic literature review	**Gap of knowledge***
Aims, Objectives, Questions	**Empirical research***, Research aim, Research question, Description, Exploration	Subquestion, Objective, Demonstration, Evaluation	Analytical / theoretical research, Desk study, Prediction, Explanation, Research acts
Research design	Case study, Research design, Delimiters, Focus	Strategies of inquiry, Resource planning, Qualifiers, Scope, Context, Congruence, Survey, Phenomenology, Category	Intervention, Hypothesis, **Experiment***, Independent and dependent variables, Control group, Experimental group, Alignment, Construct
Theoretical frameworks	**Theory***, Concept	Model, Theoretical framework	Conceptual framework
Research philosophy		**Epistemology***, Subjectivity, Intersubjectivity	Ontology, Mind-dependence, Mind-independence, Realism, Relativism, Postpositivism, Critical theory, Constructivism
Data collection	Data types, Data formats, **Qualitative data***, **Quantitative data***, Data collection method, Interview, Observation, **Primary data***	Discrete, Continuous, Secondary data, Computer-generated data, Social networks, Questionnaire, Input, Output, Parameter	Demographic data, Simulation, Emulation, Benchmarking
Sources of information	Selection of informants, Exploratory sample, Convenience sampling, Purposeful sampling strategies	Nonprobability sampling, Sample, Population, Systematic sampling, Data saturation, Stratified sampling, Comprehensive sampling, Automatic data collection, Log files	**Probability sampling***, Representative sampling
Research ethics	Research ethics, Plagiarism, **Informed consent***, Anonymity	Data protection, Security	Research permits, Disclosure, Non-disclosure, Authorship, IPR, Conflicts of interest
Data analysis	Data analysis method, Qualitative analysis, Coding, Memoing, Classifying, Transcript of data	Quantitative analysis, Descriptive statistics, Types of measurement, Midpoints, Spread of data, Statistical significance, Data visualization	Inference, **Inferential statistics***, Hypothesis testing
Quality measures	Rigor, Confirmability, Trustworthiness, Credibility, Transferability, Dependability, Peer checks, Member checks, Bracketing	Reproducibility, Measurability, **Bias***, Generalizability, Reliability, Validity	Triangulation, Testability
Reporting	Abstract, Citation, Bibliography, Paraphrasing, Verbatim quote, Tenses, **Rich description***, Practical contribution	Congruence, Facts, Interpretations, Layers of data	Theoretical contribution, IMRAD, Style manual

* A candidate for threshold concept

Table 3: A Survey of Concepts from Basic to Advanced

Midpoints, Spread of data, Statistical significance, Coding, Memoing, Classifying, Rich description, Data visualization

Quality measures

Some of the most difficult new concepts to students is concerned with the self-evaluative aspects of a research study. Validity and reliability—the "twin pillars of science"—can be broken into a complex variety of concepts, and the four criteria of qualitative research—credibility, confirmability, transferability, and dependability [12]—each have their own nuances. The number of possible sources of bias, such as design, sampling, and nonresponse bias, is equally large and often those concepts are difficult to apply to research studies.

Core Concepts: Rigor, Reproducibility, Testability, Triangulation, Measurability, Bias, Generalizability, Reliability, Validity, Confirmability, Trustworthiness, Credibility, Transferability, Dependability, Member checks, Peer checks, Bracketing

Reporting

Compiling the pieces of research together into a coherent, well aligned report requires yet another set of conceptual and technical elements: those related to technical and academic writing. Congruence (compatibility and consistency of research elements) is a measure of conceptual and terminological rigor in a research report. Proper quoting, paraphrasing, and citing requires understanding of why literature references are necessary. Academic writing, as well, has a great impact on the readability and credibility of a report.

Core Concepts: Abstract, Citation, Bibliography, Paraphrasing, Verbatim quote, Congruence, Tenses, Facts, Interpretations, Rich description, Theoretical and practical contribution, Layers of data, IMRAD, Style manual

4. DISCUSSION

The amount of new, conceptually difficult knowledge makes methodology courses hard for computing students, and it makes course design a challenge for educators. A conceptual analysis of the course contents, explication of learning objectives, and identification of threshold concepts plays a key role in developing methodology courses. This essay presents a set of core concepts in methodology education in computing and proposes candidates for threshold concepts (Table 3). The essay also gives examples of learning objectives for methodology education in computing (Tables 1 and 2). Our proposals, however, are only applicable to DSV's social and human-oriented computing research, and are analytical instead of empirically grounded. The next steps in our project are to empirically evaluate the perceived difficulty of each of those concepts, to analytically establish the connections between the concepts, to survey the extent to which the same difficulties are found in other computing institutions, and to propose educational interventions for resolving the difficulties with those concepts.

5. REFERENCES

[1] J. Biggs and C. Tang. *Teaching for Quality Learning at University: What the Student Does*. Open University Press, New York, NY, USA, 4th edition, 2011.

[2] J. Carreira and J. G. Silva. Computer science and the Pygmalion effect. *Computer*, 31(2):116–117, 1998.

[3] J. W. Creswell. *Qualitative Inquiry and Research Design: Choosing Among Five Approaches*. Sage Publications, Thousand Oaks, CA, USA, 3rd edition, 2007.

[4] J. W. Creswell. *Research Design: Qualitative, Quantitative, and Mixed Methods Approaches*. Sage Publications, Thousand Oaks, CA, USA, 3rd edition, 2009.

[5] J. C. Cronjé. The ABC (aim, belief, concern) instant research question generator. Unpublished Manuscript, 2012.

[6] P. J. Denning, C. Chang, and CC2001 Joint Task Force. Computing curricula 2001: Computer science volume. pdf, March 2001.

[7] D. G. Feitelson. Experimental computer science: The need for a cultural change. Unpublished Manuscript, December 3, 2006, 2006.

[8] P. Fletcher. The role of experiments in computer science. *Journal of Systems and Software*, 30(1–2):161–163, 1995.

[9] R. L. Glass. A structure-based critique of contemporary computing research. *Journal of Systems and Software*, 28(1):3–7, 1995.

[10] R. L. Glass, V. Ramesh, and I. Vessey. An analysis of research in computing disciplines. *Communications of the ACM*, 47(6):89–94, 2004.

[11] M. Goldweber, J. Impagliazzo, I. A. Bogoiavlenski, A. G. Clear, G. Davies, H. Flack, J. P. Myers, and R. Rasala. Historical perspectives on the computing curriculum. *SIGCUE Outlook*, 25(4):94–111, 1997.

[12] E. G. Guba and Y. S. Lincoln. Competing paradigms in qualitative research. In N. K. Denzin and Y. S. Lincoln, editors, *Handbook of Qualitative Research*, pages 105–117. SAGE, London, UK, 1994.

[13] J. Gustedt, E. Jeannot, and M. Quinson. Experimental methodologies for large-scale systems: A survey. *Parallel Processing Letters*, 19(3):399–418, 2009.

[14] C. G. Hempel. *Aspects of Scientific Explanation And Other Essays in the Philosophy of Science*. The Free Press, New York, NY, USA, 1965.

[15] P. Johannesson and E. Perjons. A design science primer. Unpublished Manuscript, February 25 2012.

[16] C. Marshall and G. B. Rossman. *Designing Qualitative Research*. Sage Publications, Thousand Oaks, CA, USA, 4th edition, 2006.

[17] G. McKee. Computer science or simply 'computics'?, the open channel. *Computer*, 28(12):136, 1995.

[18] J. H. F. Meyer and R. Land. *Threshold Concepts and Troublesome Knowledge: Linkages to Ways of Thinking and Practicing within the Disciplines*. Number 4 in Occasional Reports. ETL Project, Universities of Edinburgh, Coventry and Durham, 2003.

[19] J. H. F. Meyer and R. Land. Threshold concepts and troublesome knowledge: An introduction. In J. H. F. Meyer and R. Land, editors, *Overcoming Barriers to Student Understanding: Threshold Concepts and Troublesome Knowledge*, pages 3–18. Routledge, London, UK, 2006.

[20] D. Perkins. Constructivism and troublesome knowledge. In J. H. F. Meyer and R. Land, editors, *Overcoming Barriers to Student Understanding: Threshold Concepts and Troublesome Knowledge*, pages 33–47. Routledge, London, UK, 2006.

[21] G. Pólya. *How to Solve It*. Penguin Books Ltd., London, UK, 2nd edition, 1957.

[22] K. Popper. *The Logic of Scientific Discovery*. Routledge, London, UK, 1959.

[23] V. Ramesh, R. L. Glass, and I. Vessey. Research in computer science: An empirical study. *The Journal of Systems and Software*, 70(1–2):165–176, 2004.

[24] J. J. Randolph. *Multidisciplinary Methods in Educational Technology Research and Development*. HAMK University of Applied Sciences, Hämeenlinna, Finland, 2008.

[25] J. J. Randolph. A guide to writing the dissertation literature review. *Practical Assessment, Research & Evaluation*, 14(13):1–13, 2009.

[26] Swedish National Agency for Higher Education. National qualifications framework. Technical Report 12-5202-10, Högskoleverket, May 2011.

[27] M. Tedre. Methodology education in computing: Towards a congruent design approach. In *Proceedings of ACM Computer Science Education (SIGCSE) 2013 Conference*, pages 159–164, Denver, CO, USA, March 6–9 2013. ACM.

[28] M. Tedre and N. Moisseinen. Experiments in computing: A survey. *The Scientific World Journal*, 2014(# 549398):1–11, 2014.

[29] M. Tedre and J. Pajunen. An easy approach to epistemology and ontology in computing theses. In *Proceedings of the 13th Koli Calling International Conference on Computing Education Research*, Koli Calling '13, pages 97–104, New York, NY, USA, 2013. ACM.

[30] M. Tedre and E. Sutinen. Three traditions of computing: What educators should know. *Computer Science Education*, 18(3):153–170, 2008.

[31] I. Vessey, V. Ramesh, and R. L. Glass. Research in information systems: An empirical study of diversity in the discipline and its journals. *Journal of Management Information Systems*, 19(2):129–174, 2002.

[32] G. H. von Wright. *Explanation and Understanding*. Routledge & Kegan Paul, London, UK, 1971.

[33] M. V. Zelkowitz and D. R. Wallace. Experimental validation in software engineering. *Information and Software Technology*, 39(11):735–743, 1997.

[34] M. V. Zelkowitz and D. R. Wallace. Experimental models for validating technology. *Computer*, 31(5):23–31, 1998.

Leveraging Open Source Principles for Flexible Concept Inventory Development

Leo Porter
Mathematics and Computer
Science Department
Skidmore College
Skidmore, NY
leo.porter@skidmore.edu

Cynthia Taylor
Computer Science
Department
Oberlin College
Oberlin, OH
ctaylor@oberlin.edu

Kevin C. Webb
Computer Science
Department
Swarthmore College
Swarthmore, PA
kwebb@cs.swarthmore.edu

ABSTRACT

Concept Inventory (CI) assessments, which target high-level learning goals, have proven highly valuable for higher education research. These assessments have helped to evaluate pedagogical practices among individual instructors, both within and across institutions, and have hence elevated the level of discourse on education within the community. The success of CIs in physics has inspired similar developments in computer science, with a few CIs now developed for computer science courses. However, the development of a CI typically follows a burdensome process, requiring a significant investment to produce a single CI that may be difficult to deploy due to institutional curricular differences. Furthermore, as our field continues to be shaped by technological advances, a path to faster, more modular CI development is critical.

This paper proposes an alternative CI development model and continues the discussion within the community about the need for, and path to, concept inventories throughout the computer science curriculum. Specifically, we explore the implications of an open collaboration system for CI development that would mimic the principles common to open source software communities, which have regularly demonstrated their ability to produce high-quality results.

Categories and Subject Descriptors

K.3.2 [**Computer and Information Science Education**]: Computer Science Education

General Terms

Human Factors

Keywords

Concept Inventory, Assessment, Community Discussion

1. INTRODUCTION

In this paper, we propose an alternative process for the development of *Concept Inventories* (CIs). A Concept Inventory is an assessment mechanism consisting of a series of forced-choice questions, given as both a pre- and post-test. Unlike traditional assessment mechanisms such as final exams, CIs are designed to measure the success of the course in raising the level of students' conceptual knowledge, rather than assessing individual students. By focusing on the common concepts, CIs are applicable to similar courses taught by different instructors or at different institutions.

CIs provide valuable insight into how students conceptualize course content by focusing on student understanding of core concepts, as opposed to relying on detailed calculations or rote memorization. In recent years, concept inventories have gained traction in the sciences as mechanisms for exposing student misconceptions before and after instruction, contrasting instructor and student views of classroom material, and measuring course effectiveness.

Moreover, as standard assessment tools, CIs enable comparison of pedagogical techniques between courses, previous semesters, or across multiple institutions. In physics, where CI adoption has been most prominent, work with the Force Concept Inventory [18] led to a dramatic revamping of the way introductory physics lectures are taught, resulting in significant gains in student learning [10, 15].

Previously, the Delphi Process has been proposed as a rigorous method for developing concept inventories [13] that aims for consensus among a panel of fifteen to twenty subject-area experts. The process requires panelists to identify key concepts, propose assessment questions, and iterate though multiple rounds of refinement in which questions are scored across several metrics. Experts involved in the Delphi process are often compensated for their time, which makes developing a concept inventory a difficult proposition without significant financial support. The end result of this method is a rigorously-evaluated concept inventory, and while we strongly believe in the process's efficacy, its overhead is relatively high. The time and effort required to develop concept inventories in this manner is daunting enough to effectively hamper the development of new concept inventories, computer science topics included.

Additionally, CI development practices for other disciplines may not properly address the needs of computer science. Unlike a physics course on Newtonian mechanics where key topics are well established, curricular differences between institutions commonly lead to topics appearing in different courses (e.g., recursion may appear early in a functional programming CS1 but might not appear until CS2 at institutions that teach CS1 using an iterative language). As such, constructing a concept inventory as a collection of independent, topic-based modules may be more appropriate than a whole-course CI. Moreover, the content of courses may change as our field advances and/or technology changes. For example, while single-chip multiprocessors are a key topic in computer architecture classes today, the topic would have scarcely been mentioned ten years ago. As such curricular shifts occur, the field needs a mechanism by which CIs can similarly adapt.

In this paper, we propose an alternative concept inventory development process inspired by the open source software model. In recent years, the open source community has demonstrated the effectiveness of rapid project development by incorporating large groups of contributors with varying levels of expertise [24, 27]. We believe that by applying similar multi-author development models to the construction of computer science concept inventories, the educational community will benefit from high-quality, modular concept assessments with significantly increased course coverage.

With this paper, we aim to incite discussion surrounding concept inventories in the computer science community and solicit involvement from the community. We are not presenting results or arguing that this is a solved problem with a single correct approach. Rather, we examine the advantages of this approach, describe our goals and expectations for the resulting concept inventories, and explore the potential challenges (e.g., validation, and versioning) of the design space.

2. MOTIVATION

Concept inventories have proven to be essential in measuring student conceptual understanding in the physical sciences. In this section, we advocate CI adoption in computer science and characterize early efforts toward developing inventories for upper-division CS courses.

2.1 Value of CIs

Many STEM fields have adopted concept inventories with positive results [18, 20]. Unfortunately, the adoption of CIs in computer science, a field that has been defined by (and prides itself on) rapid improvement, remains slow. While the currently developed CIs for computer science are excellent [11, 28], they only cover a small number of courses and, in some cases, have limited availability.

The lack of concept inventories plainly reduces the potential for informed discussion in the computer science education community. A significant percentage of work in our field reports solely on student satisfaction. While satisfaction is a relevant and meaningful metric, it has limited value when reported in isolation. Ultimately, the most important metric for the success of a pedagogical practice or educational tool is *student learning*.

Recognizing the value of reporting on student learning, some work has succeeded in producing controlled studies across multiple courses using similar or identical final exams as the metric of student learning success. However, even this metric leaves room for criticism as the quality and content of the final exam is often unknown or focused on other aspects of the course (e.g., calculations rather than high-level concepts). As an established set of educational benchmarks, concept inventories would elevate the level of discourse considerably and enable stronger educational claims by CS education researchers.

2.2 Related Work

Concept inventories are now widely used in a variety of disciplines [12] to assess the impact of pedagogical methods. In the field of computer science, concept inventories have been created for digital logic [16, 17] using the Delphi process, algorithms and data structures [11], and introductory courses [13, 14, 19]. Although these CIs are a good start, the majority of computer science topics remain without concept inventories.

Other work in computer science education research has examined student learning using assessments not developed using a CI development process (such as the Delphi process) [6, 8, 21–23, 25, 28–31]. These works have successfully underscored the need for more established assessment mechanisms in computer science by providing important intuition as to student understanding.

In both formal CIs and other assessment mechanisms, findings often demonstrate that students understand far less than instruc-

Table 1: Post-test results from various concept assessments in computer science. The only available data from an assessment using the Delphi Process is [17].

Exam Content	Correctness (avg.)
BASIC Programming (Table II in [6])	21%
Number and Date Sorting [8]	59%
Code Comprehension/Tracing [21]	60%
Value and Reference Assignment [22]	63% and 17% (resp.)
Write Calculator Program [23]	21%
Fundamental Intro. Concepts [31]	42%
Digital Logic CI [17]	55%
CS1 Language Independent CI [30]	34%

tors expect [21, 23, 30, 31]. Table 1 provides results from the concept assessments. These results serve to underscore the importance of established assessment mechanisms, which facilitate meaningful comparisons between curricular and pedagogical computer science practices. Despite the Delphi process being a standard CI development method, we note that (to the best of our knowledge) many more of the non-Delphi-developed concept assessments were administered in courses with published results than Delphi-developed concept inventories. We argue that test availability should be a key goal of concept inventory development.

2.3 Preliminary work

Absent vetted CIs in Operating Systems and Computer Architecture, we have recently developed basic concept tests for these topics [26, 32]. This work applies to the present discussion, as these concept assessments were developed by just a few experienced instructors, who did not follow the Delphi Process, but nevertheless offered insight into student understanding of course content.

The concept assessment in computer architecture was designed by two experienced instructors who are published researchers in computer architecture. We designed the questions with the intent that *every* student successfully completing an architecture class should be able to answer the question correctly. The CI was run in four different courses by four different faculty at two different institutions under different conditions (as an online pre-test and as an online post-test before the end of the term, in an in-class final review session, and on the final exam). Although results on different questions varied somewhat by course, the CI revealed two interesting findings. First, there were questions for which students performance did not improve significantly from pre-test to post-test. Additionally, across these different classes, institutions, and instructors, students answered only 56% of questions correctly.

To see if such results are common in upper-division computing courses, we have similarly developed a concept test for Operating Systems following a similar methodology. Across three different instructors and four different courses at two institutions, we have found similar results to the architecture study. Students do not demonstrate significant improvement between the pre- and post-test for some questions, and on average, students answer 55% of the questions correctly.

Despite these CIs not being developed using a standard CI development process, we believe that the results are nonetheless hugely informative for instructors. That students are misunderstanding nearly half of the tested core concepts in upper-division classes is worrisome. Under the status quo, their conceptual difficulty might have gone unnoticed. With the introduction of a concept inventory, instructors can repeatedly collect student performance data, enabling them to more easily guide modifications to their courses and/or pedagogical practices. This is the true value of such evaluation mechanisms: *they provide instructors with a motivation to improve and a means to measure improvement.*

Undoubtedly, because these inventories were not rigorously vetted, their results come with some caveats. Our experience in developing them informs our belief that the availability of a respectable CI, even an imperfect one, strongly outweighs having no inventory at all. We believe this presents an opportunity to employ the collective insight of our community. With open access and contributions from community members, the quality of our inventory tools will only get better. This motivates our analogy to open source software, and in the remainder of this paper, we discuss the goals and design challenges of our proposal.

3. GOALS

To guide the design of collaborative concept inventories, we turn to the open source software community for inspiration. We aim to formulate a development process for concept inventories that leverages community involvement to quickly create and deploy a concept inventory. Ideally, any interested instructor should be able to use the test in their class and compare the results with results from other classes. Additionally, instructors should be able to contribute new questions and suggest modifications to existing ones based on their experience with the concept inventory and their classes. In this section, we describe our vision, goals, design requirements for cooperative CI development.

The following objectives are critical to the construction of a community-driven concept inventory:

Customizable. As topics appear in different courses based on differences in computer science program curricula, an assessment for a course should be customizable to the content of that course. This customizability may be at a module level (e.g., a module on sorting) or at an individual question level (e.g., a question on inheritance). At either level, assessment results will then need to be associated with the context/course in which the assessment was given.

Collaborative. Much of the value of concept inventories comes from their ability to enable comparisons across courses, instructors, and institutions. However, to fully realize this potential, a CI needs as many participants as possible. We believe that open instructor access to CI questions and response data, including instructors who do not identify as CS education researchers, is paramount to establishing the collaborative support environment around a CI.

Any interested instructor should be able to contribute to the development of a concept inventory, by contributing new questions or recommending changes to existing questions. Ultimately, as the number of CI users and contributors increases, so does the quality and availability of questions and response data, which enhances the overall impact and utility to the CS community. Thus, it should be straightforward for instructors to use a concept inventory in their class, make their results available to other instructors, compare their results with others, and contribute feedback, adjustments, or new questions for future inclusion.

Adaptable. Unlike introductory Newtonian physics, which has been relatively quiescent for decades, the technology-driven computer science discipline has evolved rapidly in recent years. Such an accelerated progression suggests that we need flexible assessment tools. Thus, inventories should be developed as dynamic exams, with a clearly-defined procedure for making modifications in response to deployment data or new technologies.

High-quality. A concept inventory requires high-quality questions if instructors and education researchers are to draw reliable conclusions from the results. "Linus's Law" [27], which states that a large enough developer base will efficiently detect and correct

software bugs, is an essential underpinning of the open source software world. The open source community has repeatedly demonstrated the ability to produce high-quality software, and we believe the same principles will serve the CI development process.

We propose leveraging the adaptable nature of community-driven project development to iteratively reexamine and refine CI questions. Thus, inventory development should converge on a set of questions and presentation style that are clear, accessible to students, and carefully crafted to elucidate concept comprehension.

Maintainable. Maintaining the quality of collaborative concept inventories will require an organized management infrastructure. Like open source software, the availability of simple tools to document and support development will lower the barrier to entry for new contributors and help to cultivate a CI's community. Thus, an inventory's development process should clearly track question contributions, collaborator discussions, alteration history, and recorded response data with low administrative overhead.

4. DESIGN

Our proposal to accelerate the development process of computer science concept inventories is not without obstacles, and in this section, we examine the design space of our approach. Since this is a discussion paper describing a space of potential choices (rather than describing an existing solution), we opt to explore potential options, rather than prescribe solutions. Ultimately, the goal is to see a variety of CIs developed across many computer science subject areas, and we recognize that each may make different design decisions.

4.1 Composition and versioning

The need for CIs to be developed openly and iteratively is critical to our *collaborative* and *adaptable* design goals. To support these goals in a realistic fashion, the community will require CI tracking and revision history.

The first point of contention we envision with respect to inventory composition is version control granularity:

> **Should a concept inventory be a loosely related set of questions or a holistic exam?**

One design option is to represent a concept inventory not as a synoptic test, but as a collection of questions, some of which may be available in multiple versions. Instructors may choose which of the set of questions available for their class they will use in the concept inventory they give, and which version of each question.

This model enables instructors to mix-and-match self-contained questions that are independently versioned. By allowing instructors to choose the questions that best fit their courses, this model helps to address the diversity in course material coverage. The potential trade-off is that collected responses would only be comparable per-question, rather than representative of student performance across a holistic CI. This complicates comparing results, as instructors who wish to make direct comparisons would need to purposely select the same set of questions.

On the other hand, a holistic approach simplifies data comparison but requires a stronger consensus from the community regarding question inclusion and may reduce a CI's dynamism. Continuing our open source analogy, we believe that a holistic CI development method might resemble the branched structure [9] common to many software development projects. A CI developed in this fashion might consist of core set of "stable" questions augmented by "experimental" questions that help to inform future revisions. Opting for a hybrid model, the experimental questions could be optionally chosen by instructors to help tailor the CI to their course.

How do changes get integrated into a release of a concept inventory?

The field of computer science is by nature constantly evolving, and with it some of the core concepts in our courses may change (e.g., energy consumption and related concepts have become a critical to systems design in the past decade). This necessitates concept inventories that are capable of adapting to the current knowledge in the subject area. The CI development process must balance the trade-off between frequent updates, which complicates data comparisons, and remaining unchanged, which runs the risk of becoming outdated.

This issue is particularly important for holistic CI development, which requires a procedure for transitioning questions from "experimental" to "stable". We envision a core group of test developers who curate the stable version and decide when to announce a new release. As instructors use a CI and provide feedback on the questions, the developers may utilize a mechanism to automatically move questions into the stable group based on quantitative instructor evaluations. Alternatively, they might employ a scheduled release cycle for new stable versions, and at that point the top-rated questions become the new stable test.

How are versions managed?

With the ability to update questions comes the need to reference specific versions of a question. Version control is a common and well-understood problem in our field, and numerous solutions, such as CVS, Subversion and Git already exist [1, 3, 5]. However, all of these systems specialize in maintaining code rather than text documents. One way to deal with this might be to simply split up each question into a separate file for ease of editing.

There is also the need to keep results associated with a specific version of the test or question. This necessitates a strong set of version numbers that are easy to reference and associate with data. Likewise, instructor feedback and discussions will also need to be associated with specific versions.

4.2 Instructor Access

Who should be given access to read and write concept inventory materials?

Central to the idea of an open source concept inventory is the ability for any interested and experienced instructor to contribute to it. However, by nature a concept inventory must be more restricted than a typical open source project, as the questions cannot be publicly available. This necessitates an approval process for access, at the very least verifying that the requester is a course instructor or researcher, and not a student attempting to locate test questions.[1]

There must be some way to verify that someone attempting to gain access to a CI is actually an instructor. The standard practice in the physics community involves password protected documents, for which instructors acquire the password by sending an email to the CI maintainers with their name, institution, and website. However, this requires instructors to be separately approved for each individual concept inventory. An alternative system might make use of a cryptographic key system, in which instructors could be verified once, and then simply provide their key afterwards.

Once instructors are approved to access a CI, they might automatically be approved to contribute, or there may be some further application process. Depending on their frequency, contributions may need to be voted on democratically or submitted to a group of maintainers prior to inclusion in the public CI repository.

---

[1]Ideally, a CI should be used as an educational metric, and not for credit, disincentivizing students from attempting to gain access.

4.3 Leadership and Quality

Who should have leadership roles in concept inventory development, and what should these roles be?

We imagine most concept inventories will have some small group of instructors who do most of the management of the concept inventory, either because they are doing research involving the concept inventory, or because it is for a class they frequently teach. How much control this group has over the concept inventory will naturally vary. One compromise between fully open source CI development and the traditional Delphi process might be to carefully select a group, consisting of both pedagogy researchers and experts in a subject area, to maintain the concept inventory. This approach could help to bootstrap new inventories during their initial development.

How will test questions be validated?

Traditionally, CI questions have been validated by a number of methods, including having students perform think-alouds in order to check if questions are misleading or rely on concepts other than what they are designed to measure, and comparing student performance on CIs to performance on final exams. This validation is not incompatible with open source CI design. Once questions are submitted, they can be validated via think-alouds or other methods, and the results of that validation used to improve the questions. Contributors can indicate if questions have been validated, and how. Instructors can choose to use only validated questions, or to include newer questions that have not yet been validated as well.

How can we assure a high-quality CI?

The rigorous structure of the Delphi process was developed specifically to assure an accurate concept inventory that assesses key concepts agreed upon by experts in the field. Without this structure, we run the risk of developing concept inventories that lead to misleading results or focus on the wrong concepts. We believe that despite this risk, quality concept inventories can be developed via open source development methodologies. Open source software projects have shown their ability to produce quality products, and we believe that open source CI development will produce better end results with more community member involvement. It is reasonable to assume that those researchers and instructors who take a leadership role in the development of concept inventories will work to assure their quality. Ultimately, we believe that even imperfect concept inventories will still provide some standard way to assess student learning, something we currently lack in a large number of computer science courses.

4.4 Response data

In addition to versioning and access control, a successful CI repository will need to record metadata (e.g., usage frequency or question development discussions) and student response statistics. We believe that collected CI results should be made available, in an anonymized form, for use by the broader computer science community. For this design aspect, we hope to steer the discussion toward several questions, the first of which is:

How much data should we collect, and what kinds?

The granularity at which we collect results is important, especially if instructors are including different questions within the versions of the CI that they administer. As instructors, we would like to easily compare results across the test as a whole, individual questions, and individual versions of questions. One solution would be for raw scores for each question to be collected each time a test was given, and those scores associated with that version of the question. Collecting results on the granularity of individual versions of questions will allow instructors to compile results for the questions as a whole, and different versions of the test.

Tagging questions with metadata such as subject area could also allow comparison across subjects. For example, an instructor may wish to measure the correlation between results from a specific question with others that assess a related concept. However, this will require instructors to be willing to contribute their data in this more detailed form. Additionally, more fine-grained data may be more difficult to anonymize, especially if it is possible to track how an individual did on each question, even if their name is removed. This becomes especially of concern when results from small classes are contributed.

Another tactic would be to only compare results from stable versions of the test, which would allow instructors to contribute their results as a whole. However, this means that an instructor can no longer compare across different test versions, and means that even when the same individual question is in multiple stable versions of the test with the same format and wording, we can no longer compare results for that question across versions.

There is also the issue of collecting meta-data about the questions. Since the concept inventory is being continually developed, feedback from instructors who have given the question to their classes would be extremely valuable. This could take the form of a simple "up vote/down vote," long form comments, and ideally the distribution of how their class performed on the question. Questions for which answers vary wildly may indicate a poorly worded or unclear question. This kind of empirical data can be collected and analyzed in order to validate test questions.

How should response data be collected and anonymized?

In the collection of response data, we need to anonymize data to protect student privacy, but also make sure we retain enough data to make the results as useful as possible. Information like the type of institution where the concept inventory was given, the experience level of the instructor, and what pedagogical techniques were used in the class will all make the data more useful for potential comparisons.

One solution to streamline both data collection and anonymization could be to administer the exam via the response data collection system. For example, an instructor could set up an account with the system (at which point items like institutional characteristics could be provided) and then request a web-link for their students to take the exam. Students could then take the exam on-line with results (potentially non-anonymized) sent to the instructor. That data could then be automatically anonymized by the system and incorporated into the collected data (with instructor permission).

Should we incentivize participation?

The more CI results aggregated for a subject area, the larger the impact it will have on the CS community. To aid in data collection, it may be beneficial to incentivize instructors to share their collected CI data. For example, a CI might only release questions to instructors who will pledge to contribute their results or aid in question development. Likewise, a CI may choose to only share previously-recorded results with instructors who commit to making their own results available. Whatever the model, it is important that the barrier to entry is not so high as to dissuade instructors from pursuing the concept inventory.

4.5 Pre- and Post-tests

How should a CI be administered?

Instructors traditionally administer concept inventories as a pre- and post-course assessment. Pre-tests help pinpoint misconceptions that may interfere with new student learning and identify existing knowledge that can be leveraged when explaining new subject material [7, 8, 19]. Comparisons between the pre- and post-test enable instructors to assess student learning gains.

Unfortunately, for many upper-level computer science classes, converting conceptual vocabulary into "plain English" that students can understandable at the start of the course is often a daunting task. While some concepts lend themselves easily to analogies (for example, tickets versus guest lists to represent capabilities and access control lists when discussing file protection), this can lead to students answering based on details of the chosen analogy, rather than the underlying concept. On the other hand, if a CI is written in technical prose, students may be intimidated by the prospect of an incomprehensible test on the first day of class. It may be desirable to administer only accessible questions as a pre-test, followed by a post-test including those and other more technical questions.

4.6 Intellectual property

How should a concept inventory be copyrighted or licensed?

Finally, CI developers must answer questions of copyright and ownership. Will individual instructors own questions they contribute? Will the test as a whole have a single copyright? If so, who will own the copyright?

Current licenses that allow for sharing and modification of work, such as the Creative Commons license [2], may be a practical solution. We believe that the chosen license should allow modification of the work, to prevent the concept inventory from becoming locked by one group of people (in the parlance of the open source community, it should be possible to fork a version). There are also questions of whether commercial use should be permitted and how to copyright development metadata. A license such as the Open Data Commons [4] may be more reasonable for sharing results.

5. CONCLUSION

The overarching objective of our concept inventory (CI) proposal is to enhance CS education, and the research surrounding it, by enabling data-driven comparisons of different pedagogical techniques. Preliminary concept inventories for CS have exposed the value of measuring student understanding of fundamental subject area concepts. The available results strongly suggest that students are *not* mastering the ideas that every student *ought* to know after completing the corresponding course. CIs represent reliable tools for measuring this high-level mastery, and their results provide desperately-needed factual data for informing pedagogical changes to improve student concept mastery.

We believe that a comprehensive collection of concept inventories would serve as a critical step towards achieving this lofty goal. CIs in other STEM disciplines, most notably physics, have already demonstrated a significant and lasting impact on educational methods and research in their fields. If we know it will be effective, why *shouldn't* we adopt a similar approach?

Some of those already working on CI development have followed the traditional Delphi Process development cycle which aims to ensure CI quality by requiring consensus from a panel of experts. Unfortunately, necessitating such formality is expensive and requires a significant time commitment. We laud the recent efforts by computer science education researchers in rigorously producing

CIs for computer science classes. However, most of the courses in our field still have no such exam available. Thus we advocate an alternative: reducing CI developmental rigidity in favor of an agile process that encourages broad collaboration and adapts to changes in technology and course content.

In this paper, we explored the application of open source software principles to computer science concept inventory development. The open source development model offers three promising advantages over current CI practices: (1) a collaborative development strategy capable of producing a quality product, (2) a clearly defined path for revision when content changes, and (3) a means to manage versioning of questions/modules/exams in order to compare results for research purposes.

This work identifies clear goals for developing high-quality, collaborative concept inventories whose open-access and availability will strongly support CS education research. We propose a basic framework for "open source" CI development, identify the obstacles faced by such a framework, and sketch the design space and trade-offs necessary to make our vision a reality. We believe that the design challenges of our proposal are surely tractable for a highly-motivated community like ours.

Ultimately, we hope that this paper will intensify the discussion of concept inventories in computer science, inspire new thinking about concept inventory development, and elicit increased participation in CI development from the CS education research community. The best way for an open development process to succeed is with your help!

6. ACKNOWLEDGMENTS

Thank you to the anonymous reviewers for their suggestions. This work was supported in part by NSF grant 1140731.

7. REFERENCES

[1] Concurrent versions system. http://cvs.nongnu.org/.

[2] Creative commons. http://creativecommons.org/.

[3] Git version control. http://git-scm.com/.

[4] Open data commons. http://opendatacommons.org/.

[5] Subversion. http://subversion.tigris.org/.

[6] P. Bayman and R. Mayer. A diagnosis of beginning programmers' misconceptions of basic programming statements. *Communications of the ACM*, 26(9), 1983.

[7] J. Bonar and E. Soloway. Preprogramming knowledge: A major source of misconceptions in novice programmers. *Human-Computer Interaction*, 1(2):133–161, 1985.

[8] T.-Y. Chen, G. Lewandowski, R. McCartney, K. Sanders, and B. Simon. Commonsense Computing: Using student sorting abilities to improve instruction. In *SIGCSE*, 2007.

[9] J. Corbet. A guide to the kernel development process. https://www.kernel.org/doc/Documentation/development-process/.

[10] C. H. Crouch and E. Mazur. Peer Instruction: Ten years of experience and results. *American Journal of Physics*, 69(9), September 2001.

[11] H. Danielsiek, W. Paul, and J. Vahrenhold. Detecting and understanding students' misconceptions related to algorithms and data structures. In *SIGCSE*, 2012.

[12] D. Evans, G. Gray, S. Krause, J. Martin, C. Midkiff, B. Notaros, M. Pavelich, et al. Progress on concept inventory assessment tools. In *IEEE Frontiers in Education*, 2003.

[13] K. Goldman, P. Gross, C. Heeren, G. Herman, L. Kaczmarczyk, M. C. Loui, and C. Zilles. Identifying important and difficult concepts in introductory computing courses using a Delphi process. In *SIGCSE*, 2008.

[14] K. Goldman, P. Gross, C. Heeren, G. L. Herman, L. Kaczmarczyk, M. C. Loui, and C. Zilles. Setting the scope of concept inventories for introductory computing subjects. *ACM Transactions on Computing Education (TOCE)*, 10(2):5, 2010.

[15] R. Hake. Interactive-engagement versus traditional methods: A six-thousand-student survey of mechanics test data for introductory physics courses. *American Journal of Physics*, 66:64, 1998.

[16] G. Herman and J. Handzik. A preliminary pedagogical comparison study using the digital logic concept inventory. In *IEEE Frontiers in Education*, 2010.

[17] G. Herman, M. Loui, and C. Zilles. Creating the Digital Logic Concept Inventory. In *SIGCSE*, 2010.

[18] D. Hestenes, M. Wells, and G. Swackhamer. Force Concept Inventory. *The Physics Teacher*, 30, March 1992.

[19] L. C. Kaczmarczyk, E. R. Petrick, J. P. East, and G. L. Herman. Identifying student misconceptions of programming. In *SIGCSE*, 2010.

[20] J. C. Libarkin and S. W. Anderson. Assessment of learning in entry-level geoscience courses: Results from the geoscience concept inventory. *Journal of Geoscience Education*, 53(4), 2005.

[21] R. Lister, E. S. Adams, S. Fitzgerald, W. Fone, J. Hamer, M. Lindholm, R. McCartney, J. E. Moström, K. Sanders, O. Seppälä, et al. A multi-national study of reading and tracing skills in novice programmers. *SIGCSE*, 2004.

[22] L. Ma, J. Ferguson, M. Roper, and M. Wood. Investigating the viability of mental models held by novice programmers. *ACM SIGCSE Bulletin*, 39(1), 2007.

[23] M. McCracken, V. Almstrum, D. Diaz, M. Guzdial, D. Hagan, Y. B.-D. Kolikant, C. Laxer, L. Thomas, I. Utting, and T. Wilusz. A multi-national, multi-institutional study of assessment of programming skills of first-year cs students. *SIGCSE*, 2001.

[24] A. Mockus, R. T. Fielding, and J. D. Herbsleb. Two case studies of open source software development: Apache and mozilla. *ACM Transactions on Software Engineering and Methodology (TOSEM)*, 11(3):309–346, 2002.

[25] R. Pea. Language-independent conceptual "bugs" in novice programming. *Journal of Educational Computing Research*, 2(1):25–36, 1986.

[26] L. Porter, S. Garcia, H.-W. Tseng, and D. Zingaro. Evaluating student understanding of core concepts in computer architecture. In *Proceedings of the 18th Annual Conference on Innovation and Technology in Computer Science Education*, 2013.

[27] E. Raymond. The cathedral and the bazaar. *Knowledge, Technology & Policy*, 12(3):23–49, 1999.

[28] A. Tew and M. Guzdial. Developing a validated assessment of fundamental CS1 concepts. In *SIGCSE*, 2010.

[29] A. E. Tew. Assessing fundamental introductory computing concept knowledge in a language independent manner. *Georgia Institute of Technology*, 2010.

[30] A. E. Tew and M. Guzdial. The fcs1: a language independent assessment of cs1 knowledge. In *SIGCSE*, 2011.

[31] A. E. Tew, W. M. McCracken, and M. Guzdial. Impact of alternative introductory courses on programming concept understanding. 2005.

[32] K. C. Webb and C. Taylor. Developing a pre-and post-course concept inventory to gauge operating systems learning. In *SIGCSE*, 2014.

Advanced Data Analytics Education for Students and Companies

Maija Marttila-Kontio
University of Eastern Finland
School of Computing
70200 Kuopio, Finland
+358403553756
maija.marttila@uef.fi

Mikko Kontio
University of Eastern Finland
School of Computing
70200 Kuopio, Finland
+358503464385
mikko.kontio@uef.fi

Virpi Hotti
University of Eastern Finland
School of Computing
70200 Kuopio, Finland
+358405629192
virpi.hotti@uef.fi

ABSTRACT

In this paper we introduce a regional education project and a positive experience of quick implementation of a new training package enabled by public funding from the European Social Fund. The project focuses on advanced data analytics (ADA) in business management.

In the project, advanced data analytics is taught to both students at University of Eastern Finland and to their potential employers at the local organizations. The university teaching favors effective teaching techniques instead of conventional teaching methods, and the same topics are taught to participants from local organizations as shorter versions. The organizations also have an important role in calibrating the teaching via discussions and maturity reviews.

Even-though the project is regional there has been great nationwide interest in the project. This indicates the general need for improving know-how on ADA both at universities and in companies and organizations.

Categories and Subject Descriptors

K.3.2 [**Computers and Education**]: *Computer science education*; J.1 [**Administrative data processing**]: *Business*

General Terms

Management, Measurement, Economics, Experimentation

Keywords

Advanced data analytics, advanced data analytics education, business intelligence, data science, data science education, management.

1. INTRODUCTION

In 2012, Davenport and Patil wrote in [1] that "there are no university programs offering degrees in data science". At the time, media had for some time been announcing a serious shortage of "multi talent data scientists" and "BI geeks".

Some universities and colleges reacted fast to offer courses – mainly online– in "Big Data analytics", "Data science", "Advanced data analytics", "Big Data and MBA", or "Business Intelligence", to mention a few. Coursera [2] represents one of the most popular massive open online course platforms offering a variety of data science and analytics online courses. Currently only few universities have master's program on some of the subjects listed above while most universities are not able to answer market's needs for data scientist, business analysts, data architects, data guru's, etc.

Literature does not offer a unique definition for data science or advanced (data) analytics but a proper one is by Dhar's [3]: "Data science is a study of the generalizable extraction of knowledge from data". We started to use advanced data analytics (ADA) to describe the paradigm shift (i.e., from statistical hypothesis testing to automatically gathered data and machine learning) whereas we do not necessarily avoid the term data science.

In Finland, the ministry of employment and economics has published a report of 21 paths to a Frictionless Finland" establishing "a roadmap for long-term efforts to make Finland a leader in information technology applications over the next ten years." [4] In the report, Big Data and data analytics education and know-how were raised into the main focus. For the reason, the Ministry of Employment and Economy recently organized a survey for finding out the state of BI and data analytics education in Finnish universities and other educational organizations (the report is published only in Finnish). We (i.e., Eastern Finland University, Department of Computer Science) were the only educational organization having a 25-credit Big Data/Advanced data analytics -training package available.

Designing and implementing a new master's program is a resource and time consuming task with great amount of bureaucracy, which is why a master's program is hard to change, remove, or start on the fly. Despite starting to arrange an ADA master's program, we did faster approach by applying a funding for designing and implementing an ADA education. The funding was approved by the local Centre for Economic Development, Transport and the Environment (EDTE Centre). The organization controls money coming, among others, from the European Social Fund.

The funding from EDTE Centre is mainly targeted for developing the local business, not university courses. In our case, this was not a problem. On the contrary, this was a great opportunity to design university courses in tight collaboration with local companies. Furthermore, there is a lot of work to be done until CEOs (chief executive officer), CIOs (chief information officer) and other data-driven decision makers have adapted advanced data analytics as a tool for competitive advantage. It is not relevant to educate a data scientist or data analysts if potential employers do not see the need for hiring one.

The paper is organized as follows. In Section 2, we give a short introduction to data science. The content of the project is represented in Section 3. In Section 4, we give our conclusion.

2. ADA's VARIOUS SUBSTANCE FIELDS

Over the years ADA has been successfully used in many substance fields from financial services to baseball management [5]. As ADA and Big Data has increasingly gained media attention, more and more substance fields have started to experiment with it. Next we describe some of the interesting ideas reported in academia and business literature.

2.1.1 Financial services and investing

Financial institutions have been one of the earliest ADA's adapters. In the past, they have mostly used numerical data, but using only numerical data is not good for some problems like predicting mergers and acquisitions (M&A) [6, 7]. This is for two reasons: first the numerical datasets of M&A cases are quite limited, and second, the textual data available from social media is ignored [8]. Sakaki et al. [7] proved that mining data from social media worked in detecting events and signals. Xiang et al. [8] built on top of this and successfully demonstrated a supervised approach to predicting M&A with factual and topic features using profiles from Crunchbase and news articles from TechCrunch.

2.1.2 Baseball management

Another interesting case is in the area of sports management. For a long time the normal way to build and manage a baseball team was to use scouts, i.e. experienced talent seekers searching for young talents and then hope that the player is developed up to his talents. Lewis documents the well-known case of Billy Beane, the general manager of the Oakland Athletics, building and managing a baseball team in financial trouble by using statistics and a scientific approach to baseball. As several authors have pointed out, the big outbreak of this approach was to successfully challenge many of the traditional unsupported practices of baseball.

2.1.3 Customer relationship management

Businesses have had customer relationship management (CRM) solutions for almost as long as corporate computing has been available [11, 12]. Recently ADA has been able to introduce solutions to some of the problems basic CRM solutions don't answer, such as predicting churn (customers leaving for a competitor) for subscription-based businesses [13]. ADA can offer solutions by applying a machine learning approach to historical training data. Another business problem related to marketing is micro-segmentation [14, 15]. Traditional or manual segmentation of large groups of customers into obvious segments (by age, location, income, etc.) creates too large and vague segments where most customers inside a certain segment do not respond well to the marketing messages. By applying ADA, an algorithm can find thousands of segments based on multivariate analysis and can automatically create pricing or recommendations for these micro-segments [13, 16]. This is a technical solution to the mass-customization to the level of one [14] introduced.

2.1.4 Health and wellbeing

Health and wellbeing have had several interesting adaptations of ADA [17]. Google announced that it could predict the outburst of influenza epidemics by analyzing search engine query terms [18]. The previous way was to collect data from healthcare professionals and then aggregate that data, which took weeks. By analyzing search query terms the predictions are almost real-time.

The previously collected medical data can be used to improve hospital (or doctoral) work. Panicker [17] explains the advantage of mining all previous historical health care data of symptoms, images, etc. to improve the quality of diagnosis.

3. THE CONTENT OF THE TIETÄVÄ PROJECT

The overall structure of the one and a half year educational project is presented in Figure 1. The structure is formed by three main parts, namely 1) education for university students, 2) education for local companies and organizations, and 3) tight collaboration between the students and companies. The collaboration gradually increases within the semesters. Our goal is to get students to make their internships and master's thesis to the companies and organizations. Hereafter we use the term 'organization' for both companies and public organizations.

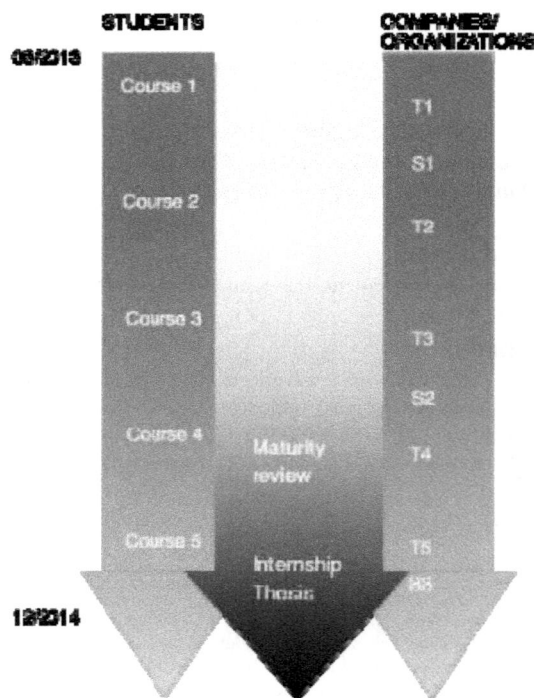

Figure 1. The project brings together the university education and the needs of organizations by offering 1) a training package to students and 2) themed courses, seminars, business intelligence maturity reviews and student internships to the organizations.

The education for university students consists of a training package of 25 academic credits (ECTS). From fall 2013 to the end of the year 2014 we organize five ADA courses, each of them five ECTS. Because the courses are closely related to each other, we offer it as a training package.

For the local organizations, we organize three seminars (S) and five themed trainings (T). Themed trainings are based on the five ADA courses, where the first themed training is a summary of the first ADA course, etc. Seminars are open for everyone who is interested in the topic. For improving ADA knowledge in an organization we will also make visits to the organizations for measuring the level of current data analytics utilization.

3.1 Training the trainers first

As mentioned previously, it is hard for universities and colleges to quickly answer markets increasing demands for educating new kinds of talents, such as data scientists. While money is often the scarcest resource, the second place comes to the teaching staff who should manage the whole scientific field in question. In this case, project team members should cover the fields of statistics, computer science and business management as well as teaching. While the three of us together have a strong background in computer science, MBA, degrees in mathematics, management, pedagogy or statistics, we realized that there still are some holes to be filled until we are ready to educate data scientist and data analysts.

Fortunately, part of the Tietävä project funding is targeted for the project team education. So far, we have participated in several commercial courses by SAS Institute to learn how to use SAS data analytics programs (i.e. SAS Enterprise Miner, SAS JMP, SAS Visual Analytics). Participation in top conferences and summits has also brought valuable information to be forwarded to students and organizations.

3.2 The ADA training package for university students

In the spring of 2013 students at the University of Eastern Finland were able to apply to the ADA training package. Since the programming skills were mandatory, 25 computer science master's degree students were approved. The number of 25 students was critical because our computer lab takes only 25 students.

The main educational goal of the training package is to introduce and motivate students to fearlessly play with all kinds and types of data. As Davenport and Patil have described it in [1], "more than anything, what data scientist do is make discoveries while swimming in data". This means gathering, exploring, cleaning, modifying, analyzing and making insight based on the previous procedures. Most of all, it requires open mind and good storytelling skills [19]. Therefore, our pedagogical approach is to create an atmosphere as supportive and explorative as possible. This means getting rid of conventional university teaching methods.

A conventional university course often consists of lectures and labs followed by the final exam. In our computer science department, a course of 5 ECTS consists approximately of 30 hours of lectures (theory) and 16 hours of labs (practice). During university lectures, interaction usually remains low. A course teacher can notice student's learning rate only during the labs –if taught by herself/himself– or, in the worst cases, not until the final exam. Furthermore, when speaking especially of modern data analytics, "skills cannot easily be acquired from books or in a classroom setting" as mentioned in [20]. Designing a well functioning and motivating course structure was, therefore, played a key role during a course design process.

The structure of an ADA course is illustrated in Figure 2. A course lasts 7-8 weeks (numbered circles on the left hand side). Instead of lectures and labs, an ADA course consists of four face-to-face training days taking place every second week. Each training day lasts 7.5 hours. Typical training day is a mixture of theory, practice and exploration in the fields of computer science, statistics and business management.

To achieve a good learning atmosphere leading to effective learning, we use pedagogic methods, such as, collaborative learning [21,22], pair programming [23], and learning by doing [24]. During the day, we are aloud to find something we haven't even planned. This approach draws us near to the ideology where data scientist is thought as "part analyst, part artist"[25].

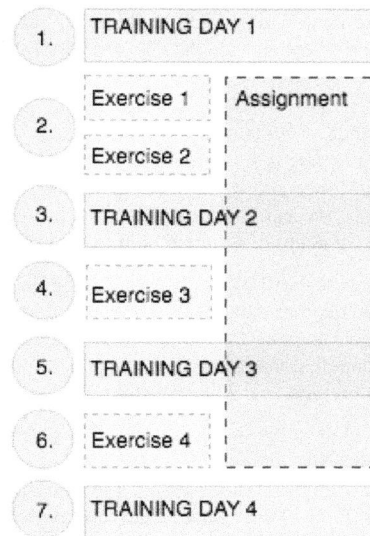

Figure 2. An ADA course consists of four training days, four home exercises and one larger assignment.

Because there are no lectures in conventional sense, part of ADA theory is leaved to a student's independent study days. In Figure 2, numbered exercises represent these studies. In each training day (except the last) students receive a new exercise (two at the first day) to be accomplished independently or in study groups. Students return their exercises in to Moodle learning environment before the next training day. The exercises are graded in Moodle and the exercise topic is discussed at the next training day.

In addition to home exercises a student does a wider assignment. To accomplish the work, a student should manage at least the basics of the ADA course. The assignment (made independently or as a group) is returned to Moodle before the last training day. The assignment is graded and the topic is discussed at the last training day. By this way, students will get valuable feedback about their work. This also decreases the number of questions about the given grades.

Next we present the content of the ADA courses. In each course, the main content, motivating questions and objectives are given.

3.2.1 Course 1: "Introduction to advanced data analytics"

The course introduces the big picture of advanced data analytics and different kinds of data sources. The terms of advanced data analytics and analysis methods are introduced. Students also learn the basics of descriptive statistics.

During the course, we will discuss the following questions: What key performance indicators (KPIs) are? What are the different concepts and definitions of data? How to learn to ask from the data, and what data can tell us? Where can data be beneficial? What kind of data there is? How could and should business management and data be connected?

After completing this course, a student can use Excel Power Pivot and JMP Add-ins in Excel for producing visualized description from analyzed data. The student understands the different sources of data, and how these sources can be used in business and business management. The student should also have a motivation to think and improve the way data is used in modern business management.

3.2.2 Course 2: "Methods",

The focus of the course is set on data and its structure, format and sources. We introduce basic tools for gathering, modifying and analyzing data so we can start to play with it. Also, inferential statistics and the concept of a statistical model are introduced.

During the course, we will discuss the following questions: Where and how can you capture data? How do you do data management? What kind of data exists? Can data be classified? What are the indicators and data that best support management processes? How does data mining and machine learning support a prediction process?

After completing the course, a student can make statistical presentations and interpretations using, for example, Excel, SAS JMP, SPSS program. She/he understands the typical sources and formats of data. The student also understands the difference between both structured and unstructured and internal and external data. Furthermore, the student should understand the main idea of statistical modeling, especially where to use predictive analytics and how it can be done.

3.2.3 Course 3: "Big data and cloud computing"

In this course, we introduce the principles and basic concepts of Big Data and utilization of cloud resources for managing vast amounts of data. We introduce basic tools, such as, NoSQL, Hadoop (plus Hive, Pig, etc.), and the principles of MapReduce. In addition to commercial cloud services (e.g., Amazon Web Services, Azure, Google, Rackspace) we use our own private cloud especially implemented for this course. In this course, we encourage students to discuss and evaluate the potentiality of Big Data in business and scientific research. On the part of statistics, we introduce the theory and practice of multivariate analysis.

During the course, we will discuss the following questions: Where and how Big Data is produced? Why do we need cloud services for managing Big Data? What are the types of cloud services? Does everyone need Big Data? How Big Data can be used for competitive advantage and business management? Where and why do we need multivariate analysis?

After completing the course, a student can acquire, modify, and analyze Big Data in the cloud. The student should understand the concept and significance of Big Data, how Hadoop and MapReduce work, how cloud services work and how cloud services relate to Big Data. A student also understands the purpose of multivariate analysis.

3.2.4 Course 4: "Interpretation of analysis"

This course is for considering and evaluating the results of advanced data analysis. This is not an easy task, since gaining insight from an analysis is always dependent on the interpreter. In this course, we go deeper into the visualization techniques and their utilities.

During the course, we will discuss: How can data be interpreted? What could be the most effective visualization technique for making interpretation easy for target audience? Who will interpret the data? What is a good way to visualize data?

After completing the course, a student manages different types of visualization techniques. The student also understands importance of using the right kind of visualization technique considering the data and the target audience.

3.2.5 Course 5: "The tools"

This course is the final data playground. Everything learned so far is pieced together to an analysis machine. Here, the focus is on the data integration and data architecture of the analysis machine.

During the course, we will discuss: What parts an analysis machine contains. What is the typical architecture of an analysis machine? How to integrate data sources, analysis tools, and target applications?

After completing the course, a student understands the complete architecture of an analysis machine (from data gathering to the final point of making interpretations from data analysis).

3.3 Lesson learned so far

At this point, we are about to start the third ADA course. According to students' feedback, the courses one and two went well. Both, the ADA as a subject, and the course structure were thanked. Most of all, the student's appreciated the absence of a final exam. Quoting anonymous feedback: "It is easy in practice to show how to ride a bike but it could be painful and useless to describe it on paper." Another interesting pedagogical thing is that students find it refreshing to have three teachers doing lessons and training in turn. While one of us had his/her training turn, the other two were just "hanging around the computer lab". Without planning, it this could have made the atmosphere more open and not so serious.

After two courses, we have learned that the hardest thing for students is to learn the basics in statistics. Most of our students do not have a strong background in (any kind of) mathematics. As we have noticed self-efficacy and motivation pose bigger problems than the subject being too complex to understand.

Referring to the course structure represented in Figure 2, we need to adjust the timing of the assignment. Students do not have enough time to accomplish the work by the last training day. We have decided to move the deadline after the last training day. The assignment will be discussed at the beginning of the next course.

3.4 Education and cooperation with the local companies

Cooperation with the local organizations is important for two reasons: first to raise awareness and understanding of the possibilities of ADA, and second to get the feedback of challenges and the state of their current use of data analytics. This feedback is then used in the course design. With raising awareness of the possibilities of ADA, we aim to create more demand for our students in the near future in the local job market.

To the members of local organizations, we have three offerings: themed courses, seminars, and business analytics maturity audits. Each of these is designed to reach different people in the organization's hierarchy. Next we present these three elements.

3.4.1 Themed courses

Themed courses are one or two-day courses that contain the most important elements of each of the five academic courses described in 3.2. Themed courses are targeted to experts working in middle management or expert level at the local organizations, who are involved in product development, IT development, or general IT related business development. The courses are designed to have a combination of theory and hands-on practices so that the participants would learn new concepts, widen their view on the possibilities of ADA, and have a change to try something concrete. The discussions during the presentations, hands-on practices, and breaks are a good way to get a realistic image of the situation in these organizations.

3.4.2 Seminars

Seminars are half-day events that introduce the topics of the courses from the management's point of view and on a higher level of abstraction than the themed courses. Seminars are targeted to managers in leadership and a decision-making role in the local organizations. Seminars consist of inspirational talks and presentations by project members and guest speakers from other organizations or technology vendors. As the seminars are targeted to different people than the themed courses, the discussions and feedback from the seminars has contained a different perspective.

3.4.3 Business analytics maturity reviews

Organizations often have difficulties in assessing how well they are doing in a certain area or process. Maturity models are frameworks that make it possible to evaluate the level of professionalism compared with the general body of the model and to other organizations that have used the model [26]. The project offers business analytics maturity reviews for local organizations. The maturity reviews serve two purposes: first the organizations see how well they are doing business analytics and what they should do to get better, and second it gives the project team a relaxed and organized framework to talk with the organizations about their situation and possibilities.

4. CONCLUSION

Resources play a crucial role in the implementation of a new university training package or master's program. A fast and easy way to pilot a new training package is to apply funding outside the university (e.g. European Social Fund). As presented in the paper, this –in addition to learn and teach state-of-the-art scientific subject– opens a great possibility to test new and more innovative pedagogical approaches and teaching methods. Our students have found the used methods (such as collaborative learning and the structure of the courses) refreshing. Tight cooperation with the local organizations has also brought teaching and learning into more expedient levels. Internships and master's thesis to be done at the organizations were important criteria for our students to apply for our training. So far we have lots of information requests from the organizations for talented students for internships and master's thesis.

Cooperation with the local organizations has so far proved to be a good way for two-way communication. The project team has been able to address the local organizations' needs, techniques, and tools in teaching. This is important, because it calibrates the students' skills with the requirements of the local organizations, making it easier for the students find internships and then get to work. Representatives of the local organizations and technology partners have also visited our lectures as guest speakers, sharing real-life cases and recent improvements in technology.

While organizing the seminars, we have run into a problem of how to get the top management of the local organizations to get interested and participate. At this point of the project, we have found that discussions with the local organizations, especially while doing the business analytics maturity reviews, has offered good opportunities to discuss the possibilities of ADA with the management. This has raised the awareness of ADA and in turn makes it easier to get participants to the seminars and to the themed trainings. Hopefully it will also make it easier for the students to get internships and finally jobs.

We have encountered some problems on the availability of the produced material posed by the funding rules. The funding rules require that all produced learning material should be available for everyone interested. Although the teachers have made the material themselves, approximately only 10% of the material can be published as such on the Internet. This is due to university publication rules that conflict with the financier's rules and general copyright rules. So far, we have not yet found a proper solution to the problem.

5. ACKNOWLEDGMENTS

The Tietävä project is funded by European Social Fund via the Centre for Economic Development, Transport and the Environment at Northern Savonia.

6. REFERENCES

[1] Davenport,T. and Patil,D. 2012. *Data Scientist: The Sexiest Job of the 21st Century*, Harvard Business Review, 10/2012.

[2] Coursera 2014. URL: https://www.coursera.org/

[3] Vasar D. 2013. Data Science and Prediction, *Communications of the ACM, 56(12) pp. 64-73.*

[4] Ministry of Employment and the Economy of Finland. 2013. *21 paths to a Frictionless Finland. Report of the ICT 2015 Working Group.*

[5] Silver, N. 2012. The Signal and the Noise, *Penguin Books, London.*

[6] Wei, C.-P., Jiang, Y.-S., and Yang, C.-S. 2009. *Patent analysis for supporting merger and acquisition (m&a) prediction: A data mining approach.* Lecture Notes in Business Information Processing 22(6):187–200.

[7] Sakaki, T., Okazaki, M., and Matsuo, Y. 2010. Earthquake shakes twitter users: real-time event detection by social

sensors, *Proceedings of the 19th international conference on World wide web* (WWW'10), 851–860.

[8] Xiang, G., Zheng, Z., Wen, M., Hong, J. I., Rosé, C. P., & Liu, C. 2012. *A Supervised Approach to Predict Company Acquisition with Factual and Topic Features Using Profiles and News Articles on TechCrunch.* Proceedings of the Sixth International AAAI Conference on Weblogs and Social Media, pp.607-610.

[9] Lewis, M. 2009: *Moneyball: The Art of Winning an Unfair Game.* W. W. Norton & Company.

[10] Cullen, F,T., Myer, A.J. and Latessa, E.J. 2009. Eight Lessons from Moneyball : The High Cost of Ignoring Evidence-Based Corrections, Victims & Offenders: *An International Journal of Evidence-based Research, Policy, and Practice*, 4:2, 197-213.

[11] Brown, S.A. 1999. Customer Relationship Management: A Strategic Imperative in the World of e-Business. John Wiley & Sons, Inc. New York.

[12] Peppard, J.2013. Customer Relationship Management (CRM) in financial services, European Management Journal, Volume 18, Issue 3, June 2000, Pages 312-327.

[13] Provost, F. and Fawcett, T.2013. Data Science for Business, What you need to know about data mining and data-analytic thinking. O'Reilly, Sebastopol.

[14] Kotler, P. 1998. From mass marketing to mass customization, *Strategy & Leadership*, Vol. 17 Issue: 5, pp.10 – 47.

[15] Funk, D. 2002. Consumer-Based Marketing: The Use of Micro-Segmentation Strategies for Understanding Sport Consumption. International Journal of Sports Marketing & Sponsorship (IJSMS), 4(3), 231 - 256.

[16] Segaran T.2007. Programming Collective Intelligence. O'Reilly, Sebastopol.

[17] Panicker, R. 2013. Adoption of Big Data Technology for the Development of Developing Countries. In Proceedings of National Conference on New Horizons in IT-NCNHIT (p. 219).

[18] Ginsberg J., Mohebbi M.H., Patel R.S., Brammer, L., Smolinski M.S, Brilliant L. 2009. Detecting influenza epidemics using search engine query data. Nature. 2009;457:1012-14.

[19] Kwan-Liu M., Liao, I., Frazier, J., Hauser, H., Kostis, H.-N., 2012. "Scientific Storytelling Using Visualization," *Computer Graphics and Applications, IEEE* , vol.32, no.1, pp.12-19.

[20] Hauder,M., Gil, Y., Sethi, R., Liu, Y., and Jo, H. 2011. *Making data analysis expertise broadly accessible through workflows.* In Proceedings of the 6th workshop on Workflows in support of large-scale science (WORKS '11). ACM, New York, NY, USA, 77-86.

[21] Laal, M. and Laal, M. 2012. Collaborative learning: what is it?, *Procedia - Social and Behavioral Sciences*, Volume 31, 2012, Pages 491-495,

[22] Laal, M. 2013. Positive Interdependence in Collaborative Learning, *Procedia - Social and Behavioral Sciences*, Volume 93, 21 October 2013, Pages 1433-1437.

[23] Williams, L. and Kessler, R. 2002. *Pair Programming Illuminated.* Addison-Wesley Longman Publishing Co., Inc., Boston, MA, USA.

[24] Surya Kiran Reddy, K., Kode, S. 2010. Enhancing the Learning Experience by Addressing the Needs of the Learner Through Customization and Personalization in the Learning by Doing Methodology, *10th International Conference on Advanced Learning Technologies (ICALT), 2010 IEEE*, pp.274-275, 5-7 July 2010

[25] IBM, 2013. *What is a data scientist* URL: http://www-01.ibm.com/software/data/infosphere/data-scientist/

[26] Lahrmann, G., Marx, F., Winter, R., and Wortmann, F. 2010. *Business intelligence maturity models: an overview.* In VII conference of the Italian chapter of AIS (itAIS 2010). Italian chapter of AIS, Naples.

Peer Instruction: a Link to the Exam

Daniel Zingaro
OISE
University of Toronto
Toronto, ON, Canada
daniel.zingaro@utoronto.ca

Leo Porter
Dept. of Mathematics and Computer Science
Skidmore College
Saratoga Springs, NY, USA
leo.porter@skidmore.edu

ABSTRACT

In computer science, the active learning pedagogical practice of Peer Instruction (PI) has been shown to improve final exam performance, reduce student failure rates, and improve student retention. PI consists of two major parts: group discussion and follow-up instructor intervention. We expect that PI performance as a whole will correlate with final exam performance, but it is unclear whether or how each piece of PI is involved in these relationships. In this work, we use isomorphic questions to isolate the effects of peer discussion and instructor intervention, and examine scores on a final exam and its code-writing and code-tracing questions. We find that both pieces of PI correlate with the final exam as a whole, code-tracing question (similar to PI questions), and code-writing question (not similar to PI questions). This is further evidence that both PI components are important to the success of PI.

Categories and Subject Descriptors

K.3.2 [**Computer Science Education**]: Computer and Information Science Education

Keywords

peer instruction; clickers; final exam

1. INTRODUCTION

Concerns that our computer science students are failing at alarming rates [2] and that many of our students are not demonstrating acceptable learning outcomes [7] have spurred the CS research community to examine how we might respond as teachers. Prompted by research from other disciplines such as psychology and physics education, CS researchers have begun questioning the lecture as the pedagogical basis of CS courses. This is evident in the recent interest in inverted classrooms [8] and in-class collaboration [6], each

ITiCSE'14, June 21–25, 2014, Uppsala, Sweden
Copyright 2014 ACM 978-1-4503-2833-3/14/06 ...$15.00.
http://dx.doi.org/10.1145/2591708.2591711 ...$15.00.

of which decenters the lecture as the core element of teaching. One particularly promising alternative to lecture is Peer Instruction (PI) [3, 15]. In a PI class, students participate in multiple iterations of individually answering a question (using a clicker), discussing that question in a group, answering the question again, and then participating in an instructor-led classwide discussion of the question.

Recent research has shown PI to offer a number of benefits over traditional lecture in CS courses. For example, PI can contribute to substantially lower failure rates [12] and improved retention of majors [13]. In addition, similar to other collaborative learning domains [6], students report being particularly engaged in PI classes [14].

As the momentum in favour of new pedagogies builds, it is paramount that we measure student learning. A growing body of research therefore seeks to verify that students learn from the PI process. Some of this work uses isomorphic (same-concept) questions to measure performance before and after peer discussion [11]. Such questions have been used to demonstrate that students learn from the peer-discussion part of the PI process. Other work shows that students in a PI class outperform students in a matched lecture class [16, 20]. As yet, no work has investigated links between PI performance and final exam performance. To be sure, we expect such links to exist — we know that PI is correlated with enhanced performance — but it is not clear whether the peer discussion, the instructor intervention, or both, are responsible for these expected links.

We examine student performance during the in-class PI process using isomorphic questions and use regression modeling to determine whether this performance predicts final-exam grades. We anticipate there to be a great deal of noise between a student demonstrating learning a concept in a class during the early weeks of a term and the final exam months later, due to other in-class content, laboratory assignments, programming assignments, outside-class discussions, studying, programming practice, etc.

Despite this noise, we expect, and find, that students who come to class already prepared to answer questions correctly do better on a final exam consisting of code-tracing and code-writing questions. We also find, controlling for baseline performance, that student learning during the PI process, both from peers and from the instructor, relates to higher exam scores. This is the first work, to our knowledge, that directly connects learning during the in-class PI process with student performance at the end of the term. We discuss the elements of PI that we believe are particularly valuable and address potential threats to validity.

2. BACKGROUND AND LITERATURE REVIEW

2.1 Active Learning in Computer Science

Computing educators have long used active and collaborative learning techniques outside of lecture, most notably in the use of pair programming [9]. Recently, notions of an "inverted classroom" have brought active learning to the forefront of CS lectures as well. An inverted classroom involves asking students to prepare for lecture, perhaps by reading, watching a video, or exploring programming techniques [8]. The justification is that our contact time with students is minimal, so it should be used in ways that maximize the utility of the instructor. Students know how to read but may not know how to integrate their reading with other disciplinary knowledge, hence the divide between reading before lecture and instructor-led learning during lecture.

Other disciplines, such as physics and psychology, have rich histories of pedagogical interventions that are presently being exercised in computing courses. For example, think-pair-share (TPS) is a popular cooperative learning technique that has students individually ponder, discuss with ad hoc groups, and then share with the entire class. Recent work has found that students are engaged in each of the three phases of the technique [6] and that much of this engagement is combined with active learning such as discussing with peers and contributing to discussion. PI has much in common with TPS and other active learning pedagogies through its focus on group discussion and conceptual understanding.

2.2 Peer Instruction

Peer Instruction (PI) focuses students on several conceptual multiple choice questions ("conceptests") per class meeting. The PI protocol includes the instructor posing a multiple choice question, giving students a minute or two to respond with a clicker, and providing time for students to discuss in groups and submit a second response. Then, the instructor leads a wrap-up discussion of the particular concept, and moves on to a mini-lecture or the next PI conceptest.

Do students learn from PI in CS? It is interesting to trace the progression of research on this question. Initial studies demonstrated that students' more often answered correctly in the second vote (the group vote) compared to the first vote (the individual vote) [15, 19]. This might mean that students are learning from group discussion, but it could also mean that students are copying from neighbors. To distinguish these alternatives, other research has used isomorphic questions where students vote a third time on a new question very similar to the first. As students vote individually on this "isomorphic vote", students are unable to passively copy from neighbors. These isomorphic studies use common terminology that we will also use below, so we introduce these terms:

- Q1: the individual vote on the first question.

- $Q1_{ad}$: the group vote on the first question. This occurs after students have discussed the question in groups.

- Q2: the individual vote on the second (isomorphic) question.

Porter et al. [11] used isomorphic questions to study PI learning in Computer Architecture and Theory of Computation. They particularly focused on those students who incorrectly answered Q1 and correctly answered q_1ad, since these are the students that may have learned (or copied) during the peer discussion. The authors found that 76% and 62% of these students correctly answered Q2, suggesting that real learning was happening during peer discussion.

Of course, the complete PI cycle — including Q1, peer discussion, and Q2 — occurs within a few minutes, and all measurements have been taken during this small time window. That is, learning might be happening, but is the learning enduring? A logical follow-up to the work of Porter et al. [11] is to examine the link between Q2 and the final exam, when Q2 represents learning from various parts of the PI process. Students' correctness on Q2 should correlate with correctness on the final exam to the extent that peer- and instructor-based learning are long-lasting. We follow this line of inquiry in the present paper.

3. METHOD

3.1 Study Context

Data for this study comes from a CS1 taught in Python at a large campus of a Canadian research university. The course uses Python 3 and studies traditional CS1 topics in the following order: introduction, functions, booleans, conditionals, while- and for-loops, lists (including nesting and aliasing), dictionaries, file I/O, testing and test coverage, introduction to object-oriented programming, and introduction to sorting and complexity. 131 students wrote the final exam.

The course took place over 12 weeks, with 3 50-minute lectures per week. Prior to each lecture, students were required to read 10-15 pages of the textbook and submit answers to three questions as part of a reading quiz. Reading quizzes are common and recommended for use in PI classes to bootstrap the discussion process in lecture [3, 5, 21]. The reading quizzes were marked based on completion (not correctness) and were worth 4% of students' final grade; in-class clicker participation accounted for a further 5% of students' grade. The course instructor was a senior education graduate student with significant PI and CS teaching experience, and had taught CS1 using PI several times. New PI materials were developed for this course offering and are freely available for anyone's use [1].

In addition to facilitating PI questions, the instructor live-programmed during lecture to model code-writing. Students also pair-programmed in weekly labs (supported by TAs) and completed two larger programming assignments. This skill-based focus on code-writing was meant to complement the conceptual focus of PI [22].

3.2 Question Administration

The course instructor developed pairs of isomorphic questions, generally using one pair per lecture. (The other PI questions in each lecture were of the standard PI format, with no isomorphic question.) To verify the isomorphic nature of the questions, the instructor sent the proposed isomorphic questions to a colleague experienced in CS1, PI, and isomorphic question administration. Questions were modified as necessary so that both parties agreed that they were

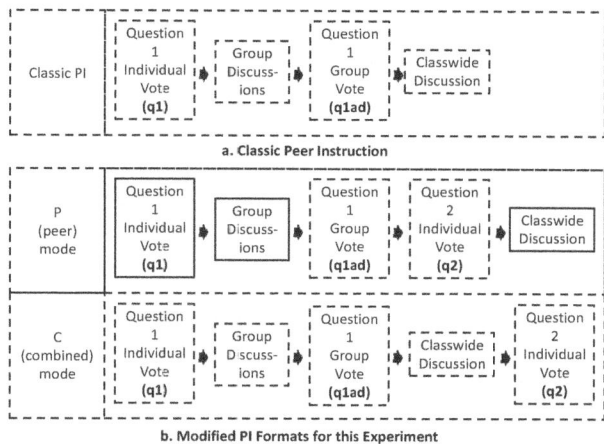

Figure 1: The P (Peer) and C (Combined) administration modes used in this study and [23].

suitably similar and of comparable difficulty. Additional controls (below) were added to help ensure isomorphicity.

For each isomorphic pair, three student votes were taken; we use the notation introduced above and refer to these votes as Q1, Q1$_{ad}$, and Q2, with the first two votes taken on the first question and the third vote taken on the second. Note that the histogram of responses was never shown between Q1 and Q1$_{ad}$.

We are interested in the relationship between Q2 and the final exam score when Q2 represents learning from the full PI cycle and when Q2 represents only the effect of peer discussion. To this end, we ran half of the isomorphic questions as follows:

Combined: students individually answered Q1, engaged in peer discussion, and answered Q1$_{ad}$. Then, the instructor displayed the histogram for Q1$_{ad}$ and proceeded to explain the question, its distractors, and its correct answer. Following instructor intervention, Q2 was shown on which students voted individually. This mode is identical to that of [23].

We ran the other half of the isomorphic questions so that Q2 measured **only** the peer-based learning, not the instructor-imparted learning. That is, these isomorphic questions were run as follows:

Peer: students were shown Q1, individually answered, engaged in peer discussion, and answered Q1$_{ad}$. Then, students were immediately presented with Q2 and voted individually. Note that between Q1$_{ad}$ and Q2, there was no instructor intervention at all, and that the correct answer to the first question was not displayed. This mode is identical to that of [11, 23].

See Figure 1 for these two administration modes and how they compare to classic PI.

We included the following experimental controls in order to validate isomorphic questions, avoid mode biases, and eliminate poor questions:

- A colleague was engaged in the validation of isomorphic questions (explained earlier).

- The presentation order (Q1 and Q2) within each question pair was randomized at the start of class.

- The choice of whether to run an isomorphic pair as Peer or Combined was randomized at the start of class.

- We removed questions that were too easy — operationalizing this as Q1 of 80% or above — as these questions leave little room for learning [17].

In the Combined mode, we expect that Q2 will be a close approximation to what students know of the concept being tested, since no further class time was spent explicitly discussing the question's topic. Most certainly, CS1 topics recur repeatedly throughout the course, so students would have seen the questions from the PI conceptests throughout the semester. But the concept itself was never explicitly tested and discussed again in isolation. In the Peer mode, by contrast, we expect that Q2 performance will less faithfully represent what students ultimately come to know, since Q2 in this mode does not measure learning from instructor follow-up. When correlating PI performance to final exam performance, therefore, we expect that Peer correctness will relate to the final exam score and that Combined will have additional predictive power over and above Peer.

3.3 Final Exam Questions

The final exam for the CS1 studied here consisted largely of code-writing questions. Such exams are common in CS1, to the extent that research finds many exams consisting mostly or entirely of code-writing questions [10]. Researchers argue that these exams offer students minimal opportunities to demonstrate elements of knowledge as opposed to coherent and complete knowledge structures. For example, progress on the way to being able to write code might not be evident in students' responses if we skip the preliminary steps and ask only for written code. To be sure, we are not advocating code-heavy exams: our final exam was produced in such a way for a different project involving between-lecture comparisons on a "traditional" CS1.

That said, the exam does contain some non-code-writing questions, and we used this limited variety to delineate performance on the final exam. We use three final exam measures in our correlations of PI scores and exam scores:

- The final exam score as a whole out of 100. The exam contained ten questions: one tracing, one sorting, one object-oriented programming, one describing code, and six mostly or completely code-writing. The mean was 38.69 with standard deviation 22.63.

- The score on a code-tracing question containing six questions each worth two marks (mean 4.23, standard deviation 2.95). The questions involved short code segments that added up integers in a loop or manipulated a Python list or dictionary; some of the questions involved nesting or aliasing. These questions are in many ways similar to PI questions: they are small, require students to trace/understand existing code (common in PI questions), and focus on single concepts. For example, one of the subparts asked students for the output of this code segment, focusing on aliasing:

```
composers = ['Kondo', 'Tamura']
composers2 = composers
composers2[0] = 'Ito'
composers2[1] = composers[0]
print(composers)
print(composers2)
```

Final Exam Topics	Block 1 Q1 Alone	Block 2 Q1, Q2 Peer	Block 3 Q1, Q2 Peer, Q2 Combined
Overall R^2	0.21	0.30	0.34
Code-Tracing R^2	0.13	0.16	0.19
Code-Writing R^2	0.16	0.22	0.25

Table 1: R^2 values for each statistical model predicting various facets of final exam performance. Across each row, the change in R^2 between adjacent columns is statistically significant.

- The score on a code-writing question worth 10 marks (mean 3.07, standard deviation 3.03). Students were given a "compressed string" like:
  `abc#2,3#5,2`
  and had to decompress it to `abcabcab`. The `#x,y` directives mean "go back x characters and copy y characters from there". Note that this question is not similar to PI questions, as it is difficult to ask students to write code in a multiple choice format [22].

4. RESULTS

Multiple regressions were used to test relationships between final exam grades and PI performance. We performed three sets of regressions: one for the final exam at large, one for the code-tracing question, and one for the code-writing question. In each case, we included our predictors in three blocks:

Block 1. We first added two covariates: the number of Peer questions answered correctly and the number of Combined questions answered correctly. We expect that these two predictors will significantly predict exam score because they represent incoming ability prior to each lecture. The more questions that students answer correctly before any peer discussion or instructor intervention, the better they should do on the final exam.

Block 2. In this block, we add the number of Peer Q2 questions that each student answered correctly. If the R^2 change from Block 1 to Block 2 is significant, it suggests that what students learn in the Peer mode (from Q1 to Q2) impacts performance on the final exam. Note that the Block-1 predictors are also included in this model and control for Q1 performance.

Block 3. In this block, we add the number of Combined Q2 questions that each student answered correctly. If the R^2 for this model is significantly larger than the R^2 for Block-2, it suggests that Combined questions correlate with exam performance over and above the relationship between Peer and exam performance.

Of primary interest is whether the change in R^2 (i.e. the change in variance explained) is significant when moving from the Block-1 model to the Block-2 model, and from the Block-2 model to the Block-3 model. We find that for each of the three regression analyses (entire final exam, code-tracing, and code-writing), each of the changes in R^2 is statistically significant.

These R^2 changes are in Table 1. The first row of the table gives the R^2 values for the final exam as a whole. We see that Q1 explains 21% of the variance, Q2 Peer increases this to 30%, and Q2 Combined increases this further

	Block 1	Block 2	Block 3
Q1 Peer	5.07 (2.01)*	3.87 (1.92)*	2.04 (1.99)
Q1 Combined	7.24 (2.01)*	4.29 (2.04)*	3.53 (2.01)
Q2 Peer		7.62 (1.95)*	4.37 (2.23)
Q2 Combined			6.56 (2.38)*
R^2	0.21	0.30	0.34

*$p < 0.05$

Table 2: Statistical models predicting overall final exam performance

to 34%. In terms of the significance of these R^2 changes, we find that the Block-2 model explains significantly more variance than the Block-1 model ($p = .0001$), and the Block-3 model explains significantly more variance than the Block-2 model ($p = .007$). This means that Peer questions correlate with final exam grade (controlling for baseline performance), and Combined questions also correlate with final exam grade (controlling for baseline performance and Peer performance).

The second row of the table gives the R^2 values for code-tracing, and they tell a similar story as the row above. The R^2 values increase from left to right, showing that adding Q2 Peer and then Q2 Combined both increase the proportion of explained variance. Specifically, the Block-2 model explains significantly more variance than the Block-1 model ($p = .041$), and the Block-3 model explains significantly more variance than the Block-2 model ($p = .023$).

Finally, the third row of the table gives the R^2 values for code-writing. Again, the Block-2 model explains significantly more variance than the Block-1 model ($p = .003$), and the Block-3 model explains marginally more variance than the Block-2 model ($p = .055$).

In Table 2, Table 3, and Table 4, we give the coefficients for each block for the overall, code-tracing, and code-writing regressions, respectively.

One might argue that Combined questions explain new variance (over and above Peer questions) simply because adding the Combined questions more accurately models how much students know. That is, perhaps we could have replaced Combined questions with more Peer questions to see the same effect. While that may be true, we document an interesting finding here to the contrary. If we add the Combined questions to the regressions first, and then add the Peer questions second, the Peer questions do not significantly increase the model R^2, though the first is marginal ($p = .053$, $p = .60$, and $p = .113$, respectively). What this means is that, controlling for the Combined questions, the Peer questions do not further improve our final exam pre-

	Block 1	Block 2	Block 3
Q1 Peer	0.52 (0.28)	0.43 (0.28)	0.21 (0.29)
Q1 Combined	0.73 (0.28)*	0.51 (0.29)	0.42 (0.29)
Q2 Peer		0.56 (0.28)*	0.17 (0.32)
Q2 Combined			0.79 (0.34)*
R^2	0.13	0.16	0.19

$^*p < 0.05$

Table 3: Statistical models predicting final exam code-tracing performance

	Block 1	Block 2	Block 3
Q1 Peer	0.59 (0.28)*	0.45 (0.27)	0.27 (0.29)
Q1 Combined	0.86 (0.28)*	0.53 (0.29)	0.46 (0.29)
Q2 Peer		0.84 (0.28)*	0.51 (0.32)
Q2 Combined			0.66 (0.34)
R^2	0.16	0.22	0.25

$^*p < 0.05$

Table 4: Statistical models predicting final exam code-writing performance

dictions. Combined questions seem to subsume the variance explained by the Peer questions, lending support to the hypothesis that measuring the full PI process in the Combined mode affords more predictive accuracy than does the Q2 measure in the Peer mode.

5. ANCILLARY ANALYSES

As $Q1_{ad}$ could represent learning from peer discussion, we decided to investigate $Q1_{ad}$ as a predictor of final exam performance. $Q1_{ad}$ necessarily conflates active learning with passive peer influence, so we suspected that it would have a weak or null relationship with the final exam (over and above the relationship between Q1 and the final exam). Using the Peer and Combined isomorphic questions as above, we performed three regressions: one for the final exam as a whole, one for the code-tracing question, and one for the code-writing question. In each case, we included Q1 and $Q1_{ad}$ as predictors. Q1, as expected, was a significant predictor in each case, but in no case was $Q1_{ad}$ a significant predictor. That is, $Q1_{ad}$ gives us no predictive power over and above Q1. We then repeated this analysis using the complete dataset of Q1 and $Q1_{ad}$; i.e. using all PI questions from the semester rather than just the Peer and Combined questions. For the final exam as a whole, code-tracing question, and code-writing question, we similarly see no positive and significant increment in R^2 when adding $Q1_{ad}$ to the models.

6. DISCUSSION

In this paper, we have shown that the learning conferred through the PI process is evidenced in higher scores on the final exam. In addition, both key portions of the PI process — peer discussion and instructor intervention — contribute to the relationship between PI correctness and final exam score.

We believe that these findings are both interesting and surprising. PI questions are not like code-writing questions. Indeed, in this PI offering, there were no PI questions that asked students to write code. (The reason is that students used clickers; while such devices allow students to submit numbers or select among multiple choice responses, they do not permit code-entry.) There were questions that asked students to fill-in the missing code and choose the correct code, but this is not the same as writing code from scratch [4]. PI questions are much more similar to code-tracing than they are to code-writing. Yet, we find relationships between PI correctness and both code-tracing and code-writing questions on a final exam. The latter relationship is a welcome surprise to us. We expected PI correctness to correlate with similarly small "chunks" on the final exam, but not to correlate much with code-writing questions. It has been argued that code-writing is at the top of a hierarchy of tasks that includes code-reading, code-tracing, and code-explaining [18]. It is encouraging that PI performance not only correlates with questions similar to PI questions, but also to dissimilar code-writing questions.

One might wonder whether it is simply the number of PI questions being answered, or indeed the number of lectures attended, that is responsible for the observed significant relationships. This is certainly part of the story, because Q1 significantly predicts final exam score. However, recall that we have controlled for Q1 in our regressions, as we investigate the additional predictive power of Q2. That is, for students who answered the same number of Q1 questions correctly, those who answer more Q2 questions correctly do better on the final exam.

Note that in this paper we are not comparing the effectiveness of PI to some other pedagogical method. In particular, we could imagine using a pre-test, post-test design in a lecture course, possibly finding that post-test scores explain final exam variance over and above pre-test scores. In addition, we cannot preclude the possibility that the students that learn from PI are simply those students that would have learned the material regardless of intervention. That is, the increase from Q1 to Q2 could simply represent the learning that would have occurred by these "potential learners" in some other learning setting (such as self-guided reading or lecture). That said, we believe that PI itself is at least partly responsible for the correlations between learning and exam performance. We found that gains from the Combined mode were related to final exam performance once we had controlled for Peer performance. We deem it unlikely that students in a lecture-only or self-guided configuration would exhibit both the peer-based and instructor-based learning gains that are associated with PI. That is, PI seems to aggregate learning from both peers and instructor, and we suggest that this pairing is powerful for both engendering and holding learning.

7. CONCLUSION

Prior Peer Instruction research has demonstrated that students score higher on the group vote than the individual vote, learn from group discussion as measured by isomorphic questions, and outperform lecture-taught peers. In the present work, we complement these findings with an analysis of the relationship between in-class clicker correctness and scores on the final exam. Using isomorphic questions and two modes of question administration, we find that learning from peers and learning from the instructor are each correlated with final exam scores. Furthermore, instructor-based learning is seen even when controlling for peer learning, suggesting additional benefits over and above the peer portion of PI. That is, while prior work has shown that PI students demonstrate learning when tested immediately after discussion, the present work shows that relationships between PI learning and performance are long-lasting. PI learning correlates with both code-tracing and code-writing on exams, even though the latter are far-removed from the types of questions we ask using PI. Future research should continue with a more fine-grained analysis of final exam performance, using exams that tap the wide array of question types that CS1 students should be able to answer. In addition, we urge the community to investigate the mechanisms through which PI learning correlates with final exam performance in order to deepen our understanding of potential causal processes.

8. ACKNOWLEDGMENTS

Thank you to the reviewers for their helpful suggestions. This work was supported in part by NSF grant 1140731.

9. REFERENCES

[1] Peer instruction for computer science. `peerinstruction4cs.org`, 2013.

[2] J. Bennedsen and M. E. Caspersen. Failure rates in introductory programming. *SIGCSE Bulletin*, 39:32–36, 2007.

[3] C. H. Crouch, J. Watkins, A. P. Fagen, and E. Mazur. Peer instruction: Engaging students one-on-one, all at once. In E. F. Redish and P. J. Cooney, editors, *Research-Based Reform of University Physics*. American Association of Physics Teachers, College Park, MD, USA, 2007.

[4] P. Denny, A. Luxton-Reilly, and B. Simon. Evaluating a new exam question: Parsons problems. In *Proceedings of the Fourth International Workshop on Computing Education Research*, pages 113–124, 2008.

[5] S. Esper, B. Simon, and Q. Cutts. Exploratory homeworks: An active learning tool for textbook reading. In *Proceedings of the Eighth international Workshop on Computing Education Research*, 2012.

[6] A. Kothiyal, R. Majumdar, S. Murthy, and S. Iyer. Effect of think-pair-share in a large cs1 class: 83% sustained engagement. In *Proceedings of the Ninth international Workshop on Computing Education Research*, 2013.

[7] R. Lister, B. Simon, E. Thompson, J. L. Whalley, and C. Prasad. Not seeing the forest for the trees: novice programmers and the SOLO taxonomy. *SIGCSE Bulletin*, 38(3):118–122, 2006.

[8] K. Lockwood and R. Esselstein. The inverted classroom and the cs curriculum. In *Proceedings of the 44th ACM technical symposium on Computer Science Education*, pages 113–118, 2013.

[9] C. McDowell, L. Werner, H. E. Bullock, and J. Fernald. Pair programming improves student retention, confidence, and program quality. *Communications of the ACM*, 49(8):90–95, 2006.

[10] A. Petersen, M. Craig, and D. Zingaro. Reviewing cs1 exam question content. In *Proceedings of the 42nd ACM technical symposium on Computer science education*, pages 631–636, 2011.

[11] L. Porter, C. Bailey-Lee, B. Simon, and D. Zingaro. Peer instruction: Do students really learn from peer discussion in computing? In *Proceedings of the Seventh international Workshop on Computing Education Research*, 2011.

[12] L. Porter, C. B. Lee, and B. Simon. Halving fail rates using peer instruction: A study of four computer science courses. In *Proceedings of the 44th ACM technical symposium on Computer science education*, pages 177–182, 2013.

[13] L. Porter and B. Simon. Retaining nearly one-third more majors with a trio of instructional best practices in cs1. In *Proceedings of the 44th ACM technical symposium on Computer science education*, pages 165–170, 2013.

[14] B. Simon, S. Esper, L. Porter, and Q. Cutts. Student experience in a student-centered peer instruction classroom. In *Proceedings of the Ninth International Workshop on Computing Education Research*, 2013.

[15] B. Simon, M. Kohanfars, J. Lee, K. Tamayo, and Q. Cutts. Experience report: Peer instruction in introductory computing. In *Proceedings of the 41st SIGCSE technical symposium on Computer science education*, pages 341–345, 2010.

[16] B. Simon, J. Parris, and J. Spacco. How we teach impacts student learning: peer instruction vs. lecture in cs0. In *Proceedings of the 44th ACM technical symposium on Computer science education*, pages 41–46, 2013.

[17] M. Smith, W. Wood, K. Krauter, and J. Knight. Combining peer discussion with instructor explanation increases student learning from in-class concept questions. *CBE-Life Sciences Education*, 10(1):55–63, 2011.

[18] A. Venables, G. Tan, and R. Lister. A closer look at tracing, explaining and code writing skills in the novice programmer. In *Proceedings of the Fifth International Workshop on Computing Education Research Workshop*, pages 117–128, 2009.

[19] D. Zingaro. Experience report: Peer instruction in remedial computer science. In *Proceedings of the 22nd World Conference on Educational Multimedia, Hypermedia & Telecommunications*, pages 5030–5035, 2010.

[20] D. Zingaro. Peer instruction contributes to self-efficacy in CS1. In *Proceedings of the 45th ACM technical symposium on Computer Science Education*, 2014.

[21] D. Zingaro, C. Bailey-Lee, and L. Porter. Peer instruction in computing: the role of reading quizzes. In *Proceedings of the 44th ACM technical symposium on Computer Science Education*, pages 47–52, 2013.

[22] D. Zingaro, A. Petersen, Y. Cherenkova, and O. Karpova. Facilitating code-writing in pi classes. In *Proceedings of the 44th ACM technical symposium on Computer Science Education*, pages 585–590, 2013.

[23] D. Zingaro and L. Porter. Peer instruction in computing: The value of instructor intervention. *Computers & Education*, 71:87–96, 2014.

Comparing Outcomes in Inverted and Traditional CS1

Diane Horton
Dept of Computer Science
University of Toronto
dianeh@cs.toronto.edu

Michelle Craig
Dept of Computer Science
University of Toronto
mcraig@cs.toronto.edu

Jennifer Campbell
Dept of Computer Science
University of Toronto
campbell@cs.toronto.edu

Paul Gries
Dept of Computer Science
University of Toronto
pgries@cs.toronto.edu

Daniel Zingaro
Dept of Mathematical and
Computational Sciences
Univ of Toronto Mississauga
daniel.zingaro@utoronto.ca

ABSTRACT

We compare a traditional CS1 offering with an inverted offering delivered the following year to a comparable student population. We measure student attitudes, grades, and final course outcomes and find that, while students in the inverted offering do not report increased enjoyment and are no more likely to pass, learning as measured by final exam performance increases significantly. This increase is not simply a function of a more onerous inverted offering, as students report spending similar time per week in the traditional and inverted offerings. Contrary to our hypotheses, however, we find no evidence that the the inverted offering disproportionally helps beginners or those not fully fluent in English.

Categories and Subject Descriptors

K.3.2 [**Computers and Education**]: Computer and Information Science Education—*Computer Science Education*

Keywords

inverted classroom; flipped classroom; CS1; novice programming

1. INTRODUCTION

It has long been understood that learning programming requires active and often collaborative engagement in the activity. For example, pair programming has shown significant benefits [7] and is argued to contribute, among other best-practices, to retention [9]. Interestingly, this focus on active and collaborative learning has been much less prevalent in lectures than labs. Only recently, notions of an "inverted classroom" have brought active learning to the forefront of CS lectures as well. An inverted classroom involves asking students to prepare for lecture, perhaps by reading, watching a video, or exploring programming techniques (for examples,

Traditional		Inverted	
Labs (9)	9%	Labs (2)	4%
Online Exercises (4)	12%	Online Exercises (8)	16%
Assignments (2)	20%	Assignments (3)	21%
		Lecture Prep	5%
Midterm	14%	Midterm	10%
Final Exam	45%	Final Exam	44%

Table 1: Marking schemes.

see [12, 3]) so that lecture time can be spent on activities that are cognitively rich.

Recently, researchers have begun investigating possible benefits of inverted activities in CS lectures. In a pilot experience report, it was found that students frequently engage with the pre-class activities and appreciate the flexibility of watching videos on their own time [6]. Interestingly, there was no evidence that inverted activities require more time of students than do traditional courses.

In the present paper, we seek to complement such experience reports through a comparison of a traditional and inverted CS1 in terms of student attitudes, pass rates, and final exam grades. We find little difference in terms of attitudinal variables but do find a significant increase in final exam grades. We discuss relevant threats to validity and interpret our findings for the wider discussion of inverted lectures in CS.

2. THE COURSE

The CS1 course studied here, offered at a research-intensive North American public university, uses the Python programming language and takes an objects-early classes-late approach. The course was taught in a traditional style in fall 2012, with four lecture sections and a peak enrolment of 834 students. In the subsequent fall term in 2013, the course was taught in an inverted style with five lecture sections and a peak enrolment of 1067 students. In both offerings, the same topics were covered to the same depth and students were expected to achieve the same level of mastery.

In the traditional offering, there were three hours of lecture per week and attendance was not required. The graded activities included weekly supervised pair-programming labs, four automatically-marked online exercises, two large programming assignments, a midterm, and a final exam.

In the inverted offering, the students watched roughly one hour of video every week to prepare for lecture. The videos were crafted to follow the same content and teaching style as in the traditional offering, and contained embedded multiple choice and short answer questions. There were three hours of inverted lectures per week and attendance was not required. During these lectures, students worked on hands-on activities, many of which had previously been used as examples in the traditional lectures. Every lecture, roughly one TA per 75 students helped answer questions. Because TA resources were redirected to the inverted in-class activities, the labs were no longer sustainable. Instead, students attended labs only for the first two weeks and then individually completed a weekly set of online exercises for the rest of the term. These exercises were similar to the online exercises from the traditional offering, but were smaller and more frequent. More details are available in [2], which describes an earlier inverted offering of this same course.

In the inverted offering, the graded activities included the two supervised labs, in-video quiz questions (marked for participation rather than correctness), eight online exercises, three large programming assignments, a midterm, and a final exam.

3. THE STUDY

We wanted to know whether inverting our course would lead to a better completion rate and superior learning. We also wanted to know how student behaviour would change and whether the inverted approach would affect the student experience. In particular, we were interested in determining whether students in the inverted offering would perform better, attend class even though lecture videos were available online, enjoy the course more, and think the quality of their learning experience was better. We also wondered whether students in the inverted offering would find the lectures to be less helpful than those in the traditional offering and would find the online materials to be as helpful as lectures in the traditional offering. Last, we were interested in whether particular subgroups — English-language learners (ELL) and beginners (people with no programming experience) — would each demonstrate different outcomes as compared to the general population.

We examined outcomes both in terms of successful completion of the course and how well students learned the material. We used the final exam rather than overall course grades as a measure of learning because it is more comparable across terms.

To examine possible attitudinal and experiential differences, we administered pre- and post-course surveys during the second and final weeks of the semester, respectively. Surveys were done on paper during lecture and conducted by a faculty member not involved in the course.

In addition to the surveys, lecture attendance was counted weekly, enrolment was tracked throughout the course, and the University's standard course evaluations were collected. The relevant outcome questions from the post-course survey and the course evaluations are shown in Table 2. All questions were answered on five-point scales.

4. THREATS TO VALIDITY

As in much in situ research, a number of factors threatening the study's validity were beyond the researchers' control.

	Trad	Inv	Total
Gave consent	554	747	1301
Complete data (Pool 1)	209	276	485
Complete data (Pool 2)	542	694	1236

Table 3: Number of participants.

Where possible, decisions were made to keep the offerings as similar as possible, but the students' best interests were our primary concern.

Two changes to the course work could invalidate comparisons across offerings. The inverted offering had more assignments, as noted above, and the overall difficulty of the assignments was unintentionally higher. The assignments covered the same concepts but were longer, requiring students to use each concept more often and in different contexts. On the other hand, the weekly online exercises in the inverted offering involved less work than the 2-hour weekly labs and the four online exercises in the traditional offering. We believe that, overall, the changes made the coursework in the inverted offering at least as difficult as in the traditional offering.

Although overlapping, the set of course instructors was not the same across the two offerings.[1] As a result, it is possible that any differences in outcomes between offerings is due to instructor differences rather than to inverted teaching. The fact that all instructors in both offerings had taught the course before mitigates this threat to some degree.

It was not possible to use a common exam in the two course offerings because the university makes past exams available to students. Instructors attempted to produce an exam with comparable content; then, for the purposes of this study, independent experienced CS1 instructors evaluated the difficulty. As discussed in section 5.2, we concluded that the exam was at least as difficult in the inverted offering as in the traditional offering.

5. RESULTS AND DISCUSSION

In total, 1307 students gave informed consent to participate in the study. We removed six subjects who enrolled in both offerings because including the same subjects in the two comparison groups would invalidate the assumption of independence in our linear regressions. We used complete-case analysis, removing subjects with incomplete data on any question used in any hypothesis. However, we had to apply this principle to two different but overlapping subsets of our total population. For most hypotheses, we needed data from both the pre-course survey and the post-course survey. "Pool 1" (see Table 3) includes students who completed both, provided answers to the necessary questions, and submitted at least one piece of course work. It would be inappropriate to use this pool, however, for hypotheses concerning pass rates or course attendance ratios: Pool 1 excludes almost all students who dropped the course and therefore did not complete the final survey. For these hypotheses, we used Pool 2, which excludes only those students

---

[1]One instructor was common to both, and taught over 56% of the students in each offering. However, we could not address this threat to validity by considering only her students, because timetabling constraints can cause CS majors to cluster in particular course sections.

Name	Exact Question
Enjoyment	How much did you enjoy this course compared to other university courses you have taken?
Difficulty	How difficult is this course compared to other university courses you have taken?
Time	How much time did you spend on this course compared to other university courses you have taken?
More	Would you like the university to offer more of its courses in this format, with some material presented online and more active learning in lectures?
Lectures Help	How much did attending lectures help you in CSC108?
Online Helps	How much did the online course materials help you in CSC108?
Quality	Overall, the quality of my learning experience in this course was ...

Table 2: Wording for each of the key outcome questions on the post-course survey and the course evaluations.

who submitted no work or did not answer the pre-survey question about prior-experience.[2]

Most students who intend to pursue a degree in computer science and have little or no prior programming take CS1 in the fall term. For our first comparison of inverted and traditional teaching in CS1, discussed in [2], data on comparable terms was not yet available. The present study extends that preliminary work by comparing two consecutive fall terms, so that the populations are as similar as possible. A Pearson's Chi-squared test confirms that there is no evidence of a significant difference in the proportion of students without prior programming experience between the traditional and inverted offerings ($p = 0.1425$ for Pool 2 participants and $p = 0.4424$ for Pool 1).

5.1 Attendance and Role of Online Materials

In the inverted offering, lecture attendance was optional in the sense that neither attendance nor participation in the in-lecture activities contributed to students' grades. This is consistent with the traditional offering and was intended to benefit students with some prior programming experience: with the core concepts taught through online materials, these students might not need to attend lecture, particularly at the beginning of the course. In fact, the instructors encouraged students to use the online exercises as a measure of their mastery of that week's material: if, after watching the videos, students could successfully complete the online exercises and felt that they fully understood the concepts, they could feel guilt-free about missing class. We also hoped that this would make the classroom less intimidating for novices.

Given the availability of high quality online materials that were created specifically for this course and our "permission" for strong students to skip class, we expected lower attendance in the inverted offering. Our preliminary results reported in [2] do indeed show lower attendance in an inverted offering than a traditional offering. However, the comparison in that paper was across terms where the populations can be expected to differ due to the structure of our CS program. In the present work, we have more comparable populations, as noted above. Again, we find lower attendance in the inverted offering, in a pattern similar to that shown in [2]. Average attendance rates were 69% and 74% in the inverted and traditional offerings, respectively.

One of the significant features of inverted teaching is that students participate in supported practise throughout the term. We expected that this would differentially benefit beginners, and hypothesized that during the inverted offer-

	Gender		Prior Experience		English-language Proficiency	
	F	M	Beg	Non-beg	Fully	Not Fully
Trad	50%	42%	44%	46%	52%	33%
Inv	47%	43%	41%	47%	50%	37%

Table 4: Attendance rates on the day of the post-course survey for various categories of student.

ing beginners would therefore be more likely to attend lectures than experienced students. We also hoped that our instructions to use the online exercises as an indicator of their need to attend class would lead to more beginners attending. Although our weekly attendance figures are based on head counts, which don't allow correlation to individual data about prior experience, we do know who was in attendance on the day of the post-course surveys. While this is a single sample of attendance, the instructors report that as the course progressed, it was largely the same group of students who regularly attended class and therefore the attendance roster on the post-survey day is representative of the average attendance roster.

Table 4 shows attendance rates (percentage of those enrolled who attended lecture) for various subgroups including beginners and non-beginners. Contrary to our hypothesis, the attendance rate among beginners was slightly lower in the inverted offering (41%) than in the traditional offering (44%). At the same time, the attendance rate among non-beginners was slightly higher in the inverted course (47%) than in the traditional course (46%).

Considering only the inverted offering, the difference in attendance rates between students with prior programming experience (47%) and beginners (41%) was not statistically significant according to a Pearson's Chi-squared test.

In addition to affecting attendance, we expected the quality of the online materials and the optionality of lectures to cause a shift in what students found most helpful. A t-test reveals that students' rating of the helpfulness of lecture in the inverted offering was lower than in the traditional offering (mean 3.89 vs 4.36, $p < 0.001$). For the inverted students, the online materials were more helpful than the classroom lectures (mean 4.15 vs 3.88, $p < 0.001$), although not as helpful as lectures for students in the traditional offering (mean 4.15 vs 4.37, $p = 0.01$).

Online video lectures can be viewed any number of times, paused as needed, and offer captioning as well as the ability to view at different speeds. All of these features may be of particular value to students with lower English-language proficiency. We hypothesized that the difference in helpfulness ratings between online materials and class lectures

---

[2]These students were effectively removed from Pool 1 also, as they would not have completed the post-course survey.

	Traditional	Inverted	Wilcoxon Test
Difficulty	2.70	2.94	significant ($p = .01$)
Time	3.11	3.29	insignificant ($p = .07$)

Table 5: Difficulty and time spent.

would be especially pronounced for students who self-report that they are not fully fluent in English. However, a t-test did not support this hypothesis.

5.2 Exam Grades

Both offerings included a 3-hour final exam. The exams were written on paper without any aids and contained a variety of question styles such as code writing and tracing.

In the traditional offering, the average on the final exam was 66.2%; the average in the inverted offering was 74.3%. To determine whether this indicates a significant difference, we used multiple regression; the model is in the left-hand column of Table 7. The model includes the offering (traditional or inverted), prior experience, and their interaction. As shown for the offering row, students in the inverted offering scored significantly higher on the exam ($b = 6.8$, $p = 0$) than students in the traditional offering.

Note that different exams were used in the inverted and traditional offerings, so it is necessary to examine their difficulty to have confidence in the above finding. Comparison of two different CS1 final exams has been done previously by Simon et al [10] in an evaluation of a media-computation version of CS1. Their comparison focused on the percentage of questions that covered core concepts (e.g., loops, if statements, arrays, etc.) and on the difficulty of questions, which was measured by the number of core concepts needed to solve each question.

For our comparison, we had two senior instructors (including one of the authors) who did not teach this course in either offering evaluate the difficulty of each question. The two instructors were presented with the exam questions from the two offerings with all identifying information removed. That is, they did not know the offering for each exam question. The instructors rated each question for difficulty on a scale from 1 to 5, taking into account whatever they felt contributed to question difficulty. Factors that influenced the ratings included whether the question involved multiple concepts, style of question (for instance, whether it involved writing code or showing comprehension of code), and code complexity. The two instructors worked independently and did not discuss or share their ratings with each other. They each concluded that the exam from the inverted offering was no easier than the exam from the traditional offering. With an exam that is no easier and a higher average mark, we conclude that students in the inverted offering demonstrated superior understanding.

As discussed in section 4, we believe that the inverted term work was at least as difficult as the term work from the traditional offering. We were suspicious that the increase in learning may have been the result of students simply spending more time on the more difficult course work. Would students in a traditional offering have learned as much if we found another way to compel them to invest more time in the course? Table 5 reports the means for the difficulty and time questions from the post-surveys as well as the p values for Wilcoxon Rank Sum tests on these samples. Stu-

dents rated the inverted offering as more difficult by a small but statistically significant margin. Echoing a previous finding [6], however, the students do not report a statistically significant difference in time spent on the course.

Finally, one might speculate that harder course work may have encouraged weaker students to drop before the exam. We cannot explicitly identify "weaker" students among those who do not write the exam, but if we examine drop rates of beginners among the two offerings, we see no significant difference. Thus, the higher exam average is not due to an elevated drop rate among beginners in the inverted offering.

5.3 Completion Rates

At first glance, the notion of failure rate seems straightforward: the number of students who fail divided by the number in the class. However some students enroll only briefly in the class, possibly dropping before even submitting a single piece of work. Others receive special permission to drop the course after the official drop deadline. Still others persist in the course until the final exam and then miss the exam. Some percentage of these receive permission to write a deferred examination and go on to pass or fail. The numbers of students in these categories can be sufficiently large to influence the reported statistics.

In the first attempt to seriously evaluate CS1 failure rates, Bennedsen and Caspersen [1] surveyed institutions around the globe asking faculty to provide numbers for the following categories: *fail* (students who failed the course), *pass* (students who passed the course), *abort* (students who drop the course before the final exam), and *skip* (students eligible to write the final exam who did not write it). Their reported failure rate is calculated as

$$\textit{fail} / (\textit{fail} + \textit{pass} + \textit{abort} + \textit{skip}).^3$$

At many institutions, the size of this *skip* category can be quite large. Ultimately the students in this category may pass, fail, or abort the course, but their status is typically unknown at the time of many studies.

In a retrospective study of ten years of CS1 offerings, Porter et al [8] define the failure rate as

$$\textit{fail} + \textit{abort} / (\textit{fail} + \textit{pass} + \textit{abort}).$$

However, their definition of *abort* does not include students who dropped before the official course drop deadline near the third week of their term.[4] Porter and Simon [9] consider retention in the program rather than course failures, drops, or passes. Relevant here is their choice for the total population (the denominator). They present results using all students enrolled at the peak enrolment date, as well as a variation that considers only those students enrolled after the drop deadline. Kinnunen and Malmi [5] argue that a high number of students drop the course immediately after registration and consequently report a drop rate that considers only students who submitted at least one piece of work.

Like Kinnunen and Malmi, we have a number of students who enrol only briefly in the course and submit no work. As noted, we removed these students from our analysis.

Because our data on grades is collected at the time of initial grade submission, the number of students in the *skip* category is significant: 19 (traditional) and 27 (inverted).

---

[3] M. E. Caspersen, personal communication

[4] L. Porter, personal communication

	Pass	Fail	Abort	Skip	Pass rate	Pass rate among completers
All Participants						
Trad	426 (79%)	47 (9%)	50 (9%)	19 (4%)	81%	90%
Inv	532 (77%)	64 (9%)	71 (10%)	27 (4%)	80%	89%
Beginners Only						
Trad	186 (67%)	31 (11%)	41 (15%)	19 (7%)	72%	86%
Inv	250 (66%)	48 (13%)	55 (14%)	27 (7%)	71%	84%

Table 6: Student outcomes by category. See section 5.3 for definitions of pass rate and pass rate among completers.

Each of these students will eventually earn a pass, fail, or abort, but this outcome is not yet known. For this reason, we remove *skip* students from both the numerator and denominator. Using the terms from [1], and after filtering out students who submitted no work, we define two variations of pass rate:

$$pass\ rate = pass\ /\ (pass+fail+abort),\ \text{and}$$
$$pass\ rate\ among\ completers = pass\ /\ (pass+fail)$$

We hypothesized that both the pass rate and the pass rate among completers would be higher in the inverted offering than in the traditional. Table 6 shows the numbers of students in each outcome category and the corresponding rates. Both rates were marginally but not statistically significantly higher in the traditional offering.

We further hypothesized that, among beginners, the pass rates would be higher in the inverted term than in the traditional. Again the two pass rates are almost identical for the different offerings.

5.4 Levelling the Playing Field

We had several hypotheses related to the differential effects of the inverted course on two types of students: beginners and English-language learners (ELL).

Beginners

Considerable research shows that students with no prior programming experience ("beginners") perform more poorly than students with experience [11, 4]. In the inverted offering, students participated in supported classroom practise three times a week and prepared for these activities by watching videos. We suspected that this increased opportunity for engagement and feedback would particularly help beginners struggling to get a foothold in a new field.

A multiple regression was used to test relationships between final exam grade and experience (beginner or non-beginner), the course offering (traditional or inverted), and the interaction of experience and offering. Our hypothesis was that the interaction would be significant, and that it would suggest that the gap between beginners and non-beginners in the traditional offering would be larger than in the inverted offering. The model is given in Table 7 (left-hand column).

The interaction is insignificant, and so the hypothesis is unsupported. That is, beginners perform more poorly than non-beginners in both inverted and traditional offerings.

ELL Students

As explained previously, we suspected that the nature of the inverted activities would particularly advantage ELL students. A multiple regression was used to test relationships between final exam grade and the course offering (traditional or inverted), English proficiency (fully fluent or not fully fluent), and the interaction of English proficiency and offering. Our hypothesis was that the interaction would be significant, and that it would suggest that exam grades depend less on English fluency in the inverted offering compared to the traditional offering. The model is given in Table 7 (middle column). As with the hypothesis above, the interaction is insignificant, and so our hypothesis is unsupported. In both the inverted and traditional offerings, those with limited English fluency perform more poorly than fully-fluent students.

5.5 Self-Reported Experience

We have seen that exam grades were improved by the inverted approach. We hoped that, in addition, students would find it a superior experience. However, requiring the inverted activities in every lecture may have been uncomfortable for those who did not continuously commit time to keeping up in the course because it forced them to come to terms with what they could and could not do. Even those who didn't attend lectures could not evade this, because students were required to submit weekly exercises for credit. We were aware that some students might enjoy the course less as a result.

In spite of these expectations, we hypothesized that students' responses to the questions about enjoyment and quality of learning experience would be higher in the inverted offering compared to the traditional offering, and that beginners in particular would enjoy the inverted offering more than the traditional offering. To investigate these hypotheses, we examined survey data and course evaluation data.

We used multiple regression to test relationships between enjoyment and experience (beginner or non-beginner), offering (traditional or inverted), and the interaction of experience and offering. The model is given in Table 7 (right column). There was no overall effect of the offering, and no qualifying interaction with prior experience. Therefore, the inverted offering did not increase student enjoyment of the offering or the enjoyment of beginners in particular. We also examined student survey responses in the inverted offering to a question asking them whether they wanted more inverted lectures in the future. Unsurprisingly based on the enjoyment data just reported, regressing student desire for more inverted lectures on prior experience yielded an insignificant model and we do not report it here.

The results on the *Quality* question on the course evaluations also show no difference between traditional (mean 3.88) and inverted (mean 3.81) offerings.

6. CONCLUSIONS

In this paper, we offer a comparison of a traditional and inverted offering of a CS1 course. We sought to understand the implications of inverting a CS1 in terms of attitudinal variables, grade-based outcomes, and pass rates. Our in-

	Grades 1	Grades 2	Enjoyment
(Intercept)	50.10 (1.17)*	49.30 (1.06)*	4.17 (0.10)*
prior_exp	−5.38 (1.74)*		−0.45 (0.14)*
offering	6.76 (1.58)*	4.76 (1.43)*	−0.09 (0.13)
prior_exp:offering	−1.56 (2.31)		0.06 (0.19)
english		−5.30 (1.92)*	
english:offering		3.65 (2.53)	
R^2	0.11	0.07	0.04
Adj. R^2	0.10	0.06	0.04
Num. obs.	475	475	485

$^*p < 0.05$

Table 7: Regression models. The baseline for each factor is as follows: prior_exp yes, offering traditional, English proficiency fluent. a:b indicates an interaction between predictors a and b.

terest was in global effects on all students, and effects on two particular subsets of students: beginners and English-language learners. In contrast to our hypotheses, we found little difference in student attitude between the two offerings, and little difference in student pass rates. However, we did find a significantly higher grade on the exam in the inverted offering compared to the traditional offering. We are further encouraged by the fact that students did not feel that they invested more time in the inverted compared to the traditional offering. That is, we suggest that inverted CS1 courses can yield exam-inferred learning gains without requiring greater student time investments and while maintaining positive student attitudes.

As this area of research in CS education is relatively new, much further work is required. Some of our validity concerns could be further addressed through within-semester comparisons of traditional and inverted offerings. In addition, researchers might collect more fine-grained data from student interviews in order to further understand some of the findings here. For example, are there effects on beginners that are present but not captured through our survey methodology? As we have found positive support for inverting a CS1 here, we urge further exploration of this promising pedagogy for future CS courses.

7. ACKNOWLEDGMENTS

We thank Professor Jim Clarke for his help reviewing the exam questions.

8. REFERENCES

[1] J. Bennedsen and M. E. Caspersen. Failure rates in introductory programming. *SIGCSE Bull.*, 39(2):32–36, June 2007.

[2] J. Campbell, D. Horton, M. Craig, and P. Gries. Evaluating an inverted CS1. In *Proceeding of the 45th ACM Technical Symposium on Computer Science Education*, SIGCSE '14, pages 307–312, New York, NY, USA, 2014. ACM.

[3] S. Esper, B. Simon, and Q. Cutts. Exploratory homeworks: An active learning tool for textbook reading. In *Proceedings of the Eighth international Workshop on Computing Education Research*. ACM, 2012.

[4] D. Hagan and S. Markham. Does it help to have some programming experience before beginning a computing degree program? *SIGCSE Bulletin*, 32:25–28, 2000.

[5] P. Kinnunen and L. Malmi. Why students drop out CS1 course? In *Proceedings of the second international workshop on Computing education research*, pages 97–108, 2006.

[6] K. Lockwood and R. Esselstein. The inverted classroom and the CS curriculum. In *Proceeding of the 44th ACM Technical Symposium on Computer Science Education*, SIGCSE '13, pages 113–118, New York, NY, USA, 2013. ACM.

[7] C. McDowell, L. Werner, H. E. Bullock, and J. Fernald. Pair programming improves student retention, confidence, and program quality. *Commun. ACM*, 49(8):90–95, Aug. 2006.

[8] L. Porter, C. Bailey Lee, and B. Simon. Halving fail rates using peer instruction: a study of four computer science courses. In *Proceeding of the 44th ACM Technical Symposium on Computer Science Education*, SIGCSE '13, pages 177–182, New York, NY, USA, 2013. ACM.

[9] L. Porter and B. Simon. Retaining nearly one-third more majors with a trio of instructional best practices in CS1. In *Proceeding of the 44th ACM Technical Symposium on Computer Science Education*, SIGCSE '13, pages 165–170, New York, NY, USA, 2013. ACM.

[10] B. Simon, P. Kinnunen, L. Porter, and D. Zazkis. Experience report: CS1 for majors with media computation. In *Proceedings of the Fifteenth Annual Conference on Innovation and Technology in Computer Science Education*, ITiCSE '10, pages 214–218, New York, NY, USA, 2010. ACM.

[11] D. Zingaro. Peer instruction contributes to self-efficacy in CS1. In *Proceeding of the 45th ACM Technical Symposium on Computer Science Education*, SIGCSE '14, pages 373–378, New York, NY, USA, 2014. ACM.

[12] D. Zingaro, C. Bailey-Lee, and L. Porter. Peer instruction in computing: the role of reading quizzes. In *Proceeding of the 44th ACM Technical Symposium on Computer Science Education*, SIGCSE '13, pages 47–52, New York, NY, USA, 2013. ACM.

CaptainTeach: Multi-Stage, In-Flow
Peer Review for Programming Assignments

Joe Gibbs Politz
Brown University
joe@cs.brown.edu

Daniel Patterson
Brown University
dbp@dbpmail.net

Shriram Krishnamurthi
Brown University
sk@cs.brown.edu

Kathi Fisler
WPI
kfisler@cs.wpi.edu

ABSTRACT

Computing educators have used peer review in various ways in courses at many levels. Few of these efforts have applied peer review to multiple deliverables (such as specifications, tests, and code) within the same programming problem, or to assignments that are still in progress (as opposed to completed). This paper describes CaptainTeach, a programming environment enhanced with peer-review capabilities at multiple stages within assignments in progress. Multi-stage, in-flow peer review raises many logistical and pedagogical issues. This paper describes CaptainTeach and our experience using it in two undergraduate courses (one first-year and one upper-level); our analysis emphasizes issues that arise from the conjunction of multiple stages and in-flow reviewing, rather than peer review in general.

Categories and Subject Descriptors

K.3.2 [**Computers and Education**]: Computer and Information Science Education

Keywords

Peer-review, Learning environments, Testing

1. INTRODUCTION

Peer review has various educational roles, including encouraging reflection and metacognition [10], fostering critical-thinking skills [5], and assisting in producing feedback or grades in large courses [6, 8]. Many faculty have experimented with peer review within computing courses, both introductory and upper-level. The vast majority of these efforts have applied peer review (a) after the assignment has been turned in, and (b) to one deliverable within the assignment. There are, however, strong arguments for relaxing each of these constraints.

Reviews would ideally help students improve their work: just as students utilize office hours and discussion boards, peer reviews can provide valuable diagnostic information.

This is perhaps especially true for programming assignments, whose problem specifications imply several objective criteria. If a student misunderstood a programming problem, peer-review while the assignment is open (henceforth *in-flow* reviewing) could help the student get back on track before the deadline. Naturally, this only works if students complete assignments early enough to receive and act on feedback. One way to accomplish this is to decompose assignments into multiple stages that each have concrete deliverables (e.g., requiring tests before code), and reviewing after each stage.

In Fall 2013, we experimented with multi-stage, in-flow peer review in two undergraduate courses (one a freshman honors course that emphasized data structures[1], the other an upper-level programming languages course[2]). We built an enhanced programming environment, CaptainTeach, to support the reviewing process. For the programming assignments in this paper, CaptainTeach used the programming language Pyret[3], whose design supports multi-stage reviewing (Section 3 discusses how).

CaptainTeach's novelty stems primarily from its integration of two ideas: (1) peer review and (2) decomposition of programming assignments into multiple deliverables that checkpoint student understanding of the assignment. Students submit and review others' work on each step before being allowed to submit work on subsequent steps. This paper focuses on logistical and policy considerations around multi-stage, in-flow reviewing for programming courses. Our evaluation focuses on whether this model is feasible and useful from a students' perspective. Section 6 contrasts CaptainTeach to other peer-review practices from the literature.

2. DECOMPOSING PROGRAMMING PROBLEMS FOR REVIEW

CaptainTeach strives to use peer review to help students adjust their work on an assignment before the due date. While reviewing complete drafts of programs is certainly possible, we'd like to help students catch their mistakes even earlier, before producing a complete program. In CaptainTeach, we design assignments to have sequential, reviewable deliverables and have students review one another's work at these intermediate stages. We explain how we decompose assignments for CaptainTeach through an example.

Consider this data-structure programming problem:

---

[1] http://cs.brown.edu/courses/cs019/2013/
[2] http://cs.brown.edu/courses/cs173/2013/
[3] http://pyret.org/

> Write a program that takes a binary tree of numbers and produces a list containing those numbers according to a pre-order traversal of the tree.

Before a student can write a correct solution to this problem in any setting, she must be able to (1) develop and use a binary-tree data structure and (2) understand the term "pre-order traversal". In our experience, students who come to office hours with "code that doesn't work" are often stuck on one of these two more fundamental problems.

The *How to Design Programs* [4] methodology provides a generalizable "design recipe" for staging programming problems such as this. The full recipe asks students to approach a problem through seven ordered steps (paraphrased here for an experienced computer science audience; the presentation for beginners is worded differently):

1. Create the data structures needed for the input.
2. Create concrete instances of the data structure.
3. Write a type signature and summary of the function.
4. Write a set of test cases for the function, including the code needed to call the function on concrete inputs and the concrete answer that the function should produce (typically using the concrete data from step 1).
5. Write a skeleton of code that traverses the input data structure (but omits problem-specific logic).
6. Add problem-specific logic to the traversal skeleton.
7. Run the tests (from step 4) against the function.

Each step yields a concrete artifact that targets a different aspect of the problem; if a student is unable to produce one of the artifacts, he is likely to have trouble producing a correct and justifiable final program. When we work with *How to Design Programs* in person, we take students through each of these steps: a student asking for help must show each step before we will help with a later step (meaning we do not look at code—a step 6 concern—until the prior steps are done). In our long experience using this curriculum, many errors in student programs manifest in one of the early steps. Thus, the early steps are vital for making sure that students understand the problem.

In theory, one could build a programming environment that asks students to submit work for each step separately, optionally with reviewing on each step (though peer-review on all steps would almost certainly be too cumbersome). In our courses, we chose a coarser granularity. We provided the data structures (step 1) and function header (step 3), because having consistent shapes, field names, and function headers reduces confusion and enables one person's tests to probe another's code. Students submitted work twice per problem: in the first stage, they submitted black-box test cases (step 4) and any defined constants used in their test cases (step 2). In the second stage, they submitted their implementations (combining steps 5 and 6); we assumed that students ran their code against their own tests (step 7) before submitting. On one assignment, we used a three-stage process in which students also developed their own data structures (step 1) as the first stage.

The split in CaptainTeach of tests before implementations reflects software-engineering practices such as test-first development. In CaptainTeach, we use tests to checkpoint students' understanding of a problem: if a student misunderstands a question, misses a corner case, or misuses a data structure, his test cases usually reflect this error.

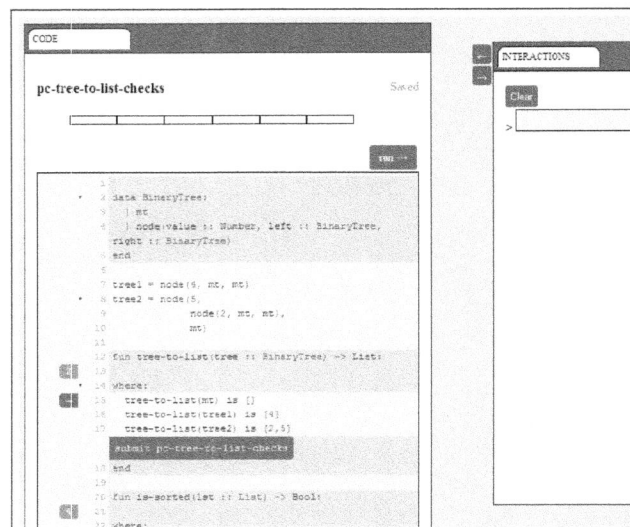

Figure 1: CaptainTeach enabled for writing tests.

3. CaptainTeach: THE TOOL AND ITS REVIEWING WORKFLOW

CaptainTeach typically takes students through a prescribed sequence of four core steps on each programming problem:

1. submit a test suite for review
2. review 2–3 other students' test suites
3. submit an implementation for review
4. review 2–3 other students' implementations

Students get reviews from others on their own work as each individual review is completed. Students can update their submissions until the assignment closes, but can only submit once for reviewing (to avoid over-burdening reviewers). Section 4 discusses grading of submissions. This section focuses on the interface, reviewing process, and language issues.

Figure 1 shows the interface when a student first starts a problem in CaptainTeach (through a web browser). In the right half of the page, students can evaluate expressions at a prompt: this is a standard interactive read-eval-print-loop (REPL). The left half of the page is the editing area, with the shaded portions locked to prevent editing. The data structure definition appears first (locked, so that everyone uses the same one), followed by an open area where students can define examples of the data structure. The next shaded area gives the name and type signature for the function. That area ends with a keyword **where**, which marks the start of test cases for the function. Students can enter their tests in the unshaded area that follows. Just under the test area is a button for submitting tests for review.

Markings in the leftmost portion of the editing area show students where they are in the sequence of steps. The arrow marks the area that students are currently expected to edit (though they may edit in any unshaded area). Numbered tags next to shaded areas show the order in which other areas will open for editing.

Once a student submits tests for review, her editing page gets additional tabs for others' work that she needs to review, as seen at the top of Figure 2. Her own code is still accessible in the CODE tab, but she will not be able to edit

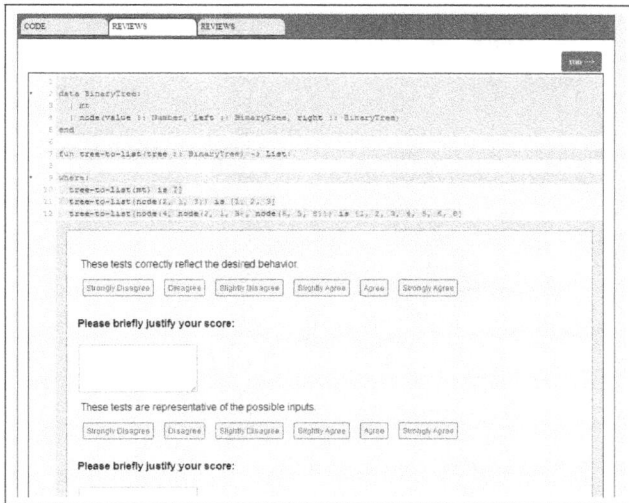

Figure 2: Interface for reviewing others' tests.

her implementation until after she submits reviews for each REVIEWS tab. The figure shows the review form for test cases. There are two prompts, each asking for a Likert-scale rating and free-form comments. One prompt asks about the correctness of the tests, while the other asks about test coverage. The button to submit the review has been truncated from the image, but appears below the lower prompt.

Once the student has submitted reviews for each tab, the area for her implementation unlocks in her CODE tab (the interface is identical to Figure 1 except the area marked with 2 is no longer shaded and the progress tags have changed). The review form for implementations also has two prompts, one about correctness and one about design and structure:

- "This code correctly implements the desired behavior."
- "This code is structured well."

Though CaptainTeach could be applied to any language, it works especially well with Pyret. In most languages, testing is a library feature so the environment must necessarily guess the loci of tests (which may even be split across files). In contrast, Pyret has linguistic support for testing in the form of where (and another kind of block indicated by check), so the environment can unambiguously identify where the tests should go, enabling it to lock and unlock portions of the editor, and also report test failures more accurately.

4. LOGISTICS AND POLICIES

Multi-stage, in-flow reviewing raises several logistical and policy questions. Some affect the design of CaptainTeach, while others impact course policies.

Whether to Synchronize Deadlines Per Stage.

With multi-stage reviewing, instructors can either allow students to complete stages at their own pace or synchronize the class through a separate due date per stage. We chose the former, so that peer-review would not constrain students' workflows. Section 5 reports timing patterns in how students submitted across stages.

Non-synchronized submission could block progress for students who submit first. We seeded CaptainTeach with several solutions, both good and bad, to give early-submitters something to review. In practice, multiple students submitted initial stages around the same times, so each students' work was sent out for review fairly quickly.

Grading and Reviews.

Other work on peer-review has unsurprisingly observed that students take reviewing more seriously when reviews themselves are graded or count towards course grades. We did not grade reviews, and used a combination of human TAs and results from an automated testing harness to determine actual grades for code submissions.

We motivated good reviewing in several ways:

- Students had to submit reviews in order to submit subsequent stages of the assignment or revisions to their own submission for the same stage.
- If students gave a bad review score to a good seed (or vice-versa), CaptainTeach told them so immediately. The seed solution and their review were accessible from their assignment page, so they could discuss their review with TAs if necessary.
- The recipient of a review could give *review feedback* to the reviewer, indicating if the review was helpful. This feedback consisted of both a Likert-scale rating and free-form comments.

The course staff also spot-checked reviews of seed solutions for general content and tone. This process never identified problems, so the staff used it only lightly later in the courses.

Potential for Plagiarism.

Showing students examples of others' work while an assignment is open might invite plagiarism. Students can copy code they are reviewing and paste it into their own solutions; also, nothing prevents students from helping one another by pasting their own solutions into reviews.

We could integrate code-similarity detection tools into CaptainTeach, but have chosen to not do so. Plagiarism has not historically been a problem in these courses, and they are small enough that human TAs can flag blatant plagiarism. More importantly, instead of fighting an uphill battle, we adopt the following two perspectives on plagiarism enabled by CaptainTeach:

First, we designed our grading policies to mitigate the effect of copying. For each deliverable (tests and implementation), students have two official submissions: one submitted for review and the final version (whatever was present when the assignment closed). Any influence from other students would reflect in the latter, but not the former. When grading assignments, the initial submission was weighted heavily (75% versus 25%): this allows students to benefit from reviewing insights, but does not allow someone to pass the course on the work of others. This also nudges students to submit what they believe is a quality submission before taking up valuable reviewing resources.

This ratio does hurt the student who does poorly at first, having significantly misunderstood the assignment, but uses reviewing as intended to correct their mistakes before the final submission. Having students submit tests first ameliorates this impact, as significant misconceptions about the problem should manifest in the test cases, before the student submits a correspondingly incorrect implementation. In addition, given that there were multiple course assignments, a significant misconception on one or two assignments would be unlikely to adversely impact the overall course grade. Finally, these discrepancies are easy to notice when making up final grades.

Second, at a more principled level, we (controversially!) view code availability as a valuable learning opportunity for students, in that it reflects modern software practice. Sites such as StackOverflow and blogs give programmers ready access to code for various tasks; the problem for users is to assess whether the code they find is worth copying. Captain-Teach anonymizes the work being reviewed, so students cannot rely on the reputation of authors when deciding whether to follow ideas seen in other students' work; instead, they must judge the code itself. If they make a correct judgement, this demonstrates learning and a corresponding improvement in their grade. However, they may also copy a wrong solution (even one we used to seed the system, which can look quite convincing!), so copying blindly is perilous.

Disrupting Mental Flow.

The reviewing process interrupts students as they work on an assignment. This interruption could be helpful, as it potentially reveals errors before students begin implementation. The interruption could also be disruptive, as students have to wrap their heads around someone else's solution between phases of working on their own.

We suspect that being asked to review would be most disruptive in the midst of working on the program body. However, test-first approaches develop tests with no dependency on an implementation. This means that when reviewing test cases, students have just finished a standalone test-writing activity, and are presumably about to transition to solution strategies. Therefore, we hope the timing of the first review minimizes disruption and maximizes reflection, and we did not receive student complaints about it.

In feedback given during the semester, students raised one concern about the mental burden of reviewing: they wanted to review work from the same students across the multiple stages. Currently, CaptainTeach assigns reviews based on submission time, and does not retain reviewer-reviewee pairs across steps. Student felt they could reuse mental effort across the review stages had they been reviewing work from the same authors. The downside to this proposal lies in timing: students might receive feedback later if they have to wait for their original reviewers to submit work. This is an interesting design choice to explore in the future.

In a similar vein, students requested an additional round of back-and-forth with their reviewers to seek clarification on comments. We had considered but not implemented this out of concern that it would be too distracting and time-consuming. In an open discussion on the system, however, students felt that one additional *optional* round would have struck an appropriate balance.

5. EVALUATION

CaptainTeach presumes that peer-reviewing helps students get quick feedback on their work (both through reviews and through self-assessment after seeing the work of others). To understand how the multi-stage aspect of CaptainTeach worked in practice, we analyzed the timings at which students completed each stage relative to the overall assignment due date, as well as student opinions on the relative value of reviewing across the stages.

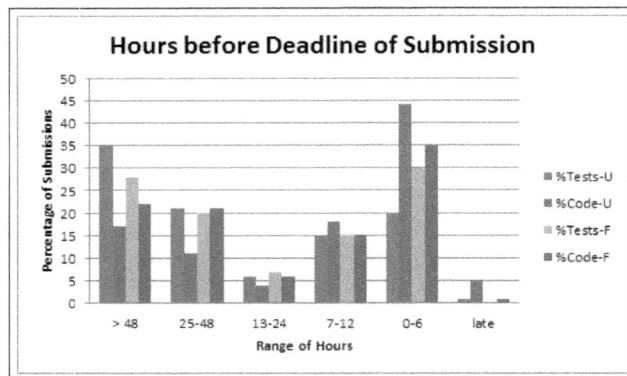

Figure 3: Bars show the percentage of submissions made within the range of hours on the x-axis. "U" and "F" in the legend refer to the upper-level and freshman course, respectively.

The freshman course used CaptainTeach on 4 assignments, with 2, 4, 6, and 17 reviewed steps. The upper-level course used it on 8 programming assignments, each with 2 reviewed steps, and 5 written assignments, each with a single reviewed step. For the 2-step assignments, the steps were (1) tests for, then (2) implementation of a single function. Assignments with 4 (resp. 6) steps, had 2 (resp. 3) sequential instances of writing tests for, then implementation of, a single function. For the 17-step assignment, students first wrote a data definition, and then wrote 8 functions in tests-then-code style.[4]

5.1 Submission and Reviewing Behavior

Figure 3 shows how far in advance students submitted each of tests and code in each course. With the exception of code in the upper-level course, more than half of the students submitted at least 12 hours before each assignment was due, with noticeable differences between test- and code-submission times in the upper-level course.

We also examined how long students had to wait to receive reviews on submitted work. The following table shows summary statistics on (a) the hours between artifact submission and receipt of *all* reviews, and (b) the hours before the receipt of the *first* review. These data show that students do get some feedback reasonably quickly. In future work, we will look at whether early feedback differs in review helpfulness or quality compared to later feedback.

Course	Stage	All Reviews (hrs to receipt)		First Review (hrs to receipt)	
		Mean	σ	Mean	σ
Upper	Tests	12.33	19.45	4.59	7.81
Upper	Code	11.54	20.9	4.66	11.89
Freshman	Tests	6.03	9.7	2.38	4.07
Freshman	Code	5.98	9.41	2.62	5.46

5.2 Student Reaction

Post-course, we surveyed students about the impact of reviewing on each individual assignment. We asked whether

---

[4]We deemed this assignment the hardest; students also rated it as benefitting the most from reviewing (see Section 5.2).

each of reviews received and reviews written were *not, somewhat*, or *very helpful* in improving their work. We also asked whether the review process was more helpful for *tests, code*, or *equally on both*. Each of the three questions was presented as a grid with assignment names labeling the rows and answer options labeling the columns. We received responses from 36 (of 49) students in the freshman course and 16 (of 37) students in the upper-level course.

The following table summarizes the survey results as percentages of students giving each response. The data from the freshman course reports on 3 of the 4 assignments. The omitted assignment was vastly easier than expected across the class, leaving students little to learn from the reviewing process (over 60% reported reviewing as not helpful on that assignment). The data from the upper-level course is broken into two groups of assignments: the programming assignments (reviews written on each of test cases and code), and the written assignments (one stage of reviewing only).

How helpful was (receiving/writing) reviews?					
Course	**Task**	**Not**	**Some**	**Very**
Freshman	Receiving	26%	59%	15%
Freshman	Writing	25%	45%	30%
Upper-Program	Receiving	45%	38%	16%
Upper-Program	Writing	43%	43%	14%
Upper-Written	Receiving	44%	40%	16%
Upper-Written	Writing	34%	28%	39%

The data on writing reviews on written assignments in the upper-level course particularly stands out ($\chi^2 = .05$ using the data on receiving reviews on writing assignments as expected values; this is significant at 97.5% with $df=2$). We hypothesize that this means that students felt they benefited from *seeing* each others' solutions, regardless of whether they had to write reviews on those solutions. Writing reviews is also rated "very" useful more often than receiving reviews within the freshman course. We are not sure how to interpret the difference in "not" ratings between the freshman and upper-level course: upper-level students may simply be more comfortable rating an aspect of the course negatively than students in their first semester; other hypotheses are also plausible.

On one assignment (in the freshman course), the "very" and "somewhat" percentages were identical on the helpfulness of writing reviews ("very" was lower in all other programming assignments in both courses). This was the only assignment in which we had students review not just tests and code, but also a *data definition*. The data definition was the first step of the problem: the students first defined a representation of a tree zipper, and then wrote various tree operations using the definition. Picking a good representation strongly guides an implementation towards a correct solution, and many representations cannot have implementations that are efficient (the assignment mandated big-O time bounds on the tree operations). In future work, we need to have students review data definitions on more problems, to help us assess whether the utility of reviewing varies across more than two problem stages.

In the future, we need to better understand the conditions that made the process more or less helpful. At mid-semester, students reported frustration trying to provide useful reviews on work that looked good overall: a student who did well might find the process unhelpful because the reviewers had offered little in the way of comment. Ratings of

"not helpful" from students who submitted good work would mean something quite different than from students who submitted work with noticeable flaws. Deeper insight about the effectiveness of reviewing will come from analyzing the accuracy of students' reviews relative to the quality of the submitted work. We intend to provide a detailed analysis on these quantitative issues in future work.

On the question of whether reviewing is more useful on test cases or code, the two courses yielded opposite responses. The following table summarizes the percentages of students in each course choosing each option, averaged across the assignments for that course (omitting writing assignments).

Which of test or code reviews was more helpful?			
Course	**Tests**	**Code**	**Equally**
Freshman	24%	49%	28%
Upper	49%	27%	24%

All but one assignment in each course had subtleties that testing could expose. These results could simply reflect better appreciation of testing among upper-class students; future work should correlate these ratings with surveys of student attitudes towards testing in the vein of Buffardi and Edwards's work [1]. The upper-level course results, which emphasize the value of reviewing tests, particularly support CaptainTeach's multi-stage approach.

6. RELATED WORK

There is extensive literature on the benefits and pitfalls of peer-review in higher education and in computer science. We do not review the general literature here. Rather, we focus on research that touches on our foci: online reviewing, in-flow reviewing, multi-stage reviewing, or reviewing test cases. Topping's 1980–96 literature survey on peer review in higher education [11] predates uses of review in CS courses similar to in-flow and multi-stage reviewing.

Søndergaard [10] uses in-flow peer review in a compilers course. Students review after completing three compiler stages but before two others. Surveys show 68% of students agreeing that peer review helped improve their own work, 63% agreeing that it improved their ability to reflect on their own learning and skills, and 89% reporting value in seeing other groups' solutions.

Expertiza [7] allows for multiple rounds of revision and review, but on complete submissions, rather than on intermediate stages of assignments as in CaptainTeach. Expertiza also allows students to review one another's reviews, and these meta-reviews are used in assessing grades. CaptainTeach also allows students to give feedback on reviews, but we do not use the review process in assigning grades.

Hundhausen, et al. [5] use code reviews to help students develop soft skills in CS1. They study several variations such as on-line versus face-to-face, inclusion of a moderator, and re-submitting work after review. Their reviews do not consider testing. Their online process has students submit reviews individually, with an optional subsequent period for group discussion of reviews. They view the failure to require group discussion as more critical than the decision to conduct reviews online. The complaints made by our students are similar to ones they report.

Reily, et al. [8] study the accuracy, effectiveness, and impact of post-flow peer-review of programming assignments in an introductory Information Systems course. Their process requires submitting at least 3 (later 5) concrete test cases as part of each review. Reviews also include Likert and open-response questions on various code characteristics. The sample review report in their paper suggests that their test cases were higher-level than ours, and at least some of them would be tested through manual interaction with a UI. In contrast, our test cases are for individual functions, and are expressed entirely in code. Their evaluation does not consider the role of testing in reviews, focusing instead on aggregation of reviews for accuracy and impact.

Zeller [13] presents the Praktomat system for submitting, automatically testing, and code-reviewing assignments. The reviewing is of whole assignments, with no in-flow component. In addition, only the final submission is assessed, rather than intermediate submissions. To combat plagiarism they personalize assignments, which results in a different reviewer experience from CaptainTeach as reviewers are longer reviewing the same problem they just solved.

Clark [2] presents a methodology where students are put in pairs or groups to review and test one another's solutions. This happens after an entire program has been created, but the projects run over a semester, giving this an in-flow feel. Students can use the outcomes of the review and peer tests to improve their solutions. The authors state that this caused students to work more steadily and consistently across the term of the long project.

Wang, et al. [12] use a workflow of early submission, followed by peer review, followed by resubmission, with the goal of getting students to do work earlier. They report that 88% (N=79) of their students "believed that their time management ability has been improved" after doing 10 assignments through this workflow. If we take the early test submissions in our data as an indication of good time management, this suggests similar results to our findings. While they have multiple steps of review possible before instructor review, students still submit the entire assignment at once, in contrast to the staged assignments of CaptainTeach.

Smith, et al. [9] use peer testing in a freshman honors data-structures course. After submitting a pair-programmed assignment, each pair tests code submitted by four other pairs. Students have three days to provide detailed reviews. Pairs then evaluate the reviews, summarize what they learned, and can submit updated solutions. To prevent copying, the course staff obfuscate and compile programs before distributing them. Our approach is much lighter-weight: it uses black-box tests primarily to diagnose whether students understand a problem and its corner cases, and expects students to spend much less time performing reviews. We would expect our students to learn less about testing per se than under Smith's approach, though we would expect them to gain a similar appreciation for good test cases.

Kulkarni, et al. [6] study how to scale peer-assessment to large online courses, where face-to-face reviewing is not feasible. To calibrate student reviews for accuracy, students first review one of a handful of assignments that have been assessed by TAs. Per assignment, students only review peers after writing a review whose score approximates that of the TAs. This approach takes training of reviewers more seriously than our approach of spot-checking reviews on seeded solutions, but the stakes are higher in Kulkarni's work as they use peer assessments for actual grades. Their rubrics are more detailed and structured, in part due to their more open-ended assignments. They also experiment with different formats to prompt for better reviews.

Buffardi and Edwards [1] study student engagement in *test-driven development* (TDD). We use tests first, but do not rigorously follow the details of TDD. Neither this paper nor Edwards' other research on testing uses peer review on tests. In a control-group-based study, they do not find significant differences in attitudes towards TDD in students who received feedback (hints) from automated test analysis, versus those who received generic hints not driven by tests.

Denning, et al. [3] explore lightweight in-class peer review. This provides students immediate, high-level feedback and helps instructors assess a class's understanding of a problem. In-class reviews are much lighter-weight than those in CaptainTeach, and done on problems that allow for such quick review. This work shares our goal of quick-turnaround reviewing while problems are fresh in students' minds.

Acknowledgments.
This work was partially funded by the US National Science Foundation and by Google. We thank the staff of Brown's CSCI 0190 and CSCI 1730 for their invaluable assistance, and the students for their forbearance.

7. REFERENCES

[1] K. Buffardi and S. H. Edwards. Impacts of adaptive feedback on teaching test-driven development. In *SIGCSE Technical Symposium on Computer Science Education*, 2013.

[2] N. Clark. Peer testing in software engineering projects. In *Australasian Computing Education Conference*, 2004.

[3] T. Denning, M. Kelly, D. Lindquist, R. Malani, W. Griswold, and B. Simon. Lightweight preliminary peer review: does in-class peer review make sense? In *SIGCSE Technical Symposium on Computer Science Education*, pages 266–270, 2007.

[4] M. Felleisen, R. B. Findler, M. Flatt, and S. Krishnamurthi. *How to Design Programs*. MIT Press, 2002.

[5] C. D. Hundhausen, A. Agrawal, and P. Agarwal. Talking about code: Integrating pedagogical code reviews into early computing courses. *ACM Transactions on Computing Education*, 13(3), Aug. 2013.

[6] C. Kulkarni, K. P. Wei, H. Le, D. Chia, K. Papadopoulos, J. Cheng, D. Koller, and S. R. Klemmer. Peer and self assessment in massive online classes. *ACM Transactions on Computer-Human Interaction*, 2013.

[7] L. Ramachandran and E. F. Gehringer. Reusable learning objects through peer review: The Expertiza approach. In *Innovate: Journal of Online Education*, 2007.

[8] K. Reily, P. L. Finnerty, and L. Terveen. Two peers are better than one: Aggregating peer reviews for computing assignments is surprisingly accurate. In *Proceedings of the ACM International Conference on Supporting Group Work*, 2009.

[9] J. Smith, J. Tessler, E. Kramer, and C. Lin. Using peer review to teach software testing. In *International Computing Education Research Conference*, 2012.

[10] H. Søndergaard. Learning from and with peers: The different roles of student peer reviewing. In *ACM SIGCSE Conference on Innovation and Technology in Computer Science Education*, pages 31–35, 2009.

[11] K. Topping. Peer assessment between students in colleges and universities. *Review of Educational Research*, 68(3):249–276, 1998.

[12] Y. Wang, H. Li, Y. Sun, J. Yu, and J. Yu. Learning outcomes of programming language courses based on peer code review model. In *International Conference on Computer Science & Education*, 2011.

[13] A. Zeller. Making students read and review code. In *ACM SIGCSE Conference on Innovation and Technology in Computer Science Education*, 2000.

Enhancing Syntax Error Messages Appears Ineffectual

Paul Denny, Andrew Luxton-Reilly, Dave Carpenter
Dept. of Computer Science
The University of Auckland
Auckland, New Zealand
{paul, andrew}@cs.auckland.ac.nz, dcar111@aucklanduni.ac.nz

ABSTRACT

Debugging is an important skill for novice programmers to acquire. Error messages help novices to locate and correct errors, but compiler messages are frequently inadequate. We have developed a system that provides enhanced error messages, including concrete examples that illustrate the kind of error that has occurred and how that kind of error could be corrected. We evaluate the effectiveness of the enhanced error messages with a controlled empirical study and find no significant effect.

Categories and Subject Descriptors

K.3.2 [**Computers and Education**]: Computer and Information Science Education—*computer science education*

General Terms

Design, Human Factors

Keywords

debugging; errors; syntax error; error messages; feedback; novice; programming

1. INTRODUCTION

Despite numerous studies on debugging, it remains a difficult skill for novices to acquire [12]. Code written by students can be filled with errors, and poor debugging skills can lead to frustration and the introduction of new errors [13]. Furthermore, very few students who have trouble debugging code are able to perform well in a course [1].

Although Fitzgerald et. al [7] found that construct-related bugs (i.e. those that are due to misunderstanding or confusion about the language) are easier to fix than those which are language independent, syntax errors can still be major obstacles that slow the progress of novice programmers. As Kummerfeld and Kay [11] note, "Syntax error correction is the first step in the debugging process. It is not possible to

ITiCSE'14, June 21–25, 2014, Uppsala, Sweden.
Copyright 2014 ACM 978-1-4503-2833-3/14/06 ...$15.00.
http://dx.doi.org/10.1145/2591708.2591748.

continue program development until the code compiles. This means it is a crucial part of the error correction process."

Denny et. al [5] explored the frequency with which students encountered compilation errors when writing relatively short fragments of code. In their study, although successful solutions consisted of a median of only 8 lines of code, approximately 70% of students experienced four or more consecutive syntax errors even when the compiler output was being shown to them. Students in the lowest performance quartile of the course encountered particular difficulty with syntax. In some cases, even after a significant amount of time and effort, students were observed abandoning an exercise when they were unable to write a compiling submission and receive feedback on the logic of their code.

Our experience is that syntax errors can be a significant barrier to student success. One example typifying the extent of this problem involves a student who spent close to 2 hours attempting to test whether the sum of two numbers was even or odd. The student was trying to solve the following exercise using an online tool in which all compilation attempts were captured:

> *Complete the isOddSum() method in Java. This method should calculate the sum of the two input values and return true if the sum is an odd number, and false if the sum is an even number. For example, the sum of 10 and 20 is 30, an even number, so the method call isOddSum(10, 20) should return false.*

To begin the exercise, the student was provided with the method signature as follows:

public boolean isOddSum(**int** a, **int** b)

The student made 31 distinct code submissions in their attempt to solve this exercise. As shown in Figure 1, which plots the time at which each submission was made, the student appeared to work fairly conscientiously on this problem.

Their first submission, made at approximately 8:35pm, is shown in Figure 2. There are many syntax errors in this code: the cast is performed incorrectly, the assignment operator is being used where an equality test is needed, semicolons are missing, the second keyword "if" has a capital letter, the return variable "sum" is declared with the wrong scope and is not the correct type as required by the method.

Over the next hour and a half the student made progress towards correcting these errors, and the second to last submission they made, at approximately 10:15pm is shown in Figure 3.

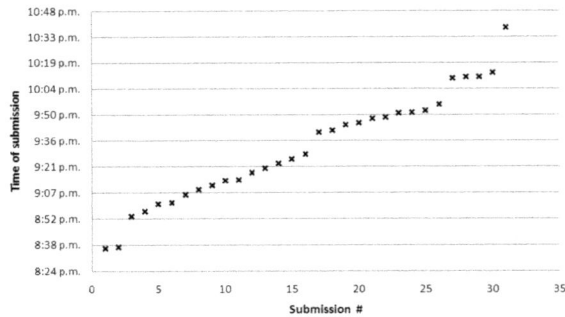

Figure 1: Time at which successive attempts were made

```
if((a=2*int( a/2))&&(b=2*(int b/2))) {
    int sum=a+b
}
If(sum=2*int(sum/2)) {
    sum=0
}
return sum
```

Figure 2: Student X's first attempt at the isOddSum() exercise

```
int sum = 0;

if(a==2*(a/2)) {
    if(b!=2*(b/2)) {
        sum = a+b;
    }
} else {
    if(b==2*(b/2)) {
        sum = a+b;
    }
}

return sum;
```

Figure 3: Student X's 30th, and penultimate, attempt at the isOddSum() exercise

```
if (n%2==0) {
    n = false;
} else {
    n = true;
}

return n;
```

Figure 4: Student X's final, and unsuccessful, attempt at the isOddSum() exercise

Although logically this code is not correct (for example, both branches of the condition assign the same value to the return variable), only one syntax error remains (the type of the return value does not match the return type of the method) and as a result the compiler would generate a "Type mismatch" error message. However, at this point the student appears to give up on this approach and approximately 20 minutes later made their final submission to this exercise, which was again both syntactically and logically incorrect, as shown in Figure 4.

It is unfortunate that this student was not able to resolve their syntax errors, as this meant they never received feedback on the logical correctness of their code. Providing targeted help to get students over this problematic syntax hurdle is the primary motivation behind our current work.

In this paper we report on an attempt to improve novice debugging performance by providing enhanced syntax error messages, directly within the development environment, that include a more verbose description of the error than the standard Java compiler. Inspired by the work of others in this area, our enhanced feedback also displays an example of code that contains the same kind of error, and a corresponding corrected version, along with details of how the example code could be corrected. We evaluate the effectiveness of the enhanced error messages with a controlled empirical study involving first year students. Our main research question is: "Does the enhanced feedback have any measurable impact on how effectively students resolve syntax errors in their code?".

2. RELATED WORK

A number of other attempts to provide enhanced feedback have been reported in the literature.

Kummerfeld and Kay [11] observe that students struggle to correct syntax errors, and speculate that perhaps the in-comprehensibility of the compiler error messages contribute to the difficulties. They provided students with a reference guide that catalogues common compiler errors. Each error message is explained and illustrated with an example of code that contains the error, and how the error could be corrected. A qualitative study of debugging behaviour involving students with access to the reference guide showed that some students seemed to not understand the syntax error until they looked at the example code. This suggests concrete examples are important for teaching syntax errors.

Code Analyser for Pascal (CAP) was developed to provide automated feedback on program syntax, logic and style errors [15]. The CAP tool performed static analysis of the code and provided feedback about what was wrong, why it was wrong and how to fix the problem. The feedback messages often included correct exemplar code for students to model. Students who used the tool reported that they valued CAP as a learning tool, and instructors reported that they spent less time grading because CAP improved the quality of student programs. However, the author observed that some students did not read the error messages, and others became dependent on the error messages for debugging.

Gauntlet [8] provides enhanced feedback by searching student's Java code for a number of commonly encountered syntax and semantic errors and presenting them to students in a more colloquial manner. After using the Gauntlet system in classes at the United States Military Academy for 18 months, teaching staff noted that the work produced by students was of a higher quality and that their workload was reduced, as fewer students were visiting them in their office hours looking for assistance. However, it became apparent that Gauntlet was not addressing the most common errors encountered by students because the errors supported by Gauntlet were chosen by instructors based on personal experience rather than empirical data [9].

Dy & Rodrigo [6] investigated automating the detection of non-literal Java errors where following the compiler's suggested correction will create a different error. They analysed data collected from student compilations to determine the most common errors, and developed an error detector that could automatically detect the kind of error based on the compiler message and the source code. This detector could, in principle, be used to provide enhanced feedback which may help students to correct common errors, but the system has not yet been deployed in a classroom context.

Toomey [16] modified the BlueJ environment to provide more detailed error messages, along with examples of incorrect and correct code related to the error message. However, this work has not (to our knowledge) been published or evaluated.

Carter & Blank [2] report on the design of an intelligent tutoring system that provides enhanced error messages similar to those we present here. The intelligent tutoring system is currently being developed and as yet no evaluation of the enhanced error messages has been performed.

It should be noted that few of the previous reports have attempted to rigorously evaluate the effectiveness of enhanced error messages in classroom contexts, and none of them provide empirical data on the impact that the error messages have on student debugging performance.

3. ENHANCING ERROR MESSAGES

We decided to implement an enhanced feedback system to users of CodeWrite [4]. CodeWrite is a web-based tool in which students complete a series of exercises that require them to write the body of a method in Java. The header of the method is always provided. Code is entered directly in the browser and is compiled and run against a set of test cases automatically. When code fails to compile, CodeWrite passes the first two compiler-generated error messages back to students. Limiting the number of errors shown to students is consistent with other well-known Java teaching environments such as BlueJ [10], and is intended to help students focus on a single error at a time.

The first step in building the enhanced feedback module was to create a recognizer that parsed both the submitted source code and the raw compiler messages, to categorize the messages according to error type. We began by examining previous student submissions (from the Second Semester 2012) that failed to compile in order to find common patterns in the code. The data set that we analysed to create the recognizer had 12369 submissions containing syntax errors.

The compiler error messages could be used to correctly identify some of the errors (approximately 78%), but the message alone was not sufficient to distinguish between some other kinds of errors. For example, consider the following two code fragments:

```
int x = 10;
int z = int x;
```

and

```
int x = 10;
int y = 20;
int z = Math.min(int x, int y);
```

In both cases, the compiler generates exactly the same error message:

Syntax error on token "int", delete this token

Although both problems are similar, if we can determine that the errant type appears prior to a parameter being passed to a method, we are able to provide more contextual feedback that includes a discussion of how to correctly pass inputs to methods via parameters.

To categorize the errors that had ambiguous compiler messages, we performed a static analysis of the code using regular expressions to match commonly occurring patterns of code that caused errors. This approach successfully identified another 14% of the total errors. We stopped adding new error types to the recognizer after the recognizer was capable of categorizing the errors present in 92% of the submissions from the 2012 data set, and each remaining error type was present in only a few submissions.

Once the error had been detected by the recognizer, we extracted the line containing the error from the code so that it could be highlighted in the feedback to aid the student in locating the error. Our recognizer identifies 53 different types of syntax errors, which we have classified into 9 different categories. Table 1 summarises the different categories of error and the number of errors included in each category.

Category	N
Incorrect return statements	3
Misused or unmatched braces or parenthesis	10
Variable or type cannot be resolved	2
Type mismatches	2
Incorrect if statements	9
Incorrect method calls	8
Missing or unexpected character e.g. semicolon	6
Incorrect assignment/creation of variable/object	9
Other	4

Table 1: Number of errors in each category identified by the error recognition module

The feedback provided by the enhanced feedback module typically contains the line that the error occurs on (as extracted by the recognizer) and a detailed explanation of what is most likely causing the syntax error. The enhanced feedback also includes a table showing two code fragments side by side, the first of which includes a simple syntax error of the type that has been recognised and the other showing the corrected version of the code with the syntax differences highlighted. The final column of this table provides an explanation of the error in the first code fragment and describes how it has been corrected in the second.

Consider the method definition below, in which the compound conditional statement is missing surrounding parentheses.

```
public boolean validScore(int score)
{
    if (score < 0 ) || (score > 100)
        return false;
        return true;
}
```

The raw error message produced by the compiler for this code is shown in Figure 5. In contrast, the enhanced feedback is shown in Figure 6 and represents an example of an error in the "*Incorrect if statements*" category listed in Table 1.

```
if (score < 0 ) || (score > 100)
Syntax error on token "||", if expected

1 problem (1 error)
```

Figure 5: An example of an original error message

4. EVALUATION

To evaluate the effectiveness of the enhanced feedback, we trialled the modified CodeWrite tool in an introductory programming course (CS1) in the Summer Semester 2013 at The University of Auckland. The Summer Semester course covers the standard CS1 curriculum at an accelerated pace with 6 lectures and 2 laboratories per week over a 6 week period compared with the standard 3 lectures and 1 laboratory per week over a 12 week period in other semesters.

Students were required to successfully answer 10 exercises in CodeWrite for 1% of their final grade. This activity spanned the second and third weeks of the six week course. As the students were still in the first half of their course, the exercises covered expressions, conditionals and methods from the java.lang.String and java.lang.Math classes, but did not cover arrays and loops.

In total, there were 90 students in the class, but only 83 contributed at least one submission. Students were randomly allocated to a control group (N=42) that received raw compiler feedback, or an intervention group (N = 41) that received the enhanced feedback. Both groups completed the same exercises.

We classify every student submission into one of the three types shown in Table 2.

Type	Explanation
P	the submission compiles and all tests pass
F	the submission compiles but fails at least one of the tests
X	the submission does not compile

Table 2: Types of student submissions

Once a student submits their code they receive instant feedback on its correctness. In the case of an "F" submission, the student is shown the passing and, importantly, failing test cases. In the case of an "X" submission, they are shown either the raw compiler error message or the enhanced feedback produced by our module, depending on the group to which they have been assigned.

Our main goal in this project was to improve the effectiveness of student debugging. In particular, we wanted to help those students who tended to repeatedly submit non-compiling code, apparently unable to resolve the syntax errors they encountered. To evaluate the enhanced feedback, we investigated whether it had any impact on:

- the number of consecutive non-compiling submissions made while attempting a given exercise,
- the total number of non-compiling submissions across all exercises, and
- the number of attempts needed to resolve the most common kinds of errors.

5. RESULTS

5.1 Did the enhanced feedback reduce the number of consecutive non-compiling submissions?

As mentioned earlier, a previous study by Denny et. al [5] revealed that the majority of students experienced a "syntax issue", in which code was unsuccessfully compiled at least 4 consecutive times before syntax errors were resolved. We were particularly concerned about students (such as Student X mentioned in the introduction) who were unable to correct the syntax errors in their code using compiler messages.

We looked at the submissions made to each exercise separately. For each student, we classified their sequence of submissions to a given exercise using the categories described in Table 2. For example, a sequence such as "XXXXFXXP" indicates that a student submitted code that failed to compile 4 times in a row, followed by code that compiled but failed one or more test cases, followed by two submissions of code that failed to compile before finally submitting code that compiled and passed all the test cases.

For each exercise, we captured the degree to which a given student was stuck with a "syntax issue" by recording the longest sequence of consecutive "X" submissions the student made to that exercise. We then compared these values for all students in the control group with all students in the intervention group using a two-sample t-test. Although data items varied considerably, Shapiro-Wilk tests indicated normality of the data in most cases. For two of the exercises, in which the data was particularly skewed with a few students encountering a large number of consecutive syntax errors, the data was log transformed prior to testing (results shown in the log p column). Table 3 summarizes the results, giving both the mean and standard deviation (in parentheses) for each exercise. There were no significant differences between groups.

Ex	$\mu_{control}(\sigma)$	$\mu_{enhanced}(\sigma)$	p	log p
1	9.72 (12.5)	6.74 (9.82)	0.25	
2	2.05 (2.20)	3.68 (3.83)		0.08
3	9.65 (11.8)	8.79 (10.1)		0.89
4	4.46 (5.01)	6.24 (8.38)	0.25	
5	5.73 (8.08)	6.35 (7.99)	0.73	
6	3.83 (5.77)	3.44 (5.61)	0.77	
7	4.63 (5.43)	5.16 (7.44)	0.72	
8	2.14 (6.69)	1.69 (2.89)	0.70	
9	3.07 (7.26)	2.34 (3.79)	0.57	
10	8.80 (20.7)	4.56 (7.92)	0.23	

Table 3: The longest consecutive sequence of submissions that failed to compile for the control group ($\mu_{control}$) compared with the intervention group ($\mu_{enhanced}$) that received enhanced feedback.

5.2 Did the enhanced feedback reduce the total number of non-compiling submissions?

To determine if the enhanced error messages made a difference to the total number of non-compiling submissions, we compared the mean number of submissions of each type made by students in each group. Table 4 gives the total number of submissions of each type for the control and in-

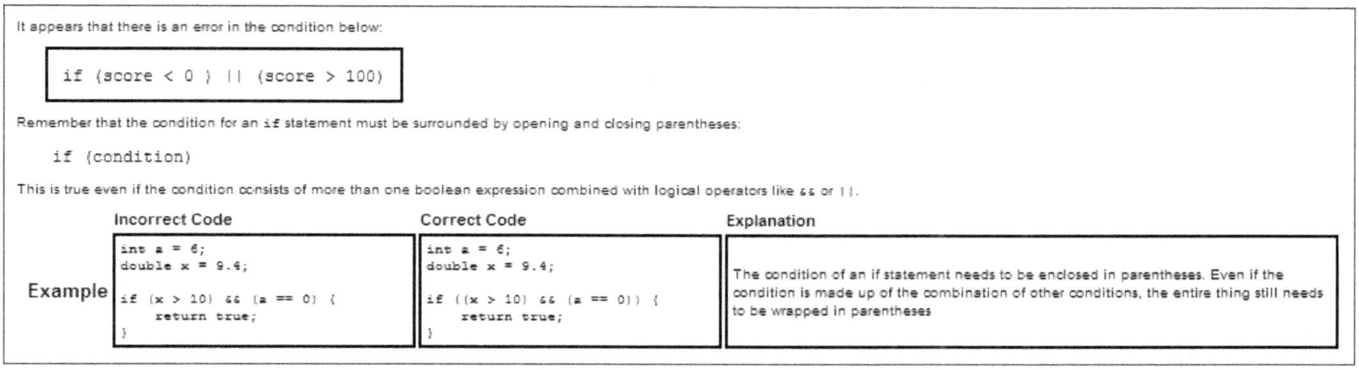

Figure 6: An example of an enhanced error message

tervention groups (means and standard deviations are in parentheses).

Type	Control	Intervention
P	**450** ($\mu, \sigma = 10.7, 3.36$)	**434** ($\mu, \sigma = 10.6, 4.00$)
F	**1892** ($\mu, \sigma = 45.0, 49.4$)	**1656** ($\mu, \sigma = 40.4, 52.8$)
X	**3343** ($\mu, \sigma = 79.6, 86.0$)	**2760** ($\mu, \sigma = 67.3, 68.8$)

Table 4: Summary of submissions of each type for the control group (raw error messages) and the intervention group (enhanced error messages). Totals are in bold, means and standard deviations are parenthesized

Although students viewing the enhanced error messages made fewer non-compiling submissions overall, the variance of both groups was high, and the difference between the means was not significant (p = 0.9471).

Note that the number of submissions with logic errors (i.e. submissions that compiled, but failed one of the tests) was also lower among the intervention group, but the difference between means was not significant (p = 0.9941)

5.3 Did the enhanced feedback reduce the number of attempts needed to resolve the most common kinds of errors?

For this question we have looked more in depth at the three most common syntax errors as reported by Denny et al. [3]. Each of these syntax errors are investigated separately:

1. Cannot resolve identifier
2. Type mismatch
3. Missing semicolon

A submission is said to have a syntax error of a particular type when the error is first reported in response to compilation. The error is said to have been resolved when the syntax error is no longer reported to students in the feedback for that submission. We measured the average number of compiles that it takes a student to resolve each type of error. Having calculated the average number of compiles for each student, we compare the mean of these averages for the control group and the intervention group.

For each syntax error investigated, we found that the average number of compiles for students to resolve the error varied greatly. In order to perform a two-sample t-test on the data, we first performed a log transformation to make

the variances approximately equal. Table 5 summarizes the results of the t-tests. In each case, a t-test for a difference between the means of the logged data did not result in a significant p-value, so we have no evidence that the enhanced feedback affects the average number of compiles needed to resolve any of these common syntax errors.

Syntax error	$\mu_{con} - \mu_{enh}$	p
Cannot resolve identifier	0.15	0.2369
Type mismatch	-0.15	0.2783
Missing semicolon	-0.10	0.4449

Table 5: The difference between the means of the control group (μ_{con}) and the intervention group receiving enhanced feedback (μ_{enh}) for the average number of compiles required to resolve each type of error

6. DISCUSSION

Although we anticipated that the enhanced error messages would help students to identify and correct errors, analysis of the data shows no significant (or practical) effect. Each student experienced approximately 70 submissions that failed to compile, but the enhanced error messages did not appear to reduce the number of "syntax issues" experienced, the total number of compilations required to solve all problems, or to help resolve the most common errors encountered. In essence, we found no empirical evidence to support the use of enhanced error messages.

There are a number of reasons why the enhanced error messages may not have helped students. It is possible that the majority of errors may have been simple enough to solve without the enhanced messages. For example, missing semicolons represent one of the more common student errors and the corresponding error message generated by the compiler, *"Syntax error, insert ; to complete statement"*, may provide adequate information to most students without the need for additional explanation. The cases for which the enhanced messages are particularly useful may be too infrequent in our data to yield significant results.

Another explanation for our findings is that students in the intervention group did not pay much attention to the additional information in the enhanced error messages. This is consistent with findings by Kummerfeld and Kay [11], who

277

note that some students did not use their reference guide that helped explain the likely cause of the errors encountered, and with the observation of Schorch who states "Some students do not read the CAP error messages fully and thus are probably not learning as much as we would like" [15].

The enhanced error messages we provided were more verbose than the raw error messages and although they may have provided an opportunity to learn about the likely cause of the error, students may have been resistant to reading additional detail beyond the simple compiler output, especially when they encountered the same error multiple times.

A third possible explanation was that the enhanced feedback did not provide examples and explanations that students could relate to their own code. The examples were intended to illustrate the kind of situation that might cause an error of the type encountered by a student, but it relies on students understanding the idea and transferring the knowledge to their own situation.

One possible threat to the validity of our findings is that the raw compiler feedback shows up to two compiler errors, while the enhanced feedback module displays only one error message to reduce the complexity for students. This may allow some students to correct two errors at once while using the raw compiler messages, or may possibly confuse other students by presenting more than one error to correct. However, it should be noted that previous research by Denny et al. [3] found that most (approximately 70%) submissions that failed to compile had only one syntax error.

In future, an observational study of how students are using the enhanced feedback in practice may shed some light on the reasons why our implementation was unsuccessful. We note that further study of enhanced error feedback would be valuable for systems (such as our own, and that of Cloud-Coder [14]) intended to support short exercises and practice in environments outside of typical supervised laboratories where personal debugging support is limited.

7. CONCLUSIONS

Syntax errors are one of the biggest problems for students learning to program. They slow students' progress and prevent them from getting feedback on the logic of their code. As educators, we have a limited amount of time to spend with each student so providing students with automated and useful feedback about why they are getting syntax errors is very important.

Although a number of researchers have previously investigated the use of enhanced compiler feedback, few provide any quantifiable results. We built an enhanced feedback module that recognises syntax errors and generates more descriptive feedback on what caused the error. The enhanced feedback module was evaluated using a controlled empirical study in which the debugging behaviour of students receiving enhanced feedback was compared with that of students receiving standard compiler feedback.

Despite our initial prediction that the enhanced feedback would improve students' performance, our results show that there was no significant benefit for students that received the enhanced feedback. This is a somewhat surprising result that warrants further investigation. It does, however, signify that the development of teaching resources need to take account of student behaviour and that innovations intended to support student learning should be evaluated in the context of real classroom situations.

8. REFERENCES

[1] M. Ahmadzadeh, D. Elliman, and C. Higgins. An analysis of patterns of debugging among novice computer science students. In *Proc. ITiCSE '05*, pages 84–88, 2005. ACM.

[2] E. Carter and G. D. Blank. A tutoring system for debugging: status report. *J. Comput. Sci. Coll.*, 28(3):46–52, Jan. 2013.

[3] P. Denny, A. Luxton-Reilly, and E. Tempero. All syntax errors are not equal. In *Proc. ITiCSE '12*, pages 75–80, 2012. ACM.

[4] P. Denny, A. Luxton-Reilly, E. Tempero, and J. Hendrickx. Codewrite: Supporting student-driven practice of java. In *Proc. SIGCSE '11*, pages 471–476, 2011. ACM.

[5] P. Denny, A. Luxton-Reilly, E. Tempero, and J. Hendrickx. Understanding the syntax barrier for novices. In *Proc. ITiCSE '11*, pages 208–212, 2011. ACM.

[6] T. Dy and M. M. Rodrigo. A detector for non-literal java errors. In *Koli Calling '10*, Koli, Finland, October 28–31, 2010. ACM.

[7] S. Fitzgerald, G. Lewandowski, R. McCauley, L. Murphy, B. Simon, L. Thomas, and C. Zander. Debugging: finding, fixing and flailing, a multi-institutional study of novice debuggers. *Computer Science Education*, 18(2):93–116, 2008.

[8] T. Flowers, C. Carver, and J. Jackson. Empowering students and building confidence in novice programmers through gauntlet. In *Frontiers in Education, 2004. FIE 2004. 34th Annual*, pages T3H/10–T3H/13 Vol. 1, 2004.

[9] J. Jackson, M. Cobb, and C. Carver. Identifying top java errors for novice programmers. In *Frontiers in Education, 2005. FIE '05. Proceedings 35th Annual Conference*, pages T4C–T4C, 2005.

[10] M. Kölling, B. Quig, A. Patterson, and J. Rosenberg. The bluej system and its pedagogy. *Computer Science Education*, 13(4):249–268, 2003.

[11] S. K. Kummerfeld and J. Kay. The neglected battle fields of syntax errors. In *Proc. ACE '03*, vol 20, pages 105–111, Australia, 2003. ACS.

[12] R. McCauley, S. Fitzgerald, G. Lewandowski, L. Murphy, B. Simon, L. Thomas, and C. Zander. Debugging: a review of the literature from an educational perspective. *Computer Science Education*, 18(2):67–92, 2008.

[13] L. Murphy, G. Lewandowski, R. McCauley, B. Simon, L. Thomas, and C. Zander. Debugging: the good, the bad, and the quirky – a qualitative analysis of novices' strategies. In *Proc. SIGCSE '08*, pages 163–167, 2008. ACM.

[14] A. Papancea, J. Spacco, and D. Hovemeyer. An open platform for managing short programming exercises. In *Proc. ICER '13*, pages 47–52, 2013. ACM.

[15] T. Schorsch. Cap: an automated self-assessment tool to check pascal programs for syntax, logic and style errors. In *Proc. SIGCSE '95*, pages 168–172, 1995. ACM.

[16] W. Toomey. Bluej with modified error subsystem. *http://minnie.tuhs.org/Programs/BlueJErrors*, 2011.

A Qualitative Think-Aloud Study of Novice Programmers' Code Writing Strategies

Jacqueline Whalley
School of Computer and Mathematical Sciences
Auckland University of Technology
Auckland, New Zealand
+64 9 9219608
jwhalley@aut.ac.nz

Nadia Kasto
School of Computer and Mathematical Sciences
Auckland University of Technology
Auckland, New Zealand
+64 9 9219999
nkasto@aut.ac.nz

ABSTRACT

This paper presents part of a larger long term study into the cognitive aspects of the early stages of learning to write computer programs Tasks designed to trigger learning events were used to provide the opportunity to observe student learning, in terms of the development and modification of cognitive structures or schemata, during think aloud sessions. A narrative analysis of six students' attempts to solve these tasks is presented. The students' progression in learning and attitudinal approaches to learning is examined and provides some insight into the cognitive processes involved in learning computer programming.

Categories and Subject Descriptors

K.3 [Computers & Education]: Computer & Information Science Education – Computer Science Education

Keywords

Vygotsky, think aloud, schemas, novice programmers.

1. INTRODUCTION

Educators are well aware, that for novices learning to program is particularly difficult. Many studies have pointed to the fact that students cannot write code, cannot read and reason about code and cannot problem solve. While we still do not fully understand the cognitive processes involved in learning to program, we know that at the earliest stages of learning to program, novice programmers have few schemas available in their long-term memory. Therefore, their knowledge is fragile and the *intrinsic cognitive load* [7] is high. This high cognitive load means that many novice programmers focus on the programming language syntax and programming concepts and as a result find the extra load of problem solving impossible. Some researchers have also explored the idea of attitude to learning, and learner types and their relationship to the ability to learn programming. Other researchers have focused on a student's ability to reason about code in relation to Neo-Piagetian levels of development [12].

In this study we are attempting to move beyond the notion of a level of development and attempting to explore the process of learning. In order to do this we have taken inspiration from psychological theories of learning to design a research instrument to trigger learning events which result in changes of knowledge structure or adjusts the incoming information to a current knowledge structure. These cognitive structure changes are often explained using the notions of "assimilation to" and "accommodation of" cognitive schema. Assimilation and accommodation are common themes within the psychological study of learning. Assimilation relates to a process of modifying (usually by expanding) an existing cognitive structure (or schema) so that a new piece of information fits within that structure [2]. Accommodation occurs when the new information is too complex to be integrated into the existing structure - this means that, cognitive structures change in response to the new information or even that a new structure is formed [7].

Another theory of learning, developed by Vygotsky [14], included the notion of a *zone of proximal development* (ZPD). ZPD has been defined as "the distance between the actual developmental level as determined by independent problem solving and the level of potential development as determined through problem solving under adult guidance, or in collaboration with more capable peers" ([14], p86). Vygotsky believed that when a student is at the ZPD for a particular task, providing the appropriate assistance will give the student enough of a "boost" to achieve the task. The ZPD has over time become synonymous in the literature with the term *scaffolding* However, Vygotksy did not use this term in his writing. *"Scaffolding"* was first used by Wood, Bruner and Ross who defined it as a "process that enables a child or novice to solve a problem, carry out a task or achieve a goal which would be beyond his unassisted efforts" ([15], p.89). Regardless the term 'Vygotsky scaffolding' has been used by researchers' to describe an approach to teaching that provides resources (tools, strategies and guides) and support to students as they learn new concepts with the aim of providing students with a higher level of understanding than they could obtain via independent study. As the students develop skills in those areas, the supports are gradually removed so that eventually the student can accomplish a task with no assistance. Our research method, discussed in the following section, uses a post-task scaffolding technique to assist the participants/students who appear to be outside of their ZPD on a task.

2. METHOD

2.1 Think Aloud Sessions

One-on-one think-aloud sessions were conducted with volunteer students from an introductory Java programming course in 2013. The sessions, held once a week for 10 weeks, were recorded using a video camera and typically lasted about 60 minutes. In these sessions the students were asked to complete a series of code writing tasks, on the computer, while thinking out loud following the protocols developed by Ericson and Simon [2]. van Someren, Barnard and Sandberg [13] also provide an excellent guide to the think aloud method. The goal of any protocol for think-aloud is to minimise the cognitive effort in verbalization in order to enable the participants to articulate their thinking process and to ensure undue bias is not introduced by the observer/interviewer.

The participants were first given practice and coaching in thinking aloud and the tasks reported in this paper were undertaken in sessions 4-6 once the students were comfortable with the environment and process. Despite this coaching, during a pilot study, we found that the cognitive load involved in writing code meant that some of the participants found it almost impossible at the time to articulate their thinking and had to be prompted to continue thinking aloud. For this reason the following retrospection phase [13] was added. During each think-aloud session the interviewer made notes and specifically noted pauses in the think-aloud session and on fragments of the think-aloud session that sounded incomprehensible, very incomplete or very confused. As soon as a think-aloud on a task was completed the interviewer undertook a retrospective interview with the participant which was triggered by video replay of their think-aloud response in order to try to establish what their thinking was during pauses in their verbalization. Finally a discussion of the protocol and the task was undertaken in which the student was provided with tutoring on the task. Notes of any tutoring activity including artefacts such as trace tables and teaching examples were recorded when appropriate using a Wi-Fi Smartpen and a digital notebook which allows for synchronized visual and audio files to be captured and replayed.

2.2 The Course

The course adopted a back to basics procedural approach (similar to that suggested by Reges [4]) except that the learning was supported by an in-house micro-world called Robot World in the BlueJ IDE. Initially, the students were provided with a small number of predefined methods that allowed the robot to navigate the world and pick up a beeper. Throughout the course the students were required write small pieces of code (procedures) within a provided method stub in the robot world. The assessment for the course was made up of a series of on-line computer based programming tests and a series of regular take home programming tasks.

2.3 The Participants

Six participants that represented the top three quartiles of the cohort were selected for this study.

Table 1. Participants by quartile

Alias	Quartile
Tom	4 (top)
Zain	4
Jim	3
Michelle	3
Mark	2
Barry	2

These participants were all novice programmers and had not previously studied computer programming. The participants from the lower quartile ($Q1$) were not selected because we were unable to elicit adequate think-aloud data typically because of the level of interviewer intervention necessary and the high cognitive effort required by the students owing to their fragile knowledge. In order to preserve student anonymity each student was given an alias (Table 1).

2.4 Tasks

The three tasks, discussed in this paper, were designed in order to be able to observe the processes of learning by providing small incremental increases in the conceptual complexity of the task. The idea was that each subsequent question would build on a concept already covered and assessed in the course in such a way that the learner would be expected to have to either fit the new knowledge to their existing schema or reorganise their cognitive structure by connecting it with some aspect of their existing knowledge (or "schema") and creating a product of learning as a newly reorganised cognitive structure (or "schema").

2.4.1 Question 1

This question asked students to write a procedure to calculate the length of a single corridor. In order to solve this problem they needed to move the robot which was located at the start of the corridor and count the number of cells the robot travelled until it reached the end of the corridor. An example scenario with a corridor of length 10 was provided to the students (Figure 1).

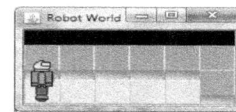

Figure 1. An example world for question 1

The students had already been given this question as part of their coursework so it should have been familiar to them. In this question we were checking whether or not the students had an existing cognitive schema for counting the length of the corridors.

2.4.2 Question 2

This question followed on from Question 1 and had not been previously seen by the students. The question asked the students to compare the length of two corridors and print out a message that either said the corridors were of equal length or gave the length of the longest corridor. The corridors were always at the same locations and were connected in the same way; only the length of the corridors changed (Figure 2).

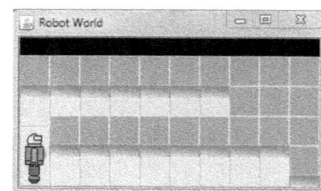

Figure 2. An example world for question 2

To solve this problem the students were expected to make use of their existing schema for calculating the length of a corridor (Question 1) as well as a schema to find the higher of two integer numbers. In a previous session all the participants had been evaluated to ensure that they were able to write procedures to compare two integer numbers and either:

- print that they were equal,
- print the higher of the two values,
- or print the lower of the two values.

The students had also written code in class and in formative and summative assessments that required the use of selection statements. But they had not had to put together selection and the notion of counting the length of corridors so these concepts should be represented by separate cognitive schemas.

2.4.3   Question 3
In this scenario there were any number of (obviously limited by the dimensions of the world) interconnected n corridors but they were always connected at the same point (column 0, as shown in Figure 3). The length of each of the corridors changed randomly each time the robot world was created. The students were again asked to write a program that calculated the length of the longest corridor, and then displayed the message:

This question, which was new to the students, required them to take the concepts and knowledge, which we assume had been developed in the process of solving the previous two questions, and modify that knowledge (or "schemata") to solve the problem.

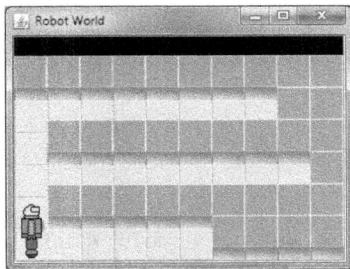

Figure 3. An example world for question 3

3. RESULTS AND INTERPRETATION
What follows is a discussion of the results from transcribing and observing the think-aloud responses and retrospections for each question.

In the discussion and interpretation of our results we use the term *redirected* to refer to a situation in which the participant is prompted to re-examine their solution and is able to recognise any errors in their solution and fix those errors without any support or instruction being provided. In such a situation we believe that the participant is within their ZPD because they are able to solve the problem alone and without scaffolding. The term *scaffolded* is used to refer to a situation where after simple redirection the participant is unable to solve the problem alone, and therefore it is not within their ZPD, and the interviewer provides support to the participants to assist their learning with the aim of extending their ZPD. The scaffolding employed is known as *soft scaffolding* where scaffolds are provided that "are dynamic, situation-specific aid provided by a teacher to assist the learning process" [1].

3.1 Question 1
Tom, Zain and Mark recalled that they had seen question 1 before.

Mark: "*I've seen this problem before*"

Zain, Tom and Mark, after stating that the task was familiar immediately, started to code their solutions without hesitation or verbalisation.

Both Zain and Mark recalled the correct solution. Zain was the only participant to check that his solution was correct without prompting. He was observed mentally tracing through the code using the example world provided prior to running his solution and by moving his finger along the example corridor and tapping rather than by using pen and paper. In the retrospection he was asked what he was doing to which he replied that he was "*checking my answer*".

Although Tom retrieved an existing schema it was flawed. He had missed the subtly of having to start the counter at 1 (to allow for the robot sitting in the first square) rather than 0. On completing the code Tom was so confident of his solution he did not even run it to check the output was correct.

Tom: "*Yes... [pause] ... that's right*"

Once Tom had finished the task the interviewer questioned his assertion that his answer was correct.

Interviewer: "*Are you sure it's correct?*"
Tom: "*I'll trace my solution*"

On running his code Tom realised there was an error and proceeded to hand execute (trace) his code. Tom realised his mistake and was able to fix the bug in his solution. In this case Tom was *redirected* by the interviewer in order prompt him to re-examine his solution.

Jim, Barry and Michael could not recall having seen the problem before. After some time considering the problem Jim recalled a schema which he had seen in class.

Jim: "*I don't know how to do this... [long pause]...need to count the of squares...in the lecture we got how to count numbers*"
"*I need to start at 0 and loops ... make the robot move forward ...when to stop?*"

Jim seemed to be trying to tailor his count the number of integers schema and adapt it to the new situation of counting the length of a corridor. Jim was able to tailor his schema to the robot world and correctly implement the robot navigation and counting of the squares however he failed to notice that he should have also tailored his counter schema, by starting at 1, in order to allow for the robot being already instantiated in the world in the first square.

Interestingly Barry and Michelle also used the same approach as Jim and retrieved the 'counting integers' schema. The students did not recognise that their program would not work and did not attempt to verify the correctness of their solutions. All three students were *redirected* by the interviewer who asked them if they thought they should do anything to check that their solution was correct.

Barry was so focused on the task that he did not think aloud but the code he wrote used the same semantics as that written by Jim and contained the same error. Barry had to be *redirected* and then *scaffolded* for him realise that he should trace through his code to check if there was an error.

Interviewer: "*Are you sure your answer is correct?*"
Barry: [without hesitation] "*yes*"
Interviewer: "*What should the length of the corridor be?*"
Barry: [pauses] "*five*"
Interviewer: "*What is the length your code finds?*"

Barry: [traces code and realises that his code would produce a corridor of four and quickly identifies the source of the error and fixes it independently] ..."*the first will not count*".

Jim did not know how to verify his solution so the interviewer suggested that he might trace through his code to check. Jim did not know how to begin to do this so the interviewer modelled (*scaffolded*) a desk check by writing a trace table, stepping through the written lines of code and drawing a representation of the robot moving down the corridor for two iterations. Jim then independently traced through the remaining iterations using his own doddles and the code written on paper (Figure 4), rather than on the computer, to reach the end of the corridor and before the last iteration realised his mistake and noted the change in his trace code.

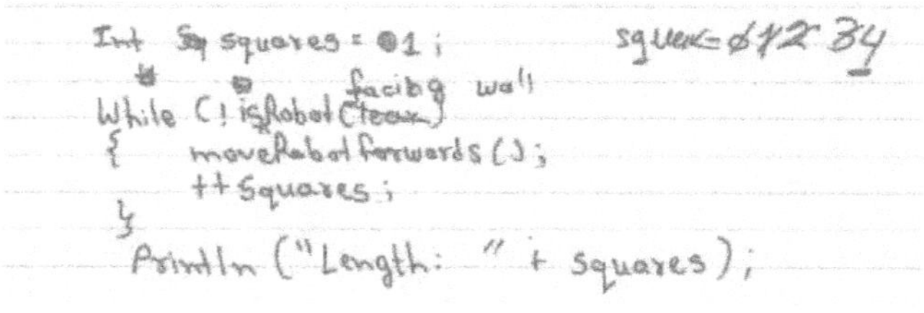

Figure 4. Jim's trace for question 1

Jim: "*oh!...initial location does not count*"
Jim: "*[I should] ....read the question properly*"

Michelle did not retrieve a fully formed schema for counting the length but instead appears to have retrieved sub-plans and joined those plans in order to build the schema. Firstly she recognized the need to iterate in order to move the robot forward then she realised a counter was required. She was unable to identify the counter error without assistance and therefore required scaffolding in order to solve the problem.

Michelle: "*I will go with the while loop*"... [wrote a while statement stub] ... "*we have to use length*" ... [added the length variable] ... "*I will initialize the length by zero*" ... "*move robot forwards*" ... [added method call to move the robot to loop body then added increment for length and finally added the print statement]

Michelle did not identify the counter error.

Interviewer: "Are you sure your answer is correct?"
[long pause] "How long is the example corridor?"
Michelle: "*if move forwards 0,1,2,3,4 so it will be equal 4*"
Interviewer: "*I don't get that are you sure four is right?*"
Michelle: "*yes*"... [pointing to example] ..."*0,1,2,3,4*"..."*4*"
At this point the interviewer pointed to the figure and counted the length of corridor *1,2,3,4,5*.

Michelle: "*it is five ok... [pause] ... then I need to initialize the counter to one*"

It appears that Michelle with scaffolding was able to tailor her schema to fit this new situation even though this change was shown to be fragile when she attempted question 2.

3.2 Question 2
This task required the retrieval of the length counting schema that should have been developed while working on the first task as well as a schema for comparing two numbers. All of the students in the study had also previously successfully, without redirection or scaffolding, answered a code writing question that required the

values of two numbers to be compared. It was a common and highly repeated task to move the robot back to its starting position in the exercises given to the students throughout the course.

Tom and Mark both jumped into programming a solution without redirection or scaffolding and with minimal verbalisation.

Tom began by initialising the two variables to keep track of the length of both of the corridors. He then without hesitation wrote the code to loop and count the length of the first corridor followed by an iterative statement to return the robot to its starting position then oriented and moved the robot ready to count the next corridor. He then copied and pasted the counting length loop and renamed the variable to count the length of the second corridor. He then correctly compared the two lengths. Finally Tom ran the unit tests to verify the correctness of his solution. We conclude from this that Tom could not only retrieve the three schema required to solve the problem but was also able to merge and tailor his schema. In order to do this he is likely to have restructured or accommodated his existing cognitive structures because he had not previously seen a problem like this so could not have already formed such a knowledge structure.

Jim and Zain immediately recognised the link between this task and the previous task.

Jim: "*I need to use the program for counting the length of one corridor, and if-else*".
Zain: "*I know how to calculate the distance*"

Michelle repeated the length counter initialisation error which she had made in question 1. This indicates that her knowledge of the tailored schema developed in answering question must have been fragile. Zain also made this error when he hadn't in task 1 and when returning the robot back to its starting position he forgot to update the loop stepper. When questioned about this in the retrospection he mentioned that he had been so focused on comparing the numbers he had forgotten. However, unlike Michelle, Zain ran the supplied unit tests and was able to identify and fix the error without redirection or scaffolding.

Jim clearly had a fragile knowledge of the required schema and was unsure even how to start solving this task. From the outset Jim required assistance from the interviewer. Unlike the other students who all attempted to use existing knowledge to build a solution Jim took a more top down approach and thought about using two robots, one to count each corridor. At this stage in the course the creation of objects had been back boxed and students were unaware of constructors and treated methods as procedures.

Interviewer: "Is this like anything else you've seen?"
Jim: "*I can measure the length of one corridor.*"
Interviewer: "Is there anything else you might need?"
Jim: "*Add if statement as well?*"
Jim: "*I don't know how to create the second robot.*"
Interviewer: "*Anything else you should add?*"
Jim: "*Two variables*"

The interviewer had to explain to Jim that he did not necessarily need two robots to solve the problem. Jim now had a plan of how to solve the problem but struggled to implement the comparison of the lengths and required the interviewer to supply tutoring and revision of selection statements as well as help in debugging his solution in order to complete the task.

Barry retrieved the plan for counting the length of a corridor and repeated it twice in his code but could not move beyond this point.

Barry: "*I'm confused*".
Interviewer: "*What do you think the problem is?*"
Barry: "*I do not know. I'm confused*"

At this point Barry gave up on the task and did not wish to continue.

3.3 Question 3

The students in the top quartile of the course Zain and Tom were once again able to solve the third task without assistance. Both students formulated a plan for solving the problem before they attempted to write the code on the computer. Zain had errors in his solution but, unprompted, tested his solution found two errors and was able to fix the bugs.

Tom: "*First, I need to count the length of the first corridor and store it in the counter in order to compare it with the length of other corridors*".

Mark on the other hand found that his solution was incorrect when he ran the unit tests and then began a process of random permutation of the code he had written with no success. When the interviewer attempted to redirect him and provide assistance he gave up on the task and was not receptive to assistance. Mark failed to solve the problem.

Barry attempted to solve the problem by immediately coding the corridor length algorithm. From that point he began tinkering in an attempt to solve the problem. This approach introduced several bugs and he gave up and was unreceptive to redirection and scaffolding.

Barry: "*I'm confused I give up*".
Barry failed to solve the problem.

Michelle once again repeated the corridor length counter initialisation error but discovered her error in this instance without redirection. Despite correctly recalling the schemata required to solve the problem she was unable to combine them to reach a solution without scaffolding.

3.4 Participants

3.4.1 Attitudinal changes

It is worth commenting on the changes which were observed in terms of attitude and learning approaches as the students progressed through the three tasks. We observed the same learning behaviours as those identified by Perkins et al [7]. Perkins described the following types of learners:

- *Stoppers* - stop and give up in the face of difficulty

- *Movers* - can use feedback about errors effectively and have the potential to solve a given problem and move on

- *Tinkerers* - cannot trace/track their program, can make changes more or less at random, and like stoppers have little effective chance of progressing.

Both Mark and Barry are students who performed in the lower middle quartile of their class. Both students, when a task fell outside of their ZPD, resorted to behaving as *tinkerers* and writing by random permutations and when that failed became *stoppers*.

Of the upper middle quartile students Jim and Michelle were consistently movers and despite difficulty persevered and were able to complete the tasks with redirection and scaffolding.

Zain did not seem to have moved outside of his ZPD for the three tasks. He was clearly a mover but he exhibited attitudinal traits that were beyond Perkin's definition for a mover. In our study movers is a broad category; some movers did not exhibit any planning tendencies while others planned in detail. Because planning is a desirable practice which we are trying to teach novice programmers, we coined the term planner in order to differentiate between movers that plan before coding and movers who do not plan. We observed that Zain was also a planner as for each task he planned out his solution prior to coding the solution on the machine. In his planning activities he also took steps to verify the correctness of his plan before moving to the code writing stage. His plans typically were a mixture of pseudo code and java syntax. To check the solution he stepped through the plan, in essence, desk checking the plan.

Tom did not plan his solutions for the first two tasks but on the final task planned prior to writing the code. He is clearly a *mover* and a *planner* but unlike Zain only resorts to planning as the task becomes more difficult for him.

3.4.2 Progression in learning

Figure 5 provides a summary of the progression in learning for each student as they progress through the three tasks. Arrows indicate learning taking place and the fill of each circle indicates the level of instructional intervention required to get the student to be able to solve a problem.

Jim and Michelle appear to be very similar. This could be because they have similar general programming competence as measured by their performance on the course or it could be a result of their receptiveness to learning to program.

In the case of Mark when the tasks were within his ZPD he exhibited mover behaviour but as soon as the task became too difficult for him to undertake independently he became a *stopper*. We did not explore the reasons for Marks change in receptiveness to learning and it is possible that external factors contributed to this change. It is worth noting that when Mark was given a question that asked him to reason about a piece of code that found the largest of two numbers he was only able to explain the code line-by-line and was unable to explain the overall purpose of the code. Previous research has found that being able to reason about code is an indicator of a student's readiness to write code [5], [3].

4. CONCLUSION

This paper presents, due to space limitations, a small snippet of a larger program of research. It confirms earlier observations by Perkins at al. [9] of behavioural and attitudinal approaches to learning to program and their affect on learning. Our findings also suggest that the students do have a ZPD and that with the right behavioural approaches to learning the students ZPD can be expanded.

We also think it worth noting from the methodological perspective that for almost all novice programmers thinking aloud is a difficult and cognitively demanding task. They are already challenged by the leaning of programming and for many trying to think aloud as well is simply too difficult. We have found that the only way to get sufficient depth of information about a student's thinking is to video the student and then use that video as a point of reference for retrospection.

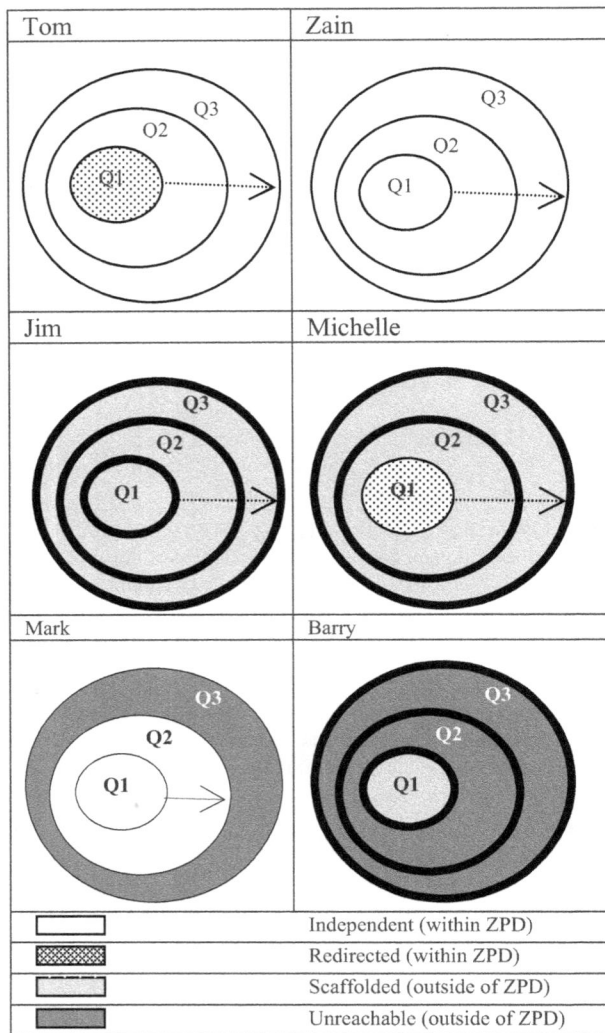

Figure 5. Progression of learning for each participant

☐	Independent (within ZPD)
▨	Redirected (within ZPD)
☐	Scaffolded (outside of ZPD)
■	Unreachable (outside of ZPD)

5. ACKNOWLEDGMENTS

We would like to thank the student volunteers who gave time to this study and to Donna Teague (QUT) and Dr. Robert Wellington (AUT) for their advice on method.

6. REFERENCES

[1] Brush, T. A., and Saye, J. W. 2002. A Summary of Research Exploring Hard and Soft Scaffolding for Teachers and Students Using a Multimedia Supported Learning Environment. *The Journal of Interactive Online Learning.* 1, 2, Retrieved on January 16, 2014 from http://www.ncolr.org/jiol/issues/PDF/1.2.3.pdf.

[2] Ericsson, K. A., and Simon, H. A. 1993. *Protocol Analysis: Verbal Reports as Data.* Cambridge, MA: Massachusetts Institute of Technology.

[3] Lister, Ray, Fidge, Colin J., & Teague, Donna M. (2009). Further evidence of a relationship between explaining, tracing and writing skills in introductory programming. In *Proceedings of the 2009 ACM SIGCSE Annual Conference on Innovation and Technology in Computer Science Education, Association for Computing Machinery*, Paris, France, 161-165.

[4] Mayer, R. E. 1977. *The Sequencing of Instruction and the concept of Assimilation-To-Schema, Instructional Science.* 6, 369-388.

[5] Mosemann, R., and Wiedenbeck, S. 2001. Navigation and comprehension of programs by novice programmers. *Proceedings 9th International Workshop on Program Comprehension (IWPC 2001)*, 79–88.

[6] Murphy, L., Fitzgerald, S., Lister, R.F., and McCauley, R. 2012. Ability to 'explain in plain English' linked to proficiency in computer-based programming, In *Proceedings of the 9th annual International Conference on Education Research (ICER '12)*. ACM, New York, NY, USA, 111-118. DOI= http://doi.acm.org/10.1145/2361276.2361299.

[7] Paas, F., Renkl, A. & Sweller, J. 2004. Cognitive load theory: Instructional implications of the interaction between information structures and cognitive architecture. *Instructional Science, 32*, 1-8.

[8] Pattis, R.E.1981. *Karel the Robot: A Gentle Introduction to the Art of Programming.* New York, NY, USA: John Wiley & Sons, Inc.

[9] Perkins, D., Hancock, C., Hobbs, R., Martin, F. and Simmons, R. 1989. Conditions of learning in novice programming, in `Studying the Novice Programmer', Lawrence Erlbaum Associates, New Jersey, 261-279.

[10] Reges, S. 2006. Back to basics in CS1 and CS2. In *Proceedings of the 37th SIGCSE technical symposium on Computer science education (SIGCSE '06)*. ACM, New York, NY, USA, 293-297. DOI= http://doi.acm.org/10.1145/1121341.1121432.

[11] Spencer, K. 1991. *The Psychology of Educational Technology and Instructional Media*, Liverpool, United Writers Press.

[12] Teague, D. Corney, M., Ahadi, A. and Lister, R. 2013. A Qualitative Think Aloud Study of the Early Neo-Piagetian Stages of Reasoning in Novice Programmers. In *Proceedings of the 15th Australasian Computing Education Conference (ACE 2013)*, Adelaide, Australia. CRPIT, 136, ACS, 87-95.

[13] van Someren, M. W., Bartnard, Y .F., and Sandberg, J. A. C. 1994. *The think Aloud Method: A practical guide to modelling cognitive processes.* Academic Press, London.

[14] Vygotsky, L. S. 1978. *Mind in society: The development of higher psychological processes.* Cambridge, MA: Harvard University Press.

[15] Wood, D., Bruner, J. S. and Ross, G. 1976. *J. Child Psychol. Psychiat.,* 17, 89-100.

Programming: Reading, Writing And Reversing

Donna Teague
Queensland University of Technology
Brisbane, Qld, Australia
d.teague@qut.edu.au

Raymond Lister
University of Technology, Sydney
Sydney NSW Australia
raymond.lister@uts.edu.au

ABSTRACT

In this paper, we look at the concept of *reversibility*, that is, negating opposites, counterbalances, and actions that can be reversed. Piaget identified reversibility as an indicator of the ability to reason at a concrete operational level. We investigate to what degree novice programmers manifest the ability to work with this concept of reversibility by providing them with a small piece of code and then asking them to write code that undoes the effect of that code. On testing entire cohorts of students in their first year of learning to program, we found an overwhelming majority of them could not cope with such a concept. We then conducted think aloud studies of novices where we observed them working on this task and analyzed their contrasting abilities to deal with it. The results of this study demonstrate the need for better understanding our students' reasoning abilities, and a teaching model aimed at that level of reality.

Categories and Subject Descriptors

K.3 [**Computers & Education**]: Computer & Information Science Education – *Computer Science Education*

General Terms

Measurement, Performance, Experimentation, Human Factors

Keywords

Neo-Piagetian theory, programming, novice programmers, think aloud, reversibility.

1. INTRODUCTION

Piaget used an experiment using a bottle of coloured water which he rotated at various angles under cover so only the outline of the bottle could be seen. He asked children to draw the changing water level as he rotated the bottle back and forth, hence testing their understanding of the effect of reversing a process or effect.

We can think of *reversibility* in a programming context as cancelling an effect by reversing the steps in order to revert to an original state. We followed Lister's [4] suggestion of providing code that rotates the values in an array in one direction with the task being to write code that rotates the values in the opposite direction, as shown in Figure 1. As the programming languages varied between semester offerings of our units, some students completed these exercises in C#, rather than Python (see C# solution in Figure 2). At our institution, we tested students' ability to reason about reversibility in this way, across several cohorts. Our students were introduced to lists and indexing in week 2 of semester, and start working with loops by week 5.

The purpose of the block of code below is to take a list of `numbers` containing five integers and to move all elements of the list one place to the ***right***, with the ***rightmost*** element moving around to the ***leftmost*** position.

```
temp = numbers[len(numbers) - 1]
for index in range(len(numbers) - 1, 0, -1):
    numbers [index] = numbers [index - 1]
numbers [0] = temp
```

For example if `numbers` initially has the value `[1,2,3,4,5]` then after the code has executed, it would contain `[5,1,2,3,4]`. If we were to show the effect of moving all the elements of a list in this way in a diagram, it would look something like this:

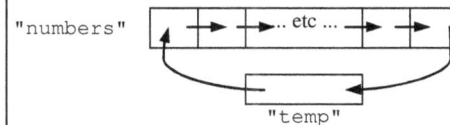

Note that `range(len(numbers)-1,0,-1)` produces a list containing numbers from one less than the length of the list down to one. For example for `numbers` defined above, the following list would be produced `[4,3,2,1]`.

Write Python code that does the opposite of the above code. That is, write code to move all elements of the list `numbers` one place to the ***left***, with the ***leftmost*** element being moved to the ***rightmost*** position.

Sample Python Solution:
```
temp = numbers [0]
for index in range (len(numbers) -1):
    numbers [index] = numbers [index + 1]
numbers [len(numbers) - 1] = temp
```

Figure 1: Reversibility Task – Python

Sample C# Solution:
```
int temp = values[0];
for (int i = 0; i < values.Length -1; i++)
    values[i] = values[i + 1];
values[values.Length - 1] = temp;
```

Figure 2: Reversibility Task - C# Sample Solution

We tested our students with this task at the end of each of our first and second programming units and we were astounded by the consistently poor results (see Table 1 below). In fact, after an additional semester of learning programming, students were no more likely to be able to complete this task. We had simply asked them to modify some relatively familiar code to change its functionality—and they could not. The *best* results achieved by any of our cohorts was 68% incorrect answers. That is, less than a third could write that code.

Table 1: Cohort Testing of Reversibility Task

Weeks of programming instruction completed	Number of students	Percentage wrong
12	71	92%
12	322	68%
24	68	79%
24	60	85%
20	82	78%

While grading these tasks we ignored minor syntax issues like missing brackets or colons, misplaced indenting, inconsistent variable names etc. However, the 5 criteria which we deemed necessary in order to mark as correct were:

a) line 1: correct value stored in temporary variable
b) line 2: correct `for` loop structure
c) lines 2 & 3: use of valid range of subscripts
d) line 3: correct rotation direction
e) line 4: correct relocation of temporarily stored value

To understand why so many students could not correctly complete a task which we thought was relatively simple, we called for volunteer students to take part in studies where we gave them this reversibility task to complete while thinking aloud. We then interpreted our data using the neo-Piagetian theoretical framework.

2. NEO-PIAGETIAN STAGES

Neo-Piagetian theory was developed as a response to problems identified in classical Piagetian theory. Both classical and neo-Piagetian theories describe cognitive development in terms of sequential, cumulative stages. However, unlike classical Piagetian theory, Neo-Piagetian theory is not age-related and applies equally to adults. Furthermore neo-Piagetian theory describes cognitive development as a person acquires knowledge in a specific domain. The cognitive structures become more complex through exposure in the domain, which explains why someone is capable of reasoning at different levels of abstraction in two different domains (e.g. Math and literature). Lister [4] proposed that these stages are evident in the novice programmer.

At the least mature stage, *sensorimotor*, there are plenty of misconceptions about programming which are not necessarily applied consistently. The sensorimotor programmer at best possesses fragile domain knowledge as disjointed snippets which he finds difficult to piece together in any satisfactory manner. At this stage the novice is focused on the mechanics and syntax of the language, and tasks like tracing code require considerable cognitive effort. He manipulates code by trial and error.

At the next more mature stage, *preoperational*, a novice is able to more reliably trace code, but any attempt to reason about it is only intuitive. Misconceptions that remain are at least applied consistently. A preoperational novice writes and traces code with heavy reliance on and reference to specific values. They are incapable at this stage of seeing a relationship between different parts of code, or of seeing how the *parts* fit into the *whole*. A novice at this stage does not really understand actions so their thinking is dominated by static images rather than mental representations of change [2]. In terms of the reversibility problem in Figure 1 and Figure 2, a preoperational novice does not immediately see the relationship between the code they were given and the code they must write. While preoperational students may eventually produce a correct solution to this problem, they will only do so after considerable effort.

By the time a novice programmer reaches the *concrete operational* stage, they are able to start reasoning at a more abstract level. Tracing for understanding and verification of code can be short-circuited because they are now capable of reasoning about code in abstract, rather than specific, terms. Concrete operational novices have developed for the first time an ability to see the *whole* and its *parts* at the same time. It is also at this stage that we are capable of conceiving the idea of inverse, nullifying actions that change something back to its original state [1]. In terms of the reversibility problem in Figure 1 and Figure 2 the concrete operational novice *does* see an immediate relationship between the code they were given and the code they must write. They can usually write their answer without hesitation.

We do not however suggest that there is necessarily a quantum leap from one stage to the next, or that we can classify novices as being at one particular stage of development. Rather than a one-way staircase model of development, we adopt the overlapping wave metaphor of Siegler [7], where as a person acquires knowledge and skills in a new cognitive domain, they exhibit a changing mix of reasoning strategies from different stages. Firstly they reason predominantly at a sensorimotor level but as they build schemas and develop skills in the domain they reason less at that level and more at the next more mature level, and so on. In this way, multiple ways of reasoning can coexist.

3. THINK ALOUD STUDIES

Using this neo-Piagetian framework we gathered think aloud data from students as they completed the exercise in either Figure 1 or Figure 2 to help us understand why many students could not reverse the effects of a piece of code.

3.1 Think Aloud Results

We discovered that our think aloud students exhibited behaviours representing a broad range of neo-Piagetian stages, but that a student's cognitive maturity was not necessarily commensurate with the amount of progress they had made through their programming course. We now focus on a small yet representative selection of these students, summarized in Table 2. We have chosen three students who were clearly demonstrating characteristics of one of the first three neo-Piagetian stages (sensorimotor, preoperational or concrete operational), and one that seemed to be on the cusp of progressing from preoperational to concrete operational. For each student, Table 2 shows the aggregate number of weeks they have completed of programming instruction.

Table 2: Think Aloud Performance on Reversibility Task

Alias	Weeks of instruction	Time taken (m:s)	Neo-Piagetian Stage
S1	45	3:51	Concrete
S2	11	14:58	Preop-Concrete
S3	9	13:20	Preoperational
S4	14	11:15	Sensorimotor

3.2 Analysis of Think Alouds

In this section we dissect the think aloud transcripts of those four sessions, which illustrate why students struggle with this reversibility problem. We document these excerpts in a format similar to that used by Lewis [3] and more recently by Teague and Lister [8] who separated the interview data from its analysis in order to help the reader better follow the participant's progress during the session.

Pauses in speech are marked "...", as are placeholders for deleted utterances which we deemed unnecessary for inclusion as those utterances add nothing to the context of the think aloud session.

We start our think aloud sessions with one which exemplifies a concrete operational student, or in other words, a student capable of operating at a fairly mature level.

3.2.1 S1 - Concrete – Week 45: C#

3.2.1.1 Summary

S1 had little difficulty completing this task. He read the question and jumped straight into writing his solution. He completed the exercise in less than 4 minutes.

3.2.1.2 Data

S1 started writing his solution by copying the given code. Before completing the first line he realized he had copied too much (i.e. the index of the rightmost element of the array) and immediately self-corrected. As he changed the subscript to 0, as shown in Figure 3, he said:

S1: *I want ... to get... 0 because we want the first thing to be at the end*

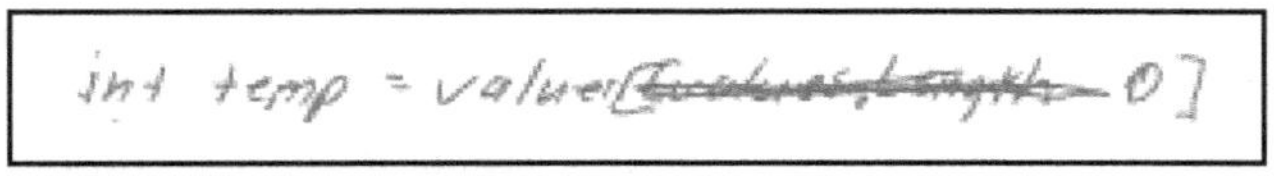

Figure 3: S1 - Temporary storage of first element [*correct*]

He then completed the two lines of the for loop, correctly, without hesitation, as shown in Figure 4. S1 gave an abstract explanation of the reassignment of values which would affect movement in the correct direction:

S1: *... and now I simply grab what is one ahead of it and move it back 1 so ... values ... at i is assigned ... values at ... i plus 1 which is going to the next one over ....*

Figure 4: S1 – Loop header and body [*correct*]

He then completed the final line, as shown in Figure 5, and uttered:

S1: *to finish it all off we just update the last one ... which is ... values dot um ... length minus 1 ... is assigned temp.*

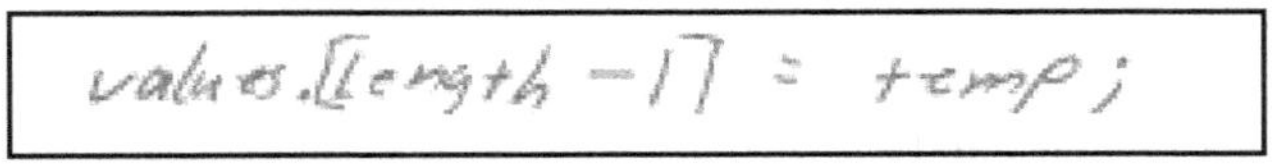

Figure 5: S1 - Relocation of temporary value [*correct, except for minor syntax issue (missing array name)*]

3.2.1.3 Analysis

S1 illustrates what most computer educators expect from their students. The abstract manner in which S1 described code is consistent with someone operating at the concrete operational level. He does not rely on tracing with specific values in variables or specific indexes in order to understand code, nor does he refer to specific values when writing code.

3.2.2 S2 – Preop-Concrete – Week 11: Python

3.2.2.1 Summary

S2 read the question text very slowly, then partially copied the given code and started annotating it. He drew arrows to indicate the direction of movement of the values and added specific values with which to trace that movement. After taking more than four and a half minutes to do this, he started writing his solution. He used diagrams and specific values to partially trace his code and, except for an off-by-one error, his final solution was correct. He articulated that he found the exercise troublesome. He had taken nearly 15 minutes.

3.2.2.2 Data

On reading the first line of the given code S2 immediately articulated an abstraction:

S2: *Temp equals list of numbers ... at a place one before the end*

This abstraction was off-by-one, yet a note he wrote soon after (see Figure 6) was accurate.

Figure 6: S2 - Abstraction of temporary storage in given code

He read the for loop structure and was temporarily troubled by the syntax of the Python range function for which the interviewer supplied an explanation. However soon after reading and copying down the loop, he summarized its purpose:

S2: *So that moves everything over one way*

He then drew two arrows pointing to the right (see Figure 7), correctly indicating the direction of that movement.

Figure 7: S2 - Annotation of given code

S2 started writing his code for the solution, quickly self-correcting any errors. As shown in Figure 8, he left blank the range of indexes to be iterated over, as well as the index of the value to be assigned inside the loop. He drew circles around both these blank parts after saying:

S2: *... figure that out later*

He completed the storage of the first value to temp and its subsequent reassignment into the last element without hesitation.

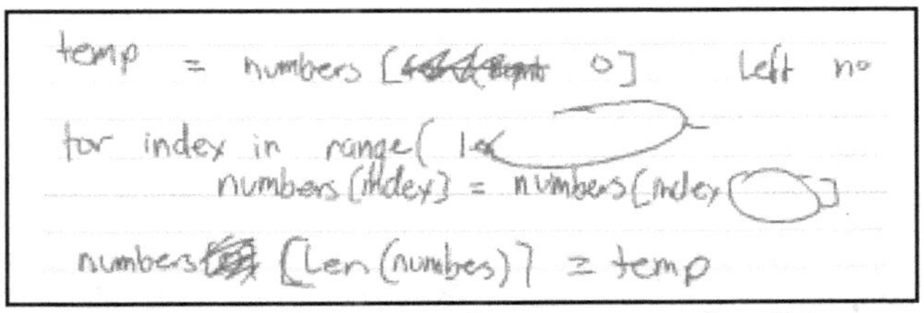

Figure 8: S2 - Initial attempt [*correct, except for off-by-one error, and incomplete*]

S2 said that he had forgotten the syntax of the loop structure so the interviewer intervened with syntactic help. Then S2 contemplated the assignment statement inside the loop:

S2: *It's really frustrating now because it's an easy one ... so if it's on 4, it'll put ... 3 in 4's spot but I want to put 4 in 3's spot ... so if we go the other way ... want to ... make 0 go to 1, make 1 go to 2 ... no that's what's happening isn't it already.*

The interviewer then suggested that he draw a diagram. His first diagram shown in Figure 9 reflected the given code with the addition of index numbers 4 and 3.

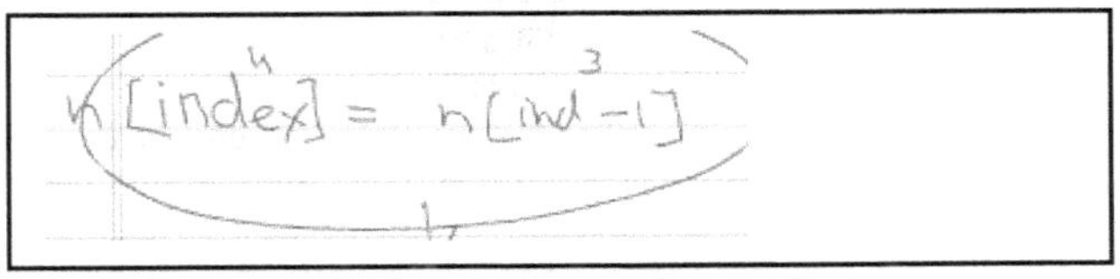

Figure 9: S2 - Annotation of given code

S2: *so if it's 4 ... so in place 4 we want 3 ... that's what the original does*

He then drew (see Figure 10) what he wanted his solution to do.

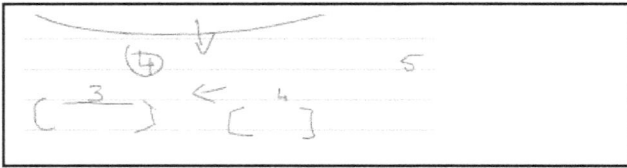

Figure 10: S2 - Annotation of proposed code

S2: *I want ... if it's 4 ... I replace 3 ... of index ... to have ... place 4's value ... is that right [pause 12 seconds] 3 ... that's moving it left ... so that's what I want.*

S2 was able to then complete the code which was correct, apart from two off-by-one errors.

S2: *I had a lot of trouble with that one*

3.2.2.3 Analysis

S2 completed the temporary storage of the end value and its reassignment at the other end before completing the loop. Once he had determined the indexes involved in the reassignment, he was able to complete the loop header, but he was only able to resolve this uncertainty with the use of diagrams and specific index values.

Unlike S1 who used no specific values while reasoning about the given code or writing his solution, S2's reliance on specific values to formulate code is indicative of preoperational thinking. However, those operating at a *purely* preoperational level also find it necessary to trace code (or an algorithm) in its entirety, whereas S2 was manifesting nascent concrete operational skills by needing only a *partial* trace of the movement of values for verification.

3.2.3 S3 –Preoperational – Week 9: Python

3.2.3.1 Summary

S3 took nearly 13 and a half minutes to complete this task.

She wrote an initial solution which contained a correct `for` loop (except for off-by-one error) but which also contained the first and last line which were copied from the given code. She then corrected the first and last lines.

3.2.3.2 Data

S3 did not read the question out loud. She simply said enigmatically:

S3: *list of numbers*

After a long pause (68 seconds) she wrote her first line of code and then after another long pause (57 seconds) annotated her code by writing numbers above that line (see Figure 11).

Figure 11: S3 - Temporary storage [*incorrect*]

After yet another pause (34 seconds) she started writing the `for` loop, as shown in Figure 12. She hesitated when deciding the range of the iteration but finally settled on it iterating from index 1 to the end of the array.

Figure 12: S3 - Loop structure [*correct*]

S3 then wrote the body of the `for` loop as shown in Figure 13. However this line of code and the `for` loop header in combination produce an off-by-one error.

Figure 13: S3 - Loop body [*correct, in isolation, except for minor syntax issue (missing bracket)*]

Then she wrote an incorrect version of the final line of her code as shown in Figure 14.

Figure 14: S3 - Relocation of temp value [*incorrect*]

After a long pause of over 5 minutes, she was prompted by the interviewer to talk about what she was thinking.

S3: *Um ... so I'm just trying to work out the ... temp variable, make sure that I've got it picking up the right number ... equals ... numbers um ... [sigh] so just going to change that to ... 0 ... have to pick up the 5*

As she completed this utterance and changed her code, she also added a comment to her first line (see Figure 15).

Figure 15: S3 – Revised temporary storage [*correct, but the comment refers to a specific set of data values*]

S3 re-read the loop structure she had written, and reasoned about its correctness:

S3: *so skipping the first number in the list ... to um the end of the list ... the index 0 here um ... would be 1 equals numbers at the index plus 1 so in this case ... the first time around ... we're going to get ... 1 ... and then the second time around it will be 1 so we'll get 2 ... and 3 and then 4*

She wrote "1,2,3,4" in the body of the loop as a comment as shown in Figure 16.

Figure 16: S3 - Commented loop body [*correct, except the comment refers to specific data values*]

S3: *cross that out because that doesn't work ... in range ... it's already got the plus 1*

After the above utterance, she then changed her loop to correct the off-by-one error.

S3: *and then ... numbers ... mm*

S3 paused for 54 seconds.

S3: *I've done it wrong [laugh] That's alright ... just leave me with it ... I'll work it out*

S3 then altered her last line of code as shown in Figure 17.

Figure 17: S3 - Revised relocation of temporary value [*correct, except for off-by-one error*]

S3 then reviewed her first line of code and added to the comment (see Figure 18).

S3: *ok so 1 2 3 4 ... equals ... temp is 5*

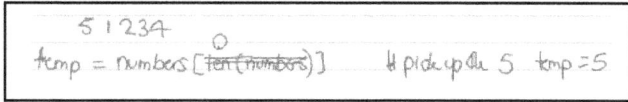

Figure 18: S3 - Revised comment

S3: *i'm saying its 5 ... so if... index is 1 it's going to be ... index is 0 ... going to be 1 ... 1 2 3 4 ... gets around to 5*

3.2.3.3 Analysis

In her initial solution, S3's first and last lines of code were incorrect in that they moved the rightmost element to the leftmost position, while her loop was moving values from left to right. This is a classic indication of preoperational thinking, where two pieces of the code are written which are conceptually incompatible.

S3 focused on the salient aspect of the task. That is, she focused on the reversal of the direction of rotation. This is in contrast to S2's approach which saw him initially focus on the temporary storage and relocation of the first value. In both cases however, the novices focused on detail which obscured the big picture. This behaviour is characteristic of preoperational reasoning.

While S3 did work with specific values including annotations to her code, her focus was frequently upon the collective direction of movement of those values. Thus she was reasoning at a slightly higher level than the movement of a single specific value at a time, but at a much lower level than S1 who traced abstractly.

3.2.4 S4 - Sensorimotor – Week 14: Python

3.2.4.1 Summary

S4 had previously attempted this exercise two weeks prior to this session. At that earlier session, his solution had amounted to little more than a near-copy of the given code, except for removing the minus operator from the first line, which he believed to be responsible for the direction of rotation.

In the session detailed here, he struggled to even trace the code given in the question, which explains why he had previously not been able to write the reversal. He talked about the code in terms of individual symbols, with the focus clearly on syntax. S4 was unable to offer much explanation about the purpose of the code. He simply reiterated the question text.

3.2.4.2 Data

S4 read the first line of given code, but he gave an incorrect articulation of the code's purpose:

S4: *numbers in brackets length of numbers minus 1 is assigned to temp ...so what's really being assigned is ... ah ... I guess what was said up the top ... well moving 5 one [place] to the ... right most number to the left most position*

The interviewer gave S4 a trace table with three columns headed `temp`, `index` and `numbers`. The initial value of `numbers` was recorded for him by the interviewer as "[1,2,3,4,5]". No other data values were provided. When asked to trace the given code, he said:

S4: *So numbers, length of numbers minus 1, so I think, ... well one off the length of numbers could mean there's only four numbers ... soooo ... that would be 1,2,3,4.*

Figure 19 shows what he then wrote in the trace table. Note that he has placed a list of values in the variable `temp` which indicates a misconception about the first line of code.

Figure 19: S4 - trace table line 1 [*incorrect*]

He continued with the trace as shown in Figure 20. Note that S4 incorrectly updated the temp variable (which is not even mentioned in the `for` loop) instead of the `numbers` list.

Figure 20: S4 - trace table complete

S4's think aloud session lasted for more than 11 minutes and the entire session consisted of attempting to trace the given code. He did not attempt to write a solution.

3.2.4.3 Analysis

S4 read the code symbol by symbol: *"numbers in brackets length of numbers minus 1"*. He did not provide any interpretation of the code or embellish on its purpose at all. Contrast that with S2 who articulated the same line as *"numbers ... at a place one before the end"*. S4 was not reasoning about the code at all, let alone as a whole. He was, as a child would when reading words, not connecting them into sentences. This behaviour is representative of someone at the sensorimotor stage of development.

S4 manifested a number of misconceptions, such as assigning a list to the variable `temp` and updating `temp` within the loop.

4. CONCLUSION

Listening to our think aloud students articulate about code provides evidence about their ability to reason abstractly. S4 used only specific values when he referred to elements and indexes in the array. S3 used specific values for both indexes and list elements as she developed her code. S2 referred to specific index numbers when he discussed the movement of values, but had the ability to talk purely in abstract terms (*"Temp equals list of numbers ... at a place one before the end"*). S1 mostly reasoned in the abstract (*"grab what is one ahead of it and move it back"*).

There is stark contrast between the performance of S4 and any of the other think aloud participants. Readers might conclude that this student showed little innate ability for programming, and that he would have most likely failed to progress much further in Computer Science studies. Conversely, S1 possessed exactly those abstract reasoning skills that would allow him to master programming at a high level. In fact, S4 is the same student as S1! The think aloud sessions with this student occurred one year apart.

Novice programmers show increased competencies with programming tasks as their ability to reason abstractly matures. But why is it that some of our students are working at such an immature level of abstract reasoning for so long? We believe that many students remain at the sensorimotor and preoperational levels because all the instruction they receive is at the concrete operational level. In other words, as Shayer [6] put it:

Think hard about the ways that your target students can process reality, and give them learning experiences which are accessible to them.

Students at the earlier sensorimotor and pre-operational stages require exposure to programming tasks *at those levels* before they can be expected to reason abstractly about programming. Vygotsky's [9] theory of "zone of proximal development" might suggest pushing the boundaries of students' current ability to reason, but to expect students to work with concepts as yet *far* out of their cognitive reach may also retard their progress by depleting both their confidence and motivation.

5. PEDAGOGICAL IMPLICATIONS

S1 represents the students to which we currently teach: students who are operating comfortably at the concrete operational level. It is at this stage when they can reason abstractly and work with concepts like reversibility. They are capable of dealing with non-trivial programming tasks.

How should we teach students at the preoperational level like S2 and S3? These two are probably more representative of our students. They are reliant on specific values to reason about code and require exposure to small tasks which are constituted from a minimal number of parts.

Other studies have found a relationship between reading and explaining skills and the ability to write code ([10], [11], [12]). Tracing code requires students to draw on the programming knowledge they accumulated at the sensorimotor level and explaining the purpose of code forces them to conceive a 'big picture', rather than remain focused on individual lines of code. Therefore, the progression of preoperational students into more mature concrete operational reasoning could be scaffolded with a sequence of these types of tasks that culminate in something like the reversibility question in Figure 1 and Figure 2.

... knowledge is not at all the same thing as making a figurative copy of reality for oneself, but that it invariably consists in operative processes leading to a transformation of reality, either in actions or in thought ... [5].

How then should we teach students at the sensorimotor level, like S4? These students have little hope of progressing until the misconceptions have been addressed. Many of these misconceptions can be identified and eliminated by a vigilant tutor or TA, but if left untendered can fester into a quagmire of confusion and frustration. Sensorimotor novices should be exposed to only very small tasks with single elements on which to concentrate. We believe that at the sensorimotor level in particular, greater emphasis should be placed on reading and tracing code until misconceptions have been addressed. It is only then that students can be expected to start constructing their own snippets of code.

It is yet unknown how long it takes to progress from one neo-Piagetian stage to the next, but it is clear from this research that it is different for every student. What we do know is that the stages are sequential and cumulative. Therefore, we must allow students to master programming skills using the type of reasoning indicative of the earlier stages of development before exposing them to significantly more abstract concepts. The pedagogical challenge now is in the identification of students' operational levels so we can facilitate a match of the appropriate levels with the learning material.

The reader may well be inclined to discount our results as unique to our institution. However, we challenge such academics to examine their own students' ability to solve the same problem and report their findings.

6. ACKNOWLEDGMENTS

We would very much like to thank the students who took part in this study and the academics who allowed us to test their cohorts of students. In particular our gratitude goes to the think aloud participants who attended each week, especially those who participated for multiple teaching periods.

7. REFERENCES

[1] Flavell, J. H. (1977). *Cognitive Development*. Englewood Cliffs, NJ: Prentice Hall.

[2] Huber, L. N. (1988). Computer Learning Through Piaget's Eyes. *Classroom Computer Learning, 6*(2), 39-43.

[3] Lewis, C. M. (2012). *The importance of students' attention to program state: a case study of debugging behavior*. Paper presented at the 9th Annual International Conference on International Computing Education Research (ICER 2012), Auckland, New Zealand.

[4] Lister, R. (2011). *Concrete and Other Neo-Piagetian Forms of Reasoning in the Novice Programmer*. Paper presented at the 13th Australasian Computer Education Conference (ACE 2011), Perth, WA.

[5] Piaget, J. (1974). *Science of Education and the Psychology of the Child*: Grossman. pp 72.

[6] Shayer, M. (1987). Neo-Piagetian Theories and Educational Practice. *International Journal of Psychology, 22*(5-6), 751-772.

[7] Siegler, R. S. (1996). *Emerging Minds*. Oxford: Oxford University Press.

[8] Teague, D., & Lister, R. (2014). *Manifestations of Preoperational Reasoning on Similar Programming Tasks*. Paper presented at the Australasian Computing Education Conference (ACE 2014), Auckland, New Zealand.

[9] Vygotsky, L. S. (1978). *Mind in society: The development of higher pyshcological processes*. Cambridge, MA: Harvard University Press.

[10] Lister, R., Adams, E. S., Fitzgerald, S., Fone, W., Hamer, J., Lindholm, M., et al (2004). *A Multi-National Study of Reading and Tracing Skills in Novice Programmers*. SIGSCE Bulletin, 36(4), 119-150.

[11] Philpott, A., Robbins, P., & Whalley, J. (2007). *Accessing the Steps on the Road to Relational Thinking*. Paper presented at the 20th Annual Conference of the National Advisory Committee on Computing Qualifications (NACCQ'07), Port Nelson, New Zeland.

[12] Lopez, M., Whalley, J., Robbins, P., & Lister, R. (2008). *Relationships between Reading, Tracing and Writing Skills in Introductory Programming*. Paper presented at the 4th Annual International Conference on International Computing Education Research (ICER 2008), Sydney, Australia.

Identifying Computer Science Self-Regulated Learning Strategies

Katrina Falkner, Rebecca Vivian and Nickolas J.G. Falkner
School of Computer Science, University of Adelaide
Adelaide, SA, Australia, 5005
katrina.falkner@adelaide.edu.au, rebecca.vivian@adelaide.edu.au,
nickolas.falkner@adelaide.edu.au

ABSTRACT

Computer Science students struggle to develop fundamental programming skills and software development processes. Crucial to successful mastery is the development of discipline specific cognitive and metacognitive skills, including self-regulation. We can assist our students in the process of reflection and self-regulation by identifying and articulating successful self-regulated learning strategies for specific discipline contexts. However, in order to do so, we must develop an understanding of those discipline-specific strategies that are successful and can be readily adopted by students.

In this paper, we analyse student reflections from an introductory software development course, identifying the usage of self-regulated learning strategies that are either specific to the software development domain, or articulated in that context. This study assists in the understanding of how Computer Science students develop learning skill within the discipline, and provides examples to guide the development of scaffolding activities to assist learning development.

Categories and Subject Descriptors

K.3.2 [**Computing Milieux**]: Computers and Education-Computer and Information Science Education

General Terms

Human Factors

Keywords

Computer Science Education, Self-regulation strategies

1. INTRODUCTION

Introductory programming courses pose many challenges for students, as a large number enter Computer Science (CS) programs with little or no prior discipline experience. Students are required to master a wide range of discipline, cognitive and metacognitive skills and studies show that our

students continue to struggle with mastering these skills, both in terms of the development of programming skills and awareness and mastery of the software development process [8, 7]. In order to be successful, students need the required discipline knowledge as well as strategies for cognitive development and self-regulation [20]; Sheard et al [15] highlight the fact that development of deep learning strategies, self-regulation, abstract thinking and metacognitive strategies are vital in order to assist students in achieving success. A self-regulating student will set their goals, marshal their resources and then manage their time effectively [14] - without this fundamental level of metacognition they cannot direct their knowledge in a useful and constructive manner.

A significant aspect in the development of self-regulating learning (SRL) strategies is the ability to monitor and reflect upon those strategies within a discipline context, enabling the individual to identify their success or failure, identify strategies to apply in specific contexts and develop new strategies [3, 18]. Allwood [1] identifies that novices tend to use more general strategies rather than the more powerful specialised strategies employed by experts. The transition from novice to expert is assisted by reflection on prior successes and failures [13], followed by analysis of potential areas for improvement. Before we can assist our students in the process of reflection and self-regulation, we must identify and articulate successful SRL strategies for the CS context [6]. Therefore, we must develop an understanding of those discipline specific strategies that can be successfully learnt and adopted by students [10].

In this paper, we analyse students' reflections on their SRL processes as applied to introductory software development. Using a grounded theory model of qualitative analysis, we are able to identify SRL strategies that are specific to CS, expressed in the students' own words and relative to their own experiences. In our previous work, we establish that students who have a less developed understanding of software development and are less successful in their programming activities have a higher reliance upon generic self-regulatory mechanisms, and are unable to articulate discipline-specific techniques to improve their processes. In this paper, we extend this work through a detailed analysis of the nature of these discipline-specific SRL strategies and how these strategies contribute to their learning.

We adopt a mixed methods approach to our study, combining qualitative and quantitative data collection, driven by grounded theory [19], using an open coding process to analyse and identify representative strategies within our case study. In our study, 85 students, who were enrolled in an introductory software development course, participated in a multi-part reflection process, documenting their software development and learning processes and their perceived successes and failures. We identify that while some students are able to articulate mature SRL strategies that are embedded within their discipline, others struggle to understand how their learning may be adapted to the specific requirements of their discipline. In our conclusions, we propose the need for targeted scaffolding to address this issue.

2. RELATED WORK

Zimmerman [20] defines self-regulated learners as those that 'plan, set goals, organise, self-monitor and self-evaluate'. Research suggests that the development of SRL strategies is a complex issue, associated with the perceived purpose of engagement with the activity, the student's self-perception of their ability, and the situated context of the activity - these three factors impact upon the self-regulation strategies that the student then considers relevant for application [9]. Lichtinger and Kaplan [6] call for the identification of domain and context-specific purposes of engagement, and the articulation of types of SRL strategies that would be desirable for students within that domain. Further, the development of effective domain-specific SRL strategies, such as domain-based design and planning, can assist in the application and development of other SRL strategies [16].

Novices in any area lack the detailed, well-organised domain knowledge that is necessary to produce effective problem solving processes - this may be seen in software development as opportunistic and arbitrary design and implementation [11]. Novice problem solvers struggle to understand conceptually difficult problems, due in part to their lack of deep discipline knowledge, and tend to approach the problem using known techniques from their knowledge of programming languages, and a process of 'impasses and local repairs' [16]. As they are unskilled in planning, novices also tend to delay planning relevant to the problem solving process itself until it is absolutely necessary, imposing further delays in their development of that skill set.

There has been considerable work exploring mental models and learning strategies associated with introductory programming, although little explicitly addresses SRL strategies applicable to the software development process itself. Bergin et al [2] explore the relationship between SRL and introductory programming performance, specifically the use of metacognitive strategies, finding that students who perform well in programming tasks also exhibit frequent use of metacognitive behaviours. Violet [17] explores the co-operative development of metacognitive strategies for an introductory computer science course, involving students in both the development of the strategy and the identification of modelling and coaching procedures designed to guide students through the strategy. The strategy introduced builds upon theories of social constructivism and cognitive development, and follows a simple five-step process of software design. They found that this instructional approach resulted in significant changes in students' cognitive learning outcomes.

Caruso et al [4] explore a grounded theory analysis of students' reflections on their software development process, identifying a focus on non-discipline aspects of self-regulation and an inability to develop appropriate plans for improving their SRL strategies. Hanks et al [5] identify similar results in a 'saying is believing' experiment where students completing a course on introductory programming were asked to provide advice for the next cohort. Hanks et al report a combination of general advice (63%), attitudinal advice (34%) and programming-specific advice (23%), identifying a relative dearth of work on discipline-specific strategy.

3. METHODOLOGY

In this paper, we undertake a quantitative and qualitative analysis of student reflections on their software development processes and SRL strategies in order to identify those strategies that are specific to CS. We explore the identification of such strategies within a case study of an introductory software development course. The research question that we ask is: *what SRL strategies do first-year programming students articulate as using in programming assignments and which are specific to CS?*

3.1 Research Method

An instrumental case study was a suitable approach for answering our research question as it allows us to use a particular case as an illustration to identify and elaborate SRL strategies within software development. Case studies capture the complexities of a phenomenon; such detailed observations cannot be captured in surveys or experimental designs [12]. Although still a small sample size, the number of participants in our study, 85, is sufficient, with samples sizes for qualitative research ranging from 1 to 99, with an average sample size of 22.

This project has adopted a mixed-method case study design where both quantitative and qualitative data were collected. The data were subjected to grounded theory analysis, starting with a process of open coding, before proceeding to axial coding. Grounded theory involves the establishment of a coding framework and analysis environment derived from the data itself. Grounded theory differs from other types of qualitative analysis in that a specific, structured coding framework is not employed. The first stage in grounded theory development is open coding, where the data is broken down into distinct segments in order to obtain the full collection of ideas and concepts present in the data, without regard to how it will be used. Subsequently, axial coding is employed, where the coding framework developed during the open coding stage is refined and reorganised into specific categories, informed by theoretical frameworks and comparison within the data. There are significant advantages in the adoption of a grounded theory approach, in contrast to directed content analysis with an established coding framework, including removing the potential to force fit observations into existing categories and misclassification. However, we subsequently align our coding framework with that of Zimmerman [20] in order to aid comparison.

The case considered in this research project is an introductory software development course at the University of X. Students within this course have completed 1-2 prior programming courses, providing them with competencies in the application and tracing of fundamental programming constructs, and design skills within small scale problem solving. The learning objectives for this course include awareness and application of simple data structures, related algorithms and algorithm complexity, and initial experiences in medium-scale problem solving and software engineering. Students are assessed on the functional outcome of their programming assignments, and their process, via design documents and

Table 1: CS-specific SRL strategies and their indicated frequency (total count = 255).

Category	Freq	%Freq
Development Process	255	54.5%
Use diagrams to describe or explain design	119	25.4%
Use design to understand problem or code	45	9.6%
Develop design before coding	22	4.7%
Document design or code for future use	20	4.3%
Validate design	18	3.9%
Comprehensive test cases	15	3.2%
Develop design concurrently with coding	9	1.9%
Develop design after coding	4	0.9%
Use design principles or standards	3	0.6%
Decompose problem	53	16.24%
Use decomposition to develop testing strategy	53	11.9%
Create plan from design	20	4.49%
Time Management	72	15.4%
Prioritisation	63	13.5%
Design as aid to time management	8	1.7%
Allocate time for prototyping	1	0.2%
Assess Difficulty	54	11.5%
Algorithm complexity	23	4.9%
Prototyping and experimentation	12	2.6%
Use design to assess difficulty	10	2.1%
Number of concepts, stages or components	7	1.5%
Need for design driven by complexity	2	0.4%
Build Knowledge	10	2.2%
Practice writing code	10	2.2%

Table 2: General SRL strategies and their indicated frequency (total count = 455).

Strategy	Freq	%Freq
Assess Difficulty	127	27.9%
Identify new knowledge that is needed	42	9.2%
Assess own ability	24	5.3%
Assess difficulty - no specific strategy	23	5.1%
Understand question	20	4.4%
Compare with previous	12	2.6%
Specification – length, assessment	5	1.1%
Ask friends	1	0.2%
Time Management	105	23.1%
Fixed timetable - sufficient	59	13.0%
Time Estimation	26	5.7%
Overestimate time	16	3.5%
Time management - no specific strategy	4	0.9%
Build Knowledge	81	17.8%
Talk to friends or lecturers	42	9.2%
Access resources	39	8.6%
Decompose problem	72	15.8%
Create plan from specification	58	12.7%
Decompose - no specific strategy	12	2.6%
Frequent accomplishment	2	0.4%
Personal Management	70	15.4%
Reflection and changing strategies	49	10.8%
Self assessment	10	2.2%
Avoid sources of anxiety	8	1.8%
Avoid working late	2	0.4%
Reduce distractions	1	0.2%

descriptions of testing strategies. In addition, the course includes two structured reflective exercises requiring students to describe their software development processes and how they have changed. These exercises provide a small contribution, less than 2% in total, to their final grade.

3.2 Coding Framework

The basic unit of analysis in this project were coding units [19], including sections of text responses, of any size. Within the open coding stage, sections of text, such as a sentence, word or phrase, were coded while the selection represented a single idea or concept related to SRL strategy. In excess of 300 pages from 85 student reflections were coded using the qualitative software NVivo (version 10) defining an initial set of 78 distinct codes. The researcher methodically worked through the student reflections, coding their observations either to existing nodes within the framework or to a newly created node, identifying a description of the newly created node and exemplar. During the axial coding stage, the researcher worked in collaboration with the project team to iteratively refine the established codes into categories, merging codes where appropriate, informed by existing coding categories related to SRL as defined by Zimmerman [20] and identifying discipline-specific categories as derived from the data (see Table 1).

The content analysis frequencies, combined with qualitative examples of student descriptions of their behaviours and strategies, are discussed further below.

4. QUANTITATIVE ANALYSIS

Our analysis reveals that students utilise a range of SRL strategies, including general strategies, strategies that are adapted and articulated within the context of CS, and strategies that are specific and newly introduced to address the learning challenges of CS. Further, we are able to categorise these strategies as (a) those that were perceived to lead to success, and (b) those that led to failure.

Tables 1 and 2 present the identified strategies associated with successful behaviour, classified as either CS-specific or general strategies. Table 1 identifies a clear focus on software design processes, with a dominant use of diagrams to help describe or explain their software design, and the development of sub-goals based on their software designs (and subsequent software decomposition). Prioritisation is also indicated as a key strategy - in this case referring to the prioritisation of design activity over subsequent implementation and testing activities. Assessing problem difficulty is a crucial step in planning and goal-setting, with several CS-specific strategies identified within this category. Table 2 reports the identified general SRL strategies; these strategies were frequently articulated within the CS context, with contextual description added to illustrate how the strategy was employed or modified within the domain.

Students also indicated strategies that led to unsuccessful behaviours. The majority of these strategies are general strategies, and are frequently in direct opposition to a contrasting strategy found to be successful. Table 3 presents those general strategies found to be unsuccessful by students, focusing primarily on poor time management, inadequate goal setting and insufficient planning strategies. Interestingly, students identified poor strategies associated with focusing their activity based on the assessment, i.e. directing their effort based on how many marks individual parts of the assignment were worth. As a smaller fraction of the marks was associated with design than implementation functionality, as a consequence, these students did not place a high priority on undertaking design activities, and typically developed a design document subsequent to the completion and testing of their code. Table 4 describes the CS-specific strategies associated with failure, reflecting this observation.

We further analysed the successful SRL strategies (both general and CS-specific) in terms of their relationship with the coding framework established by Zimmerman [20] (see Table 5). Approximately 50% of the strategies identified correspond to those identified by Zimmerman, with the majority (28.9%) related to goal-setting and planning.

Table 3: General unsuccessful SRL strategies and their indicated frequency (total count = 222).

Strategy	Freq	%Freq
Time Management	*115*	*51.8%*
Poor prioritisation of competing demands	42	18.9%
Underestimated time	33	14.9%
Poor time management	14	6.3%
Fixed timetable - insufficient	11	5.0%
Procrastination	5	2.3%
Time management - no specific strategy	5	2.3%
Avoiding difficult tasks	4	1.8%
Assume nothing will go wrong	1	0.5%
Assess Difficulty	*57*	*25.7%*
Underestimated complexity	35	15.8%
Lack of fundamental skills	13	5.9%
Misunderstand requirements	7	3.2%
Did not assess difficulty	2	0.9%
Personal Management	*33*	*14.9%*
Assessment achievement focus	31	14.0%
No reflection leading to change	2	0.9%
Build Knowledge	*10*	*4.5%*
Did not seek help or ignored help	8	3.6%
Not attending class	2	0.9%
Decompose problem	*7*	*3.2%*
Did not decompose	7	3.2%

Table 4: CS-specific unsuccessful SRL strategies and their indicated frequency (total count = 70).

Strategy	Freq	%Freq
Development Process	*70*	*100.0%*
Coding before Design	40	57.1%
Incomplete design	29	41.4%
Insufficient testing	1	1.4%

5. QUALITATIVE ANALYSIS

Our analysis so far indicates that students recognise and report both general and CS-specific SRL strategies. In this section, we explore further the key categories of CS-specific strategies that we have identified.

5.1 Design as Strategy

Design is a challenging process for our students to learn as they transition from novice to expert programmers [11], with many of our students fixating on design as an artefact rather than a process or strategy in itself [Reference withheld]. The lack of understanding that design is a process means that students struggle to form consistent strategies to assist their process. Many students were able to articulate the importance of completing a design prior to initiating code implementation, represented as a positive tradeoff between spending time initially in the design phase to save time later in the code implementation and testing phases (prioritisation); however, they were less consistent in the adoption of strategies that reflected this understanding.

A small number of students initially indicated that they completed their design (as an artefact) subsequent to the completion of their task - they indicated that this was successful in that they completed their task, but also indicated that they were not able to conceptualise any strategies to help them explore and develop an appropriate mental model for the design process. In these cases, teaching assistants would provide an initial set of strategies that students could try, such as creating class diagrams, flow charts of process, and algorithmic descriptions. Use of diagrams was clearly identified as the most useful strategy in our case study, sug-

Table 5: Reclassification of strategies according to Zimmerman

Strategy	Freq	%Freq
Other	418	49.7%
Goal-setting and planning	243	28.9%
Organising and transforming	58	6.9%
Seeking information	44	5.2%
Seeking social assistance	43	5.1%
Reviewing records	12	1.4%
Environmental restructuring	11	1.3%
Self-Evaluation	10	1.2%
Self-consequences	2	0.2%
Keeping records and monitoring	0	0.0%
Rehearsing and memorising	0	0.0%

gesting the introduction of appropriate diagramming processes as an appropriate scaffolding technique.

> 'This was the first time I used diagrams to aid in design. I initially did this as I was aware the tutors were expecting to see it but I actually found it very useful. Particularly for inheritance I found that using a diagram easily allowed for a visual representation of the relationships between classes and enabled me to mentally encapsulate the project to see where polymorphism could be used.'

This typically resulted in increased awareness of the utility of these strategies for their adoption in future tasks, and a reconceptualisation of design as a strategy in itself to assist understanding of the problem. Some students expressed quite mature strategies for their development process, citing the use of formal design principles, design tools such as UML and comprehensive test case development.

> 'It was helpful to look back to the design while writing code to compare the initial design to the product in progress and record alterations and trace the repercussions of these alterations.'

5.2 Decomposition

Many students reported strategies to assist in decomposing a problem into sub-goals, including general strategies based on using available resources to guide their decomposition, or through the use of their design activity to produce a decomposition plan.

Many students identified that setting sub-goals and problem decomposition was an appropriate strategy, but felt that they did not have the required skills to do this. As the assignments were described in a stepwise fashion, the students quickly identified that they could substitute the assignment specification for a plan even though this was not the intention of the lecturer and rarely suitable. This behaviour effectively interfered with a significant goal of the assignment - to establish design skills, and provides support for explicit scaffolding around design activities.

> 'For a more systematic approach on an assignment, I usually chose to break an assignment into tasks according to the given tasks that has been listed out in the assignment question. Since they are listed out by an experienced programmer, the steps are always helpful in a way that they guide me in completing the assignment.'

As students developed more experience with software development, they were able to identify more mature strategies for setting sub-goals, as indicated below. This strategy exhibits an understanding of the crucial requirement of design activity as part of the planning process.

> 'At the start of the semester, I followed the 'Stage' system given in assignments. I would complete coding one stage at a time. This was an effective way to ensure I would get maximum marks for the work I did, even if I didn't finish everything on time. Once I became more confident in my ability to always complete assignments on time, I decided that this was not the most efficient way to code. From then on I coded one class at a time. Once each class was working, I could treat it as a 'black box' and did not need to return to it for further modifications. Treating my assignments as a whole project rather than stages reduced the need to modify my design or code from earlier stages to adapt to requirements for later stages.'

The adoption of decomposition strategies reflected awareness of the relationship between software decomposition and testing strategies, i.e. performing unit-based testing or test-driven development as a natural result of decomposition.

> 'This allowed me to test the code in small segments and to assess if my plan was really the best way handle the 'lower' classes before writing the 'higher' classes.'

5.3 Time-management and Planning

Students expressed a strong reliance on fundamental goal-setting and planning strategies as supporting their learning, with time management and prioritisation identified as key to success. We are able to identify both simplistic and mature strategies in relation to goal-setting and planning. A considerable number of students indicate a strategy based on fixed time management - always commencing their work on a fixed day, rather than varying their timetable according to the difficulty of the task.

> 'I often started to do my assignments on the day just before the due day.'

Students also identified a fixed timetable strategy as leading to failure, with the difference being the amount of time allocated. Students who initially worked to a fixed timetable but were not successful identified that the issue was one of insufficient time, and responded by increasing the time allotted to their work, although still retaining a fixed timetable.

> 'After [practical X] I realised that I couldn't just run head first into every practical two days before it was due.'

> 'I believe that if I set myself out to complete the assignment a day or two before the due date then even if I didn't complete it but still got as far as I did normally, it would allow me the next two days to fix up and make sure maybe get the rest of the practical done.'

Students identified more mature goal-setting and time management strategies that were tightly linked to their software development process, identifying CS-specific strategies in assessing task difficulty that assisted in their planning.

5.4 Assessing Task Difficulty

A significant factor in students' planning is the ability to accurately assess the difficulty of the required task. Again, the strategies identified varied in maturity, with some use of simplistic strategies for assessing task difficulty, such as being guided by the length of the question, the marking scheme or the deadline, and some CS-specific strategies, such as counting the number of functions or software objects to be developed.

> 'Reading the question and searching for the number of functions required was generally a good indicator'

Students identified the need to analyse the complexity of the algorithms needed for the task, however, teaching assistants needed to demonstrate strategies for how they would do this, such as assessing their own familiarity with the concepts of algorithms required, comparison with previous work, or identification of new skills needed.

Further, students identified that the activity of design forms a crucial part of this goal-setting process, rather than being solely part of the task itself. This distinction is crucial in establishing the purpose of design as a process rather than as an artefact for assessment. Prioritising design in their time management led to successful code implementation and testing, and ultimately, successful completion of the assignment.

> 'Once a proper design had been written up, the real scope of the project became clear and allowed me to assess the difficulty of it and to more accurately estimate the time that I would require to complete it.'

At the more mature level, strategies that explored the use of prototyping and experimentation as a crucial aspect of understanding the task, and accordingly necessary for understanding both the design complexity and algorithmic complexity were also identified. Teaching assistants supported this through suggestions to compare and contrast design choices, leading to the need for small-scale prototyping and evaluation.

> 'I assessed the difficulty of an assignment, along with how I would approach the problem by researching, experimenting and prototyping.'

6. CONCLUSIONS

In our analysis, we identify examples of successful SRL strategies within the context of introductory software development, consisting of general strategies reconceptualised within the CS context, and CS-specific strategies. These strategies provide guidance in the development of scaffolding activities to assist in learning the process of software development, specifically:

- The introduction of diagrams, i.e. class diagrams or flow charts, as an explicit, early design activity.

- Assessment of task difficulty, incorporating the identification of needed skills, leading to the development of time management and sub goal planning.

- Explicit conceptualisation of design as part of the software development process, linked to the above activities, and viewed as an iterative process.

- Explicit inclusion of experimentation as part of design, incorporating activities that require students to explore alternative designs, and their evaluation and comparison.

Caruso et al [4] identify that students must develop their own strategies in response to their own experiences. In our work, we have identified that explicitly scaffolding strategy-related activities can assist in this process. We intend to explore explicit scaffolding related to the successful SRL strategies identified in this study, specifically the introduction of scaffolded design activities [17] to assist in understanding and assessing problems, prototyping and experimentation with design choices, design as decomposition, and creating informed time management plans.

Allwood [1] identifies that novices tend to devote less time to understanding and exploring the problem, and instead try to move immediately to solving the problem using a known solution. It is apparent in our analysis that the process of understanding programming problems, involving assessing task difficulty, design choices and planning, is complex with many different, inter-related strategies employed by our students and requires explicit scaffolding for development.

The frequent adoption of design-based decomposition as a planning strategy warrants further discussion. Although a successful strategy for many students, particularly through related adoption of frequent testing strategies, it was also evident that students were regularly completing each individual component, i.e. function or class, without necessarily thinking about how that component related to the whole. This supports previous studies, which found that novices did not consider how individual components would interact with other components, and did not have a clear holistic understanding of their solution, which is in contrast to behaviours exhibited by experts [1, 11]. Accordingly, there is motivation to explore appropriate scaffolding to help students visualise component interactions and to explicitly address integration concerns at early stages.

7. REFERENCES

[1] C. Allwood. Novices on the computer: a review of the literature. *International Journal of Man-Machine Studies*, 25:633–658, 1986.

[2] S. Bergin, R. Reilly, and D. Traynor. Examining the role of self-regulated learning on introductory programming performance. In *Proceedings of ICER'05*, pages 81–86, 2005.

[3] R. Cantwell and P. Moore. The development of measures of individual differences in self-regulatory control and their relationship to academic performance. *Contemporary Educational Psychology*, 21:500–517, 1996.

[4] T. Caruso, N. Hill, T. VanDeGrift, and B. Simon. Experience report: Getting novice programmers to think about improving their software development

process. In *Proceedings of SIGCSE'11*, pages 493–498, 2011.

[5] B. Hanks, L. Murphy, B. Simon, R. McCauley, and C. Zander. Cs1 students speak: Advice for students by students. In *Proceedings of SIGCSE'09*, pages 19–23, 2009.

[6] E. Lichtinger and A. Kaplan. *Self-Regulated Learning*, chapter Purpose of engagement in academic self-regulation, pages 9–19. Jossey-Bass, 2011.

[7] R. Lister, E. Adams, S. Fitzgerald, W. Fone, J. Hamer, M. Lindholm, R. McCartney, E. Mostrom, K. Sanders, O. Seppala, B. Simon, and L. Thomas. A multi-national study of reading and tracing skillls in novice programmers. *SIGCSE Bulletin*, 36(4):119–150, December 2004.

[8] M. McCracken, V. Almstrum, D. Diaz, M. Guzdial, D. Hagen, Y. Kolikant, C. Laxer, L. Thomas, I. Utting, and T. Wiusz. A multi-national, multi-institutional study of assessment of programming skills of first-year cs students. *SIGCSE Bulletin*, 33(4):125–140, 2001.

[9] S. Paris and J. Turner. *Student Motivation, Cognition and Learning: Essays in Honor of Wilbert J. McKeachie*, chapter Situated Motivation, pages 213–237. Hillsdale, N.J.: Erlbaum, 1994.

[10] V. Ramalingam, D. LaBelle, and S. Wiedenbeck. Self-efficacy and mental models in learning to program. In *Proceedings of ITiCSE'04*, pages 171–175, 2004.

[11] P. N. Robillard. The role of knowledge in software development. *Communications of the ACM*, 42(1), January 1999.

[12] M. Sandelowski. Sample size in qualitative research. *Research in Nursing & Health*, 18(2):179–183, 1995.

[13] D. Schon. *The Reflective Practitioner: How Professionals Think in Action*. Basic Books, 1983.

[14] G. Schraw, K. Crippen, and K. Hartley. Promoting self-regulation in science education: Metacognition as part of a broader perspective on learning. *Research in Science Education*, 36(1-2):111–139, 2006.

[15] J. Sheard, Simon, M. Hamilton, and J. Lönnberg. Analysis of research into the teaching and learning of programming. In *Proceedings of ICER'09*, pages 93–104, 2009.

[16] M. Veenman, J. Elshout, and J. Meijer. The generality vs domain-specificity of metacognitive skills in novice learning across domains. *Learning and Instruction*, 7(2):187–209, 1997.

[17] S. Violet. Modelling and coaching of relevant metacognitive strategies for enhancing university students' learning. *Learning and Instruction*, 1:319–336, 1991.

[18] P. Winne. Inherent details in self-regulated learning. *Educational Psychologist*, 80:284–290, 1995.

[19] Y. Zhang and B. Wildemuth. *Application of social research methods to questions in information and library science*. Westport Conn: Libraries Unlimited, 2009.

[20] B. Zimmerman. A social cognitive view of self-regulated academic learning. *Journal of Educational Psychology*, 81(3):329–339, 1989.

Motivational Active Learning – Engaging University Students in Computer Science Education

Johanna Pirker
Graz University of Technology
Institute for Information Systems and
Computer Media
Inffeldgasse 16c, Graz, Austria
0043-316-8735625
jpirker@iicm.edu

Maria Riffnaller-Schiefer
Graz University of Technology
Institute for Information Systems and
Computer Media
8010 Graz
riffnaller@student.tugraz.at

Christian Gütl
Graz University of Technology
Institute for Information Systems and
Computer Media
Curtin University, Perth, Western
Australia
School of Information Systems
0043-316-8735604,
cguetl@iicm.edu

ABSTRACT

Attracting and engaging computer science students to enhance their mathematical and algorithmic thinking skills are challenging tasks. In winter 2013 we introduced a new teaching format for a course, which combines theory in computer science with hands-on algorithmic challenges, mathematical thinking activities, and collaborative problem-solving. Therefore, we introduced the pedagogical model Motivational Active Learning (MAL), which is grounded in MIT's successful format for teaching physics, Technology-Enabled Active Learning (TEAL), and combines it with motivational strategies usually used by game designers. Results from the initial setup in class reveals that students indeed assessed the course structure as more interactive and motivating compared to other similar courses. In this paper we discuss the course design, issues, and the impact, and analyze the first results in detail.

Categories and Subject Descriptors

K.3.2 [**Computer and Education**]: Computer and Information Science Education – *computer science education*.

General Terms

Measurement, Design, Experimentation, Human Factors.

Keywords

Active Learning, CS Education, Interactive Learning, Pedagogy, Gamification, Game-based learning, Motivation.

1. INTRODUCTION

In computer science (CS) education an important issue is the successful transfer of not only theoretical concepts, but also teaching skills such as computational and mathematical thinking and creative problem-solving. However, many pedagogical approaches are still auditory, abstract, deductive, passive, and sequential [1] and fail in teaching how to solve problems, and recite the solutions instead [7]. This leads to student frustration,

high drop-out rates, and does not match the objectives of engineering education. In the last decade, especially in STEM fields, there is a growing interest in developing new teaching models based on constructivist models such as interactive engagement, problem-based reasoning, and collaborative problem-solving strategies [9],[12].

One successful implementation of interactive and collaborative learning activities is the way physics is taught at the Massachusetts Institute of Technology (MIT). The format is grounded in interactive engagement strategies and integrates hands-on experiments, collaborative experiences, interactive visualizations and simulations, and mini lectures with concept quizzes (used with personal response systems). Analyses have shown that the failure rate has decreased and learning gains have doubled [21]. TEAL achieves student motivation also by integrating collaborative activities, such group discussions. The importance of such motivating and engaging activities in education is well known and many studies promote cooperative learning strategies in order to enhance the students' motivation and raise the attendance rate [1],[19]. A rather new approach to engage students to achieve better learning gains and to push their own personal boundaries is the integration of gamification aspects to create a motivational atmosphere through constant feedback, mini challenges, and positive reinforcement [18]. In this paper, we present our pedagogical approach MAL (Motivational Active Learning), which is grounded in TEAL and combines it with motivational gamification design aspects. We conducted an initial study with one class of 28 students. The aim of this paper is to analyze the study outcomes and discuss the impacts, prospects, and issues of this model and its concepts. The remainder of the paper is organized as follows: we will first present background information and related work in the fields of active learning and gamification in education. After that, we will present the concepts of MAL and will then show a first study setup and its outcomes.

2. THEORETICAL BACKGROUND

Many authors have discussed different learning approaches to make education for students more attractive and help them to *"learn more, learn it earlier and more easily, and [...] learn it with a pleasure and commitment"* [4]. In the last decades, especially in the STEM domain physics education, many innovative interactive teaching styles have emerged. Quantitative research promotes the effectiveness of different active learning models using strategies such as collaborative learning methods or computers as auxiliary device for learning. Following we present and discuss a selection of related important pedagogical approaches with focus on interactive and engaging aspects.

2.1 Active Learning Formats

Interactive Engagement (IE) challenges students in face-to-face lectures to solve problems together. A study with 6000 students shows that IE strategies are superior to support the students' problem-solving abilities and their conceptual understanding [9]. Following different formats grounded in IE strategies and active learning are presented.

Peer Instruction (PI) is a teaching model for physics education introduced by Mazur at Harvard. To design a large-scale course to be more interactive and personal, students use personal response systems (PRS) to answer small multiple-choice questions in the lecture. Afterwards they discuss the questions with their peers and can revise their answer [13]. Many authors also report of successful integrations of PI in CS courses. Porter and Simon used a format grounded in PI, media computation (learning computation through digital media manipulation), and pair programming (solving programming exercises in pairs). They report reduced dropout rates, increased student pass rates, and an absolute improvement of more than 30% in programmatic retention among students in a CS1 course [17].

Scale-Up (Student-Centered Activities for Large Enrollment for Undergraduate) is an interactive learning approach, which integrates typical small class elements into large enrollment passive physics courses. Scale-Up combines lecture (discussion), polling questions, laboratory experiments, discussion, and problem solving to create an interactive learning environment. Students work in homogeneous groups of three and each student has a special role. Each group sits on a rounded table together with two other groups (nine students on each table) [8]. The special classroom features whiteboards on the walls, portable whiteboards, a computer/laptop for each group, and a class presentation system. Research has shown that this interactive learning environment has positive effects on the students learning process. As a result, Scale-Up improves problem solving skills and conceptual understanding of the students. They noted also a positive effect on the grades in follow up classes [2].

Studio-Physics is another example for an active learning approach. Kohl and Kuo transformed the traditional physics course at the Colorado School of Mines into a Studio-Physics course. Modern information technologies were used together with traditional techniques for experiments, hands-on activities, and problem solving tasks. Some of the activities were done in homogeneous groups so that students could learn from each other. Activities include in-class activities like conceptual questions as well as home assignments. An important element of Studio-Physics is the scaffolding system, which iteratively improves the students' problem-solving skills. A study has shown that the students' grades have improved. However, they also noted that there is no automatic improvement without also adapting the curriculum to the new learning approach [11].

Technology-Enabled Active Learning (TEAL) is based on the ideas of Studio-Physics and Scale-Up and integrates activities like desktop experiments, reflection/preparing tasks, discussions, and lectures interrupted by conceptual questions. The learning environment of the classroom is similar to Scale-Up. Students are sitting on a round table and work in groups of three to nine. TEAL combines collaborative activities with modern technologies such as networked laptops, whiteboards, and PRSs to foster *visual*

skills and conceptual understanding. Researches have shown that TEAL improves conceptual understanding of students and has a long-term learning effect. [5].

It can be emphasized, that a learning approach which combines collaborative working, different kinds of activities, and problem solving tasks with modern information technologies, can lead to positive learning effects. However, Dori et al. found that students show some resistance against new learning approaches which are in contrast to traditional approaches [6]. Therefore, in the next section, we will analyze pedagogical models grounded in gamification and game design to reduce the students' resistance and, instead, to motivate the students to actively participate in the course.

2.2 Gamification of Instructions

Motivation is the most important driver for successful learning. Many authors promote the effectiveness of educational computer games as powerful and motivational learning tools. Papasterigou for example describes the successful implementation of a digital game for learning computer memory concepts which not only achieved better learning gains, but also enhanced the students' engagement (equally for boys and girls) [16].

Recently, also gamification strategies were more and more involved in educational models to engage in particular intrinsic motivation. In comparison to learning games, gamification uses game design elements, such as leaderboards, badges, constant feedback, and points. It is defined as the use of "*game design elements in non-game contexts*" [3]. Quest to Learn (Q2L) is an entire curriculum model in New York City based on gamification strategies. Instead of homework, Q2L promotes mission-and challenge-based units. These quests especially involve game strategies such as collaboration, role-playing, or simulations. The learning experience focuses on hands-on problem-solving approaches [1]. Instead of frustrating and stressing student with failure rates at exams, Q2L uses a point system where students are rewarded for putting extra effort to account for mistakes and not punished for failing one single exam. They can constantly try to level up to master a course and can focus on the course content instead of stressing over their grades [15].

However, competitive gamification strategies do not attract all learning types and can lead to student frustration instead of motivation. Different studies comparing competitive, individual, and cooperative learning strategies report the most successful outcomes by cooperative strategies [10]. Therefore, in the educational domain it is important to not only integrate competitive game elements such as leaderboard information, but also collaborative elements such as working together as a group towards points and helping each other by achieving common goals.

In the next section we propose a pedagogical model integrating interactive and collaborative aspects from the learning format TEAL and combine it with engaging competitive game mechanics.

3. MOTIVATIONAL ACTIVE LEARNING

Motivated by the positive impacts on students' learning outcomes of different innovative learning formats such as TEAL, we designed an initial version of a pedagogical model combining different interactive strategies and concepts with game-design aspects. *Motivational Active Learning (MAL)* aims to help students understanding the concepts in an engaging way.

3.1 Objectives

Hand in hand with designing an actual course in the CS domain, the objectives of the initial pedagogical model were to:

- Design a course combining (1) theoretical background and concepts, (2) algorithmic understanding, and (3) analytical understanding of mathematical models

- Engaging students by interactivities and motivational activities

- Increase the students' activities and motivation for hands-on exercises

The single elements and activities of the course format to achieve those goals include a variety of question types and interactive tasks. Based on TEALs example each lecture is organized into mini lectures, each one starting with a concept question and ending with a small concept quiz to be able to observe the learning progress of the students and adapt the speed accordingly.

The course structure is designed to balance hands-on problem-solving activities, necessary abstract theories, and creative tasks and assignments to address the different learning styles of students. Table 1 lists the different activity types. Automatic assessment systems deliver immediate feedback, assignments such as discussion question, however, need a manual grading.

Table 1. Content types and their feedback options

Content Type	Feedback	Definition
Lecture Block	-	The lecture is divided into different blocks. Learning content and concepts are presented on power point slides.
Recap Quiz	Immediate	A small quiz at the beginning of each lecture about last lectures content
Concept Question	Overview statistic	Ungraded question about a new concept.
Concept Quiz	Immediate	Questions based on previous concept question.
Discussion Questions	Deferred	Peer / group discussions about new concepts / ideas / issues
Research Questions	Deferred	Internet research assignments for peers / small groups
Programming Exercises	Deferred	Programming exercises to practice learned concepts
Small Calculation Tasks	Immediate	Very small calculation tasks to practice learned concepts
Advanced Calculation Task	Deferred	More complex calculation tasks to practice learned concepts
Reflection Quiz	Immediate	A small quiz after each lecture to revise the content
Reflection Forum	Deferred	In an online forum groups should discuss last lectures' content and issues

Quizzes, assignments, or results of group activities such as discussion or research outcomes are submitted in an accompanying e-learning system (e.g. Moodle) to be able to track the students' progress in-time. This also enables the possibility of giving immediate feedback (by automatic question assessment) on their knowledge and skill improvement by automatically awarding points and giving motivational feedback (by assigning badges and tracking leadership information), which does not affect their grading, but triggers competitive motivation. Most of the assignments are designed to be revisable, so that they can achieve more points by working harder for it.

Summarizing, the main features of MAL include:

- Collaborative Learning: Students solve tasks in small subgroups (2 or 4 depending on the activity)

- Constant interactions: Concept questions, small quizzes and discussion questions are used to stimulate the interactions between instructor and students (see Figure 1, left for exemplary course material)

- Immediate feedback: The majority of the small tasks and quizzes deliver immediate feedback on their task performance

- Motivational feedback: Badges for special activities and leaderboard information deliver motivational feedback, by triggering competitive motivators or positive enforcements

- Errors are allowed: Students are able to revise assignments and repeat quizzes

- Adaptive class design: Learning progress during and after class allows in-time adaption the individual learning speed of the class.

The next section describes the first integration of MAL into a CS course with focus on mathematical and algorithmic concepts.

3.2 The Setting

MAL was first introduced in the course 'Information Search and Retrieval (ISR)' in the winter term 2013 at Graz University of Technology. The objective of the course is to build a knowledge base in selected theory and practice in searching and retrieving information with focus on the mathematical and algorithmic concepts. The content includes topics such as indexing and searching models, retrieval algorithm, or query languages. Hence, in each lecture it is necessary to combine theoretical background with algorithmic or mathematical concepts. The course was split into seven lecture blocks. To study the progress of the students and to support activities delivering immediate feedback the course was accompanied by the learning management system Moodle. Hence students had to bring their own technical devices such as laptops or tablets to the course. The course content was presented using power point slides. Figure 1 shows a typical course setup.

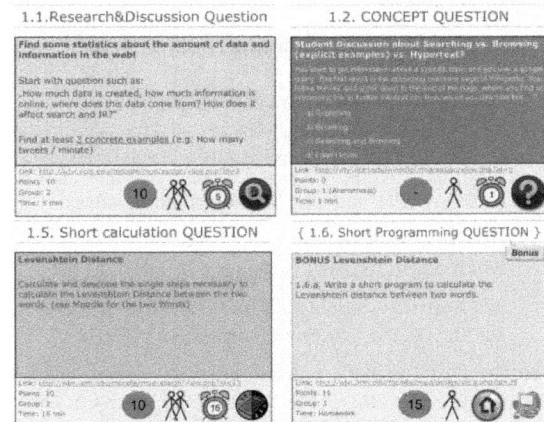

Figure 1. Slides of different question types

Special activities were highlighted by different colors and symbols (see Figure 2). Depending on the content type, students worked individually, in groups of two, or in groups of four. The group formation did not change to ease group assessment. Quizzes were designed as individual tasks, most hands-on exercises were conducted with peers (group size 2). Most assignments were started during class and students had the possibility to finish them as homework. Beside in-class assignments they also had to submit homework assignments, which were to one part compulsory and to another part bonus tasks.

To track in-class activities, an external observer was taking notes and tracking the student activities. Hence, a detailed breakdown of the single lectures into the different content parts was possible. Figure 3 shows exemplary the percentage of different activities in lecture 1. It shows a mixture of different kind of activities such as lecture, questions, discussion, calculation, and programming tasks. Although the lecture part was predominant, figure 4 shows the special combination of lecture and interactivities for all lectures in more detail.

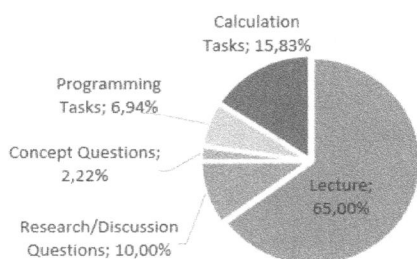

Figure 2. Percentages of activities in lecture 1

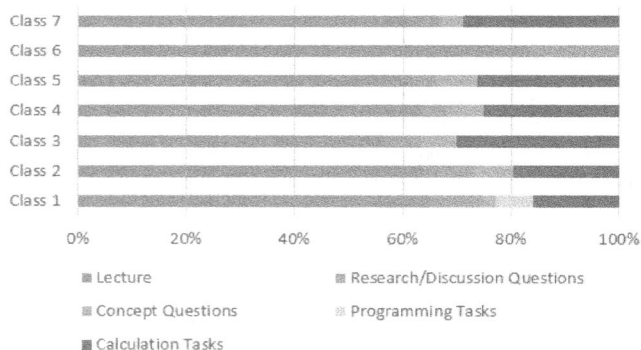

Figure 3. Overview of content distribution in the lectures

3.3 Materials and Methods

To evaluate MAL we conducted an initial study with the ISR course in winter 2013. The research goals were defined as:

- Evaluate the students' understanding of the course content

- Analyze the students' engagement and motivation

- Analyze the students' attitude towards the new model and the used e-learning environment

To evaluate these goals we used qualitative and quantitative methods. Also a field observation during the course was used to analyze the students' behavior and engagement during the course.

Before the start of the course we polled the students of the course via a web-based survey to learn about their expectations towards the course, their usual learning habits and motivation, their previous knowledge about the course content, and experiences with similar learning methods. The survey consisted of Likert-scale (1 strongly disagree, 5 I strongly agree) and open-ended questions. During the course we measured the students' learning progress using small quizzes and concept questions. We collected qualitative data by observing their activity and active participation and taking according field notes. After the course and finishing the grading, we invited the students to complete a web-based post-questionnaire which should shed light on the students' motivation during the courses and their attitude towards the class structure and its content. Therefore the post-questionnaire consisted of reflection about the different content and activity types (see Table 1), their experiences of collaborative assignments, and questions focusing on gamification aspects. Additionally, we added 30 rating questions based on the Advanced Motivation Scale, which is used to measure different types of intrinsic and extrinsic motivation and amotivation [22].

4. FINDINGS

28 students started the ISR course, one student dropped out. The pre-questionnaire was completed by 26 (6 female) of 28 students between the ages of 22 and 31. The post-test was completed by 21 (5 female) of 27 students. In this paper we will focus on the outcomes of the post-questionnaire.

Experiencing Cooperative Learning.

The tasks were balanced between assignments to be completed alone, collaborative assignments in pairs, group discussions in groups of 2, and collaborative assignments in groups of 2-4. We asked the students about their motivation towards these settings. The majority of the students stated to prefer activities in teams and stated to experience advanced learning gains through group assignments. *"The group assignments during classes were the best concept. It was good to use the concept just learned to remember it better, but also eventual misunderstandings could be discussed"*

Table 2. Survey results of cooperative learning experiences.

	Arith. Mean	Std Dev
I prefer activities in teams.	3.38	1.32
I prefer activities in groups of 2 over activities in groups of 4	4.1	1.3
I would have liked more activities in a team of four than in a team of two	2.33	1.62
I would have liked more single activities in this course	2.57	1.29
The topics were easier to understand in groups of 2	3.9	1.48
The topics were easier to understand in groups of 4	2.95	1.28
The topics were easier to understand alone	2.29	1.19
I prefer to be graded / get points individually	3.05	1.32
I prefer to get feedback individually	3.24	1.18
I learned more in group assignments than in individual assignments	3.38	1.12

The results have shown that students prefer tasks in groups of two over individual tasks. (see Table 2) But it was difficult for students to solve tasks in group of four people. In-class we observed, that even for tasks meant to be solved in groups of four, they preferred to work in groups of two and merged their results at the end. However, the results show, that the learning styles of the single students differ dramatically. Even though the standard deviation states, that the majority of 21 students prefer assignments in teams of two over teams of two, 5 students would prefer bigger groups.

Experiencing Motivation.

Asking students what they did like in the course, many of them immediately mentioned to receive points instead of grades. *"[I liked] the chance to improve already graded work. It was also a motivating thing to immediately see received points"; "[I liked] 2nd chances"; "[I like that it is] hard to fail this course and hard to get lost and procrastinate".* The study results show, that students enjoyed the new grading system (see table 3). They prefer getting points over grades and were motivated to finish further assignments to receive additional points. Another important feature was the grading book. However, the study data show that the students' engagement by the ranking information differed a lot. 5 students agreed to get motivated to conduct further assignments, while 6 students disagreed. This is in line with our observation of the necessity of attracting different learning styles and integrating both, cooperative and competitive activities. The results also show that earning badges was neither important nor attractive to many students. However, badges can be used as positive enforcement and to give students an overview of their achieved masteries.

Table 3. Survey results of cooperative learning experiences.

	Arith. Mean	Std Dev
I liked getting points rather than grades for exercises.	3.95	1.12
I was motivated to do the bonus assignments	3.57	1.25
I liked earning badges	2.52	1.21
Earning badges was not important to me	4.38	1.24
I used the grading book to view my points	4.67	0.58
I used the grading book to view my ranking	3.67	1.35
I was interested in the ranking information	3.33	1.43
Seeing my own ranking motivated me to conduct further assignments	2.81	1.6

Experiencing Interactivities.

Asking students open-ended questions about their attitude towards the course many mentioned the positive impression of the interactive content: *"I liked the interactivity of the course. It was not like in other assignment-based courses, where exercises must be done at home and then presented. There was time for researching or calculations, and then the results were discussed."; "I liked the interactive learning. The structure of the course, some parts lecture, immediately followed by exercises, was nice."* However, many students criticized classes with a large number of exercises. We also found that students get frustrated if they have to solve too many different kind of tasks in one lecture. First, they are stressed because of the short time and cannot finish the task in class. Additionally, if students are interrupted in

performing the tasks, they cannot concentrate on new content. They still think about the solution path of the unfinished task. Fortunately, due to the adaptive course design it was possible to revise the course structure accordingly.

Designed for Adaptability.

An important part of the course was the constant attention to the students' feedback during and after lecture. Using the concept questions it was possible to adapt the learning content to their current knowledge base and allowed the instructor to slow down or skip topics accordingly. Also, after each block we asked for feedback about the effort of the past lecture to adapt the lectures to the average class speed. According to the students' feedback this was an important step towards interactive, adaptable, and flexible class design: *"It was hard to follow all the stuff showed in the lecture, but the lecturer obviously read the feedback after each block and slowed down a little bit at the end which was much better"*

Assessing Learning Progress.

The learning progress was measured in-class before and after each mini-lecture. Students had also the possibility to revise the quizzes and assignments. Figure 5 shows the learning progress of the students, comparing the results of the first concept question with their answer after hearing the mini-lecture and their final answer after revising the question at home.

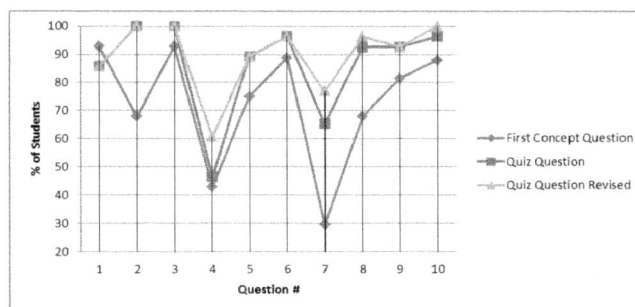

Figure 4. Comparison of learning progress

4.1 Challenges and Solutions

Students had to finish a quiz to recapitulate the content of the previous lecture at the beginning of each lesson. We have found that the communication between instructor and students is lost, if the recap quiz is the first part of the lecture. If the instructor discusses the main elements of last lecture with the students and the recap quiz follows afterwards, the loss of interaction can be prevented.

One of the major challenges is the balance of presenting abstract concepts and interactive assignments. Also, attracting students with different learning styles is a challenging task. Having an adaptive teaching model helps in changing teaching speed and style accordingly, but also requires a customizable model for the course content. The studied showed that students preferred small calculation and programming examples over complex ones. For the next phase we will split them down into smaller, but more examples with the focus of having one project that grows with each exercise.

A severe issue in this course was the grading effort of assignments. At this point we only automated the correction of quizzes and small calculation assignments. In the next phase we will focus on further automatic assessment of programming and calculation assignments.

Learning in groups was analyzed as valuable model for achieving optimized learning gains. However, the attitude of the students towards group sizes varies. For the next course we are planning to use working groups of three students. This has some advantages over groups of two people. For example if one student misses a lecture, no student must work alone and the group is still able to finish the tasks in time. Also the grading time of the class can be decreased. Also, the current course format is especially design for small classes. Constant interactions with the instructor and peers require larger courses (100+) to be split into smaller classes.

5. CONCLUSION

In this paper we have presented the learning format Motivational Active Learning based on interactive and collaborative learning strategies grounded on TEAL combined with engaging gamification mechanics. In an initial study we evaluate the attitude of the students towards MAL and its learning concepts. Stuart and Rutherford have shown that students are able to concentrate for a maximum of 10-15 minutes [20]. In contrast, we found that students are able to follow a more theoretical lecture in combination with some discussion questions for even three hours. One reason for the long lasting concentration could be that in an interactive learning environment, students are more focused because there could be a new activity at any time. This result is important because McConnell has shown that learning content, which is difficult to understand, should be presented in form of a lecture [14]. The teaching format was a good fit for the course content, which integrated theory, mathematical concepts, and algorithms. The combination of interactive and engaging strategies motivated students to finish more assignments on their own accord. Giving students points instead of grading them with traditional grades was an important step towards positive enforcement. To attract different learning types it was important to integrate both, and collaborative learning activities. The adaptive course content allows instructors to adjust the speed and difficulty to the class' learning style and level. Future work includes the adaption of the group size, an elaborate badge design, the reduction of assignments sizes, and the automation of assignment assessment.

6. ACKNOWLEDGMENTS

This work is a work in progress and was first introduced at a poster at SIGCSE14. At this point we want to thank our students at TU Graz who have participated in this project.

7. REFERENCES

[1] Augustine, D.K., Gruber, K. D., & Hanson, L. R. 1990. Cooperation works! Educational Leadership, 47

[2] Beichner, R.J. and Saul, J.M. 2003. Introduction to the SCALE-UP (Student-Centered Activities for Large Enrollment Undergraduate Programs) Project. In Proceedings of the International School of Physics "Enrico Fermi", Varenna, Italy.

[3] Deterding, S. and Khaled, R. 2011. Gamification: Toward a Definition. In CHI'11 Gamificatoin Workshop. ACM

[4] DiSessa, A. A. 2000. Changing Minds: Computers, Learning, and Literacy. MIT Press, Cambridge, MA.

[5] Dori, Y.J. and Belcher, J. 2005. How Does Technology-Enabled Active Learning Affect Undergraduate Students' Understanding of Electromagnetism Concepts? The Journal of the Learning Sciences, Vol. 14(2), 243-279.

[6] Dori, Y.J., Hult. E., Breslow, L., and Belcher, J.W. 2007. How much have they retained? Making Unseen Concepts Seen in a Freshman Electromagnetism Course at MIT. Journal of Science Education and Technology, 16(4), 299 – 323.

[7] Freedman, R. A. 1996. Challenges in Teaching and Learning Introductory Physics. In From High Temperature Superconductivity to Microminiature Refrigeration (pp. 313-322).

[8] Gaffney, J.D.H., Richards, E., Kustusch, M.B., Ding, L., and Beichner, R.J. 2008. Scaling Up Education Reform. Journal of College Science Teaching (Mai/June), 18-23.

[9] Hake, R. 1988. Interactive-engagement versus traditional methods: A six-thousand-student survey of mechanics test data for introductory physics courses. American Journal of Physics, 66 (1), 64-74.

[10] Johnson, R.T., Johnson, D. W., and Stanne, M. B. 1986. Comparison Of Computer-Assisted Cooperative, Competitive, And Individualistic Learning. In American Education Research Journal, Vol. 23, No 3. 382-392.

[11] Kohl, P.B., and Kuo, H.V. 2012. Chronicling successful secondary implementation of Studio Physics. American Journal of Physics. Vol. 80(832), 832-839 http://dx.doi.org/10.1119/1.4712305

[12] MacKay, B., and College, C. 2006. Interactive Engagement. (Science Education Resource Center at Carleton College) Retrieved 9 2012, 1, from http://serc.carleton.edu/introgeo/models/IntEng.html

[13] Mazur, E. 1996. Peer Interaction, A User's Manual. Prentice Hall.

[14] McConnell, J.J. 1996. Active learning and its use in Computer Science. Integrating technology into Computer Science Education, 6/96, Barcelona. 52-54.

[15] McGonigal, J. 2011. Reality is broken: Why games make us better and how they can change the world. Penguin Press.

[16] Papasterigiou, M. 2009. Digital Game-Based Learning in high school Computer Science education: Impact on educational effectiveness and student motivation. Computers & Education 52. 1-12.

[17] Porter, L. and Simon. B. 2013. Retaining Nearly One-Time more Majors with a Trio of Instructional Best Practices in CS1. In SIGCSE'13 Proceedings, Denver, Colorado, Usa.

[18] Shantanu S. February 14, 2012. "Motivating Students and the Gamification of Learning". Huffington Post.

[19] Slavin, R. E. 1990. Cooperative learning. New Jersey: Prentice-Hall.

[20] Stuart, J. and Rutherford, R. 1978. Medical Student Concentration During Lectures. The Lancet, Vol. 2, (September), 514-516.

[21] TEAL-Project. 2006. Retrieved 06 2012, from http://icampus.mit.edu/projects/TEAL.shtml

[22] Vallerand, R., Pelletier, L. Blais, M., Briere, N., Senecal, C., and Vallieres, E. 1992. The Academic Motivation Scale: A Measure of Intrinsic, Extrinsic, and Amotivation in Education. Educational and Psychological Measurement, 52, 1003-1017.

Study on Difficulties and Misconceptions With Modern Type Systems

Ville Tirronen
Department of Mathematical Information Technology
University of Jyväskylä, Finland
ville.e.t.tirronen@jyu.fi

ABSTRACT

Functional programming is often presented as an advantageous programming paradigm by its advocates, but many students and teachers consider it to be hard to learn. One particular hurdle in learning functional programming is mastering the modern type systems employed in these languages. In this article, we identify student difficulties with means of multiple choice questions embedded into the on-line materials of an introductory functional programming course. The most prevalent misconceptions were confusing with parametric polymorphism with subtyping, the assigning too much meaning to variables names, and confounding general language patterns with special cases.

Categories and Subject Descriptors

K.3.2. [**Computers and education**]: Computers and Information Science Education – *Computer Science Education*

Keywords

Functional Programming, Misconceptions, Type systems, Experiment

1. INTRODUCTION

Functional programming (FP) languages are proposed to have many benefits for both experienced programmers as well as for beginners [8]. For the beginners, such languages offer a familiar algebraic execution model and simple semantics and for the experts, they offer a way to write both concise and robust programs.

A large part of the benefits in many FP languages is due to elaborate type systems that provide ubiquitous formal checking for programs and allow expert programmers to specify their intent with high precision. Regardless of their usefulness, type systems have also been reported as significant source of difficulties for beginner programmers [12], while many textbooks on functional programming [1, 10, 15] largely elide the behaviour of the type system and

ITiCSE'14, June 21–25, 2014, Uppsala, Sweden.
Copyright is held by the owner/author(s). Publication rights licensed to ACM.
ACM ACM 978-1-4503-2833-3/14/06 ...$15.00.
http://dx.doi.org/10.1145/2591708.2591726.

rely on examples and intuitive understanding. In our experience, this approach is not sufficient and does, in part, lead to greater student dropout.

We opine that the language of types present in modern FP languages is complex enough to be considered as topic of its own. These type system have clear semantics, rules and a 'behaviour' which could be visualized in variety of ways [20] or be considered through the models such as notional machines (see [21]), similar to how programming languages in general are often considered.

Difficulties of learning to program are often explained by prevalence of 'non-viable' mental models that students hold [13]. Identification of student misconceptions and the mental models held by the students can be seen as a necessary condition for helping the problem students. In the present article, we study the student answers to multiple choice questions embedded in our course materials and present hypotheses of non-viable mental models that occur when learning type systems. With this article, we wish to inform other educators of the common mistakes we see in our courses and to present hypotheses of their origin and of the means for alleviating them.

2. RELATED WORK

Motivation for stronger emphasis in teaching type systems arises from studies such as the one presented by Heeren et al. [9]. This study consists of an extensive collection of statistical information of student actions when using a custom build Haskell environment. The authors document the rates of different compilation errors and note that roughly 50% of compilation attempts succeed and that 50% of these failed attempts are due to type errors.

Likewise, Chambers et al. [5] present a study in which experienced programmers with no functional programming background were observed during five project sessions. On basis of their study, the authors conclude that more than half of the programming errors made are caught during compile time. Although the authors do not document the exact sorts of errors, they refer to difficulties with the Haskell type system, higher order functions and algebraic constructs such as monads.

Difficulties in teaching type systems are also discussed in many experience reports on teaching FP. For example, Joosten and Berg [12] report the associativity of the function type seems to be a commonly misunderstood and functions with multiple parameters cause difficulties due the use currying. Similar experiences are reported by Clack and Myers

[6] who note that students are prone to confusing the type of a function with the type returned by the function.

In addition to the technical issues arising from complex type systems, issues with motivation can also be an important factor for student success in this area. From the viewpoint of the beginner student, the skill of using types does not result in immediate benefits in the same way as learning to use a new program construct or a library. Further, as noted by Wallingford [24], the inexperience of many FP teachers can cause many students to learn only the surface features of FP, which can be insufficient to motivate learning the intricasies of the type system. Motivational concerns are also discussed by Chakravarty et. al. [4], who state that students' preconceptions against FP, such as perceiving the type system as needlessly complex, diminish students' learning efforts.

In contrast to the above studies which are concerned with teacher experiences and compiler error frequencies, the present article investigates student difficulties with the type system on basis of data drawn from questions designed for finding misconceptions.

3. THE LANGUAGE OF TYPES

Since Haskell and other FP languages are relatively undiscussed in this community, this section presents a small synopsis of the type system utilized in these languages.

Haskell is a statically typed language in which every program expression has a type that is known at the compile time. For large part, these types are deduced by the compiler but they can be also specified in the source code for purposes of documentation and to ensure the programmers intent.

The primitive types found in Haskell programs are similar to those of the mainstream languages such as Java and they consist of such things as `Int`s, `Bool`s, and `String`s. The rest of the Haskell type system is, however, quite different from that of the mainstream languages. Many languages define more primitive types for things like objects and function pointers, whereas Haskell defines *type constructors* which are used to compose pre-existing types into more complex types. The the most common example of a type constructor is the function arrow '->', which is used to construct function types. The function arrow can be used to, for example, denote the type for functions that map `Int`s to `String`s by writing `Int -> String`. `[Int]`) or pairs (ie. `(Int,String)`), are predefined while many more can be defined by the user both in infix and prefix forms.

In contrast to the mainstream type systems, the type constructors, such as the `->` do not place restrictions on the types being composed and can be used recursively. For example, the type `Int -> (Int -> Int)` is a valid Haskell type which denotes a function from `Int`s into functions `Int -> Int`. Unfortunately for beginner Haskell programmers, such compositions are the standard way of defining multiparameter functions in Haskell and thus the complex types like the above must be taught on day one.

Another aspect that is different from the mainstream languages is that Haskell uses a different kind of polymorphism. Instead of the usual subtyping schemes (ie. `Integer` is an `Object`) Haskell supports *parametric polymorphism*. Parametric polymorphism bears a slight similarity to generics of Java or C# and is indicated by the use of type variables. For example, the function that calculates length of a list containing *any* type of an element is denoted as `[a] -> Int`.

One semantically correct way of understanding type variables is that when a variably typed value is written in the code, the type variables are instantiated to concrete types. For example, when the `length` function is used in the code with lists containing `Int`s, it's type becomes `[Int] -> Int`. The difference to subtyping becomes obvious when considering a type such as `Int -> a`. In Haskell, such type would denote a function that takes an `Int` and returns *whatever* type the programmer wants. This function could be used as `Int -> Bool`, or as `Int -> [String]` or even as `Int -> Email`. A function of type `Int -> a` is clearly impossible to implement sensibly.

The compositional nature and the flexibility of the type system allows the programmer to define many similar looking but drastically different types. In caricature, any sequence of valid type names interspersed with arrows and balanced parentheses is a valid Haskell type. This can confuse beginners, who can, for example, mistakenly write `(Int -> Int) -> Int` in place of `Int -> (Int -> Int)`. While the latter type declares a two parameter function, such as addition of two integers, the former does nothing of the kind. If an unfortunate student tries to implement function of the former type there will be no end to their troubles.

4. STUDY SETTING

The data for our experiment on student misconceptions with types was collected during 8 week, 5 ects, introductory functional programming course. The course is elective for students of Department of Mathematical Information Technology at the University of Jyväskylä and the participants usually have taken CS1 and CS2 courses prior to participating. The course has traditionally been well received and attended by increasing number of students every year. Overall, 88 students enrolled on the studied course instance and 29 of them completed the course on schedule. Regardless of the popularity of the course, we have experienced constant difficulties in teaching the topic of types and have speculated that these difficulties cause many students to drop out.

One specific aspect of our courses is that we increasingly rely on the students potential for self-regulated and self-directed learning [11]. Besides of the many benefits gained by emphasising student self-regulation (see, e.g. [16]), there are also difficulties: not all students are naturally self-directed and some may be unable to exert proper control over their learning and environment [3]. For example, we have observed that students with weak self-regulation skills naturally postpone learning difficult topics such as types. We find that, especially with the more difficult topics, it is important to provide support when self-direction is required [3, 11].

One way of supporting self-regulation is to provide tools for formative assessment for the students. That is, students should be provided with means of assessing their knowledge and getting feedback on their performance. As part a of such support, we have embedded multiple choice questions with an instant feedback mechanism to our teaching material.

The questions in the teaching material consist of multiple multiple choice (MMC) where the student checks all choices that correctly complete the stem of the question. In our personal experience, we found that MMC style questions are easier to design than traditional single choice questions.

For many of the questions, we could create the set of choices by enumerating the student mental models observed during previous iterations of the course or presented in the literature.

We also wish to relate our use of multiple choice questions to the constructivist idea of *cognitive conflict*, which emphasizes the importance of expressly challenging the pre-existing ideas held by the student. It is thought that such challenges prompt the student to re-evaluate and rebuild their cognitive models [18]. This cognitive remodelling is conditioned by not only by the fact that the student understands the conflict between their prior conceptions and the information presented, but also by student motivation and how relevant they perceive the problem to be [7]. We hope to provide relevant cognitive conflicts by first challenging the student with appropriate questions and providing immediate feedback. We also hope, as the student is already engaged with the studying the course material, that there will be enough motivation to respond to the conflict by knowledge building activities.

5. DATA COLLECTION

We gathered the data for this study by tracking student activity with the multiple choice questions in our online course material during the 8 week course. This study also includes data from an 8 week grace period after the course, during which students could submit missing parts of their work. The questions were answered anonymously and without an effect to grading. Students were also allowed to answer to the same question multiple times.

In total, we collected 1152 answer patterns during the course. Of the collected answers, 737 contained a mistake. In 56 of these cases the students had not answered the question at all. The remaining incorrect answers formed 270 distinct answer patterns, each of which was coded by the author (the course instructor) using an (open) coding scheme, where each of the answer patterns was first coded with codes emerging from the data. The codes were then subsequently consolidated to reduce their number and the coding procedure was repeated with the consolidated codes to ensure validity.

The coding was was validated by presenting a random subset of 30 answer patterns to be analyzed by colleague who had earlier taught the same course. The results of both codings could be unified, though no formal statistical test was employed to verify this. The codings were informed by the previous experience in teaching the course and were done under the assumption that each of problematic answer sequences could be explained by one or more non-viable mental models. As expected, we found that majority of the incorrect answer patterns could not be explained by a single code and several answer patterns (84) were inconsistent with any feasible hypothesis we could generate.

6. CODING OF STUDENT MISTAKES

The results of the coding are presented in the following list along with their intended meaning. The numbers after the description describe how frequently each of the codes appeared in the data. The numerator of the fraction is the absolute number of answers labeled with the given code and the denumerator gives the total number of answers where the code could have been appared. For example, the code

AssumesSubtyping appeared in 44 answers out of total 50 answers to such questions where this code was applicable. Some of the codes are used to describe both type and value level mistakes with both types of mistakes contributing to the in the given frequencies. Codes that were used to describe less than 5 answers were left out from the list.

AssumesSubtyping Student answer is not correct under parametric polymorphism but is consistent with subtyping. For example, student may indicate that function returning type `[a]` can be implemented by returning a list of `Integers`. $(44/50 = 0.88)$

DoesNotRecognizeTypeVar Student fails to recognize lowercase words in type expressions as type variables. $(67/109 = 0.61)$

NameOfFunctionCannotBeNameOfTypeVar Student fails to recognize that type variables and values occupy different name spaces by indicating that a name of a common value cannot be used as the name of a type variable. $(59/109 = 0.54)$

ArrowAintTypeConstructor Student fails to recognize the function arrow '`->`' as a type constructor. $(40/78 = 0.51)$

AlphaEquivalence The student thinks that the names of type variables are not interchangeable. $(55/112 = 0.49)$

DoesNotRecognizeParametricTypeVars Student has failed to recognize that the type variables can be also used to abstract over parametric types. $(45/109 = 0.41)$

SameVariableCanHaveDifferentTypeVars Student thinks that a single value level value can be described by multiple different type variables. For example, student can claim that a pair `(x,x)`, where `x` is a value level variable, can be typed as `(a,b)`. In few extreme cases, students seem to assume that each instance of the variable *must* correspond to a different type variable. $(19/50 = 0.38)$

MetaSyntax Student has confused the meta syntax in the instructional material with the actual syntax of the Haskell language. $(107/290 = 0.37)$

MistakenAssociativity Student has made a mistake regarding associativity or precedence of operators. Common instance of this error is to mistake between `(a -> b) -> c` and `a -> b -> c`. $(91/261 = 0.35)$

ConfusesListsWithTuples Student thinks that `[Int, Int, Int]` is a type. $(36/109 = 0.33)$

DoesNotRecognizeNeedForConstraint Student does not recognize a need for typeclass constraint. $(19/63 = 0.30)$

StringAintAList Student has failed to note that Haskell strings are represented as lists of characters. $(10/50 = 0.25)$

InsufficientGeneralization Student has difficulties in recognizing general patterns. For example, some students answered that `Int -> Int -> Int -> Int` is the same as `Int -> Int -> (Int -> Int)` but refused to accept that `Int -> (Int -> (Int -> Int))` is also an equivalent expression. $(40/207 = 0.19)$

DoesNotRecognizeParametricTypes The student does not acknowledge parametric types to be valid types (ie. `Wibble Foo`), except in cases where the parametric type is well known (i.e. `Maybe`). $(18/109 = 0.17)$

DifferentTypeVariablesMustBeInstantiated Differently The student thinks that different type variables must be instantiated differently. $(12/96 = 0.13)$

TroubleWithParens Student seems confused about parentheses and is willing to accept expressions such as 1(+2+3) as valid. (10/86 = 0.12)

ConfusesFunctionInputWithResult Student confuses the domain and a codomain of the function type. (Ie. indicating that giving `String` to function `Int -> String` yields an `Int`.) (12/109 = 0.11)

ConfusesValuesWithTypes Student confuses value level expressions with type level expressions. (8/109 = 0.07)

7. CATEGORIES OF STUDENT DIFFICULTIES

After the open coding process we sorted the resultant codes into two main categories. First of the categories consists of codes that arise from difficulties with formal languages, and second which involves mistakes with the semantics of the type system. After sorting the codes, we found that our categorization is a subset of the classification given by du Boulay [2] and that presenting our emergent classification in terms of this previous study would help to clarify its meaning. The classification of student difficulties given by du Boulay consists of five parts, the second and the third of which correspond to our own classification:

1) *Orientation* and finding out what programming is about.
2) Understanding the **notional machine**, or the general properties of the machine one is attempting to control.
3) Difficulties with formal **notation**.
4) Insufficient knowledge about standard *structures* and patterns applied in programming tasks.
5) Difficulties in mastering the *pragmatics* of programming, such as testing and debugging.

Placing our issues under this framework reveals that issues within our introductory course are related more to early understanding of the type system than to difficulties in applying it in practise. On the flip side, we also find that the issues discovered during the open coding process are helpful in understanding how du Boulays categorization applies to type systems. In the following sections, we further divide the two main categories into themes which allow us to conjecture about the underlying misconceptions leading to the observed difficulties.

7.1 Issues with the notional machine of type systems

Based on the collected data, we can propose two hypothetical misconceptions relating to the notional machine of Haskell types. Firstly, we found evidence that points to confusion between two different kinds of polymorphism schemes commonly employed in programming, the subtyping based polymorphism as used in Java or C# and the parametric polymorphism which is employed in ML style languages. Secondly, we discovered that several issues with (type) variables could be explained by a misconception where student assumes the intent of the programmer to have a semantical meaning in program execution.

7.1.1 Subtyping in place of parametric polymorphism

Almost all students made mistakes in questions related to parametric polymorphism and similar problems were frequently observed during the supervised sessions of our course.

The problems with polymorphism were known to us from previous instances of the course. This preconception led us to explore the hypothesis that many students confuse parametric polymorphism with subtyping. The following codes relate to this issue:

- *AssumesSubtyping*
- *SameVariableCanHaveDifferentTypeVars*
- *DoesNotRecognizeNeedForConstraint*

These codes and their relatively high prevalence seems to be simplest to explain with the hypothesis that the student has confused type variable with the notion of *root class* of subtyping based object oriented languages. For example, consider the failure to recognize that a function returning value of type `[a]` cannot be implemented by returning an `Integer`. This is easy to explain with the misconception that the type variable represents the root class, or the supertype of all types. Under this model, `Integer` would be a subtype of root type represented by the type variable and everything would work properly.

Mending this issue can be difficult due strong student preconceptions and we speculate that doing this effectively requires us to explicitly teach the behaviour of the notional machine of the Haskell type systems. For this reason, we have begun devising an algebra-like way of demonstrating the inner workings of the type system [22]. We also recommend taking inspiration from the graphical notation for type systems presented by Ruehr [20].

7.1.2 Teleological interpretation of variable names

Since variables are notoriously difficult to teach in elementary algebra [19, 23] it seems no wonder that they also present a prevalent difficulty when teaching programming. In many cases, computer science teachers are even worse off than mathematics teachers, since the concept of variables in computer science almost always mixed with sequencing and mutability. In functional programming, the situation is again confused by reverting back to mathematical variables instead the, often recently learned, programmers' variables. Mathematical variables play a large role in type expressions and we discovered several codes related to difficulties with them:

- *AlphaEquivalence*
- *DifferentTypeVariablesMustBeInstantiatedDifferently*
- *NameOfFunctionCannotBeNameOfTypeVar*
- *ConfusesFunctionInputWithResult*

Besides the earlier interpretation that these codes result from confusion between parametric polymorphism and subtyping, we can alternatively propose that they occur because students assign too much meaning for variable names. According to this hypothesis, the first of the above codes could result from a teleologically confused thinking – since programmers choose variable names according to their intended purpose, different variable names must then signify different intent and a different program. The second code can also be understood according to this theory by proposing the following logic: if the two variables are named differently the programmer must have intended their contents to be different. The same hypothesis can also be used to explain why students are unwilling to accept type variables that share a name with a well known function. If the name is taken to signify the meaning of a symbol, it is natural to assume that symbols with known functionality cannot be used as variables.

In the extreme case, confusing the type of a function with the type of its result (cf. [6]) can be seen as instance of this mistake. In this case student may reason that if a function returns a number it is intended to be used as a number.

The teleological misconception is implicitly addressed in our course where students are taught to evaluate simple expressions by hand. This should be enable them to easily check whether two expressions have the same meaning. Why do students then make such elementary mistakes in the multiple choice questions? One explanation for this is to propose that students do not engage such problems with an analytical mindset, but instead apply a less laborious heuristic: the expressions *look* different so the student thinks that they *are* different (cf. [14] p. 85).

7.1.3 Insufficient abstraction

Many of our students seemingly had difficulties in using correct level of abstraction in many programming tasks. This difficulty is reflected in the following codes:

- *DoesNotRecognizeParametricTypeVars*
- *AlphaEquivalence*
- *InsufficientGeneralization*

Many instances of insufficient abstraction relate directly to 'unexpected' language features, exemplified by the prevalent difficulties with parametric type variables. This abstraction is similar to abstracting over the content of a container, such as writing `List<T>` in Java with the twist that instead of abstracting over the content, parametric type variables abstract over the container class: `<T>Integer`. The latter behaviour is expressly forbidden in Java, and we suspect that this prior knowledge makes parametric type variables hard for the students to understand.

Other instances of insufficient abstraction are harder to explain by conflicting prior knowledge. In these cases, the students seemingly had difficulties in discriminating the underlying abstract pattern of the language and worked according to limited set of special cases they had learned. For example, many of our students were unable to recognize similarity between pieces of code where the names of bound variables were different. Similarly, we saw cases where student has applied some fact, such as associativity of an operator, correctly in simple cases, but had failed to do the exactly same transformation inside a longer expression. In our view, this phenomenon is best described by the concept of fragile knowledge discussed by Perkins et al. [17].

7.2 Issues with syntax and formal languages

Several of the our codes can be recognized as a general ineptitude with a formal languages. Part of these difficulties arise from unfamiliarity with formal languages in general while another set of difficulties results from unawareness of specifics of the Haskell language. Finally, we observed a third class of difficulties related to correctly identifying the proper classes of syntactic elements of the language.

7.2.1 Unfamiliarity with formal languages

The students' general unfamiliarity with formal languages is evident from the following codes:

- *MetaSyntax*
- *TroubleWithParens*
- *AlphaEquivalence*

Difficulties represented by these codes, such as systematically confusing the symbols of meta language used to describe the workings of program code with symbols of the programming language or the inability to use parenthesis and variables properly are certainly encountered in any field where formal languages are used.

7.2.2 Failing to recognise the structure of the language

Some of the codes indicate difficulties in connecting the symbols with their proper syntactic class, which is exemplified by errors such as confusing value and type level expressions. These relevant codes are:

- *ConfusesValuesWithTypes*
- *ArrowAintTypeConstructor*

Some of these difficulties may be specific to ML-like languages. The syntactic forms in these languages are very symmetrical and designed to be combined in many different ways and the resulting structure does not often offer 'signposts' such as keywords or semicolons to help the student to navigate the code. As a concrete example, consider a function call, such as `atan2(a,b+c)`, written in Java language. The Haskell version, `atan2 a (b+c)`, offers much less explicit structure; there are no parentheses to indicate the arguments and there is no comma to separate the different arguments. In our personal teaching experience, lack of these signposts is a major source of errors. Students write the above expression almost invariably, and incorrectly, as `atan2 a b+c`.

We conjecture that the lack of structural signposts also intensifies the semantic difficulties exhibited by our students. Many students expect to find structural markers such as commas and parenthesised function arguments and finding none of these they assign their role to specific operators and symbols. For example, mistaking the function arrow to be special syntax could explain the various difficulties the students had with types of higher order functions.

7.2.3 Unfamiliarity with Haskell

Some of the codes reflect unfamiliarity with constructs specific to the Haskell language. These codes are:

- *DoesNotRecognizeTypeVar*
- *StringAintAList*
- *DoesNotRecognizeParametricTypes*
- *DoesNotRecognizeParametricTypeVars*
- *MistakenAssociativity*
- *ConfusesListsWithTuples*

These codes indicate failure to recognize the common idioms of the language and recalling facts such as how `Strings` are represented and whether brackets or parentheses are used to denote tuples.

Although these codes arise from mere unfamiliarity with the language does not mean that these difficulties are harmless. For example, the difficulties arising from lack of structural signpost to help students discover the structure of the code is further exacerbated by Haskells' relatively high reliance of infix operators. Relying on infix operators to structure the code requires the student to recall the levels of precedence assigned to them for understanding the code. For instance, the prototypical beginner mistake of writing `atan2 a b+c` instead of `atan2 a (b+c)` is nothing but a mistake in operator precedence.

8. CONCLUSIONS

In this article, we studied beginner student answers to multiple true/false questions embedded in our course material. By using a simple coding scheme, we identified several patterns of student mistakes regarding the Haskell type system. We further sorted the results of the coding process into several categories in order to present theories of the misconceptions that could explain the identified student difficulties.

The most evident misconceptions were confusion between parametric polymorphism and subtyping, the general concept of variables and tendency to see parts of the general structure of the language as isolated special cases. One important lesson seems to be that due to lack of fixed structure and tendency for complicated and nested expressions in functional languages, significant effort must be spent to familiarize students with formal languages and syntax.

The identification of misconceptions and the resulting theories naturally beg the question "what next?". In this regard our answer is simple: the misconceptions detected with the multiple choice questions are re-embedded into our course material as more precise and explanatory multiple choice questions. Regarding the theoretical framework of conceptual change, this allows us to induce relevant cognitive conflicts in our teaching materials. When answering, the student has already engaged with the material and most likely has at least external motivation to also engage in knowledge building activity when the course material system throws up a red flag.

9. REFERENCES

[1] Bird, R. 1998. *Introduction to functional programming using Haskell*. Prentice Hall Europe.

[2] Boulay, B.D. 1986. Some difficulties of learning to program. *Journal of Educational Computing Research*. 2, 1 (1986), 57–73.

[3] Candy, P.C. 1991. *Self-direction for lifelong learning. a comprehensive guide to theory and practice*. ERIC.

[4] Chakravarty, M. and Keller, G. 2004. The risks and benefits of teaching purely functional programming in first year. *Journal of Functional Programming*. 14, 1 (2004), 113–123.

[5] Chambers, C., Chen, S., Le, D. and Scaffidi, C. 2012. The function, and dysfunction, of information sources in learning functional programming. *Journal of Computing Sciences in Colleges*. 28, 1 (2012), 220–226.

[6] Clack, C. and Myers, C. 1995. The dys-functional student. *Funtional programming languages in education*. Springer. 289–309.

[7] Duit, R. and Treagust, D.F. 2003. Conceptual change: a powerful framework for improving science teaching and learning. *International journal of science education*. 25, 6 (2003), 671–688.

[8] Felleisen, M., Findler, R.B., Flatt, M. and Krishnamurthi, S. 2004. The structure and interpretation of the computer science curriculum. *Journal of Functional Programming*. 14, 4 (2004), 365–378.

[9] Heeren, B., Leijen, D. and IJzendoorn, A. van 2003. Helium, for learning haskell. *Proceedings of the 2003 ACM SIGPLAN workshop on Haskell* (2003), 62–71.

[10] Hudak, P. 2000. *The haskell school of expression: learning functional programming through multimedia*. Cambridge University Press.

[11] Isomöttönen, V. and Tirronen, V. 2013. Teaching programming by emphasizing self-direction: How did students react to the active role required of them. *ACM Transactions on Computing Education (TOCE)*. 13, 2 (2013), 6.

[12] Joosten, S., Berg, K. and Hoeven, G. 1993. Teaching functional programming to first-year students. *Journal of Functional Programming*. 3, 1 (1993), 49–65.

[13] Kaczmarczyk, L.C., Petrick, E.R., East, J.P. and Herman, G.L. 2010. Identifying student misconceptions of programming. *Proceedings of the 41st aCM technical symposium on computer science education* (2010), 107–111.

[14] Kahneman, D. 2011. *Thinking, fast and slow*. Macmillan.

[15] Lipovaca, M. 2012. *Learn you a haskell for great good!: a beginner's guide*. no starch press.

[16] Minnaert, A. and Janssen, P.J. 1998. The additive effect of regulatory activities on top of intelligence in relation to academic performance in higher education. *Learning and Instruction*. 9, 1 (1998), 77–91.

[17] Perkins, D. and Martin, F. 1986. Fragile knowledge and neglected strategies in novice programmers. *first workshop on empirical studies of programmers on empirical studies of programmers* (1986), 213–229.

[18] Posner, G.J., Strike, K.A., Hewson, P.W. and Gertzog, W.A. 1982. Accommodation of a scientific conception: Toward a theory of conceptual change. *Science education*. 66, 2 (1982), 211–227.

[19] Rosnick, P. 1981. Some misconceptions concerning the concept of variable. *The Mathematics Teacher*. 74, 6 (1981), 418–450.

[20] Ruehr, F. 2008. Tips on teaching types and functions. *Proceedings of the 2008 international workshop on functional and declarative programming in education* (2008), 79–90.

[21] Sorva, J. 2013. Notional machines and introductory programming education. *ACM Transactions on Computing Education*. 13, 2 (2013), 8:1–8:31.

[22] Tirronen, V. and Isomöttönen, V. To appear. Teaching types with a cognitively effective worked example format (tentatively accepted). *Journal of Functional Programming*. (To appear).

[23] Trigueros, M. and Ursini, S. 2003. First-year undergraduates' difficulties in working with different uses of variable. *CBMS issues in mathematics education*. 8, (2003), 1–26.

[24] Wallingford, E. 2002. Functional programming patterns and their role in instruction. *Proceedings of the International Conference on Functional Programming, Pittsburgh* (2002).

Interdisciplinary Connections
in a Mobile Computing and Robotics Course

Stan Kurkovsky
Computer Science
Central Connecticut State University
1615 Stanley Street, New Britain, CT 06050, USA
kurkovsky@ccsu.edu

ABSTRACT

Using robots and mobile devices in education can serve as a foundation for hands-on studies encompassing many different disciplines including computer and electrical engineering, computer science, mathematics, and physics. Educational robots and mobile technology have been shown to be successful in promoting student interest in these and other STEM (Science, Technology, Engineering, and Mathematics) disciplines. This paper describes an experience of using robotics and mobile computing in an upper-level Computer Science course. Our discussion focuses on leveraging the inherent symbiosis of these two topics to explore the connections between computing and other disciplines through experiential learning.

Categories and Subject Descriptors

K.3.2 [**Computers and Education**]: Computer and Information Science Education – *Computer science education, Curriculum*

Keywords

Android; mobile computing; mobile application development; Sphero; robotics

1. INTRODUCTION

Computing can no longer be considered as a standalone area of study. Instead, the definition of Computer Science (CS) is expanding to emphasize solving practical problems that are directly related to other disciplines. Robotics can make it easier to illustrate the synergistic application of concepts from computing, engineering, physics, and mathematics in different educational settings ranging from elementary school to the university level. Due to their tangible nature, robots and mobile devices have inherent intellectual and emotional qualities that appeal to a diverse array of learners of varying age, gender, or academic interest. Currently, robotics and mobile application development are widely used as a motivational tool to promote STEM disciplines in introductory courses, in summer camps, middle and high schools, as well as entry-level college courses [9,14].

Despite the success of using robotics and mobile computing to attract students to STEM disciplines, these two areas remain under-utilized in CS education. There are very few university-level programs in computing that offer courses in robotics or include robotics-related material beyond the entry-level 'teaser' courses [12]. Furthermore, adding robotics-related material in upper-level courses could provide an excellent environment to illustrate the interdisciplinary nature of modern practical problems solved by computing professionals.

This paper describes the author's experience to fill this void by using a simple robot in combination with mobile devices in a Systems Programming course. This experience explored the symbiotic relationship of robotics and mobile computing that offered ample opportunities to present students with simple, yet inherently interdisciplinary problems that helped students witness many connections between computing and other disciplines.

2. COMPUTING AND INTERDISCIPLINARY PROBLEMS

The need to prepare computer science graduates to work in interdisciplinary projects has long been recognized. In 1996, writing about the strategic directions for CS education, Tucker [18] suggested: "new curricula should be developed that stress the interactions between computer science and other disciplines." Today, more than ever, it is vital for CS programs to produce graduates that are able to meet the challenges of solving practical interdisciplinary problem. In fact, a report from the National Science Foundation [17] indicates: "Future generations of the U.S. science and engineering workforce will need to collaborate across national boundaries and cultural backgrounds, as well as across disciplines."

Both computing industry and research institutions are confronted with an increasing number of problems that are interdisciplinary by their nature. Yet, as Amoussou et al [1] point out, "we have created disciplinary silos of expertise needed to solve problems that are deep and highly focused." The next generation of computing professionals employed in the industry and computer scientists working on research projects must be capable to resolve the challenges stemming from the interdisciplinary nature of emerging problems. To achieve this, we must provide our current students with a rich variety of skills in interdisciplinary computing. Current research literature offers many examples of involving students into interdisciplinary research projects and interdisciplinary tracks, or programs. Examples of cross-connected disciplines include bioinformatics [4,10,20], geographic information technology [3,20], and physics [11]. Furthermore, interdisciplinary research projects have been successfully used to recruit and retain underrepresented students. For example, Beck et al [4] report a great success in using bioinformatics research projects to attract female students to computing and to encourage them to continue their studies at the graduate level.

Although student research projects provide an excellent environment for exploring interdisciplinary connections, it is important to provide students with an opportunity to experience the connections between computing and other disciplines in regular (not research-oriented) and lower-level courses. By doing so, students will gain cross-cutting computing skills and will be better prepared to tackle full-scale interdisciplinary projects later in their studies or after graduation.

3. INTERDISCIPLINARY NATURE OF ROBOTICS AND MOBILE DEVICES

Current publications describing the use of robotics and mobile devices in the computing curriculum emphasize their role to improve student motivation, the use of these devices as a learning context, as well as an outreach mechanism to attract elementary, middle, and high school students, including non-CS college-level students to computing and other STEM disciplines [7,15,16].

As an inherently interdisciplinary area, robotics integrates a wide spectrum of computing sub-disciplines (computer architecture, artificial intelligence, software engineering, embedded systems, etc.), along with mechanical and electrical engineering, physics, and mathematics. Consequently, studying robotics may help students witness and understand a strong symbiotic relationship among several STEM disciplines. Furthermore, using programmable devices such as robots or smartphones has been shown to stimulate student creativity and problem-solving skills [2,19]. Hands-on experimentation with tangible real-world objects supports the principles of constructionist teaching and learning, which helps students organize and transfer theoretical knowledge to practice through experience. Programmable devices are not only fun to work with; they also provide an excellent platform for a holistic combination of practice and theory [8].

3.1 Robots and Mobiles in a Single Course

This work explores the combination of robotics material with mobile computing, which has been already advocated for [6,13]. In particular, this paper focuses on the experience of teaching robotics within the frameworks of a Systems Programming course, which includes topics on machine and operating system organization, hardware/software interfaces, hardware-specific constraints on software applications, and using application programming interfaces and system libraries for the design and development of systems applications. Implementing a range of capabilities in a complex hardware/software system requires students to utilize their skills and knowledge from such core competencies as software and system design, software engineering, and mathematical foundations of computing.

Both robots and mobile devices such as smartphones or tablets are perfect examples of systems with extreme integration: they combine a processor, at least one type of communication interface, and a diverse range of sensors within a single functional unit. Although the two types of devices have different design objectives (robots: electromechanical capabilities; mobiles: communication and computation), they share many common features. As a result of extreme integration, robots and mobiles represent a good example of a cross-disciplinary learning context, which extends far beyond computing alone. On the one hand, studying mobile computing and robotics requires students to have a good working knowledge of computer architecture, operating systems, and computer networking, and also reinforces the idea that none of the above areas of computing can exist in isolation from the others. On the other hand, both mobile computing and robotics help illustrate strong connections between computing and

other STEM disciplines, such as physics, mechanical and electrical engineering, and mathematics.

Android and Sphero were used as the device platforms. Android was chosen as the mobile application development platform due to a number of factors: a) most students already have a good working knowledge of Java; b) application development environment, such as Eclipse, is supported on many operating systems; c) there are little to no associated costs; and d) Android devices suitable for development are readily available to many, if not all, students.

Figure 1. Sphero and its internals.

Sphero shown in Figure 1 is a small ball-shaped robot manufactured by Orbotix and marketed as a gaming and entertainment device. Two internal motors enable Sphero to roll on a flat surface in any direction. Sphero is equipped with an accelerometer, gyroscope, and Bluetooth connectivity, which allows it to communicate with other devices via an open low-level API. High-level SDKs for iOS and Android provide a way to control the robot via an external application running on a mobile device. Our previous work [13] provides a detailed justification for the choice of Sphero as a hardware platform and explains why it is indeed well suited to teach robotics. Our previous work also offers an in-depth discussion of advantages and disadvantages of combining robotics and other topics such as mobile computing in a single course along with a detailed survey of the existing work on integrating robotics material within other topical courses. While the previous work aimed to make the case for integrating robotics-related topics into other courses, this paper focuses on exploring the benefits of pairing robotics with mobile computing and application development. Most importantly, this work emphasizes how hands-on experiences can help students gain better understanding of the existing connections between computing and other related disciplines, such as physics, mathematics, and engineering.

3.2 Hands-on Experiences

Experiential learning focuses on providing students with hands-on experiences in a practical project with tangible outcomes; it provides a rich and rewarding environment that motivates students to strive for success. Project-based learning [5] emphasizes creating functional artifacts that embody the knowledge acquired by students. By creating tangible results through design, development and experimentation, students are able to improve their competence in applying the acquired knowledge and skills, develop and reinforce their problem solving abilities, and practice creativity.

Table 1. Hands-on activities in the Android+Sphero course.

Lab/project	Objectives, topics and related areas
Android GUI	Objective: Build a simple Android app with a few different controls (layouts). Information technology: Software package dependencies; installing and using Eclipse. Software engineering: Model-View-Controller (MVC) pattern and how it is used in Android.
Mini web browser	Objective: Use Android intents to pass and process queries between different user activities and Android services. Operating systems: Inter-process communication. Computer networking: HTTP protocol and request handling. Human-computer interaction: Limitations of mobile user interfaces and interaction modalities.
Context-sensitive help system	Objective: Create a query-based system for retrieving text articles based on keywords. Database systems: persistent data storage and manipulation, SQL. Artificial intelligence: natural language processing.
Android sensors	Objective: Implement a shake counter. Physics: Laws of motion, acceleration, and gravity. Electrical engineering: Implementation of an accelerometer. Human-computer interaction: How to account for physical differences in motion produced by different users.
Intro to Sphero	Objective: Understand the role of each of Sphero's internal components. Electrical engineering: Functionality and integration of electronic and mechanical components inside the robot. Computer networking: Bluetooth protocol and its implementation in Android and Sphero.
Robotic motion	Objective: Learn how to programmatically communicate with Sphero and control its motion. Mechanical engineering: Two-wheeled support for lateral and circular motion. Physics: The force of friction, the role and impact of floor traction at low speeds.
Etch-a-sketch	Objective: Use Sphero as a 3D joystick and stream its sensor data to an Android device to implement an Etch-a-Sketch app. Linear algebra: 3D rotation matrix (roll, pitch, yaw). Embedded systems: Processing hardware sensor data in real time. Data structures: Maintaining a constantly changing non-graphical memory representation of the drawing.
Collision detection	Objective: Detect and study the collisions of Sphero with stationary and moving objects. Physics: Inertia and mass. Digital signal processing: Detecting meaningful changes in real-time accelerometer data. Game design: Design an Android app that would take advantage of Sphero collision detection for entertainment purposes.
Robot race (course project)	Objective: Enable Sphero to behave autonomously by following a complex script. Robotics: Use a set of well-defined commands to control the motors of the robot enabling it to move at given speeds: roll along a straight line of a given length, roll along an arc with a given radius and angle; turn in place; and change the LED color. Operating systems: Design and implement a real-time multithreaded controller. Human-computer interaction: Design a user-friendly mobile interface for script editing, storage, and retrieval. Programming languages: Design and implement a simple parser for custom scripts to control the robot. Computer networking: Use an HTTP-based connection to retrieve text-based scripts from a URL; implement asynchronous data transfer between the robotic sensors and a mobile device over Bluetooth. Linear algebra: Transform the robot's coordinate system and an absolute heading into a coordinate system with a relative heading; transform an arbitrary circular arc into a sequence of straight lines; convert the robot's odometry into real-world speed metrics. Physics: Understand and account for the effects of floor traction at low speeds.

The Android+Sphero course described here was structured around a number of hands-on lab projects, which, as a rule, were offered once a week. Each lab typically required students not only to practice the theoretical topics and skills emphasized by the most recent course material, but also required students to reach further into other topics of computing, or required students to apply the knowledge and skills from other STEM disciplines. These connections are summarized in Table 1. As illustrated by the topics listed in the table, especially towards the end of the course, the hands-on activities required students to branch out into the related STEM disciplines in order to fully understand the requirements of each activity and successfully reach its objectives.

The final project played an integral role in this course. As shown in Table 1, the objective of the project is to design and develop a complex software system that meets a set of specified requirements with the features ranging from providing a high-level user interface, meeting mid-level data storage considerations, to ensuring a correct low-level interaction with a hardware controller. Furthermore, students are required to make design choices to balance the complexity of the system by

distributing its features across various levels of architecture granularity and abstraction paradigms.

The functionality of the project had many layers, but its core was formed by the student implementation of four basic commands to control the robot:

- *Roll* to move the robot along a straight line to the specified distance at the given speed;
- *Turn* to make the robot rotate in place to the specified angle;
- *Arc* to roll the robot along a segment of the circle with the given radius, angle, and speed; and
- *Color* to change the robot's internal LED color to the specified RGB value.

This course project emphasized the importance of evaluating the trade-offs resulting from different design choices at many levels of the system's architectural design. The robot's Arc command could serve as a good example. One way to make the robot follow the path shaped as a segment of the circle is to approximate it by executing a repeating sequence of two other commands, Roll and

Turn. This approach may be easier to implement because reusing two much simpler commands results in breaking down the complexity of the Arc command. At the same time, some computations will be required to derive the length of the Roll and the angle of the Turn to correctly approximate the Arc with the given radius and the overall angle. On the other hand, the Arc command can be implemented by programming the robot at the lower level by indirectly accessing its two motors. Once the robot starts moving straight, a periodic adjustment of its heading would accomplish the objectives of the Arc command. This approach will require converting the linear speed of the robot to tangential speed and sending a sequence of heading adjustment commands in real time. Although the two approaches to implementing the Arc command would typically result in achieving the same overall goal, the original design choices have a significant impact on the outcome. The first approach is a discrete approximation of the curved path and is much simpler to implement. The second approach results in a continuous motion of the robot, but requires a substantial amount of experimentation and testing to get it right.

4. DID STUDENTS SEE THE CONNECTIONS?

The Systems Programming course combining mobile computing and robotics was offered in the Fall 2012 and again in the Fall 2013 semester. In order to better understand the effectiveness of combining these two topics in a single course and leveraging their symbiotic relationship to illustrate the connections between many STEM disciplines, students were asked to complete pre- and post-course surveys. Some of the results are presented here.

Table 2. Student demographics.

Characteristic	2012	2013
Course enrollment	22	23
Male	19	21
Female	3	2
Freshmen	0	0
Sophomores	1	0
Juniors	6	8
Seniors	15	15
Completed surveys	20	20

The objective of this study was to determine whether this course made a positive impact on the students' perception of computing as an area of study and practice, which is concerned with solving interdisciplinary problems. Both at the beginning and at the end of the semester during both course offerings, students were presented with a list of topics and subjects both within and outside of computing, as shown in Table 3. Using a five-point Likert scale, students were asked to rate whether the knowledge and skills in the corresponding areas is useful in a) projects involving robotics, and b) projects involving mobile application development.

Table 3. Pool of topics and subjects used in the study.

Algorithms;	Database systems;
Artificial intelligence;	Electrical engineering;
Assembler language;	Embedded systems;
Compiler construction;	Human-computer interaction;
Computer architecture;	Mathematics;
Computer graphics	Mechanical engineering;
Computer networking;	Object-oriented programming;
Computer security;	Operating systems;
Computer vision;	Physics;
Data structures;	Software engineering.

The difference between the pre-course and post-course results was assessed using a one-tailed t-test to determine those areas in which the changes in student responses were statistically significant. Table 4 and Table 5 show the results of statistical analysis indicating the values for the mean and standard deviation in student responses in both pre- and post-test groups, the change in student response (Δ), as well as the t and p values obtained from the t-test. Student responses from the Fall 2012 and Fall 2013 were merged together into the corresponding pre- and post-test sets of results to increase the pool size for the resulting n=40 (Table 2). For the sake of brevity, these tables only contain data for the items with any statistical significance ($p < 0.05$ and $p < 0.1$).

Table 4. Connections and effects of robotics.

Item descriptor		Mean	SD	Δ	t	P
Computer vision	pre-test	3.40	1.19	0.45	1.812	0.085
	post-test	3.85	0.81			
Electrical engineering	pre-test	3.90	1.12	0.50	2.058	0.053
	post-test	4.40	0.75			
Embedded systems	pre-test	3.00	1.34	0.80	2.329	0.030
	post-test	3.80	1.28			
Mathematics	pre-test	3.85	0.99	0.55	2.377	0.028
	post-test	4.40	0.75			
Mechanical engineering	pre-test	3.65	1.09	0.50	1.805	0.086
	post-test	4.15	1.18			
Physics	pre-test	3.40	0.99	0.80	3.204	0.004
	post-test	4.20	0.83			

4.1 Connections and Effects of Robotics

As a result of completing this course, students were able to better see the importance of skills and knowledge in several of the areas listed in Table 3 when applied to the projects involving robotics. The analysis of pre- and post-test student responses (Table 4) indicates that there was a statistically significant change ($p < 0.05$) in the following areas:

Embedded systems. A number of student activities focused on working with the Sphero's on-board sensors, understanding their functionality, as well as processing the real-time data received from these sensors and making the system react in response to changes in the sensor readouts. During lectures, students were introduced to the high level overview of Sphero architecture with a particular emphasis on the features supporting real-time communication between the robot and other devices. In the Etch-a-sketch lab (Table 1), students disabled the robot's stabilization mechanism to make the robot function as a 3D joystick. Real-time accelerometer data was streamed from Sphero and processed on an Android device to analyze the movements of the robot in space and create an on-screen drawing.

Mathematics. The final course project provided ample opportunities for students to apply some of their math skills. In order to enable the robot to follow the script and navigate the racetrack, the robot's coordinate system and its absolute heading needed to be transformed into a coordinate system with a relative heading. As described in Section 3.2, one of the most challenging parts of the project was implementing the Arc command, which could be done by transforming an arbitrary circular arc into a sequence of straight lines.

Physics. Sphero's shape and mechanics have a significant impact on how the robot moves and interacts with the environment. Due to the lack of a direct contact of Sphero's wheels with the floor surface, traction with the floor is not always perfect, especially on hard surfaces and at low speeds. Also, hard surfaces often do not provide enough traction when the robot starts moving at a high speed. These factors had a significant impact on implementing the robot's motion commands in the final project: students had to conduct many experiments to ensure that the robot behaves consistently at different speeds and on different floor surfaces. During the collision detection lab, students were able to gain hands-on experience with the effect of inertia and mass on the spikes of accelerometer readouts as the collision was registered. Consequently, students had a great deal of in-depth experimentation with Sphero's on-board accelerometer and gained a thorough understanding of the role of gravity on the process of detecting collisions.

As a result of their experiences in this course, students could also better see the importance of these three areas, although with a weaker statistical significance ($p<0.1$):

Electrical and **mechanical engineering.** In order to gain a full mastery of both high-level and low-level features of the robot, students had to get a good grasp on the functionality and integration of electronic and mechanical components inside the Sphero. In particular, to be able to correctly implement the Turn and Arc commands of the final project, students needed a good understanding how the two motors can support both lateral and circular motion of the robot.

Computer vision. Sphero is equipped with an accelerometer and a magnetometer, and these are the only sensors that it can use to perceive the surrounding environment. Although students in this course did not have any experience working with light sensors or with implementing computer vision algorithms, they successfully used the accelerometer for sensing collisions with surrounding objects. As a result, they gained a thorough appreciation for the importance of computer vision in the robotics projects.

Table 5. Connections and effects of mobile computing.

Item descriptor		Mean	SD	Δ	t	P
Computer architecture	pre-test	2.90	0.91	0.50	1.839	0.081
	post-test	3.40	1.27			
Human-computer interaction	pre-test	4.40	0.75	0.35	2.187	0.041
	post-test	4.75	0.44			
Operating systems	pre-test	3.40	1.14	0.45	1.751	0.095
	post-test	3.85	0.99			
Physics	pre-test	2.25	0.91	0.60	2.287	0.033
	post-test	2.85	1.09			

4.2 Connections and Effects of Mobile Computing

Similarly to robotics, mobile computing and application development were also a fertile ground for making connections between computing and other disciplines. The experiences of this course helped students better see the importance of the areas described below when applied to projects involving mobile application development. The analysis of pre- and post-test student responses (Table 5) indicates that there was a statistically significant change ($p<0.05$) in the following areas:

Physics. Prior to being introduced to Sphero, students had to complete a lab exploring the use of sensors that an Android device is equipped with. For example, students had to use the accelerometer to detect a situation when the device is in a free fall or to determine whether the device is being shaken. During such hands-on experiences, students applied such physics concepts as acceleration, motion, and gravity to solve a practical computing problem.

Human-computer interaction (HCI). As the data shown in Table 5 suggests, students came into the course with a preconception that the skills and knowledge in the area of HCI are important in mobile application development. A statistically

significant change in the student feedback indicates that the experience of this course reinforced this concept even further. Students were able to consider many limitations and features of mobile devices from the software developer's perspective. In particular, the limitations of a small screen, a lack of or a very small size of the physical keyboard are the most obvious constraints. Voice and gesture interaction, tactile feedback, and physical device manipulation are among the interaction modalities that mobile application developers must be proficient with. In particular, in one of the labs students needed to learn how to account for physical differences in motion produced by different users when implementing a device shake counter. Although HCI is an interdisciplinary field by its very nature, it was not our objective to determine whether students were more interested in the computing or social, engineering, and design aspects of HCI.

As a result of their experiences in this course, students could also better see the importance of these three areas applied in a mobile application development project, although with a weaker statistical significance ($p<0.1$):

Operating systems and **computer architecture.** Mobile application development provides ample opportunities to learn about many aspects of the inner workings of a computing device. For example, communication between components and services receives a substantial emphasis in this course in order to fully explain the fundamental Android principle of using intents. The concept of activity lifecycle also plays a fundamental role in Android. This concept is reinforced within every single lab, thus giving students a substantial exposure to the principles of process management in an operating system. A continued emphasis on the constrained hardware resources available in a mobile device helps students gain a better understanding of computer architecture principles in order to become effective mobile application developers.

5. CONCLUSION

The need to produce computing professionals who are ready to tackle interdisciplinary problems has been recognized by the industry, academia, and the government. So far, most educational efforts concentrated on offering interdisciplinary research projects, as well as interdisciplinary tracks and programs. The objective of this work was to show that interdisciplinary connections could be successfully made in a standalone CS course. The success of this effort could be demonstrated not only through the statistical analysis presented above, but also by quoting the students who answered a number of open-ended questions included in the post-test survey instrument. The following two student answers exemplify the underlying opinion that students expressed when asked to describe the connections between CS and other disciplines:

CS embodies all the best parts of engineering and math, specifically creative problem solving, but is infinitely more rewarding because it is relevant to modern society.

I believe that the knowledge of math and physics is necessary for anyone who studies CS.

Incorporating experiential learning activities focused on programming robotic and mobile computing devices helped achieve many of the course goals. Most importantly, by participating in hands-on learning activities involving a complex tangible system, students were able to apply their knowledge and skills from a range of STEM disciplines: computing, mathematics, physics, as well as mechanical and electrical engineering. As a result, students could witness the application of these interdisciplinary connections in a practical setting. The post-test survey asked students whether this course changed their opinion about these connections; the following quote embodies the underlying theme in the student responses:

I saw the connections from the beginning, but the course helped demonstrate them in a tangible way.

6. ACKNOWLEDGMENTS

The author would like to thank all students enrolled in the course described in this paper, as well as the Orbotix team for providing Sphero robots, guidance, and valuable feedback.

7. REFERENCES

[1] Amoussou, G.-A. Boylan, M., Peckham, J. 2010. Interdisciplinary computing education for the challenges of the future. In *Proceedings of the 41st ACM technical symposium on Computer science education* (SIGCSE '10). ACM, New York, NY, USA, 556-557.

[2] Apiola, M., Lattu, M., Pasanen, T.A. 2010. Creativity and intrinsic motivation in computer science education: experimenting with robots. In *Proceedings of the 15th annual conference on Innovation and technology in computer science education* (ITiCSE '10). ACM, New York, NY, USA, 199-203.

[3] Barr, J., Erkan, A. 2012. Educating the educator through computation: what GIS can do for computer science. In *Proceedings of the 43rd ACM technical symposium on Computer Science Education* (SIGCSE '12). ACM, New York, NY, USA, 355-360.

[4] Beck, J., Buckner, B., Nikolova, O. 2007. Using interdisciplinary bioinformatics undergraduate research to recruit and retain computer science students. In *Proceedings of the 38th SIGCSE technical symposium on Computer science education* (SIGCSE '07). ACM, New York, NY, USA, 358-361.

[5] Blumenfeld, P., Soloway, E., Marx, R., Krajcik, J., Guzdial, M., Palincsar, A. 1991. Motivating project-based learning: Sustaining the doing, supporting the learning. *Educational psychologist, 26,* 3-4, 369 398. 1991.

[6] Bogle, S.A., Potter, W.D. 2011. Using robot based learning to enhance CS curriculum delivery, In *Proceedings of the 11th IEEE International Conference on Advanced Learning Technologies (ICALT)* (Jul. 2011), 576-578.

[7] Burd, B., Barros, J., Johnson, C., Kurkovsky, S., Rosenbloom, A., Tillman, N. 2012. Educating for mobile computing: addressing the new challenges. In *Proceedings of the final reports on Innovation and technology in computer science education 2012 working groups* (ITiCSE-WGR '12). ACM, New York, NY, USA, 51-63.

[8] Cielniak, G., Bellotto, N., Duckett, T. 2013. Integrating mobile robotics and vision with undergraduate computer science. *IEEE Trans. on Education*, 56, 1 (Feb. 2013), 48-53.

[9] Doerschuk, P., Liu, J., Mann, J. 2009. INSPIRED broadening participation: first year experience and lessons learned. In *Proceedings of the 14th annual ACM SIGCSE conference on Innovation and technology in computer science education* (ITiCSE '09). ACM, New York, NY, USA, 238-242.

[10] Doom, T. Raymer, M. Krane, D. Garcia, O. 2003. Crossing the interdisciplinary barrier: a baccalaureate computer science option in bioinformatics, *IEEE Transactions on Education*, 46, 3, 387-393, Aug. 2003.

[11] Gentile, L., Caudill, L., Fetea, M., Hill, A., Hoke, K., Lawson, B., Lipan, O., Kerckhove, M., Parish, C., Stenger, K., Szajda, D. 2012. Challenging disciplinary boundaries in the first year: a new introductory integrated science course for STEM majors. *Journal of College Science Teaching*, 41, 5, 44-50, May 2012.

[12] Kay, J.S. 2011. Contextualized approaches to introductory computer science: the key to making computer science relevant or simply bait and switch? In *Proceedings of the 42nd ACM technical symposium on Computer science education* (SIGCSE '11). ACM, New York, NY, USA, 177-182.

[13] Kurkovsky, S. 2013. Mobile computing and robotics in one course: why not? In *Proceedings of the 18th ACM conference on Innovation and technology in computer science education* (ITiCSE '13). ACM, New York, NY, USA, 64-69.

[14] Lee, I., Martin, F., Denner, J., Coulter, B., Allan, W., Erickson, J., Malyn-Smith, J., Werner, L. 2011. Computational thinking for youth in practice. *ACM Inroads*, 2, 1 (Feb. 2011), 32-37.

[15] Major, L., Kyriacou, T., Brereton, O. P. 2011. Systematic literature review: Teaching novices programming using robots, In Proceedings of 15th Annual Conference on *Evaluation & Assessment in Software Engineering (EASE 2011)*, 21-30, Apr. 2011.

[16] McGill, M.M. 2012. Learning to Program with Personal Robots: Influences on Student Motivation. *Trans. on Computing Education*. 12, 1 (Mar. 2012).

[17] National Science Foundation. 2006. *Investing in America's Future: Strategic Plan 2006–2011*. Arlington, VA.

[18] Tucker, A.B. 1996. Strategic directions in computer science education. *ACM Comput. Surv.* 28, 4 (Dec. 1996), 836-845.

[19] Wolber, D. 2011. App inventor and real-world motivation. In *Proceedings of the 42nd ACM technical symposium on Computer science education* (Jun. 2011). ACM, New York, NY, USA, 601-606.

[20] Zhang, M., Lundak, E., Lin, C.C., Gegg-Harrison, T., Francioni, F. 2007. Interdisciplinary application tracks in an undergraduate computer science curriculum. *In Proceedings of the 38th SIGCSE technical symposium on Computer science education* (SIGCSE '07). ACM, New York, NY, USA, 425-429.

Teaching a Core CS Concept through Robotics

Stéphane Magnenat
Autonomous System Lab
ETH Zurich, Switzerland
stephane@magnenat.net

Jiwon Shin
Dept. of Computer Science
ETH Zurich, Switzerland
jiwon.shin@inf.ethz.ch

Fanny Riedo
Lab. de Systèmes Robotiques
EPFL, Lausanne, Switzerland
fanny.riedo@epfl.ch

Roland Siegwart
Autonomous System Lab
ETH Zurich, Switzerland
rsiegwart@ethz.ch

Morderchai Ben-Ari
Dept. of Science Teaching
Weizmann Inst. Sci., Israel
moti.ben-ari@weizmann.ac.il

ABSTRACT

We implemented single-session workshops using the Thymio-II—a small, self-contained robot designed for young students, and VPL—a graphical software development environment based upon event handling. Our goal was to investigate if the students could learn this core computer science concept while enjoying themselves in the robotics context. A visual questionnaire was developed based upon the combined Bloom and SOLO taxonomies, although it proved difficult to construct a questionnaire appropriate for young students. We found that—despite the short duration of the workshop—all but the youngest students achieved the cognitive level of Unistructural Understanding, while some students achieved higher levels of Unistructural Applying and Multistructural Understanding and Applying.

Categories and Subject Descriptors

K.3.2 [**Computers & Education**]: Computer and Information Science Education - *Computer Science Education*; I.2.9 [**Robotics**]

General Terms

Human Factors

Keywords

robotics in education, Thymio II, Aseba, VPL, event-action pair

1. INTRODUCTION

Outreach programs are widely used to expose young people to *science, mathematics, engineering, technology (*STEM*)* in general and to *computer science* (CS) in particular. These programs are intended to motivate them to consider further STEM studies, as well as to raise the level of their self-efficacy.

ITiCSE'14, June 21–25, 2014, Uppsala, Sweden.
Copyright is held by the owner/author(s). Publication rights licensed to ACM.
ACM 978-1-4503-2833-3/14/06 ...$15.00.
http://dx.doi.org/10.1145/2591708.2591714 .

Technologies used in outreach programs include kinaesthetic activities such as Computer Science Unplugged [1], and visual programming environments such as Alice [10] and Scratch [7]. Robotics activities are very popular [3], because they reify the abstract behaviour of algorithms and programs as concrete artefacts that appeal to young people. We believe that even within the context of an outreach program, an attempt should be made to teach core CS concepts, so that the children have an insight on what CS truly is, beyond superficial interaction with computers.

This paper describes an outreach program that used the Thymio II educational robot and the Visual Programming Language (VPL) of the Aseba development environment. VPL supports one programming construct, *event-action pairs*, created by dragging and dropping graphical blocks. The concept of event handling is a core CS concept widely used for structuring software and Bruce et al. proposed that it be the basis of teaching CS1 [2]. We designed the outreach sessions to introduce this concept, taking advantage of the fact that a robot is a physical device that—when paired with VPL—makes this concept accessible in a concrete way.

The robot and the environment were demonstrated by the first three authors at several public events in the past [6, 9]. Feedback from the events informed the subsequent development of VPL. The EPFL robotics festival in 2013 allowed the first and third authors to test VPL with hundreds of participants and to demonstrate that it was well accepted and understood by children 6–11 years old. We decided to pursue this outreach program with a focus on teaching a core CS concept during a single workshop. This paper describes the development of the content of the sessions, observational evidence of the success of the program, and pilot research used to check the level of understanding achieved by the participants.

Section 2 describes the robot and the software environment, while Section 3 presents the outreach workshops. The design of the questionnaire is explained in Section 4. The results of the analysis, the discussion and the limitations of the research appear in Sections 5–7. Section 8 describes our plans for the future.

2. THYMIO II AND ASEBA

The Aseba programming environment [5] was designed and constructed at the Swiss Federal Institute of Technology (EPFL in Lausanne and ETH in Zürich). The Thymio II robot [6, 9] was created by EPFL and ECAL (University of

Arts and Design) in Lausanne. The robot is small ($11 \times 11 \times 5$ cm), self-contained and robust with two independently-driven wheels for differential drive:

The robot has five proximity sensors on the front and two on the back, and two sensors on the bottom that measure the ground reflectivity. There are five capacitive buttons on the top, a three-axis accelerometer, a microphone, an IR sensor for a remote control and a thermometer. For output, in addition to the two motors, there are RGB LEDs at the top and bottom of the robot, as well as monocoloured LEDs next to the sensors, and a sound synthesizer.

The specifications of the hardware can be downloaded under the CreativeCommons Attribution-ShareAlike license. The robot is affordable, priced at 99 CHF (about 80 Euros) plus tax and shipping (http://www.mobsya.org/en-shop). The Aseba software is open source under the LGPL license. Software, documentation, projects and tutorials can be found at http://thymio.org.

The Aseba programming environment has two modules: a classical interactive developement environment called Studio and a visual programming interface call VPL. The Aseba programming language is based on the construct **onevent**, which is used to create event handlers for the sensors. The Studio environment features a display of the sensor values that is *dynamically refreshed*; this enables the user to learn about how the sensors work in practice before writing a program. Aseba programs are downloaded through a USB cable, which also recharges the internal battery. Once the program is loaded, the robot can run untethered.

VPL is a component of Aseba for visual programming designed to be accessible to young children. The environment is minimalistic and the block icons are large. Figure 1 shows the environment and a program for following a line of black electrician's tape on a white floor. On the left is a column of *event blocks* and on the right is a column of *action blocks*. By dragging and dropping one event block and one action block to the centre pane, an *event-action pair* is created. Both event and action blocks are parametrized, enabling the user to create many programs from the small number of blocks.

VPL programs are automatically compiled into Aseba programs. When the program is run, all the event-action pairs run concurrently.

In the event-action pair:

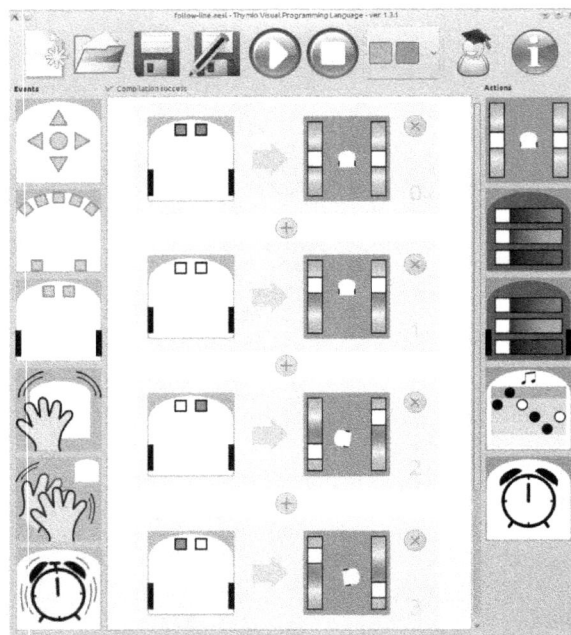

Figure 1: The Aseba/VPL environment

the event is "the right ground sensor detects the white floor and the left sensor detects the black tape," and the action is "the right motor is set to fast forward and the left motor to fast backwards." The result is that *if* the event occurs, the robot turns to the left.

A reference manual and a tutorial for VPL are available at https://aseba.wikidot.com/en:thymioprogram.

3. THE OUTREACH PROGRAM

Although many CS concepts are abstract, we believe that they are accessible to young children if reified in a context. We investigated whether the concept of *event handler* could be successfully taught using the Thymio II robot and VPL.

3.1 Population

Three workshops were held in Switzerland:

- A workshop of three 45 minutes sessions was given at a primary school in Lausanne to 20 students aged 8–9, 10 boys and 10 girls.

- A 1.5-hour workshop was given in Zürich to 40 children aged 10–15, 30 girls and 10 boys. Six teaching assistants coached these students, and the first two authors observed and provided minor support.

- A 1.5-hour workshop was given at a teacher-training school in Liestal (near Basel) to 10 students aged 22–30, 8 women and 2 men. The first author coached this workshop.

3.2 The robot tasks

The students were introduced to the Thymio-II hardware and the VPL software, and requested to solve tasks, which were based on the following specific learning objectives:

- Understand the concepts of event, action and event-action pair. (Advanced blocks for timers and states were not taught in these workshops.)

- Understand that an event specified in an event block occurs *conjunctively*, when all the conditions on the sensors specified in the block occur.

- Understand that the events specified in different event-action pairs occur *disjunctively*, so that if more than one event occurs, all the associated actions take place concurrently.

- Create a program given a detailed description of what it should do, such as "the robot should become red when the left button is touched."

- Create a program given an abstract description, such as "explore a labyrinth while avoiding walls."

In the second and third workshops, a sequence of predefined tasks was presented to the participants. These were intended to gently introduce them to the capabilities of the Thymio robot and the VPL environment. The tasks were:

1. The robot becomes red when the left button is touched and green when the right button is touched.

2. The robot changes colour and plays music when tapped; it changes colour again when the rear button is touched.

3. The robot moves in a direction that depends on which button is touched (left, right, front); it stops when the rear button is touched.

4. The robot changes colour depending on which front sensor detects a finger. The lights turn off if both the leftmost and rightmost sensors are covered.

5. The robot detects a light or dark ground and changes its colour accordingly.

6. The robot follows a line on the ground.

7. The robot moves forward and stops at the edge of the table. This should also work if the robot approaches the edge at an angle.

8. The robot navigates a labyrinth without touching its walls; it stops when there is a black tape on the ground.

The first two tasks use only the most basic capabilities of the robot and are used to familiarize the students with the system. Tasks 3–5 introduce the students to the semantics of the sensors (conjunctively within a single block and disjunctively among multiple blocks), and require them to create a program from a detailed specification. Tasks 6–7 are abstract descriptions of advanced robotics behaviours that require the students to design and implement an algorithm. Although the behaviours are advanced, the high expressivity of the event-handling architecture of Aseba means that the implementations require only a handful of event-action pairs, so the tasks are within the capabilities of the students.

4. THE QUESTIONNAIRE

To measure the level of understanding of the CS concept, we constructed a questionnaire using the taxonomy of cognitive levels proposed in [8]. We restricted ourselves to the following cognitive levels:

- Unistructural Understanding and Applying (UU, UA).

- Multistructural Understand, Applying and Creating (MU, MA, MC).

The definitions are given in [8, pp. 5,7]:

- Unistructural: A local perspective where mainly one item or aspect is used or emphasized. Others are missing, and no significant connections are made.

- Multistructural: A multi-point perspective, where several relevant items or aspects are used or acknowledged, but significant connections are missing and a whole picture is not yet formed.

- Understanding: The ability to summarize, explain, exemplify, classify, and compare CS concepts, including programming constructs.

- Applying: The ability to execute programs or algorithms, to track them, and to recognize their goals.

- Creating: The ability to plan and produce programs or algorithms.

In the context of VPL, unistructural sometimes refers to an individual block, but mostly to an individual event-action pair composed of two blocks, since there is little meaning to the blocks outside a pair. Multistructural refers to the behaviour of a program composed of more than one pair.

We drafted a questionnaire with eleven questions: three UU, two MU, two UA, two MA and two MC. Three of the authors and one colleague independently assigned cognitive levels to the questions, and consensus was obtained on all questions except for one at the MU level; this question was dropped from the questionnaire. The questionnaire was then translated from English into French and German for use in the workshops. It is available at https://aseba.wikidot.com/en:thymiopaper-vpl-iticse2014.

We observed that the questionnaire was too difficult for the reading ability of the young students at the Lausanne workshop, so only observations are reported for this workshop.

5. RESULTS

5.1 Observations

5.1.1 The Lausanne workshop

We initially observed a relatively high variability between the students. This put a strain on the teacher who had to deal with many questions at the same time. The problem was alleviated by pairing faster students with slower ones and explicitly asking the faster to coach the slower. The slower student was in control of the mouse, while the faster student explained which block must be used and why.

The students reported that VPL was easy and comfortable to use. When asked if something should be changed in VPL, they claimed that the music block was not "fashionable" enough and that it lacked a volume control. We asked whether they built their programs by copying an existing one, creating their own program or by trial and error; we found that most used trial and error.

For this age group, we found that while children can understand and use the VPL interface, they seemed to lack the capability to think about programs abstractly.

5.1.2 The Zürich workshop

The students who attended the workshop in Zürich were a bit older than those of the first workshop and had more personalized attention: one teaching assistant for every 5–7 children. We observed that they worked in groups of two or three, that most groups worked well together, and that no individual dominated the others. We observed a variability in the performance of the groups that seemed to stem from the motivation and interests of the students. In some groups, students were actively engaged in playing with the robot and VPL, and programmed complex behaviors. In a couple of other groups, children showed a lack of interest and struggled to program even the simplest behaviors such as making the robot move forward or changing the robot's body colour when a button is touched.

After the workshop, one parent wrote that she was grateful for the workshop because it increased her daughter's motivation for study, something that she felt it is difficult for parents to do. In fact, the girl decided on the spot that in the future she *must* study at ETH! Admittedly, this is a transient anecdote but it is encouraging for the potential of a robotics outreach program to influence motivation.

Confusing concepts.

The students struggled with the compilation error caused by redundant event-action pairs (cf. the result of the questionnaire discussed below). They were also confused that the robot would not stop unless a motor action with null speed was programmed. The horizontal and ground sensor event blocks were problematic because they can be programmed to cause an event to occur when something is detected or not detected. For the horizontal sensor, an obstacle will cause the *IR light to be reflected*, while for the ground sensor, at the end of the table, the *IR light is no longer reflected*. The students simply believed that an event will occur when "something happens," without realizing that in one case the event occurs when light is reflected and in the other when it is not reflected. We believe that with more explicit instruction and with more practice, the students will be able to learn to use these sensors correctly.

5.1.3 The Liestal workshop

The students in this workshop were pre-service teachers who were less excited by the robot than the children in the other workshops. Some were reluctant to follow the tasks, and one person complained that the workshop required logical thinking, something this person expressed to dislike to carry out. One person asked for a comparison against other products such as the LEGO Mindstorms, a question we could only answer informally.

The fact that the workshop took place during the last two weeks of the semester as the exams approached was probably a factor in the relative lack of interest by these students.

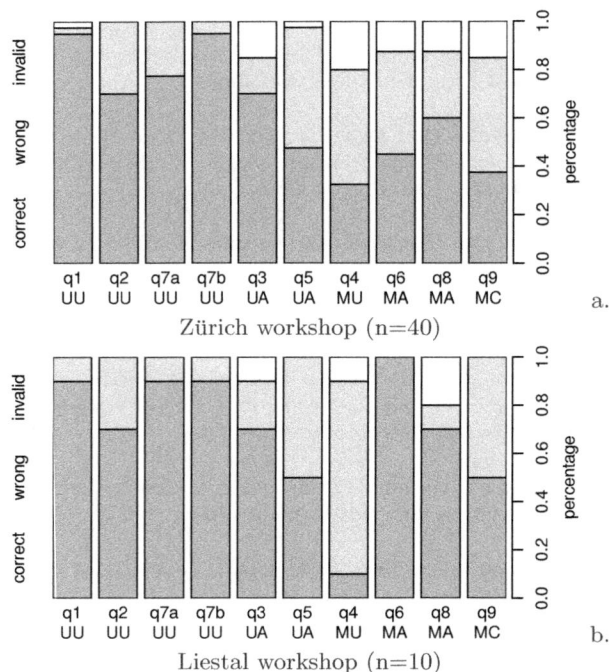

Figure 2: Ratio of correct answers per question.

5.2 The questionnaire

5.2.1 The Zürich workshop

Figure 2(a) shows the results of the questionnaire, ordered by the cognitive level of the taxonomy. There is a bar for each question which is also labeled with its cognitive level. Each bar is divided into three sections: one for correct answers, one for incorrect answers and one for invalid answers (when no answer was given, when multiple answers were given, or when the answer was unreadable).

Questions at level UU were answered correctly by most students, but they had difficulty with the higher levels. It is interesting that the scores are similar for UA and MA, from which we conclude that the task of tracking execution, not the number of event-action pairs, is the prime factor that makes a question difficult. Question 5 at the UA level concerned the ground sensor block, which was problematic as previously mentioned, and only 47 % of the students gave the correct answer. The results were better for question 3, the other UA question.

Figure 3 shows the detailed answers for questions 4 and 9, which posed the greatest difficulty for the students. For question 4 (Appendix A), most students chose the correct answer, while the other answers were distributed relatively equally over the other alternatives. This question was testing the syntactic concept that a valid program cannot contain identical event-action pairs. Since this issue had not been explicitly mentioned, the result is not surprising. The problem could be overcome by explicit instruction and by teachers drawing students' attention to the VPL error messages.

For question 9 (Appendix B), the answer *(a)* was chosen more often than the other wrong answers. This is understandable because the correct answer was *Either (a) or (c)*,

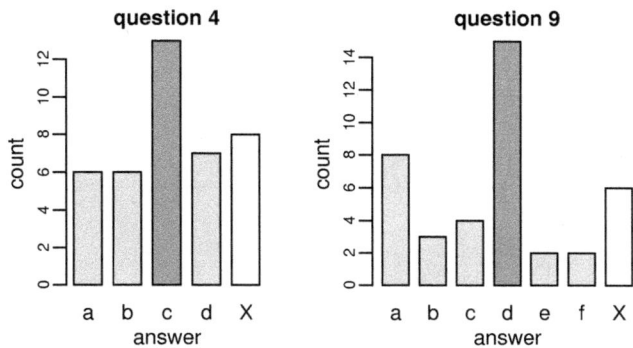

Figure 3: Answers chosen for questions 4 and 9 (X invalid) at the Zürich workshop. The correct answer has the darkest shade.

so *(a)* was partially correct. In addition, there were quite a few invalid answers for this question. We concluded that the logical reasoning required was beyond the ability of this age group and we will change the question in the future.

For questions 6 and 8, the errors were spread over all possible alternatives; we attribute this result to the complexity of the questions.

5.2.2 The Liestal workshop

The results of the questionnaire are displayed in Figure 2(b). These results are similar to the ones of the Zürich workshop with the exception of questions 4 and 6. Question 4 asked about the syntax error, but the students did not encounter this error in their work and so were confused by the question. Question 6 referred to a simple program, but the answers were complex sentences; we conjecture that their success can be attributed to the relatively advanced linguistics capabilities of these adult students.

6. DISCUSSION

The self-contained and inexpensive Thymio II robot was attractive to the young students and enabled them to construct interesting and meaningful projects during the short workshops. We believe that the success of the students in completing robotics projects will increase their self-efficacy and their motivation to engage with STEM.

The Aseba VPL software environment was easy for the students to use. The event-action pair is the *only* construct in VPL, which simplifies teaching, even though the core CS concept it implements is advanced.

We attempted to go beyond observations and to obtain quantitative evidence for the cognitive level achieved by the students, using a questionnaire built according a taxonomy that integrated the Bloom and SOLO taxonomies [8].

The visual language of VPL facilitated the construction of the questionnaire, but also highlighted the importance of ensuring that a questionnaire is age-appropriate. Our questionnaire was relatively accessible to students aged 10–15, but was too hard for students aged 7–9.

In the age group 10–15, most students achieved the level of Unistructural Understanding: they understood the concept of event-action pair and that events happen asynchronously and concurrently. Roughly half demonstrated the levels of Unistructural and Multistructural Applying. We observed

similar scores for Applying at both the Unistructural and Multistructural levels. This is interesting because it shows that what is difficult for children is not the high-level understanding of how a program works, but rather the details of the interactions between the different blocks, especially for different parameters. This comes from the fact that a robot is an autonomous agent and to understand how it works one has to reason logically about the behaviours of the robot and its interactions with the environment.

Question 5 was designed to check the understanding the conjunctive semantics of the sensors within a single event block; although students were confused on how to set the parameters to distinguish between white and black, most understood correctly the *and* between the sensors, validating our third objective.

We measured the level Creating with one question to which 40 % of the students gave the correct answer. Many students did create non-trivial programs, so we concluded that the fourth and fifth objectives were achieved by roughly half the participants. We believe that longer workshops spread out over several days would enable most students to achieve the higher cognitive levels.

We agree with Lister and Leaney [4] that not every student should be expected to achieve the same level:

> Weaker CS1 students are simply required to demonstrate knowledge and comprehension; the ability to read and understand programs. Middling students attempt traditional tasks, while the stronger students are set openended tasks at the synthesis and evaluation levels (p. 143).

In our program, it is not so much a matter of weaker vs. stronger students, but more a matter of a wide variation of the cognitive and emotional development to be expected in young students. We are satisfied with an outcome where most students achieve the lower two levels, many achieve also the middle two levels and a few the top levels.

We found it difficult to construct questions that are appropriate for very young students. To overcome this, it is possible that the taxonomy may need to be modified or replaced with a different one.

7. LIMITATIONS OF THE RESEARCH

Due to the lack of sufficient time and budget to prepare for the workshops, they suffered from logistic issues and from inadequate preparation of the assistants. The workshops were held in various locations, with different teachers, in two languages and with different age groups. We observed that the Thymio II robot and the VPL programming environment were easily and enthusiastically used by all age groups; however, the various contexts of the workshops meant that the populations cannot be compared. Furthermore, a single workshop is not sufficient for enabling young children to think about their program in an abstract way.

We did not compare the use of the Thymio and VPL environment to other robotics environments or to other contexts such as visual programming environments.

8. CONCLUSION

We have shown that the Thymio II educational robot and the Aseba/VPL visual programming environment can be used in short outreach workshops with children. The workshops demonstrated that a core CS concept—event handling—can be successfully taught to young students. We plan to continue our research by improving the VPL interface and by designing instruments that can measure CS learning in various age groups.

9. ACKNOWLEDGEMENTS

We wish to thank Philippe Rétornaz, Michael Bonani, Florian Vaussard and Francesco Mondada for their contribution to the Thymio II robot and their feedback on VPL; Nathalie Bonani and Christina Rothen for giving us access to their students and providing valuable feedback; Hanna Behles and Gregory Hitz for help with translation; and Stefan Bertschi for technical support. Finally, we thank the participants to the workshops for their cooperation. This work was supported by the Swiss National Center of Competence in Research "Robotics" and "ERC Grant no. 291389".

10. REFERENCES

[1] T. Bell, L. Lambert, and D. Marghitu. CS Unplugged, outreach and CS kinesthetic activities. In *Proceedings of the 43rd SIGCSE Technical Symposium on Computer Science Education*, SIGCSE '12, pages 676–676, 2012.

[2] K. Bruce, A. Danyluk, and M. Thomas. *Java: An Eventful Approach*. Prentice Hall, 2006.

[3] K. P. King and M. Gura, editors. *Classroom Robotics: Case Stories of 21st Century Instruction for Millennial Students*. Information Age Publishing, 2007.

[4] R. Lister and J. Leaney. Introductory programming, criterion-referencing, and bloom. In *Proceedings of the 34th SIGCSE Technical Symposium on Computer Science Education*, SIGCSE '03, pages 143–147, 2003.

[5] S. Magnenat, P. Rétornaz, M. Bonani, V. Longchamp, and F. Mondada. ASEBA: A Modular Architecture for Event-Based Control of Complex Robots. *IEEE/ASME Transactions on Mechatronics*, PP(99):1–9, 2010.

[6] S. Magnenat, F. Riedo, M. Bonani, and F. Mondada. A programming workshop using the robot "Thymio II": The effect on the understanding by children. In *IEEE Workshop on Advanced Robotics and its Social Impacts (ARSO)*, 2012.

[7] J. H. Maloney, K. Peppler, Y. Kafai, M. Resnick, and N. Rusk. Programming by choice: Urban youth learning programming with scratch. In *Proceedings of the 39th SIGCSE Technical Symposium on Computer Science Education*, SIGCSE '08, pages 367–371, 2008.

[8] O. Meerbaum-Salant, M. Armoni, and M. Ben-Ari. Learning computer science concepts with Scratch. *Computer Science Education*, 23(3):239–264, 2013.

[9] F. Riedo, M. Chevalier, S. Magnenat, and F. Mondada. Thymio II, a robot that grows wiser with children. In *IEEE Workshop on Advanced Robotics and its Social Impacts (ARSO)*, 2013.

[10] S. H. Rodger, J. Hayes, G. Lezin, H. Qin, D. Nelson, R. Tucker, M. Lopez, S. Cooper, W. Dann, and D. Slater. Engaging middle school teachers and students with Alice in a diverse set of subjects. In *Proceedings of the 40th SIGCSE Technical Symposium on Computer Science Education*, SIGCSE '09, pages 271–275, 2009.

APPENDIX

A. QUESTION 4

Is something **wrong** with this program?

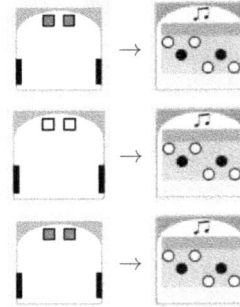

(a) Yes, you **can't have** two event-action pairs with exactly the **same event**.

(b) Yes, you **can't have** two event-action pairs with exactly the **same action**.

(c) Yes, you **can't have** two event-action pairs that are **exactly the same**.

(d) No, **Nothing is wrong** with the program.

The question is categorized as Multistructural because it asks to consider several pairs, and as Understanding because there is no need to trace the execution nor is creativity necessary to answer the question.

B. QUESTION 9

The following program causes the robot **approach a wall** and to **stop when** the robot **hits** the wall:

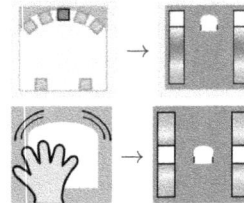

Which two event-action pairs must be **added** to the program so that the robot turns the **top light red** when it **detects the wall** and **plays** music when it **hits the wall**?

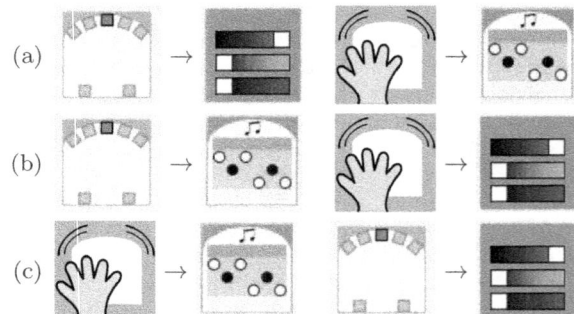

(d) Either (a) or (c)

(e) Either (a) or (b)

(f) Either (b) or (c)

This question is categorized as Multistructural because it asks to consider several pairs, and as Creating because students must plan what the robot has to do.

Three Views on Motivation and Programming

Amber Settle (moderator)
DePaul University
College of Computing and Digital
Media
243 S. Wabash Avenue
Chicago, IL 60604

asettle@cdm.depaul.edu

Arto Vihavainen
University of Helsinki
Department of Computer Science
P.O. Box 68
(Gustaf Hällströmin katu 2b)
Fi-00014 University of Helsinki

avihavai@cs.helsinki.fi

Juha Sorva
Aalto University
Department of Computer Science and
Engineering
P.O. Box 15400
FI-00076 Aalto, Finland

juha.sorva@aalto.fi

OVERVIEW

Teaching programming is one of the most widely studied areas in computing education. Part of the reason for this may be the difficulty students experience when learning programming which makes it a challenging endeavor for instructors. There is a relationship between student motivation and success in learning to program [1], and motivation is also important in the bigger picture for computing educators, having inspired two ITiCSE working groups [2]. What is perhaps surprising is that motivation does not play an equal role in the various subfields of programming education.

In this panel we discuss three areas of programming education, emphasizing the importance of, or in some cases the lack of attention to, student motivation. The first panelist will consider task design, and particularly what we can do to motivate students to learn to program in CS1 courses. Here instructors must pay careful attention to the level of difficulty of tasks as well as the way in which they prompt students in their course activities. A balance between challenge and support must be found to enable students to reach their potential in the crucial first class. The second panelist will discuss program visualization tools. Motivation is related to perceived relevance: a tool is only likely to be helpful if students see it as useful in relation to their existing goals. The perceived relevance of visualization tools and students' motivation to use them might be boosted by training students to explain visual examples to themselves and by increasing students' sense of ownership over what is being visualized. The third panelist considers the teaching of recursion. Although recursion is one of the most difficult ideas programming students encounter, motivation is a little-discussed topic in the literature. Information about the few studies that have considered motivation is presented, along with ideas as to why motivation does not play a larger role in the area.

Categories and Subject Descriptors

K.3.2 [**Computer and Information Science Education**]: Computer science education

ITiCSE'14, June 21–25, 2014, Uppsala, Sweden.
ACM 978-1-4503-2833-3/14/06.
http://dx.doi.org/10.1145/2591708.2591709.

Keywords

CS1, motivation, programming, recursion, visualization

1. ARTO VIHAVAINEN

Students' effort correlates with success [13], and students' motivation, or the lack of it, has been pointed out as one of the major reasons for attrition in CS1 courses [5]. Effort and motivation go hand in hand. As learning programming requires constant practice, maintaining the students' motivation is of utmost importance. Motivation can be supported from multiple directions: the learning material and tasks, the interaction with peers and course staff, and the visibility of the learning progress.

Motivation can be undermined by providing incorrectly timed tasks that the students are not able to accomplish with their existing skill set, or simply by small verbal cues. For example, if a student is struggling with a task, responding with a "do your best"-comment that is often considered as one of the first choices for an educator, results in a lower performance when compared to providing a clear goal such as "try to do at least 80% of the task" [6]. The tasks at hand must, however, support such a goal.

On the other hand, setting high goals may also be detrimental. When students have not yet mastered the elementary routines, high goals may decrease students' performance, as their cognitive resources are mostly allocated to learning the routines. However, as the student starts to master the basic tasks and is able to move forward from the declarative state of learning, explicitly setting high goals can lead to an increase in performance.

In this part of the panel, we review motivational theories in the light of introductory programming education, and discuss good practices for designing programming tasks for different phases of an introductory programming course.

2. JUHA SORVA

Program visualization (PV) software can be used to illustrate the dynamics of program execution and related concepts (e.g., references, the call stack) [10]. However, beginner programmers do not always understand what a visualization tool has to offer and may not connect what they learn through the visualizations to their programming practice [11]. Although students often report that they "like" such visualizations, they may be unmotivated to use visualization tools in constructive ways even when they are motivated to learn to program.

In the literature on PV for beginners, the topic of motivation has not usually been at the forefront, but it has been approached through the notion of *engagement*: what a student does with a visualization is expected to be key to the visualization's impact [8, 10]. For instance, manipulating a visualization or answering questions about it is expected to be more effective than just viewing it. Even then, interacting with graphics alone does not always bring students to see the *relevance* of the graphics.

This part of the panel will discuss the perceived relevance of PV tools and argue that we should look to integrate PV tools into pedagogies that improve students' motivation to use them. Two possible paths for such work will be proposed: 1) There is some evidence that even a modest training effort can help learners explain given examples better to themselves [9]. Students could be trained to be better at studying PV examples, improving their ability to benefit from PV and their motivation to use it. 2) Researchers and teachers who use educational PV should explicitly acknowledge that it is not only how you engage with a visualization that matters but also how you engage with what is being visualized: when a student has a higher sense of ownership over the code or algorithm being visualized, the use of PV is more likely to be motivating and meaningful.

The attendees will be invited to discuss these ideas and to share their own.

3. AMBER SETTLE

Teaching recursion has long been an area of interest for computing educators. Some of the earliest articles on the subject appeared in the 1980s and, as might be expected in an area that spans over 30 years, the focus of each researcher varies. Novel pedagogical approaches, useful and illuminating problems, helping students to attain accurate mental models, assisting non-traditional populations in understanding recursion, and the impact of recursion outreach activities are some of the main themes in the computing education literature, which includes well over forty articles.

Only a small fraction of the articles directly consider motivation. Gunion and her collaborators studied elementary and middle-school students in an extracurricular program focusing on recursion and found that the activities improved student interest in computing [4]. A study focusing on whether to teach iteration or recursion first noted that the motivation levels of the two populations had differed, making definitive conclusions difficult to draw [7]. Researchers involved in the Game2Learn project directly considered motivation in creating and measuring the impact of a game for learning recursion [3]. One author suggested that graphical problems more easily solved using recursion than iteration would be motivating for students [12].

What remains unclear in a survey of the literature is why motivation plays such a small role in teaching and learning recursion. One hypothesis is that recursion is a more advanced topic in the curriculum, one that students only encounter after they have committed to computer science. It may also be that effectively teaching recursion in such a way to produce accurate mental models remains an open question, and that fundamental problems in pedagogy are more interesting for researchers. Unfortunately, it is easy to find holes in each of these arguments, leaving a satisfying answer to the question out of reach. Attendees at the panel will be encouraged to share their views on the topic.

4. REFERENCES

[1] A. Carbone, J. Hurst, and D. Gunstone. An explanation of internal factors influencing student learning of programming. In *Proceedings of the 11th Australasian Computing Education Conference*, ACE '09, New York, NY, 2009. ACM.

[2] Carter, J. et al. Motivating all our students? In *Proceedings of the 16th Annual Conference Reports on Innovation and Technology in Computer Science Education – Working Group Reports*, ITiCSE '11, 2011.

[3] A. Chaffin, K. Doran, D. Hicks, and T. Barnes. Experimental evaluation of teaching recursion in a video game. In *Proceedings of the 2009 ACM SIGGRAPH Symposium on Video Games*, New York, NY, 2009. ACM.

[4] K. Gunion, T. Mildford, and U. Stege. Curing recursion aversion. In *Proceedings of the 14th Annual Conference on Innovation and Technology in Computer Science Education*, ITiCSE '09, New York, NY, USA, 2009. ACM.

[5] P. Kinnunen and L. Malmi. Why students drop out CS1 course? *In Proceedings of the Second International Workshop on Computing Education Research*, ICER '06, pages 97-108, New York, NY, USA, 2006. ACM.

[6] E.A. Locke, K.N. Shaw, L.M. Saari, and G.P. Latham. Goal setting and task performance: 1969-1980. *Psychological bulletin*, 90(1): 125, 1981.

[7] C. Mirolo. Is iteration really easier to learn than recursion for CS1 students? In *Proceedings of the International Computing Education Research Workshop*, ICER '12, New York, NY, USA, 2012. ACM.

[8] T.L. Naps, G. Rößling, V. Almstrum, W. Dann, R. Fleischer, C. Hundhausen, A. Korhonen, L. Malmi, M. McNally, S. Rodger, and J.Á. Velázquez-Iturbide. Exploring the role of visualization and engagement in computer science education. *SIGCSE Bulletin*, 35(2): 131-152, June 2003.

[9] A. Renkl, R. Stark, H. Gruber, and H. Mandl. Learning from worked-out examples: The effects of example variability and elicted self-explanations. *Contemp. Educ. Psychol.*, 23(1):90-108, 1998.

[10] J. Sorva, V. Karavirta, and L. Malmi. A review of generic program visualization systems for introductory programming education. *ACM Transactions on Computing Education*, 13(4):15:1-15:65, Nov. 2013.

[11] J. Sorva, J.Lönnberg, and L. Malmi. Students' ways of experiencing visual program simulation. *Computer Science Education*, 23(3):207-238, 2013.

[12] B. Stephenson. Using graphical examples to motivate the study of recursion. *Journal of Computing Sciences in Colleges*, 25(1):42-50, 2009.

[13] P.R. Ventura. Identifying predictors of success for an objects-first CS1. *Computer Science Education*, 15(3):223-243, 2005.

ITiCSE: The Next Decade

Arnold Pears
Uppsala University
Arnold.pears@it.uu.se

Alison Clear
CPIT
Alison.clear@cpit.ac.nz

Lillian (Boots) Cassel
Villanova University
Lillian.cassel@vilanova.edu

Ernesto Cuadros-Vargas
Universidad Catolica San
Pablo
ecuadros@spc.org.pe

Valentina Dagiene
Vilnius University
valentia.dagiene@mii.vu.lt

Cary Laxer
Rose-Hulman Institute of
Technology
laxer@rose-hulman.edu

ABSTRACT

This year marks the 19th ITiCSE conference. This panel will provide conference delegates, both frequent attendees and those new to ITiCSE the opportunity to reflect on the conference's success as one of the premier international computer science education conferences and to discuss potential future directions for the conference.

Categories and Subject Descriptors

K.3.2 [**Computer and Information Science Education**]: [Computer Science Education]

Keywords

ITiCSE Conference

1. INTRODUCTION

The Innovation and Technology in Computer Science Education (ITiCSE) conference has now been in existence for 19 years with the first conference being held in Barcelona, Spain in 1996. The conference is usually held in late June early July and has been primarily held in Europe with only two exceptions, Turkey in 2010 and Israel in 2012. It is normally hosted by the University of the Chair of the conference. The program consists of keynote speakers, academic papers, panels, posters and tips and techniques. The conference has always been of a high standard with an average accept rate of papers over the past 18 years of 37.5

The ITiCSE conference has two unique features; Working Groups and the afternoon of excursions. The Working groups are formed early in the year of the conference and start work electronically in April. The participants arrive early at the conference and work face to face for the Saturday and Sunday before the conference proper and then continue for the three days of the conference. They are required to produce a report that is then reviewed before publication later in the year. The afternoon of excursions, while being an opportunity to see the sights of the beautiful cities in which ITiCSE has been held, also provides a special opportunity for delegates to meet each other and discuss future research and collaborations that benefit the whole of the SIGCSE community. Many collaborations have been born from these excursions.

As ITiCSE is a truly international conference, it is a perfect opportunity for computing academics from around the world to meet, discuss, collaborate, and share similar experiences and new ideas.

Now that ITiCSE is moving into the third decade of existence, this panel will provide an opportunity to reflect on the past, look at the factors that have worked, propose new ideas and discuss the future plans for this exciting, collaborative and innovative conference.

ITiCSE'14, June 21–25, 2014, Uppsala, Sweden.
ACM 978-1-4503-2833-3/14/06.
http://dx.doi.org/10.1145/2591708.2617812.

Making the Hardware-Software Connection with PLP

Sohum Sohoni
Department of Engineering
College of Technology & Innovation
Arizona State University
sohum.sohoni@asu.edu

ABSTRACT

In this paper, we describe a novel platform for Computer Science and Engineering education that helps students to connect software concepts with the underlying hardware. Students often learn about programming languages, computer architecture, assembly languages and compilers in isolation, and fail to see the connections between the hardware and the software. The Progressive Learning Platform (PLP) was designed for students to anchor their conceptual learning about microprocessors and computer architecture, and for them to see the connections between assembly language and tradeoffs in architecture. The long-term vision for PLP is to be a free and scalable platform for face-to-face and online education in computing worldwide.

Categories and Subject Descriptors

K.3 [**Computers and Education**]: K.3.1 Computer Uses in Education- *Collaborative learning;* K.3.2 Computer and Information Science Education- *Computer science education*

Keywords

Active Learning, Integrated Learning, Computer Architecture, Assembly Language, CSE Education, Microprocessors, Computer Organization, Progressive Learning Platform, PLP.

1. PLP HARDWARE AND SOFTWARE

The PLP processor has an instruction set architecture (ISA) similar to the MIPS processor, but with a further reduction in the ISA. The PLP system utilizes Field-Programmable Gate Array (FPGA) development kits. Currently the platform targets the Digilent Nexys 2 and Nexys 3 development kits. The HDL for the reference PLP CPU is defined behaviorally and special structures such as block RAMs are generically defined to aid in proper inference for a number of targets. PLP is designed to be highly portable, and the Verilog code for the PLP CPU is open source and free to download. Details of the PLP hardware are available on the website [1] and in prior publications [2, 3].

PLPTool, the PLP simulation and visualization suite, was designed for a Microprocessors course to allow students to write, test, and debug assembly programs written in the PLP ISA. PLPTool also has a detailed simulator that features a watcher window, a CPU view showing the disassembly and the contents of all the CPU registers, and a memory visualizer. For an instructor, PLPTool can illustrate important concepts in an interactive way. For example, instead of using five PowerPoint slides to show how a stack grows and ebbs, one can use PLPTool and the memory visualizer. PLPTool is written in Java to be

ITICSE '14, Jun 21-25 2014, Uppsala, Sweden
ACM 978-1-4503-2833-3/14/06.
http://dx.doi.org/10.1145/2591708.2602678

platform-agnostic, and is open source and free to download. A screenshot of PLPTool with the memory visualizer is shown below.

2. PLP-BASED COURSES

PLP is currently used at Arizona State University in a Microprocessors course and a Computer Architecture course. Details of its use in these courses can be found in prior publications [3, 4]. The PLP website [1] also provides the syllabi, course projects, lectures, and other useful course materials. It has also been used in a graduate level computer architecture course, and can be used in Compilers and Operating Systems courses.

3. STUDIES CONDUCTED

We have conducted a number of initial studies of PLP in the classroom. The qualitative and quantitative methods used in these studies range from pre-post tests to linguistic analysis of student reflection essays and focus group interviews. Details of these studies are available in prior publications [3, 5]. The findings showed a significant improvement in student learning outcomes in both the cognitive and affective domains.

4. ACKNOWLEDGMENTS

This work was supported in part by NSF EEC 1136934/1305100.

5. REFERENCES

[1] *Progressive Learning Platform Website* https://plp.asu.edu

[2] D. Fritz, W. Mulia and S. Sohoni, "The progressive learning platform," in *Workshop on Computer Architecture Education,* San Antonio, TX, 2011.

[3] W. Mulia, D. Fritz, S. Sohoni, K. Kearney and M. Mwavita, "PLP: A Community Driven Open Source Platform for Computer Engineering Education," *International Journal of Engineering Education,* vol. 29, pp. 215, 2013.

[4] S. Sohoni, D. Fritz and W. Mulia, "Transforming a microprocessors course through the progressive learning platform," in *ASEE Midwest Section,* Russelville, AR, 2011.

[5] R. Damron, S. Sohoni, K. Kearney and Y. Cho, "Impact of PLP on student learning: Initial results," in *ASEE Annual Conference,* Atlanta, GA, 2013.

Supporting Communication within Industrial Doctoral Projects: the Thesis Steering Model

Ilona Heldal
School of Informatics
University of Skövde
+46 500 448382
ilona.heldal@his.se

Eva Söderström
School of Informatics
University of Skövde
+46 500 448347
eva.soderstrom@his.se

Lars Bråthe*, Robert Murby*
*retired from
Volvo Powertrain AB
lars.brathe@gmail.com
robert.murby@swipnet.se

ABSTRACT

This study presents the Thesis Steering Model (TSM), an instrument supporting systematic communication and collaboration between the different stakeholders involved in industrial doctoral projects. The results describe TSM and illustrate its introduction for seven doctoral projects within a postgraduate school in applied informatics. The experiences from the first two years in use are: enhanced communication, mutual understanding of academic and business values, and opportunity to the doctoral students to build a research identity associated to their own project.

Categories and Subject Descriptors

K.3.2 [**Computer and Information Sciences**]: Information Systems – *Computer science education, Curriculum, Information systems education.* K.6.1 [**K.6.1 Project and People Management**]: Information Systems – *Management techniques.*

Keywords

Postgraduate education; intercultural collaboration; knowledge formation; knowledge transfer; models and instruments in education.

1. INTRODUCTION AND AIMS

A possible way that promotes knowledge transfer between universities and commercial organizations are industrial doctoral projects. These projects are anchored and initiated in problems identified by business organizations, further discussed and developed by researchers from associated research areas and last approximately five years. Although, there are a number of benefits of such interdisciplinary projects, there are also associated problems, often originating in difficulties in communication or coordinating activities due differences between the cultures, interests and goals [1].

The hypothesis behind this study was that considering industrial process steering instruments [2] together with requirements on the doctoral project from academia enables communication between the industrial and academic partners and focuses their attention on

the actual issues at the accurate phases of a doctoral project. Therefore, the management of the industrial research school in Applied Informatics developed the Thesis Steering Model (TSM) based on the academic requirements and commonly used project steering instrument at different Volvo companies, the Information Systems Global Development Process [2]. This paper presents TSM as an instrument supporting systematic communication of the academic requirements and of the business values.

2. TSM – BASICS AND INITIAL RESULTS

There are a number of collaborative activities within industrial doctoral projects that need to be supported, and which guarantee high scientific values and the production of business values during the doctoral process. TSM breaks down the doctoral process into sub-processes in order to enable structural analysis.

TSM has seven gates: start gate (SG), vision gate (VG), concept gate (CG), development gate (DG), follow-up gate (FG), report gate (RG) and end gate (EG). Each project group plans a gate meeting where different values are explicitly analyzed (business value, research quality management, examination management and project values). Only after a common agreement at a gate meeting can the group involved in the doctoral project and management 'open the gate' for continuing the project. At the SG the partners need to approve the business and the scientific level of the project area and formally start a pre-study. The pre-study ends with the VG where multiple project visions are examined. At the CG, visions are reduced to the three-five most interesting ideas to be investigated further. At the DG, one research question has to be prioritized. A doctoral project may contain several FGs. The FG is usually situated near the licentiate thesis. The RG approves that the research is ready to build a complete report, while the EG approves scientific quality, current business values and also valuates future business expectations. An initial overview of the last two years eleven meetings for seven doctoral projects finds TSM useful. Even it does require extra resources, but can detect problems and discuss solutions in the right time, at the right cost with respecting quality and content requirements and empower doctoral students to better master their own projects.

3. REFERENCES

[1] Wallgren, L. and Dahlgren, L.O. 2007. Industrial doctoral students as brokers between industry and academia, Industry and Higher Education, 21(3).

[2] Eneroth, T., Hellsten, P. and Hamilton, S. 2009. Get Connected. Culture in Projects at Volvo. Technical Report.

Structuring Software Engineering Learning within Open Source Software Participation

Heidi J. C. Ellis
Western New England University
011-413-782-1748
ellis@wne.edu

Gregory W. Hislop
Drexel University
011-215-895-2179
hislop@drexel.edu

ABSTRACT
Software engineering students need to understand the major phases of software development such as requirements elicitation, design, etc., as well as the documentation that supports these activities. Students also need to understand the critical need for excellent communication both within development teams as well as with customers, managers, and other stakeholders. Student participation in Free and Open Source Software (FOSS) projects provides an opportunity for students to gain a range of software engineering knowledge and skills via interaction with software professionals. However, many FOSS projects have minimal or incomplete documentation and frequently the documentation that does exist lacks organization. This presentation demonstrates the use of IEEE standard-based document templates within a FOSS project to scaffold student learning.

Categories and Subject Descriptors
K.3.2 [**Computers and Education**]: Computer and Information Science Education – *computer science education.*

General Terms
Human Factors.

Keywords
Humanitarian Free and Open Source Software, Student Learning.

1. INTRODUCTION
One of the challenges in educating software engineering students is providing them with real-world and professional experience. Participation in Free and Open Source Software (FOSS) projects allows students to learn directly from professionals in a vertically integrated development environment containing developers with a range of backgrounds and experiences. However, FOSS projects typically have an informal documentation structure that differs from the more organized approach usually used in industry. For instance, many FOSS projects do not have formal requirements, design or testing documents. This means that students participating in FOSS projects may not understand the importance of providing a concise set of requirements so that all stakeholders can agree on the functionality of a product. Document templates are one way of providing some scaffolding for students to help

them understand, structure, and better communicate information for the software development process.

This presentation discusses the use of IEEE standard-based templates (http://xcitegroup.org/softhum/doku.php?id=f:templates) to improve student understanding of and communication about software. Where possible, the templates are scaled down versions of IEEE standard documents for major software life cycle artifacts that contain a fully fleshed-out structure for the document along with extensive comments by the instructor about the intention and contents of the sections. Templates provide guidance and structure for student learning within the somewhat informal culture of FOSS projects in a variety of ways including:

Structuring large documents – Students must learn to organize information so that it is understandable by the intended audience. The templates help students organize work and practice presenting material in an orderly fashion and at varying levels of detail.

Reviewing complex documents – Students must learn how to analyze and evaluate documents. Template structure allows students to evaluate content at a variety of levels of abstraction. The common structure also makes it easier for students to review each other's documents, and easier for students to grasp document excerpts presented in class.

Planning team work – One key skill that students need in order to become skilled professionals is the ability to work within a team. Team interactions require communication and inter-personal skills. Templates provide a common base of understanding that teams can use as a way to structure communication. The templates help students understand their tasks in more detail before starting. They provide information for planning the work, and help the team talk about the document more easily.

The presentation includes an overview of the concept and approach to scaffolding student learning by using templates including presenting the contents of one template in enough detail for participants to understand what the template provides and how it would be used. The discussion will also include experience in using this approach in several FOSS projects including discussing the instructional techniques used, and perceived problems and benefits. The use of templates to organize smaller course deliverables such as homework will also be discussed.

2. ACKNOWLEDGMENTS
This material is based on work supported by the National Science Foundation under Grant CNS-0939059, DUE-1225708, 1225738, and 1225688. Any opinions, findings and conclusions or recommendations expressed in this material are those of the author(s) and do not necessarily reflect the views of the National Science Foundation (NSF).

AsseSQL: an Online, Browser-based SQL Skills Assessment Tool

Julia Prior
School of Software
Faculty of Engineering and IT
University of Technology, Sydney
Australia
Julia.Prior@uts.edu.au

1. THE TOOL

AsseSQL is an online, browser-based SQL query assessment tool, developed in-house.

2. GOAL

To assess students' SQL query design and construction skills in a manner that more authentically mirrors how these skills are applied in professional practice.

3. APPLICATION

With manual assessment, it's difficult for students to know if they have the query design correct, or if their query returns the correct results.

One of the difficulties for a student is conceptualising and visualising the result of an executed SQL statement. Constructing queries online, executing them, visually verifying the result and, if necessary, modifying the query until it gives the correct result further internalises the query formulation skill. Immediate feedback is an important component in the learning and assessment loop.

Each student doing the online SQL test is presented with a different mix of questions from a question pool for a given database, although the same mix of difficulty levels is used for all students. For each question, the expected result table is shown. Students can attempt the questions in any order, and can resubmit answers as often as they wish. They can see their results immediately and able to revise and resubmit solutions.

AsseSQL is primarily an assessment tool – it is not meant as a learning or mastery tool, although students are able to practice doing SQL tests online as much as they want to prior to the formal, graded test. Much of the learning takes place in tutorial/seminar sessions where the students learn how to design and construct SQL queries methodically. They learn collaboratively in small groups, using large pieces of paper to record 'dry runs' of their query answers to exercises, as well as executing their queries directly in the database system.

4. RESULTS

A few thousand students have now used this assessment tool over ten years. Every student who does the test completes a feedback form. Student feedback is still overwhelmingly positive, primarily for the reason that they are assessed as they will use their SQL skills in professional practice. Most students view AsseSQL as a fair, consistent assessment approach.

Following are some of the topics that I will expand upon in my presentation:

- 2002 – I designed the online SQL test software with colleague, and initial online tests taken by 500 students;

- 2003 – first feedback from students analysed and concomitant changes;

- 2004 – we demonstrate that the way that students are assessed affects the way that they learn prior to the assessment;

- 2008 – increased security for the system and added GUI interface for test setup and administration;

- 2010-2011 – I ran several online tests remotely without any technical hitches; and

- 2012/13 – computer system issues became dominant.

AsseSQL has been a successful way of assessing students' skills. The Tips, Techniques and Courseware session is an opportune time to reflect on its use, the challenges and possible changes.

ITICSE'14, June 21–25, 2014, Uppsala, Sweden.
ACM 978-1-4503-2833-3/14/06.
http://dx.doi.org/10.1145/2591708.2602682

Automatic Evaluation of Students' Programs

Tonci Dadic
University of Split
Faculty of Science
Split, Croatia
+385 95 905 3400
tdadic@pmfst.hr

Vlado Glavinic
University of Zagreb
Faculty of Electrical
Engineering and Computing
Zagreb, Croatia
+385 1 612 9955
vlado.glavinic@fer.hr

Marko Rosic
University of Split
Faculty of Science
Split, Croatia
+385 21 385 009
marko.rosic@pmfst.hr

ABSTRACT

Our component for tutoring systems automatically verifies small programs avoiding false alarms, and delivers corrections and educational help. It compares students' programs against models calculating semantic program distances.

Categories and Subject Descriptors

K.3.1 [**Computers and Education**]: Computer Uses in Education – *Computer assisted instruction.*

Keywords

Symbolic execution, semantic program distance, automatic debugging.

1. INTRODUCTION

Logical errors in novice programs are individual and may differ very much. In a traditional classroom, teachers have to localize and explain errors to each student. Introducing a computerized system capable of localizing and explaining such errors, the teaching process can be improved significantly. Automatic evaluation of students' programs in introductory programming courses motivated us to design a system that should verify students' programs avoiding false alarms, correct bugs, and redirect students' thinking process in order to achieve correct programs.

2. PROGRAM EVALUATION

Difficulties in evaluating students' programs arise because of many different, but equivalent implementations. Variants of program may implement different algorithms. For example, both quotient and remainder of an integer division can be calculated by *div* and *mod* operators, but also by repeated subtraction. Additionally, the same algorithm may be implemented using different instructions, different variable names, temporary variables, as well as different signatures of functions and procedures.

Corrections of a student's program and delivered help have to accommodate to the student's intention, hence the system has to recognize the intended solution variant. In this respect, we extend the notion of string and tree editing distance [1] to that of semantic distance of programs, which is defined as the minimal number of modifications of a target program to make it equivalent

to the model. By modification we mean the change, insertion and deletion of tokens. Moving an instruction from one position to another is a program modification as well. E.g. the semantic distance of a student written inequality $!(a-b<0)$ from the respective model $a>b$ is one, as some equivalent model expressions are *(i)* $a-b>0$ and *(ii)* $!(a-b<=0)$. Obviously, the student's intention was to write the expression *(ii)*, which becomes equivalent to the model by modifying the inequality symbol. The semantic distance of instructions of the same type is based on distances of the respective expressions.

2.1 Formal verification

Human programming experts prepare the models that define acceptable solutions for a given problem. The models include logical formulas of post-conditions. The automatic formal verification includes the following steps:

- symbolic interpretation of student's program, resulting in logical formulas over the final state of variables,
- mapping of student's variables to model variables,
- rewriting post-conditions using student's variables, and
- checking satisfiability of post-conditions by using the SMT solver[2].

A symbolic variable state represents an arbitrary value from the domain defined by the data type, so that the automatic formal verification is implementation independent and checks all paths of a program.

2.2 Corrections and help

The model defines both elements of correct implementation and common bugs with attached descriptions in natural language. In order to find corrections and deliver educational help, the system provides:

- generation of equivalent model expressions based on identities of algebra and propositional logic,
- semantic distance calculation,
- instructions mapping of student's program to model, such that the distance of two programs is minimal, and
- corrections, and delivery of educational help that is the description given by the model.

We call this process program recognition based on semantic distance.

3. REFERENCES

[1] Bille, P. 2003. Tree Editing Distance, Alignment Distance and Inclusion, IT University of Copenhagen, ISBN 87-7949-032-8.

[2] Bjorner, N. and De Moura, L. 2009. Z3: Applications, Enablers, Challenges and Directions, In CFV '09 Sixth International Workshop on Constraints in Formal Verification

ITICSE'14, June 21–25, 2014, Uppsala, Sweden.
ACM 978-1-4503-2833-3/14/06.
http://dx.doi.org/10.1145/2591708.2602683

ALGO-RYTHMICS: Science and Art without Ethnic Borders

Zoltan Katai
Sapientia University
Târgu-Mureş/Corunca, şoseaua Sighişoarei 1C. Romania.
+40 727 370 346
katai_zoltan@ms.sapientia.ro

ABSTRACT

The "2013 Best Practices in Education Award" (organized by Informatics Europe) was devoted to initiatives promoting Informatics Education in Primary and Secondary Schools. We briefly present the AlgoRythmics project (part of one of the winning proposals), consisting of six "sorting-dances" and an online e-learning tool which effectively exploits the didactical value of the dance-choreographies.

Categories and Subject Descriptors

K.3.2 [**Computers and Education**]: Computer and Information Science Education – *computer science education.*

Keywords

Intercultural Computer Science Education; Innovative Methods.

1. THE SOFTWARE TOOL

The e-learning environment we designed (http://algo-rythmics.ms.sapientia.ro) introduces users to the mini-world of sorting algorithms. Users are invited (see Figure 1):

- to watch stimulating illustrations of the algorithms as Central European folkdance choreographies;

- to watch expressive computer animations of the algorithms;

- to orchestrate the algorithms on random sequences stored in white- and black-arrays;

- to watch a suitable parallel simulation of the six algorithms.

Figure 1. Dancing/Animating/Simulating.

2. IMPLEMENTED EDUCATIONAL PRINCIPLES

Educational principles we have proposed to implement:

- Generating and sustaining motivation: surprising science-art and modern-traditional combinations; moderate-progressive challenge; genuine active involvement;

- Balanced involvement of both sides (academic/artistic) of the brain;

- The more senses involved – the more effective the learning;

- Sequenced multiple representations (gradual shift from concrete to abstract): dancer/white-box/black-box sequences.

3. THE IMPACT

To make the algo-rythmics environment more accessible to the worldwide teaching-learning community we posted the videos on YouTube (youtube.com/AlgoRythmics) (we also created facebook.com/AlgoRythmics).

Extracts from the feedback we received (4 years, 207 countries):

- views: 2,292,892; estimated minutes watched: 2,197,234; likes: 16,858; dislikes: 225; subscribers: 6,036; SHAREs: 6,595.

- The words 'like' 'awesome' 'great' 'best' 'nice' 'brilliant' 'love' 'epic' 'cool' 'amazing' 'excellent' 'fantastic' etc have appeared hundreds of times in users' comments.

Some recent comments:

- I've been using these videos in my class, and my students loved it. Also, check their website for some great hands-on sorting tasks. Great job, Algo-rythmics!

- This has got to be the greatest math's lesson I've ever had!

- I've never enjoyed studying for finals more... I wish my teacher had used this in class.

- This is awesome! Make me want to go implement Quick-sort in every language I know even a little bit.

- The only true international language!

- Who said programming is boring?

- Showed it to the kids and they loved it!

4. FUTURE PLANS

Among our future plans are:

- to create the "heap-sort dance" and the parallel versions of quick- and merge-sort dances;

- to develop another software unit that supports students in coding the sorting strategies they have just learned;

- to develop a one semester curriculum to promote algorithmic thinking in all students at all levels.

A Social Platform Supporting Learning through Video Creation by Students

Jaime Urquiza-Fuentes, Jorge Castellanos,
Isidoro Hernán, Estefanía Martín
LITE Group, Universidad Rey Juan Carlos
C/Tulipan, s/n, 28933 Madrid
{jaime.urquiza,jorge.castellanos,isidoro.hernan,
estefania.martin}@urjc.es

Pablo A. Haya
Instituto de Ingeniería del Conocimiento
Universidad Autónoma de Madrid
C/Francisco Tomás y Valiente,11, 28049 Madrid
pablo.haya@uam.es

ABSTRACT
This courseware contribution describes the work done based on a social networking platform for educational purposes. The main task of the students will be creating videos related to concepts of inheritance. One of the main roles of the platform is to facilitate communication and discussion among students during the video creation process. Students thought that private discussion forums and video rating were the most useful tools. In addition students are satisfied with the learning experience.

Categories and Subject Descriptors
K.3.1 [**Computer Uses in Education**]: Collaborative learning.
H.5.1 [**Multimedia Information Systems**]: Video.

General Terms: Human Factors.

Keywords: Educational Platforms, Video Based Learning, Social Networks.

1. INTRODUCTION
CSCL is a possible approach to foster students' active engagement in their own learning process. Social networks represent a natural extension of CSCW. Its educational use has followed different approaches. There are no clear results about their educational impact. But in general, it seems that user satisfaction is good and students' involvement in educational tasks is greater.

This contribution presents an educational platform based on a social network approach. The development of this tool is part of the JuxtaLearn project (http://www.juxtalearn.org). One of the main objectives of the project is to facilitate video creation by students in a collaborative environment. In order to facilitate the work among the members of the working group, and the subsequent discussion with the rest of the community (course, class, ...), we have used an educational platform based on the social networks approach that will support part of these tasks.

2. DESCRIPTION OF THE PLATFORM
The design of the platform is based on the Elgg environment (http://www.elgg.com), it allows the creation of social platforms with standard tools: forums, chats, content, summary, etc. In addition, it can be adapted to specific features of the platform to be developed. The aim of our platform is to facilitate video creation and sharing, and support subsequent discussions among the students. Thus, the general idea of the platform is based on social networks adapted to the educational scope.

The landing page of the platform shows a summary of the activity carried out by all groups. The style of this page is similar to the Facebook wall. The main idea is to provide an interaction style similar to the social networks' one. The platform provide a set of tools, some of them belong to the Elgg core distribution, while others are installed as plug-ins to extend the platform.

The platform provides standard tools such as message boards, file upload, private messaging among users, blog, content search, tag cloud, photo gallery and chat.

In addition, we extended the features of the platform with the following tools. The *Groups* tool allows student groups management. Each group has access to several private spaces for: files, videos, photos, images and discussion forums. The *embedded videos* tool allows the inclusion of video files embedded within contents posted by users of the community in different sections of the platform. The *voting system* allows students to rate the content posted by others using both: a five values scale and the "like" button. Thus, each element could be associated with an average score that would qualify it. The *event calendar* can be accessed by all the users, but it also allows the creation of custom calendars for each group. The *wallnote* is a micro-blogging system that allows the students communicate with the rest of the community using short text message, like Twitter. *Twitter* and *Facebook connect*, allow students to access the platform using their identification via Twitter or Facebook. Finally, the *bookmark tool* allows students and groups to identify interesting sites and share them with the community.

3. A FIRST EXPERIENCE
We have used this platform in an object oriented programming course, with 28 students, focusing on the inheritance topic. The students produced 13 videos and gave their opinion about the experience. The best graded tools were the private (group) discussion forums, the comments from their peers and the voting tool with the five values scale. They thought that this kind of activities was helpful for them. Finally, they highlighted that the script production step was more important than the video creation.

4. ACKNOWLEDGMENTS
The research leading to these results has received funding from the European Community's Seventh Framework Programme (FP7/2007-2013) under grant agreement n° 317964 JUXTALEARN.

ITICSE '14, Jun 21-25 2014, Uppsala, Sweden
ACM 978-1-4503-2833-3/14/06.
http://dx.doi.org/10.1145/2591708.2602685

Team Based Learning in Theoretical Computer Science

Nathaly Verwaal
University of Calgary
2500 University Drive NW
Calgary AB, Canada
1.403.210.8485
verwaal@cpsc.ucalgary.ca

ABSTRACT

Design and Analysis of Algorithms are generally acknowledged to be vital to the formation of fully rounded Computer Scientists, because abstract design approaches are applicable to all areas of Computer Science. Yet, designing and analyzing algorithms remains one of the main areas in which Computer Science students struggle. Students perceive the subject as being both extremely difficult (low student efficacy) and of little value, and students often repeat the course multiple times before they are able to earn a passing grade. We've introduced the team based learning approach into our Design and Analysis of Algorithms course in 2013 with the aim of increasing both the value that students see in the material, their perceived efficacy and to improve the depth of their learning.

Categories and Subject Descriptors

K.3.2 [Computers and Education]: Computer and Information Science Education – *computer science education.*

General Terms

Algorithms, Theory.

Keywords

Team-based learning, theory, algorithms, design.

1. INTRODUCTION

At the University of Calgary, Computer Science 413 (CPSC 413), "The Design and Analysis of Algorithms I" is a required course for a Computer Science degree. It has three main components: designing algorithm using formal and systematic approaches including Divide and Conquer, Dynamic Programming and Greedy Algorithms; analyzing proposed algorithm using proofs of correctness and asymptotic run-time analysis; classifying computational problems by introducing complexity classes P, NP and NP-Complete.

The course is a core component to the formation of Computer Scientists, yet both formal and informal student reports indicate that students perceives the subject as being both extremely difficult and of little value, and students often repeat the course

ITICSE '14, Jun 21-25 2014, Uppsala, Sweden
ACM 978-1-4503-2833-3/14/06.
http://dx.doi.org/10.1145/2591708.2602686

multiple times before they are able to earn a passing grade. This leads student to focus on passing the course rather than deep learning and they do not apply the concepts to further Computer Science courses or problems encountered during their careers.

2. CHANGES IN TEACHING APPROACH

Several attempts have been made to redesign the course CPSC 413 to change student perceptions and improve their learning experience. Students responded positively when instructors related problems examined in the course to problems encountered in more usual hands-on scenarios. This explicitly helps illustrate the connection between abstract formulation and specific application of a problem. Students also found it helpful when instructors demonstrated the creative process when designing algorithms. These past modifications have only minimally addressed the issue of students undervaluing the importance of designing and analyzing algorithms. We consistently receive feedback from students that they feel they have learned nothing of value, even when they provide positive feedback on the teaching approach used by the instructor.

According to Ambrose et al.[1], to change student perceptions of CPSC 413, students need to: see a strong commitment from the instructors to make this course approachable and valuable; experience an environment where they feel they can succeed; work in an environment where they feel safe to make mistakes and understand the opportunities to learn generated from these mistakes; practice formulating practical problems into abstract problems to link to the practical application of the material; experience a level of challenge that is appropriate to their abilities and previous experiences; and have flexibility and control over the course material.

We've introduced the team based learning approach into our Design and Analysis of Algorithms course in Fall 2013 since this teaching strategy has shown great success in meeting these goals. This session will report on the tools used to deliver a team-based learning version of the course, the methods used to evaluate the effectiveness of the delivery, the results that were observed and plans for further course development.

3. BIBLIOGRAPHY

[1] Ambrose, S. A., Bridges, M. W., DiPietro, M., Lovett, M. C., and Normal, M. K. 2010. *How learning works: 7 research-based principles for smart teaching.* Jossey-Bass.

[2] Halpern, D. F. and Hakel, M. D. 2003. Applying the science of learning to the university and beyond: Teaching for long-term retention and transfer. *Change.* 35,4 (2003), 36-41.

[3] Michaelsen, L. K.,Bauman Knight, A., Fink, L. D. 2002. *Team-based Learning: A Transformative Use of Small Groups.* Praeger Publishing

CaptainTeach: A Platform for In-Flow Peer Review of Programming Assignments

Joe Gibbs Politz
Brown University
joe@cs.brown.edu

Shriram Krishnamurthi
Brown University
sk@cs.brown.edu

Kathi Fisler
WPI
kfisler@cs.wpi.edu

1. INTRODUCTION

Peer review is effective for teaching students to evaluate approaches to problems, fostering collaboration, and assessing other students' work. Peer review often happens after assignments are turned in, on complete artifacts that other students have created. We've been experimenting with a different style of peer review, which we call *in-flow* reviewing, in which programming assignments are broken into reviewable stages. After students complete each stage they review one anothers' work, allowing for feedback early on in the assignment.

We've built a system, dubbed CaptainTeach, for exploring in-flow reviewing for both programming and written assignments. In our demonstration and tutorial, we will show what the student experience looks like for a CaptainTeach assignment, explain the interface that instructors have for creating assignments in CaptainTeach, outline some of the mechanisms for anonymously assigning reviews and distributing feedback, and discuss future directions for the tool. We give a brief introduction to each of these facets in this document.

2. STUDENT EXPERIENCE

The CaptainTeach environment contains embedded editors for students to create and submit their assignments. It currently supports both programming assignments in Pyret (http://pyret.org), and open-response questions, written in plain text. In either case, when the student logs in and visits an assignment page, they are presented with one or more editors for the different steps in an assignment.

Upon submitting a step of an assignment, students are presented with several other students' work along with a review rubric. Depending on the type of problem, they are given a rubric with different questions. We have currently designed questions for test suites, data definitions, function implementations, and open response questions.

3. INSTRUCTOR EXPERIENCE

Assignments for CaptainTeach are written in a custom

markup language for describing problems, their steps, and their reviews. For example, a fragment of the markup for a two-step assignment looks like:

```
@code-assignment["cs01-bst-to-list" #:reviews 2]
 @name{Binary Search Trees}
 @library-part{
   data BinTree: mt | node(value, left, right) end }
 @fun-part["tree-to-list"]{
   @header{tree-to-list(tree :: BinTree) -> List} } }
```

Here, a teacher describes an assignment with a predetermined data definition (the `library-part` defining `BinTree`), and a function to write, called `tree-to-list`. CaptainTeach will take this specification and create an assignment with two steps, one for writing a test suite for the function and one for writing its implementation. After each step, students will be presented with two reviews (`#:reviews 2`). Several parts of this markup are customizable, to allow instructors to write assignments with different numbers of reviewable steps and different styles of review.

4. REVIEW DISTRIBUTION

We've experimented with two different styles of review distribution in CaptainTeach. In one style, the first review a student gets is always an instructor-provided solution, and students know this. The solution is designed to let students practice reviewing before they give one another feedback. In another style, instructor-provided solutions are mixed in randomly with student solutions, so any given solution may come from another student or be a known-good or known-bad solution written by the instructor.

Reviews between students are always anonymous. Currently, we have distributed solutions for review in a simple time-ordered queue: when a student submits, they get the most recently-submitted solutions with no reviews to review first. This has a fairness guarantee for timeliness of feedback, but other distribution orders are possible: we could distribute randomly, or based on assigning reviews based on students' performance.

5. FUTURE WORK

We are currently working to generalize the interface to work with more kinds of assignments (for example, projects hosted on Github in an arbitrary language). We also want to build infrastructure for doing controlled A/B tests of different review styles and rubrics within a course population, which requires a more sophisticated assignment specification language.

Learning Computer Programming
A Study of the Effectiveness of a COAC#

Jakeline Marcos-Abed
Computer Science Department
Tecnológico de Monterrey (ITESM)
Monterrey, N.L. México
jakeline@itesm.mx

ABSTRACT
The learning of computer programming is difficult for many students, particularly to learn Iterative Control Structures and Data Structures. In order to improve the understanding of Loops, Strings and Arrays, a tool called COAC# was developed, to show in a graphic and animated form the loop functionality. Together with a practice, COAC# was used with a set of test cases so that the student can understand the result associated with each test case. This work in progress measures the effectiveness of COAC# tool, comparing the student's answers in a practice versus their performance in exams.

Categories and Subject Descriptors:

K.3.2 Computer and Information Science Education. Computer Science Education.

Keywords: loops; repetition; iterative control structures; computer languages; programming fundamentals; CS1.

1. INTRODUCTION
One of the most powerful concepts in any programming language is repetition or "loops". This is one of the elements that allow a program to do much more than just performing a simple calculus.

When enrolled in CS1, students solve daily life arithmetic problems, trying to translate their solution to the programming language they are learning. But things get complicated when they start to use loops, as they fail to associate their traditional arithmetic solutions to the code they write.

2. LEARNING COMPONENTS IN CS1
One of the problems students have to face is to think in the code they are writing, the syntax and semantics of the loop structure and choose the right value for initialization, the right condition and the right increment, in order to repeat some instructions, or exit the loop and move to the next statement.

According to this, learning components for CS1 are a combination of: logic, syntax-semantic rules, an IDE and too much practice.

3. DEVELOPING A TOOL CALLED COAC#
COAC# is a visual application created to facilitate the learning path of programming languages. Initially, this application was developed for C# -this is the reason for the name COAC#, and later on the C++ and JAVA versions were added.

The application consists of simulating the execution of a code fragment, dividing the screen in 4 parts [1]:
1. The code written in programming language, whether it is C#, C++ or JAVA.
2. The results of the code execution, displayed in a black textbox that simulates a console.
3. The animated flowchart diagram, which makes it easy for the user to choose or set certain values for the variables and certain conditions for the loop.
4. And how the values are changing in "memory".

4. USING COAC# WITH A SET OF TEST CASES
Students from a CS1 class, were assigned to complete a practice using the COAC# tool. This practice includes a series of test cases with open-ended questions for each topic, which students should analyze and answer correctly.

5. PRELIMINARY RESULTS
COAC# tool, plus a practice with several test cases integrated, may help students on their performance in CS1. However, it can be misused because anyone, even those without programming skills, can answer the place-value questions in the practice, simply by recording the results of the automated tool.

The hypothesis here is that, in order to have COAC# to help students, it is recommended not only execute the COAC#, but guide students using this tool, so that:
- Students see how COAC# operates, executing the coach many times with different values.
- Students answer place-value questions with specially designed test cases for the COAC#.
- Students answer open-ended questions, understanding what the COAC# is doing and why. This will give more detail about a student's true learning.

Preliminary results show that those students, who use the COAC# and respond the practice with long answers, express in a better way the knowledge they have internalized, and thus, get better grades in their exams.

ITICSE '14, Jun 21-25, 2014, Uppsala, Sweden.
ACM 978-1-4503-2833-3/14/06.
http://dx.doi.org/10.1145/2591708.2602652

6. REFERENCES
[1] Marcos-Abed, J. (2014). Using a COAC# for CS1. WCCCE'14, Richmond, British Columbia, Canada. http://dx.doi.org/10.1145/2597959.2597971

AlgoTouch: A Programming by Demonstration Tool for Teaching Algorithms

Patrice Frison
Université de Bretagne Sud
Campus de Tohannic
56000 Vannes, France
Patrice.Frison@univ-ubs.fr

ABSTRACT

AlgoTouch is a tool that helps teachers explain to beginner programmers how to design basic algorithms. The main idea behind the tool is that the teacher can directly manipulate variables, indexes and arrays in order to execute the core of an iteration. The system offers possibilities for recording and replaying. A complete algorithm can be designed and executed without writing a single line of code. This poster explains the goals of the project and the main features of the tool.

Categories and Subject Descriptors

D.1.7 [**Programming techniques**]: Visual Programming; D.2.6 [**Programming Environments**]: Programmer workbench

General Terms

Algorithms; Design; Languages; Human Factors

Keywords

Algorithm visualization; Direct manipulation; Novice programming environment; Programming by demonstration

1. INTRODUCTION

As opposed to many student-centered systems, AlgoTouch is designed to help teachers illustrate the design of array iterative algorithms (mainly searching and sorting). One of the most important features is the possibility to use the system in real time. Unlike MatrixPro [1] which has been designed to demonstrate general data structures and algorithms, AlgoTouch is dedicated to designing simple single loop algorithms.

Teachers usually start with an introduction of the design principle of an algorithm and show how it works, visually, either on a blackboard (white board) or with slides (possibly animated). For instance, using the blackboard, the teacher

ITICSE '14, Jun 21-25 2014, Uppsala, Sweden
ACM 978-1-4503-2833-3/14/06.
http://dx.doi.org/10.1145/2591708.2602654 .

shows an array of ten values and simulates the algorithm. He draws variables in which to store temporary results and indexes for the array elements. The difficulty is to animate the algorithm, which generally results in confusion. With slides, the task is a very tedious and various cases must be anticipated. If a student comes up with an unexpected case, slides are useless and the teacher has to go back to the blackboard. AlgoTouch has been designed to help overcome these two difficulties.

2. ALGOTOUCH PROTOTYPE

AlgoTouch uses the blackboard metaphor *i.e.* direct manipulation (on the screen) of programming objects (variables, indexes, arrays). By simple touch gestures, the teacher can move these elements, drag and drop values into variables or arrays, increase index values, make comparisons, calculate basic expressions. He can also record a sequence of actions, replay the recorded sequence, and finalize the loop construction (adding exit cases).

In fact when the record mode is activated, a program is created and built as the teacher "plays" with the algorithm elements. The recorded program may contain some empty blocks corresponding to alternative cases. These blocks will be filled when executing the program on a new test case — blocks are recorded in real time as in the Pygmalion system [2].

A prototype has been implemented as Proof Of Concept. Most of the features presented in this paper are available in a Java/Swing version. AlgoTouch is simple to use. The teacher can show the "live" design of any simple algorithm on arrays since the whole process does not take long. Should the algorithm not operate properly, the teacher may record it again — which is highly valuable from a pedagogical point of view. We plan to experiment AlgoTouch with our students in the Spring term. Ultimately the AlgoTouch project aims at developing an Android version for tablets so as to implement multi-touch gestures.

3. REFERENCES

[1] V. Karavirta, A. Korhonen, L. Malmi, and K. Stålnacke. MatrixPro - A tool for on-the-fly demonstration of data structures and algorithms. In *Proceedings of the Third Program Visualization Workshop*, pages 26–33, The University of Warwick, UK, July 2004.

[2] D. C. Smith. Pygmalion: An executable electronic blackboard. In *Watch what I do*, pages 19–48. MIT Press, 1993.

Evolving Synchronous Online Graduate CS Education

J. Mark Pullen
Department of Computer Science
George Mason University
4400 University Drive, Fairfax VA 22030
+1.703.993.1538
mpullen@netlab.gmu.edu

Priscilla M. McAndrews
C4I Center
George Mason University
4400 University Drive, Fairfax VA 22030
+1.703.993.1728
pmcandre@netlab.gmu.edu

ABSTRACT

The authors have supported online distance education delivery of the Master of Science in Computer Science degree at George Mason University for the past decade. We have focused on simultaneous online and classroom delivery, using an open-source hybrid approach combining synchronous classroom capture with the popular Moodle learning management system. Our program has been challenged to change its mode of operation to survive administration plans for growing asynchronous distance education in our institution. We report here on results of our efforts in rising to this challenge: technology enhancements to reduce support requirements and student surveys to understand the best new directions for the program.

Categories and Subject Descriptors

K.3.1 **[Computing Milieux]:** Computer Uses in Education – distance learning

General Terms

Management, Performance, Human Factors.

Keywords

Internet distance education, synchronous, asynchronous.

1. INTRODUCTION

The authors have been responsible for supporting online distance education (DE) delivery of the Master of Science in Computer Science (MSCS) degree at George Mason University for the past decade [1,2]. Our program has been challenged to change its mode of operation to survive administration plans for growing asynchronous distance education in our institution. We report here on results of our efforts in rising to this challenge.

2. REDUCING SUPPORT COSTS

We call our approach *simulteaching*. It features significant flexibility for the regional student, who is able to avoid commuting to class on most or all occasions, while allowing the needs of online students and classroom students to be met simultaneously with a single presentation. A related benefit is the ability to offer online courses that would not attract sufficient enrollment for a separate online section. In addition to immediate

online delivery, the class, as captured in the classroom and transmitted online, is recorded for later playback.

Our hybrid, Moodle-based, open-source software has been tuned to the needs of simulteaching and includes features that reduce requirements for instructor attention to the system operation. Other features include support for a separate projector whiteboard so that classrooms students are not burdened with details of the instructor interface. In the last year, we have added these new features:

- Auto-configuration to classroom facilities
- Automatic upload and posting of class recordings
- Auto-preparation of open standard slide file sets
- Improved floor control to reduce need for monitoring

3. STUDENT ATTITUDE SURVEY

In order to understand how our online courses met students' needs, we performed an in-depth survey resulting in the following findings:

- Students reported no significant difference in learning experience for online versus classroom.
- Overall experience in classroom was rated better than online by a modest fraction of students.
- Interaction with instructor was found somewhat less effective online, but acceptable.
- Interaction with fellow students was notably less effective online, but this resulted in little dissatisfaction.
- Preponderance of students reported that their grades were the same with online or classroom attendance.

The changes described here made our program more supportable and cost-effective. We seek to sustain the advantages of simultaneous classroom and synchronous delivery in an environment where asynchronous distance education rapidly is becoming the norm.

4. REFERENCES

[1] Pullen, J., R. Simon, and P. McAndrews, An Online Graduate Computer Science Program Delivered Via Simulteaching, *Advanced Technology for Learning* Vol 2 No 3 (Jul. 2005) 148-155, ACTA Press, Calgary, AB

[2] Pullen, J., Pros and cons for teaching courses in the classroom and online simultaneously, ACM ITiCSE 2012, Haifa, Israel

Automated Assessment of UML Activity Diagrams

Michael Striewe, Michael Goedicke
Paluno – The Ruhr Insitute for Software Technology
University of Duisburg-Essen
Essen, Germany
michael.striewe@paluno.uni-due.de,
michael.goedicke@paluno.uni-due.de

ABSTRACT

Current approaches to automated assessment of UML diagram mainly focus on static analysis. As this may be insufficient for behavioural diagrams, this contribution presents an approach to dynamic checks of UML Activity Diagrams. The approach makes use of trace generation and sequence alignment and shows fair results in preliminary experiments.

Categories and Subject Descriptors

K.3.1 [**Computers and Education**]: Computer Uses in Education—*Computer-assisted instruction (CAI)*

General Terms

Design, Languages

Keywords

Modeling; E-Assessment; UML Activity Diagrams; Feedback Generation

1. INTRODUCTION

Introductory courses to system modeling using the UML are a typical part of computer science curricula. If many students attend these courses, detailed feedback to solutions of modeling exercises cannot be provided with short response times. To help in this problem, some approaches exist that enable automated assessment of particular diagram types of the UML [1, 3] or static analysis of UML diagrams in general [4, 2]. However, the behavioural diagrams of the UML do not only have static properties, but also dynamic semantics. As with programming exercises, which are typically checked both statically and dynamically, these kinds of diagrams should also be checked in two ways. Hence this contribution presents work in progress towards fully automated checks of UML behavioural diagrams using UML Activity Diagrams as sample instance.

ITiCSE'14, June 21–25, 2014, Uppsala, Sweden.
ACM 978-1-4503-2833-3/14/06.
http://dx.doi.org/10.1145/2591708.2602657.

2. TRACE-BASED CHECKING

Checking diagrams dynamically means to compare the semantics of the solution to reference semantics. The semantics of UML Activity Diagrams are in general defined by token flows: Tokens represent objects, dates, or control and are passed from one activity to another via the edges in the diagram. The sequence of activities that accept a token on its way from its creation to a final node can be considered as a trace. Forks may occur that cause several tokens to be passed around in parallel. The resulting trace thus contains parallel sequences that need to be reduced to sequences deterministically before traces can be compared. Then the solution trace and the reference trace can be aligned using algorithms from sequence alignment as used in bioinformatics, e.g. Ukkonen's algorithm [5]. This algorithm uses a scoring function that adds positive scores for matches of sequence elements, and subtracts scores for mismatches or gaps. Based on the individual alignments an overall match score for all sequences generated by one solution can be computed and used for feedback generation.

3. PRELIMINARY RESULTS

Experiments with solutions from a bachelor degree course on UML modelling showed satisfying results with the feedback quality. In particular, the approach was able to accept solutions using alternate modeling approaches (such as using interrupt sections instead of decision nodes) without problems. However, the approach still shows some weaknesses with respect to mismatches of activity names.

4. REFERENCES

[1] J. Soler, I. Boada, F. Prados, J. Poch, and R. Fabregat. A web-based e-learning tool for UML class diagrams. In *Education Engineering (EDUCON), 2010 IEEE*, pages 973–979, 2010.

[2] M. Striewe and M. Goedicke. Automated checks on UML diagrams. In *Proceedings of the 16th Annual SIGCSE Conference on Innovation and Technology in Computer Science Education, ITiCSE 2011, Darmstadt, Germany, June 27-29*, pages 38–42, 2011.

[3] P. Thomas, N. Smith, and K. Waugh. Automatic Assessment of Sequence Diagrams. In *Proceedings for 12th CAA Conference*, 2008.

[4] P. Thomas, N. Smith, and K. Waugh. Automatically assessing graph-based diagrams. *Learning, Media and Technology*, 33(3):249–267, 2008.

[5] E. Ukkonen. Finding Approximate Patterns in Strings. *Journal of Algorithms*, (6):132–137, 1985.

Learning within a Professional Environment: Shared Ownership of an HFOSS Project

Heidi J. C. Ellis
Stoney Jackson
Western New England University
011-413-782-1748
ellis@wne.edu; stoney.jackson@wne.edu

Gregory W. Hislop
Drexel University
011-215-895-2179
hislop@drexel.edu

Darci Burdge
Lori Postner
Nassau Community College
011-516-572-7383
darci.burdge@ncc.edu; lori.postner@ncc.edu

Joanmarie Diggs
Igalia, S.L.
Spain
jdiggs@igalia.com

ABSTRACT

Curriculum guidelines for both Computer Science and Software Engineering emphasize the need for student experience working on a sizeable, real-world project. This poster presents student experience in a Humanitarian Free and Open Source Software (HFOSS) project that is jointly maintained by the GNOME Accessibility Team and three academic institutions. In this environment, students enjoy apprenticeship learning and learn directly from professionals within an active project. Results from a survey on student self-reported software engineering learning, attitude towards computing, and career plans are presented.

Categories and Subject Descriptors

K.3.2 [**Computers and Education**]: Computer and Information Science Education – *computer science education.*

General Terms

Human Factors.

Keywords

Humanitarian Free and Open Source Software, Team Projects.

1. INTRODUCTION

MouseTrap is an application for users with disabilities that uses a webcam to track movement of the forehead or other body part and translate that movement into on-screen cursor movement. This project is being jointly developed by the GNOME Accessibility Team and faculty and students at Western New England University, Drexel University, and Nassau Community College. This effort is part of an ongoing research study into student and faculty learning via student participation in HFOSS [1,2].

Students participated in the MouseTrap project as either part of a Software Engineering class or an internship. A survey was used to

elicit student opinion on three aspects of their experience in MouseTrap:

1. Attitude towards computing
2. Software Engineering learning
3. Major and career plans

Survey results indicate that students gained a variety of software engineering knowledge that spanned tools, process, and professional issues. Students appeared to gain a better understanding of the scope of computing and how their efforts could positively impact users.

Survey results also indicate that students enjoy learning within the professional community of an HFOSS project. Student feedback included the comment: "Not many people can say they got help from big contributors to GNOME and it was probably one of the coolest experiences I've had in my field."

The project also appeared to impact not only what students learned, but the learning process itself. Students appeared to better understand the need for learning throughout their career with one student saying: "This experience has been invaluable and will change how I continue to learn as a Software Engineer throughout my career."

The poster will present the MouseTrap project, ways that students contributed to the project, and survey results indicating student opinion of the experience.

2. ACKNOWLEDGMENTS

This material is based on work supported by the National Science Foundation under Grant Nos. - CNS-0939059, DUE-1225708, DUE-1225738, and DUE-1225688. Any opinions, findings and conclusions or recommendations expressed in this material are those of the author(s) and do not necessarily reflect the views of the National Science Foundation (NSF).

3. REFERENCES

[1] Ellis, H.J.C., Hislop, G.W., Rodriguez, J.S., and Morelli, R.A. 2012. Student Software Engineering Learning via Participation in Humanitarian FOSS Projects *119th Association for Engineering Education Annual Conference and Exposition.*

[2] Ellis, H.J.C., Jackson, S., Burdge, D., Hislop, G.W., and Diggs, J. 2013. Developing HFOSS Projects Using Integrated Teams Across Levels and Institutions, *14th Annual Conference in Information Technology Education.*

SHAvisual: A Secure Hash Algorithm Visualization Tool

Jun Ma, Jun Tao
Department of Computer Science
Michigan Technological University
Houghton, MI
{junm,junt}@mtu.edu

Melissa Keranen
Department of Mathematical Sciences
Michigan Technological University
Houghton, MI
msjukuri@mtu.edu

Jean Mayo, Ching-Kuang Shene, Chaoli Wang
Department of Computer Science
Michigan Technological University
Houghton, MI
{jmayo,shene,chaoliw}@mtu.edu

ABSTRACT

This poster presents a visualization tool SHAvisual for instructors to teach and students to learn the SHA-512 algorithm visually with demo and practice modes. This poster will also discuss some findings of classroom use and student reactions, which are very positive and encouraging.

Categories and Subject Descriptors

K.3.2 [**Computers and Education**]: Computer and Information Science Education

General Terms

Algorithms, Security

Keywords

Cryptography, visualization

1. INTRODUCTION

Cryptography is the foundation upon which secure communication rests and the topic is now a component in many courses, such as Computer Security, Network Security and Cryptography. The diversity of courses that cover cryptography together with its mathematical sophistication makes teaching this topic challenging. Students have diverse backgrounds and abilities and the time that can be devoted to the topic varies based on the focus of the course. We have developed a visualization tool, SHAvisual, that helps students learn the SHA algorithm. We believe this tool will help instructors manage the classroom time devoted to this algorithm and will substantially enhance independent study for interested students.

Software tools for demonstrating cryptography algorithms have started to appear in recent years. Although SHA plays an important role in cryptography, not many visualization tools include SHA. The web-based applet SHA1-VA [1] was claimed by the authors as the first interactive software to demonstrate the SHA-1 algorithm step by step. Our SHAvisual and SHA1-VA are significantly different. First, SHA1-VA is for SHA1 while SHAvisual is designed for a more advanced algorithm, SHA-512. Second, SHAvisual has the demo and full modes separately. Third, the practice mode in SHAvisual provides instructors a convenient check for teaching effectiveness. Finally, SHA1-VA presents the algorithm with a few graphical demonstrations, while SHAvisual shows each component individually with a better and more graphical presentation in a straightforward way.

2. CONTENT OF POSTER

This poster will explain our new tool SHAvisual for learning the SHA-512 algorithm. It will discuss some preliminary classroom evaluation and self-study assessment by students who were not taking the course and only used SHAvisual for self training through reading some documents and web sites. A live demonstration will be available. This tool is one component of a larger NSF project to develop a set of materials for teaching cryptography. Electronic versions of the SHAvisual, as well as the other tools developed as part of this NSF project, will be available at www.cs.mtu.edu/~shene/NSF-4.

3. SIGNIFICANCE AND RELEVANCE

Our work focuses on two fronts: the tool must be easily used for demonstration by instructors in the classroom, showing the algorithm step by step, and the tool can be used for self training by students who wish to learn the basic cryptography methods. Our tool is designed to match the layout of those found in most cryptography and/or data security textbooks to minimize user confusion. Since there are not many published visualization tools for the SHA algorithms, our work is not only relevant to this conference but also helpful to those who are teaching cryptography and data security courses and to students who may need additional aid to learn cryptography methods.

4. REFERENCES

[1] D. B. Nasr, H. M. Bahig, and S. S. Daoud. Visualizing Secure Hash Algorithm (SHA-1) on the Web. In *Proceedings of International Conference on Active Media Technology*, pages 101–112, 2011.

Acknowledgements

This work is supported by the National Science Foundation under grants DUE-1140512, DUE-1245310 and IIS-1319363.

Learning Outcomes using Objectives with Computer Science Students

Jose Amelio Medina
Computer Science
Department.
University of Alcalá.
Spain
+34 91 885 66 68.
josea.medina@uah.es

Juan Jose Sanchez
Computer Science
Department.
University of Alcalá.
Spain
+34 91 885 65 33.
juanjo.sanchez@uah.es

Eva Garcia-Lopez
Computer Science
Department.
University of Alcalá.
Spain
+34 91 885 66 68.
eva.garcial@uah.es

Antonio Garcia-Cabot
Computer Science
Department.
University of Alcalá.
Spain
+34 91 885 66 68.
a.garcia@uah.es

ABSTRACT

One of the main problems that exist when subjects are taught in technical degrees and new technologies are used is how could students be motivated to avoid abandonment In this paper we present our experience in training process with the aid of e-lerning platforms.

The course has been planned with ambitious but achievable goals, and other techniques such as gamification and teamwork. This allowed getting good results, the average grade obtained by the students increased 5%, and the number of students who have not passed the course has been reduced.

Categories and Subject Descriptors

K.3.2 [**Computers and Education**]: Computer and Information Science Education – Computer science education

General Terms

Experimentation, Theory..

Keywords

Experience; Motivation; Objective; GPU; Scala; GWT;

1. INTRODUCTION

Nowadays classroom training process is increasingly being supported by e-learning tools. Most of the training process involves students and this leads in some cases to a loss of their motivation or even to abandon the course [1].

The objective of this paper has been to develop an experiment centered in a classroom course in which different techniques such as gamification [3], teamwork and individual goals [2] (among others) have been applied with the purpose of increasing students' motivation who participated.

2. DESIGN OF THE EXPERIENCE

For the experiment, we focused on a course titled "Advanced programming extension" of the Computer Science Degree in our institution. This course is composed of three units: in the first one GPU Computing is taught; in the second one, functional programming in Scala; and in the third one Cloud Computing.

Due to its configuration, this is one of the most complicated courses, which can lead to an important loss of motivation and, in some cases, its abandonment.

We focused on the optimization of the training process in order to achieve the competences needed, causing students' interest in the course, directing and maintaining their effort through the course with the aim of achieving the predetermined learning objectives.

The instruments used to validate the training process were the analysis of data collected during the course from practical works, theoretical tests, classroom participation and participation in forums, and those obtained from a final survey about each unit in which the course is divided.

3. RESULTS

The results were satisfactory, since the average grade of students increased 5% over the previous year. The satisfaction of the students with the course was very high, as can be seen in surveys, getting an overall score of 4.36 on a 5 points Likert scale; and the participation in the survey was 97.61%.

Finally, the evaluation process of the course has been fussy and, due to the training process followed, there were no suspended students. The motivation is reflected in the participation of the students until the end of the course, since although 52% of the students had passed it before finishing it, they participated actively in all tasks, works and assessments until the end.

4. REFERENCES

[1] Alderman, M. K. (1999). Goals and goal setting. *Motivation for achievement: possibilities for teaching and learning.* New Jersey: Lawrence Erlbaum Associates.

[2] Alderman, M. K. (2004). *Motivation for Achievement. Possivilities for Teaching and Learning* Lawrence Erlbaum Associate, Mahwah, New Jersey London

[3] Domínguez, A., Saenz-de-Navarrete, J., de-Marcos, L., Fernández-Sanz, L., Pagés, C., Martínez-Herráiz, J.J. 2013 Gamifying learning experiences: Practical implications and outcomes Computers & Education. 63. pp. 380-392.

ITICSE'14, June 21–25, 2014, Uppsala, Sweden.
ACM 978-1-4503-2833-3/14/06.
http://dx.doi.org/10.1145/2591708.2602666

Remote Pair Programming (RPP) in Massively Open Online Courses (MOOCs)

Jonathan McKinsey
UC Berkeley
Department of EECS
mckinsey@berkeley.edu

Samuel Joseph
Hawai'i Pacific University
Department of CS
sjoseph@hpu.edu

Armando Fox
UC Berkeley
Department of EECS
fox@berkeley.edu

Daniel D. Garcia
UC Berkeley Department of EECS
ddgarcia@berkeley.edu

ABSTRACT

Pair programming, a form of collaborative learning where two programmers work on the same computer, enhances learning in novice programmers and improves code quality in experienced programmers. Remote pair programming (RPP) brings the pedagogical technique of pair programming to the distributed online environment of Massively Open Online Courses (MOOCs). edX's CS169 Software as a Service MOOC successfully uses a Google+ community for students to generate their own RPP events or join events created by their peers. This paper examines survey results summarizing the RPP experiences and RPP technologies of student pairings in the Fall 2013 offering of CS169. In the future, the aim is to generalize RPP methodology through analyzing RPP sessions, expand applications of RPP to other MOOCs and traditional classrooms, and compare its effectiveness to in-person pair programming.

Author Keywords

Remote Pair Programming; Virtual Pair Programming; Distributed Pair Programing; Collaborative Learning; Massively Open Online Course; Online Education; CS Education; RPP; MOOC.

ACM Classification Keywords

K.3.1 Computer Uses in Education; K.3.2 Computer and Information Science Education.

ITICSE '14, Jun 21-25 2014, Uppsala, Sweden
ACM 978-1-4503-2833-3/14/06.
http://dx.doi.org/10.1145/2591708.2602667

Impact of Reward Structures in an Inverted Course

Diane Horton
Department of Computer Science
University of Toronto
dianeh@cs.toronto.edu

Jennifer Campbell
Department of Computer Science
University of Toronto
campbell@cs.toronto.edu

ABSTRACT

The inverted or flipped classroom [4] has been shown to be effective in computer science [5, 2, 1]. Inverted teaching depends on students engaging in both pre- and in-lecture activities. What reward structure will motivate students to do so? We report on our experience with inverted teaching for a one-month unit in a third-year database course.

1. INTRODUCTION

The context for this study was a third-year introductory database course offered during the winter of 2013 at the University of Toronto. A four-week segment in the middle of the course was inverted. Students prepared for lecture by reading portions of the textbook or watching videos on a MOOC platform [6] and completing a small set of exercises designed by the instructor. In lecture, students participated in active learning exercises. Both the preparatory and in-lecture exercises were graded. To free the TA time required for this work, the homework assignment on that topic was not graded. Instead, a TA was available to provide students with support and feedback on it.

To assess the impact of our reward structures, we examined grades and attendance, and surveyed students in the final week of the course. 82 of 208 students enrolled (39%) completed the survey and gave informed consent to participate in our study.

2. RESULTS

Small grade reward, high participation

Although the lecture preparation exercises were worth only 1.25% of the course grade per week, approximately 82 to 86% of students enrolled at the time completed each set. As a result, students invested more time overall on preparation for lecture: 76% reported spending more or much more time preparing for lecture during the inverted portion of the course than during the traditional portion. A small grade reward was also sufficient to motivate students to attend lecture and complete in-lecture exercises. The nine sets of these exercises were worth a total of only 5%, yet each was completed by 76 to 80% of those enrolled. For comparison, in an inverted CS1 that did not give credit for in-lecture exercises, only 57% on average even attended lecture in one offering [1], and 69% in another offering [3].

Side effect: more learning in lectures

A strong majority of students (68%) reported that they learned a bit more or much more from lectures in the inverted portion of the course than in the traditional portion, while only 10% reported learning less or much less. This was correlated with spending more time preparing for lecture in the inverted portion of the course ($r = .47, p < .001$).

No grade reward, varied outcomes

Reallocation of resources to inverted activities meant that one assignment was not graded, yet 79% of students reported completing at least some of it. Not surprisingly, doing more work on the assignment was correlated with earning higher grades on the test questions covering the material, and on the course ($r > .33$ and $p < .003$ in each case). Still, even those who did little work on the assignment earned reasonable grades, probably due to their work on the pre-lecture and in-lecture activities. Those who reported doing no work at all on the assignment, however, had a failing average on the final exam questions on the topic.

3. REFERENCES

[1] J. Campbell, D. Horton, M. Craig, and P. Gries. Evaluating an inverted CS1. In *Proceedings of the 45th ACM Technical Symposium on Computer Science Education*, SIGCSE '14, pages 307–312, New York, NY, USA, 2014. ACM.

[2] J. A. Day and J. D. Foley. Evaluating a web lecture intervention in a human-computer interaction course. *IEEE Transactions on Education*, 49(4):420–431, 2006.

[3] D. Horton, M. Craig, J. Campbell, P. Gries, and D. Zingaro. Comparing outcomes in inverted and traditional CS1. In *Proceedings of the 19th Annual Conference on Innovation and Technology in Computer Science Education*, ITiCSE, New York, NY, USA, 2014. ACM. To appear.

[4] M. J. Lage, G. J. Platt, and M. Treglia. Inverting the classroom: A gateway to creating an inclusive learning environment. *The Journal of Economic Education*, 31(1):30–43, Jan. 2000.

[5] K. Lockwood and R. Esselstein. The inverted classroom and the CS curriculum. In *Proceedings of the 44th ACM Technical Symposium on Computer Science Education*, pages 113–118, 2013.

[6] J. Widom. Introduction to databases. https://class2go.stanford.edu/db, January 2013.

ITiCSE'14, June 21–25, 2014, Uppsala, Sweden.
ACM 978-1-4503-2833-3/14/06.
http://dx.doi.org/10.1145/2591708.2602671.

A Small Scale Project to Investigate the Current and Potential Use of Collaborative Tools at Sheffield Hallam University

Presenters:

Thomas Gibson
Sheffield Hallam University, UK-
tomgibson.home@yahoo.co.uk

Cheryl Middleton
Sheffield Hallam University, UK-
cmscm2@exchange.shu.ac.uk

ABSTRACT
This poster presents key findings based on a current project exploring the further use and deployment of new and developing collaboration tools in undergraduate distance learning and on-campus courses based at Sheffield Hallam University (SHU). An extensive report and tool base has been produced to make recommendations of collaborative technologies to support teaching delivery and assessment of courses at undergraduate level. Initial primary research has been carried out to evaluate pros and cons of existing tools currently used in group and self-based assessment in undergraduate modules.

1. INTRODUCTION
An essential process of this project was the design and deployment of extensive surveys to explore staff and student perspectives of different aspects of collaboration and group working. Small samples of this research and questions that were asked are detailed in the next section. Completion of these surveys was undertaken by 75 students and 25 staff members to provide interesting insights of the differing staff/student perspectives relating to learning processes, collaborative technologies and group working challenges and experiences [1].

2. KEY FINDINGS
Question to students – Do you use any collaboration tools to help you with your group work within modules? The popular tools include Facebook, Google Docs and Blackboard, as illustrated in the chart below:

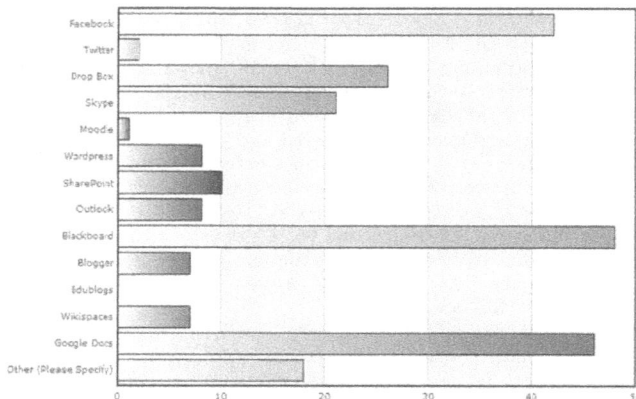

Question to staff – Do you use any collaboration tools to help you support group work within modules? The popular tools include Blackboard, Outlook and Drop Box, as illustrated in the chart below:

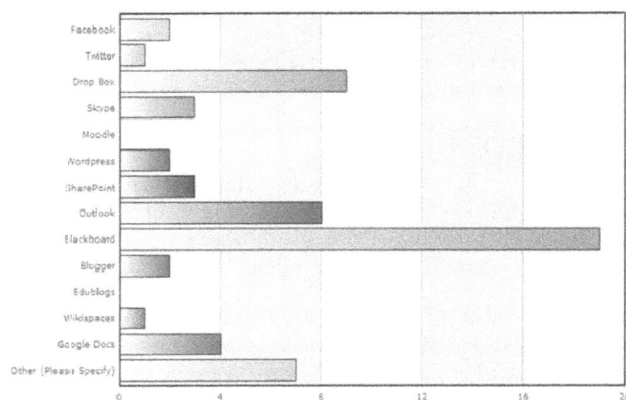

3. RECOMMENDATIONS
The prototype created for this project is currently subject to further work and deployment for exploring how collaboration and group working tools can support assessed group work [1].

Categories and Subject Descriptors
H.5.2 [USER INTERFACES]: *prototyping*;
K.3.1 [COMPUTERS AND EDUCATION]: Computer Uses in Education - *Collaborative learning, Distance learning*

General Terms
Design

Keywords
Collaboration; Technology Enhanced Learning

4. REFERENCES
[1] Gibson, T (2013). *The development of an online e-learning prototype to encourage student collaboration and demonstrate the potential of using Technology Enhanced Learning to support Distance learning modules at Sheffield Hallam University.* Bsc Thesis, Sheffield Hallam University, Uk. Prototype available at:
http://homepages.shu.ac.uk/~srdtmg/Prototype/index.htm

Enhancing the Information Assurance and Security (IAS) in CS Education with Mobile-device based Hands-on Labs

Minzhe Guo,
Prabir Bhattacharya
University of Cincinnati
2600 Clifton Ave.
Cincinnati OH 45221
guome@mail.uc.edu,
bhattapr@ucmail.uc.edu

Kai Qian,
Chia-Tien Dan Lo
Southern Polytechnic State University
1100 South Marietta Pkwy
Marietta, GA 30060
kqian@spsu.edu,
clo@spsu.edu

Xi He
Department of Computer Science
Georgia State University
Atlanta, GA 30302
xhe8@student.gsu.edu

ABSTRACT

To enhance the Information Assurance and Security in computer science (CS) education and to prepare students for the challenges of security issues, this paper presents our ongoing work on developing mobile-based hands-on security learning modules that will be integrated into existing courses in CS curriculum.

Categories and Subject Descriptors

K.3.2 [**Computers and Education**]: Computer and Information Science Education – Computer Science Education.

General Terms

Design, Security.

Keywords

Android, CS Education, Information Assurance and Security.

1. INTRODUCTION

As the need for cybersecurity increases in all areas, the demand for professionals with knowledge in the areas of Information Assurance and Security (IAS) is also growing dramatically. IAS has become one of the core Body of Knowledge in the latest ACM recommendation for computer science (CS) undergraduate education [1], which covers both techniques and policies intended to protect information systems by ensuring their confidentiality, integrity, and availability. However, the practice of IAS education in CS curriculum is still insufficient. An important step for broadening IAS education is to expose CS students to IAS concepts and practices more often in their coursework. Therefore, as an alternative to the practice of offering a dedicated IAS course, we propose to investigate the integration of IAS into various existing CS courses in order to increase students' exposure to IAS related materials, improve their security awareness, and enhance their understanding of course subject relevant security concepts and practices. A distinct feature of our

approach is that we build security concepts and practices into mobile-device-based hands-on learning modules. This will not only enable students to learn course-relevant security knowledge with hands-on practice, but also provide them an opportunity to obtain experience in mobile programming. We choose the Android based mobile devices for the development, since it is popular, low cost, and open-source; in addition, it uses Java as the programming language, which is widely used in CS1 and CS2.

2. HANDS-ON LEARNING MODULES

We are developing a set of hands-on learning modules for IAS education (Table 1). Each module emphasizes the security knowledge that is closely related to a course or a few courses. Each module includes a pre-lab (concept introduction) on the subject and several Android based hands-on labs. Some of the modules have been developed and implemented in a network security course and a mobile security course. The student feedback is positive. More modules will be developed and more course integrations will be implemented and evaluated.

Table 1. Learning Modules under Development

Knowledge Area	Learning Module	Tentative Course for Integration
Foundational concepts in Security	Access control	Operating System, Database
Defense secure programming	SQL injection	Database, Programming
	Race condition	Operating System, Parallel Computing
Threats and Attacks	Malware	Programming
	Phishing	Human-computer Interface
Cryptography	Cryptographic primitives	Network

3. ACKNOWLEDGMENTS

This work is based in part upon work partially supported by the National Science Foundation under Grant No. DUE-1244697. Any opinions, findings, and conclusions or recommendations expressed in this material are those of the author(s) and do not necessarily reflect the views of the National Science Foundation.

4. REFERENCES

[1] The ACM/IEEE Joint Task Force on Computing Curricula. 2013. Curriculum Guidelines for Undergraduate Degree Programs in Computer Science. Available at http://goo.gl/hjLaEk, Dec. 20.

ITICSE '14, Jun 21-25 2014, Uppsala, Sweden
ACM 978-1-4503-2833-3/14/06. ...$15.00.
http://dx.doi.org/10.1145/2591708.2602673

ACM IT Curricular Guidance

Robert D. Campbell
CUNY Graduate Center
365 Fifth Avenue
New York, NY USA
+1 212 817 7350
rcampbell@gc.cuny.edu

Cindy S. Tucker
Bluegrass Comm. & Tech. College
500 Newtown Pike
Lexington, KY USA
+1 859 246 4634
cindy.tucker@kctcs.edu

Cara Tang
Portland Community College
12000 SW 49th Avenue
Portland, OR USA
1+ 971 722 4447
cara.tang@pcc.edu

ABSTRACT
As directed by the ACM Education Board, the ACM Committee for Computing Education in Community Colleges (CCECC) is finalizing its curricular guidance for associate-degree Information Technology (IT) programs, consisting of core IT learning outcomes with associated assessment metrics. The competency model, influenced by international perspectives, is available from www.capspace.org, and waits Ed Board approval in Q3 2014.

Categories and Subject Descriptors
K.3.2 [**Computers and Education**]: Computer and Information Science Education – *Curriculum*

General Terms
Standardization, Measurement

Keywords
Two-Year College, Education, Information Technology, Assessment

1. BACKGROUND
The CCECC is nearing completion of the 2011 directive by the ACM Education Board that an associate-degree IT curricular task force be constituted to produce IT curricular guidance and measurement that are:

- Built from the ground up on a framework of learning outcomes.
- Constituted by core IT competencies assembled into a competency framework.
- Influenced by the current and future needs of business and industry, by certifications and related curricula, by government and standards bodies, and by new and emerging technology.
- Designed in a manner that provides for staying power, breadth and adaptability.
- International in application.
- Accompanied by well-designed assessment rubrics and meaningful evaluation metrics.

In pursuing this charge, the ACM CCECC followed a multiphase process of collaboration and debate among representatives from two-year college faculty, business and industry, and certification/standards bodies, including peer dissemination and public comment on draft results, and oversight by a team of experts in student assessment.

ITICSE '14, Jun 21-25 2014, Uppsala, Sweden
ACM 978-1-4503-2833-3/14/06.
http://dx.doi.org/10.1145/2591708.2602653

2. RESULT
The final product is a set of well-vetted student learning outcomes that express core IT competencies across all IT-related associate-degree programs representing both the technical and behavioral. The 50 learning outcomes span the first three levels of Bloom's Revised Taxonomy [1]. Each student learning outcome is accompanied by a structured, three-tier assessment rubric, giving further clarity and meaningful evaluation metrics for the outcomes. The assessment rubrics facilitate integration of the learning outcomes into assessment-based curricula, which are typical among associate-degree and career-preparatory programs. To make the collection of student learning outcomes more accessible to various constituent groups, the CCECC has categorized them in accordance with a variety of existing ontologies and frameworks, including the SIGITE 2008 "Curriculum Guidelines for Undergraduate Degree Programs in Information Technology" [4], the U.S. Department of Labor Competency Model [2], the European e-Competence Framework [3], the Common Criteria for Information Technology Security Evaluation (in alignment with ISO/IEC 15408:2005), CSTA Standards, and Bloom's Revised Taxonomy [1].

3. FOLLOW-UP OPPORTUNITIES
As follow-on to the recent public dissemination of the *ACM Associate-degree Curricular Guidance for Information Technology: A Competency Model of Core Learning Outcomes and Assessment*, the presenters will seek champions of and course examples for the guidance. Champions are organizations that appreciate the importance of robust associate-degree IT programs, make a commitment to the academic foundations of IT students, and promote education that meaningfully prepares graduates as future employees and practitioners. This guidance and related resources are now available from capspace.org.

4. REFERENCES
[1] Anderson, Lori, et al. *Taxonomy for Learning, Teaching, and Assessing: A Revision of Bloom's Taxonomy of Educational Objectives*. Boston. Allyn and Bacon, 2000.

[2] Employment and Training Administration, U.S. Department of Labor 2012. *Information Technology Competency Model*.

[3] European Commission Enterprise and Industry CEN. *European e-Competence Framework 2.0: A Common European Framework for ICT Professionals in all Industry Sectors*. 2010

[4] Lunt, B., et. al. 2008. *Information Technology 2008: Curriculum Guidelines for Undergraduate Degree Programs in Information Technology*. ACM Special Interest Group for Information Technology Education.

[5] Klee, K. et. al. *Guidelines for Associate-Degree Programs to Support Computing in a Networked Environment*. 2000. ACM Committee for Computing Education in Community Colleges.

Capstone Projects in Computer Science: Evaluated by Stakeholders

Juan J. Olarte, César Domínguez, Francisco J. García-Izquierdo, Arturo Jaime

Dpto. Matemáticas y Computación. University of La Rioja, 26005 Logroño. Spain

{jjolarte, cesar.dominguez, francisco.garcia, arturo.jaime}@unirioja.es

ABSTRACT

This study evaluates several aspects related to capstone projects in a computer science degree: level of advisor involvement, type of student, and type of project. We consider the points of view of students, advisors, and evaluation committees. Students claimed the level of advisor involvement to be significantly greater than that perceived by the advisors themselves. Regarding students skills, we found no significant differences between the opinions of advisors and students. And lastly, students have a significantly better opinion about their projects than advisors do.

Categories and Subject Descriptors

D.2.9 [**Management of Computing and Information Systems**]: Project and People Management – *Life cycle, management technique, systems development.*

General Terms

Management; experimentation.

Keywords

Capstone project; computer science degree.

1. INTRODUCTION

Computer science degree programs [1] often expect students to undertake a capstone project integrating the specific knowledge and skills acquired over the course of their studies, along with other orthogonal skills required by professional work. The project generally comprises the life-cycle of an information system development. An advisor guides the student and supervises the process. Although the scope may vary, a considerable proportion of projects follow comparable guidelines. When the project is completed, students present a portfolio compiling the written deliverables and the product itself (when appropriate). Finally, students give an oral presentation on the project to a committee of three professors. Each project is graded by both the advisor and the committee.

This study compares the points of view of students, advisors and evaluation committees regarding capstone projects. Three questionnaires were developed to survey each stakeholder.

2. RESULTS AND CONCLUSIONS

We successfully gathered the surveys corresponding to 36 projects developed during the last academic year.

Level of advisor involvement: Our questionnaires addresses the primary facets of project supervision [2]: technology, initial arrangements, keeping the project alive, execution, meetings, management, and reports. Students indicated a level of advisor involvement significantly greater than that perceived by the advisor. This is a telling observation, since it is difficult for advisers to strike the proper balance between encouraging student autonomy and monitoring project development. Consequently, advisors could slightly reduce the level of monitoring in the future

Student skills: The questionnaires assessed the autonomy, project management, meetings/communication, technology, methodology, and writing skills of students. We did not find significant differences between the opinions of students and their advisors, although students' opinion is slightly higher regarding all the aforementioned items.

Project features: We also evaluated the need for training, product usefulness, project complexity, technological innovation, and scope. The surveys of advisors and committees solicited the project grade. We found significant differences among the three points of view regarding scope, complexity, and usefulness of the product (the latter showed only a significant tendency). Students had a better opinion of their projects than the other stakeholders. In fact, there were significant differences between student and advisor perspectives on all these project features, except for the need for training and technological innovation. Committees held a better opinion –but not significant– of the projects than advisors (except for the need for training). However, committees proposed slightly lower grades than advisors. It appears that the views of committees and consultants on projects were very similar, while students deemed their work to be of a higher quality. Students' lack of a comparative overview of other projects may explain this difference of opinion. Students consider only their own project while professors review multiple projects developed during multiple academic years. Another factor that may explain this result is that students may have failed to adequately demonstrate the strengths of their work to the other stakeholders.

ACKNOWLEDGEMENTS

Partially supported by University of La Rioja (APIDUR 12/13)

3. REFERENCES

[1] ACM/IEEE-CS, *Computer Science Curricula 2013*.

[2] Domínguez, C., Jaime, A., García-Izquierdo, F.J., Olarte, J.J. "Supervision Typology in Computer Science Engineering Capstone Projects". *J Eng Educ*. 4: 679-697, 2012

Code Reading Exercises Using Run Time Traces

Michael Striewe, Michael Goedicke
Paluno – The Ruhr Insitute for Software Technology
University of Duisburg-Essen
Essen, Germany
michael.striewe@paluno.uni-due.de,
michael.goedicke@paluno.uni-due.de

ABSTRACT

Programming requires both to write code and to read code. In debugging tasks, students can use supporting tools that create additional artefacts like visualizations or traces, but these again need to be read and understood. This contribution presents a concept of code reading exercises that asks students to create the same artefacts for given code as they would use for debugging their own code.

Categories and Subject Descriptors

K.3.1 [**Computers and Education**]: Computer Uses in Education—*Computer-assisted instruction (CAI)*

General Terms

Languages

Keywords

Programming; E-Assessment; Reading Code; Feedback Generation

1. INTRODUCTION

In programming, it is not only important to write code, but also to know how to read code: Reading code is necessary to be able to learn from examples; debugging own code requires to read it in order to check where it deviates from the intended behaviour; and collaborative exercises and team projects require to read code written by others.

The first aspect can be tackled by quizzes, where students demonstrate their understanding by answering questions about a given piece of code. The second aspect is often supported with respect to debugging, e.g. by providing additional artefacts such as visualizations [1] or traces [2]. However, this in turn requires the ability to understand these artefacts. Hence it is desirable to train students in reading code by asking them to create these artefacts. It can be assumed that this in turn will help them to also use these artefacts in debugging tasks. As visualizations and traces can be created automatically, automated feedback generation is possible. This contribution elaborates on the use of traces as one possible realization of this concept that has so far been implemented as a prototype in an e-assessment system.

2. EXERCISE DESIGN AND INTERFACE

The user interface for this kind of exercise consists of two parts: In the upper section, a piece of source code is presented to the students. In the lower part, a skeleton of a trace table is provided. It provides a column for line numbers and allows students to insert an arbitrary number of additional columns for each variable used in the source code. In addition, students can add an arbitrary number of lines to the trace. With this interface, students are able to create a complete trace table for the given piece of code and some given input. Notably, exercises can be generated from submissions to other programming exercises, thus also tackling the third aspect mentioned in the introduction. Moreover, one exercise can be attended repeatedly for different inputs that result in different traces.

3. FEEDBACK OPTIONS

Feedback can be based on different observations: The number of columns or the name of columns can be wrong, which indicates errors in understanding the variables used in the program code. The number of lines or the sequence of line numbers can be wrong, which indicates errors in understanding the control flow of the program. Finally, individual values in the trace table cells can be wrong, which hints towards errors in understanding data flow or the semantics of individual operations. All observations can be made automatically by comparing the student's response to an automatically created trace for the same piece of code.

4. REFERENCES

[1] A. Moreno, N. Myller, E. Sutinen, and M. Ben-Ari. Visualizing Programs with Jeliot 3. In *Proceedings of the Working Conference on Advanced Visual Interfaces*, AVI '04, pages 373–376, New York, NY, USA, 2004. ACM.

[2] M. Striewe and M. Goedicke. Using Run Time Traces in Automated Programming Tutoring. In *Proceedings of the 16th Annual SIGCSE Conference on Innovation and Technology in Computer Science Education*, *ITiCSE 2011, Darmstadt, Germany, June 27-29*, pages 303–307, 2011.

ITiCSE'14, June 21–25, 2014, Uppsala, Sweden.
ACM 978-1-4503-2833-3/14/06.
http://dx.doi.org/10.1145/2591708.2602658.

The Challenge of Teaching Students the Value of Programming Best Practices

Daniel Toll, Tobias Olsson,
Anna Wingkvist
Dept. of Computer Science
Linnaeus University
Kalmar, Sweden
daniel.toll|tobias.ohlsson|anna.wingkvist@lnu.se

Morgan Ericsson
Dept. of Computer Science and Engineering
Chalmers University of Technology and
University of Gothenburg
Gothenburg, Sweden
morgan@cse.gu.se

ABSTRACT

We investigate the benefits of our programming assignments in correlation to what the students learn and show in their programming solutions. The assignments are supposed to teach the students to use best practices related to program comprehension, but *do the programming assignments clearly show the benefits of best practices?* We performed an experiment that showed no significant result which suggests that the assignments did not emphasise the value of best practices. As lecturers, we understand that constructing assignments that match the sought after outcome in students learning is a complex task. The experiment provided valuable insights that we will use to improve the assignments to better mirror best practices.

Categories and Subject Descriptors

K.3.2 [**Computers and Education**]: Computer and Information Science Education

Keywords

Experimentation, Maintainability, Type Safety, Comments

1. INTRODUCTION

We have observed that students are reluctant to accept and incorporate best practices, such as source code comments and type safety. We attempt to design our programming assignments to stress their importance and value. For example, a programming assignment should be easier to solve if it relies on programming best practices.

In order to validate our assignments, we constructed a 2×2 factorial experiment[1] to validate if a programming assignment illustrates the value of best practices, such as comments and explicit types. The students were given a system with or without comments and explicit types and a maintenance task they should perform. They where also asked to track and report the time it took for them to complete the task. The course context formed and restricted the design of the experiment. Approximately 50% of the students that attended the course are (on-line) distance students. This required the experiment to be distributed in both time and place, and is thus similar to a field experiment with less control of the environment.

2. DISCUSSION

We found no significant difference between the variants, so this assignment does not emphasise best practices in a good way. We consider the experiment a valuable lesson on how hard it is to make realistic assignments and predict the learning outcome. The maintenance task was not specifically chosen to exemplify the need for comments or typed arguments, but rather as a realistic change scenario that relied on a system we had access to.

The experiment made us realise three important aspects of best practices and how students form strategies to counter the absence of these. First, it is not only the use of a best practice, such as writing comments or not, that matters but also the quality of the comments and the combination with other best practices such as good naming strategies. Second, several students reported that reading code was a good experience. Perhaps the value of best practices is not as direct as we expected. Third, students used different strategies to approach the source code before making changes. Some read the entire source code, while others searched and injected their change in a very limited part of the code. We also found that there are interesting interactions between best practices, for example how types, comments and naming practices can provide redundant information.

We will continue with similar assignments to provide students with an opportunity to work with larger source code bases and reflect on code quality. We plan to perform an updated version of the experiment during the next course iteration. To better show the need for a specific best practice, we should customise the assignments so best practices are essential.

3. REFERENCES

[1] C. Wohlin, P. Runeson, M. Höst, M. C. Ohlsson, B. Regnell, and A. Wesslén. *Experimentation in Software Engineering: An Introduction.* Kluwer Academic Publishers, Norwell, MA, USA, 2000.

Playing with Metaphors: A Methodology to Design Video Games for Learning Abstract Programming Concepts

Jeisson Hidalgo-Céspedes, Gabriela Marín-Raventós, Vladimir Lara-Villagrán

Centro de Investigaciones en Tecnologías de la Información y Comunicación (CITIC), Universidad de Costa Rica
{jeisson.hidalgo, gabriela.marin, vladimir.lara}@ucr.ac.cr

ABSTRACT

Learning to program a computer is a difficult task for many Computer Science students. Constructivism theory states that learning is unavoidably done through association of new concepts with existing ones. In order to learn abstract programming concepts, like memory indirection and execution threads, students must build them upon life experience concepts. We hypothesize that easing the association process by using metaphors, and letting students program them directly through video games, can foster learning of abstract concepts. We propose a methodology to design video games under this principle, and provide an example using metaphors for difficult abstract programming concepts.

Categories and Subject Descriptors

K.3.2 [**Computers and education**]: Computer and Information Science Education – *Computer science education*

Keywords

Learning; programming language; video game; metaphor

1. PLAYING WITH METAPHORS

Constructivism theory states learning is done by association of new concepts with existing ones [1]. When learning computer programming, students must mentally construct abstract concepts like pointers and threads, by associating them with other concepts acquired in their life experience. Because abstract concepts cannot be experienced by the senses, students must resort to imagination in order to make these associations. When left to the imagination alone, these associations can be weak or incorrect.

Association of abstract computer concepts can be established with ordinary concepts through *metaphors*. Teachers can use verbal or illustrated metaphors, as Waguespack did with programming concepts [3], and Forišek and Steinová with algorithms [2], without empirical evaluation of their strategies. Constructivism theory states students learn in active state; in other words working directly with the metaphors in order to deduce, by themselves, the fundamental principles of abstract concepts through ordinary concepts. We hypothesize that representing metaphors of abstract programming concepts in a video game, and letting students program them directly, can help students learn them better.

Video game related systems such as Robocode, Greenfoot, CodeCombat, and CodeSpells, have been developed for learning

ITiCSE '14, Jun 21-25 2014, Uppsala, Sweden.
ACM 978-1-4503-2833-3/14/06.
http://dx.doi.org/10.1145/2591708.2602661

computer programming. But their game concepts (tanks, crates...) are not direct metaphors of abstract programming concepts. We propose a methodology for developing video games where objects represent simultaneously both worlds: a familiar real life concept and an abstract programming concept. When students follow natural gameplay rules for those objects, they automatically learn abstract programming rules. We illustrate our five step methodology with an example of a puppetry game:

1. *Choose the abstract concepts to represent with metaphors.* We chose the concepts of *concurrency* and *memory handling* in C++ because they were reported as the most difficult and useful topics to learn by our surveyed students.

2. *Find colloquial concepts that resemble abstract ones.* We found puppetry fits the selected concepts (Figure 1). A puppeteer resembles an execution thread that follows a script (code segment). Puppets placed in the scenery (dynamic heap segment) must be controlled through strings (pointers) from the puppeteer's working area (stack segment). Each puppet must be handled by an independent puppeteer (concurrence). Large puppets, like Chinese dragons, must be controlled by two or more puppeteers (shared memory).

3. *Build a game idea with colloquial concepts.* We have designed a game that empowers students to be active playwrights, which build their own theatre plays.

4. *Support other abstract concepts, if applicable.* Our metaphor can also support *debugging* (e.g. run the script step by step) and *inheritance and polymorphism* (e.g. create new puppets).

5. *Implement and evaluate the game idea.*

Using this methodology, the puppetry metaphor was constructed and validated by professors. We are working on getting additional metaphors validated or, even better, generated by students.

2. REFERENCES

[1] Bogoyavlensky, D.N. and Menchinskaya, N.A. 2011. La psicología del aprendizaje desde 1900 a 1960. *Psicología y pedagogía*. Ediciones Akal. 119–188.

[2] Forišek, M. and Steinová, M. 2012. Metaphors and analogies for teaching algorithms. *SIGCSE '12*, 15.

[3] Waguespack, L.J. 1989. Visual metaphors for teaching programming concepts. *ACM SIGCSE Bulletin*, 141–145.

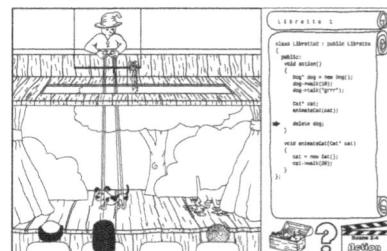

Figure 1. Paper prototype of the game (script text not important)

An Interactive Visualization Method of Constructionist Teaching and Learning of Geometry

Egle Jasute
Vilnius University Institute of Mathematics and Informatics
Akademijos str. 4
LT-08663 Vilnius, Lithuania
Phone: (+370~5) 21 09 300
egle.jasute@mii.vu.lt

ABSTRACT

Today's youth has grew up with digital technology and has lived immersed in environments populated by computers, videogames, digital music players, video cameras, cell phones, and thousands of other toys and tools of the digital age. It is probably for this reason that the authors are persuaded that education in XXI century should be directed to use digital resources as well as digital ways of teaching in all subjects. Mathematics among the other disciplines needs digitization and the paper deals with the development of dynamic sketches for geometry teaching and learning. Dynamic geometry education is important for pupils to develop visualization and spatial thinking. The attention is paid to the constructionist learning model for learning geometry developed by Baytak (2011) [1]. The model is extended and adapted for teaching geometry with dynamic geometry software at a lower and upper secondary school level. In order to help the teachers to use the dynamic geometry and other information technologies is developed an interactive geometry visualization method. The method is based on abstract data type theory. Four abstract data types have been developed and defined using algebraic specifications. The development of a dynamic sketch's scenario with the implementation of these abstract data types is presented in details. An example of creating an interactive microworld, using the abstract data types, is presented and discussed as well.

Categories and Subject Descriptors

D.3.3 [**Programming Languages**]: Language Constructs and Features – *Abstract data types*;
K.3.1 [**Computer and Education**]: Computer Uses in Education – *Computer-managed instruction (CMI)*

General Terms

Algorithms

Keywords

Dynamic geometry; constructionist learning; abstract data type.

1. INTRODUCTION

The problem domain of our work is intersection of fields of information visualization, informatics theory and informatics application. The external domains such as psychology, pedagogic, and mathematics education have influence on our problem too (see Figure 1).

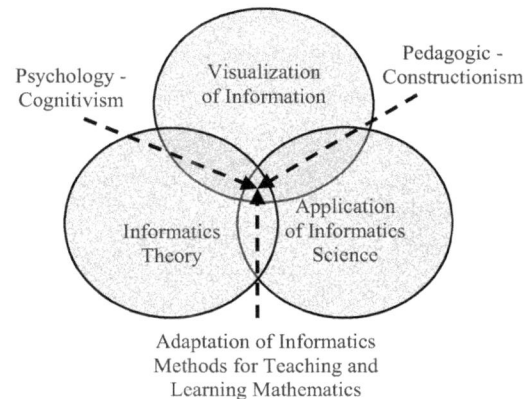

Figure 1. Research domain

When we solve informatics problem we have to take in an account the pedagogical context of the result. The solution of problem gives us two results [2]:

- The theoretical result – method developed by adapting ADT – in Informatics;
- The practical result – an interactive digital learning tool – in teaching and learning mathematics.

Consequently the psychological and pedagogical approaches were studied. Problems related with our research of this approach were recognized and described.

2. REFERENCES

[1] Baytak, A. *An investigation of the artifacts, outcomes, and processes of constructing computer games about environmental science in a fifth grade science classroom.* Phd Thesis. BiblioLabsII, 2011. ISBN-13: 9781243722775

[2] Dagiene, V. & Jasutiene, E. Developing Dynamic Sketches for Teaching Mathematics in Basic Schools. *The 17th ICMI (International Commission on Mathematical Instruction) Study: Technology Revised.* Hanoi University of Technology, Vietnam, 2006. 120–127.

Using Reflections in a Program Integrating Course

Viggo Kann
KTH, Royal Institute of Technology
Stockholm, Sweden
viggo@nada.kth.se

ABSTRACT

A program integrating course runs over several years, shows the main thread of the program, and its purpose is to enable students to become more professional in handling their studies, at the same time as the course has a positive effect on the mentors, other courses and the program itself. This is achieved through regular reflection seminars where students meet in small cross-grade groups with a professor as a mentor.

Categories and Subject Descriptors

K.3.2 [**Computers and Education**]: Computer and Information Science Education—*Computer science education*

General Terms

Human Factors

Keywords

program integration; reflection; motivation

1. THE INTEGRATING COURSE

The *Program Integrating Course* runs during the three first years of the five year Computer Science and Engineering program at KTH. The course uses reflections as the main educational instrument. The students learn why the compulsory courses are compulsory in the program and how these relate to each other, how they should select courses and specialization to become well-prepared for their future employment, and how to study to gain the most from the program. The program integrating course each year simply consists of four one-hour seminars in groups of about a dozen students, a third each of first, second and third year students, together with a professor as a mentor. Since the program is quite large there are 39 parallel groups and 13 professors as mentors.

ITiCSE '14, Jun 21-24 2014, Uppsala, Sweden
ACM 978-1-4503-2833-3/14/06.
http://dx.doi.org/10.1145/2591708.2602664.

Each seminar has a theme (e.g. plagiarism and responsibility, studying abroad, procrastination, quality in education), some links to texts to read or videos to look at, and some questions to think about. The students write a 600 word reflection on the theme and also on their current courses and studies. Finally they should read each others' reflections and discuss them at the seminar.

2. EXPERIENCES

We have found this model extremely fruitful. The students learn very much from each other in the discussions. The course has been useful in the following ways.
1. academic introduction to the program
2. increased understanding of the program
3. connections between teachers and students
4. stimulation of the exchange of experiences of students from different years
5. training in written and oral communication and reflection
6. covering of subjects that other courses are not covering
7. information about selection of courses and specialization as well as studies abroad
8. follow-up of results of the academic studies
9. education of the professors involved in the program
10. evaluation of the program for quality enhancement

3. REFLECTIONS

Asking computer science students to write reflections is a delicate task [1]. The design and administration of the course is very important, because otherwise the students might think of the course as bothersome and fuzzy. Much effort has been made to motivate the existence of the course and the use of reflections as the main working tool.

In order to inspire the students to improve their reflection abilities, we ask the second and third year students to reflect at the third and fourth levels in the framework defined by Hatton and Smith [2]. Our impression is that the first-year students really are learning how to improve their reflections by reading the reflections by the second and third year students. We will try to validate this in a research project the coming year.

4. REFERENCES

[1] O. Barzilay, O. Hazzan, and A. Yehudi. Evaluation of a software engineering course by reflections. In *ITiCSE '09*, pages 273–277. ACM, 2009.

[2] N. Hatton and D. Smith. Reflection in teacher education: towards definition and implementation. *Teaching and Teacher Education*, 11(1):33–49, 1995.

Mastering Model-Driven Engineering

Håkan Burden
Computer Science and Engineering
University of Gothenburg
Gothenburg, Sweden
burden@cse.gu.se

Tom Adawi
Engineering Education Research
Chalmers University of Technology
Gothenburg, Sweden
adawi@chalmers.se

ABSTRACT

The challenge of transforming the understanding of a problem into a validated solution is not a trivial task. Using the conceptual framework of cognitive apprenticeship we show two ways to guide novices towards becoming masters in model-driven engineering.

Categories and Subject Descriptors

K.3.2 [**Computer and Information Science Education**]: Computer Science Education

General Terms

Design,Theory

Keywords

Cognitive Apprenticeship; Pair lecturing; Executable models

1. COGNITIVE APPRENTICESHIP

In software development the process of understanding a problem and defining a solution implies interacting with other stakeholders as well as validation of the implementation. Mastering this process is not necessarily an easy task. In the context of teaching Model-Driven Engineering, MDE, it is not obvious for all students how to develop and validate different solutions. Cognitive apprenticeship [1] aims to verbalize how masters step-by-step formalize their understanding into a solution. In this way the tacit knowledge as well as the alternative routes are made explicit to the apprentices who learn from imitating and reflecting on the practice of the master.

2. TEACHING MDE

The only way to validate a sketch or blueprint model is by manual inspection which requires the skills of a master. We therefore employed an executable modeling language that supplied the students with continuous validation [3]. Using the terminology of cognitive apprenticeship teacher-student time was used for *modelling* and *coaching* while *scaffolding* and *exploration* distinguished the work the students did on their own. The project demonstration at the end of the course was an opportunity for us as teachers to ensure the students reflected on their own ability. In total 43 out of 50 projects delivered executable models that met the design criteria within the designated time frame. Our own evaluation of the models gave that the quality in terms of details and consistency had improved in general and in some cases went beyond what we thought possible, given the context.

While the introduction of executable models improved the students modeling we still found that the students struggled to apply the lecture content to their project. Lectures tend to present a neat solution to a problem and in the case the process for obtaining the solution is given that is also given as a straight-forward process. What we wanted to do was to increase the interaction with the students in order to adjust the lecture content to their needs since students learn more when they are actively involved during lectures.

Pair lecturing lets us do just this [2]. In the context of cognitive apprenticeship we used the lectures to *model, articulate, reflect* and *explore* different ways of modelling. In this way we make explicit our own individual cognitive processes in interaction with the students. Regarding the pros and cons of pair lecturing the students found that too many opinions could be confusing while they appreciated that complicated concepts were explained twice and in different ways by the two teachers. As teachers we found that we were out of comfort zone since we could not predict where the student interaction would take us. The most important change for us was the new possibility for *reflection*.

3. REFERENCES

[1] J. S. Brown, A. Collins, and P. Duguid. Situated cognition and the culture of learning. *Educational Researcher*, 18(1):32–42, Jan-Feb 1989.

[2] H. Burden, R. Heldal, and T. Adawi. Pair Lecturing to Model Modelling and Encourage Active Learning. In *Proceedings of ALE 2012, 11th Active Learning in Engineering Workshop*, Copenhagen, Denmark, June 2012.

[3] H. Burden, R. Heldal, and T. Siljamäki. Executable and Translatable UML – How Difficult Can it Be? In *APSEC 2011: 18th Asia-Pacific Software Engineering Conference*, Ho Chi Minh City, Vietnam, December 2011.

ITiCSE'14, June 21–25, 2014, Uppsala, Sweden.
ACM 978-1-4503-2833-3/14/06.
http://dx.doi.org/10.1145/2591708.2602665.

The Effect of Computer Science on the Learning of Computational Physics

Rivka Taub   Mordechai (Moti) Ben-Ari   Michal Armoni

Department of Science Teaching
Weizmann Institute of Science
234 Herzel st.
Rehovot, 76100, Israel
{rivka.taub,moti.ben-ari,michal.armoni}@weizmann.ac.il

ABSTRACT

Computational science is a growing scientific field that involves the design of computational models of scientific phenomena. This field combines science, computer-science (CS), and applied mathematics in order to solve complex scientific problems. In the past few years computational science is being taught in secondary schools, leading researchers to wonder about the effect of combining disciplines on students' learning. The current research is conducted in the context of a high school computational science course and investigates: the physics conceptual learning that the students achieve; the learning processes the students undergo and the effect of CS on those; the problem-solving abilities they acquire and the effect of CS on those. Findings indicate that students' conceptual understanding of physics and their problem solving abilities were enhanced and significantly influenced by CS, which served as a reflective tool representing the students' physics knowledge.

Categories and Subject Descriptors

K.3.2 [Computers and Education]: Computer and Information Science Education – *Computer Science Education.*

General Terms

Design, Human Factors.

Keywords

Computational science, simulation design.

1. INTRODUCTION

Computational science deals with the construction of computational models. It is an interdisciplinary field that combines computer science and applied mathematics, in order to understand and solve complex scientific problems. Studies show that computational environments foster students' scientific understanding [2]. The current research aimed to explore whether and how, among other reasons, the elements of the computational environment foster scientific understanding and problem-solving abilities.

Specifically, it investigated the way the discipline of CS affects physics conceptual understanding and problem-solving abilities.

2. METHODOLOGY

This research took place in a course on Computational Science intended for talented high-school students, where the students learned how to program computational models of physics phenomena.

We observed and recorded the work of pairs of 10th and 11th grades students while designing simulations of physics phenomena. In order to analyze the learning processes the students went through, three theoretical perspectives were used: understanding performances [4]; knowledge integration [3]; problem solving strategies of experts vs. novices, as appear in the literature [1].

3. FINDINGS

Students' conceptual understanding in physics was significantly enhanced. Moreover, it was influenced by the discipline of CS, which represented physics knowledge and enhanced reflection on it. Knowledge representation was achieved through three CS knowledge domains: structural knowledge, procedural knowledge, and systemic knowledge. Reflection was achieved through a fourth domain of execution. The influence of CS was apparent in all four phases of the knowledge integration process.

Students' problem-solving abilities were improved during the programming process. For example, students' became more independent in their physics learning, in part due to the immediate feedback they received from the simulation's execution. In addition, they learned to focus on physical principles instead of on specific cases, since the simulation is required to handle all cases.

4. REFERENCES

[1] Chi, M. T. H., Feltovich, P. J., and Glaser, R. 1981. Categorization and representation of physics problems by experts and novices. *Cognitive Science*, 5, 121-152.

[2] Chabay, R., & Sherwood, B. 2008. Computational physics in the introductory calculus-based course. *American Journal of Physics*, 76, 307.

[3] Linn, M. C., & Eylon, B.-S. 2011. *Science learning and instruction: taking advantage of technology to promote knowledge integration.* New York: Routledge.

[4] Perkins, D.1993. Teaching for understanding. *American Educator*, 17(3), 28-35.

Algorithmic Thinking for ALL: a motivational perspective

Zoltan Katai
Sapientia University
Târgu-Mureş/Corunca, şoseaua Sighişoarei 1C. Romania.
+40 727 370 346
katai_zoltan@ms.sapientia.ro

ABSTRACT

We proposed to investigate whether properly calibrated learning tools can effectively promote algorithmic thinking among both (S)ciences and (H)umanities oriented students. Our investigation revealed that there are no unbridgeable motivational differences between the way these two learning communities relate to e-learning processes aimed at promoting algorithmic thinking.

Categories and Subject Descriptors

K.3.2 [**Computers and Education**]: Computer and Information Science Education – *computer science education.*

Keywords

Algorithmic thinking; Motivation.

1. THE "TWO CULTURES"

Algorithmic thinking is an important ability in an information based society, one that all should possess. Based on the concept of "two cultures" introduced by Snow [1], some authors speak about sciences and humanities oriented people as being characterized by different ways of viewing the world and different approaches to problem solving. Since designing and implementing effective differentiated teaching-learning strategies may involve substantial additional costs, we propose a learning environment potentially more efficient for *both* learning communities.

Since motivational research lacks studies that focus on the impact that orientation (sciences/humanities) has on motivation for algorithmic thinking, we proposed to analyze specific motivational challenges that instructional designers might face in developing algorithmic thinking promoter learning environments.

2. THE EXPERIMENT

The e-learning environment we designed aimed to introduce students to the mini-world of sorting algorithms. Forty-eight first-year undergraduate students participated in the experiment (25: S-students; 23: H-students). Students from both groups were invited

- to watch an exciting illustration of bubble-sort algorithm as a folkdance choreography;
- to watch an expressive computer animation of the algorithm;
- to interactively reconstruct the operation (compare, swap)

sequence of the observed animation;

- to orchestrate the algorithm on a random sequence;
- to orchestrate the algorithm on a black-box sequence;
- to watch a nice parallel simulation of six sorting algorithms.

Specific questionnaires were designed to detect both the level and type of student motivation during the e-learning session: how they were thinking/feeling before and after the session and between the consecutive stages. We focused predominantly on assessing the motivational contributions of the generated (situational factors) positive/negative emotions, challenge and active involvement during the e-learning experience.

3. CONCLUSIONS

The main conclusion of this study is that there are no unbridgeable motivational differences between the ways H- and S-students relate to algorithmic thinking promoter e-learning tools. Although S-students' motivational-scores were consistently superior to those of their H-colleagues there was strong correlation between them, and any differences diminished as both groups advanced through their e-learning tasks. (see Figure 1)

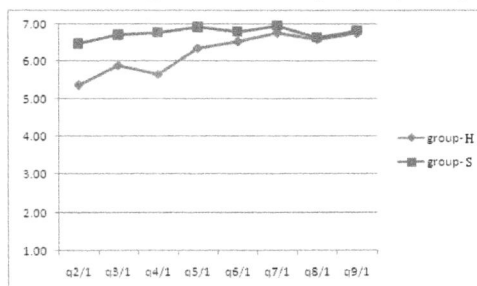

Figure 1. Students' response scores on a 7-point scale.

The results stress the highly significant role of genuine active involvement. Besides its motivational contribution it helped students to effectively recognise the logic of the strategy: it unmasked false perceptions of understanding (especially in the case of H-students); it revealed typical misconceptions that some students held regarding the viewed algorithm.

This study should encourage curriculum developers and instructional designers to analyze the possibility of designing and developing algorithmic thinking promoter e-learning courses for all students.

4. REFERENCES

[1] C. P. Snow. *The two cultures and the scientific revolution.* Cambridge University Press, New York, 1959.

Mining Job Ads to Find What Skills are Sought After from an Employers' Perspective on IT Graduates

Morgan Ericsson
Dept. of Computer Science and Engineering
Chalmers University of Technology and
University of Gothenburg
Gothenburg, Sweden
morgan@cse.gu.se

Anna Wingkvist
Dept. of Computer Science
Linnaeus University
Växjö, Sweden
anna.wingkvist@lnu.se

ABSTRACT

We mine job ads to discover what skills are required from an employers' perspective. Some obvious trends appear, such as skills related to web and mobile technology. We aim to uncover more detailed information as the study continues to allow course content to better match the expressed needs.

Categories and Subject Descriptors

K.3.2 [**Computers and Education**]: Computer and Information Science Education

General Terms

Data mining

Keywords

Data mining, classifieds, skills

1. INTRODUCTION

The need to understand what skills a graduate should possess naturally arise when we seek to update our undergraduate education in software engineering. There exist a number of suggestions, such as the SoftWare Engineering Body Of Knowledge (SWEBOK) and the ACM/IEEE Computing curricula guidelines. These provide lists of skills on a quite specific level (e.g., "Requirements traceability in architecture"). The suggestions are helpful, but lack contemporary [2] trends (the SE curricula was last updated 2004) and do not include actual tools and technologies. Based on discussions with potential employers it is clear that graduates need to be familiar with current technology and know the principles behind them to get hired.

To better understand what skills employers require, we data mine employee wanted ads. There exist several studies of wanted ads, e.g., Litecky et al. [3] and Aken and Michalisin [1], but these are limited to specific countries, time,

and questions. Since our main target is job ads in Sweden/Swedish, we cannot reuse tools and techniques directly.

2. A CORPUS OF RELEVANT IT ADS

During the first week of March 2014 more than 20,000 new classifieds were registered at Arbetsförmedlingen, the largest Swedish public employment service. There is a RESTful API[1], which can be used to automatically fetch ads that match certain criteria, e.g., job type. The ads are available via the API while they are active, i.e., until the last application date. To get a larger corpus, we fetch new ads once a week and store them in a local database. We limit ourselves to IT related ads. We started the collection process early January 2014 and we currently have approximately 3,600 ads.

3. MINING THE CORPUS

Our current focus is to gather data, so we only have preliminary mining results. Not surprisingly, many of the ads require skills related to web and mobile, such as Javascript, ASP.NET or Objective-C. We find that skills related to revision control, such as Git are quite common. We do cover the latter in our current program, but we lack courses that focus on mobile and web. While these are obvious trends, and something we should cover, we think that mining ads can uncover less obvious trends as well.

There are several challenges related to gather and store data, such as how to anonymise it, exactly what to gather, etc. For example, after two months we realised that we would like to gather all ads to be able to find specific skills required for IT. When it comes to data processing, many of the suggested approaches and tools are designed for English, so we need to adjust them to Swedish.

4. REFERENCES

[1] A. Aken and M. D. Michalisin. "The impact of the skills gap on the recruitment of MIS graduates". In: *Proc. ACM SIGMIS CPR*. 2007, pp. 105–111.

[2] P. Kruchten. "The Biological Half-Life of Software Engineering Ideas." In: *IEEE software* 25.5 (2008), pp. 10–11.

[3] C. Litecky et al. "Mining for computing jobs". In: *IEEE Software* 27.1 (2010), pp. 78–85.

ITiCSE'14, June 21–25, 2014, Uppsala, Sweden.
ACM 978-1-4503-2833-3/14/06.
http://dx.doi.org/10.1145/2591708.2602670.

---

[1]http://api.arbetsformedlingen.se

Brain-based Teaching in Programming Courses

Barbara Sabitzer
Alpen-Adria-Universität Klagenfurt
Universitätsstraße 65-67
9020 Klagenfurt, Austria
+43(463)27003517
barbara.sabitzer@aau.at

Stefan Pasterk
Alpen-Adria-Universität Klagenfurt
Universitätsstraße 65-67
9020 Klagenfurt, Austria
+43(463)27003517
stefan.pasterk@aau.at

ABSTRACT

Brain-based teaching is neither a method nor a concept. It is rather a way of teaching that tries to support the whole learning and memory process by considering how the brain works. The concept of "Brain-based Programming" is one attempt of putting neurodidactical principles into practice in order to improve the learning outcomes in introductory programming courses. In the pilot project this aim could be achieved [1] and the results of the ongoing study in three of seven parallel groups confirm the success in part.

Categories and Subject Descriptors

K.3.2 [**Computer and Information Science Education**]

General Terms

Human Factors.

Keywords

Computer science education, brain-based learning, neurodidactics.

1. INTRODUCTION

Proposals for brain-based teaching come from the field of neurodidactics that combines findings of brain and memory research, didactics, pedagogy and psychology. The original aim was to support children with learning difficulties. Therefore, it seems reasonable to apply neurodidactical principles in all subjects when learning is considered difficult, e.g. in Computer Science. Integrating brain-based teaching methods in introductory courses can improve the learning outcomes as shown in the project "Brain-based Programming", described below and more detailed in [1].

2. BRAIN-BASED TEACHING

2.1 Brain-based Programming

Brain-based Teaching includes various concepts and methods proposed by neurodidactics. One example is "Brain-based Programming", a new teaching concept for introductory programming courses. It has been developed during a pilot project of the same name and was implemented as a didactical experiment in one of seven parallel practical courses of "Introduction to structured and object-based programming" at our university. Usually they have a high failing rate (50% -70%); hence, the project aimed at improving the learning outcomes by considering neurodidactical principles in the teaching methods (e.g. discovery learning, cooperative learning, peer tutoring, questioning, pair-programming) as well as in the design of material (e.g. reading corners, step-by-step exercises, competence-oriented mini exercises with solutions). [1]

ITICSE'14, June 21–25, 2014, Uppsala, Sweden.
ACM 978-1-4503-2833-3/14/06.
http://dx.doi.org/10.1145/2591708.2602674

2.2 Methods and Results

To compare the learning results in the different groups the achieved points in the mid-term and final exams (the same for all) as well as the students' grades were compared. In the pilot project the experimental group reached a better average grade, more students successfully completed the course and female students could benefit even more than males. [1].

In the current semester the concept is tested in three of seven parallel courses with different teachers and the results of the mid-term exam confirm the success of the pilot project. Table 1 shows the number of the students in the different experimental (EG) and control groups (CG) as well as the results of the mid-term exam: the average points (max. 25) and grades (1=best, 5=failed). The learning outcomes in the experimental groups with an average of 20.8 points (grade 2.0) were significantly better than in the control groups (17.98 points, grade 2.5). A T-test for independent samples proves that the students of the brain-based groups (EG1-3) were significantly better than those of the control groups. The effect size Cohens d = 0.42 shows a small effect in favor of the brain-based teaching method. This effect is even higher regarding the results of the female students (Cohens d = 0.6). Females seem to benefit more from cooperative learning; perhaps they are used to solve problems by discussing them [2]. In the final exams the difference between experimental and control groups was not so clear. More students of the brain-based groups (EG) completed the course with success (52% in the EG, 41% in the CG) and in average they reached more points than those of the control groups (EG=10.73; CG=8.82 points). But, the difference is not significant (T= -1.545; p=0.124). Possible reasons for the significant effect in the mid-term exam may be a probable positive effect of previous knowledge or less complex tasks. Regarding the final results of the course, an overall effect (Cohens d = 0.41) confirms the effectiveness of the brain-based methods.

3. DISCUSSION AND OUTLOOK

The results of the study demonstrate that it is worth continuing the neurodidactical approach in teaching programming. This regards lesson structure, teaching methods as well as the design of appropriate material. In a follow-up project the concept is being adapted for and tested in further subjects at university and secondary school level. Then a closer look at specific aspects like the use of pattern recognition in classroom, the impact of cooperative methods and gender aspects will be taken.

4. REFERENCES

[1] Sabitzer, B., Strutzmann, S. 2013. Brain-based Programming. In *Proceedings of IEEE Frontiers in Education, October 2013*, Oklahoma City, Oklahoma, US.

[2] Schinzel, B. (1993). Zur Gleichstellung von Frauen und Männern in der Informatik. In *Frauen in Mathematik und Informatik* (pp. 94–106). Retrieved on 10/01/2014 from http://www.careerbench.uni-freiburg.de/cms/fileadmin/publikationen/users/schinzel/publikationen/curriculum.pdf

Why Is Programming So Hard to Learn?

Gillian Bain & Ian Barnes

Moray College, University of the Highlands and Islands, Elgin, Scotland

Gillian.Bain.Moray@uhi.ac.uk & Ian.Barnes.Moray@uhi.ac.uk

ABSTRACT

We present preliminary results of an ongoing study into the barriers to student learning in programming. Unlike similar studies, we look at students who have not previously been high achievers in the education system. The key barriers identified so far are poor problem solving strategies and emotional issues caused by previous educational experiences.

Categories and Subject Descriptors

K.3.2 [**Computers and Education**] Computer and Information Science Education — *Computer science education*

Keywords

Programming, student learning, difficulties.

1. INTRODUCTION

We believe that the world-wide shortage of programmers will not be solved just by studying and improving learning for traditional university students; we need to extend the invitation to a wider range of potential programmers. This study differs from other similar research because most students come to the University of the Highlands and Islands via non-traditional routes.

2. PREVIOUS WORK

Previous research [3, 5] has had only a limited effect on success rates in programming courses. Studies often look at individual aspects in isolation; however students need to put together several new areas of knowledge/skill. In terms of Bloom's taxonomy [1], programming students need to reach Levels 3, 4 and 5 (apply, analyse, evaluate) early, yet many are only comfortable operating at Level 1 (remember) and sometimes Level 2 (understand).

3. METHODOLOGY

We used semi-structured interviews (adapted using the protocol of Boustedt *et al.* [2]), followed by a questionnaire. The purpose of the interviews was to identify a concept or topic that the student found difficult, and explore what problem-solving strategies they used in their attempt to get unstuck. The questionnaire asked students to rate the difficulty of a list of concepts identified by us.

4. RESULTS

We identified a major issue with problem-solving strategies: 50% had no strategy beyond "Google it". Students do not connect topics: 53% thought that their "difficult" topic was unrelated to the rest of the subject, and 46% thought understanding it did not help them with understanding other topics. An unexpected finding was that many students found the interview itself helpful—even cathartic—and seem to have benefited simply from the opportunity to reflect and talk about their experience privately, and instead of focussing on a particular immediate problem (as happens in the classroom environment), to step back and instead look at their strategies and reactions to difficulties encountered.

5. ANALYSIS

We found big differences between traditional students and those who come to us by non-traditional routes. Students who have not succeeded at school and come through vocational courses find everything more difficult, rate their own ability lower, and tend to adopt a more passive learning approach. Many students could not let go of previous bad experiences, often from school. These had an important and lasting effect on their approach to learning. This effect was strongest with "second chance" students, those who had not succeeded in education before coming to college. These emotional responses are a major barrier to learning. This finding goes beyond the results of previous related studies [4].

6. CONCLUSION

Our main conclusion from this preliminary study is that the main obstacles are poor problem solving strategies and emotional barriers caused by past experiences.

7. FUTURE WORK

We plan to continue this work, using the results obtained so far as a baseline for experimentation with teaching and learning techniques. We hope to add a longitudinal aspect following students through the system. The study will also be extended to other UHI partner colleges offering computing.

8. ACKNOWLEDGEMENTS

This work was supported by the Moray College UHI Research Committee.

9. REFERENCES

[1] Bloom, S. 1956. *Taxonomy of educational objectives: the classification of educational goals, Volume 1.* D McKay, New York.

[2] Boustedt, J., Eckerdal, A., McCartney, R., Moström, J.E., Ratcliffe, M., Sanders, K. and Zander, C. 2007. Threshold concepts in computer science: Do they exist and are they useful? In Proceedings of the 38th SIGCSE technical symposium on Computer science (Covington, Kentucky, USA, March 7-10 2007) SIGCSE '07. ACM, New York.

[3] Boyle, R., Carter, J. and Clark, M. 2002. What makes them succeed? Entry, progression and graduation in computer science. *Journal of Further and Higher Education.* 26, 1, 3-18.

[4] Chang, S.E. 2004. Computer anxiety and perception of task complexity in learning programming-related skills. *Computers in Human Behaviour.* 21, 713-728.

[5] Pears, A., Seidman, S., Malmi, L., Mannila, L., Adams, E., Bennedsen, J., Devlin, M. and Paterson, J. 2007. A survey of literature on the teaching of introductory programming. *SIGCSE Bull.* 39, 4 (December 2007), 204-223.

Mastery Grids: An Open-Source Social Educational Progress Visualization

Tomasz D. Loboda
tol7@pitt.edu

Julio Guerra
jdg60@pitt.edu

Roya Hosseini
roh38@pitt.edu

Peter Brusilovsky
peterb@pitt.edu

School of Information Sciences
University of Pittsburgh
Pittsburgh, PA 15260

ABSTRACT

Many pieces of educational software are underused by students. Open learning model and social visualization are two approaches which have been helpful in ameliorating that low usage problem. This article introduces a fusion of these two ideas in a form of social progress visualization. A classroom evaluation indicates that this combination may be effective in engaging students, guiding them to suitable content, and enabling faster content access.

Categories and Subject Descriptors

H.5.2 [**Information Interfaces and Presentation**]: User Interfaces—*Graphical user interfaces (GUI)*; K.3.1 [**Computers and Education**]: Computer Uses in Education

General Terms

Design, Human Factors

Keywords

social progress visualization, evaluation, classroom study

1. INTRODUCTION

Over the last 30 years researchers and practitioners have developed a range of advanced educational tools for computer science education (CSE) such as animations, simulations, programming problems, and self-assessment questions. Unfortunately, their benefits observed in the lab do not always translate into broad educational impact [1]. One of the reasons for this seems to be low usage by students which afflicts advanced CSE tools the most because the majority of these tools are crafted to support knowledge enhancement through self-study which makes it hard to mandate and control their use.

Past research has identified two technologies which aim for ameliorating this low usage problem: Learner knowledge visualization (or open learner modeling) which acknowledges students progress and highlights gaps in their knowledge and social visualization based on the ideas of social comparison [3] allowing one to compare oneself to one's peers or the entire class.

The work presented here proposes a progress visualization approach that combines the two approaches in the form of open-source social progress visualization called Mastery Grids.

2. POSTER CONTENT

The poster presents the user interface of Mastery Grids (MG) as well as the results of its evaluation. MG presents students with a number of grids which visualize the progress they and their classmates make. That progress is tracked according to topics (e.g., "Arrays") and resources (e.g., annotated examples). Students access activities by interacting with the grids.

To examine the role of Mastery Grids as both a visualization and a content access interface we gave students an alternative way of accessing content through a simple two-level hierarchy of HTTP links. Both interfaces were used in three courses in the Fall 2013 term at the School of Information Sciences, University of Pittsburgh.

The evaluation revealed that the majority of the students chose to use MG even though it was not required. Additionally, students using MG answered more questions, tried more examples, inspected more example line comments, and got a higher correct question answer ratio. Furthermore, MG helped students be more productive by allowing them to access questions at a higher rate. We also found that students who performed more educational actions in MG got a significantly better final grade. Finally, subjective responses revealed a generally positive reception of MG but also allowed us to identify features which require more work and a potential redesign.

3. REFERENCES

[1] T. Naps, G. Rößling, J. Anderson, S. Cooper, W. Dann, R. Fleischer, B. Koldehofe, A. Korhonen, M. Kuittinen, C. Leska, M. McNally, L. Malmi, J. Rantakokko, and R.J. Ross. Evaluating the educational impact of visualization. *ACM SIGCSE bulletin*, 35(4):124–136, 2003.

[3] L.A. Festinger. Theory of social comparison processes. *Human relations*, 7(2):117–140, 1954.

Permission to make digital or hard copies of part or all of this work for personal or classroom use is granted without fee provided that copies are not made or distributed for profit or commercial advantage and that copies bear this notice and the full citation on the first page. Copyrights for third-party components of this work must be honored. For all other uses, contact the Owner/Author. Copyright is held by the owner/author(s).
ITiCSE'14, June 21–25, 2014, Uppsala, Sweden.
ACM 978-1-4503-2833-3/14/06.
http://dx.doi.org/10.1145/2591708.2609840

Author Index

www.ingramcontent.com/pod-product-compliance
Lightning Source LLC
Chambersburg PA
CBHW080713220326
41598CB00033B/5400